international business **law**

international business law

Bryan Mercurio
Leon Trakman
Meredith Kolsky Lewis
Bruno Zeller

OXFORD
UNIVERSITY PRESS
AUSTRALIA & NEW ZEALAND

OXFORD
UNIVERSITY PRESS
AUSTRALIA & NEW ZEALAND

253 Normanby Road, South Melbourne, Victoria 3205, Australia

Oxford University Press is a department of the University of Oxford. It furthers the University's objective of excellence in research, scholarship, and education by publishing worldwide in

Oxford New York

Auckland Cape Town Dar es Salaam Hong Kong Karachi
Kuala Lumpur Madrid Melbourne Mexico City Nairobi
New Delhi Shanghai Taipei Toronto

With offices in

Argentina Austria Brazil Chile Czech Republic France Greece
Guatemala Hungary Italy Japan Poland Portugal Singapore
South Korea Switzerland Thailand Turkey Ukraine Vietnam

OXFORD is a trademark of Oxford University Press in the UK and in certain other countries

First published 2010

National Library of Australia Cataloguing-in-Publication entry

International business law / Bryan Mercurio ... [et al.].

9780195560176 (pbk.)

Includes index.

Business law.
International business enterprises—Law and legislation.
Commercial law.
Foreign trade regulation.

Mercurio, Bryan.

343.087

Edited by Natasha Broadstock
Cover design by Canvas Group
Text design by Sardine Design
Typeset by diacriTech, Chennai, India
Proofread by Stephen James
Indexed by Puddingburn Publishing Services
Printed in Hong Kong by Sheck Wah Tong Printing Press Ltd

brief contents

expanded contents

table of cases

Note: cases in bold are extracted cases.

table of statutes

Commonwealth

International

Japan

Mexico

South Africa

Switzerland

preface

Many successful businesses today have some form of international presence, whether it is simply through selling their products or marketing their services abroad or through deeper integration such as sourcing materials from, or even producing their products, overseas. As the world becomes even more deeply integrated, the global market expands and the importance of international business to domestic firms equally increases. For this reason, businesses cannot simply choose to comply with their domestic laws and ignore foreign or international law. Businesses must have at least a basic understanding of the other legal systems that can impact upon international business. It is the role of the lawyer to appreciate the differences, effects and consequences of non-domestic laws and to advise their clients accordingly.

The aim of this book is to demonstrate the possibilities and risks that exist in international business while also highlighting and addressing the various legal consequences that may eventuate. The target of the book is Australian law and business students, and every chapter is written to be directly relevant to those students. But this does not mean that the book relies solely on Australian examples and case extracts. Indeed, notwithstanding the Australian emphasis, we have made the book accessible for students from other countries. Materials and commentary from a variety of jurisdictions are used to emphasise and reinforce important legal provisions affecting international transactions, as well as to highlight the similarity of both business interests and legal issues around the world. Importantly, international organisations, treaties, conventions and agreements are also discussed in detail, as they play a vital role in the regulation of international business transactions.

This book is necessarily selective, and only covers the issues that are most relevant and important to business. These include the international sale transactions of goods, insurance, financing, customs and import and export regulation, intellectual property, agency and distributorships, licensing, franchising and dispute settlement. Each chapter aims to familiarise readers with the legal issues and to provide the relevant context and background for readers to more fully understand the issues. It should be stressed that it is simply not possible in an introductory textbook to cover *all* of the issues. The knowledge, background and context provided in the chapters (through commentary, extracts, illustrations and examples) enable readers to grasp the major issues and to delve more deeply into particular issues raised, should they wish to.

It should also be recognised at the outset that the field of international business is changing rapidly, as are some areas of law. As far as possible this book identifies the uncertainties that arise from such fluidity. As the world attempts to recover from the current financial and economic crisis, which began in earnest in 2008, further changes will inevitably follow. International business responds to economic (among other) cycles and world leaders (and economists) are still in the early stages of determining what influence the global economic recession will have on the regulation of international business. What is likely to evolve over the next few years are tighter regulations governing the free flow of goods and services over national borders, new forms of national and regional protectionism and domestic and international instruments and institutions directed at both enforcing and harnessing such regulatory measures. These changes will no doubt impact business interests and influence the legal framework.

This book is the product of extensive industry and academic consultation and would not have been possible without the insight and helpful comments of all those who were consulted. The authors also wish to acknowledge the support and assistance of the many people who have assisted in the development of this book. We are especially grateful to everyone at Oxford University Press, and in particular to Karen Hildebrandt for her unwavering support, patience and guidance. Without her, this book simply would not have been produced. We also wish to thank Michelle Head and Tim Campbell for seeing this project to completion, Natasha Broadstock for her editorial work, the two anonymous referees for their important contributions, and all the others who have read or commented on the draft chapters.

Finally, it should be noted that Bryan Mercurio primarily authored chapters 1, 4–5 and 8–10 and contributed to chapters 3 and 11. Leon Trakman primarily authored chapters 11–13. Meredith Kolsky Lewis primarily authored chapters 6–7. Bruno Zeller primarily authored chapters 2–3 and contributed to chapter 1.

Bryan Mercurio
Leon Trakman
Meredith Kolsky Lewis
Bruno Zeller
30 June 2009

acknowledgments

The author and the publisher wish to thank the following copyright holders for reproduction of their material.

American Review of International Arbitration, for Leon Trakman, '"Legal Traditions" and International Commercial Arbitration' (2006)17(1) *American Review of International Arbitration* 1, reprinted by permission of ARIA, Columbia University; Buckley Ross P., 'A Comparative Analysis of the Standard of Fraud Required under the Fraud Rule in Letter of Credit Law', by Buckley Ross P. & Gao Xiang (2003) 13 *Duke Journal of Comparative & International Law* 293; Cengage Learning Services, for the extract from Michael J. Trebilcock & Robert Howse, *The Regulation of International Trade*, 2nd edn, Routledge, London 1999, pp. 213–17, reprinted by permission; Chow Daniel C.K., for 'Congressional-Executive Commission on China Dirksen Senate Office Building', 16 May 2005, Statement of Professor Daniel C.K. Chow, Counterfeiting in China, available from the CECC website and reprinted by permission of Prof Chow; Commonwealth of Australia, for excerpts from the Australia Group (AG) website, [www.australiagroup.net]; 'Pineapple prepared or preserved in containers exported from the People's Republic of China and the Philippines', Review of Ministerial decision to impose dumping duties, 21 February 2007; 'Intellectual Property and Competition Review Committee', Review of Intellectual Property Legislation under the Competition Principles Agreement (Ergas Committee) (2000) 22–4; and Thomas Westcott, 'Foreign investment issues in the Australia–United States Free Trade Agreement, all copyright Commonwealth of Australia, reproduced by permission; Commonwealth of Australia, for excerpts from the *Australian Tariff Act*. All legislative material herein is reproduced by permission but do not purport to be the official or authorised versions. It is subject to Commonwealth of Australia copyright; Copyright Clearance Centre, for John H. Jackson & Andreas F. Lowenfeld, 'ASIL Insights: Helms-Burton, the U.S., and the WTO' (March 1997)' reprinted by permission of CCC; Copyright Clearance Centre and American Journal of International Law, for Joseph A. LaNasa, III, 'Rules of Origin and the Uruguay Round's Effectiveness in Harmonizing and Regulating Them' (1996) 90 *American Journal of International Law* 625, reprinted by permission of CCC; Copyright Clearance Centre and Case Western Reserve Journal of International Law, for the extract from Keith E. Maskus, 'Intellectual Property Rights and Economic Development' (2000) 32 *Case Western Reserve Journal of International Law* 471, 499–502, reprinted by permission of CCC; Copyright Clearance Centre and Columbia Business Law Review, for the extract from Guo Qingjiang, 'Barriers to Technology Transfer' (1987) 1987 *Columbia Business Law Review* 117, 127–31; Earthscan Ltd, for Duncan Brack, 'Multilateral Environmental Agreements: An Overview', in Halina Ward & Duncan Brack (eds) *Trade, Investment and the Environment*, The Royal Institute of International Affairs/Earthscan Publications Ltd, London 2000, pp. 122, 125–9. Reproduced by permission of Earthscan Ltd, [www.earthscan.co.uk]; Erbisch Frederic, for excerpts from 'Sample Licensing Agreement', by Dr Frederic Erbisch, Director (Retired), Office of Intellectual Property, Michigan State University

(United States); Federal Court of Australia, for the extract from *Agro Holdings Ltd v Flexi-Coil* (Australia) Pty Ltd [1999] FCA 1658; *Fordham Intellectual Property Law Journal*, for 'The New Campaign against Counterfeiting and Piracy' (2004) 14 *Fordham Intellectual Property, Media & Entertainment Law Journal* 955, copyright © 2004, Fordham IPLJ; *Huston Law Review*, for the extract from Kyle Roane, Note, '*Hanil Bank v Pt. Bank Negara Indonesia (Persero)*: Continuing the Quandary of Documentary Compliance under International Letters of Credit', 41 *Hous. L. Rev.* 1053 (2004), reprinted by permission; ISIS, for the material by the Institute for Science and International Security (ISIS), reprinted by permission; Lexis Nexis Australia, extracts from the *Australian Law Decisions* and *Australian Law Reports*, reprinted by permission; Melbourne International Law Journal, for Gavin Griffith and Andrew D. Mitchell, 'Contractual Dispute Resolution In International Trade: The UNCITRAL Arbitration Rules (1976) and the UNCITRAL Conciliation Rules (1980)', © 2007 Melbourne Journal of International Law. This article was originally published in (2002) 3 *Melbourne Journal of International Law* 184. Reprinted with permission; *Northwestern Journal of International Law & Business*, for Warren Pengilley, 'International Franchising Arrangements and Problems in Their Negotiation' (1985) 7 NW. J. INT'L L. & BUS. 185, 185–207. Reprinted by special permission of Northwestern University School of Law, *Northwestern Journal of International Law and Business*; OECD, for the extract from OECD (2007), 'The Economic Impact of Counterfeiting and Piracy: Executive Summary', pp. 25–8, reprinted by permission; Scott M. Thompson, for 'The Hamburg Rules: Should They Be Implemented in Australia and New Zealand?' (1992) 4 *Bond Law Review* 168, 171–7, reprinted by permission of the author; Spaulding Barry R., 'Understanding Foreign Direct Investment', by Jeffrey P. Graham and R. Barry Spaulding, 2004; Texas International Law Journal and Prof. Weintraub, for the extract from Russell J. Weintraub ©, 'Choice of Law for Quantification of Damages: A Judgment of the House of Lords Makes a Bad Rule Worse', as originally published in the *Texas International Law Journal*; Thomson Reuters Australia, for extracts from *Administrative Appeals Reports* and *Commonwealth Law Reports*. Reproduced with permission of Thomson Reuters (Professional) Australia Limited, [www.thomsonreuters.com.au]; UNCITRAL, for excerpts from UNCITRAL Arbitration Model Law (1985, amended in 2006), reproduced by permission; United States Court of Appeals 5th Circuit, for *Croft & Scully Co. v M/V Skulptor Vuchetich et al.*, US Court of Appeals, Fifth Circuit (1982); Vindobona Journal, for Roberto Bergami, 'eUCP: A Revolution in International Trade?', © 2004 Roberto Bergami. This article was first published in *The Vindobona Journal of International Commercial Law and Arbitration* 2004, vol. 8(1), pp. 23–36, and has been reprinted with the kind permission of the MAA; World Trade Organisation, for excerpts from: GATT articles; 'Trade and foreign direct investment' 9 October 1996; WTO's Agreement on Subsidies and Countervailing Measures (SCM Agreement); and Australia—Measures Affecting Importation of Salmon (WT/DS18/AB/R. 20 October 1998), all reproduced by permission.

Every effort has been made to trace the original source of copyright material contained in this book. The publisher will be pleased to hear from copyright holders to rectify any errors or omissions.

about the authors

Bryan Mercurio is a Professor of Law at the Chinese University of Hong Kong. He previously taught at the University of New South Wales, where he held the position of Director, International Trade and Development Project at the Gilbert + Tobin Centre of Public Law. He has also held visiting positions at the Center for International and Comparative Law at St Louis University School of Law, The George Washington University Law School, the Institute for International Economic Law at the Georgetown University Law Center, and the National University of Singapore. Bryan is currently a Fellow of the Tim Fischer Centre for Global Trade and Finance, a founding member and steering committee member of the Asian International Economic Law Network, an Associate Member of the Asian WTO Research Network and a member of the Founding Committee of the Society of International Economic Law (SIEL). He remains on the Executive Board of the SIEL.

Leon Trakman is the Immediate Past Dean and Professor of Law at the University of New South Wales. He has taught at the University of California, Davis, Dalhousie Law School, Wisconsin Law School, University of Cape Town, Tulane Law School and McGill Univesity. He is author and editor of six books and over a hundred articles and papers on contract law, dispute resolution and trade law. Trained as an international commercial arbitrator and mediator, he has also served extensively as a trade adjudicator, appointed by US, Canadian and Mexican governments under North American Free Trade Agreement. He holds masters and doctorate degrees from the Harvard Law School.

Meredith Kolsky Lewis is a Senior Lecturer on the Victoria University of Wellington Law Faculty and is Co-Director of the New Zealand Centre of International Economic Law (NZCIEL). Previously, Meredith was a senior associate practising litigation and international trade with Shearman and Sterling LLP in Washington DC and Tokyo. Meredith is the New Zealand alternate member of the International Trade Law Committee of the International Law Association; a Founding Executive Committee member and currently the Secretary of the Society of International Economic Law; and a member of the Asian WTO Research Network. She has provided trade-related technical assistance in both Vietnam and Indonesia, and has provided training on various WTO issues for the New Zealand Ministry of Foreign Affairs and Trade. She is a past Editor-in-Chief of the *New Zealand Journal of Public and International Law*.

Bruno Zeller joined the Victorian Law School in 2000 and was promoted to Associate Professor in 2006. He teaches International Trade Law, International Arbitration, Conflict of Laws and Maritime Law. Currently he is researching the design of effective dispute-resolution mechanisms to resolve disputes in carbon trading. Since 2006 he has also been an Adjunct Professor at Murdoch University, Perth, and he is also currently an associate in the Institute for Logistics and Supply Chain Management at Victoria University. He was appointed Arbitrator by the Maritime Law Association of Australia and New Zealand (MLAANZ) in 2008. He is also a member of the International Law Section of the Law Council of Australia.

CHAPTER 1

introduction

1.1 Aims of this book

This book aims to introduce and clarify some of the most important issues relating to international business law (also referred to as international commercial law or even international trade law). It is written in a clear and instructive manner, with extensive commentary and analysis as well as case and journal extracts used as an illustrative teaching tool. It is written with students in mind and will primarily cater to students in an introductory course at the undergraduate or postgraduate level. This book will also be useful to practitioners seeking insight into certain unfamiliar issues.

There is some disagreement as to what areas should be covered in an introduction to international business law course and what should be left for other subjects. The reason is that courses with identical titles sometimes cover vastly different subject matter. After careful consideration, we have selected topics that represent the types of issues a lawyer practising in the area will likely encounter. We have therefore not attempted to cover in any substantive detail the issues more associated with 'public' international trade law, most notably the World Trade Organization (WTO). Instead, WTO issues will only be described in detail where they are directly relevant to traders.

This decision was taken for two reasons. First, this book focuses on 'private' international trade law; that is, the law as it relates to international traders. Lawyers representing clients engaged in cross-border trade consult and work with the relevant national law or regulation (and oftentimes have little time to consider why the law is drafted in a particular manner). 'Public' international trade law is simply not directly relevant to the day-to-day practice of most lawyers practising in the area. Furthermore, public international law such as WTO disputes are argued on a government-to-government level and private parties are not involved in these disputes. Put another way, the WTO agreements may directly impact upon and shape national legislation, but it is the national legislation that traders must comply with. This is not to denigrate 'public' international trade law in the slightest. In fact, the second reason why this book will not focus on 'public' international trade law is because such subject matter now serves as a separate course offering at most law schools. A decade or so ago, it was common to merge public and private international trade law into a single course. Today, the opposite is true and it is indeed the rare institution that still attempts to cover both public and private international trade law in a single course.

1.2 The applicable law

One interesting aspect of international business law must be noted at the outset: there is no 'international law' that directly governs international transactions and no 'international court' that can be asked to rule on such disputes. Both domestic and international sales transactions rely on a domestic law, and a domestic court or tribunal must have the required authority to settle a dispute. Simply stated, a dispute involving an international transaction will be settled by relying on a domestic law.

Depending on the domestic laws of the jurisdiction selected in the contract or otherwise deemed to be governing the contract, the applicable laws may be the same whether the dispute is domestic or international in nature, or they may be entirely different. As an example, in a domestic sales contract in Australia, the various state *Sale of Goods Acts* as well as the common law will apply, whereas in an international sales contract only the *Sale of Goods (Vienna Convention) Acts* will apply to the exclusion of all other domestic laws. However, as a general rule, the international community recognises that disputes which are 'international' in character require uniform solutions, and hence treaties and conventions have been formulated in an attempt to facilitate the smooth flow of trade and reduce the costs and burdens of enforcement. This book will specifically address some of the treaties and conventions in detail.

Treaties and conventions are the result of diplomatic conferences, where national representatives under the auspices of international bodies such as the United Nations Commission on Trade Law (UNCITRAL) discuss and negotiate a treaty. Once the terms of an international treaty have been agreed upon, the treaty will be open for signatures by nations. Importantly, the Australian Constitution does not allow for treaties to become part of the domestic law merely by an executive signature (unlike other countries, such as Italy), but requires the treaty to be passed though parliament. This process is called the ratification process. A convention is, in general, preceded by enabling legislation; that is, enabling legislation places the convention within the domestic law. For example, the various state *Sale of Goods (Vienna Convention) Acts* contain a section stating that the relevant Act takes precedence over any other laws in force. The convention must be added as agreed upon by the diplomatic conference; it cannot be amended in any way unless the convention itself allows for reservations. However, the more significant point may be that just because a nation has signed a treaty, this does not mean that the treaty is in force or otherwise applicable in that nation.

There is another matter that needs to be considered. Private organisations such as the International Chamber of Commerce (ICC) and UNCITRAL may draft model laws (such as Incoterms—generally accepted interpretations of commercial terms—by the ICC or the Model Law on International Arbitraton by UNCITRAL). These laws are 'soft laws'—they do not form part of the 'official' body of law of any country. In other words, they are not in and of themselves governing law. Two options, however, are open to nations:

- First, a country may incorporate the model laws into its own legal regime because they are either deemed to be better laws than those currently on offer, or they fill a gap (it may also be that there is no need for countries to 'reinvent the wheel' when a perfectly sufficient model law exists). The Model Law on Arbitration is such an example, as it forms part of the *International Arbitration Act 1974* (Cth) in Australia. Because it is a model law it can be changed as deemed necessary by the particular country adopting it. In practice, this is often the case as domestic legislatures frequently deem it necessary to localise the law.

- The second way of applying the soft law of model laws is to incorporate the soft law into a contract (such as Incoterms). Courts will almost always respect the wishes of parties and hence in any dispute the terms in a contract will be given primacy as long as it is not in conflict with a mandatory law. The law is always in reserve if the contract has not specifically made provisions to cover a particular aspect. Simply put, the contract will govern the issues as noted, and if the contract is silent the domestic law will be used to cover the gaps left by the contract. Many of the soft laws (such as Incoterms) have even become customary laws due to their widespread use. However, a caution is necessary, as despite the status of customary law they still do not form part of a domestic legal regime.

In order to determine which country's law is applicable, a special branch of law will assist the courts to determine the relevant substantive law. This special branch of law is often deemed to be the rules on conflict of laws. This book does not intend to discuss conflict of laws in detail, but it is necessary to briefly mention the issue at this point. Conflict of laws is, at its most basic level, a doctrine that allows a court to determine whether it has jurisdiction to decide the matter before it. The court that is seized of jurisdiction will then, pursuant to its conflict of laws rule, apply the applicable substantive law to the matter. Of course if an appropriate contractual clause has been drafted, the contractual wishes will almost always be honoured (unless, of course, they breach mandatory domestic laws).

Another point is worth noting at this juncture. While this book will deal mostly with substantive black letter law, it will also discuss soft laws (such as Incoterms and the UCP 600—Uniform Customs and Practice for Documentary Credits) when they are relevant to the daily life of traders. The difference is that black letter law has passed through the Australian Parliament, while the source of soft laws is not a parliament but rather the incorporation of the soft laws into the contract. Where relevant (such as in the chapters on courts and arbitration), another branch of law will be discussed, namely procedural law. Procedural law, unlike substantive law, merely instructs the parties as to the procedure to commence either litigation or arbitration. Only once a court or arbitral tribunal has been properly constituted, using procedural laws, will it be able to discuss and rule on the merits of the case.

The next section provides more detail on the types of issues lawyers practising in the area face and, correspondingly, what will be covered in this book.

1.3 The typical transaction

In this section, we will review some of the elements present in a typical domestic transaction before turning to the similarities and differences of an international transaction.

In a typical domestic transaction, the legal representative acting on behalf of a client selling goods from New South Wales (NSW) to a buyer in Queensland encounters few situations or complications that are not present if the buyer is also based in NSW. However, note that this is not a blanket rule. From a legal point of view, NSW and Queensland are sovereign states and hence, as far as state legislation is concerned, they can pass laws as they see necessary. In general, states do take note of the laws of the other states but variations can occur (and can sometimes be significant). From this point of view, a transaction between NSW and Queensland must be treated in the same fashion as a transaction between, say, France and Australia; therefore, caution is warranted when dealing with inter-state transactions.

Perhaps the most significant practical feature of an inter-state transaction will be which law to apply and which court or tribunal will be the appropriate forum in case of a dispute. Even this, however, will likely not be too problematic; while the law might differ slightly (and even importantly) in the varying Australian jurisdictions, all lawyers practising law in Australia will have similar legal training or skills, be familiar with the same documents, and could relocate across Australia. The state law societies recognise this through the mutual recognition provisions, which make it extremely easy for a licensed lawyer in one state to acquire a licence to practise in another state.

Both a NSW-to-Queensland and a NSW-to-NSW transaction would likely be a standard documentary sale transaction, meaning that payment would probably be made upon the presentation of documents by the seller to the buyer, and not upon inspection of the goods after they have arrived (meaning the buyer and seller do not meet to exchange the goods at the same time as the money).

If the transaction involves a substantial amount of money, a letter of credit would likely be used to reduce risks and avoid a situation where the seller or buyer has possession of both the goods and the money at the same time. The use of a letter of credit means that an additional player or two are added to the transaction: the buyer seeks out an issuing bank—a bank that must issue the letter of credit for the benefit of the seller (and guarantee payment when the goods are turned over to a carrier for delivery)—and the seller can insist upon the use of a confirming bank (also called an advising bank) to guarantee that the letter of credit will be honoured once the necessary conditions therein are fully complied with. In a domestic transaction, the seller would likely accept the letter of credit issued by another Australian bank (regardless of its location within Australia) without the use of a confirming bank closer to NSW.

The particulars of the sales contract will likely be easy to negotiate—the contract will be in written in English, the currency of payment will almost certainly be in Australian dollars and both parties will probably be familiar with the standard sales documents.

As stated above, the international transaction contains a number of similarities with the domestic transaction, but also includes a number of differences (and complications). In an international transaction, the parties will encounter differing business practices, cultural etiquette and legal systems. These complications are multiplied when a party is located in a developing country. For instance, developing country ports may be less efficient, with outdated and inefficient infrastructure, which makes the loading and unloading of goods more difficult. These circumstances also make the loading and unloading of goods more expensive, as the longer goods sit at the port or on the vessel, the higher the risk of damage to the goods, and this in turn increases the costs of insurance. Customs agents at several developing country ports are also known to regularly charge 'unofficial' tariffs in order to facilitate the inspection process more quickly and smoothly. Failure to pay the (corrupt) officer may result in the goods either sitting in customs for an extended period of time, or being denied entry/exit for no legitimate reason.

Another potential trouble spot for traders is that the documents and terms might differ from the familiar depending upon the host nation of the other party involved in the transaction. For instance, even common commercial terms such as CIF or FOB may have different meanings and place different risks on the parties in each nation (the use of ICC Incoterms would help in this situation, and this is discussed in more detail in Chapter 3). In addition, if the buyer to the transaction is unfamiliar with the seller, the buyer may want a third party to inspect the goods before receipt to ensure the goods delivered are the goods ordered. While this can also occur in a domestic transaction, it is more likely in an international transaction. The addition of an inspection reduces the risk of fraud or otherwise receiving non-confirming goods, but it also adds to the cost of the transaction.

In an international transaction, the parties will likely use a letter of credit to facilitate payment. The documentary sale works in the same manner as it does domestically, but is more complicated and risky when the transaction is international. For instance, the seller will almost certainly insist upon the use of an confirming bank, and both parties will want to use a bank in their own location. Thus, in a transaction between a Thai buyer and a NSW seller, the buyer will likely use a Thai bank as the confirming bank, while the seller will almost certainly require that a NSW bank be used to confirm the letter of credit. The use of a confirming bank by the seller adds to the certainty of payment and reduces its risk. For example, in case of a dispute the NSW seller would not want to go to Thailand to challenge the decision of the Thai bank. The NSW seller would much prefer to go to a NSW bank to present the documents for payment—thus avoiding having to send the documents to an agent in Bangkok to present to the Thai bank and being able to enforce any claim it has against the NSW bank in a NSW court (or through local arbitration).

International transactions also increase the risks that loss or damage will occur when transporting the goods. Put simply, the greater the distance the goods have to be transported, the greater the risk of loss. While this is true even with a shipment of goods from Sydney to Perth, the risks are usually greater with shipments crossing into international waters, as well as the waters of other nations. Of course, it should be noted that a sea-going shipment from Sydney to Perth may cross into the jurisdictional waters of another country, which could present additional risks, difficulties and costs. In such a circumstance, the parties could choose to ship the products over land or by air and avoid the added risks and difficulties. This luxury is not afforded to most internationally shipped goods. Other common risks involved in international carriage of goods by sea is that a vessel carrying goods from one country to another may stop in a number of different foreign ports before reaching its final destination. These stopovers create even more risks and potential difficulties.

The issue is that the shipper (the person responsible for arranging shipment of goods) will enter into a contract with the carrier. That relationship—that is, the contractual obligations of the parties—is subject to the laws and rules applicable to outgoing vessels. While all nations have legislation concerning the international carriage of goods at sea, these laws can differ considerably as they are based on different rules (the Hague Rules, the Hamburg Rules or the Hague-Visby Rules).

In an international transaction, both the buyer and the seller must also ensure that they fully understand the customs laws governing the exportation and importation of the goods at issue. Tariffs and non-tariff barriers may make the sale of goods to a particular foreign market uneconomical, or they may even effectively prohibit the sale. Furthermore, both parties must be certain that they comply with all relevant importation/exportation procedures, including obtaining the proper documentation and complying with quarantine standards.

The NSW seller may insist on being paid in Australian (or US) dollars when dealing with the Thai buyer, due to the stability of these currencies. However, it must be remembered that even if a foreign buyer agrees to pay the purchase price in Australian dollars, its government might impose exchange restrictions that prohibit hard currency from leaving the country. These concerns, as well as many others, must be taken into consideration before signing a sales contract.

The above issues relate to the commercial sale of goods, but this is only the first part of international business law. Quite naturally, as business interests and market share expand, so does the nature of a company's presence. Thus, if our NSW seller sells a sufficient quantity in a certain country or region, it may establish a representative office in the targeted foreign market. As opportunities grow, the company may wish to make use of an agent or distributorship to further develop the business. The laws and regulations governing both transactions are quite different, as are the potential risks.

Thus far, our NSW-based company has increased its operations from an isolated or occasional foreign sale to using an agent or distributorship to increase sales in a foreign market. The next step in the progression is manufacturing the product abroad. The choices here start with licensing a foreign company to manufacture (and likely distribute) the product abroad. Licensing can create a revenue stream with little effort, but it does mean that the NSW-based company will have to give up some control over its product. Licensing also creates its own risks, and will likely invite government scrutiny. Alternatively, our company may decide that its range of products and services are suitable for franchising; that is, expanding its business by allowing others to use its business format in exchange for a fee and continuing royalties. Another possibility would be the riskier, but potentially more lucrative, step of investing directly in to the foreign market. This can occur in a number of ways, such as through a joint venture agreement with a local partner or as a wholly owned foreign enterprise.

In each case, our company must carefully research its target market by doing such things as studying bank reports and country-specific studies, as well as making use of government and business organisations (such as Austrade) and, if possible, commissioning its own feasibility studies. It is important that our company be well-informed of the legal regime of the targeted country.

The method of penetration that is selected can have a major impact on the success or failure of the venture. Our company should understand that the choices it makes will depend largely on the legal regime of the targeted country. For instance, the company will be subject to certain local laws that will be mandatory—that is, they cannot be contracted out—including but certainly not limited to the relationship with its foreign employees. Other undertakings, such the enforceability of contracts, will also be subject to the foreign laws. In addition, tax liabilities will play a major role in determining which method of penetration is most suitable. International agreements (such as the WTO) are also relevant and important in determining the level and extent to which a foreign company can penetrate another's market.

During this entire process, our company must ensure that its intellectual property rights (IPRs) are protected abroad. Issues such as whether its IPRs are recognised or enforced aboard could be crucial to the success of the venture. Our company must know how to protect its rights, as well as how it can attempt to combat counterfeiting and piracy.

Finally, our company must prepare for the possibility of a dispute with the other party to the transaction. Our company would be wise to address such issues as the forum for dispute settlement and the law governing the contract in the sales agreement. Contract law differs widely between countries in both procedural and substantive ways, and the frustrations and added costs associated with navigating a foreign legal system (particularly one in a developing country) can be significant. For this reason, our NSW-based company may wish for any dispute to be heard in a NSW court, with NSW law governing the contract. The other side, for obvious reasons, may not agree to such an arrangement. The parties may decide to avoid the courtroom and include an arbitration clause in the contract. Even then, the parties should decide on a forum as well as the rules governing the arbitration.

These are just a few of the differences that can arise in a commercial sale of goods where the seller and buyer are in different countries. The differences tend to focus on the legal and economic systems of the countries involved, but cultural differences can also play a part (ranging from minor embarrassment to more serious consequences). For example, where is it appropriate to talk about business? What strategy should be used (adversarial or consensual)? Is business discussed over food? Are gifts appropriate (or necessary)? Do spouses come to post-meeting dinners? How are business cards offered and accepted? How should you sit?

1.4 Book coverage

The above description of a typical transaction outlines the issues covered in this book.

Part I focuses on the international sales of goods. Chapter 2 covers the application of contract law to international trade matters. Among other things, the chapter will introduce and discuss some of the more relevant aspects of the Convention on Contracts for the International Sale of Goods (CISG), an increasingly important convention. Chapter 3 introduces the laws and regulations covering the international carriage of goods by sea. The focus is on essential concepts and terminologies, such as charterparties, bills of lading, insurance and Incoterms.

Part II, comprising only Chapter 4, exposes the reader to the most common payment options, while at the same time showing how these options interact with the international business transaction. The chapter begins with a brief overview of the payment risks of conducting international business transactions, before detailing the main payment options, most notably the letter of credit.

Part III focuses on import and export regulations. Chapter 5 provides an overview of customs law, particularly focussing on selected issues of importance to international traders, namely product classification, tariff barriers, rules of origin and valuation of the goods. Chapter 6 focuses on non-tariff barriers to trade, such as anti-dumping laws, safeguards, subsidies and quarantine laws. Chapter 7 looks at barriers to the exportation of goods, such relevant multilateral treaties and arrangements, as well as domestic legislation.

Part IV focuses on intellectual property and the transfer of technology. Chapter 8 overviews the various forms of intellectual property rights before providing detailed analysis of three contemporary issues relevant to international business: pirated and counterfeit goods, parallel imported goods and compulsory licenses. Chapter 9 concentrates on licensing, with particular focus on the licensing of technology. Chapter 10 explains the concepts of agency, distributorship and franchising, with particular emphasis on the risks associated with franchising abroad, as well as the associated intellectual property risks.

Part V, comprising only Chapter 11, details the procedural and substantive issues, as well as the perceived benefits and risks surrounding foreign direct investment.

Part VI concludes this book with two chapters focusing on dispute resolution. Chapter 12 introduces the issues involving dispute resolution through the courts, while Chapter 13 focuses on arbitration as a means of resolving disputes.

PART I

International Sales of Goods

CHAPTER 2

considerations in the international sale of goods

Pierre Degas, a French importer, ordered 50 000 hats from John William, an Australian hat manufacturer. The order was that 10 000 black 'Bushman' hats were to be delivered 'on or about' 10 January, and a further 10 000 brown 'Outback' hats were to be delivered before 20 January. The remainder of the hats were to be delivered in equal parts made up of 'Bushman' and 'Outback' models, and this delivery was to arrive in Paris exactly on 3 March for a hat exhibition to last one day only, namely on 4 March. Pierre informed John that all the hats were to be used for the exhibition, although he also mentioned that he intended to send some of the earlier delivery as 'samples' to his trade contacts.

The first delivery of 10 000 hats did not arrive at all, but 20 000 hats arrived on 19 January. On 30 January, Pierre heard through the trade that John was in financial difficulty and there was a possibility that he would not be able to deliver the remainder of the hats on time. Pierre was further informed that John had started to sell all his stock and that manufacturing had ceased.

In a state of panic, Pierre opened some of the delivered boxes to check on the quality of the hats and discovered that the total delivery consisted of brown 'Outback' hats. On 10 February he wrote to John complaining about the delivery and asking for a substitute delivery of 10 000 black 'Bushman' hats. He furthermore told John that he wished to cancel his order for further delivery, as he had lost confidence in John's ability to deliver on time.

2.1 Introduction

Everyone in business understands that a simple sales transaction involves a buyer and a seller. It is also understood that if the transaction goes awry, then the law will assist in resolving the dispute if a mutually agreed solution cannot be reached by the parties. Most business people are also aware that litigation is not the only way to resolve a dispute and that several alternative dispute resolution (ADR) mechanisms (such as mediation and arbitration) are available. This is true of both domestic and international transactions. However, despite looking similar, not all the features of domestic sales transactions are duplicated when goods cross borders. International sales contracts are subject to completely different legal regimes to domestic ones.

Furthermore, an international sale leads inevitably to interrelated problems affecting customs duties, letters of credit and third party obligations, just to mention a few.

Two examples illustrate this point:

EXAMPLE 1: If John from Melbourne sells faulty goods to Betty from Melbourne, then Betty will simply access the Victorian legal system and use Victorian law in order to remedy the situation. Both John and Betty are under the jurisdiction of the Victorian legal system, and recourse to the courts is automatic and the claim cannot be rejected (this is not to say that Betty will automatically win the case, only that she will have her day in court). Enforcement of any judgment is also simply done by the Victorian legal system.

EXAMPLE 2: If John from Melbourne sells faulty goods to Betty from Germany, the first question would be which legal system will apply (the Australian legal system or the German system); that is, the question Betty would need to resolve is which court will seize jurisdiction. Even if the German court seizes jurisdiction, the question for the court would be which law it applies. In this situation, German domestic laws and the application of German choice of laws rules would need to be consulted. Another question would be how Betty could enforce a German judgment in Australia.

The main point of Example 2 is that there is no international commercial court. An international dispute must either be heard in a domestic system using domestic laws or through commercial arbitration (via agreement of the parties). Enforcement, if necessary, will be in another legal system pursuant to the rules of that particular system. Thus, just because (for example) an Australian court renders a judgment, it does not necessarily follow that the judgment will be enforced in a foreign country. Instead, the foreign law must be consulted to find out how—and even whether—the Australian decision can be enforced in the foreign country against one of its citizens.

In the first instance, the plaintiff is able to select the jurisdiction in which it wishes to bring the complaint. These issues are further discussed in Chapter 12, but for the time being it is sufficient to merely understand that these considerations need to be carefully thought through before a decision is made to ask a particular court to seize jurisdiction.

A further point needs to be considered: once a dispute is heard in either a domestic or foreign jurisdiction, the question is not only how the dispute is to be settled using substantive rules (in our case, contract law). The court or tribunal must also apply the procedural rules that allow it to review the substantive matter (in our case, breach of contract). The most common rule is that the law of the forum—that is, where the dispute is being heard—will supply the procedural rules (and, in some circumstances, the conflict of laws rules). This chapter is not concerned with procedural matters, and instead merely discusses the substantive part of the resolution of a trade dispute, namely the breach of a contract itself, or contract law.

The chapter will discuss the application of contract law to international trade matters. Specifically, the usefulness of the Convention on Contracts for the International Sale of Goods (CISG) will be highlighted.[1] In particular the following will be discussed:

---

1 The CISG is not discussed fully in this book. Only some pertinent parts are covered in order to give the reader guidance in the application of the convention. Many books are available if a detailed understanding and knowledge of the CISG is required, such as J Felemegas (ed), *An International Approach to the Interpretation of the United Nations Convention on Contracts for the International Sale of Goods (1980) as Uniform Sales Law*, Cambridge University Press, Cambridge, 2006; B Zeller, *CISG and the Unification of International Trade Law*, Cavendish, London, 2009.

- formation of the contract
- interpretation of the convention and the contractual obligations
- obligations of the buyer
- obligations of the seller
- breach of a contract.

In order to appreciate the importance of soft laws, especially in arbitration and as a tool in the interpretation of contractual obligations, the chapter will also cover the development of uniform soft laws, such as the UNIDROIT Principles and the Principles of European contract law.

2.2 The typical international sales transaction: the contract

An international contract by definition contains several other contracts. This can be illustrated by the problems associated with the goods leaving the seller's sphere of control. For instance, when does risk pass? Who bears the costs? These issues inevitably lead to interrelated problems affecting customs duties, letters of credit and third party obligations, which makes enforcement difficult and costly. It is therefore important for a contract to contain clauses that govern all foreseeable eventualities. The reason is very simple—courts in most countries will first look to the contract when resolving a dispute, and will only apply the applicable rules of the domestic law if the contract does not cover a particular eventuality. There is one caveat: the contract will not govern if the jurisdiction contains a mandatory law that cannot be voided or otherwise avoided. For instance, in Australia most of the consumer protection sections in the *Trade Practices Act 1974* (Cth) cannot be derogated by contract and any attempt to do so would be void. If a mandatory law does not apply, however, the law is essentially the fall-back position in cases where the contract is silent. To illustrate, consider the situation where an Australian seller and a French buyer agree that all disputes must be heard in Singapore using English law. As this is the contractual choice of the parties and the clause is not in breach of any Singaporean law, the courts in Singapore will readily enforce the clause. The principle of party autonomy dictates that courts simply follow the wishes of the parties to the contract.

It should be apparent that most potential situations and problems can be overcome if a contract is properly drafted. The contract can—and often does—prescribe the governing law as well as the forum. For instance, a model commodity contract reads as follows:

> Buyers and Sellers agree that, for the purpose of proceedings either legal or by arbitration, this contract shall be deemed to have been made in England, and to be performed there ... and the Courts of England or Arbitrators appointed in England ... shall ... have exclusive jurisdiction over all disputes which may arise under this contract. Such disputes shall be settled according to the law of England, whatever the domicile, residence or place of business of the parties to this contract may be or become ...[2]

2 Domicile clause 31 in Grain and Feed Trade Association 100.

This clause operates to solve disputes at a place where—economically speaking—there is absolutely no connection. Most businesses are multinationals operating outside England in matters that have absolutely no connection to England. The drafters of the model commodity contract, however, recognise this and have constructed the clause in such a way as to overcome any potential problems, not only with the actual sales contract, but with all disputes capable of being resolved in England.

2.3 Unification in international trade law

Understanding and applying a foreign law is obviously not an easy task. Making matters even more complicated is the fact that conflict rules are not the same in all countries. It is therefore not surprising that efforts have been made to unify the rules governing international trade law.

Unification of international trade law has its roots in what is arguably the single most notable development in the last 40 years in economic terms: globalisation. Globalisation has increased the importance of cross-border trade in a number of ways. First, it has contributed greatly to the internationalisation of trade and hence to the unification and harmonisation of laws. Even small businesses that in the past concentrated on domestic trade are now looking at export and import opportunities. Second, the process of transplanting the domestic laws of one jurisdiction into that of another has extended to uniform laws. Modernisation of legal systems in many cases has resulted in the transplantation of branches of laws. Examples include Turkey adopting the Swiss civil code and Japan adopting the German civil code. In fact, Turkey still considers decisions of the Swiss Federal Court to apply to its own domestic system. Hence it can be argued that Turkish contract law is identical to Swiss contract law. Furthermore, the development and enlargement of trade blocs cannot be underestimated in producing or at least attempting to produce unified laws—not on a global scale, but within their own sphere of influence. The European Union (EU) is an excellent example of where a serious attempt has been made to not only increase the trading bloc, but also to unify areas of law within the trading bloc and remove barriers to trade. It should also be mentioned that several countries, such as Germany, now adopt large tracts of international conventions for use in their domestic systems. For instance, in its efforts to update its civil codes, Germany adopted large parts of the CISG for use in its law governing sales of goods domestically. All these developments were basically driven by political ambitions and desires. Prior to 1935, an idea that held the world was divided into states with their own independent economic, social and legal systems would not have attracted much attention. In 1935, however, a revolution in substantive law began (and is yet to run its course), with Professor Ernst Rabel starting the debate regarding the introduction of a worldwide uniform sales law.[3] At that time, the application of private international law or conflict of laws was considered too complicated and abstract

3 E Rabel, 'Der Entwurf eines Einheitlichen Kaufgesetzes' (1935) 9 *Rabels Zeitschrift* 1.

(it had the reputation of being the 'nuclear physics of jurisprudence');[4] thus, it was not considered relevant for the correct application of the proper domestic law to the matter at issue. Instead, scholars were merely debating the possibility of applying foreign laws within their jurisdiction. The question or possibility of a uniform international law was a novel approach.

The first tentative steps towards unified international trade laws resulted in the realisation that the conflict of laws rule using nationality as a connecting factor would lead to different results according to the different domestic laws in use. For instance, in France and Italy, domestic law was always kept in 'reserve', should the judge experience problems applying foreign laws. This approach can be countered with the approach still in use in Australia, where a foreign law has to be proven as a matter of fact and not law. Unless a party introduces evidence as to the foreign law, an Australian court would commence with the position that Australian law is the same as the applicable foreign law.

Kötz, among others, advocated strongly that the solution to the harmonisation problem was the creation of certain 'general principles' which could be used to create the foundation for harmonisation or unification of international laws. Significantly, Kötz argued that the teasing out (*Ermittlung*) of general principles is a task not only for legal academics, but also for judges.[5] These issues have now come to fruition with the creation of international unified laws in the form of treaties and model laws such as the CISG, which is the focal point of this chapter.

It might be argued that, once contract practices have been identified, an international law can be put into effect. Looking at this question, Honnold asks: 'Can clear, predictable international law be made from the divergent rules of dozens of domestic legal systems, rules built with local idioms for which there are no equivalent terms in other languages?'[6] Honnold answers his question by stating: 'unhappily no, but that is not the end of the story'.[7] It must be remembered that any kind of legal regulation is a potential source of unpredictability, but the transnational nature of international business provides an additional source or dimension to the difficulty of securing predictability.

The solution is found in the work done by Kötz, as well as the earlier work of Rabel.[8] In essence, an autonomous contract has to be constructed which will not alleviate all the problems but will provide the commercial community with a framework. Within that framework at least one problem of municipal law can be eliminated, namely the divergence of idioms that require local knowledge and contribute towards cross-border legal risks.

Rabel gave the initial impetus followed by other projects, notably the United Nations-drafted CISG, the UNIDROIT Principles and the Principles of European contract law.

4 H Kötz, 'Allgemeine Rechtsgrundsatze als Ersatzrecht' (1970) 34 *Rabels Zeitschrift* 663 at 663.

5 Ibid at 677.

6 J Honnold, 'Goals of Unification–Process and Value of the Unification of Commercial Law: Lessons for the Future Drawn from the Past 25 Years' (1992) 25th UNCITRAL Congress 11 at 11.

7 Ibid.

8 See note 3 above.

2.3.1 The CISG

Drafted by a diplomatic conference under the auspices of the United Nations Commission on International Trade Law (UNCITRAL) and adopted by the conference on 11 April 1980, the CISG attempts to apply a uniform standard to the multinational sales of goods.

In Australia, as with many other nations, a convention such as the CISG must be ratified before it forms part of domestic law. A further complication in the Australian context is the fact that the sale of goods is not constitutionally within the ambit of the Federal Government, thus all Australian states needed to include the CISG in their domestic laws prior to its application within Australia. Such action was executed by all states and territories between 1986 and 1987 by ratifying the CISG in their respective parliaments. As a result the *Sale of Goods (Vienna Convention) Acts* were introduced by each state as the governing law in relation to international sales. In 1989, and in conformity with constitutional requirements, the Federal Government also gave effect to the CISG.[9]

It must also be noted that the CISG is not a foreign law that needs to be proven as fact in a court; rather, it is part of the domestic system of law. As a result of the ratification process dictated by Australian federalism, the CISG forms part of state law. As the law is not devised by domestic legislatures, conventions must be placed within the ambit of domestic law in order to avoid inconsistencies and conflicts. The enabling legislation always precedes the actual convention, which is added to the legislation. The difference is easily detectable, as the enabling legislation is divided into sections whereas the convention utilises articles. Whether we look at the enabling legislation or the convention itself, both carry the full weight of the law. The Commonwealth also had to include a section in the *Trade Practices Act 1974* (Cth) (s 66A), which states that the CISG takes precedence over provisions of the *Trade Practices Act*, as well as providing that where the Act would apply were it not for a term in the contract, that term is overridden and the Act does apply.

A further point needs to be taken into consideration when viewing the CISG; namely that the convention is the product of a diplomatic conference and hence is by definition a compromise solution. This does not mean that the rules of law are vague or incapable of meaning. On the contrary, the drafting of the CISG is a blend of civil and common law legal principles, and the drafters consciously avoided the use of terms that have domestic connotations. What this does mean is that the CISG must be read and applied without domestic methods and connotations in mind, and this is enshrined in the CISG (Article 7).

On the negative side, the drafters of the convention could not agree on certain terms and hence the CISG is not a code. It contains gaps that must be filled by the relevant applicable domestic law, which can be and has become problematic. The ramifications and correct applications of the CISG are discussed below in detail.

2.3.2 UNIDROIT Principles of International Commercial Contracts

In addition to official efforts to create uniform laws, many organisations also attempted to institute change in the application of laws that govern international contracts. Unlike

9 Australia, however, filed an Article 93 declaration excluding some territorial islands from the application of the CISG (none of which has had any great practical significance).

their 'official' counterparts, organisations such as the International Institute for the Unification of Private Law in Rome 'merely' comprise academics and professionals. As such, the corresponding results from such organisations (including the UNIDROIT Principles of International Commercial Contracts (2004)) are not laws, which are open for ratification, but are regulations that can be termed soft laws or 'model laws', in that they do not form part of a municipal system of law. However, this is not to say that they lack credibility or have no influence at all. Any rules—whether they are black letter rules or soft laws—can form part of the terms of a contract. Courts will always follow the wishes of the contractual party and the black letter law merely is a fall-back position that fills gaps left open by a contractual document. The only exceptions to party autonomy are mandatory laws which cannot be excluded. Hence documents such as the UCP 600[10] and Incoterms are widely applied to the exclusion of domestic laws. Because there is a wide body of legal and academic writing, the rules are predictable and the results foreseeable.

Courts are starting to address—at least in a questioning way—the advantages the UNIDROIT Principles offer when interpreting contracts. Courts in many jurisdictions have referred to the Principles on several occasions. Three decisions are of interest: two from England and one from New Zealand. It is particularly instructive to note the views expressed in *Hideo Yoshimoto v Canterbury Golf International Ltd.*[11] In that case, the New Zealand Court of Appeal found it necessary to refer to the UNIDROIT Principles and the CISG as it grappled with difficulties in interpreting a contract. Specifically, the advantages of Article 4.3 of the Principles were explained as allowing the court a more realistic approach in the interpretation of contracts. However, the court did not apply the Principles, or the CISG for that matter, as it was not prepared to go beyond these declarations. The court commented:

> But while this Court could seek to depart from the law as applied in England and bring the law in New Zealand into line with these international conventions, I do not think it would be permitted to do so by the Privy Council.[12]

There is arguably sufficient evidence that domestic systems have considered the Principles in the process of 'creeping' transplantation. Bonell points out that the Principles are useful as a means of interpreting and supplementing the otherwise applicable law in cross-border transactions.[13] The argument Bonell advances is that even if the CISG is applicable, the UNIDROIT Principles can be used as a guide to clarify otherwise unclear matters where the CISG is either silent or not explicit. Furthermore, nothing would prevent a domestic seller or buyer from including the UNIDROIT Principles as clauses into the contract. The interesting part would be that the contract could not be interpreted using the parol evidence rule, as the contract via the UNIDROIT Principles contains a valid interpretative rule that must be used. This is so because the parol evidence rule is not a

10 Uniform Customs and Practice for Documentary Credits.

11 (2000) NZCA 350.

12 Ibid at para 90. At the time of this decision, the Privy Council was still the highest appellate court for New Zealand.

13 M Bonell, 'The UNIDROIT Principles and the CISG-Sources of Inspiration for English Courts?' *Uniform Law Review* 2006-2, Volume XI at 305.

mandatory domestic law; hence the contract takes precedence over the fall-back position, namely the common law or any other statutes.

The UNIDROIT Principles and the CISG have also found their way into UK case law, despite the fact that the UK has failed to ratify the CISG (even though the UK was very proactive in the drafting process). In *ProForce Recruit Ltd v Rugby Group Ltd*[14]—a domestic case—Lord Justice Mummery noted:

> careful consideration may have to be given to the aims to be achieved by contractual interpretation and the precise extent to which the law requires an objective interpretation. It may be appropriate to consider a number of international instruments applying to contracts. It is sufficient to take two examples. The UNIDROIT Principles of International Commercial Contracts give primacy to the common intention of the parties and on questions of interpretation require regard to be had to all the circumstances, including the pre-contractual negotiations of the parties (art 4.3). The UN Convention on Contracts for the International Sale of Goods (1980) provides that a party's intention is in certain circumstances relevant, and in determining that intention regard is to be had to all relevant circumstances, including preliminary negotiations.

Similar sentiments were expressed in another UK domestic case by Lady Ardon in *The Square Mile Partnership Ltd v Fitzmaurice McCall Ltd.*[15] It certainly can be argued that the UK courts are increasingly becoming aware of the need to 'modernise' contractual interpretation in order to stay in step with international developments.

It should be noted in passing that many legal practitioners are familiar with arbitration and many institutional arbitration rules specifically allow the arbitrators to use soft laws if the parties authorise the tribunal to do so. For example, the ACICA[16] rules as well as the Swiss Rules of International Arbitration have clauses that state: 'The arbitral tribunal shall decide as amiable compositeur or ex acquo et bono only if the parties have expressly authorized the arbitral tribunal to do so'[17]. Simply put, the black letter law is always assumed to be applicable unless the parties decide otherwise. However, the choice is there and if the parties wish to do so, they can move to a soft law, which is then applicable as the substantive law of the contract, and hence avoid the application of a particular domestic law.

2.3.3 A Comparison of the UNIDROIT Principles and the CISG

The Secretariat Commentary to the CISG strongly suggests that the CISG achieved as much as it could, given the political nature of the negotiations. UNIDROIT recognised that there were shortcomings in the CISG and decided to abandon the idea of a binding instrument in favour of a soft law. The UNIDROIT Principles address substantially the same issues as the CISG, and either refine some of the uncertain provisions by adding more detail, or add topics that were not covered by

---

14 2006 EWCA Civ 69 at para 57; available at [www.unilex.info/case.cfm?pid=1&do=case&id=1119&step=FullText].

15 A3/2006/0290e; see also [http://cisgw3.law.pace.edu/cases/061218uk.html].

16 Australian Centre for International Commercial Arbitration.

17 Swiss Rules, Article 33.

the CISG. The advantage of the UNIDROIT Principles is the underpinning idea of the drafters that:

> while as a rule preference was given to solutions generally accepted at international level (common core approach), exceptionally solutions best suited to the special needs of international trade were preferred even though they represented a minority view at domestic law level (better rule approach).[18]

Given the above, it is not surprising to see that a number of national legislatures have adopted the UNIDROIT Principles in their modernisation efforts.

The real issue is the nature of the relationship between the UNIDROIT Principles and domestic law (which includes the CISG for signatory countries). The starting point is the fact that the UNIDROIT Principles are soft law; hence, they do not form part of a domestic law. However, nothing stops a party from including the UNIDROIT Principles as contractual terms into an international contract pursuant to the principle of party autonomy. This chapter will thus investigate how the UNIDROIT Principles can be applied in conjunction with the CISG.

It is obvious that a contract cannot exist in a legal vacuum, and that it requires a legal system for support—hence a system of law will be applicable. Indeed, some municipal systems of law specifically address this point, as does Germany in Article 27(2) of the BGB (the *Bürgerliches Gesetzbuch*—the civil code of Germany).

A system of law must be either expressly stated or determined by a relevant choice of law rule. If, say, the law of Germany or Australia is chosen, the obvious solution is that it includes the CISG. The contract now rests on, first, the contractual terms; second, the CISG as the governing law; and finally, the domestic law as the fall-back position to fill any gaps left in either the contract or the CISG.

Courts and tribunals have used the UNIDROIT Principles under several circumstances. Parties have selected the UNIDROIT Principles to supplement the CISG, and the UNIDROIT Principles have also been used as gap fillers for the CISG.[19] Most obvious is the use of the UNIDROIT Principles to assist in the understanding of the CISG where the CISG is not clear.

Thus, two situations can arise where the UNIDROIT Principles can be of assistance: first, as an express term in the contract and, second, to inform courts and tribunals in their interpretation of the CISG. It is perfectly admissible for a party to include the UNIDROIT Principles as contractual clauses. After all, contractual obligations are negotiated by both parties and find expression in the contractual terms insofar as they regulate the risk and rights and obligations of the parties. It is the expression of the wishes of the parties that is protected by the courts; whether the parties write up their own terms and conditions or rely on a template such as the UNIDROIT Principles is irrelevant.

It is, therefore, of value to investigate the most important provisions of the CISG against the solutions offered by the UNIDROIT Principles.

---

18 M Bonell, 'Towards a Legislative Codification of the UNIDROIT Principles?', in C Anderson & U Schröter (eds), *Sharing International Commercial Law across National Boundaries*, Hill Publishing, London, 2008, p 63.

19 J Gotanda, 'Using the UNIDROIT Principles to Fill Gaps in the CISG', in D Saidov and R Cunnington (eds), *Contract Damages: Domestic and International Perspectives*, Hart Publishing, Oxford, 2008, p 115.

2.3.3a Damages[20]

This comparative discussion will first focus on Article 74 of the CISG as it is applicable in most circumstances, regardless of whether a contract is avoided. The remainder of this section covers provisions dealing with avoidance, and situations where the contract is still in force and damages or other remedies are sought. This discussion is not a complete comparative analysis of all relevant articles. Instead, it focuses on the key provisions within the broad area of damages.

Article 74 provides:

> Damages for breach of contract by one party consist of a sum equal to the loss, including loss of profit, suffered by the other party as a consequence of the breach. Such damages may not exceed the loss which the party in breach foresaw or ought to have foreseen at the time of the conclusion of the contract, in the light of the facts and matters of which he then knew or ought to have known, as a possible consequence of the breach of contract.

It has been suggested that Article 74 leaves many practical issues open or unresolved, including:

> the time at which damages are to be calculated, the liability and calculation of future damages, contributory conduct of the claimant that increases the amount of damages, saved expenses, loss of an opportunity or chance, penalty clauses and proof of damages.[21]

If we compare the CISG to the relevant articles of the UNIDROIT Principles, two important aspects are shared by these instruments: first, full compensation is envisaged—that is, the aggrieved party should be put in the same position that party would have been in had the contract been performed; second, irrespective of any remedy described in Article 45 of the CISG, the aggrieved party never loses the right to claim further damages pursuant to Article 74, up to the limit of full compensation. Furthermore, the foreseeability principle as embodied in Article 74 is also contained in Article 7.4.4 of the UNIDROIT Principles. However, there is a difference between the two articles: the term 'possible consequence' in the former and the word 'likely' in the latter. Some authors have noted that the CISG uses a broader term. The UNIDROIT Principles note that:

> the test [for foreseeability as described in Article 7.4.4] is what a normally diligent person could reasonably have foreseen as the consequences of the non-performance in the ordinary course of things and the particular circumstances of the contract, such as the information supplied by the parties or their previous transactions.[22]

Arguably, the test is not significantly different from the test in the CISG; hence, in both instruments the subjective and objective tests are applied.

---

20 For more detailed analysis, see B Zeller, *Damages under the Convention on Contracts for the International Sale of Goods*, 2nd edn, Oxford University Press, Oxford & New York, 2009.

21 S Eiselen, 'Measuring Damages for Breach of Contract: Remarks on the Manner in which the UNIDROIT Principles of International Commercial Contracts may be Used to Interpret or Supplement Article 74', in J Felemegas (ed), *An International Approach to the Interpretation of the United Nations Convention on Contracts for the International Sale of Goods (1980) as Uniform Sales Law*, Cambridge University Press, Cambridge, 2007, p 211.

22 UNIDROIT Principles, 2004, Rome, 239.

From this point of view, it can be argued that the UNIDROIT Principles have the same underlying general principles as the CISG regarding compensation for losses in relation to a breach of contract. It follows that the UNIDROIT Principles can assist in clarifying uncertainties within the CISG.

However, there is a difference between the remedial schemes of the CISG and of UNIDROIT Principles Article 7.4.2. The CISG endeavours to grant full compensation to the aggrieved party pursuant to Article 74, which is limited only by the exceptions to be found within the four corners of the CISG. The most notable limitations are the mitigation factor and Article 5, which excludes compensation for death and personal injury 'caused by the goods to any person'. The UNIDROIT Principles define full compensation much more broadly.

Article 7.4.2 of the UNIDROIT Principles notes that the aggrieved party is 'entitled to full compensation for harm sustained'. It can be argued that 'harm' is a much broader term than simple 'loss' or 'lost profits'. This view is enforced by subparagraph (2), which specifically states that 'such harm may be non-pecuniary and includes, for instance, physical suffering or emotional stress'.[23] In the 2004 edition of the UNIDROIT Principles, the non-pecuniary rule is explained as being primarily applicable to artists, outstanding sportspersons, and consultants. Not surprisingly, the examples do not include the sale of goods, and hence it can be safely assumed that this particular rule in the UNIDROIT Principles would not be applicable to the CISG. However, it has been argued that the provisions in the UNIDROIT Principles can be applied in circumstances where Article 5 of the CISG has to be interpreted. The argument is that Article 5 should not be interpreted restrictively; hence, personal damage, such as damage to reputation, should be included within the sphere of the CISG.[24]

It has been argued that the CISG contains an apparent gap, namely that it does not deal with future damages. The UNIDROIT Principles specifically mention that 'compensation is due only for harm, including future harm that is established with a reasonable degree of certainty'.[25] The issue is that any harm must be established with a reasonable degree of certainty; hence speculative assertions are to be discarded by courts and tribunals. Arguably, the CISG does by implication deal with future harm in the form of loss of profits. To establish with a reasonable degree of certainty that a profit is possible, and that a loss of that profit will occur owing to the breach of the contract, contains in itself an element of uncertainty, as not all business ventures end up with profits. For example, if goods are not delivered and the intention was to sell the goods on, the profit is easily determinable by taking the invoices into account. If, on the other hand, goods are bought and put into stock, the only matter that is certain is that an attempt will be made to sell the goods; any loss of profit as a result of market fluctuations is a future harm, and hence can and must be established with a reasonable degree of certainty. The UNIDROIT Principles can assist in the interpretation of the CISG, and in this case all uncertainties can be removed.

---

23 Ibid, 236.

24 See Eiselen above note 21.

25 UNIDROIT Principles, Article 7.4.3.

2.3.3b Principles of European Contract Law[26]

As another development to the UNIDROIT Principles, the European Commission and other organisations supported a project to draw up a set of contract laws and principles. These rules are now the culmination of work that started in 1982. Not unlike the UNIDROIT Principles, the rules have been drawn up by an independent body of experts from each member state of the EU.

The Principles of European Contract Law, Parts I and II (PECL I and II), cover the core rules of contract, formation, authority of agents, validity, interpretation, contents, performance, non-performance (breach) and remedies. The Principles, previously published in Part I (1995), are included in a revised and reordered form. Part III covers plurality of parties, assignment of claims, substitution of new debt, transfer of contract, set-off, prescription, illegality, conditions and capitalisation of interest.

PECL is of specific interest in the EU as the European Parliament has twice called for the creation of a unified European Civil Code. No doubt PECL—and to a lesser degree the CISG as well as the UNIDROIT Principles—will form the nucleus of a possible unified sales law in the EU, and possibly in Europe.

At the beginning of the project doubts were expressed that the Amsterdam Treaty does not allow the EU to prepare a unified contract law, which in essence would form part of the EU Civil Code. In 1999, the decision was made that the European Commission and the Council of Ministers should prepare a study to establish whether a soft law or comprehensive and binding EU legislation on the law of contract should be prepared. The matter appears to be resolved in favour of the creation of a black letter law.

The Commission on European Contract Law

With a few exceptions, the members of the Commission of European Contract Law have been academics, but many of the academics are also practising lawyers. The members have not been representatives of specific political or governmental interests, and they have all pursued the same objective: to draft the most appropriate contract rules for Europe.

In some respects the Principles may be compared with the US Restatement of the Law of Contracts, which was published in its second edition in 1981. Like the Restatements, the articles drafted are supplied with comments and notes. The Restatements consist of non-binding rules, or soft law. They purport to restate the common law of the USA. The Principles are also soft law, but their main purpose is to serve as a first draft of part of a European Civil Code. Furthermore, a common law does not exist in the EU. The Principles have therefore being established by a more radical process. No single legal system has been their basis, as the Commission considered all the systems of the member states (but it must be noted that not every domestic system influenced every issue). The rules of legal systems outside of the European Communities were also being considered, as were the US Restatement of the Law of Contracts and existing conventions, such as the CISG. Some of the Principles reflect ideas that have not yet materialised in the law of any state. In short, the Commission has tried to establish those principles that it believed to be best under the existing economic and social conditions in Europe.

26 This part relies heavily on—and has drawn in parts directly from—the website of the Commission on European Contract Law [http://frontpage.cbs.dk/law/commission_on_european_contract_law/].

The Commission attempted to draft short rules which are easily understood by prospective users of the Principles, such as practising lawyers and business people. The Commission has made an analysis of the extent to which Part 1 of the Principles is applicable to the more important commercial contracts for the provision of goods and services of various kinds and the transfer of rights (licence agreements, etc.). Although the Principles cannot provide the appropriate solution to all of the issues raised by every one of these specific contracts, the Commission has found them applicable to the great majority of issues.

The Commission has made an effort to deal with those issues in contract which face business life of today and which may advance the trade, especially the international trade. However, the Principles are not intended to apply exclusively to international transactions.[27]

2.4 Applicable law: formation of contract

As noted above, an international contract is always subject to a particular and applicable domestic law. The conflict of laws rules, as briefly discussed, will assist any court to arrive at that decision. It should be clear that it is important to read the clause first before drawing any conclusions. However, in the end, whether the court determines the applicable law or the contractual clause has resolved this matter, the fact remains that knowledge of a governing domestic law needs to be sufficient in order to understand either its application or—at the drawing stage of the contract—which law suits the particular contractual purpose best.

In Australia—and in the states in particular—three areas of law influence sales contracts: the common law, the various legislation—state or federal—and the CISG. Remember, unless incorporated into the contract by the parties, the UNIDROIT Principles and PECL are soft law and can at best only be used as governing law in arbitration proceedings. Where soft law has been incorporated into the contract, it forms part of contractual terms; such terms would therefore need to be dealt with by a domestic court, supplemented where needed by domestic law.

2.4.1 The CISG

The CISG is divided into four parts. Part I deals with the sphere of application, Part II with the formation of the contract, Part III the sale of goods, and Part IV the final provisions. Simply put, the CISG applies in all cases of international sale of goods, unless explicitly excluded by contract, because of the enabling legislation enacted by the Australian states. For instance, s 6 of the Victorian enabling legislation, the *Sale of Goods (Vienna Convention) Act 1987*, states: 'The provisions of the Convention prevail over any other law in force in Victoria to the extent of any inconsistency.' Moreover, Article 1 of the CISG, which forms part of the Australian Acts, states in the pertinent part:

27 See [http://frontpage.cbs.dk/law/commission_on_european_contract_law].

(1) This Convention applies to contracts of sale of goods between parties whose places of business are in different States:
  (a) when the States are Contracting States; or
  (b) when the rules of private international law lead to the application of the law of a Contracting State.

Thus, Article 1 specifically states that the CISG regulates international sales and that it must prevail over any other law in Victoria (or any signatory country), unless of course the parties have by an express clause in the contract excluded the CISG pursuant to Article 6. Article 6 allows parties to exclude the CISG, or derogate from or vary the effect of any of its provisions. In other words, the CISG automatically applies unless otherwise stated. Unfortunately, not all municipal courts or even the legal profession as a whole are fully aware of this point, and tend to ignore the fact that the CISG is the governing law in relation to international sales of goods. For instance, in *Perry Eng P/L (Rec and Man appt'd) v Bernold AG No. SCGRG-99–1063*,[28] a plaintiff in Australia attempted to sue a Swiss firm by relying on the South Australian *Sale of Goods Act*, because the 'choice of law' clause in the contract noted that the law of South Australia was to apply. As Judge Burley correctly pointed out, the CISG is part of the law of South Australia, and hence the CISG and not the *Sale of Goods Act* is applicable. This case is an illustration and warning to those who ignore the CISG or are not aware that an international sale is governed by the CISG. However, what is surprising is that the earlier four appearances by *Perry Engineering* were not as forcibly rejected. Judge Burley commented that: 'The statement of claim has been drawn up on the assumption that the South Australian *Sale of Goods Act* applies. This seems to me to be fatal to the plaintiff's ability to proceed to judgment ...'.[29]

The following extract provides more detail of a typical dispute where, unfortunately, the complainant failed to refer to the CISG as the proper law and instead relied on the sales law governing domestic transactions, and the court had to dissect the transaction and apply the correct law.

Asante Technologies, Inc v PMC-Sierra, Inc

US [Federal] District Court for the Northern District of California, 30 July 2001

I. Introduction

This lawsuit arises out of a dispute involving the sale of electronic components. Plaintiff [buyer], Asante Technologies Inc, filed the action in the Superior Court for the State of California, Santa Clara County, on February 13, 2001. Defendant [seller], PMC-Sierra, Inc, removed the action to this Court, asserting federal question jurisdiction pursuant to 28 USC section 1331. Specifically, [seller] asserts that [buyer's] claims for breach of contract and breach of express warranty are governed by the United Nations Convention on Contracts for the International Sale of Goods ('CISG'). [Buyer] disputes

28 [2001] SASC 15 (1 February 2001). [http://cisgw3.law.pace.edu/cases/010201a2.html].

29 Ibid.

jurisdiction and filed this Motion to Remand and for Attorneys' Fees. The Court conducted a hearing on June 18, 2001. Based upon the submitted papers and oral arguments of the parties, the Court DENIES the motion to remand and the associated request for attorneys' fees.

II. Background

The Complaint in this action alleges claims based in tort and contract. [Buyer] contends that [seller] failed to provide it with electronic components meeting certain designated technical specifications. [Seller] timely removed the action to this Court on March 16, 2001.

[Buyer] is a Delaware corporation having its primary place of business in Santa Clara County, California. [Buyer] produces network switchers, a type of electronic component used to connect multiple computers to one another and to the Internet. [Buyer] purchases component parts from a number of manufacturers. In particular, [buyer] purchases application-specific integrated circuits ('ASICs'), which are considered the control center of its network switchers, from [seller].

[Seller] is also a Delaware corporation. [Seller] asserts that, at all relevant times, its corporate headquarters, inside sales and marketing office, public relations department, principal warehouse, and most design and engineering functions were located in Burnaby, British Columbia, Canada. [Seller] also maintains an office in Portland, Oregon, where many of its engineers are based. [Seller's] products are sold in California through Unique Technologies, which is an authorized distributor of [seller's] products in North America. It is undisputed that [seller] directed [buyer] to purchase [seller's] products through Unique, and that [seller] honored purchase orders solicited by Unique. Unique is located in California. Determining [seller's] 'place of business' with respect to its contract with [buyer] is critical to the question of whether the Court has jurisdiction in this case.

[Buyer's] Complaint focuses on five purchase orders. Four of the five purchase orders were submitted to [seller] through Unique as directed by [seller]. However, [buyer] does not dispute that one of the purchase orders, dated January 28, 2000, was sent by fax directly to [seller] in British Columbia, and that [seller] processed the order in British Columbia. [Seller] shipped all orders to [buyer's] headquarters in California. Upon delivery of the goods, Unique sent invoices to [buyer], at which time [buyer] tendered payment to Unique either in California or in Nevada.

...

[Buyer] now requests this Court to remand this action back to the Superior Court of the County of Santa Clara pursuant to 28 USC section 1447(c), asserting lack of subject matter jurisdiction. In addition, [buyer] requests award of attorneys fees and costs for the expense of bringing this motion.

III. Standards

A defendant may remove to federal court any civil action brought in a state court that originally could have been filed in federal court. When a case originally filed in state court contains separate and independent federal and state law claims, the entire case may be removed to federal court.

The determination of whether an action arises under federal law is guided by the 'well-pleaded complaint' rule. The rule provides that removal is proper when a federal question is presented on the face of the Complaint. However, in areas where federal law completely preempts state law, even if the claims are purportedly based on state law, the claims are considered to have arisen under federal law. Defendant [seller] has the burden of establishing that removal is proper. If, at any time before judgment, the district court determines that the case was removed from state court improvidently and without jurisdiction, the district court must remand the case.

The Convention on Contracts for the International Sale of Goods ('CISG') is an international treaty which has been signed and ratified by the United States and Canada, among other countries. The CISG was adopted for the purpose of establishing 'substantive provisions of law to govern the formation of international sales contracts and the rights and obligations of the buyer and the seller.' The CISG applies 'to contracts of sale of goods between parties whose places of business are in different States ... when the States are Contracting States.' Article 10 of the CISG provides that 'if a party has more than one place of business, the place of business is that which has the closest relationship to the contract and its performance.'

IV. Discussion

Defendant [seller] asserts that this Court has jurisdiction to hear this case pursuant to 28 USC section 1331, which dictates that the 'district courts shall have original jurisdiction of all civil actions arising under the Constitution, laws, or treaties of the United States.' Specifically, Defendant [seller] contends that the contract claims at issue necessarily implicate the CISG, because the contract is between parties having their places of business in two nations which have adopted the CISG treaty. The Court concludes that [seller's] place of business for the purposes of the contract at issue and its performance is Burnaby, British Columbia, Canada. Accordingly, the CISG applies. Moreover, the parties did not effectuate an 'opt out' of application of the CISG. Finally, because the Court concludes that the CISG preempts state laws that address the formation of a contract of sale and the rights and obligations of the seller and buyer arising from such a contract, the well-pleaded complaint rule does not preclude removal in this case.

A. FEDERAL JURISDICTION ATTACHES TO CLAIMS GOVERNED BY THE CISG

Although the general federal question statute, 28 USC at 1331(a), gives district courts original jurisdiction over every civil action that 'arises under the ... treaties of the United States,' an individual may only enforce a treaty's provisions when the treaty is self-executing, that is, when it expressly or impliedly creates a private right of action. The parties do not dispute that the CISG properly creates a private right of action. Therefore, if the CISG properly applies to this action, federal jurisdiction exists.

B. THE CONTRACT IN QUESTION IS BETWEEN PARTIES FROM TWO DIFFERENT CONTRACTING STATES

The CISG only applies when a contract is 'between parties whose places of business are in different States.' If this requirement is not satisfied, [seller] cannot claim jurisdiction under the CISG. It is undisputed that [buyer's] place of business is Santa Clara County, California, USA. It is further undisputed that during the relevant time period, [seller's] corporate headquarters, inside sales and marketing office, public relations department, principal warehouse, and most of its design and engineering functions were located in Burnaby, British Columbia, Canada. However, [buyer] contends that, pursuant to Article 10 of the CISG, [seller's] 'place of business' having the closest relationship to the contract at issue is the United States.

...

[Buyer emphasises] the purchase orders submitted by [buyer] to Unique Technologies, a nonexclusive distributor of [seller's] products. [Buyer] asserts that Unique acted in the United States as an agent of [seller], and that [buyer's] contacts with Unique establish [seller's] place of business in the US for the purposes of this contract.

... [Buyer] provides no legal support for this proposition. To the contrary, a distributor of goods for resale is normally not treated as an agent of the manufacturer. Agency results 'from the manifestation of consent by one person to another that the other shall act on his behalf and subject to his control, and consent by the other so to act.' [Buyer] has produced no evidence of consent by [seller] to be bound by the acts of Unique. To the contrary, [seller] cites the distributorship agreement with Unique, which expressly states that the contract does not 'allow Distributor to create or assume any obligation on behalf of [seller] for any purpose whatsoever.' Furthermore, while Unique may distribute [seller's] products, [buyer] does not allege that Unique made any representations regarding technical specifications on behalf of [seller]. Indeed, Unique is not even mentioned in the Complaint. To the extent that representations were made regarding the technical specifications of the ASICs, and those specifications were not satisfied by the delivered goods, the relevant agreement is that between [buyer] and [seller]. Accordingly, the Court finds that Unique is not an agent of [seller] in this dispute. [Buyer's] dealings with Unique do not establish [seller's] place of business in the United States.

[Buyer's] claims concern breaches of representations made by [seller] from Canada. Moreover, the products in question are manufactured in Canada, and [buyer] knew that [seller] was Canadian, having sent one purchase order directly to [seller] in Canada by fax. [Buyer] supports its position with the declaration of Anthony Contos, [buyer's] Vice President of Finance and Administration, who states that [buyer's] primary contact with [seller] 'during the development and engineering of the ASICs at issue ... was with [seller's] facilities in Portland, Oregon.' The Court concludes that these contacts are not sufficient to override the fact that most if not all of [seller's] alleged representations regarding the technical specifications of the products emanated from Canada. Moreover, [buyer] directly corresponded with [seller] at [seller's] Canadian address. [Buyer] relies on all of these alleged representations at length in its Complaint. In contrast, [buyer] has not identified any specific representation or correspondence emanating from [seller's] Oregon branch. For these reasons, the Court finds that [seller's] place of business that has the closest relationship to the contract and its performance is British Columbia, Canada. Consequently, the contract at issue in this litigation is between parties from two different Contracting States, Canada and the United States. This contract therefore implicates the CISG.

C. THE EFFECT OF THE CHOICE OF LAW CLAUSES

[Buyer] next argues that, even if the Parties are from two nations that have adopted the CISG, the choice of law provisions in the 'Terms and Conditions' set forth by both Parties reflect the Parties' intent to 'opt out' of application of the treaty. Article 6 of the CISG provides that 'the parties may exclude the application of the Convention or, subject to Article 12, derogate from or vary the effect of any of its provisions.' 15 USC App, Art 6. [Seller] asserts that merely choosing the law of a jurisdiction is insufficient to opt out of the CISG, absent express exclusion of the CISG. The Court finds that the particular choice of law provisions in the 'Terms and Conditions' of both parties are inadequate to effectuate an opt out of the CISG.

Although selection of a particular choice of law, such as 'the California Commercial Code' or the 'Uniform Commercial Code' could amount to implied exclusion of the CISG, the choice of law clauses at issue here do not evince a clear intent to opt out of the CISG. For example, [seller's] choice of applicable law adopts the law of British Columbia, and it is undisputed that the CISG is the law of British Columbia. Furthermore, even [buyer's] choice of applicable law generally adopts the 'laws of' the State of California, and California is bound by the Supremacy Clause to the treaties of the United States. Thus, under general California law, the CISG is applicable to contracts where the contracting parties are from different countries that have adopted the CISG. In the absence of clear language indicating that both contracting parties intended to opt out of the CISG, and in view of [seller's] Terms and Conditions which would apply the CISG, the Court rejects [buyer's] contention that the choice of law provisions preclude the applicability of the CISG.

D. FEDERAL JURISDICTION BASED UPON THE CISG DOES NOT VIOLATE THE WELL-PLEADED COMPLAINT RULE

The Court rejects Plaintiff [buyer's] argument that removal is improper because of the well-pleaded complaint rule. The rule states that a cause of action arises under federal law only when the [buyer's] well-pleaded complaint raises issues of federal law. Anticipation of a federal preemption defense, such as the defense that federal law prohibits the state claims, is insufficient to establish federal jurisdiction. Even where both parties concede that determination of a federal question is the only issue in the case, removal is improper unless the Plaintiff's complaint establishes that the case 'arises under' federal law.

It is undisputed that the Complaint on its face does not refer to the CISG. However, Defendant [seller] argue[s] that the preemptive force of the CISG converts the state breach of contract claim into a federal claim. Indeed, Congress may establish a federal law that so completely preempts a particular area of law that any civil complaint raising that select group of claims is necessarily federal in character.

It appears that the issue of whether or not the CISG preempts state law is a matter of first impression. In the case of federal statutes, 'the question of whether a certain action is preempted by federal law is one of congressional intent. The purpose of Congress is the ultimate touchstone.' Transferring this analysis to the question of preemption by a treaty, the Court focuses on the intent of the treaty's contracting parties.

In the case of the CISG treaty, this intent can be discerned from the introductory text, which states that 'the adoption of uniform rules which govern contracts for the international sale of goods and take into account the different social, economic and legal systems would contribute to the removal of legal barriers in international trade and promote the development of international trade.' The CISG further recognizes the importance of 'the development of international trade on the basis of equality and mutual benefit.' Id. These objectives are reiterated in the President's Letter of Transmittal of the CISG to the Senate as well as the Secretary of State's Letter of Submittal of the CISG to the President. The Secretary of State, George P Shultz, noted:

> Sales transactions that cross international boundaries are subject to legal uncertainty—doubt as to which legal system will apply and the difficulty of coping with unfamiliar foreign law. The sales contract may specify which law will apply, but our sellers and buyers cannot expect that foreign trading partners will always agree on the applicability of United States law ... The Convention's approach provides an effective solution for this difficult problem. When a contract for an international sale of goods does not make clear what rule of law applies, the Convention provides uniform rules to govern the questions that arise in making and performance of the contract.

The Court concludes that the expressly stated goal of developing uniform international contract law to promote international trade indicates the intent of the parties to the treaty to have the treaty preempt state law causes of action.

V. Conclusion

For the foregoing reasons, Plaintiff [buyer's] Motion to Remand is DENIED ...

... ...

This extract illustrates the simple fact that the CISG cannot be ignored and that ignorance of the CISG can result in unnecessary expenses for clients, courts and entire legal systems.

A further point needs to be noted. The CISG only applies to the sale of goods and, pursuant to Article 3, sales where the party who orders the goods supplies a substantial part of the material, or where the obligation of the party furnishing the goods consists to a great extent in the supply of labour or other services. Thus, for example, if A orders a machinery shed and part of the contract is that B not only supplies the material, he also erects the shed, the question of whether or not the CISG applies depends on the split between the cost of material and the costs of labour. If labour is the preponderant part of the total contact cost, the CISG does not apply. The word 'preponderant' has often been interpreted by courts as meaning more expensive. For example, the Swiss Appellate Court Zug noted:

> Apart from being obliged to effect delivery, [seller] had an obligation to install the stove. Such contracts generally fall within the scope of application of the CISG since the installation is often of only minor relevance when compared to the whole transaction volume. Even if, pursuant to [seller]'s offer, the installation took three days for a technician, this does not imply that the installation should be regarded as more expensive than the delivered good itself. Therefore, the present dispute is to be governed by the provisions of the CISG. The question of applicable law must be settled *ex officio*. Thus, it is irrelevant that [buyer] did not contest the applicability of the CISG.[30]

2.4.2 Basic considerations

2.4.2a Formation of contract

Interpretation

Before the details of the CISG can be discussed it is imperative to understand that the CISG cannot be interpreted with the tools available within the domestic system. Instead, the CISG incorporates its own interpretative article. Article 7 states:

> (1) In the interpretation of this Convention, regard is to be had to its international character and to the need to promote uniformity in its application and the observance of good faith in international trade.
>
> (2) Questions concerning matters governed by this Convention which are not expressly settled in it are to be settled in conformity with the general principles on which it is based or, in the absence of such principles, in conformity with the law applicable by virtue of the rules of private international law.

This article contains important, if not mandatory, rules regarding the application as well as the interpretation of the CISG.

Article 7(1) contains two basic rules. As the CISG is international in character, the first mandate is to 'promote uniformity in its application'. This simply provides that any interpretation of a contract must be undertaken free from any recourse to domestic

30 Switzerland, 19 December 2006, Appellate Court Zug, available at [http://cisgw3.law.pace.edu/cases/061219s1.html].

law and principles. Simply put, academic writing and international judgments form the authoritative base to resolve any ambiguities. Of interest is a judgment of the German Federal Supreme Court. It noted:

> The Court of Appeal's legal starting point was correct, namely that the merits of the purchase price demand at issue in the proceeding are governed by provisions of the CISG because both contract parties are domiciled in different contract states (Art 1(1)(a) CISG). However, insofar as the Court of Appeals refers to the Panel judgments of April 16, 1969 (BGHZ 52, 51), in analysing the question whether, at the time the risk passed, the delivered meat conformed with the contract within the meaning of Arts 35, 36 CISG, it ignored the fact that these decisions were issued before the CISG went into effect in Germany and refer to § 459 BGB. The principles developed there cannot simply be applied to the case at hand, although the factual position—suspicion of foodstuffs in trans-border trade being hazardous to health—is similar; that is so because, in interpreting the provisions of CISG, we must consider its international character and the necessity to promote its uniform application and the protection of goodwill in international trade (Art 7(1) CISG). The provisions of the CISG are, therefore, generally autonomous, ie, by themselves and within the overall context of the Convention, without recourse to the rules developed regarding the standards of the non-uniform national laws.[31]

Unfortunately, in Australia most cases misinterpret or misapply Article 7(1). For instance, in *Playcorp Pty Ltd v Taiyo Kogyo Limited*[32] the defence first argued correctly that Japan is not a signatory to the CISG, which makes Article 1(1)(a) inapplicable. However, as the defendant submitted to a Victorian court and hence to Victorian domestic law, Article 1(1)(b) should be applied and thus the CISG was the governing law. The plaintiff and the court, however, directly breached the mandate expressed in Article 7 by using terms contained in s 19 of the *Goods Act 1958* (Vic), such as 'fitness for purpose' and 'merchantable', as opposed to terms contained in the CISG. The Court noted specifically:

> It was not suggested that there was any material difference or inconsistency between the provisions of art 35 and s 19(a) and (b) and because of that and the way the case was conducted, it is unnecessary to consider whether there is. Counsel proceeded on the basis that there was no material difference or inconsistency.[33]

Such ethnocentric views are not in line with the international document. The 'dualism' of legal principles has been influenced by transplantations of legal documents as well as conventions and treaties. Transplantation is simply the 'taking over' of either a law of a country or a particular text in a convention and adapting it to domestic situations. To that end legal principles have influenced directly or indirectly the way contracts are and need to be interpreted. One example will briefly illustrate the transplantation effects on our domestic system, namely the Warsaw Convention. It is now established that in certain circumstances where a law has been transplanted, techniques other than the ones explored in Australia can be used.

The Australian High Court has recognised that the 'goal' of international law is the mandate of uniformity. It is encouraging to note that the High Court understands

---

31 Germany, 2 March 2005, Federal Supreme Court [http://cisgw3.law.pace.edu/cases/050302g1.html].

32 [2003] VSC 108 (24 April 2003).

33 At 235.

that uniformity of law is an important feature which contributes towards certainty and predictability in international trade. In a domestic matter the High Court noted: 'decision must be reached by this court with close attention to any relevant developments of international law, including decisions of the municipal courts of other states parties'.[34]

The Australian High Court went even further and clearly stated that 'no differentiation could be drawn on the basis that it was not obligatory for Australia to apply the language of the Warsaw Convention to domestic carriage by air within Australia'.[35]

The mere fact that the Warsaw Convention was transplanted into Australian domestic law was sufficient for the High Court to abandon ethnocentric interpretation in favour of an international one. Arguably, a reason not to adopt an international interpretation would be difficult to maintain and would run contrary to the objective of certainty.

The second important article in relation to the interpretation of contracts is Article 8, which must be read in conjunction with Article 7. Whereas Article 7 basically mandates the way the CISG must be interpreted, Article 8 takes a micro view, namely it explains how contractual dealings between parties need to be interpreted.

Simply stated, Article 8 negates the parol evidence rule of the common law, and establishes that pre-contractual, contractual and post-contractual statements and conduct can be taken into consideration when interpreting a contract. This article is a very important one as it lays the cornerstone of contractual obligations. It states:

> (1) For the purposes of this Convention statements made by and other conduct of a party are to be interpreted according to his intent where the other party knew or could not have been unaware what that intent was.
> (2) If the preceding paragraph is not applicable, statements made by and other conduct of a party are to be interpreted according to the understanding that a reasonable person of the same kind as the other party would have had in the same circumstances.
> (3) In determining the intent of a party or the understanding a reasonable person would have had, due consideration is to be given to all relevant circumstances of the case including the negotiations, any practices which the parties have established between themselves, usages and any subsequent conduct of the parties.

The key criterion embedded within Article 8 is that the intention of the parties must be understood by all, or at least the other party should have been aware of that intent. Article 8(2) in essence reflects the parol evidence rule, as the interpreter will consider the objective intent of the parties. This article makes it clear that the reasonable person test is applied only if the other party is not aware or could not have been aware.

This was confirmed in *Guang Dong Light Headgear Factory Co Ltd v ACI International, Inc*, where the court noted:

> The plain language of the CISG requires the Court to evaluate a party's subjective intent, so long as the other party was aware of that intent. Otherwise, paragraph two of article 8 applies. ACI argues that despite the plain language of the sales contracts, the subjective intent

34 *Air Link Pty Limited v Paterson* [2005] HCA 39 (10 August 2005) at [40].

35 Ibid at [49].

> of the parties was to treat these forms as mere confirmations of orders between ACI and China Pearl.[36]

Subsection (3) simply describes the relevant circumstances the interpreter can rely upon in order to determine the intent of the parties, namely the negotiations, practices they have established, trade usage and, most importantly, subsequent conduct of the parties.

The leading case on this point is *MCC-Marble Ceramic Center v Ceramica Nuova D'Agostino.*[37] The facts of the case are simple: a buyer unfamiliar with the Italian language orally negotiated a contract in English, and signed the seller's standard agreed terms, which were written in Italian. Under the signature, in Italian, was a note indicating that the buyer was also agreeing to be bound to the terms on the reverse side of the order.

In interpreting Article 8, the court noted that the criterion in Article 8(1) was not met as the buyer was not aware, nor could it have been aware, of the conditions on the reverse side of the order form. The court noted:[38]

> article 8(3) of the CISG expressly directs courts to give 'due consideration ... to all relevant circumstances of the case including the negotiations ...' to determine the intent of the parties. Given article 8(1)'s directive to use the intent of the parties to interpret their statements and conduct, article 8(3) is a clear instruction to admit and consider parol evidence regarding the negotiations to the extent they reveal the parties' subjective intent ...

The court endorsed the position that 'the parol evidence rule is not viable in CISG cases in light of Article 8 of the Convention'.[39]

It must be remembered that in common law the textual approach is slowly being replaced by the contextual one. In other words, the parol evidence rule is not as strictly applied as it has been in the past, as the courts have realised that the parol evidence rule—that is, the textual approach—does not reflect the actual intent of the parties. By eliciting the objective as well as the subjective intent of the parties, the CISG gives true meaning to the contractual obligations of the parties.

Creation of a contract

Unlike the common law, the CISG does not include 'consideration' or the 'intention to create legal relations' in its regime, and there is no reference to a statute of frauds or to the parol evidence rule.[40] Most of these omissions are filled in by other parts of the CISG, such as Article 8, which allows (for the purposes of determining the intent of a party) for all relevant circumstances related to the formation of the contract to be taken into consideration; and Article 11, which allows a contract to be concluded or evidenced without need for 'writing.' Furthermore, the CISG has also embedded good faith as a principle in its regime. Good faith not only instructs the courts and tribunals to interpret

---

36 United States, 28 September 2007, Federal District Court [http://cisgw3.law.pace.edu/cases/070928u2.html]. See also *MCC-Marble Ceramic v Ceramica*, United States, Eleventh Circuit Court of Appeals, *Federal Reporter, Third Series*, Vol 144, p 1384 (1988).

37 United States, Eleventh Circuit Court of Appeals, Federal Reporter, Third Series, Vol 144, p 1384 (1988).

38 Ibid at para 19.

39 Ibid at para 20.

40 See P Winship, 'Formation on International Sales Contracts under the 1980 Vienna Convention', in *International Lawyer 1-18* (1983), also available at [www.cisg.law.pace.edu/cisg/biblio/winship3.html].

the CISG in good faith, it also extends to the parties using good faith in their dealings. This is reinforced by Article 8, which mandates that not only objective intent of the parties, but also subjective intent, needs to be taken into consideration when interpreting contractual relations.

Under the CISG, an effective offer must be followed by an effective acceptance in order to form a contract. In other words, the CISG follows the civil law rather than the common law model, without entirely abandoning common law principles. The method of gap filling pursuant to Article 7(1) is well known in the civil law tradition where, whether statutorily provided for or informally applied, resorting to the general principles is a well-known method for filling gaps within the system. In the common law tradition, this concept is more difficult to see in action, but is not unknown. For example, s 1–103 of the US Uniform Commercial Code (UCC) provides that 'unless displaced by the particular provisions of [the UCC], the principles of law and equity ... shall supplement [the UCC] provisions'. As noted, the phrase 'principles of law and equity' has been 'understood to refer to the general body of case law'.[41]

The important point to note is that the CISG has not 'invented' a new law, but forged a compromise between the civil law and the common law. The CISG is broad in its language rather than detailed because its general principles—which are to be found within the four corners of the CISG—can be used as tools to fill the gaps. This also makes the CISG more adaptable to diverse factual situations.

Offer

The CISG, like any other system of law, distinguishes between an offer and a mere communication between business people, which in common law terms may be called an invitation to treat. The rules as contained in Articles 14 and 15 do not elaborate on what an invitation to treat is, but Article 14 supplies the test as to what constitutes an offer. Hence the simple solution is that if a communication does not pass the test as set down in Article 14, it is simply not an offer.

Article 14 states: 'A proposal for concluding a contract addressed to one or more specific persons constitutes an offer if it is sufficiently definite and indicates the intention of the offeror to be bound in case of acceptance'. Therefore a proposal only needs to include an identification of a person or persons, a clear identification of the goods, the quantity and the price in order to be termed an offer. Taking Article 8 into consideration it is not surprising that Article 14(1) also notes that the key criteria do not need to be expressly stated but can be elicited by implication from the conduct of the parties.

The offer becomes effective when it reaches the offeree pursuant to Article 15. This rule is no different from equivalent rules in most legal systems. However, the CISG does not indicate what is meant by 'reaching the offeree' specifically in cases of electronic communications. In such cases, a gap exists that needs to be filled by domestic law and in this case by the relevant *Electronic Transaction Act*. It may very well be the case that an offer reaches the offeree when it enters the server of the other party and not when

41 JO Honnold, *Uniform Law for International Sales Under the 1980 United Nations Convention*, 3rd edn, Kluwer Law International, The Hague, 1999, p 102.

it is downloaded on a particular computer. This may have a bearing on revocations or withdrawals of offers if there is a dispute as to timing.

Withdrawal, revocation and rejection of offers

The simple rule is that an offer can be revoked before it reaches the offeree. Under Article 15(2), this rule even applies to irrevocable offers, as long as the withdrawal reaches the offeree before or at the same time as the offer. Timing is simply a matter of factual determination, and not a rule of law.

Under Article 16(2), an offer cannot be revoked if a fixed time for acceptance has been set. (This deviates from the common law, as the granting of a fixed time is not a separate contract supported by consideration.) Again, the actions of the parties—whether subjectively or objectively determined—will indicate if an irrevocable offer has been sent or not. If the offeree is under the belief that the offer is irrevocable and the offeror knows or ought to have know this fact, and the offeree acts in reliance on the offer, then it cannot be revoked. Therefore, the offeree simply has to wait until either the fixed time has lapsed or the offeree rejects the offer pursuant to Article 17.

It is important to note that the CISG has brought together the differences of the common law and civil law systems. It can be argued that the CISG, as with other principles, has avoided favouring one system in preference of the other by adopting the common basis of both systems and avoiding the differences. As stated above, the common law views the granting of extra time as a new contract requiring consideration, and in French law, 'although revocation of an offer is permitted ... the offeror is bound to indemnify the offeree or to pay damages in case or revocation'.[42]

Acceptance

The rules as to acceptance can be found in Article 18. The first sentence of Article 18(1) makes it clear that the acceptance does not have to be in writing, but can be expressed by the conduct of the offeree. However, the conduct of the offeree is further defined in the second sentence, which states that 'silence or inactivity does not in itself amount to acceptance'.[43] Thus, while the CISG does not state that silence amounts to acceptance, at the same time it has not reproduced the rule as found in *Felthouse v Bindley* (more accurately that one cannot impose an obligation on another to reject an offer).[44] Whether silence or inactivity amounts to an acceptance needs to be resolved by the factual matrix of a case and in taking note of Articles 8 and 9.

An acceptance only becomes effective when it reaches the offeror within the time fixed, or at least within a reasonable time. This takes the opposite view to the common law postal rule, where acceptance is effective as soon as it is posted. The question as to the meaning of 'reaches' the address is addressed in Article 24.

---

42 G Eörsi, in *Bianca-Bonell Commentary on the International Sales Law*, GiuffrèMilan, 1987, p 154.

43 For interpretation, see *United Technologies International Inc Pratt and Whitney Commercial Engine Business v Magyar Légi Közlekedési Vállalat* (Málev Hungarian Airlines), Hungary, Metropolitan Court of Budapest, 1992, Case No 3.G.50.289/1991/32.

44 (1862) 142 ER 1037.

The question of reasonable time[45] has been fixed as depending on the mode of communication. Therefore an oral offer must be accepted immediately, unless Articles 8 or 9 again indicate that specific circumstances allow for a different interpretation of 'reasonable time'. Furthermore, in accordance with practices established by the parties or usage, an acceptance of the offer can be indicated by actually performing part of the contract, such as dispatching goods or paying the price, without having to give notice of acceptance first.

Withdrawal of acceptance

An acceptance can be withdrawn as long as the notification of withdrawal reaches the offeror prior to the indication of acceptance. Therefore, the withdrawal of the acceptance must reach the offeror before the acceptance itself, otherwise the withdrawal might constitute an unjustifiable revocation and therefore a breach on the part of the offeree.

Battle of forms

Article 19 deals with a very difficult issue: an acceptance that does not match the offer. It has been argued that Article 19 conforms to the mirror image rule (that is, that an offer must be accepted exactly without modifications—in other words, the acceptance must be a 'mirror image' of the offer). However, if the reply to the offer does contain additions, that in itself does not amount to a counter offer. The additions or variations must materially alter the terms of the offer in order to be classed as a counter offer. Article 19(3) is of assistance as it lists conditions that do materially alter the terms of the contract: price, payment, quality and quantity of the goods, place of delivery and time of delivery, extent of one party's liability to the other, and the settlement of disputes. However, this list is not exhaustive. The article uses the words 'amongst other things', indicating that the facts of each case must be taken into consideration in order to determine whether the purported acceptance in fact constitutes a counter offer.

The problem appears to arise mainly in cases where one party submits its standard terms and the other party responds by referring to its own standard terms. In the end, the question is which terms are contained in the contract. Case law on this issue seems to suggest two main doctrines: the 'last shot' and the 'knockout'. According to the last shot doctrine, the last document in the exchange of offers and counter offers is the document controlling the terms of the deal; while the knockout doctrine compares the the terms of the seller and the terms of the buyer, and only the matching terms become part of the contract. These approaches are discussed in more detail below.

Another approach suggested by some authors and case law would consider the issue as a question of validity subject to Article 4. This approach is however very limited.

The following extract from the widely cited case of *Filanto, SpA v Chilewich International Corp*[46] illustrates the problem and compares the CISG approach to that of the US UCC. In the case, the plaintiff (Filanto, an Italian shoe manufacturer) brought suit against a New York export–import firm (Chilewich) as a result of a contract signed by the defendant's London-based agent (Byerly Johnson) with the Soviet Union's Foreign Economic Association (Raznoexport) for the supply of a certain number of

---

45 Article 20 gives more details as to how the 'period so fixed' has to be calculated. It also addresses the issues of official holidays and non-business days.

46 United States, District Court, Southern District of New York, Federal Supplement, vol 789, p 1229 (1992).

shoes. The contract contained an arbitration clause, with Moscow the chosen seat of the arbitration. Chilewich and Byerly Johnson met with Filanto, presumably to negotiate a purchase to fulfil the Russian Contract, and subsequently sent Filanto the following:

> Attached please find our contract to cover our purchase from you. Same is governed by the conditions which are enumerated in the standard contract in effect with the Soviet buyers [the Russian contract], copy of which is also enclosed.

Filanto claims to have replied and specifically excluded the arbitration clause, but Chilewich claims not to have received the reply. Chilewich later sent Filanto a memorandum of understanding that again referred to the arbitration clause, to which Filanto did not immediately respond. Chilewich nevertheless opened a letter of credit in Filanto's favour, and Filanto eventually signed and returned the memorandum of understanding; however, in a covering letter Filanto stated that it would not be bound by the arbitration clause (among other clauses in the Russian contract). Filanto sent the goods and Chilewich accepted delivery. Chilewich received a second order, but claimed the boots were defective and therefore did not purchase the remaining boots to fulfil the order. Filanto filed suit in a New York court.

Filanto, SpA v Chilewich International Corp

United States, District Court, Southern District of New York, Federal Supplement, vol 789, p 1229 (1992)

[The law] to be applied in this case is found in the United Nations Convention on Contracts for the International Sale of Goods (the 'Sale of Goods Convention'). This Convention, ratified by the Senate in 1986, is a self-executing agreement which entered into force between the United States and other signatories, including Italy, on January 1, 1988 ... Since the contract alleged in this case most certainly was formed, if at all, after January 1, 1988, and since both the United States and Italy are signatories to the Convention, the Court will interpret the 'agreement in writing' requirement of the Arbitration Convention in light of, and with reference to, the substantive international law of contracts embodied in the Sale of Goods Convention.

Not surprisingly, the parties offer varying interpretations of the numerous letters and documents exchanged between them. The Court will briefly summarize their respective contentions.

Defendant Chilewich contends that the Memorandum Agreement dated March 13 which it signed and sent to Filanto was an offer. It then argues that Filanto's retention of the letter, along with its subsequent acceptance of Chilewich's performance under the Agreement—the furnishing of the May 11 letter of credit—estops it from denying its acceptance of the contract. Although phrased as an estoppel argument, this contention is better viewed as an acceptance by conduct argument, eg, that in light of the parties' course of dealing, Filanto had a duty timely to inform Chilewich that it objected to the incorporation by reference of all the terms of the Russian Contract. Under this view, the return of the Memorandum Agreement, signed by Filanto, on August 7, 1990, along with the covering letter purporting to exclude parts of the Russian Contract, was ineffective as a matter of law as a rejection of the March 13 offer, because this occurred some five months after Filanto received the Memorandum Agreement and two months after Chilewich furnished the Letter of Credit. Instead, in Chilewich's view, this action was a proposal for modification of the March 13 Agreement. Chilewich rejected this proposal, by its letter of August 7 to Byerly Johnson, and the August 9 fax by Johnson to Italian Trading SRL, which communication Filanto acknowledges receiving. Accordingly, Filanto under this interpretation is bound by the written terms of the March 13 Memorandum Agreement; since that agreement incorporates by reference the Russian Contract containing the arbitration provision, Filanto is bound to arbitrate.

Plaintiff Filanto's interpretation of the evidence is rather different. While Filanto apparently agrees that the March 13 Memorandum Agreement was indeed an offer, it characterizes its August 7 return of the signed Memorandum Agreement with the covering letter as a counteroffer. While defendant contends that under Uniform Commercial Code § 2-207 this action would be viewed as an acceptance with a proposal for a material modification, the Uniform Commercial Code, as previously noted does not apply to this case, because the State Department undertook to fix something that was not broken by helping to create the Sale of Goods Convention which varies from the Uniform Commercial Code in many significant ways. Instead, under this analysis, Article 19(1) of the Sale of Goods Convention would apply. That section, as the Commentary to the Sale of Goods Convention notes, reverses the rule of Uniform Commercial Code § 2-207, and reverts to the common law rule that 'A reply to an offer which purports to be an acceptance but contains additions, limitations or other modifications is a rejection of the offer and constitutes a counteroffer'. Although the Convention, like the Uniform Commercial Code, does state that non-material terms do become part of the contract unless objected to, Sale of Goods Convention Article 19(2), the Convention treats inclusion (or deletion) of an arbitration provision as 'material', Sale of Goods Convention Article 19(3). The August 7 letter, therefore, was a counteroffer which, according to Filanto, Chilewich accepted by its letter dated September 27, 1990. Though that letter refers to and acknowledges the 'contractual obligations' between the parties, it is doubtful whether it can be characterized as an acceptance.

...

Since the issue of whether and how a contract between these parties was formed is obviously related to the issue of whether Chilewich breached any contractual obligations, the Court will direct its analysis to whether there was objective conduct evidencing an intent to be bound with respect to the arbitration provision.

The Court is satisfied on this record that there *was* indeed an agreement to arbitrate between these parties.

There is simply no satisfactory explanation as to why Filanto failed to object to the incorporation by reference of the Russian Contract in a timely fashion. As noted above, Chilewich had in the meantime commenced its performance under the Agreement, and the Letter of Credit it furnished Filanto on May 11 itself mentioned the Russian Contract. An offeree who, knowing that the offeror has commenced performance, fails to notify the offeror of its objection to the terms of the contract within a reasonable time will, under certain circumstances, be deemed to have assented to those terms. The Sale of Goods Convention itself recognizes this rule: Article 18(1), provides that 'A statement made by or other conduct of the offeree indicating assent to an offer is an acceptance'. Although mere 'silence or inactivity' does not constitute acceptance, Sale of Goods Convention Article 18(1), the Court may consider previous relations between the parties in assessing whether a party's conduct constituted acceptance, Sale of Goods Convention Article 8(3). In this case, in light of the extensive course of prior dealing between these parties, Filanto was certainly under a duty to alert Chilewich in timely fashion to its objections to the terms of the March 13 Memorandum Agreement—particularly since Chilewich had repeatedly referred it to the Russian Contract and Filanto had had a copy of that document for some time.

There are three other convincing manifestations of Filanto's true understanding of the terms of this agreement. First, Filanto's Complaint in this action, as well as affidavits subsequently submitted to the Court by Mr Filograna, refer to the March 13 contract: the Complaint, for example, states that 'On or about March 13, 1990, Filanto entered into a contract with Chilewich…' These statements clearly belie Filanto's post hoc assertion that the contract was actually formed at some point after that date. Indeed, Filanto finds itself in an awkward position: it has sued on a contract whose terms it must now question, in light of the defendant's assertion that the contract contains an arbitration provision. This situation is hardly unknown in the context of arbitration agreements.

Second, Filanto did sign the March 13 Memorandum Agreement. That Agreement, as noted above, specifically referred to the incorporation by reference of the arbitration provision in the Russian Contract; although Filanto, in its August 7 letter, did purport to 'have to respect' only a small part of the Russian Contract, Filanto in that very letter noted that it was returning the March 13 Memorandum Agreement '*signed for acceptance*'. Exhibit A to November 28 Filograna Affidavit (emphasis added). In light of Filanto's knowledge that Chilewich had already performed its part of the bargain by furnishing it the Letter of Credit, Filanto's characterization of this action as a rejection and a counteroffer is almost frivolous.

Third, and most important, Filanto, in a letter to Byerly Johnson dated June 21, 1991, explicitly stated that 'the April Shipment and the September shipment are governed by the Master Purchase Contract of February 28, 1989 [the Russian Contract]'. Furthermore, the letter, which responds to claims by Johnson that some of the boots that were supplied were defective, expressly relies on section 9 of the Russian Contract—another section which Filanto had in its earlier correspondence purported to exclude. The Sale of Goods Convention specifically directs that 'in determining the intent of a party … due consideration is to be given to … any subsequent conduct of the parties', Sale of Goods Convention Article 8(3). In this case, as the letter post-dates the partial performance of the contract, it is particularly strong evidence that Filanto recognized itself to be bound by all the terms of the Russian Contract.

In light of these factors, and heeding the presumption in favor of arbitration, which is even stronger in the context of international commercial transactions, the Court holds that Filanto is bound by the terms of the March 13 Memorandum Agreement, and so must arbitrate its dispute in Moscow.

… … …

Although the last shot doctrine is a construction of common law, civil law courts have also relied on the doctrine. For example, in the Austrian case of *Conveyor Band*,[47] the court used the last shot doctrine to determine the applicable terms of the contract. The facts of the case are simple. As the court noted:

The case at hand was characteristic because:

- First, [seller] had made an offer based on its standard terms;
- Thereupon, [buyer] had placed an order based on its partially conflicting standard terms; and,
- Finally, [seller] had confirmed the order once again based on its standard terms.

47 Austria, 23 March 2005, Oberlandesgericht [Appellate Court] Linz [http://cisgw3.law.pace.edu/cases/050323a3.html].

> This is a situation in which [buyer] had accepted the deliveries and the [seller]'s invoices (which again made reference to [seller]'s standard terms) without further contesting or negotiating the validity of [seller]'s standard terms.[48]

The court looked at the last writing and determined it to be a counter offer. The only problem then was to determine whether the counter offer was accepted or not. The court correctly applied Article 8 to determine this issue.

An important point needs to be made here, which this case specifically highlights. If conflicting standard form contracts need to be investigated, the first point to note is whether the question is one of contract formation or whether it is one of contract interpretation. If the main issue hinges on whether or not a counter offer has been accepted, then the question of which terms are accepted has been resolved. If on the other hand both parties believe that a contract has been validly concluded, but the main issue hinges on which of the terms are applicable, then the question will arise as to whether the last shot or knockout rule will be used to settle the dispute.

As mentioned above, according to the last shot approach, the last document in the exchange of offers and counter offers is the document controlling the terms of the deal. The logic behind this is that the party who had the opportunity to object to unwanted terms but failed to do so is deemed to have accepted them.

The knockout approach on the other hand starts from a different premise. The two disputed documents—that is, the terms of the seller and the terms of the buyer—are compared and only the matching terms become part of the contract. Any terms that are 'knocked out' are treated as missing terms and are governed by the fall-back position, namely the domestic law, which is in this case the CISG. It is left to the courts to decide whether the absence of fundamental terms such a quality and price renders the contract void, or whether the CISG can supply the answer. Case law on this issue tends to be tainted by domestic law, with the inevitable result that the mandate set by Articles 7 and 8 is not followed. However, the leading case in relation to the knockout rule is the decision of the German *Bundesgericht* in the *Powdered Milk* case,[49] which is not so tainted. The court examined the facts closely and noted correctly:

> The question to what extent colliding general terms and conditions become an integral part of a contract where the CISG applies, is answered in different ways in the legal literature. According to the (probably) prevailing opinion, partially diverging general terms and conditions become an integral part of a contract (only) insofar as they do not contradict each other; the statutory provisions apply to the rest (so-called 'rest validity' theory). Whether there is such a contradiction that impedes the integration, cannot be determined only by an interpretation of the wording of individual clauses, but only upon the full appraisal of all relevant provisions.[50]

Many commentators consider the last shot approach as being 'caustic and unfair'. In support of the last shot theory, however, other commentators emphasise that the approach, although rigid, 'in addition to legal certainty … provides adequate protection

---

48 Ibid.

49 Germany, 9 January 2002, Supreme Court [http://cisgw3.law.pace.edu/cases/020109g1.html].

50 Ibid.

to the parties in the majority of cases and permits enterprises to more perfectly plan their standardized transactions'.[51] The wording of Article 19(2) seems to favour this interpretation.

As with all matters within the CISG, however, the four corners approach to statutory interpretation will dictate that, in the end, Articles 8 and 9 will have a determinative influence on the question whether terms in the purported acceptance materially alter the offer. As Professor Schlechtriem pointed out:

> [As the CISG lacks] provisions on the control on standard form contracts, I think the one tool that may come to grips with standard contracts is Art 8(2). It enables the court to ignore fine print, which is contradictory, vague, or difficult to understand by using a 'reasonable person similarly situated' standard.[52]

A further point has been considered by case law and academic writing, namely whether it is not only necessary to alert the other party of the standard terms and conditions, but also to make the text available to the other party. As one commentator notes: 'According to the almost certainly dominant position, making the text available is indispensable for the valid incorporation'.[53] A point that still has not been clarified is whether the party relying on the standard form needs to make the text available in such a language that it satisfies the user's duty to inform.[54] However it must be added that 'to make the text available' cannot be extended to physically sending the text, as long as the other party has the potential to acquire the text and has been made aware that standard terms and conditions apply. After all, the other party has a duty to investigate once they have been made aware of terms and conditions.

The above observations suggest that parties should exercise due care in drafting a contract. The CISG is helpful in filling obvious gaps, but in the end it is the intent and care of the parties—especially in the context of the battle of the forms—that will avoid the need for legal action to resolve the problem of formation of a contract.

2.4.2b Performance of the contract

Obligations of the seller

The obligations of the seller and the buyer are treated in two different chapters of the CISG, despite the fact that some of the remedies and obligations are the same. It is useful, however, to deal with the obligations of the parties separately. The CISG obviously needs

---

51 M del Pilar Perales Viscasillas, '"Battle of the Forms" under the 1980 United Nations Convention on Contracts for the International Sale of Goods: A Comparison with Section 2-207 UCC and the UNIDROIT Principles', (2001) 10 *Pace Int'l L Rev* 97, 104–36, also available at [www.cisg.law.pace.edu/cisg/biblio/pperales.html].

52 See P Schlechtriem, 'Uniform Sales Law—The Experience with Uniform Sales Law in the Federal Republic of Germany', (1991/92) 1/12 *Jurisdik Tidskrift*, also available at [http://cisgw3.law.pace.edu/cisg/biblio/schlech2.html].

53 See A. Janssen, 'The Application of the CISG in Dutch Courts', in F Ferrari (ed), *Quo Vadis CISG: Celebrating the 25th Anniversary of the United Nations Convention on Contracts for the International Sale Of Goods*, Sellier European Law Publishers, Munich, 2005, p 144.

54 Ibid, p 145.

to take into account that goods will pass national borders, and hence two obligations on the part of the seller are very important. First, the seller must deliver the goods and hand over the documents, thereby transferring the property in the goods to the seller. As pointed out in Chapter 3 of this book, the bill of lading acts among other things as a document of title, and hence if the bill of lading is not handed over the buyer cannot take possession of the goods (Articles 30–34). Second, the goods must conform to the quality and description required by the contract and must be free of third party claims (Articles 35–44).

It follows from the above that in situations where any of the obligations are not adhered to, there is a breach of contract. The remedies that flow from such a breach are described in Articles 45–52.

Delivery of goods and handing over of documents

Article 30 is a generic article and is the first in a series that explains the obligations of the buyer to 'deliver the goods hand over any documents and transfer the property in the goods to the buyer'. As noted previously, the CISG must be read within its four corners and, despite the fact that Article 30 notes that the property of the goods must be transferred to the buyer, all legal obligations emanating from this obligation have to be resolved by domestic law pursuant to Article 4(2).

The CISG also reiterates the universal principles that primacy must be given to the contract and that the CISG is the fall-back position. Article 9 of the CISG assists in this matter, as this article specifically points out that parties are bound by usage and trade terms. Therefore shipping terms (such as Incoterms) and other trade terms must be consulted first if the parties have made use of them. In addition, any problems regarding the form or validity of the documents, or the proper way to deliver documents, is within the scope of the shipping terms or other trade terms. However, failure to deliver the documents—being a breach of contract—will be governed by the CISG.

Article 31 fills the gap if no particular delivery point is contained in the contract. Correctly, the CISG distinguishes between carriage of goods, and where no carriage of goods is contemplated.

In cases of carriage of goods, the obligation of the seller is to hand the goods over to the first carrier. Again it must be noted that Article 9—and hence domestic law—will be the primary source of determining the delivery obligations of the seller. Furthermore, Article 32 also needs to be consulted, as it sets out the seller's obligations regarding shipping arrangements.

In all other cases the seller simply needs to place the goods at the buyer's disposal. The question as to the time when the seller needs to deliver the goods is primarily left to the contractual agreements, or is simply fixed as being 'within a reasonable time after the conclusion of the contract', as stipulated in Article 33.

As in most international transactions, the obligations of sellers and buyers regarding possession of the goods are controlled by documents such as the bill of lading. However such obligations are not merely restricted to shipping—they can arise in all other situations, such as while the goods are in possession of the seller. The obligations of sellers and buyers regarding documentary sales, and obligations under carriage of goods, will be discussed in depth in Chapters 4 and 3 respectively. However, note that the CISG simply sets out a fall-back position and suggests a simplified approach to the delivery and handing over of documents.

Conformity of the goods

The basic obligations of the sellers regarding their duty to deliver conforming goods are contained in Article 35. At first glance this appears to be similar to Article 19 of the *Goods Act 1958* (Vic). The Victorian Supreme Court unhelpfully commented:

> It was not suggested that there was any material difference or inconsistency between the provisions of art 35 and s 19(a) and (b) and because of that and the way the case was conducted, it is unnecessary to consider whether there is. Counsel proceeded on the basis that there was no material difference or inconsistency.[55]

The question is not whether there is an inconsistency; the simple fact is the *Goods Act* does not apply. The CISG does not use remedial terms such as 'breach of warranty or condition'. In addition, Article 35 contains an obligation that the goods must be 'packaged in a manner required by the contract'. Also, the remedial regime of Article 35 is different to the one prescribed by s 19 of the *Goods Act*. Furthermore, Article 7 makes it perfectly clear that the CISG cannot be viewed through the lens of domestic law.

In essence, the CISG not only mandates what constitutes conforming goods, but also takes account of distances and therefore added cost to both parties if the goods do not conform to the contract. Hence the CISG makes it clear that buyers must examine the goods and notify the seller of any defects as quickly as possible. Also, in line with the problem of distance and costs, the CISG in Article 37 allows the seller to cure any defects in goods already delivered as long as this does not 'cause the buyer unreasonable inconvenience or unreasonable expense'. It must be remembered that the buyer, as in all other instances, retains the right to claim damages pursuant to Article 74.

The failure to examine the goods within an acceptable period of time results in the buyer being unable to rely on breaches of Article 35. What constitutes an 'acceptable' or 'reasonable' time period has been the subject of many cases. In general, it is considered to be less than two months, unless the defects are latent ones. In essence, the courts and tribunals will look at the facts and determine what is considered to be reasonable. In the case of a delivery of Parma ham before Christmas, the court decided that examination should have been undertaken immediately and not after the festive season, when it was found that the ham was spoiled.[56] Articles 38 and 39 must also be read in conjunction with each other. Buyers wishing to rely on Article 35 must not only examine the goods within a reasonable time, they must also notify sellers of the results of this examination—that is, the exact defect—within a reasonable time.

The onerous and perhaps harsh obligations on the buyer are mitigated by Articles 40 and 44. The seller cannot rely on Articles 38 and 39 if the lack of conformity 'relates to facts of which he knew or could not have been unaware and which he did not disclose to the buyer'. Also, notwithstanding the provisions of Articles 39(1) and 43(1), buyers still

---

55 *Playcorp Pty Ltd v Taiyo Kogyo Limited* [2003] VSC 108 (24 April 2003) at 235, also available at [http://cisgw3.law.pace.edu/cases/030424a2.html].

56 *Ham Case*, Amtsgericht Riedlingen, 21 October 1994, 2C 395/93 [http://cisgw3.law.pace.edu/cases/941021g1.html].

can reduce the price or claim damages (except loss of profit) if they have a reasonable excuse why they did not give the required notice of defects to the seller within a reasonable time.[57]

Breach of the contract

As far as the remedies of the buyer are concerned, the CISG lists the remedies available to the aggrieved buyer in Article 45. Of importance is the fact that the CISG maintains and further explains the difference between a breach of contract and a fundamental breach. Simply put, if there is a breach of a contact, then in essence the contract is still afoot and the aggrieved party can claim remedies as described in Article 45. In other words, that party will be put into the same situation as if the contract had been properly performed. A breach of contract does not terminate the legal relationship between buyer and seller.

A fundamental breach on the other hand terminates the contractual relationship, and the parties revert back to where they were before the contract was entered into.

What constitutes a fundamental breach is explained in Article 25 which states:

> A breach of contract committed by one of the parties is fundamental if it results in such detriment to the other party as substantially to deprive him of what he is entitled to expect under the contract, unless the party in breach did not foresee and a reasonable person of the same kind in the same circumstances would not have foreseen such a result.

Remedies for breach

Article 45 in essence provides the 'roadmap'—that is, it is the logical starting point—for remedies for breach of contract, as subsection (1) notes that this article is available if the 'seller fails to perform any of his obligations'.

Importantly, this article makes it clear that any remedial provisions that are available within the four corners of the CISG are always to be considered in conjunction with damages pursuant to Articles 74–77. Furthermore, subsection (3) makes it clear that a court cannot grant a period of grace to a seller once the buyer resorted to a remedy for breach of contract.

Articles 46–52 set out the remedies alluded to in Article 45. A buyer can therefore simply require performance on the part of the seller or, if the goods do not conform to the contract, require substitute delivery. Substitute delivery is however only allowed if the breach was a fundamental one. In all other cases the contract is still afoot; hence alternative remedies are available, but not substitute delivery. It goes without saying that substitute delivery—even if the contract has been avoided—can only be asked for if the buyer can return the goods in the same condition as they were received; that is, if the buyer can make restitution.

Obligations of the buyer

The third matter to be considered (after delivery and conformity of goods) is the remedies for a breach of the buyer's obligations. The most obvious and important obligation of the buyer is to pay the price and take delivery of the goods.

---

57 Article 44.

Payment of price

As is customary under the CISG, the contractual terms as well as customary matters are to be considered first; but Article 54 makes it clear that the obligation of the buyer extends to taking active steps to discharge the debt. Any non-compliance with this article amounts to a breach of contract. However in some circumstances the price may not have been expressly set, or may be indefinite. In such situations, Article 55 serves as a gap filler and indicates that the parties will be bound to the price normally charged at the time the contract was concluded.

One of the problems that parties experience is when the place of payment has not been stipulated.[58] In the absence of agreement, the CISG designates the place of payment to be the place of business of the seller (Article 57(1)(a)). However, if payment is to be made against documents, then the price must be paid at the place where the documents are to be handed over (Article 57(1)(b)).

Taking delivery

Despite the brevity of Article 60, the responsibilities of the buyer in taking delivery are spelled out clearly. This article must be read in conjunction with Article 31—the seller's obligation to deliver—and hence the buyer's obligation to take delivery does not occur until the seller's obligations are fulfilled under the contract and under Article 31. On the other hand, the seller can also rely on the buyer's obligation to do 'all the acts which could be reasonably be expected of him' (Article 60(a)), which expands the seller's remedies in cases where the buyer does not cooperate with the seller. What these obligations are is usually spelt out in the contract or governed by trade usage. In subsection (b), the simple words 'in taking over the goods' hide important obligations, specifically when the contract involves the carriage of goods. As soon as the buyer takes possession of the goods the risk potentially shifts from the seller to the buyer; alternatively, if the buyer refuses to take delivery, a breach of contract has occurred.

Breach of the contract

It is not surprising that the remedies for breaches of the buyer and the seller are nearly identical, except for the fact that the buyer needs to pay the price and the seller needs to deliver the goods. It is therefore also not surprising that the wording of Article 61 mirrors that of Article 45. The major difference is that the buyer has more remedies available than the seller. This is natural, as the seller's obligations are more complicated— the seller performs the bulk of the obligations between the contractual parties—and can therefore give rise to more remedies. This relationship is reflected in the conflict of laws rules of many domestic systems, which in brief state that in the absence of a contractual clause, the governing law of the contract is the one with which the contract has its real and most important connection, which in many instances is found to be the seller's place of business.

2.4.3 Passing of risk

As mentioned above, pursuant to Article 4(2) the CISG does not concern itself with the effect 'the contract may have on the property in the goods sold'. However, also

58 For analysis, see the *Natural Gas Case*, Austria, Supreme Court, 1996, 10 Ob 518/95.

as indicated above, the CISG—like many other domestic laws—sets out the fall-back position in cases where neither the contract nor any other applicable laws are sufficient to resolve the issues.

In international trade, the allocation of risk is nearly always covered by insurance: shipping contracts in general demand that the buyer maintains insurance coverage. In addition, risk allocation is often regulated by Incoterms which, pursuant to Article 6, can be imported to derogate or vary the provisions of the CISG. (It must be noted that terms such as FOB can have a different meaning, and therefore contractual parties must clearly describe which term is applied, such as 'Incoterms 2000'.) However there are instances where the parties have not covered all eventualities regarding passing of risk, and hence the CISG needs to be consulted. In such cases, the passing of risk is governed by Articles 66–70.

Article 66 is self-explanatory as it merely reiterates a common rule, namely that the buyer needs to pay for the goods after the risk has passed to the the buyer, unless of course the buyer can show that the loss or damage is due to an act or omission of the seller.

When goods are either shipped or transhipped, Article 67 sets out the default rule in cases where the place of handing over of the goods is not stipulated. In these cases the risk passes to the buyer once the seller hands the goods over to the first carrier. In all other cases the risk passes once the seller hands the goods over to a carrier at the stipulated place. Furthermore, even if the seller still has the right to control the documents, this does not change the fact that the risk has passed once the seller discharges the duty to hand over goods to a carrier. In other words, the risk is with the party who controls the goods and the documents are merely a means by which payment can be effected. In addition, Article 67 embodies the rule that a buyer only becomes liable—that is, accepts the risk—once the goods are clearly identified.

The CISG also envisages situations where a buyer onsells goods while they are in transit. The default rule is that the risk passes to the ultimate buyer at the time of the conclusion of the contract. However in certain circumstances—not described in the CISG, but left to the courts to determine—the ultimate buyer takes on the risk retrospectively from the time when the documents were handed over to the first carrier.

In circumstances where the goods are not sold in transit or shipped, Article 69 provides that the risk passes to the buyer when the buyer picks up the goods, or the goods are placed at the buyer's disposal.

Article 70 is of importance as it describes situations where the seller has committed a fundamental breach. In short, the buyer retains all rights the buyer would have had irrespective of the fact that the risk of loss has passed already. The reason for this is that the buyer has the right to avoid the contract or can ask for substitute goods (Article 46(2)), hence shifting the risk of loss back to the seller.

2.4.4 Remedies for breach/common provisions

So far, the rights and duties of buyers and sellers, the formation of the contract, the passing of risk the question of what constitutes conformity of goods and what remedies are available in cases of breaches of contracts have all been dealt with taking into consideration whether the provision addresses the buyer or the seller. We now turn to

Articles 71–88 (Chapter V), which contain provisions that are common to the seller and the buyer.

The distinction between a fundamental breach and non-performance of the contract, which has already been highlighted, becomes important again when damages and anticipatory breaches are discussed. This is because the remedial scheme is different, and it must be understood that only under the principle of fundamental breach can a contract be terminated. A breach of contract that is not fundamental does not terminate the legal relationship between buyers and sellers.

Articles 71–88 can be divided into four categories:

- First: matters that need to be taken into consideration if a fundamental breach has occurred;
- Second: remedial matters associated with a breach of contract that does not give rise to avoidance;
- Third: exemptions; and
- Fourth: the obligations in situations where the goods have been delivered, namely the obligation to preserve the goods.

2.4.4a Anticipatory breach and instalment contracts

This chapter of the CISG starts with an important filling of a gap: what happens if there is an anticipatory breach or if there are disputes in relation to instalment contracts. The most important aspect is that a party which suspects an anticipatory breach can suspend performance, but must give the other party the opportunity to respond to their concerns. Suspension is possible for single contracts or instalment contracts. Once the concerns are satisfactorily addressed, performance must continue. However if the suspending party wrongly suspends performance, that party will be in breach of the contract and would need to pay damages.

The difference between Article 71 and 72 lies in the severity of a possible breach. If a party—pursuant to Article 72—is certain that non-performance amounts to a fundamental breach, then that party can avoid the contract. However this would not be the case under Article 71, where the breach is not to be considered fundamental.

In case of the fundamental breach of an instalment contract, Article 73 allows the aggrieved party to cancel one instalment and avoid performance of that instalment only. However, if a party has 'good grounds to conclude that a fundamental breach' of the contract as such will occur, then that party may declare the whole contract avoided.

2.4.4b Damages

The logical question that needs to be answered is what happens if a contract is breached or avoided. Article 74 is to be regarded as the general all-embracing solution to damages, as it explains the concept of calculating damages and can always be relied upon, irrespective of whether the breach is fundamental or not.

Article 74 allows an aggrieved party to claim loss of profit as well as a sum equal to the loss. In other words, the CISG will put the aggrieved party into the same position as if the contract had been properly performed. It can be said that the balance sheet approach is used. Also, damages must be a consequence of the breach and cannot 'exceed the loss which the party in breach foresaw or ought to have foreseen at the time of the conclusion of the contract'. Unfortunately, many common law lawyers and judges are under the mistaken believe that the rule in *Hadley v Baxendale*[59] is embedded in Article 74. This is not correct. *Hadley v Baxendale* stands for the contemplation rule, whereas Article 74 relies on the foreseeability rule.

Controversially, the issue of the inclusion of attorneys' fees into Article 74 has not yet been resolved, In *Zapata Hermanos*[60] a US Appellate Court ruled against the inclusion of legal costs being part of Article 74. This debate is ongoing.

In addition to Article 74, Articles 75 and 76 deal with specific calculations of loss when a contract is avoided, namely where a cover purchase has been made or where the party 'walked away' from their obligations.

If a cover purchase has been made, or the seller has resold the goods, damages are generally calculated by looking at the difference between the contract price and the price of the substitute goods. Furthermore, other damages that fall under Article 74 can still be claimed. If on the other hand no cover purchase was made—that is, the aggrieved party simply walked away from the contract—damages are the difference between the contract price and the current price at the time of avoidance. In addition, other damages can still be claimed under Article 74.

2.4.4c Exemptions

The CISG also recognises two important provisos that come into play if contracts are breached: mitigation and frustration.

The first principle, mitigation, makes sure that the party relying on the breach cannot sit on its hands but must take positive steps to minimise its losses, otherwise the party at fault can reduce the damages by the amount of loss 'by which the loss should have been mitigated' (Article 77). However, the cost of mitigation must be reasonable—in other words, mitigation at all costs is not permitted, and mitigation must be in line with the actual damages claimed. The duty to mitigate applies in all cases (that is, in the case of anticipatory breach or actual breach of a contract).[61]

The second principle, frustration, arises when one party cannot fulfil their obligation due to an impediment beyond their control (Article 79). This principle is similar to but not the same as the common law remedy of hardship or *force majeure*. Care should be taken not to confuse these principles, as under Article 7 the 'homeward trend', or ethnocentric interpretations—that is, the propensity to interpret an international convention in accordance with domestic principles and concepts—have been ruled out.

Three factors must be present in order for a party to claim frustration. First, the failure must be 'due to an impediment beyond his control'; second, at the conclusion of the contract, the impediment could not have reasonably been taken into account;

---

59 (1854) 9 Exch 341.

60 *Zapata Hermanos v Hearthside Baking*, United States, 19 November 2002, Federal Appellate Court [7th Circuit] [http://cisgw3.law.pace.edu/cases/021119u1.html].

61 For more on damages and mitigation, see *Downs Investments Pty Ltd v Perwaja Steel SDN BHD* [2000] QSC 421 (17 November 2000).

and third, again at the time of the conclusion of the contract, the party could not have 'avoided or overcome [the impediment] or its consequences'.[62] Even if there is an impediment beyond the breaching party's control, the CISG only offers limited protection.[63] The aggrieved party cannot claim any damages under Article 74, but is not precluded from relying on any other rights under the CISG.

2.4.4d Restitution

As pointed out above, avoidance releases both parties from their obligations under the contract.[64] However, the CISG recognises the principles of restitution, and the breaching party must account for all benefits it has derived from the contract.[65]

The overarching principle governing avoidance rests on whether restitution of the goods can be made, in substantially the same condition in which they were received. If that is not the case, then avoidance is not possible unless one of the exceptions applies, such as the goods have perished due to their short shelf life.

It follows therefore that goods once delivered must be preserved for the benefit of the other party. Preservation of goods does not mean that they must be stored or warehoused; they can be sold to a third party. Mitigation of losses—that is, Article 77—can also be brought into play.

2.5 Conclusion

The important conclusion is that in Australia the CISG applies to all intemational contracts for the sale of goods. This is because Australia has ratified the convention, and hence the CISG forms part of Australian domestic law. A term such as 'the law of Victoria shall apply' therefore includes the application of the CISG.

The ratification process means that an international convention or treaty has passed through the Australian Parliament in a form identical to that approved by the diplomatic conference. Any changes or reservations can only be made if they are embodied within the convention (for example, Article 96 of the CISG).

Notwithstanding, due to its political nature a convention is rarely a complete statement of the law within one discrete area. The CISG is no exception and therefore gaps exist. The drafters of the CISG accordingly included a definitional article—Article 7—whereby the CISG excludes the application of domestic case law because 'regard is to be had to its international character and the need to promote uniformity in its application'. To this end, only case law dealing with matters covered by the CISG are of persuasive character. Courts and tribunals have been (found to be) erroneous in their assumption that because the CISG tracks domestic law the matter can be proven by the application of domestic

62 For an excellent account, see *Raw Materials Inc v Manfred Forberich GmbH & Co, KG*, United States, 6 July 2004, Federal District Court [http://cisgw3.law.pace.edu/cases/040706u1.html].

63 See *Nuova Fucinati, SpA v Fondmetall International, AB*, Italy, Civil Court of Monza, 1993.

64 Article 81.

65 Article 84.

case law.[66] Article 7 also supplies an 'interpretation ladder' to fill gaps. If a gap cannot be filled by either the interpretation of the provision or by the application of general principles, then it must be filled by the application of domestic law. Conflict of laws rules at the place where jurisdiction is sought will determine the applicable substantive law that supplies the body of law governing the conflict.

It should also be noted that the UNIDROIT Principles can be used to assist in the interpretation of the CISG. The UNIDROIT Principles are only soft laws—they do not form part of our domestic system of law but they can be included in a contract as the governing terms, and then any court or tribunal must take note of the terms and implement them. This is because the contractual terms are the governing rules of any contract. This leads to an important point that needs to be taken into consideration when dealing with contract law: the domestic body of law is only the fall-back position in cases where the contract is silent. The exception is that mandatory laws will 'trump' contractual terms. In all other cases, it is the reverse.

The CISG automatically applies, hence there is no 'opt in' clause; however Article 6 allows the contractual parties to either vary or opt out of the application of the CISG. Unfortunately this happens far too often, as many legal professionals have not appreciated the possibilities the CISG can offer. Even a cursory glance at the CISG will show that the drafters have taken the best principles of the civil as well as the common law and moulded these principles into an easy-to-understand legal formwork. In the formation of contract the 'mirror image' rule has been substantially included, but the common law rule of consideration has not been included.

Perhaps an interesting point to note is Article 16, which states that an offer with a fixed time of response attached cannot be revoked before the time lapses, unlike the common law position, where revocation is possible if the time of response is not supported by consideration—which makes sense considering the international flavour of the CISG, and adds certainty to the dealings of the contractual partners.

This seems to be the hallmark of the CISG, as the drafters have recognised that added distance and costs require definite and easy-to-understand laws that give finality as quickly as possible to a contractual relationship. This is mirrored in the remedies that are available under the CISG should a contract be breached.

Of special significance is the remedy of avoidance. Only when a fundamental breach of a contract has eventuated can a contract be avoided. In all other cases the contract stays afoot and remedies such as damages and loss of profit can be claimed, but not repudiation or cancellation of the contract.

The most important point is that the CISG is a uniform international law and has been ratified by all important trading partners of Australia, with the notable exception of the UK. It makes sense therefore to base contractual relationships on a common base. The question of an information disadvantage is eliminated as both parties are dealing with the same legal framework.

Furthermore the CISG has been written without recourse to technical words and is therefore easily understood. As 'doing business' on the global stage is so much easier

66 See for example J Lookofsky & H Flechtner, 'Nominating Manfred Forberich: The Worst CISG Decision in 25 Years?', (2005) 9(1) *Vindobona Journal of International Commercial Law and Arbitration* 199–210.

in the twenty-first century, it does make sense that businesses can rely on the same legal framework, irrespective of whom they are trading with.

Questions

With regard to the case study at the beginning of this chapter:

1 Which law will apply, French or Australian law? Why?
2 Has John William breached the contract in not delivering the first 10 000 hats 'on or about' January 10? If so, what are the remedies available to Pierre Degas?
3 What are the remedies available to Pierre in relation to the delivery of the wrong batch of hats?
4 When must a buyer ordinarily have to make payment?
5 Would Article 7 of the CISG be of relevance and importance in this case? What jurisprudence would you quote to support your answer?
6 Can you think of any arguments based on Article 8 of the CISG to support your contention in relation to the decision by Pierre to cancel the contract?
7 What are the grounds on which a buyer can reject the goods?
8 Can Pierre cancel the whole contract or only the outstanding deliveries? On what grounds?
9 What actions must Pierre take if he wishes to seek damages, avoid the contract or obtain specific performance?
10 If the contract does not state the place of delivery, where are the goods to be delivered?
11 If a domestic contract contains a clause indicating in brief that it will be governed by the UNIDROIT Principles, does the parol evidence rule apply in the interpretation of the contract?

CHAPTER 3

international carriage of goods by sea

Mr Smith, an Australian manufacturer, enters into a contract to supply 40 000 cartons of Emerald Lager to Mr Longbow a Swedish importer. The cartons are to be packed into four containers. When Mr Longbow opens the containers at his premises he discovers that one container is completely empty, one contains only broken bottles and one is filled with Bear Beer and not Emerald Lager. Only the fourth container is to his satisfaction. An investigation shows that the beer was stolen from the first container while in the bonded warehouse. The bottles were broken in the second container during passage, when the container moved during a storm while on board the carrier's ship, the *SS Goodwill*. Upon inspection of the sales contract, Mr Longbow finds a clause indicating that all disputes between seller and buyer have to be resolved by arbitration, to be held in Singapore. Furthermore, the terms of the contract are: 'FAS. Melbourne Port.'

3.1 Introduction

Shipping is the most common mode of international transport, due predominantly to its ability to carry large and bulky items, and its low cost relative to other forms of transport. By virtue of having no land border—and thus no possibility of using road or rail transport—shipping is by far the most common mode of transporting goods to and from Australia. The other option, which is used mainly for some smaller, expensive and perishable items (for example, fresh, cut flowers), is air freight.

Accordingly, it is useful for every buyer and seller engaged in international trade, as well as every lawyer representing such clients, to understand the basic concepts of shipping and the legal issues raised by shipping contracts. Contracts for the sale and exportation/importation of goods differ from domestic contracts for the sale of goods in several ways. For instance, the question of the governing law should be determined by the parties. While this can be left for the courts to determine, the prudent lawyer (and client) will resolve the issue in the standard form contracts exchanged by the parties. Another concern not often accompanying domestic contracts is the inherent risks associated with distance. Such risks include the fact that in most cases—and almost always if the distance between the exporter and the importing country is great—it will be uneconomical to return the goods to the exporter. Another risk is that the goods are often entrusted into the care of more than one carrier. Moreover, multimodal contracts—that is, contracts which include carriage by road, sea and rail—are increasingly commonplace. It is therefore obvious that one simple international sales contract has several contracts embedded into it.

Above all, the greatest problem faced by international traders is that payment and delivery occur in different countries. Therefore the question of when risk and property pass from the seller to the buyer takes on far greater significance than in domestic contracts. Questions of insurance and who pays for the transport cost are also important problems that need to be settled before goods are shipped or transported to another country. Yet another problem is that some goods are frequently sold and resold over 100 times while the goods are in transit (for example, oil).

Some of the above problems are resolved through Incoterms, which will be discussed in detail at the end of this chapter. However it is sufficient to know at this stage that the two most common Incoterms incorporated into an export contract are FOB and CIF. In brief, under an FOB ('free on board') contract the seller's obligations end after the seller arranges the loading of the goods onto a nominated vessel. Under a CIF ('cost, insurance and freight') contract, on the other hand, sellers are not only obliged to take out insurance, they also need to pay and arrange for carriage. Both forms of contract regulate two important and distinctive characteristics of an export contract; namely the payment against documents and the transfer of risk on loading.

The relationship between the shipper and carrier needs to be acknowledged as well. Simply put, the shipper (which in most cases is the seller of the goods) will contract with a carrier to transport the goods to the port of destination. The bill of lading is the contractual document that in part regulates this relationship. However the underpinning minimum terms and conditions are contained within international conventions and have been given force in Australia by the *Carriage of Goods by Sea Act 1991* (Cth) (COGSA).

All the parties involved in an export transaction—that is, the buyer, the seller, the banks, the carriers and the shipper—must take account of their varied and different concerns in the same transaction. The negative domino-like effect of the contract can only be avoided if all parties think laterally across all interrelated contracts. Above all, it must be noted that the bill of lading, or any other similar document, expresses the contractual terms of the transport of goods. It is thus not an overstatement to say that the entire transaction hinges on and is tied in with the bill of lading. An understanding of the pivotal character of the bill of lading is essential to any lawyer representing an importer or exporter, no matter how small the transaction.

It needs to be understood that the shipping of goods—and in fact the carriage of goods by any mode—creates many relationships (between, at least, the seller, buyer, carriers, insurer and banks), along with the corresponding legal obligations and rights.

This chapter attempts to explore the fundamental issues present when trading goods internationally through reference to the carriage of goods by sea, including when things do not eventuate as planned. The chapter begins by defining and analysing the charterparty and bill of lading, two concepts central to the international carriage of goods by sea. It then explains the purpose of the *Carriage of Goods by Sea Act*, before briefly highlighting the salient points regarding marine insurance. The Incoterms conclude this chapter.

3.2 Charterparties and bills of lading

The bill of lading is an integral part of the carriage of goods, and it is essential that traders and their legal representatives understand the role it plays in international trade as well as the legal issues it can raise. However, as carriage of goods in many instances is carried out by a ship under charter, it is useful to understand the nature and type of charterparty before examining the bill of lading. Such knowledge will assist traders to understand who in effect is the carrier or the owner of the ship, as well as giving the exporter the possibility of chartering a ship in its own right.

3.2.1 Charterparties

A charterparty is a formal, written contract between the owner of a vessel and a person/company (the 'charterer') desiring to hire either the entire vessel or parts thereof. The charterparty will set forth the terms of the arrangement (rate of freight, ports of call, etc) as well as specifying whether the hiring is for a specific voyage or a particular time. There are two differing types of charterparty arrangements. The first is a demise charter, where the charterer hires the ship including the crew. In such a circumstance, the crew and the master are entirely under the control of the charterer. In a demise charter, a bill of lading signed by the master binds the charterer but not the owner. In all other circumstances, called non-demise charterparties, the master and the crew are under the control of the ship owner.

As mentioned, the charterer can hire the vessel for a specific voyage or for a particular length of time. Under a voyage charter, it is obviously in the interest of the charterer to pay only for the period of time when the ship is actually under sail. However, the vessel owner will want to be paid for the total time the ship is under charter. A period where the ship is 'idle' is referred to as laytime, and if laytime is outside the contractual terms, demurrage (damages) has to be paid to the vessel owner.

In a voyage charter, the first part of the voyage is the loading voyage, where the ship is required to arrive at a designated port at a fixed date or with reasonable dispatch (note however that the charterer can only nominate what is called a 'safe port'). After the loading operation, the actual carrying voyage commences, followed by the discharging operations. The shipowner must guarantee that the ship is seaworthy and that the owner will proceed without unreasonable deviations. The shipowner also has a duty to get the goods out of the hold, place them on deck or alongside the vessel and provide suitable tackle.

Under a time charter, a ship is hired out for a particular time (as opposed to a specific voyage). The time is calculated from the point at which the vessel and its crew are placed at the charterer's disposal until the vessel has been redelivered. A shipowner must use reasonable diligence to ensure that the vessel is fit for ordinary cargo service unless a specific ship has been hired, such as an oil tanker.

The question of redelivery has attracted some judicial interest, because if a voyage is delayed, an exact redelivery time will not be possible. Hence in *The Peonia*[1] it was held that a reasonable margin or tolerance is applied to cater for unforeseen but reasonable delays.

1 [1991] 1 Lloyd's Rep 100.

3.2.2 Bills of lading

As mentioned above, the bill of lading has four functions: a receipt, a document that transfers constructive possession, a document of title and, finally, evidence of the carriage contract. In addition, the bill of lading also contains clear and precise information as to the goods that are loaded onto the vessel, as well as contractual terms of the carriage.

The bill of lading originated around the fourteenth century, and by the eighteenth century acquired its current characteristics. Historically, the liability of the carrier to transport goods safely from port to port was strictly subject to common law exemptions, such as acts of God, public enemies (that is, acts of war) and inherent vice. The nineteenth century saw a shift of power from the shipper to the carrier. Freedom of contract allowed carriers to take advantage of their bargaining power, and some carriers included provisions in the bill of lading providing themselves with total immunity, even from negligent actions. It goes without saying that shippers, banks and underwriters resisted, and some nations drafted legislation that provided a degree of protection for the aggrieved parties.[2] This piecemeal attempt at legalisation, however, did not enhance the shipowners' economic ambitions. Eventually, a meeting by the shipowners, shippers, banks and underwriters in 1921 resulted in the drafting of the Hague Rules, and in 1924, the Hague Convention was signed in Brussels.

The Hague Convention aimed to introduce uniform rules relating to bills of lading and establish a protection for cargo owners. Although ratified by many nations, including Australia, the Convention was only of limited utility and contained many gaps. Throughout the Commonwealth, the common law filled these gaps. It is unsurprising, therefore, that the Convention was subject to further negotiations, two of which resulted in the Hague-Visby Rules and the Hamburg Rules.

As there is no uniform shipping law, a certain degree of complexity is apparent in every law that relates to shipping. Conflict of law rules further complicate the situation, as legislation in some nations includes mandatory rules as to the applicability of the legislation. For instance, s 11 of the *Carriage of Goods by Sea Act 1991* (Cth) (COGSA) states that parties to any sea carriage document relating to carriage from Australia to any place outside Australia are 'taken to have intended to contract according to the laws in force at the place of shipment'.

Another point worth noting is that the amended Hague Rules are not a code, and hence the common law may still be applicable.[3] Correspondingly, in Australia the rights and duties of the parties are to be found in the relevant legislation and common law, not in any convention itself. An important point needs to be made in this context—most countries base their domestic laws on the international rules, but do not entirely adopt them as governing law. This is due to a number of factors, and the broader point can be illustrated by the Australian legislative process and end result.

2 A notable example of such legislation was the *Harter Act 1893* (US).

3 Thus, for instance, the carrier or shipowner may be liable under common law, despite being protected by the amended Hague Convention under excepted perils. The carrier is considered to be a common carrier as described under common law, and may also be liable under tort for negligent acts.

In Australia, conventions are not automatically applied as 'the law of the land', despite the fact that Australia (through the executive arm of government) may have signed the convention. In order to become law, it must be ratified; that is, legislation must be passed through parliament. Federal Parliament can only ratify a convention if it has the relevant powers to enact the resulting laws. The most important Heads of Power in the Commonwealth Constitution are contained in s 51(i) (the trade and commerce power), s 51(xxix) (the external affairs power) and s 76(iii) (conferring 'admiralty and maritime' jurisdiction upon the Commonwealth). It is thus clear that the power of the Commonwealth is limited to overseas and interstate trade and commerce. However, the power of the Commonwealth can be extended to certain intra-state issues if the same issues are affecting international and inter-state matters. Furthermore, s 109 of the Constitution is clear on the issue that Commonwealth legislation takes precedence over state legislation.[4]

Based on the authority of the Constitution, Federal Parliament passed and enacted the relevant rules on the carriage of goods in COGSA. COGSA covers many aspects of shipping. However, despite ratifying the Hague Rules, COGSA does not simply adopt one of the conventions—it is instead a hybrid of the Hague and Hague-Visby Rules (with the common law also remaining a relevant consideration).[5] However, Article 2A(1) of COGSA requires that the minister must from time to time review whether the amended Hague Rules should be replaced by the Hamburg Rules. This has not yet occurred.

Thus, while the legislative framework of carriage of goods by sea is largely governed by conventions and treaties, the conventions are ratified by many countries and these documents are never the exact governing law of nations. That being said, the maritime laws of the important trading nations do not greatly differ from each other, as each is generally based on the Hague Convention, the Hague-Visby Rules or the Hamburg Rules. The differences stem mainly from the inception of the three different international conventions. The following extract compares several provisions of the two most recent conventions, the Hague-Visby Rules and the Hamburg Rules.

Scott M Thompson, 'The Hamburg Rules: Should They Be Implemented in Australia and New Zealand?'

4 (1992) *Bond Law Review* 168 at 171–7

The Australian *Carriage of Goods by Sea Act 1991* (COGSA), incorporating the Hague-Visby Rules, applies to contracts of carriage evidenced by a bill of lading 'or any similar document of title'. However a receipt as a document of title will not be sufficient to trigger the Hague-Visby Rules unless it has the character of a bill of lading. The Hamburg Rules have a wider application as they

4 As far as the physical boundaries are concerned, the state boundary finishes at the low-water mark.

5 It must also be noted that COGSA also included the Hamburg Rules, however at this stage the Hamburg Rules have not been ratified yet by Federal Parliament and are not in force in Australia. It is doubtful whether this will ever happen considering the introduction of the new UNCITRAL set of enlarged rules in relation to the international carriage of goods by sea.

apply to sea carriage regulated by 'any contract whereby the carrier undertakes against payment of freight to carry goods by sea from one port to another'.

There is no mention of documents of title. This should simplify the often contentious question as to the qualification of the documents relating to a pending dispute under the Hague-Visby regime. Even where there is no bill of lading the Hamburg Rules, unlike the Hague-Visby Rules, are able to apply as all they require is a contract of carriage. Under Article 2.3 the Hamburg Rules are expressly withdrawn from application to charterparties, or to a bill of lading issued directly to a charterer. Consequently the Hamburg Rules enjoy wide application. In Australia, inter-state and exported sea-borne cargo are covered by the Hague-Visby Rules, while the Hague Rules have similar application in New Zealand. This is in contrast to the scope of the Hamburg Rules which apply to outbound, as well as inbound cargo.

The Hamburg Rules were drafted for wider application than the existing Hague-Visby Rules. Did this concept extend to the definition of 'goods'? Under both sets of rules, 'goods' are widely defined. The COGSA expressly excludes live animals and deck cargo from being 'goods' under the Hague-Visby Rules. One change in respect to the definition of 'goods' is probably tailor-made for New Zealand and Australia. The Hamburg Rules define 'goods' as including live animals, which is beneficial to both countries which have recently developed a major export in live sheep trade with nations in the Middle East.

Interpretation under the Hamburg Rules of 'deck cargo' has arguably been left to the courts. Article 9.1 prohibits the rules from applying to deck cargo but then allows exceptions if there is an agreement with the shipper, or it is the usage of a particular trade, or it is required by statutory rules or regulations. Article 9.2 establishes that the 'agreement' must be in the appropriate clause or statement in the bill of lading or on the contract of carriage.

The main problem is with the exception of 'usage'. Since the term 'usage in the trade' is not defined, it is one area that will have to be clarified by the courts in resulting litigation. It would appear a straight forward task to nominate the sorts of cargo and containers that are acceptable in the trade for deck cargo. It is puzzling why the Hamburg Convention, when attempting to unify and clarify the risk allocation of carriage of goods by sea, would resort to vague terms such as 'usage' without addressing this issue thoroughly. Overall the Hamburg Rules have expanded on the right to carry deck cargo.

Provisions which determine who is the 'actual carrier' are clearer in the Hamburg Rules than in the current Hague-Visby Rules. The Hamburg Rules make the initial carrier, who is a party under the contract of carriage, responsible for the whole carriage even if it was performed by another subsequent carrier. This was designed to alleviate the problems that a shipper faced in determining the party liable for damages where there were numerous carriers, owners and charterers involved in the carriage of goods. Obviously the carriers objected to this provision but took solace in the fact that under Article 11 if any on-carrier was named in the bill of lading and the damage occurred when the second carrier had responsibility of the goods, the first mentioned carrier was exempt from liability. The carriers argued that they are not always in a position to state the on-carrier on the bill of lading in time to notify the shipper. Neither provision stops the initial carrier, as defendant in an action for loss or damage to cargo, joining the other carriers involved as co-defendants or as third parties to the action. Although expensive, it would allow the courts to apportion fault. Once the 'actual carrier' is determined, it is necessary to consider during which stages of the carriage the carrier is exposed to liability.

The Hague-Visby Rules apply from 'tackle to tackle', that is when the goods are physically aboard the carrier's vessel, whereas the Hamburg Rules extend the liability of the carrier to the entire period he is in charge of the goods. This is defined as 'being from the time the goods are received from the shipper or responsible third party, until the goods have been delivered to the consignee or responsible third party'. This extension of liability with which the carrier is faced under the Hamburg Rules not only codifies, but expands, the common law position that extended the Hague-Visby Rules to apply to goods under a bill of lading for an entire voyage. This entails the goods being covered while at dock and while being transferred to another vessel during part of the original voyage.

An example of this application is in the case of *The Bunga Teratsai*[6] where a container of prawns was stolen after it was discharged from the vessel onto a wharf in Sydney. The carrier's liability under the Hague Rules had ceased once the container was discharged from the vessel. Article 1 of these rules made the carrier liable from the time the goods were loaded to the time the goods were discharged, which permitted the carrier to rely on this exclusion as a successful defence. If similar facts arose under the Hamburg Rules then the decision would possibly be reversed for the carrier is liable for the loss of the goods until they are delivered to the consignee in accordance with the contract of carriage.

The carrier, when not able to deliver the goods to the consignee, is able to 'place them at the disposal of the consignee in accordance with the contract, or with the law, or with the usage of the particular trade applicable at the port of discharge'. An attempt to define 'usage of the particular trade' is another area of potential litigation. The ideals of the Hamburg Convention for uniform rules are diluted by allowing vastly differing local laws such a large scope for possible application at loading and discharge of the goods.

Probably the most fundamental change envisaged by the Hamburg Rules is in determining the general liability of the carrier. Under Article 3 of the Hague-Visby Rules the carrier has to 'exercise due diligence' at the beginning of the voyage to make the vessel seaworthy. In effect Article 5.1 of the Hamburg Rules extends this requirement of 'seaworthiness' to the entire voyage which, in light of modem technology and commercial reality, is a reasonable change. The basis of liability under the Hamburg Rules is Article 5.1 which clearly establishes a single test for carrier liability:

> The carrier is liable for loss resulting from loss or damage to the goods, as well as from delay in delivery, if the occurrence which caused the loss, damage or delay took place while the goods were in his charge as defined unless the carrier proves that he, his servants or agents took all measures that could reasonably be required to avoid the occurrence and its consequences.

This basis of liability brings the Hamburg Rules into line with the evolving trend established in other transport conventions towards carrier liability based on negligence. The burden of proof rests with the carrier to establish that he took all reasonable care to avoid the loss or that it was due to circumstances beyond his control such as 'an act of God'.

The actual 'list' of defences available to the carrier under Article 4.2 of the Hague-Visby Rules is discarded in the Hamburg Rules. Although the English courts in particular have restricted the attempts of the carrier's indiscriminate use of these defences, the loss of the defences of negligent navigation, or negligent management of the ship under the Hamburg Rules will be the ones most

6 (1989) 167 CLR 219.

sorely missed by the carriers. The defences are an archaic principle found in no other law of transport. The other defences under the Hague-Visby Rules still exist but are contained in the 'single sentence' test for liability in Article 5.1 of the Hamburg Rules as quoted above.

This was one area where the lobby groups of shippers and carriers partially agreed with each other that the reforms would increase litigation. Under the Hague-Visby Rules a majority of claims are settled without litigation as each party to the dispute can justify their position with reference to one of the defence provisions in Article 4 without the need to refer to negligence. One view is that under the Hamburg Rules, such disputes, except for the obvious cases, will involve litigation to determine if the carrier was negligent by not taking all measures reasonably necessary to avoid the occurrence and its consequences. It was argued by the carriers, that under this 'new' burden of proof, fifty years of litigation dealing with the cause and effect on cargo damage would now be re-litigated.

One obvious exception to the above progressive changes to the Hague-Visby Rules is Article 5.4 of the Hamburg Rules dealing with the defence of fire which arguably favours the carrier. Under the Hague-Visby Rules the carrier had to establish that he had used due diligence in making the vessel seaworthy prior to his invoking the exception of fire. The burden of proof as established in the new standard of carrier liability however is reversed. Instead of the carrier having to pro[ve] that 'he, his servants or agents took all measures that could reasonably be required to avoid the occurrence and its consequences,' the shipper, who does not have the evidence, has the burden of proof. Article 5.4 provides that the carrier is only liable for the loss of, or damage caused to, goods or delay in their delivery caused by fire if the claimant proves that the fire arose from the fault or neglect of the carrier or his servants or agents. There seems no logical reason why the defence of fire was treated differently by the convention.

Article 5.4(b) allows the claimant to carry out a 'survey' into the cause and handling of the fire in the preparation of his case against the carrier. The type of survey to be used is described as being 'in accordance with shipping practices' which is another qualification that could well be open to abuse and resulting litigation.

The Hamburg Rules distinguish between damage and loss from delay, liability for damage and loss caused by negligence. Damages for delay, often extremely difficult to establish, are recoverable under the Hague-Visby Rules. They were treated in a similar fashion to claims for damages, that is the plaintiff had the burden to establish that the loss was direct and foreseeable. Under the Hamburg Rules, unless the carrier takes 'all measures that could reasonably be required to avoid' the delay, he would be liable for damages. This leads to the question as to how the Hamburg Rules determine what is a 'delay' and how to determine 'damages'.

First, 'delay' under Article 5.2 occurs if the 'goods have not been delivered at the port of discharge provided for in the contract of carriage by sea within the time expressly agreed upon'. If no time was agreed upon, then the relevant time period is the time in which it would be reasonable to require a diligent carrier to complete the contract. If the goods are not delivered within 60 days after the expiry time on the contract of carriage then the goods are deemed to be lost. Secondly, under the Hague-Visby Rules, there was no limit on the damages recoverable for delay so long as they were not too remote under principles of the common law. At first the shippers probably celebrated the fact that under the provisions of the Hamburg Rules they now had 'delay' as a recognised head of damage. Any such celebrations should have been short lived as the negotiating power of the carriers enabled them to limit this liability for delay.

The Hamburg Rules limit liability for delay to 'an amount equivalent to two and a half times the freight payable for the goods delayed, but not exceeding the total freight payable under the contract of carriage of goods by sea'. There were initial industry concerns as to the interpretation of the amount of damage payable if perishable goods had been merely delayed, or if they had suffered damages as a consequence of delay. This does not seem to be an issue as the Rules provide that if both damage and delay occurs, the aggregate liability cannot exceed the liability in respect of damaged goods except as otherwise agreed. One could be excused for believing initially that this reform favours the shipper but, because of the limitation of damages, it appears to favour the carrier.

Finally, it must be noted that UNCITRAL is attempting to harmonise the various regimes adopted throughout the world through the production of a modern uniform law. In fact, the process is quite far advanced, with the draft Convention on Contracts for the International Carriage of Goods Wholly or Partly by Sea likely to be presented to the General Assembly of the United Nations for conclusion sometime in 2009. If the Convention becomes widely adopted, the governing laws will soon be altered and become more uniform throughout trading nations. On the other hand, if the Convention is not adopted by all (or even the majority of) states, the addition of the Convention will introduce another set of laws and only serve to further widen the gap between the law and practice in trading nations.

3.2.2a Receipt

The bill of lading usually contains the following information:

- Condition and quantity of the goods
- The date they are loaded onto the vessel
- The name of the vessel
- Ports of lading and discharge.

The shipper—that is, the current owner of the goods—will prepare the bill of lading and have it signed by the master of the ship. Thus, the bill of lading also serves as the record for the carrier as to the content of the ship's cargo.

A bill of lading can be issued before the goods are loaded onto the vessel; that is, it can be handed over to the carrier at the carrier's warehouse. Such a bill is normally marked as 'received for shipment', but the issue is that the buyer would not be sure that the goods were actually loaded in good order onto the ship. A bill marked 'received for shipment' can however be endorsed as a 'shipped' bill of lading, once the goods are loaded onto the ship.

Many buyers and certainly all issuing banks involved in a documentary transaction require a 'shipped', 'clean' bill of lading (see Chapter 4). A clean bill of lading is one that is marked by the ship's mate or master to the effect that they have received the goods in apparent good order and condition. By contrast, a 'claused' bill of lading is when a notation is added at the time the goods are loaded indicating that a discrepancy exists between the goods loaded and the goods listed on the bill. Claused bills of lading are generally unacceptable to third parties.[7] The remainder of this section will analyse select issues related to receipt.

7 See further *M Golodetz & Co, Inc v Czarnikow-Rionda Co, Inc (The Galitia)* (1978) 2 All ER 726 (QB).

Receipt as to quantity

As seen above, the carrier will note on the bill of lading the quantity of the goods received (among other things). Under common law, the bill of lading is prima facie evidence that the goods were shipped. The carrier has the burden of proof to show differently and it is a question of fact, not one of probability. However, as the bill of lading is a contractual document, a carrier can include clauses such as 'weight and quantity unknown' or 'said to weigh X tonnes', which in effect decrease or even exclude the carrier's liability. As an example, if the shipper indicates that it handed 300 tonnes over to the carrier, but the bill of lading contains a 'weight unknown' clause, the courts would indicate that the carrier did not accept the weight as being 300 tonnes, but only took that weight for the purpose of calculating the cost carriage.

Under Article 3(3)of COGSA, the shipper is entitled to demand the issuance of a sea carriage document (which includes a bill of lading). However the carrier is under no obligation to issue a sea carriage document if not requested to do so. The bill of lading must show, among other things, the identification marking of the goods, the number of packages or quantity or weight (as the case may be), and that the goods are in apparent good order and condition. Article 3(5) also notes that the shipper 'is deemed to have guaranteed to the carrier the accuracy at the time of shipment'. It is therefore not surprising that Article 3(3) also allows the carrier to refuse to note the condition on a bill if the carrier is not satisfied as to the accuracy of the information supplied by the shipper. The carrier is also obliged to note only one of the features and can deny knowledge of the other. To illustrate, if a bill of lading notes that 5000 sacks of sugar were loaded 'weight of 25 000 kilograms for the calculation of the freight only', the carrier's obligation is only to the 5000 sacks taken on board—it does not extend as far as the accuracy of the weight is concerned.

Receipt as to condition

The shipowner or the shipowner's agent is merely required to make a statement as to the apparent condition of the goods as far as the shipowner can judge by an outward inspection.[8] Today, with increased containerisation, the inspection is often simply as to the condition of the container, and not the condition of the goods inside the container. Masters are understandably under some pressure, as they obviously wish to avoid liability by noting any defects on the bill of lading, but also understand that a bank requires a clean bill of lading in order to finance the contract. In cases where the bill of lading differs from the actual state of the goods, the shipowner is estopped from denying the truth of the statement. The justification of the estoppel is that the assignee relied on the statement of the bill of lading, hence the principle of detrimental reliance applies. However, as pointed out previously, the estoppel only applies to those defects that would have been apparent upon a diligent and reasonable inspection. The contract of shipment as evidenced by the bill of lading can also contain clauses that exempt the shipowner from liability, such as 'condition unknown'.

As noted above, Article 3(3) allows the shipper to demand the issue of a bill indicating the condition of the goods. Pursuant to Article 3(8), clauses in the bill of lading relieving the master of liability are null and void. The master is, however, allowed

8 See for example *The David Agmashenebeli* [2003] 1 Lloyd's Rep 92 at 104ff.

to make 'marginal endorsements' to describe the actual condition of the goods. This would be the case if, as an example, the shipper informs the master that the goods are in good condition while still on the wharf, but before loading the goods are damaged. As the bill would already be issued, a marginal endorsement would clarify the matter for the master. The shipper may pressure the carrier to issue a clean bill of lading and give an assurance of indemnity, but if the carrier is aware that the condition of the goods does not correspond with the 'clean bill', then the indemnity is worthless as the carrier has committed an act of fraud. The situation is different if the carrier is not aware of the bad condition of the goods, as long as a reasonable inspection would not have revealed the damage to the goods. Pursuant to Article 3(5) the carrier can only rely on the shipper's assurance (and rely on the indemnity) in relation to 'marks, numbers, quantity and weight'.

3.2.2b Documents transferring constructive possession

Two types of bills need to be distinguished: the 'bearer bill' and the 'order bill'. Goods carried under a bearer bill can only be delivered to the named person, whereas an order bill means that anybody holding the bill of lading can gain possession of the goods. The result is that transferring constructive possession of the goods requires a different method. In the case of a bearer bill, transfer can only be effected by endorsement on the back of the bill; that is, a new bearer or name needs to be inserted or an endorsement in blank is effected. An endorsement in blank turns a bearer bill into an order bill. Therefore constructive possession occurs automatically once the bill of lading is handed to another person. The carrier as bailee must hand the goods only to the person who rightfully holds the bill of lading. As bills of lading are usually issued in sets of three or more, the carrier is best protected against misdelivery by handing the goods over only against production of an original bill of lading.

3.2.2c Document of title

As transport by ship is lengthy, sellers or buyers on occasion need to finance the purchase of goods or wish to take advantage of price fluctuation while the goods are still at sea. Bills of lading were, therefore, devised as negotiable instruments; that is, they operate as documents of title. However, only order bills are capable of operating as documents of title. Any other bills of lading (such as 'bearer bills' or 'straight bills' or, as they are sometimes called, 'waybills') lack the negotiable quality. Bills of lading are transferred by endorsement, but as they represent the goods the transferee gets 'no better title' to the goods than that held by the transferor.

Possession of the bill of lading can be equated as being the same as having actual physical possession in the following circumstances:

- First, any holder of the bill is entitled to have the goods delivered to the designated court of discharge.
- Second, the holder can merely endorse the bill and hence transfer ownership in the goods.
- Third, the bill of lading can also be used as security for a debt.

Holder of bill of lading

Endorsement, and hence transfer of ownership, must comply with four requirements:

- First, the bill is transferable on its face; that is, it must be an order bill and not a bearer bill.
- Second, the goods must be in transit; that is, the goods have left the original seller's possession and cannot be delivered yet to the ultimate buyer.
- Third, the bill of lading can only be assigned to another person by a person who holds good title over the goods.
- Fourth, the endorsement must be with the intention of transferring ownership in the goods.

Thus, in order to transfer ownership the parties must intend to have title of the goods pass to another person. Ownership will not be transferred where there is no intention for the ownership to pass (such as an in-house movement). Ownership will likewise not pass when the bill of lading is merely a temporary security for monies advanced.

Financing a contract of sale

The most common international sales require some sort of finance, unless the buyer and seller are in an established trading relationship. The usual process is that a bank will open a letter of credit. This is more fully explained and analysed in Chapter 4, but it is worth noting here that the process involves the bill of lading, the invoice and the insurance documents being handed over by the seller to the bank. Once this has been done, the bank will then pay the seller. Clearly, the bill of lading is the most important document, as from it the bank can verify all the important matters, such as that the goods have been shipped, and the quality and quantity of the goods. Therefore, a 'shipped bill of lading' is almost always required. As bills of lading are issued in multiple copies, the bank will normally require all copies to be delivered, otherwise it would be possible for another person who holds a copy to obtain the goods.

Contract of carriage

The bill of lading represents the goods during transit and therefore the holder of the bill controls the goods during transit. Furthermore, the holder of the bill is entitled to delivery of the goods at the port of discharge.

3.2.2d Evidence of the contract of carriage

Normally the reverse side of a bill of lading contains the contractual terms. However, it was held in *The Ardennes*[9] that the bill of lading is not in itself a contract between the shipper and the carrier. It is excellent evidence of the terms of the contract, but the contract itself can come into existence before the bill of lading is issued. Any previous arrangements can be produced as evidencing the intentions of the parties. In *The Ardennes* the shipper was assured that the goods (oranges) would be in London on 1 December. The goods arrived late and the carrier could not rely on the terms contained in the bill of lading.

9 [1951] 1 KB 55.

Notwithstanding this, it must be noted that an endorsee will be bound by the terms contained within the bill of lading, and hence the bill of lading is conclusive evidence of the contract of carriage. *The Ardennes* demonstrates that the bill of lading is only prima facie evidence as to the terms of the contract, and that oral evidence can be presented indicating that the contract came into existence before the bill of lading was issued. However, it is not in contention that any third party will be bound by the bill of lading, which is conclusive evidence of the terms of the contract.

3.2.2e Third party reliance on bill of lading terms

Any shipper of goods would be aware that carriers do not usually perform all the obligations themselves. Many activities are subcontracted to independent contractors, for instance stevedoring companies will load and unload ships. Many bills of lading specifically contain clauses to the effect that the carrier reserves the right to subcontract obligations relating to the carriage of goods.

Under the doctrine of privity of contract the subcontractors are often not protected by the clauses in the bill of lading. The shipper can sue the subcontractor directly in tort, but such a situation is not satisfactory for several reasons, the most important one being commercial reality. Once a contract has been agreed to, it is understood that subcontractors will have a part in the performance of the contract and hence it would be inefficient to disturb the balance of the contract.

The courts have used several mechanisms to extend the protection of the original contract to third parties, most notably bailment on terms, the vicarious immunity approach and the Himalaya clause.

Bailment on terms

The leading case is *The Pioneer Container*,[10] where the original carrier subcontracted the carriage to a sister ship. The bill of lading contained a clause entitling subcontracting 'on any terms the whole, or any part, of the carriage, loading, unloading, storing, warehousing or handling' of the goods. The sister ship issued a feeder bill[11] and also included an exclusive Taiwanese jurisdiction clause in the bill. The ship subsequently had an accident and sank; hence the plaintiffs' goods were lost. The defendant (the owner of the sister ship) relied on the exclusive jurisdiction clause.

There was no direct relationship between the plaintiffs and the defendant, and the Privy Council bridged the gap between the two parties by invoking the principle of sub-bailment. There was never any dispute as to the shipper consenting to sub-bailment. The problem simply was whether the plaintiffs were bound by the terms agreed by the head bailor and the sub-bailee. The Privy Council in brief argued that the plaintiffs were so bound, despite the fact that there was no contractual relationship between the plaintiffs and the defendant. The court stated:

> if the effect of the sub-bailment is that the sub-bailee voluntarily receives into his custody the goods of the owner and so assumes towards the owner the responsibility of the bailee, then

10 [1994] 2 AC 324.

11 For an explanation of the feeder bill, see ibid at 324.

> to the extent that the terms of the sub-bailment are consented to by the owner, it can be properly be said that the owner has authorised the bailee so to regulate the duties of the sub-bailee in respect of the goods entrusted to him, not only towards the bailee but also towards the owner.[12]

In effect, the plaintiffs consented to be bound by any terms whatsoever, and therefore they were also bound by the terms of the sub-bailee, as long as they were not unreasonable or unexpected in the context of the carriage of goods. Hence the Privy Council granted the stay and the plaintiffs were bound by the terms, despite the fact that there was no direct contractual relationship between them and the sub-bailee.

The vicarious immunity approach

The Pioneer Container established that the sub-bailee can rely on the terms contained in the sub-bailment as a defence. However the courts have been reluctant to allow the sub-bailee to rely on the terms contained within the head contract. The reason is simple: the sub-bailee is not a party to the contract between the carrier and the shipper. This has been confirmed in *Gadsden v Australia Coastal Commission*,[13] where the Court of Appeal upheld the privity of contract rule and noted that the shipowners in this case could not rely on the bill of lading as they were not party to it.

The Himalaya clause

While the privity rule was adopted, Lord Reid in *Scrutton v Midland Silicones*[14] suggested that an agency relationship between the carrier and a stevedoring company could provide an answer to the problem of allowing stevedores, engaged as independent contractors, to take advantage of the limitation clause in the contract of carriage.

Two important cases illustrate the principle of the Himalaya clause well. In *The Eurymedon*[15] the original bill of lading incorporated an express clause to the effect that any servant, agent or independent contractor would be entitled to protection under the bill of lading, and the carrier was not only contracting on his behalf but also as an agent on behalf of all the named parties in the bill of lading. The Privy Council agreed that the stevedoring company could rely on the benefits and limitations of the bill of lading.

In *The New York Star*[16] the Privy Council upheld the Himalaya clause as expressed in *The Eurymedon*. The court noted:

> the establishment of any new legal principle, as in the finding that in the normal situation involving the employment of stevedores by carriers, accepted principles enable and require the stevedore to enjoy the benefit of contractual provisions in the bill of lading.[17]

This must be contrasted with *The Starsin*.[18] In effect the Himalaya clause in this case extended a wider exemption to the independent contractor than was available to the

---

12 Ibid at 339.

13 [1977] 1 NSWLR 575.

14 [1962] AC 446.

15 [1975] AC 154.

16 [1981] WLR 138.

17 Ibid at 143.

18 [2003] 1 Lloyd's Rep 571.

carrier, and the court held that Article 3(8) of the Hague-Visby Rules rendered that particular clause void.

The Himalaya clause has to be drafted precisely, in order to achieve the stated aim of giving a third party the benefits, despite the fact that they are not a party to the contract. In *The Mahkutai*[19] the question was whether the jurisdiction clause extended to a third party. The court noted:

> [the jurisdiction] clause can be distinguished from terms such as exceptions and limitations in that it does not benefit only one party, but embodies a mutual agreement under which both parties agree with each other as to the relevant jurisdiction for the resolution of disputes. It is therefore a clause which creates mutual rights and obligations. Can such a clause be an exception, limitation, condition or liberty benefiting the carrier within the meaning of the clause?[20]

The court found that it could not, and therefore the third party could not rely on the clause. It is important to understand this distinction when a Himalaya clause is discussed.

3.2.3 Carriage of goods

3.2.3a Introduction

As the bill of lading is a contractual document, a carrier could traditionally exclude any and all of its liabilities, especially if goods were lost or damaged while at sea.

In order to redress the imbalance of bargaining power in the relationship between carrier and shipper, the Hague Rules (and likewise the Hague-Visby and Hamburg Rules) substantially curtailed the absolute power to avoid all liability. In Australia, the carrier's minimum duties—as well as limitations to liability—are contained in COGSA and supplemented by common law rules. In particular, Article 3(8) notes that a clause that purports to widen the protection of the carrier is null and void.

It is important to remember, however, that COGSA does not apply to intra-state sea-carriage (s 10).[21] Section 10 further states that the amended Hague Rules, which apply to contracts made after 31 October 1991, only apply to carriage from a port in one state to a port in another state of Australia, or to a port in a foreign country, as long as the contract is evidenced by a bill of lading or a similar sea carriage document such as a waybill.

In the 2006 update of the Hague Rules, Article 1 supplies the meanings of relevant terms, and these are important when identifying the exact situations in which the amended rules apply. The rules apply to goods of every kind whatsoever except live animals.

'Carrier' is defined as 'including the owner or the charterer who enters into a contract of carriage with a shipper'. The 'period of carriage' is further defined as covering the time 'during which a carrier is in charge of the goods'.

---

19 [1996] 3 WLR 1.

20 Ibid at 13.

21 Several states (not including Victoria) have introduced their own sea carriage of goods legislation: see for example the Tasmanian *Water Carriage Act 1918*.

3.2.3b Carrier's duties

Article 3 of COGSA sets out the duties of the carrier; in particular, the duties to make the ship seaworthy, cargoworthy and to take care of the cargo.

Article 3 points to three important aspects:

- First, in rule 1 the carrier is bound before and at the beginning of the voyage to exercise due diligence.
- Rule 7 explains the duty of the carrier after the goods are loaded.
- Rule 8 importantly points out that any clause or covenants or agreements are null and void if the terms in the contract lessen the liabilities described in Article 3. Simply put, Article 3 sets a minimum standard of liability.

Seaworthiness

At common law the duty of the carrier to provide a ship that is seaworthy was absolute. In Article 3(1), COGSA changed this absolute undertaking to one of exercising due diligence.

The definition of seaworthiness was explored in *The Aquacharm*.[22] In that case, the ship took on coal to sail from Baltimore to Tokyo via the Panama Canal. It was overloaded by the master to enter the canal and had to transfer approximately 600 tonnes of coal to another ship. As a result the ship was nine days off-hire. The question was whether the ship was seaworthy. Lord Denning noted:

> the word seaworthy in the Hague Rules is used in the ordinary meaning and not in any extended or unnatural meaning. It means that the vessel—with her master and crew—is herself fit to encounter the perils of the voyage and also that she is fit to carry the cargo safely on that voyage.[23]

The conclusion was that the offloading of the excess cargo did not fall under the term 'seaworthiness'. At the same time the court did not imply that the ship must be able to withstand all storms, but only the ordinary perils of the sea. However this must be contrasted with the events of *The Gudermes*,[24] where it was held that the ability or fitness of the ship to discharge a particular cargo—in this case oil—at the nominated port is an aspect of seaworthiness.

The obligation of seaworthiness does not only fall upon the carrier, but includes the servants, agents and independent contractors. In addition, the obligation to have a ship seaworthy is dependent on the facts at hand. The nature of the ship and cargo, whether the ship is adequately manned, and the voyage are factors that need to be taken into consideration when defining seaworthiness.

Cargoworthiness

The second duty of the carrier is to properly man, equip and supply the ship pursuant to Article 3(1)(b). This must be read in conjunction with subparagraph (c), which requires the carrier to '[m]ake the holds, refrigerating and cool chambers, and all other

---

22 [1982] 1 Lloyd's Rep 7 at 9.

23 Ibid.

24 [1991] 1 Lloyd's Rep 456.

parts of the ship in which goods are carried, fit and safe for their reception, carriage and preservation'.

Clearly, a ship needs to be seaworthy to carry cargo. *The Gudermes*[25] addressed both terms, namely seaworthiness and cargoworthiness, holding:

> Seaworthiness includes Cargoworthiness so that art III r 1 lays down an absolute obligation to provide a ship fit to carry the particular cargo on a particular voyage to the particular destination.[26]

The vessel carried fuel oil from Russia to Italy, and it is common practice to heat oil while on board in order to avoid a low pour point. Because of the low temperature of the oil, the port of destination refused to discharge the oil. The cargo had to be transferred to another ship, where it was heated and later successfully discharged. The court therefore found that the carrier failed to properly and carefully carry, keep and care for the cargo pursuant to Article 3(1).

Care of cargo

Article 3(2) follows logically: subject to any exemptions contained in Article 4, the carrier is required to 'properly and carefully handle, stow, carry, keep care for, and discharge the goods carried', as found in *The Gudermes*. However there is another point to be taken into consideration, namely the interplay between the care of cargo and the carriers immunities, as listed in Article 4 (discussed below). In *Shipping Corp of India Ltd v Gamlen Chemical Co (A/Asia) Pty Ltd*[27] two facts were clear: first, the drums of chemicals were not secured properly in the hold; and second, the ship encountered heavy weather at sea. As a result the drums broke free and were lost. The court held that the 'effect of the opening words of Art III, r 2 is to subordinate that rule to the provisions of Art IV'.[28]

3.2.3c Carrier's immunities

Article 4 of COGSA sets out excepted perils. Neither the carrier nor the ship is responsible for loss or damage resulting from perils listed in Article 4. However, the carrier is only protected by Article 4 if the ship is seaworthy.

The doctrine of excepted perils is clearly defined by case law. First, there has to be a causal connection between the loss or damage 'arising or resulting' from an unexpected peril. The loss does not, therefore, need to be the direct result of the peril.

Once the loss is established by the cargo owner, the burden of proof will shift to the carrier, who has to prove that an excepted peril existed which caused the loss.

Should the carrier satisfy this requirement, the burden shifts back to the cargo owner to show that the cause of the loss—despite the presence of an excepted peril—was caused by the negligence of the carrier. In *Shipping Corp of India Ltd v Gamlen Chemical Co (A/Asia) Pty Ltd* the shipper was unable to prove negligence and hence could not claim damages. The court noted:

---

25 Ibid.

26 Ibid.

27 (1980) 147 CLR 142.

28 Ibid at 150.

> a cargo owner must prove his loss, the carrier may then establish facts entitling him to rely upon exculpatory clauses, of which peril of the sea is one, but the cargo owner may then nevertheless succeed by proof of negligence, for example, proof of improper stowage.[29]

If the loss is caused by the presence of an excepted peril and by the negligence of the carrier, the shipper can only claim losses that were caused by the negligence of the carrier, not those caused by the perils of the seas.

3.2.3d Main excepted perils

Under Article 4(2)(a), the carrier and the ship are not responsible for loss or damage arising from 'Act, neglect or default of the master, mariner, pilot, or the servants of the carrier in the navigation or in the management of the ship'.

In *Chubu Asahi Cotton Spinning Co Ltd v Ship Tenos*[30] the question turned on the phrase 'management of the ship'. The servants of the carrier filled a hole with water which subsequently spoiled wool stored in a different cargo hole. The court distinguished between 'want of care of cargo and want of care of vessel indirectly affecting cargo', and concluded that the fault of the crew was only in relation to the care of the cargo and had nothing to do with the management of the ship.[31] The court found that there was negligence of the crew in taking care of the cargo but not in the management of the ship.

Excepted perils under Article 4(2)(c) are '[p]erils, dangers and accidents of the sea or other navigable waters'. *Shipping Corp of India Ltd v Gamlen Chemical Co (A/Asia) Pty Ltd*[32] provides a definition as to what constitutes perils of the sea or mishaps at sea. Mason and Wilson JJ pointed out that the losses or the cause of the loss or damages do not have to be extraordinary:

> Sea and weather conditions which may reasonably be foreseen and guarded against may constitute a peril of the sea ... Perils of the sea excludes only those losses which could have been avoided by the carriers' skill and prudence.[33]

Under Article 4(2)(p), 'Latent defects not discoverable by due diligence' are excepted perils. The question what can be deemed to be a latent defect was examined in *Charles Brown & Co Ltd v Nitrate Producers Steamship Co Ltd.*[34] A cargo of wheat was loaded, but upon arrival in the UK it was found that some wheat had been damaged due to leaks in the ship's hull. The leaks were caused by very fine splits in rivets in the bulkhead. It was not in dispute that the grain was loaded in perfect condition, but was damaged upon discharge. It was also not in dispute that the ship was seaworthy. The question was whether the damage was due to a latent defect in the ship, namely the leaking rivets, and therefore whether Article 4 gave protection to the carrier. The court held that:

---

29 Ibid at 145.

30 (1968) 12 FLR 291.

31 Ibid at 299 (quoting *The Ferro* [1893] Prob Div 38 at 38).

32 (1980) 147 CLR 142.

33 Ibid at 166.

34 (1937) 58 Lloyd's List LR 188.

> latent defect does not mean latent to the eye. It means latent to the senses, that is, it may be hammer tested, or there may be any other test. The only question is whether by 'latent' it means that you have to use every possible method to discover whether it exists, or whether you must use reasonable methods. I cannot myself believe that in every case it is obligatory upon a ship's officer upon the commencement of a voyage to go and tap every rivet to find if it has a defect or not. It that were so, ships would be help up in port for a very long time while the rivets were being tapped and eyes used to determine whether a defect exists or not. I think it means such an examination as a reasonably careful man skilled in that matter would make ...[35]

In summary, as long as tests are executed in a diligent and reasonable manner, a carrier can rely on Article 4(2)(p) where damage to cargo eventuates that is not due to an unseaworthy ship.

The immunities are narrowly construed, however, and carriers remain liable for failure to exercise due diligence in carrying out their fundamental duties. The following excerpt illustrates this point.

Great China Metal Industries Co Ltd v Malaysian International Shipping Corporation Berhad

[1998] HCA 65; 196 CLR 161; 158 ALR 1; 72 ALJR 1592 (22 October 1998)

In 1989, 40 cases of aluminium can body stock in coils were consigned from Sydney to Keelung, Taiwan. The respondent issued a bill of lading dated 5 October 1989, acknowledging receipt of the goods in apparent good order and condition. The vessel named in the bill as the intended vessel was the *MV Bunga Seroja*.

The shipper named in the bill was Strang International Pty Ltd ('Strang') as agent for Comalco Aluminium Ltd. Strang packed the containers in which the cargo was shipped. The appellant was named in the bill as 'the notify party' and property in the goods duly passed to it.

The bill provided that it should have effect subject to legislation giving effect to the Hague Rules. By the *Sea-Carriage of Goods Act 1924* (Cth), the Hague Rules applied to the carriage of the goods. The parties to the bill of lading were deemed by ss 4(1) and 9(1) of that statute to have intended to contract according to the Hague Rules.

In the course of its passage across the Great Australian Bight, the vessel encountered heavy weather. That weather had been forecast before the vessel left port. Some of the goods were damaged.

Although, as will appear, it is not determinative of the outcome of the appeal, the question to which submissions primarily were directed is the meaning and effect of Art IV r 2(c) of the Hague Rules that:

> Neither the carrier nor the ship shall be responsible for loss or damage arising or resulting from
>
> ...
>
> (c) perils, dangers and accidents of the sea or other navigable waters ...

35 Ibid at 188.

The appellant contended that:

- this exception (the 'perils of the sea' exception) does not apply if damage to cargo results from sea and weather conditions which could reasonably be foreseen and guarded against;
- the weather encountered by the *Bunga Seroja* was foreseen; and
- the statement of Mason and Wilson JJ in *Shipping Corporation of India Ltd v Gamlen Chemical Co (A/Asia) Pty Ltd*[36] that 'sea and weather conditions which may reasonably be foreseen and guarded against may constitute a peril of the sea' is wrong and should not be followed.

The appellant pleaded that the respondent had failed to meet its responsibility under Art III r 1 of the Hague Rules to exercise, before and at the beginning of the voyage, due diligence to make the ship seaworthy, to properly man, equip and supply the ship and to make the holds and all other parts of the ship in which the goods were carried fit and safe for their reception, carriage and preservation. It also pleaded failure by the respondent to properly and carefully load, handle, stow, carry, keep, care for, and discharge the goods carried (Art III r 2). By its defence, the respondent relied upon various immunities specified in Art IV r 2. In particular, the respondent pleaded that it was not responsible for any loss or damage to the goods arising or resulting from perils of the sea and that any damage to the goods resulted or occurred by reason of that matter.

The trial judge (Carruthers J) entered judgment for the respondent. His Honour concluded:

> In my view, the [respondent] has established to the requisite degree that the damage to the subject cargo was occasioned by perils of the sea ... In summary, the evidence satisfies me that, bearing in mind the anticipated weather conditions: (i) when the *Bunga Seroja* sailed from Burnie she was fit in all respects for the voyage; (ii) the [respondent] properly and carefully loaded, handled, stowed, carried, kept and cared for the subject cargo; and (iii) there was no neglect or default of the master or other servants of the [respondent] in the management of the ship or cargo.
>
> I am satisfied that the damage to the subject cargo was occasioned by perils of the sea, in that, the pounding of the ship by reason of the heavy weather caused the coils within the container to be dislodged and thereby sustain damage.

The New South Wales Court of Appeal dismissed an appeal. The appeal to this Court also should be dismissed.

...

In understanding the operation of the Hague Rules, there are three important considerations. The rules must be read as a whole, they must be read in the light of the history behind them, and they must be read as a set of rules devised by international agreement for use in contracts that could be governed by any of several different, sometimes radically different, legal systems. It is convenient to begin by touching upon some matters of history.

...

Because the Hague Rules are intended to apply widely in international trade, it is self-evidently desirable to strive for uniform construction of them. As has been said earlier, the rules seek to allocate risks between cargo and carrier interests and it follows that the allocation of those risks that is made when the rules are construed by national courts should, as far as possible, be uniform. Only then can insurance markets set premiums efficiently and the cost of double insurance be avoided.

36 (1980) 147 CLR 142.

In *Gamlen*, Mason and Wilson JJ note that:

> There is a difference between the Anglo-Australian conception of 'perils of the sea' and the United States-Canadian conception. According to the latter, 'perils of the sea' include losses to goods on board which are peculiar to the sea and 'are of an extraordinary nature or arise from irresistible force or overwhelming power, and which cannot be guarded against by the ordinary exertions of human skill and prudence': *The Giulia* adopting *Story on Bailments*, s 512(a). In the United Kingdom and Australia it is not necessary that the losses or the cause of the losses should be 'extraordinary' (Carver, *Carriage by Sea*, vol 1, 12th ed (1971), s 161; *Skandia Insurance Co Ltd v Skoljarev*). Consequently sea and weather conditions which may reasonably be foreseen and guarded against may constitute a peril of the sea.

When reference is made to occurrences identified as 'extraordinary', the question arises as to the nature of the relativity which is contemplated. Thus it has been said that the events which occurred 'may be considered extraordinary as compared with an even voyage upon a placid sea; and yet [they] may be an entirely ordinary occurrence as compared with transportation by sea generally'.

It may be that the difference between Anglo-Australian and American-Canadian construction of the 'perils of the sea' exception is less than might appear from reference to cases such as *The Giulia* or *The Rosalia*—both decisions of the Second Circuit Court of Appeals. In *The Rosalia* a peril of the sea was described as 'something so catastrophic as to triumph over those safeguards by which skillful and vigilant seamen usually bring ship and cargo to port in safety'. More recent authority in the United States has, perhaps, placed less emphasis on whether what happened was extraordinary and catastrophic. But whether or not that is an accurate reflection of more recent developments, there is great force in what Judge Learned Hand said in *Philippine Sugar Centrals Agency v Kokusai Kisen Kabushiki Kaisha*:

> The phrase, 'perils of the sea', has at times been treated as though its meaning were esoteric: Judge Hough's vivid language in *The Rosalia* ... has perhaps given currency to the notion. That meant nothing more, however, than that the weather encountered must be too much for a well-found vessel to withstand ... The standard of seaworthiness, like so many other legal standards, must always be uncertain, for the law cannot fix in advance those precautions in hull and gear which will be necessary to meet the manifold dangers of the sea. That Judge Hough meant no more than this in *The Rosalia* ... is shown by his reference to the definition in *The Warren Adams* ... as the equivalent of what he said. That definition was as follows: 'That term may be defined as denoting "all marine casualties resulting from the violent action of the elements, as distinguished from their natural, silent influence."' It would be too much to hope that *The Rosalia* ... will not continue to be cited for more than this, but it would be gratifying if it were not.

We agree, with respect, that perils of the sea should not be treated as having some esoteric meaning. Nor can its meaning be identified in a single all embracing definition capable of unvarying application to all circumstances. There is no single criterion which, standing alone, will identify whether what happened is or is not properly to be called a peril of the sea.

...

[T]he Second Circuit Court of Appeals said of perils of the sea, in a marine insurance case, *New Zealand Insurance Co v Hecht, Levis & Kahn*:

> We may concede *arguendo* that they cover only 'extraordinary occurrences,' ... but if so, while they do not include those injuries which are the run of all voyages, they certainly do include occasional visitations of the violence of nature, like great storms, even though these are no more than should be expected.

Thus there are statements to be found in the United States authorities that a 'perils of the sea' exception may apply even if the weather encountered was no more than expected.

Nor should statements made in the many English cases dealing with perils of the sea be read divorced from their context. Some can, we think, be seen as no more than decisions about particular facts. Others examine questions of onus of proof and concurrent causation which do not arise in this case. Particular reference need be made to only two of the English cases—*The Xantho* and *Hamilton, Fraser & Co v Pandorf & Co.* Both cases pre-dated the Hague Rules and concerned the construction of an exception in bills of lading in favour of 'dangers and accidents of the seas'. We mention *The Xantho* for the distinction drawn by Lord Herschell between perils of the sea and other losses of which the sea is the immediate cause. He said:

> I think it clear that the term 'perils of the sea' does not cover every accident or casualty which may happen to the subject-matter of the insurance on the sea. It must be a peril 'of' the sea. Again, it is well settled that it is not every loss or damage of which the sea is the immediate cause that is covered by these words. They do not protect, for example, against that natural and inevitable action of the winds and waves, which results in what may be described as wear and tear. There must be some casualty, something which could not be foreseen as one of the necessary incidents of the adventure.

The distinction drawn by his Lordship is important and must be borne in mind when considering the operation of the 'perils of the sea' exception.

The second case, *Pandorf*, is worthy of note because it shows that there may be damage resulting from a peril of the sea despite there being no great catastrophic event. It was held, there, that a cargo was damaged by 'dangers and accidents of the seas' when, during the voyage, rats gnawed a hole in a pipe thus allowing water into the hold. It is important to note, however, that it was admitted or proved that the ship was seaworthy and that the damage occurred without fault on the part of the crew. Those facts being accepted, what other explanation for the occurrence could be given save that it was a peril of the sea? If the decision appears strange to the modern eye, its oddity lies not in the conclusion reached but in the premises from which that conclusion proceeded: that the ship was seaworthy and that the loss was not caused by default of the crew. But we need not say whether those findings of fact would now be regarded as open.

Many other cases were mentioned in argument or can be found in the books. We think it desirable to touch briefly on only three other streams of authority. First, it seems that in German law, a peril of the sea need not be an extraordinary event and that a storm of a certain force is regarded as a peril of the sea. Similarly, in French law a peril of the sea need not be 'unforeseeable and insurmountable'. Finally, the Supreme Court of Canada held in *Goodfellow Lumber Sales v Verreault* that:

> even if the loss is occasioned by perils of the sea, the ship owner is nevertheless liable if he failed to exercise due diligence to make the ship seaworthy at the beginning of the voyage and that unseaworthiness was a decisive cause of the loss.

How then are these disparate streams of authority to be brought together? In our view one must begin by recognising that the inquiry is, in large part, a factual inquiry—is the carrier immune in respect of what otherwise would be its failure to discharge its responsibilities under Art III because the loss or damage to the goods arose or resulted from a cause which brings the carrier within the immunity conferred by Art IV r 2?

If cargo has been lost or damaged and if the vessel was seaworthy, properly manned, equipped and supplied, what led to the loss or damage? Did it arise or result from want of proper stowing (Art

III r 2)? Did it arise from the 'act, neglect or default of the master ... or the servants of the carrier in the navigation or in the management of the ship' (Art IV r 2(a))? Or, did it result from some *other* cause peculiar to the sea? The last is a peril of the sea.

In *Gamlen* Mason and Wilson JJ said that 'sea and weather conditions which may reasonably be foreseen and guarded against may constitute a peril of the sea'. The fact that the sea and weather conditions that were encountered could reasonably be foreseen, or were actually forecast, may be important in deciding issues like an issue of alleged want of seaworthiness of the vessel, an alleged default of the master in navigation or management, or an alleged want of proper stowage. Similarly, the fact that the conditions encountered could have been guarded against may be very important, if not decisive, in considering those issues. (Their decision may then make it unnecessary to consider the 'perils of the sea' exception.) But if it is necessary to consider the 'perils of the sea' exception, the fact that the conditions that were encountered could reasonably be expected or were forecast should not be taken to conclude that question. To that extent we agree with what was said by Mason and Wilson JJ in *Gamlen*. Such an approach, even if it is different from the American and Canadian approach, better reflects the history of the rules, their international origins and is the better construction of the rules as a whole.

The present appeal

In the present case the trial judge held that there was no breach of Art III r 1 or r 2. That is, the trial judge rejected the contentions that due diligence had not been exercised to make the ship seaworthy, to properly man, equip and supply the ship and to 'make the holds ... and all other parts of the ship in which goods are carried, fit and safe for their reception, carriage and preservation'. Indeed the trial judge found that in fact the vessel was fit in all respects for the voyage when it left port. Further, the trial judge rejected the contention that the carrier had not properly and carefully stowed the goods. It follows, as we have indicated earlier in these reasons, that the owner having failed to prove any breach of the carrier's responsibilities under Art III, the applicability of the defence of perils of the sea within the meaning of par (c) of Art IV r 2 did not strictly arise. However, in the light of the findings made at the trial, the conclusion that the damage to the cargo was occasioned by perils of the sea was correct. The fact that the weather encountered had been forecast before the vessel left port does not deny that conclusion.

It was submitted by the appellant that the master should not have left port or should have diverted so as to avoid the weather which was forecast. The former contention appears not to have been made at trial. The latter was, but was rejected. The trial judge, having heard the evidence of experts called by both parties, said that he was 'unable to conclude that any deficiencies in the conduct of the ship and her cargo by [the ship's master] have been demonstrated'. There is no basis for departing from that finding. Once it was made, the trial judge's conclusion that there was no neglect or default of the master or other servants of the carrier in the management of the ship or cargo was inevitable. To the extent that the appellant now seeks to expand its contention to include the proposition that the vessel should not have left port, it is enough to say that, if the judge's finding does not meet the contention, it is a contention that could be made only with evidence to support it and there was none.

...

The failure of the submissions by the appellant makes it unnecessary to consider grounds urged in support of the decision of the Court of Appeal by the respondent in its Notice of Contention. The appeal should be dismissed with costs.

... ...

3.2.3e Limits on liability

Even if a carrier or ship is liable to pay damages, such damages are capped. The Hague Rules set the liability limit at £100 per package or unit when shipped in 'customary freight units'. This monetary limit quickly became unacceptably low, and the Hague-Visby Rules raised the limit to '10 000 gold francs per package or unit, or thirty gold francs per kilo of the gross weight of the goods lost or damaged, whichever is higher'.[37] Damages are now capped at '666.67 units of account per package or unit or 2 units of account per kilograms of gross weight of the goods lost or damages, whichever is the higher'.[38]

Of course, this limitation can be overcome if the nature and value of such goods have been declared to the shipper before shipment and inserted in the sea carriage document; that is, if the parties agree otherwise. Moreover, the limitations do not apply if the carrier acted 'with intent to cause damage' or 'recklessly and with knowledge that damage would probably result'.[39]

What constitutes a package or a unit is defined in Article 4(5)(c), and is especially important if goods are put into containers or on pallets. If the sea carriage document is silent, then each container or pallet is to be considered a package or unit. If on the other hand the sea carriage document enumerates the packages or units contained within each container, then the number as expressed in the document is to be considered the number of packages or units. Owing to the low limits set in the Hague-Visby Rules, shippers have become creative in defining terms such as 'package' and 'customary freight unit'. In the following extract, a court agreed with the creative definitions advanced by a shipper.

Croft & Scully Co v M/V Skulptor Vuchetich, US Court of Appeals, Fifth Circuit (1982)

Appellant Croft & Scully Co appeals from a decision by the District Court limiting to $500 its recovery in an incident where the parties stipulated negligence. Finding that the District Court applied an incorrect standard in determining what constitutes a 'package' for purposes of the *Carriage of Goods by Sea Act* (COGSA), 46 USCA § 1300 et seq, we reverse and remand.

Things go better with Coke

Croft & Scully contracted to ship 1755 cases of soft drinks from Houston, Texas to the middle eastern country of Kuwait. Apparently Kuwaitis would like to be Peppers, too. Croft & Scully arranged to ship the soft drinks on board M/V *Skulptor Vuchetich*, which would arrive in Houston on December 8, 1977. Baltic Shipping Co, owner of *Skulptor*, dispatched a 20-foot steel container to Croft & Scully's supplier in Wharton, Texas. Employees of the supplier loaded the 1755 cases, each

37 Article IV rule 5.

38 The 'unit of account' is calculated by referring to the Special Drawing Rights as defined by the International Monetary Fund.

39 Article IV rule 5.

containing 4 '6-packs' or 24 cans, into the container, closed and sealed it—a real Teem effort. The supplier then trucked the container to Goodpasture's yard, near the Houston Ship Channel, which Baltic had selected as a convenient storage facility pending arrival of *Skulptor*.

During the Refreshing Pause between arrival of the container and arrival of *Skulptor*, the vessel's agent prepared a Bill of Lading and hired Shippers Stevedoring, Inc, to load the soft drink container on board *Skulptor*.

Pepsi Cola hits the spot-on the pavement

As one of the Stevedore's employees was lifting the container, with the use of a forklift, he negligently dropped it. By our calculations, 42 120 cans of soft drinks crashed to the ground, never a thirst to quench. In the Crush, the cans were damaged. The stevedore, no doubt, was in no mood to have a Coke and a smile.

Dr Pepper at 10, 2 and § 1304

Croft & Scully sued Goodpasture, Shippers Stevedoring, and *Skulptor* and her owners to pick up the Tab for its damages. The District Court dismissed the suit as to Goodpasture because it had no agency relationship with Shippers Stevedoring. Relying upon a so-called Himalaya Clause in the Bill of Lading, it granted the remaining defendants' motion for summary judgment and, finding that the container constituted a 'package' within the meaning of § 4(5) of COGSA, limited Shippers Stevedoring's liability to $500. Croft & Scully appeals. Things Go Better on appeal, and we reverse and remand.

A peek at the Himalaya Clause

Croft & Scully asserts that the Himalaya Clause limiting recovery to $500 violates public policy. That claim fails to make the grade, given our decision in *Brown & Root v M/V Peisander*, 648 F2d 415—AMC—(5th Cir 1981), upholding such a clause. Indeed, the conflict which we surmounted there does not even arise in this case. Clause 17 of the Bill of Lading makes clear provision for an increased valuation at a higher freight rate. A more unequivocal declaration, in fact, one could not find. As Croft & Scully could have availed itself of extra loss or damage protection but chose not to, the District Court correctly ruled that the Himalaya Clause applied.

Don't judge the package by its appearance

Even if liability is limited to $500 per package, Croft & Scully argues, the cardboard cases of soft drinks rather than the 20-foot container should constitute the relevant 'package'. Shippers Stevedoring responds with equal fervor that the container is the 'package'. Their argument, we think, given the recent decision in *Allstate Insurance Co v Inversiones Navieras Imparca*, holds no water, carbonated or otherwise.

We begin by pointing out that COGSA does not apply by its own force and effect, since the incident occurred in the yard and not on the vessel. Rather, the Bill of Lading incorporates COGSA. Thus, its provisions are merely terms of the contract of carriage which, like any other contractual terms, call out for judicial interpretation in case of dispute.

The District Court further observed that the Fifth Circuit had not established a test to determine what constitutes a 'package' under COGSA. Since the date of its order, this Court has formulated such a test in whose good hands the parties—and the District Court—must rest.

Allstate involved the loss of 341 cartons of stereo equipment. The shipper loaded the cartons inside a container, sealed it, and had its agent deliver it to the carrier. The carrier issued a Bill of Lading which described the contents both in number and in kind. When the container arrived in Venezuela, it was as empty as a can of soda on a hot summer day. The shipper sought recovery for its full damages, but the carrier, relying on COGSA, sought shelter in the $500 limitation. Although the District Court concluded that the container was the COGSA package, the winds of judicial change Schwepped away the $500 shelter and exposed the carrier to full liability.

Judge Anderson, writing for the Court, after reviewing the history of COGSA and decisions in other Circuits, found that each stereo carton was a discrete 'package'. He based his decision on a case in the Second Circuit, *Mitsui & Co v American Export Lines*. There Judge Friendly expressly rejected as unworkable and unsound the old 'functional economics' test, propounded in *Royal Typewriter Co, Division of Litton Business Systems Inc v M/V Kulmerland*. Instead, relying on dicta in *Leather's Best, Inc v SS Mormaclynx*, he looked to see whether the carrier had clear, unequivocal notice of the container's contents:

> Clearly the goal of international uniformity is better served by the approach in *Leather's Best* that generally a container supplied by the carrier is not a COGSA package if its contents and the number of packages or units are disclosed.

We find nothing in the Bill of Lading to indicate that the contracting parties intended some special meaning of the term 'package'. Since Croft & Scully included information about the contents of the container and their number, *Allstate* governs. Therefore, the District Court erred in granting summary judgment on the 'package' issue.

Customary freight unit

Even if the container was not a COGSA 'package', Shippers Stevedoring contends, the Court should uphold the $500 award because the container was a 'customary freight unit' within the ambit of § 4(5) of COGSA, and thus the Himalaya Clause still applies...

Caterpillar Americas Co v S/S Sea Roads, held that the 'customary freight unit' was a tractor and its parts rather than hundredweight units, 'regardless of the harshness or seeming illogic of such a result':

> With respect to the words 'customary freight unit', the authorities are conclusive that this phrase refers to the unit upon which the charge for freight is computed and not to the physical shipping unit. As thus construed, the statute gives the court the task of determining what unit was actually used by the carrier for computing the freight charge on the shipment in question. Under the statute the freight unit, if one exists, will control the question of limitation of liability, unless the freight unit employed was a mere sham, and, therefore, not a 'customary' unit within the meaning of the statute.

From these cases, we deduce that 'customary freight unit' is a question of fact that will vary from contract to contract. Of particular importance in this as in any contractual dispute, then, is the parties' intent, as expressed in the Bill of Lading, applicable tariff, and perhaps elsewhere. Indeed, the District Court so recognized: 'Further, consideration of the intent of the parties is particularly, although not exclusively, appropriate where, as in the instant cause, COGSA does not apply of its own force.'

Although Croft & Scully admitted that the freight charge was $2200, calculated on a 'flat container rate', we do not know how the parties arrived at that rate. Does it depend upon the contents, weight, value, custom of the trade, applicable tariffs, if any, or other factors? The District

Court must consider these questions on remand. If it finds that the container was a 'customary freight unit', then the Court should reinstate the $500 limitation of liability. If not, then it should hold further proceedings to determine the amount of damages. We, of course, express no opinion concerning the outcome.

Recap

We affirm the District Court's dismissal of *Goodpasture* and its conclusion that the Himalaya Clause applies. We reverse its grant of summary judgment for Shippers Stevedoring and its finding that the steel container was a COGSA package. As the District Judge never reached the important factual question whether the container of soft drink cartons was a 'customary freight unit', we remand for further inquiry into the facts and for consideration of the parties' intent, factors that will guide the trial Court in determining the meaning of that COGSA clause.

Affirmed in part, reversed in part and reaffirmed.

… … …

3.3 Marine insurance

3.3.1 Introduction

This section will not discuss general insurance principles, which should be known from the study of other subjects. In general, this section will discuss the concept of marine insurance, as well as problems associated specifically with marine insurance.

In Australia, the *Marine Insurance Act 1909* (Cth) is the relevant legislation. It should be noted that principles of marine insurance appear to be very similar in most countries. However the Act is not a code, as s 4 of notes that the rules of the common law and law merchant apply as long as there is no inconsistency with the Act. What constitutes marine insurance is defined in s 7:

> a contract whereby the insurer undertakes to indemnify the assured, in manner and to the extent thereby agreed, against marine losses, that is to say, the losses incident to marine adventure.

Being a Commonwealth act, it is of no surprise that the *Marine Insurance Act* applies to all marine losses other than intra-state matters, but includes state marine insurance that extends beyond the boundaries of a particular state.

3.3.2 Types of policies

The Act refers to five types of policies:

- Valued policy (s 33(2)): this policy requires a set amount; that is, the value to be insured is an agreed amount.
- Unvalued policy (s 34): no specific value has been agreed upon in the policy and the insurable value has to be agreed later, subject to limits of the sum insured.
- Floating policy (s 35(1)): insurance is only described in general and other matters such as the name of the ship and other particulars as they may be are left to be filled in later.

- Voyage policy (s 31(1)): this policy is specifically for a particular voyage; that is, from one place to another.
- Time policy (s 31(1)): the subject matter of the policy is insured for a specific time period, however notice as to lengthening or shortening of the period is permissible.

3.3.3 Insurance cover

Marine insurance—pursuant to s 9(2)—covers losses where 'ships, goods or any other movables are exposed to maritime perils'. 'Maritime perils' are defined in the same section as:

> the perils consequent on, or incidental to, the navigation of the seas, that is to say, perils of the seas, fire, war perils, pirates, rovers, thieves, captures, seizures, restraints, and detainments of princes and peoples, jettisons, barratry, and any other perils, either of the like kind, or which may be designated by the policy.

In *Skandia Insurance Co. Ltd v Skoljarev* [40] the court had to resolve the question of what is meant by perils of the sea, and hence whether the loss was due to the perils of the sea. The facts are simple. A ship sank unexpectedly in calm waters. The policy holder was insured against perils of the sea, and had to prove that the ship sunk due to perils of the sea and not because it was unseaworthy. Judge Mason noted:

> Although there is nothing in all this to throw the burden of proof of seaworthiness onto the insured, there is one class of case in which the insured will find it necessary to establish seaworthiness in order to prove this case. This is where the insured having no direct evidence of loss due to a fortuitous event, seeks to establish by inference a case of loss due to an unascertained peril of the sea. To justify this inference he will see to exclude the possibility of loss caused by unseaworthiness by calling evidence as to the condition of the ship.[41]

As unseaworthiness was excluded as a cause of the loss, the court inferred that the loss was caused by a peril of the sea despite the fact that the court could not ascertain what the peril exactly was.

3.3.4 Insurable interest

Due to the nature of commodity sales in particular and marine trade in general, insurable interest in brief does not need to be established at the time when the insurance is effected, but at the time when the loss occurs. Section 11(2) notes that any person interested in a marine adventure has an insurable interest. However, if the goods are insured 'lost or not lost' an insured may benefit from the insurance even if they have not yet acquired an insurable interest.

In *NSW Leather Co. Pty Ltd v Vanguard Insurance Co Ltd*[42] the question of 'lost or not lost' and insurable interest was determined. The facts again are simple. An Australian

---

40 (1979) 142 CLR 375.

41 Ibid at 391.

42 (1991) 25 NSWLR 699.

importer ordered leather form a Brazilian seller on FOB terms. Before the goods were loaded in 11 containers, thieves stole some of the leather and put seals back onto the containers. The seller was not involved and the buyer only found out after he took possession of the goods and paid the price. The court of first instance held that the buyer had no insurable interest as the contract was FOB—he only acquired the insurable interest after the goods passed the ship's rail.

On appeal, the question turned on the term 'lost or not lost.' Handley JA agreed that the FOB contract meant that the insured had not acquired an insurable interest. However he then quoted s 12, which states:

> The assured must be interested in the subject matter insured at the time of the loss … Provided that where the subject matter is insured 'lost or not lost' the assured may recover although he may not have acquired his interest until after the loss …

The loss fell upon the insured and the policy was worded appropriately, and the question of insurable interest was subordinate to the loss in such instances.

3.3.5 Loss

Generally speaking, the insurer is only liable for damages that are described in the policy and are 'proximately' caused by the insured peril. 'Proximately' means that the cause of the loss must be associated with the peril; that is, the dominant cause of the loss is associated with the insured peril.

Section 61(2) lists losses that are excluded, namely wilful misconduct of the insured, delay, and wear and tear and inherent vice of the insured items. However, as in any other insurance policies, the parties are always free to agree on contractual terms.

Losses may be total, partial or a general average loss clause may apply. In maritime matters occasions occur where, in order to preserve the property, sacrifices are made or expenditure incurred that is voluntary, such as having to abandon goods at sea in order to save the ship and other cargo. In such cases, pursuant to s 72(3) the party who suffers the loss is entitled to expect a contribution from all others who did not suffer the loss.

3.3.5a Total loss

The *Marine Insurance Act* mandates that a calculation of a total loss can be worked out on either an actual or constructive basis. It is obvious that a total loss occurs where the insured subject matter is so destroyed or damaged that it ceases to be of any value.

A constructive loss, on the other hand, mostly occurs when the subject matter cannot be preserved or saved from total loss without incurring excessive expenditure that would make a recovery economically unsound.

3.3.5b Partial loss

Obviously if a loss is not a total loss, it has to be a partial one. It follows that the insurer is only liable to the extent of the actual partial loss.

3.3.6 Subrogation

Subrogation is a vital part of insurance law. Simply put, it allows the insurer to bring action in the name of the insured. The *Marine Insurance Act* defines subrogation in s 85(1):

> [The insurer] becomes entitled to take over the interest of the assured in whatever may remain of the subject-matter so paid for, and [the insurer] is thereby subrogated to all the rights and remedies of the assured in and in respect of that subject-matter as from the time of the casualty causing the loss.

3.4 Special international trade terms: Incoterms

3.4.1 Introduction

In order to more easily facilitate the international trading of goods, traders have over the course of many years developed numerous 'trade terms' to allocate the rights and obligations between the contracting parties to a contract. As customs and terms evolved, problems developed when traders in differing regions used the same term but, due to regional variations, the meanings (and allocations of risks and responsibilities) of the terms meant different things to different traders. Such regional differences and ambiguities became a major problem and, far from more easily facilitating international commerce, the trade terms sometimes became a costly interference.

Fortunately, efforts at the international level to clarify and interpret trade terms have proven to be largely successful. The most widely used trade terms are 'Incoterms', which are drafted and revised by the International Chamber of Commerce (ICC). The ICC is a non-governmental entity founded in 1919, and is essentially a global business organisation that expresses business views. ICC activities cover a broad spectrum, including setting standards, arbitration and dispute resolution, promoting open trade and the market economy system, business self-regulation, and fighting corruption or combating commercial crime. Incoterms are sometimes updated to reflect the reality of modern transport, with the most recent revision occurring in 2000. The ICC was not the only one to draft model trade terms, but its terms prevailed and are now widely recognised and used in the industry.

First produced in 1936, Incoterms developed to provide an internationally recognisable way to easily facilitate the obligations of the buyer and seller. Such obligations include:

- What acts the seller must do to deliver;
- What acts the buyer must do to accommodate delivery;
- The costs each party must bear; and
- At what point in the delivery the risk passes from the seller to the buyer.

In most countries, including Australia, Incoterms are not part of national legislation, nor are they an international treaty. In this regard, they cannot be the 'governing law' of a contract.[43] Instead, Incoterms are a written form of *custom or usage* in the trade; that is, they are expressly incorporated into the contract (and varied if the parties to the contract so desire). Thus, even though the national laws of most countries define commercial terms, these are expressly subject to 'agreement otherwise'. Express reference to Incoterms satisfies this requirement, and courts in Australia, the USA and Europe have confirmed this interpretation.[44] Incoterms may also be implied into a contract as part of an international custom,[45] and UNCITRAL refers to Incoterms as 'widely-observed usage for international trade'. Moreover, Incoterms would likely qualify under Article 9(2) of the CISG, which recognises 'usage ... which in international trade is widely known to, and regularly observed by, parties to' international sales contracts, even if usage is not global.

In the latest version, Incoterms 2000, 13 different methods of dividing responsibilities between the buyer and the seller are used. These 13 methods are divided into four classes: E, F, C and D. The obligations, responsibilities, costs and risks on the buyer and seller differ depending upon which Incoterm is used. As will be detailed below:

- E Terms are used where the buyer will collect the goods from the seller;
- F Terms are used when the seller will load the goods onto a method of transport (carriage) provided by the buyer;
- C Terms are used where the seller undertakes to send the goods to the buyer; and
- D Terms are used where the seller must actually deliver the goods to an agreed destination.

These are also the four traditional categories at common law. It should be noted, however, that while the main responsibilities and risks are the same under common law and Incoterms 2000, there are slight variations in the finer details (for example, the extent to which goods must be insured when using a C Term is less than at common law). In order to avoid any misunderstandings, it is important to explicitly state in the contract which interpretation is to be applied. This can be done by simply stating 'Incoterms 2000' after the relevant trade term (for example, 'FOB Sydney Incoterms 2000').

Care must be taken to avoid incorporating into the sales contract terms that do not correctly represent the intentions of the parties. In this regard, it is important for each party to fully understand the terms and the consequences of misuse of the terms. Misuse normally arises when the actual intention of the party using a particular mode of transport (say, multimodal transport) was different from what is understood by the terms utilised in the sales contract (say, an Incoterm meant for port-to-port shipment).[46] Such misuse leads to disputes over which party bears the cost and risk, and inevitably raises the costs of doing business.

---

43 In some countries, however, trade terms form part of national law and their meanings cannot be varied by contract.

44 As a point of order, when Incoterms are expressly incorporated into the sales contract, the term 'Incoterms 2000' should appear after the appropriate abbreviation to avoid confusion with earlier or other interpretive terms.

45 Scholarly commentary as well as the courts of, at least, Germany and France, confirm this interpretation.

46 See *St Paul Guardian Insurance Company v Neuromed Medical Systems & Support*, GmbH, US District Court for the Southern District of New York, case no 5096 (2002).

All lawyers, not just those specialising in shipping law, should have a copy of Incoterms 2000 and fully understand the allocation of responsibility of each term prior to advising on a contract. Once incorporated into the sales contract, Incoterms become part of the contract—and like any other item in the contract, they are subject to negotiation and agreement between the parties.

As mentioned above, selecting the correct term is crucial in order for the parties to a contract to truly understand the risks and costs associated with transporting the goods from the country of export to the foreign buyer. There are no 'best' terms to use; likewise there are no terms to avoid. Each term merely allocates the responsibilities, obligations, costs and risks differently. Sellers inexperienced in the ways of international commerce may select the terms that most resemble a normal domestic sale. In such an instance, the E Terms would be selected, and the seller would only have to make the goods available for the purchaser to pick up at an agreed time. Similarly, inexperienced buyers may feel that the additional costs of using the DDP (delivered duties paid) term (D Term) is preferable to figuring out and dealing with such unfamiliar aspects as customs and import formalities. On the other hand, experienced sellers may have no trouble accepting the additional responsibilities, obligations, and risks associated with the C or D Terms when they can charge a premium for undertaking such services. Likewise, experienced buyers with contacts in the industry may feel that they are able to save money by making the carriage and insurance arrangements. Remember too that the party which undertakes to pay for the carriage contract and insurance is liable to financially benefit or be harmed by externalities, including currency fluctuations, a sudden rise (or, less likely, fall) in premiums and the like. Trade terms are all a matter of assigning duties and risks.

3.4.2 E Terms

E Terms, or EXW (ex works—named place) term, imposes the fewest duties on sellers and exposes them to the minimum amount of risk and liability of all the terms. Under the EXW term, sellers must only make the goods available at their premises (or any other agreed place) in order to fulfil their main obligations. Both the risk and the property are transferred to the buyer upon delivery. The responsibility for making all further arrangements falls to the buyer. For instance, sellers are not responsible for loading the goods onto transport or for clearing the goods for export (unless otherwise agreed).

Seller must, however, fulfil certain other obligations, for instance to supply goods that conform to the sales contract. Sellers are also required to:

- Assist the buyer in obtaining export documents, if requested (but sellers are not responsible for the costs or risks);
- Supply adequate packaging and be responsible for the costs of packaging (to the extent that the buyer advises of the method of transport and type of packaging required);
- Provide the buyer with adequate information regarding when the goods will be available (equally, buyers must provide adequate notice if they decide when delivery will take place).

Buyers are obligated to take delivery and pay for the goods at the allocated and agreed upon time. Buyers are also responsible for any additional costs resulting from their failure to take delivery as agreed as, importantly, risk passes to the buyer when the goods are placed at the buyer's disposal at the allocated and agreed upon time and place (note, not when the buyer eventually takes delivery of the goods). The sales contract should indicate whether any special delivery arrangements are needed (for example, ramps) and whether pre-shipment inspection (at the buyer's expense) is required.[47]

Buyers are also responsible for arranging and paying for the transportation of the goods and, if they so choose, for procuring insurance for the goods. In addition, buyers are responsible for clearing the goods for export, import and any transit requirements, and for paying all relevant charges. Therefore, the EXW term should not be used unless buyers are confident they can carry out all the export/import/transit formalities. Finally, buyers are responsible for paying any other associated costs relevant to the exportation of the goods, such as pre-shipment inspection, officials' charges and/or any costs incurred by the seller in assisting the buyer with the relevant formalities.

Two additional points are worth noting. First, the Incoterms do not recognise or interpret variations in the EXW term (for example, 'EXW Loaded'). Variations of the standard terms are not recommended, as their use means that parties are entering into an agreement where the interpretation of the term is unknown and subject to judicial determination; and also because such usage risks compromising the worldwide understanding of the terms. Second, as sellers fulfil their obligations under the EXW term much as they would in a domestic sale, the parties should be aware that local law could apply in determining a number of terms in the contract (for example, exclusions or limitations to liability, reasonableness, etc).

3.4.3 F Terms

F Terms are used when the contract for sale involves port-to-port carriage, where the seller is responsible for arranging and paying for pre-carriage of the goods in the exporting country. The two most common F Terms are FAS (free along side/ship) and FOB (free on board). Under the FAS term, sellers deliver the goods *alongside the ship* at the named port of shipment, and the costs and risk shift to the buyer when this occurs. The seller bears the costs and risk of loss until that time. Under the FOB term, sellers do not discharge their obligations until they *put the goods on a ship* nominated by the buyer at a port and at a time nominated by the buyer. The allocation of costs and risks are more complicated under this term and will be explained in detail below. When the principal carriage is by air, not sea, the terms 'FOB Aircraft', 'FOB Airport' or 'FCA' (free carrier—named place) should be used.[48]

The passing of risk under the FOB term is currently in somewhat of a state of flux. Traditionally, risk passes from the seller to the buyer when goods cross the ship's rail.

47 It may be wise for the seller to include a term in the contract requiring the buyer to reimburse the seller for the cost of the pre-shipment inspection if it reveals defects or anomalies in the goods.

48 Under FOB Aircraft the seller is responsible for delivering the goods onto the aircraft (and is thus responsible for obtaining and paying for export clearance and related charges), whereas with FOB Airport and FCA Airport the seller delivers the goods into the custody of the air carrier (or agent). When either of the latter two terms are used, the buyer is responsible for obtaining and paying for export clearance and related charges. Traditionally, the FOB term was only used for sea carriage.

This is, of course, an unreal concept, but Incoterms 2000 continues to use it (with a slight variation). However, some commentators and judges now interpret the term to mean that risk passes when the master of the ship is in charge of the goods. Still others interpret the term to mean that risk passes when the goods are loaded on board (considerable jurisprudence exists on this interpretation). Importantly, however, under any interpretation of the FOB term, the goods must be delivered on board to discharge the delivery obligation. The obligation to deliver the goods does not end when the goods cross the ship's rails (that is, the seller cannot simply leave the goods dangling in mid-air). At that point, however, property (and all its associated risks) passes to the buyer.

It is also important to understand that all references to the transfer of risk are expressly limited to physical loss of or damage to the goods, the so-called 'price risk'. Price risk does not cover other risks, such as delay or non-fulfilment, delivery of non-conforming goods, or failure to take delivery in accordance with the contract. (Note that this is by no means an exhaustive list of possible other risks, merely a few examples.) Therefore, even though the risk of damage or loss has passed to the buyer, the seller could still be liable and in breach of the contract. For instance, if the seller delivers non-conformity of goods or inadequately packages the goods and they are damaged during transit, the seller would still be liable for the breach of contract. The issues would be resolved by contract, the CISG or other applicable law/domestic legislation. It is therefore highly recommended that both parties should take out insurance in order to cover these risks.

There is an exception to the rules regarding the passage of risk. Where the buyer fails to nominate a ship, port and delivery time, or for some reason loading is impossible (such as when the vessel fails to arrive), the buyer is responsible for storage, and insurance and risk passes when the period for agreed shipment expires. The reason for this exception is obvious, as otherwise the risk to the seller would be extended beyond what was negotiated in the contract. This exception applies equally to the seller, meaning that the seller's failure to deliver the goods on time will result in the risk remaining with the seller beyond the date of delivery agreed in the contract.

In both FOB and FAS, the seller is responsible for the pre-delivery carriage, or pre-shipment carriage. However, the debate over the ship's rails versus on board is not only limited to the allocation of risk; it also comes into play when allocating the division of loading costs. Incoterms 2000 apportions using the old theory; that is, the seller bears the cost of loading the goods until the goods pass the ship's rails. After the goods cross the ship's rails, the buyer is responsible for paying the loading costs. Incoterms 2000 does, however, suggest the parties vary this position to reflect port-to-port differences and modern realities. With stevedores now commonly using their own or port authority equipment, division of costs should be apportioned in the sales contract (allocated as stevedoring charges). In most instances, sellers are in the better position to be familiar with port formalities and costs and should bear the costs of loading (and price their goods accordingly). It should also be noted that the terms 'FOB stowed' and 'FOB stowed and trimmed' are now commonly used to explicitly apportion the costs to the seller until delivery on board is complete. Importantly, however, allocation of costs does not change the allocation of risk. Regardless of whether the buyer or seller pays the loading costs (or it is divided in some manner), the buyer bears the risk after the goods cross the ship's rail and before they are properly loaded and stowed (that is, before the seller has discharged its obligation to deliver). Interestingly, the Guide to INCOTERMS 2000 provides for the possibility that the sales contract can stipulate that risk does not pass until the seller's delivery obligations are fulfilled, without changing the nature of FOB.

Once the goods are loaded onto the vessel, the seller is handed a mate's receipt that it provides to the buyer so that they can negotiate a contract for carriage and take delivery of appropriate shipping documents (bill of lading, etc) from the carrier. Under both FAS and FOB, the seller also supplies the buyer with the invoice and other documents evidencing conformity of the goods. Under Incoterms 2000, the seller is responsible for obtaining export clearance, and must supply the buyer with the necessary export clearance documents to enable the buyer to take delivery of the goods. As a protection measure, the seller should include an avoidance clause in the contract, in the event that exporting is difficult or suddenly prohibited (the buyer should consider the same for import clearance prohibitions). Such a clause could be seen as a *force majeure* clause, and release the seller from liability in the event of disruption.[49] From that point, the buyer is responsible for paying all subsequent costs, including stowage of goods, freight and insurance, and the costs involved in clearing the goods through customs on arrival at the final destination. Importantly, if the buyer cannot secure import clearance, it still must pay for the goods (unless the contract stipulates otherwise).

At common law, interpretive variations have developed as to what the parties intend when incorporating a simple FOB reference in a contract for sale. For instance, most jurisdictions, including Australia and New Zealand, now recognise that the responsibility of negotiating the contract of carriage can be divided differently, depending on the intention of the parties, as long as issues of risk/delivery remain unchanged, without changing it from an F Term. Such deviations were recognised in *Pyrene Co Ltd v Scindia Navigation*,[50] where Devlin J recognised three types of FOB contracts:

- The first is the classic FOB contract, which occurs when the seller negotiates the contract of carriage, with the buyer nominating a vessel.
- The second variation of FOB is where the buyer nominates the vessel and the seller is a party to the contract of carriage, and takes out the bill of lading in the buyer's name.
- The third—and now most common—form of FOB occurs with the buyer nominating the vessel and negotiating the contract of carriage.

Importantly, *Pyrene* does not suggest that the point at which risk passes (or the delivery point) changes according to whether the seller has agreed to conclude the contract for carriage. Thus, under Australian jurisdiction and Incoterms, the key principles remain that:

1 The buyer remains responsible for the costs of freight; and
2 Risk passes to the buyer when the goods cross the rail of the ship.[51]

---

49 Note that under Article 19 of the CISG, performance would only be suspended and not discharged.

50 [1954] 2 QB 402 at 424.

51 In practice, commercial realities determine who concludes the carriage contract and who bears the cost. For instance, if buyer has difficulty obtaining foreign exchange, it will want to contract so the seller pays the cost of freight and insurance—that is, the buyer will not want an FOB term, but will want a C or D Term.

To explain more fully, the seller can negotiate the carriage contract (it is usually more convenient) on the basis that the buyer is responsible for costs without changing the nature of the F Term.[52] In other words, the seller can decide to assist the buyer by negotiating the contract of carriage without there being any change in the delivery point and when costs and risks pass;[53] however, under an FOB term, the seller has no obligation to do so. Where the seller declines to negotiate the contract of carriage (and thus the buyer negotiates the carriage), the seller's responsibilities are discharged when:

1 The goods are delivered on board the nominated vessel;
2 Sufficient or 'timely' notice of the delivery has been provided to the seller of the ship's name, loading point and required delivery time;[54] and
3 Assistance has been given by the seller in obtaining the necessary documentation to enable the buyer to procure insurance and take delivery of the goods.

Of course, failure of either side to discharge their responsibilities may constitute a breach and affect both the point at which risk passes and the allocation of costs.[55]

Whenever an F Term is used, the seller remains obligated at the buyer's request, costs and risk to assist in obtaining the contract of carriage—that is, bill of lading, sea waybill or Electronic Data Interchange (EDI)[56] (if electronic documents are being used). The seller is also expected to deliver goods that conform to the sales contract, as well as supply a commercial invoice that identifies the goods shipped (as described in the sales contract), along with the other transport and related documents required under the sales contract.

It is important to realise that, just because a contract uses a particular Incoterm, this does not mean that the risks and costs associated with that particular term will apply. For example, a contract which states that it is using FOB but does not have the essential features of the FOB term (that is, risk and costs passing to the buyer when the goods cross the ship's rail) will likely not be deemed to be an F Term. Instead, a court may find that the parties have in fact divided the costs/risks very differently and substitute another term, such as a D Term (destination term). Thus, the mere use of the term is insufficient; it can be overridden if the contract apportions the risks/costs differently to what the term provides. To illustrate, in *The Julia*,[57] an Argentine seller contracted to ship grain to a Belgian buyer, CIF Antwerp, payment against the documents. However, the delivery

---

52 In practice, even where the buyer negotiates the bill of lading with the carrier, it is not unusual for the seller to be handed this document as proof of delivery. Incoterms 2000 even provides for this by requiring the seller to provide the buyer with the 'usual document' as proof of delivery.

53 Under s 35 (3) of the *Sales of Goods Act 1923* (NSW) (and unless otherwise agreed), where the seller despatches the goods by sea and it is usual to insure the goods, the buyer must be notified when the goods are despatched so as to enable insurance to be purchased. Failure on the part of the seller to do so in a sufficient and timely manner could result in the risk remaining with the seller.

54 Incoterms do not deal with the consequences of failing to nominate a ship, but at common law it is a fundamental breach of the sales contract.

55 For instance, failure of the buyer to provide sufficient or timely notice of the vessel's name and loading point would mean the buyer has to bear the risk and responsibility for consequent additional expenses of storage and insurance.

56 EDI is a system used to transfer electronic documents from one computer system to another in trade transactions.

57 *Comptoir d'Achat et de Vente du Boerenbond Belge S/A v Luis de Ridder Limitada* [1949] AC 293.

order and bill of lading contained additional conditions on the seller before 'delivery' would be deemed to occur. The outbreak of the Second World War prevented the vessel from landing in Antwerp, the vessel was diverted and the grain was sold elsewhere. Due to the additional conditions, the House of Lords ruled that payment was no longer against the documents and that the contract was no longer CIF, despite explicit reference to that term in the contract. Instead, the court ruled that a D Term governed the contract.

The situation becomes more complicated when terms provide for differing meanings depending upon the jurisdiction. For instance, the US Uniform Commercial Code (UCC) rather confusingly deviates from Incoterms 2000 when using the FOB term. Thus, in the USA, FOB could mean the place of shipment or the place of destination. To reduce uncertainty, it is advisable for the parties to explicitly include the words 'Incoterms 2000', or at least reference the Guide to Incoterms 2000 in the sales contract to reduce uncertainty.

3.4.4 C Terms

When utilised in port-to-port transport, C Terms contain two possible choices:

- CIF (named port of destination); and
- CFR (named port of destination)/C & F (named port of destination).

C Terms are the traditional alternatives to FOB, with the essential difference being that freight is paid for by the seller, who is normally expected to arrange the contract for carriage. The only difference between CIF and CFR is that in the former the seller must also procure and pay for insurance, while in the latter the seller is not required to obtain insurance. It is important to state at the outset that CIF and CFR are unsuited to multimodal transport—they are designed only for port-to-port delivery. Terms suitable for multimodal transport will be discussed in the next section.

As with the F Terms, risk under the C Terms traditionally passes from the seller to the buyer when the goods cross the ship's rail, and delivery occurs when the goods are placed on the ship. When the C Terms are used, however, property does not pass when the goods are loaded onto the ship, but instead passes on the tender of the documents.[58] The C Terms, however, contain one additional key point in the transaction: the port of destination. The port of destination is relevant in determining the terms and appropriate costs of the freight and insurance, for which the seller is responsible. This is unlike the F Terms, where the buyer is responsible for the cost of freight and for procuring insurance.[59] When making use of C Terms, the seller must pass on the additional costs for procuring transport and, if applicable, insurance to the buyer as part of the sales contract. The seller, therefore, bears the risk of loss or the financial benefits from any fluctuations

58 In actual fact, property that passes on the delivery of the documents is conditional upon the acceptance of the inspection of the goods. If the buyer rejects the goods for conformity, the property reverts to the seller.

59 It should be mentioned that even though the seller procures the insurance, the buyer should be given direct enforcement rights, as a direct relationship between the buyer (or transferee) and the carrier and insurer is essential to the smooth operation of CIF.

in currency or the cost of carriage and insurance (if applicable) following the conclusion of the sales contract; the seller cannot pass any price increases onto the buyer following the conclusion of the sales contract.

Under the C Terms, the seller must pay for export clearance and for the costs of ship loading and unloading, which may be charged by regular shipping lines. The seller must also provide a document that enables the buyer to claim the goods from the carrier. By contrast, under an F Term (unless otherwise agreed), the seller is only required to provide evidence that the goods have been delivered (for example, a mate's receipt). Of course, the seller must also hand over any other such relevant document which it receives (such as the bill of lading, if it has been received from the carrier). The buyer is responsible for a number of other expenses, such as unloading costs (such as lighterage or wharfage charges), obtaining import clearance and paying customs duties (as with the F Terms, the seller must assist the buyer, for example by providing the certificate of origin), and for all contingencies that occur after shipment and before delivery (such as strikes, collision and government directives).

As in the F Terms, under the C Terms the documents represent the goods. Again, this means that if the goods are lost or damaged prior to reaching their destination, the seller may still be entitled to collect payment upon the presentation of documents.[60] The carrier should therefore not release the goods without sighting the original bill of lading. In fast shipping lanes, this could mean that the documents may not be available until after the arrival of the goods. Not wanting to lose the advantage of a quick turnaround, carriers generally therefore prefer the use of a non-negotiable bill of lading (a sea waybill). As we shall see in Chapter 4, non-negotiable bills of lading are not suitable when banks are involved (such as in a letter of credit) as they are not deemed acceptable security; nor are they suitable if the goods are going to be sold in transit (for example, oil carried under a charterparty, or where the importer resells the goods as components to a third party who takes delivery). Non-negotiable bills of lading also make it difficult for a third party to pay for the goods prior to delivery to the original consignee.

In terms of delivery obligations, when CIF is used the seller is obligated to:

1 Deliver the documents representing the goods against which the buyer must pay;[61] and
2 Deliver goods that conform to the requirements of the sales contract.

Interestingly, and in contradistinction to the common law, under Incoterms 2000 the seller must actually ship the goods (that is, the goods must be placed on a vessel and shipped) in order for the CIF term to be used. Technically, this means that the seller cannot make use of the CIF term if it has purchased (or intends purchasing) the goods when they are in transit.

---

60 The buyer can still reject the goods in two situations: (1) where the documents tendered by the seller were either untimely or contained any discrepancies; or (2) where the seller has shipped non-conforming goods. In either situation, the buyer can reject the goods, treat the contract as repudiated and claim damages for non-delivery.

61 Merely stipulating the time at which payment will be made in the contract does not change the fact that the documents represent the goods, when risk passes, or when delivery occurs, so the term is still a C Term.

As mentioned above, the point of delivery is on board the vessel (as it is under FOB). The buyer must accept delivery and receive the goods from the carrier at the point of destination so as to allow the carrier contract to be discharged. The failure of the buyer to fulfil these obligations may result in the seller incurring additional charges from the carrier. The seller is allowed, of course, to pass these additional costs on to the buyer.

3.4.5 Multimodal terms

Multimodal terms were incorporated into Incoterms 1980 to provide for the situation where goods are not to be loaded past the ship's rails, but instead stowed in containers at an earlier stage in the transportation chain. In such cases, it is inappropriate for the ship's rail to be the division point for functions, cost and risk. Despite this, an enormous amount of containerised transport transactions occur using CIF and CFR. Usage of these particular C Terms is inappropriate, due to the fact that when containerised goods are being transported, the goods are not delivered by the seller to the port of shipment but to an inland freight-forwarding depot. Traders engaged in export transactions must be careful to utilise the Incoterm that best reflects the reality of when goods actually pass from the control of the seller.

The main difference between multimodal terms and those suitable only for port-to-port transport is that the division of responsibility comes at an earlier stage under the former, such as when the goods 'fill a container load' (FCL) or 'less than a container load' (LCL). Thus, when multimodal transportation is used, responsibility shifts at the point at which the seller delivers the goods into the transportation chain, not when the goods reach the port of delivery.

Multimodal transportation has become very popular in recent years, with goods often loaded into a container or 'break bulk' and placed on a train or a lorry, and at a later stage transported by sea to the port of destination, or simply loaded inland onto a pallet for subsequent sea or air transport. In fact, it is now quite common for transport to consist of rail or road, then sea or air, then rail or road again before the delivery is completed. In this situation, it is common for the freight forwarder to simply deliver a full container to the importer's place of business (if the container is LCL, the freight forwarder will degroup the container and separate the parcels prior to delivering the goods to the importer).

Incoterms include three terms to be used in preference to FOB or CIF when container transport is used. These terms are also applicable when goods are shipped by air (as Incoterms contain no special term for shipment by air):

- 'FCA free carrier to (... named place)';
- 'CPT carriage paid to (... named place of destination)';
- 'CIP carriage and insurance paid to (... named place of destination)'.

These terms have several unique characteristics. The first point to notice is that they refer to a 'place', not a 'port', and are thus unsuitable when a negotiable marine bill of lading is required. The terms are, however, based on the FOB and CIF terms. For instance, the buyer will pay for carriage under FCA, but the seller is responsible for the costs of carriage under CPT and CIP. Second, while 'shipped' bills of lading are normally for

FOB/CIF, combined transport trade terms usually envisage only 'received for shipment' transport documents.

Under the FCA term ('FCA free carrier to (... named place)'), 'free carrier' means that the seller has discharged its delivery obligation when it hands over the goods, cleared for export, to a carrier named by the buyer at the named place or point. Importantly, Incoterms 2000 defines a 'carrier' as 'any person' who undertakes to perform by 'rail road, sea, air, inland waterway or by a combination of such modes'. Freight forwarders are, therefore, included in the definition. The FCA term is designed for containerisation and multimodal transport, but is also appropriate in cases where a single means of transport (say, rail or air) is to be used. For example, the term is applicable where a carton manufacturer negotiates a contract to send a consignment of flattened cartons by air from Hong Kong to Sydney. In this situation, the term 'FCA free carrier to (Sydney Airport)' would be used.

Under the above circumstances, the seller is responsible for the carriage up until the goods are delivered to the air carrier or airfreight depot at the designated airport (that is, Hong Kong Airport). The seller is also responsible for appropriate packaging (if it is aware of the circumstances of transport), obtaining export clearance (and obtaining an air waybill for the buyer, if willing). Thereafter, the risk, cost of carriage and insurance passes to the buyer, who must take responsibility for obtaining quarantine and customs clearance. Therefore the risk passes at the point in which the seller delivers the goods into the transportation chain. Correspondingly, the failure of buyer to nominate the place of delivery may result in the premature passing of risk; that is, risk passing to the buyer before actual delivery occurs.

While the FCA term is similar to the FOB term, the terms 'CPT carriage paid to (... named place of destination)' and 'CIP carriage and insurance paid to (... named place of destination)' differ fundamentally from the CFR/CIF terms in a number of important ways. For instance, delivery occurs under CFR and CIF when the goods pass the ship's rails and are loaded on board the vessel at the point of shipment; but when the CPT and CIP terms are used, delivery occurs when the goods are in custody of the first carrier (who may be inland). To illustrate, under CPT/CIP, if goods are taken from an inland point by rail or road from Orange to a port in Sydney for shipment to Hong Kong, delivery occurs when the goods are handed over to the first inland rail/truck carrier (in Orange). Likewise, risk passes from the seller to the buyer at the point in which the goods are delivered to the first carrier.

In terms of cost, this difference does not alter the seller's position because under the C Terms the seller arranges and pays for freight (and insurance in CIF and CIP) to the country of destination. The CPT/CIP terms should be used when the mode of transport is air, road, unnamed or multimodal (that is, anything but sea), or by any of those methods in addition to sea. The terms are also applicable when goods are not handed over for sea transport 'over the rails', but when containers or ro-ro ('roll on, roll off') vessels are used in the sea transport.

3.4.6 D Terms

D Terms, or 'destination' or 'arrival' contracts, are used when the parties agree that the seller should be responsible for the carriage, risk and cost until the goods are delivered at a named port or named place of destination in the country of destination. The applicable terms are as follows:

- 'DES (… named port of destination)';
- 'DEQ (… named port of destination)';
- 'DDU (… named point of destination) duties unpaid';
- 'DDP (… named point of destination) duties paid';
- 'DAF (… named port of destination)'.

DES/DEQ are used when the principal carriage is by sea, whereas DDU/DDP are used when delivery is to a place inland from the port. The DAF term is used when the means of transport is by rail and, as it is not relevant for Australasian traffic, it will not be discussed further.

As just mentioned, the DES/DEQ terms are utilised when the principal means of transport is by sea. While common law has long recognised two similar terms, 'ex ship (… named port of arrival)' and 'ex quay (… named port of arrival)', using DES/DEQ has the advantage of clarity in that the Incoterms 2000 clearly spells out the responsibilities that attach to each party.

Importantly, when any D Term is used, the focus is on delivery of the goods, not the documents. In other words, in the absence of an agreement to the contrary, the buyer's obligation to pay the contract price arises when the goods (as opposed to the documents) are delivered at the destination. This does not mean that the documents are unimportant, however, as the buyer still needs the necessary documents to take possession (the freight forwarder will not release the goods until the necessary document or EDI message is received, which allows them to surrender the goods). Therefore, as with the other terms, the seller must provide the 'usual transport document' to enable the buyer to collect the goods. Unsurprisingly, under the D Terms, the seller bears risk for loss or damage until delivery is complete. The seller is also responsible for all costs until delivery is complete.

Under the DES/DEQ terms, the seller has the responsibility for negotiating the contract of carriage and can select the transport to be used, provided it is by the usual route in the customary manner. Thus, if the seller selects an unusual route or makes it difficult for the buyer to receive the goods, the additional risk and costs are on the seller.

In all D Term contracts, the point of destination should be stated in the contract. As the carriage contract is negotiated and paid for by the seller, the seller may select the point that best suits its purpose. For example, the seller may select to unload in Sydney even though the buyer is located in Victoria. If this is a problem for the buyer, the DDU/DDP terms should be selected in preference to DES/DEQ.

Destination contracts do not contain an obligation for either side to procure insurance, but it is of course advisable for both to obtain insurance. As the seller bears the risk until the goods arrive at the point of destination, the seller should build the costs of insurance into the contract price.

In order to deliver the goods, the seller must place goods 'at the disposal of the buyer' at the agreed point of destination. Under the DES term, the seller is not required to unload the goods (the goods must arrive at named port in the stipulated delivery time); while DEQ, DDU and DDP require the seller to take responsibility for unloading (the buyer takes carriage on the quay or wharf). These terms are not really suitable when the shipowner charges for discharge in its carriage price (this is more likely for a charterparty).

Under the DDU/DDP terms, the place of delivery is usually an inland freight forwarder or the buyer's place of business. When the DES, DEQ and DDU terms are utilised, the seller does not have the responsibility to pay for import clearance and related charges (usually to the freight forwarder). Under normal circumstances, if the buyer cannot obtain customs clearance and the seller cannot deliver, the risk will pass to the buyer and the seller can avoid the contract. Of course, such a circumstance is far from ideal, as the seller will have incurred charges (lost time, change in prices, opportunity costs, etc), and it may be difficult to recoup these losses in a foreign court.[62] The seller can, however, undertake the responsibility for import clearance (as distinct from paying the costs). This would, of course, shift the liability resulting from the inability to obtain customs clearance from the buyer to the seller. Under the DDP term, the seller is responsible for all such obligations and costs unless the contract specifies to the contrary (in most circumstances, however, the costs are usually divided, as the buyer knows what charges the country of destination will charge and is better able to anticipate changes and recognise anomalies). The DDP term is an arrival contract with payment being due only upon arrival of the goods.

3.5 Conclusion

The international carriage of goods by sea adds additional contracts to a sale of goods. One of the parties, normally the seller, will arrange shipment of goods with a carrier. The contract between the shipper and the carrier is documented via a bill of lading or a waybill. It should be noted that the carrier is not necessarily the owner of the vessel. The carrier may have hired the vessel by entering into a charterparty with the owner, either for a specific voyage or a specific time. It should be obvious that all the parties involved in an export transaction—that is, the buyer, the seller, the banks, the carriers and the shipper—must take account of their varied and different concerns in the same transaction. The pivotal instrument is the bill of lading.

The contract between the shipper and the carrier in essence specifies the rights and duties between the two parties and most importantly regulates the liabilities (and the exclusions) of the carrier in relation to the goods which are entrusted into its care. The duty of the carrier is to provide a seaworthy and cargoworthy vessel on which the goods can be transported. The contract is normally embedded in a bill of lading, which takes on three important functions: it serves as a receipt of the goods, it verifies that constructive possession has been transferred to the carrier, and it is a document of title—that is, the goods can only be obtained by the person who holds the requisite bill of lading.

Multimodal bills can also be devised. These allow the goods to be shipped by other means than sea transport, or in combination with sea transport. However, Australia is not,

62 It should be mentioned that some governments allow the words 'cleared for import' to be placed after the DDU term, which means the seller can proceed and clear and deliver the goods without paying any associated fees.

nor can it be, a signatory to the road or rail convention as it simply does not have any direct link to road or rail (all goods need to be put on a ship or aircraft).

Incoterms are an important tool to further define the relationship between the parties. The rights and obligations of all parties convened must be understood in order to work out whether insurance is needed and who must apply for the insurance (for instance). FAS has very different obligations in this respect to CIF. Incoterms also define the passing of risk from seller to buyer.

To conclude, the carriage of goods by sea or by multimodal means of transport involves not only a relationship between the parties but also implicates the sales contract. For this reason, the CISG or any other governing law must be read with Incoterms in mind.

Questions

With regard to the case study at the beginning of this chapter:

1 Mr Longbow is particularly concerned about the stolen goods. He cannot see any clauses in the sales contract that cover what happens in such a case, and who is responsible for covering the costs. Please advise.
2 How would you phrase a clause to cover yourself for unexpected theft of goods?
3 Can Mr Longbow take action against Mr Smith in relation to the whole matter? If yes, why? If not, why not, and who are the other possible parties?
4 a Assuming the bottles were broken while on board the ship, who should Mr Longbow sue? Will he be successful? Give reasons.
  What would your answers be if the bottles were broken while:
  b In transport in Melbourne; or
  c Being loaded onto the ship?
5 Will Mr Longbow be forced to arbitrate in Singapore?
6 If Mr Smith had the shipment insured in his name, will the company pay for the damages?
7 When transporting goods in containers, is FAS or FOB the appropriate term to use?
8 Can a ship be cargoworthy without being seaworthy?
9 If you were to sign a multimodal contact with a carrier, who is responsible for transporting the goods by truck to the wharf?
10 Why is the bill of lading such an important instrument?
11 What is the difference, if any, between a bill of lading and a waybill?
12 Why is the term 'insurable interest' of such importance in marine insurance?

PART II

Payment Options

CHAPTER 4

payment in international business transactions

BUY Pty Ltd, an Australian company based in Orange, New South Wales, requires several hundred steel beams manufactured to a certain and exacting specification. While browsing the internet, the President of BUY finds the website for SELL Corp, a Hong Kong-based manufacturer and supplier of metal works, and sends an email enquiring whether SELL Corp can meet the standard required and all other specifications.

BUY requires a credit period, but as it is unfamiliar with the various methods of payment normally involved in an international transaction, it is unsure which party must arrange and bear the costs. Nevertheless, BUY agrees that payment will be made through an irrevocable, confirmed, sight letter of credit upon the presentation of a bill of lading and other documents. BUY subsequently learns that SELL Corp has a reputation for steel that fails to meet the specific standard and grade of steel required in the contract. BUY is unsure whether SELL Corp is a reputable company, or whether it is negligent or fraudulent, and is concerned that it too might be shipped an inappropriate grade of steel. BUY wants to know what steps it could take to prevent (or delay, pending an inspection of the goods) payment on the letter of credit.

4.1 Introduction

This chapter investigates the main methods of payment most likely to be used in an international business transaction. The method of payment should be negotiated into the sales contract. Numerous payment options can be used, and the contractual choice will likely depend upon a number of considerations, chief among which is the relative bargaining power of the parties. If the parties are not familiar with each other, the seller may not want to risk extending credit to the buyer and may instead prefer to involve banks in the transaction. However, such a service is not free, and the cost should be considered and spelt out in the sales contract.

This chapter could not possibly explain all the permutations and details of every conceivable payment option. Instead, the chapter merely will expose the reader to the most common payment options, while at the same time showing how these options interact with the international business transaction.

The chapter begins with a brief overview of the payment risks involved in conducting international business transactions. It then provides a short outline of the main payment options utilised in international business before covering a few of the more prominent options in greater detail.

4.2 Overview

At a very minimum, the parties to the contract should agree on the mode of payment, the time when payment is due, the place of payment and the currency of payment.

In reaching an agreement over the payment option, the parties must consider several factors. Most notable among these factors is *risk*. Each payment option has benefits and risks for each party. There are, of course, the *general commercial* risks that occur as a result of doing business internationally: what is the nature of the relationship between the parties? How solvent and reliable is the other party? How likely is a dispute to occur? How familiar are the parties with international transactions (including customs and export/import regulations)? There are also *economic* risks which stem from a number of factors, including the economic and political situation of the countries of both parties. Other questions of economic risk include the stability of the currency, the quality of the judicial system, and the reliability and trustworthiness of the banks. Finally, there are also *financial* risks in an international business transaction, involving currency exchange rates and interest rates.

Given the above three types of risk, the seller will not want to relinquish control over the goods until it has received payment for the goods. The buyer, on the other hand, will not want to pay for the goods until it has received and inspected them. In essence, each party wants to limit its own risks.

In order to facilitate the smooth functioning of international trade, several methods of payment have been developed which attempt to reconcile some of the conflicting interests of the parties, thereby limiting the risks of both parties. Most of these methods entail the involvement of a third party (usually a bank) and the usage of documents.

4.3 Methods of payment

A bill of exchange (also referred to as a 'draft') is often used in an international transaction to facilitate payment. A bill of exchange is a written unconditional order for payment from a seller (drawer, or payee) to a buyer (drawee), directing the drawee to pay a specified amount of money in a given currency to the drawer or named payee at a fixed or determinable date (the most common form of a draft is a simple cheque). The demand for payment could be made upon sight of the draft (sight bill) or at a specified time at some point thereafter (term bill). In the latter circumstance, the buyer/drawee will need to sign the bill (accept the bill) and deliver it to the seller/drawer. The buyer will thus have received a credit for a certain period of time. The seller, having accepted the draft, can either hold onto the bill until its maturity, at which time it would present the bill to the buyer for payment, or it can onsell the bill to another person prior to maturation (this process is referred to as 'discounting the bill', as the value of the bill is often reduced below face value).

A bill of exchange is therefore a negotiable instrument that can be traded, either between parties or through the use of banks as intermediaries. A bill of exchange can even be used in conjunction with the delivery of the transport documents (it is then referred to as a 'documentary bill'). The seller can increase its security in this process by insisting that the bill is signed and guaranteed by a bank.

The five major methods of payment detailed below all can—and often do—make use of a bill of exchange. All of the methods involve varying degrees of certainty, risks and costs for both parties. Each contracting party to a sales contract must evaluate all relevant factors before determining which method is suitable for a particular transaction.

The first method of payment, *payment in advance*, is the most secure method of payment for the seller.[1] This method offers the seller minimum risk, as the seller is able to secure payment for the goods before shipment.[2] Conversely, this method is the most risky option for buyers, who must pay for the goods before they are shipped (thus leaving the seller with both the goods and the money).

A less risky option for the buyer is *payment on delivery*. Particularly suitable when the 'ex works' term is utilised in the sales contract, this method requires the buyer to pay for the goods when they are presented and delivery occurs. In order to limit its risks, the buyer could negotiate a right of inspection prior to parting with the payment.

The third payment option described is the *open account*. This option simply involves the seller sending an invoice to the buyer (either prior to or following delivery of the goods), who then pays on the account either at that time (sight payment) or at some other specified time in the future (for example, within 30 days of receiving the invoice). As this option involves the most risk to the seller, its use is limited to situations where the seller is familiar with the buyer and assured there is no (or very limited) risk of insolvency or default. *On consignment* is a form of open account that occurs when the seller agrees that the buyer may pay for goods progressively as the goods are onsold.

The fourth and fifth payment options are the most common forms of payment used in an international transaction—*documentary credits* (also called letters of credit) and *documentary collection*. Both are suitable for and commonly used when the sales contract calls for the trade terms FOB or CIF. Both methods are briefly described here, but will be more thoroughly explained below.

At its simplest, a documentary credit arrangement/letter of credit is a widely used payment option that enables the seller to receive an undertaking of payment from

---

1 Payment may be made by a variety of means, including by cheque or electronic transfer. Each payment method involves differing risks and should be fully analysed. For electronic transfers, many nations have laws on the matter. See for example the *Australian Electronic Transactions Act 1999* (Cth). See also the 1996 UNCITRAL Model Law on Electronic Transfers.

2 Another even more secure option for the seller is 'payment with order', which requires the buyer to pay for the goods prior to their manufacture.

a bank upon the fulfilment of certain conditions, namely the 'presentation of the documents'. In this arrangement, the buyer initiates the process by opening a letter of credit in the seller's favour with a bank. The seller will receive the payment from the bank when it can prove that it has shipped the goods subject to the contract. It proves this by presenting the relevant documents (set out in the letter of credit and most often including the commercial invoice, a negotiable bill of lading, certificates of quality and origin and (depending upon the shipping terms used) an insurance certificate) to the bank.[3] At this point, payment will be effected and the bank will then seek reimbursement from the buyer.

The letter of credit therefore breaks down a major risk into a smaller risk for both parties. Payment will not be made until the goods have been shipped, but shipment of the goods will effectuate payment. Thus, the documents control possession of the goods and neither party controls both the goods and the money.

As will be discussed in greater detail below, letters of credit are most often subject to the International Chamber of Commerce's (ICC) Uniform Customs and Practice for Documentary Credits (UCP), the most recent revision of which came into force 1 July 2007 (referred to as the 'UCP 600').[4] The UCP must be incorporated by reference into the contract.

A documentary collection arrangement also uses documents to effectuate payment. In this transaction, the seller normally tenders the necessary documents and instructs the corresponding bank to collect payment from the buyer. The buyer will then normally have to pay for the goods (by, for instance, a sight or term bill of exchange) prior to receiving the documents that enable it to take possession of the goods.[5] In this regard, the bank generally does not have any interest in the documents, and instead is merely acting as an agent for the seller. This method is less secure for the seller, who must actually ship the goods before receiving a guarantee of payment (from either the seller or the bank). Documentary collections can be regulated under the ICC Uniform Rules for Collection Pub No 522 (1995) if they are incorporated by reference into the contract.

It should also be mentioned that the buyer can also make use of additional mechanisms to protect itself from a breach (or fraudulent conduct) by the seller. In this regard, the buyer can reduce such a risk by having a third party set up a guarantee in favour of the buyer. The guarantee, which would have to be negotiated by contract, must officially be initiated by the seller and would only be used in the event of a breach/default on the part of the seller. The most likely mechanisms to be used are the performance bond, advance payment bond, performance guarantee and standby letter of credit.

---

3 See for example *Pavia & Co SPA v Thurmann-Neilson* [1952] 2 QB 84.

4 The UCP is developed by the International Chamber of Commerce and was first published in 1933. It has been said that the UCP has been drafted by bankers, for bankers. Exporters and importers were not consulted in the drafting. The previous version, the UCP 500, was in place 1993–2007.

5 If payment is not made, the bank will normally turn the documents back over to the seller.

4.3.1 Documentary credits

4.3.1a Introduction

The documentary credit (or letter of credit) is a common form of payment mechanism in international transactions and one that has greatly assisted the smooth facilitation and expansion of international trade. The importance of the letter of credit to international commerce cannot be understated. The Supreme Court of Western Australia recently summarised the nature of the letter of credit by stating:

> Letters of credit have been described as the 'crankshaft of modern trade'; the 'life-blood of international commerce': *RD Harbottle (Mercantile) Ltd v National Westminster Bank Ltd* [1978] QB 146 at 155 per Kerr J; and 'the life blood of commerce': *Intraco Ltd v Notis Shipping Corporation (The 'Bhoja Trader')* [1981] 2 Lloyd's Rep 256 at 257 per Donaldson LJ (who said that 'Thrombosis will occur if, unless fraud is involved, the Courts intervene and thereby disturb the mercantile practice of treating rights thereunder as being the equivalent of cash in hand') ... In *Cruickshank v Westpac Banking Corporation* [1989] 1 NZLR 114 at 121, Sinclair J said that letters of credit are regarded by the commercial and business world as 'sacrosanct' ... In *Ian Stach Ltd v Baker Bosley Ltd* [1958] 2 QB 130 at 139, Diplock J said that this kind of letter of credit is more than 'a mere method of payment' and 'creates a direct liability upon the banker independent of the contract of sale, and is an undertaking by the banker that if the seller presents the required documents in the required time he will receive payment of the contract price'. In *United City Merchants (Investments) Ltd v Royal Bank of Canada* [1983] 1 AC 168 (HL), Lord Diplock said at 183:
>
> > The whole commercial purpose for which the system of confirmed irrevocable documentary credits has been developed in international trade is to give to the seller an assured right to be paid before he parts with control of the goods that does not permit of any dispute with the buyer as to the performance of the contract of sale being used as a ground for non-payment or reduction or deferment of payment.[6]

Letters of credit have several advantages for the seller, as the seller does not have to ship the goods until a letter of credit has been properly set up and the seller has been properly advised as such.[7] Use of a letter of credit adds an additional party to the transaction, as the bank that issues the letter of credit (the 'issuing bank') provides an independent undertaking and adds another layer of security of payment for the seller. As will be more fully explored below, the letter of credit is also completely separate to the underlying sales contract, meaning payment will be made to the seller upon the fulfilment of the conditions in the letter of credit (normally, once it has provided the necessary document, including evidence that it has shipped the goods subject to the sales contract). Thus, disputes as to the fulfilment of the underlying sales contract will not interfere with the obligations under the letter of credit. This 'independence' principle is only overridden in very limited circumstances (explained below).

In order to effectuate payment, the documents tendered by the beneficiary must be made as called for in the letter of credit to the named institution/person. The letter of

6 *Ideas Plus Investments Ltd v National Australia Bank Ltd* [2006] WASCA 215 at para 33.

7 See *Bunge Corporation v Vegetable Vitamin Foods (Pte) Ltd*, QBD (Comm) [1985] 1 Lloyd's Rep 613.

credit essentially operates as conditional payment of the purchase price between the buyer and seller. Under a letter of credit, a seller must make use of this method. If for some reason the seller cannot obtain payment due to fault of its own (for example, failure to produce the correct documents), it cannot claim payment by other means (for example, by directly invoicing the buyer). The buyer is discharged from its obligations of payment.[8] However, there are some exceptions where the seller can claim payment directly from the buyer, for instance if the chosen intermediary (bank) becomes insolvent.[9]

When presenting documents to the bank for payment, the beneficiary (seller) must strictly comply with the conditions of the letter of credit. Failure to meet the conditions may result in the bank rejecting the documents, meaning the seller will not be paid. Therefore, if the seller notices any discrepancies between the sales contract and the letter of credit it must notify the buyer and either insist upon the terms as set out in the contract, or renegotiate them as per the letter of credit.

If the seller presents documents that do not conform to the letter of credit, the bank will most often confer with the buyer to see if that party will waive the discrepancy. As it is estimated that over 50 per cent of all presentations contain at least one discrepancy,[10] buyers quite often do agree to waive the discrepancy and instruct the bank to accept the presentation. In a falling market, however, the buyer can insist upon strict compliance and instruct the bank to reject the documents (the buyer can then either negotiate a lower price or purchase the goods elsewhere). With the goods already in transit, the seller is thus in a weak negotiating position.

4.3.1b Letter of credit: the transaction

Before continuing with the intricacies of the letter of credit and related jurisprudence, it is necessary to fully explain how the letter of credit transaction works.

The use and terms of a letter of credit are negotiated by contract. The process of initiating a letter of credit begins when the buyer contacts its bank and applies for a letter of credit to be opened in favour of the seller in accordance with the terms of the sales contract. The UCP must be incorporated into the contract (and is thus subject to contractual negotiation and agreement), and at that point takes precedence over other legal rules. The letter of credit will almost always incorporate the UCP. In fact, during its period of use, the UCP 500 was incorporated in over 98 per cent of all letters of credit.[11] It is expected that the UCP 600 will also be incorporated in a similar percentage of letters of credit. The UCP 600 does not, however, render domestic laws redundant in all respects, as the UCP does have gaps and domestic law fills the vacuum.

8 See *Shamser Jute Mills Ltd v Sethia (London) Ltd*, QBD (Comm) [1987] 1 Lloyd's Rep 388.

9 See *ED & F Man v Nigerian Sweets & Confectionery Co Ltd*, QBD (Comm) [1977] 2 Lloyd's Rep 50.

10 See Simplifying International Trade Ltd (SITPRO), *Report On The Use Of Export Letters Of Credit 2001/2002* (11 April 2003), at 2, 3, available at [www.sitpro.org.uk/reports/lettcredr/lettcredr.pdf]. For the 10 most frequent disrepencies, see SITPRO, *Report on the Use of Export Letters of Credit 2001/2002*, Section 4: 'The survey', available at [www.sitpro.org.uk/reports/lettcredr/lettcredrs4.html].

11 Since 2002, the eUCP has come into effect to supplement the UCP 500 and, when incorporated into the contract, provides the rules for when all or some of the documents are submitted electronically.

But it is important to remember that the UCP will override domestic law in the event of conflict, unless the conflict involves a 'mandatory' provision of domestic law.

The credit can traditionally be either revocable or irrevocable; all credits should clearly indicate the type.[12] In an irrevocable letter of credit, the issuing bank provides an undertaking to pay the beneficiary upon the fulfilment of the conditions of the credit. The credit cannot be cancelled or modified/amended in any way without agreement of the issuer, the confirming bank (if any) and the beneficiary.[13] Payment to the seller is thus assured provided the seller presents the necessary documents and otherwise acts in accordance with the terms of the credit. The revocable letter of credit can, however, be cancelled, amended or modified in any way and at any time by the issuing bank or buyer.[14] Quite clearly, a revocable letter of credit fails to provide the security needed by the seller in the transaction and is thus not normally appropriate.[15] For this reason, Article 6(c) of the UCP 500 recognised the irrevocable letter of credit as the default position (this can be amended by contract).[16] The UCP 600 goes one step further, however, and Article 3 appears to have eliminated the concept of a revocable credit altogether. Of course, the parties can still specifically provide in the credit that it is revocable, but the UCP 600 will not apply to such a credit, presumably even if it is referenced in the credit.

While the seller may accept a letter of credit from a bank in the buyer's country, this would mean that the seller must claim from that bank (the issuing bank) and, if necessary, enforce its obligations under the letter of credit in that country. For this reason, in addition to other legitimate reasons (such as a lack of knowledge of the trustworthiness, credibility and liquidity of the bank), sellers normally require the involvement of a second bank in the transaction. The second bank, normally located in the seller's country, is employed by the buyer's bank to act as a recipient of the documents.

This second bank can either act as an agent of the issuing bank or provide an undertaking of its own to the letter of credit. If the former, the bank in the seller's country does not enter into a contractual relationship with the seller; it merely advises the seller that a letter of credit has been opened in its favour and facilitates the exchange of documents against payment. In this situation, the bank is referred to as an 'advising' or 'nominated' bank.[17] While the issuing bank has an obligation to pay, the advising bank

---

12 See UCP 500, Articles 6, 8, and 9.

13 See UCP 600, Article 10. This article is similar to Article 9(d) of the UCP 500; however, that version also required the agreement of all parties, including the applicant, in order to amend a credit. Despite the wording of Article 10 of the UCP 600, many commentators still are of the opinion that agreement of the applicant is still necessary.

14 UCP 500, Article 8. This is the case even where part payment has been made in a credit involving multiple shipments of goods: see *Cape Asbestos Co v Lloyd's Bank* [1921] WN 274. However, the issuing bank must reimburse any other bank that has paid against the documents before receiving notice of the revocation: see UCP 500, Article 8(b).

15 It should be noted that some commentators have taken the position that the failure of the advising bank to inform the beneficiary of the revocation of a credit in a timely manner could expose the bank to liability in both tort and contract law. This position has no support at common law.

16 The position taken in the UCP 500 is in line with the traditional view at common law, but did reverse the rule in the UCP 400 which provided that, in the absence of an indication as to whether a credit was revocable or irrevocable, the credit was deemed to be revocable.

17 See UCP 600, Article 9.

has no obligation to pay. The credit is therefore 'unconfirmed'.[18] On the other hand, if the bank in the seller's country provides an undertaking to the letter of credit, it has entered into a contractual relationship with the beneficiary (seller) to pay the money stipulated in the letter of credit upon the fulfilment of its conditions. In this instance, the bank has 'confirmed' the credit and is referred to as the 'confirming' bank.[19] In essence, the confirming bank is providing a guarantee that the seller will be paid, even if the buyer and issuing bank become insolvent or the issuing bank refuses to honour the drafts drawn upon it. As the bank is most likely to be in the same jurisdiction as the seller, the seller should be aware of its reputation and status, as well as be in a position to have the bank's obligations enforced domestically.[20]

Once the beneficiary fulfils its obligations under the credit, payment can be effected in four different ways: sight payment, deferred payment, acceptance or negotiation.[21] More specifically, the credit could provide for payment on presentation of the documents (sight credit), or for payment at some point in the future, determinable in accordance with the stipulations of the credit (deferred payment credit). These do not involve the use of a negotiable instrument. The two other methods—acceptance and negotiable credit—do use a negotiable instrument. In an acceptance credit, the seller draws a bill of exchange (draft) on the issuing or confirming bank or directly on the buyer. In a negotiation credit, the nominated bank can negotiate (purchase) a bill of exchange drawn by the seller on the buyer or issuing bank.

Figure 4.1: Letter of credit flowchart

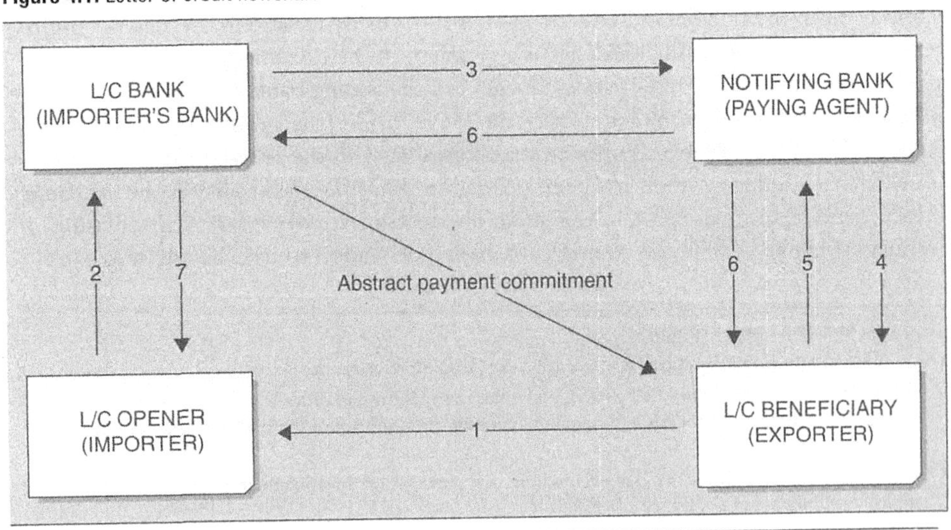

18 See *Maran Road Saw Mill v Austin Taylor & Co Ltd* [1975] 1 Lloyd's Rep 156.

19 See UCP 600, Article 8.

20 See *Panoustos v Raymond Hadley Corporation of New York* [1917] 2 KB 473.

21 See UCP 600 Arts 7a and 8a, 6b. It should be noted that the method of payment also determines which party is liable to pay any interest accruing during the transportation and delivery period of the transaction. See *Midland Bank v Seymour* [1955] 2 Lloyd's Rep 147, 165.

Without question, an irrevocable and confirmed sight credit is the most seller-friendly method as it is the most secure, and payment is effected as quickly as possible. It should however be noted that banks charge for the service of issuing and confirming/advising a letter of credit. As the service can be quite costly, the parties should consider whether it is worth the cost and, if so, assign in the contract which party is responsible for paying for the letter of credit arrangements, as well as of any confirmation of the credit that will be used (and who will pay for it).

Figure 4.1 should assist in understanding the nature of the transaction.

- In step 1, the exporter and importer sign a sales contract.
- In step 2, the importer applies to its bank (the issuing bank) to open a letter of credit.
- In step 3, the issuing bank sends the advice of the credit to the advising bank.
- In step 4, the exporter is advised of the credit.
- In step 5, after shipping the goods, the exporter presents the documents to the advising bank (the paying agent).
- In step 6, the advising bank makes the payment to the exporter (after checking the documents and confirming that they agree with the terms of the letter of credit). At the same time, the advising bank forwards the documents to the issuing bank and requests reimbursement for the amount of the letter of credit plus the bank's fees and expenses.
- In step 7, the issuing bank sends the documents to the importer and debits its account for the letter of credit amount plus the fees and expenses of the banks involved.

4.3.1c Letters of credit: the details

The question of which law governs the various parts of a documentary transaction is a complicated one, for which there is no set answer. In short, the answer depends upon what stage the transaction is at, as well as the jurisdiction where the matter is raised. Moreover, this is a mandatory law in most jurisdictions, meaning parties cannot utilise a choice of law provision to select the governing law.

In the USA, issuing and confirming banks are generally governed by the law of the jurisdiction where they are located, meaning there may be different laws for different parties to the transaction. In this regard, most courts hold that the place of performance of the letter of credit is where the bank issued the letter of credit. Under such holdings, if the law of the issuer's country would excuse the issuer's payment obligation, then the issuer's payment obligation is also excused in the USA.[22] Australian courts generally agree with this position.[23] On the other hand,

22 See *RSB Manufacturing Corp v Bank of Baroda* (In re RSB Manufacturing Corp 9 B.R. 414 (Bankr SDNY 1981), aff'd, 15 BR 650 (Bankr SDNY 1981); *Chuidian v Philippine National Bank* 734 F Supp 415 (CD Cal 1990), aff'd, 976 F2d 561 (9th Cir 1992).

23 See R Purvis & R Darvas, *The Law and Practice of Commercial Letters of Credit, Shipping Documents and Termination of Disputes in International Trade*, Butterworths, Sydney, 1975, p 153.

some US courts hold that the place of performance is where the bank is to honour the letter of credit.[24]

In the UK, the governing law is the law of where the payment (performance) is to be made (as opposed to where the payment will originate). This can be illustrated by the case of *Power Curber International Ltd v National Bank of Kuwait SAK*,[25] in which a North Carolina company agreed to sell machinery to Hammoudeh & Al Fulaij General Trading & Contracting Co WLL (Hammoudeh), a Kuwait company. The payment was assured by a $75 794.46 irrevocable letter of credit issued by Hammoudeh's bank, the National Bank of Kuwait. The bank provided that it would reimburse negotiating banks from its account held with Bank of America in New York. After Power Curber shipped the goods to Hammoudeh, a Kuwaiti court order prohibited the National Bank of Kuwait from honouring the letter of credit. When Power Curber failed to receive payment from the National Bank of Kuwait, it filed suit against the bank in the UK. In separate judgments, both Lord Denning and Lord Justice Griffiths expressly rejected the bank's argument that the proper law to apply was that of the issuer's jurisdiction—that is, Kuwaiti law—and not that of the beneficiary's, North Carolina. More specifically, Lord Denning held that unlike ordinary debts, which a debtor may pay in the place where it resides, a debt incurred under a letter of credit must be paid in 'the place where it is in fact payable against documents'.[26]

Obligation to open a letter of credit

At common law and in Australia, if the contract provides for the use of a letter of credit, the buyer is under a contractual obligation to open a letter of credit under the terms of the contract. The buyer's failure to open a proper letter of credit under the terms of the contract is a breach of the underlying contract for which the seller may generally repudiate the contract.[27] The seller can, however, choose to act upon a non-conforming letter of credit, but it must reserve the right to claim damages; otherwise it may be held to have waived the buyer's breach.[28]

Moreover, the buyer's obligation to the seller to open a letter of credit is only fulfilled when the advising or confirming bank advises the seller that the letter of credit has been opened. As the opening of the letter of credit is a condition precedent to the shipment of the goods, the failure of the buyer to open the letter of credit in the stipulated period of time may result in the seller repudiating the contract and claiming damages. Further, as the reason for the letter of credit is to provide the seller with an assurance of payment upon shipment, any obligation on the seller to load and ship the goods within a certain time period is suspended, or does not commence until the letter of credit is opened.[29]

---

24 *J Zeevi & Sons, Ltd v Grindlays Bank (Uganda) Ltd* 333 NE2d 168 (NY 1975); *Chuidian v Philippine National Bank* 976 F2d at 565–8 (Fernandez J, dissenting).

25 (1981) 1 WLR. 1233 (CA).

26 Ibid at 1240 (Lord Denning). See also ibid at 1242 (Griffiths LJ).

27 Of course, whether a repudiation is possible, or whether the contract is still valid and damages should be sought, depends on the applicable law, which would be ascertained through the relevant choice of laws rule in the chosen jurisdiction.

28 See *Sopromа SpA v Marine & Animal By-Products Corporation*, QBD (Comm) [1966] 1 Lloyd's Rep 367.

29 See the UK cases of *Kronos Worldwide Ltd v Sempra Oil Trading SARL* [2004] Int Com.LR 01/23; *Pavia & Co SpA v Thurmann-Neilsen* [1952] 2 QB 84; and *Plasticmoda SpA v Davidsons (Manchester) Ltd* [1952] 1 Lloyd's Rep 527.

Confirming the details of the letter of credit

Once the seller receives notice that the letter of credit has been opened, it must check and confirm the details of the credit. If the terms of the credit, as well as all accompanying details, are in order with the terms of the sales contract, the seller must then ship the goods.

Presenting the documents

When seeking payment following the shipping of the goods, the seller must present all of the documents specified in the letter of credit to the appropriate institution as stipulated in the credit. The most likely institutions would be the issuing bank, the confirming bank (if the letter of credit is confirmed), or another banking institution. Under the terms of the credit, the seller must present the required documents at the stipulated location and before the expiration of the credit.[30] If the credit does not assign a time period or expiry date for the presentation of the documents, Article 14(c) of the UCP 600 (formerly Article 43 of the UCP 500) provides that the date shall be no later than 21 days following shipment of the goods.

Checking the documents

Once the documents have been presented to the appropriate bank, the institution must check the documents against the terms of the credit in order to determine whether the documents comply with the credit. If the documents do comply with the terms of the credit, the bank should accept the documents and make payment. On the other hand, if the documents do not, on their face, comply with the terms of the credit, then the bank can reject the documents and refuse payment.

According to Article 14(b) of the UCP 600, banks must examine the documents within five banking days following their presentation (Articles 13 and 14 of the UCP 500 provided 'a reasonable time, not exceeding seven banking days').[31] As a result of the change, it is thought that banks will always take the five banking days to examine the documents, rather than examining them in less time if possible. Notice, as well as all of the reasons for the rejection, must be communicated to the party that presented the documents in a manner specified by Article 16 of the UCP 600.

Upon rejection, the bank will either return the documents or hold onto them at the disposal of the presenting party. This allows the beneficiary the opportunity to cure (remedy the discrepancies) and re-present the documents, so long as the time period for presentation has not expired.[32] The failure of the bank to comply with the rejection procedures set out in the UCP results in the bank being precluded from rejecting the documents.[33]

---

30 See UCP 600, Articles 6(d) and 29.

31 In previous versions of the UCP, as well as at common law (as applied in both the UK and the USA), banks have a 'reasonable time' to examine the documents. See for example *Bankers Trust Co v State Bank of India* (CA) [1991] 2 Lloyd's Rep 443. In the USA, a period of less than seven days had often been applied as 'reasonable' by the courts.

32 This is in accordance with UCP 600, Article 16 (UCP 500, Article 14).

33 See *Bayerische Vereinsbank Aktiengesellschaft v National Bank of Pakistan*, QBD (Comm) [1997] 1 Lloyd's Rep 59.

Importantly, banks must include all of the reasons for rejecting the documents within the set time period, as they will be precluded from later raising any other issue as a reason for the rejection.[34] For instance, in *Kerr-McGee v FDIC*, the issuing bank rejected the documents because the draft was in the wrong amount. After the beneficiary cured the defect, the issuing bank complained the invoice was inconsistent with the letter of credit. The court rejected the issuing bank's argument that notice of the defect in the draft constituted notice that the invoice was defective as well.[35] The rule can also be illustrated in *Bank of Taiwan, Ltd v Union National Bank*, where the issuing bank rejected the documents due to a defective bill of lading. At trial, the court precluded the issuing bank from raising additional defences: 'By formally placing its refusal to pay on one ground, the defendant must be held to have waived all others'.[36]

The bank's examination of the documents must therefore be 'thorough' and 'precise', because if the documents are not rejected in a timely fashion, the bank loses the right to reject them for discrepancies; and the bank only has this one period to identify any and all discrepancies upon which it may ever seek to rely. The practical result of such a rule does two things:

- First, it forces the issuer to raise all objections promptly.
- Second, it saves the courts from having to litigate all the subsequent thoughts that arise when lawyers become involved.

Risks to the bank

The biggest risk for the bank is that it makes payment when there were in fact discrepancies with the documents. In such an instance, the bank makes payment at its own risk. Thus, if the bank pays when there were discrepancies with the documents, or if it otherwise fails to comply with the letter of credit, it risks not being reimbursed.

---

34 Originally, this rule was based on the principle of estoppel, as the beneficiary was said to have reasonably relied on the issuer's failure to object to defective documents within a short time to its detriment, and it would be unfair to penalise that reliance. However, with the passage of time, courts have phased out any discussion of 'reliance' and 'detriment', and seemingly base their decisions only on whether the issuing banks or applicants are attempting to complain about defects after the fact for other reasons: see *Weyerhaeusen v First National Bank* 150 Or 172, 43 P2d 1078 (1935), where the court even rejected the issuing bank from raising the fact that the letter of credit was revocable, since it did not do so in the original notice of defect, even though it is doubtful there can be any 'reliance' in a revocable letter of credit. Under traditional Anglo-Australian jurisprudence, banks were only precluded from raising the discrepancies later if this denied the beneficiary the opportunity to cure the documentary defect. See for example *Westpac Banking Corp v South Carolina National Bank* [1986] 1 Lloyd's Rep 311 at 315; *Philadelphia Gear Corp v Central Bank* 717 F2d 230 at 237–40 (5th Cir 1983). But see contra *Hing Yip Hing Fat Co v Daiwa Bank Ltd* [1991] 2 HKLR 35 at 56–7. Some commentators still prefer the traditional view: see R Buckley, 'The 1993 Revision of the Uniform Customs and Practice for Documentary Credits' (1994) 28 *George Washington Journal of International Law and Economics* 256.

35 872 F2d 971 (11th Cir 1989).

36 1 F2d 65 at 66 (3rd Cir, 1924). See also *Barclays Bank DCO v Mercantile National Bank.*, 481 F2d 1224 (5th Cir 1973);

Corresponding banks have attempted to limit their risk by payment 'under reserve' against non-conforming documents. Under such a stipulation, the beneficiary is obligated to repay the money to the bank if the issuing bank rejects the documents and does not reimburse the corresponding bank.[37] Another option for the corresponding bank is to make the payment but have the beneficiary indemnify it for any loss or damage that may arise from the payment and/or defect(s) in the documents. Both options, however, involve some risk to the corresponding bank and, most importantly, the financial status of the beneficiary would have to be determined before either option is exercised.

4.3.1d Fundamental principles of the letter of credit

Two fundamental principles of the letter of credit have emerged, both at common law and now the UCP 600. These principles are:

1 The autonomy of the letter of credit; and
2 The doctrine of strict compliance.

Moreover, the fraud exception has emerged as a counter-principle, although its interpretation and use depends upon the country at issue.

Each of these three principles will now be explained and explored.

Autonomy of the letter of credit

Under the common law, the letter of credit is treated as a separate and independent undertaking from the underlying sales contract. This has been called the *principle of autonomy of the letter of credit.* The UCP 600 (Articles 4, 5 and 34) likewise applies the principle of autonomy of the letter of credit.[38]

The essence of the letter of credit transaction is its documentary character independent of the physical goods. The goods are represented by the bill of lading, which is a document of title and may often be used to finance the transaction. This was described by Lord Wright in *TD Bailey, Son & Co v Ross T Smyth &Co Ltd*:

> The general course of international commerce involves the practice of raising money on the documents so as to bridge the period between the shipment and the time of obtaining payment against documents.
>
> The documentary character of this type of bankers' credit which is used in international trade cannot be over-emphasised. The paying bank will pay the exporter because it holds the documents as collateral security and, if necessary, can take recourse to the issuing bank which, in turn can take recourse to the buyer as instructing customer.
>
> The documentary credit is autonomous and constitutes a contract between the banker and the beneficiary which is independent of the other contractual relationships between buyer and seller. The issuing bank can not refuse to perform its obligations under an irrevocable credit on the grounds that the seller has shipped defective goods, and any

---

37 See *Banque de l'Indochine et de Suez SA v JH Rayner (Mincing Lane) Ltd* [1983] QB 711.

38 It should be noted that commodity sales specifically in relation to string and circle contracts can pose different problems; these issues are not discussed in this chapter.

> dispute between the buyer and seller has to be resolved independently of the letter of credit transaction, *Hamzeh Malas v British Imex Industries* [1958] 2 QB 127.[39]

Therefore, under the principle of autonomy, any disputes relating to the underlying sales contract do not affect the letter of credit. Thus, if the presented documents on their face confirm to the terms of the letter of credit, the bank should accept the presentation and pay against the documents.

Following on from Justice Kerr's statement in *RD Hardbottle (Mercantile) Ltd v National Westminster Bank Ltd* that letters of credit are the 'life-blood of international commerce',[40] Donaldson LJ and Ackner LJ in *Intraco Ltd v Notis Shipping Corporation of Liberia ('The Bhoja Trader')* summed up the reasoning behind such a principle by stating:

> Irrevocable letters of credit and bank guarantees ... have been said to be the life blood of commerce ... thrombosis will occur if ... the courts intervene and thereby disturb the mercantile practice of treating rights there under as being the equivalent of cash in hand.[41]

This obligation on the bank is almost iron-clad, and the only exceptions are where forged or fraudulent documents have been tendered or where the underlying sales contract is illegal.[42]

Doctrine of strict compliance

Under the doctrine of strict compliance under the common law and the UCP 600, a bank can reject any document that is not in strict conformity with the terms of the credit. The reason behind such a policy is clear: banks do not deal with goods and cannot be deemed to have intimate knowledge of the underlying transaction or the trade customs or usage. Given this reality, it is unfair to have the banks decide whether similar terms or substantial compliance are appropriate.[43]

Traditionally, documents containing even the slightest discrepancy could be rejected. This position has been expressed by Lord Sumner in *Equitable Trust Co of New York v Dawson Partners Ltd* (House of Lords) in the following way: 'There is no room for documents which are almost the same, or which will do just as well.'[44] Article 18(c) of the UCP 600 (Article 37(c) of the UCP 500) is also relevant to the discussion of compliance. It states: 'The description of the goods in the commercial invoice must correspond with the description in the Credit'.

While the doctrine of strict compliance is also used to interpret Article 18(c), it has been suggested that this does not require exactly identical wording, but rather that strict compliance is directed to the substance, not merely to the identical nature of the wording. The following extract illustrates the resulting uncertainty.

---

39 (1940) 56 LTR 825 at 828.

40 [1978] QB 146 at 155.

41 [1981] 2 Lloyd's Rep 256 at 257.

42 See *The American Accord* [1982] 2 WLR 1039.

43 Article 14(a) of the UCP 600 states: 'A nominated bank acting on its nomination, a confirming bank, if any, and the issuing bank must examine a presentation to determine, on the basis of the documents alone, whether or not the documents appear on their face to constitute a complying presentation.'

44 (1927) 27 Lloyd's List LR 49 at 52.

Kyle Roane, Hanil Bank v Pt Bank Negara Indonesia (Persero): Continuing the Quandary of Documentary Compliance Under International Letters of Credit

(2004) 41 *Hous L Rev* 1053

Under the UCP compliance standard, strict compliance is not mentioned, but it has nonetheless become the standard for evaluating documentary compliance. The UCP states that

> banks must examine all documents stipulated in the Credit with reasonable care, to ascertain whether or not they appear, on their face, to be in compliance with the terms and conditions of the Credit. Compliance of the stipulated documents on their face with the terms and conditions of the Credit, shall be determined by international standard banking practice as reflected in these Articles.

Despite its reference to 'international standard banking practices,' the UCP does not provide any objective standards to define what constitutes strict compliance or standard practices.

The provision 'as reflected in these articles' suggests that the standard practices are codified only within the UCP, but unfortunately this is not the case. The UCP is not the sole source of banking practices for evaluating LCs. There are many banking practices not included in the UCP 500 that provide assistance in determining strict documentary compliance. One commentator has suggested that failure to recognize un-codified international banking practices when ascertaining documentary compliance frustrates parties' reasonable expectations because international standard banking practices are continually being developed, and failing to recognize new practices would unreasonably prevent change. However, academics have previously argued that the addition of 'as reflected in these [a]rticles' to the UCP 500 indicates that 'the words of the article do not permit expert testimony on what is standard banking practice beyond the extent to which other articles of the UCP reflect it.'

Arguably, the provision 'as reflected in these articles' is not meant to be given strict judicial construction, which would prevent the UCP from accommodating changes in international standard banking practices. Therefore, the UCP embodies both codified practices and practices yet to be codified. The evaluation of documentary compliance requires an understanding of international standard banking practices, which equally requires an awareness of the authorities on which document examiners, bankers, and lawyers can rely to formulate opinions on documentary compliance.

Although the UCP demands strict compliance of documents, some courts have interpreted the standard as 'allowing deviations that do not cause ostensible harm,' which is ultimately not functional for evaluating documentary compliance. The UCP only requires document examiners to know the function of the documents involved and the significance of the banking discrepancies; it does not require particular knowledge of the industry involved in the transaction. In the end, courts will likely be the final arbiter of international standard banking practices and will ultimately decide if a bank's decision to pay or to dishonour an LC conforms to such international practices. Thus, whether or not a court should require expert testimony on interpretations of international standard banking practices has become a highly debated issue.

One commentator has suggested that the UCP does not require courts to defer to banking experts when determining international standard banking practices and that such deference would entail a 'battle of the experts.' The courts would probably resort to simply finding whether or not the

> bank's determination of documentary compliance 'made sense.' Alternatively, another commentator has noted that using expert opinions to help determine international standard banking practices for documentary compliance would not result in a battle of the experts. However, such an interpretation is unsound because when an LC dispute reaches trial, each party will probably offer conflicting expert testimony on international standard banking practices in order to help their respective cases. Whereas the 'UCC Article 5 clearly vests ultimate determination of standard banking practice with the court, ... UCP 500, on its face, attempts to vest ultimate determination of international standard banking practice with the banking experts.'

... ...

As noted, jurisprudence on this issue is inconsistent and, for that reason, caution must be taken when identical wording is not used. For instance, in *JH Rayner & Co Ltd v Hambros Bank Ltd*,[45] Hambros opened a letter of credit that stipulated a bill of lading covering about 1400 tons of Coromandel groundnuts. The issued bill of lading described the goods as 'OTC CRS Aurhus', and in the body of the bill described them as 'machine-shelled groundnut kernels'. Despite the fact that an expert would have known that both of these expressions mean exactly the same as Coromandel groundnuts, the court upheld the bank's refusal to pay because the issuer of the bill of lading did not strictly comply with the terms of the letter of credit. While this case occurred prior to the addition of Article 37(c), the presence of this article would likely not have changed the outcome.

On the other hand, in *Soproma SpA v Marine & Animal By-Products Corporation*,[46] McNair J ordered the bank to pay even though both the sales contract and the letter of credit described the goods as 'Chilean Fish Full Meal', the sales invoice described the goods as 'Chilean Fish Full Meal, 70% protein' and the bill of lading described the goods as 'Chilean Fishmeal', holding that anyone in the trade would not expect to see a more specific description than 'Fishmeal' and thus could not reasonably object to such a description.[47]

To further illustrate the uncertainty, the court in *Beyene v Irving Trust Co* held that an unmistakably clear typographical error could not lead to a rejection of the documents. In that case, the misspelling of 'Sofan' as 'Soran' was held to be an unmistakable typographical error.[48] Likewise, 'Smith' being spelled as 'Smyth' in the letter of credit would likely produce the same result. However, the court in *Hanil Bank v Pt Bank Negara Indonesia (Persero)* ruled that a letter of credit incorrectly issued for the benefit of 'Sung Jun Electronics Co, Ltd' instead of the correct 'Sung Jin Electronics Co Ltd.' was not an insignificant error as 'Sung Jun' was not an obvious misspelling of 'Sung Jin'.[49]

The jurisprudential uncertainty in this area is unfortunate, as the number of documents containing discrepancies is astonishingly high. Thus, even though studies

---

45 [1943] 1 KB 36.

46 [1966] 1 Lloyd's Rep 367.

47 Ibid at 385–6. See also *New Braunfels National Bank v Odiorne* 780 SW 2d 313 (Tex Ct App 1989); *Voest-Alpine Trading USA Corp v Bank of China* 142 F3d 887 (5th Cir 1998).

48 762 F2d 4 (2d Cir 1985).

49 F3d 127 (1988).

show that applicants waive discrepancies in approximately 90 per cent of cases (meaning most defects are technical or minor in nature), the presentation of deficient documents remains a major problem. Further studies show that up to 70 per cent of documents presented to banks are rejected on first presentation; this not only diminishes the effectiveness of the documentary credit and has financial impact, but also increases the costs of doing business, forces companies to litigate and reduces overall profit margins.

It is also important to remember that the doctrine of strict compliance only operates with regard to the letter of credit (that is, it does not apply to the underlying sales transaction). Thus, the fact that a particular detail of the sales contract differs from the credit is irrelevant.[50] If the seller, however, does not question the alterations, it may be bound by the new terms. This has been confirmed in cases regarding alterations of terms as to when the goods are shipped,[51] a buyer's request for additional time,[52] where documents have been tendered under previous instalments[53] and where the seller has only objected to some but not all of the alterations.[54]

Fraud exception

The one exception to the principle of autonomy of the letter of credit is for fraud or illegality.[55] In such circumstances, a strict application of the autonomy principle can cause inequitable results in situations involving fraud by unjustly enriching a dishonest beneficiary. There is thus a need to weigh the importance of the independence principle against the need to discourage fraud in transactions involving letters of credit.

The fraud exception is interpreted and applied differently in all of the common law jurisdictions. It can be said, however, that common law courts have historically applied the standard now incorporated into Article 34 of the UCP 600 (essentially a reproduction of Article 15 of the UCP 500), which holds that a bank cannot be held liable for paying against the tender of forged documents when it has complied with the terms of the credit and its duty to inspect the documents.[56] Article 34 states:

> A bank assumes no liability or responsibility for the form, sufficiency, accuracy, genuineness, falsification or legal effect of any document, or for the general or particular conditions stipulated in a document or superimposed thereon; nor does it assume any liability or responsibility for the description, quantity, weight, quality, condition, packing, delivery, value

50 In this regard, the opening of a letter of credit that is not in conformity with the sales contract could be viewed as an offer to alter the sales contract. The seller can object to the alterations and hold the buyer to the terms of the original contract: see *Glencore Grain Rotterdam BV v Lebanese Organisation for International Commerce* (CA) [1997] 4 All ER 514.

51 See *Panoutsos v Raymond Hadley Corporation of New York* (CA) [1917] 2 KB 47 (CA).

52 See *Enrico Furst & Co v WE Fischer Ltd*, QBD (Comm) [1960] 2 Lloyd's Rep 340.

53 *WJ Alan & Co v El Nasr Export & Import Co* (CA) [1972] 2 QB 189.

54 *Ficom SA v Sociedad Cadex Ltda*, QBD (Comm) [1980] 2 Lloyd's Rep 118.

55 Illegality would include situations where the letter of credit was used in an illegal scheme to mislead. In such an instance, public policy dictates that payment should not be made when the letter of credit was used to secure payment against a contract that breached the law: see *Mahonia Limited v JP Morgan Chase Bank (No 1)* [2003] EWHC 1957 and *(No 2)* [2004] EWHC 1938, both QBD (Comm), where money was lent to a company, part of which was secured by a letter of credit, in order to enable the company to commit an accountancy offence.

56 See for example *Gian Singh & Co Ltd v Banque de l'Indochine* (PC) (Singapore) [1974] 2 All ER 754.

> or existence of the goods, services or other performance represented by any document, or for the good faith or acts or omissions, solvency, performance or standing of the consignor, the carrier, the forwarder, the consignee or the insurer of the goods or any other person.

The remaining portion of this section will review the state of the law in the USA, as well as extract an article which reviews the position in the UK, Canada and Australia.

4.4 A comparative analysis

4.4.1 The US position

In the USA, the independence principle is set out in Article 5-103(d) of the Uniform Commercial Code (UCC). It was, however, debated and interpreted prior to the adoption of the UCC. For instance, in *Maurice O'Meara Co v National Park Bank*,[57] the New York Court of Appeal rejected an attempt to apply the fraud exception to the independence principle, with the majority in that case finding that the bank was only concerned with the drafts and the documents accompanying them. If the documents were in order, the bank was bound to make the payment under the letter of credit even if it knew that the goods were not of the quality required by the contract.

Thus, the majority in *Maurice O'Meara* limited the bank's inquiry into possible fraudulent conduct to the documents themselves. Judge Cardozo, in dissent, suggested that if a seller presenting the draft for payment was guilty of fraud, and the bank became aware of this fraud before making payment to the seller, the bank may be entitled to refuse payment if the fraud was detected before the payment was due. In so doing, Judge Cardozo stated that the bank acts not only on the credit of its customer, but also of the merchandise.

The US position on the issue was reversed several years later as a result of the decision in *Sztejn v J Henry Schroder Banking Corporation*.[58] The court in that case stated:

> No hardship will be caused by permitting the bank to refuse payment where fraud is claimed, where the merchandise is not merely inferior in quality but consists of worthless rubbish, where the draft and the accompanying documents are in the hands of one who stands in the sale position as the fraudulent seller, where the bank has been given notice of the fraud before being presented with the drafts and documents for payment, and where the bank itself does not wish to pay pending an adjudication of the rights and obligations of the parties.

The exception recognised in *Sztejn*, however, was limited to the fraudulent conduct of the seller 'as represented in the documents'.[59] A number of cases in the USA have since

---

57 146 NE 636 (NYCA 1925).

58 31 NY Supp 2d 631 (Supreme Court, 1941) at 634.

59 Ibid at 634–5. However, it has been suggested that Shientag J nonetheless considered the performance of the underlying transaction in making his determination in that case: JJ Browne, 'The Fraud Exception to Standby Letters of Credit in Australia: Does it Embrace Statutory Unconscionability?' (1999) 11 *Bond LR* 98 at 103.

grappled with the concept of whether there should be an exception based only on fraud in the presentation of the documents required by the letter of credit, or also fraud in the underlying commercial transaction. The introduction of the UCC appeared to do little to resolve the confusion. In fact, the original version of Article 5 of the UCC merely sought to codify *Sztejn*:

> when documents appear on their face to comply with the terms of a credit but a required document ... is forged or fraudulent or where there is fraud in the transaction ... an issuer acting in good faith may honour the draft or demand for payment despite notification from the customer of fraud, forgery or other defect not apparent on the face of the documents but a court of appropriate jurisdiction may enjoin such honour.[60]

The 1995 revisions—now Article 5-109 of the UCC—resolved the ambiguities to some extent, as well as expanding the concept:

> (A) If a presentation is made that appears on its face strictly to comply with the terms and conditions of the letter of credit, but a required document is forged or materially fraudulent, or honor of the presentation would facilitate a material fraud by the beneficiary on the issuer or applicant:
>
> (1) The issuer shall honor the presentation, if honor is demanded by (a) a nominated person who has given value in good faith and without notice of forgery or material fraud, (b) a confirmer who has honored its confirmation in good faith, (c) a holder in due course of a draft drawn under the letter of credit which was taken after acceptance by the issuer or nominated person, or (d) an assignee of the issuer's or nominated person's deferred obligation that was taken for value and without notice of forgery or material fraud after the obligation was incurred by the issuer or nominated person; and
>
> (2) The issuer, acting in good faith, may honor or dishonor the presentation in any other case.
>
> (B) If an applicant claims that a required document is forged or materially fraudulent or that honor of the presentation would facilitate a material fraud by the beneficiary on the issuer or applicant, a court of competent jurisdiction may temporarily or permanently enjoin the issuer from honoring a presentation or grant similar relief against the issuer or other persons only if the court finds that:
>
> (1) The relief is not prohibited under the law applicable to an accepted draft or deferred obligation incurred by the issuer;
>
> (2) A beneficiary, issuer, or nominated person who may be adversely affected is adequately protected against loss that it may suffer because the relief is granted;
>
> (3) All of the conditions to entitle a person to the relief under the law of this state have been met; and
>
> (4) On the basis of the information submitted to the court, the applicant is more likely than not to succeed under its claim of forgery or material fraud and the person demanding honor does not qualify for protection under division (A)(1) of this section.

Thus, the courts are therefore now instructed to always examine the underlying transaction.

In the case of fraud in the underlying transaction, the beneficiary must have perpetuated the fraud in order for the presentation not to be honoured, whereas the

60 UCC, Article 5-114(2).

bank can deny payment if any of the documents required by the letter of credit are forged or materially fraudulent, even if the beneficiary did not perpetuate the fraud. The expansion of the exception in this regard may lead to more frequent payment delays and court actions seeking injunctive relief.

Another potential issue with the revised Article 5 of the UCC is its requirement that the fraud be 'material' in order to deny payment. This is a difficult standard to apply, but may have been included to ensure the standard under Article 5-109 remains high.

Under the revised Article 5, relief is not available against innocent third parties, such as when the person demanding honour is a nominated bank that has given value in good faith and without notice of the fraud. Finally, it should also be noted that Article 5 does not define the term 'fraud', but leaves the determination to local law.

Gao Xiang and Ross P Buckley, 'A Comparative Analysis of the Standard of Fraud Required Under the Fraud Rule in Letter of Credit Law'

(2004) 13 *Duke J of Comp & Int'l L* 293

The position in the United Kingdom

English courts have traditionally adopted a relatively rigid and narrow approach towards the application of the fraud rule, requiring a high standard of proof of fraud: 'clear,' 'obvious,' or 'established' fraud known to the issuer. Accordingly, fraud has been very difficult to establish in English courts. When no fraud is found to have been committed in a transaction, there is no need for a court to consider the standard of fraud or other specific issues relating to the application of the fraud rule. Since there have been only a limited number of cases in which the fraud rule is applied, the discussion of what kind of fraud can invoke the fraud rule has also appeared in just a few cases.

In *United City Merchants (Investments) Ltd v Royal Bank of Canada*, when considering the issue of third party fraud, Lord Diplock touched on the issue under discussion:

> To this general statement of principle [of independence] as to the contractual obligations of the confirming bank to the seller, there is one exception: that is, where the seller, for the purpose of drawing on the credit, fraudulently presents to the confirming bank documents that contain, expressly or by implication, *material representations* of fact that to his knowledge are untrue.

According to Lord Diplock, material misrepresentation is the kind of fraud that can invoke the fraud rule under the English law. Raymond Jack has interpreted material misrepresentation as follows: the word misrepresentation 'is very close to a statement of the elements of fraudulent misrepresentation which constitute the tort of deceit.' The tort of deceit contains the following elements: '(1) knowing the representation to be false; (2) without belief in its truth; or (3) recklessly, careless whether it be true or false.' The word 'material' means 'material to the bank's duty to pay, so that if the document stated the truth the bank would be obliged to reject the documents,' which is close to the interpretation of material fraud in Official Comment on Revised UCC Article 5, Section 109. Jack's interpretation seems to be at odds with Lord Diplock's own words, however:

> the answer to the question: 'to what must the misstatement in the documents be material?' should be: *'material to the price* which the goods to which the documents relate would fetch on sale if, failing reimbursement by the buyer, the bank should be driven to realise its security.' But this would

> not justify the confirming bank's refusal to honour the credit in the instant case; the realisable value on arrival at Callao of a glass fibre manufacturing plant made to the specification of the buyers could not be in any way affected by having been loaded on board a ship at Flexistowe on December 16, instead of December 15, 1976.

In accordance with Lord Diplock, the misrepresentation should be 'material' to the real value of the goods. Predating the bill of lading in the case was not considered material because it did not affect the value of the goods. But according to Jack's interpretation, predating the bill of lading should be considered material because the bank would have been obliged to reject the documents if the bill of lading had stated the truth of the loading date. It is, with respect, submitted that Jack's interpretation is a far better statement of principle (though not an accurate interpretation of Lord Diplock's judgment) and Lord Diplock's observation is out of step with the wider law and practice of letters of credit.

Lord Diplock's observation in *United City Merchants* that material misrepresentation is the kind of fraud that can invoke the fraud rule has been accepted by subsequent English cases. In *Themehelp Ltd v West*, one of the few English cases where an injunction was granted, the Court of Appeal followed the words of Lord Diplock quoted above with respect to the standard of fraud and affirmed the trial court's decision.

In *Banco Santander SA v Bayfern Ltd*, the confirmer discounted the obligation of a deferred payment letter of credit before its maturity. Shortly after the discounting, some of the documents presented were found to be fraudulent. Subsequently, the issuer refused to pay the confirmer. The confirmer brought the action against the issuer in the Queen's Bench Division for reimbursement and sought summary judgment, claiming it should be immune from the fraud rule despite fraud. For trial of preliminary issues, fraud was assumed to have been established in the case. The trial court ruled for the issuer on the basis of established fraud. On appeal, the decision was upheld by the Court of Appeal. Both courts cited with approval Lord Diplock's above passage relating to the standard of fraud.

'Material misrepresentation' thus appears to have been settled as the standard of fraud in the law governing letters of credit in the United Kingdom. In language the English position is close to that of the United States in Revised UCC Article 5, Section 109: 'material fraud.' As both of them have not been sufficiently tested, it is too early to make a reasonable comparison. If a comparison has to be made, however, the difference between the two appears to be that the US position is enshrined in a statute, but the UK position is embodied in the common law. This may mean that courts in the United States will 'look more on the severity of the effect of the fraud on the transaction rather than the state of fraud of the beneficiary,' whilst courts in the United Kingdom, at least if Jack is correct, will require proof of the state of the mind of the fraudster. Be that as it may, with the development of the fraud rule, the two systems are coming closer together: lower standards of fraud such as 'constructive fraud,' seem to have been abandoned by US courts following the promulgation of Revised UCC Article 5; and the more recent English cases to have applied the fraud rule seem to be shifting from the traditional rigid standard of proof, 'established' or 'clear' fraud, to the less rigid standard of proof, 'the only realistic inference ... is that of fraud.'

The position in Canada

Canadian courts have generally focused on the standard of proof rather than the standard of fraud when considering the application of the fraud rule. When considering the kind of fraud that can invoke the fraud rule, Canadian courts, like their English counterparts, are likely to ask whether 'clear or obvious' fraud or 'a strong prima facie case of fraud' has been shown, not how serious the fraud was in the sense of the standard of fraud being discussed here. Canadian courts have also considered whether the application of the fraud rule should be confined to cases of forged or fraudulent documents or extend to fraud in the underlying transaction. This is well illustrated by the case of *Bank of Nova Scotia v Angelica-Whitewear Ltd.*

In *Angelica-Whitewear*, the court considered four issues with respect to the application of the fraud rule, but the standard of fraud under discussion was not among them. When the court was considering the alleged fraud in the case, that is, the inflation of the prices in the invoice by some 17 dollars per dozen above those agreed to in the sales contract, it was not interested in how serious the fraud was, but whether the fraud (1) had been 'sufficiently established to the knowledge of the Bank before payment of the draft to make it clear or obvious to the Bank,' and (2) could 'be regarded as having made invoice 0014 a false document in so far as its representation of the applicable prices was concerned, or whether it be regarded as fraud in the performance of the underlying sales contract.' The court put the question simply, was this 'fraud of the kind that comes within the fraud exception,' which seems to indicate that fraud is a simple concept, the meaning of which is known by everybody in Canada.

Due to the general approach of the Canadian courts towards the standard of fraud, the issue, even when it is mentioned in a Canadian case, has normally been addressed in a very simple way. For example, in *CDN Research & Development Ltd v Bank of Nova Scotia*, when issuing an injunction restraining the issuer from paying the demand, Justice Galligan stated:

> It is my opinion, in this case, an injunction ought to be granted. In my view, it ought to be granted for at least two reasons. The first is that the plaintiff has made out a strong prima facie case that the demand made by the agent of the Ministry of War is fraudulent. Delivery has clearly been made and claim for a payment of a delivery guarantee necessarily implying that delivery was not made is *clearly untrue and false.*

This issue has been said to have been 'dealt with in some depth' in the case of *Cineplex Odeon Corp v 100 Bloor West General Partner, Inc.* In *Cineplex*, a limited partnership was formed to develop a multifunctional complex. The parties had entered into a number of agreements, according to which the plaintiff, Cineplex, provided a letter of credit to secure its obligations under certain agreements. Cineplex defaulted in its obligation to build the project, and the letter of credit was called upon. The plaintiff moved to enjoin payment, claiming that it was not in default in the obligation that the letter of credit was meant to guarantee, any draw by the defendants would be fraudulent and thus the fraud rule should be applied. After reviewing the facts and the principle of independence, before dismissing the plaintiff's motion, Justice Blair pointed out:

> I pause at this point to note, in passing, a factor which occasionally seems to be lost amidst the melee in these sorts of disputes which more and more are finding their way to the courts in times of economic stress: the exception is 'fraud', not something less than fraud.

Then he went on:

> In the eyes of the party seeking to prevent payment on the letter of credit, almost any conduct or position of the beneficiary which does not accord with the aggrieved party's view of the universe may appear to be fraud, and therefore justify non-payment. Such, of course, cannot be the case, given the recognized characteristics of a letter of credit ... Fraud is a straightforward five-letter word, meaning just what it says: 'fraud'. Fraud is not simply a legitimate dispute or disagreement

> over the interpretation of a contract, however one-sided that dispute may appear. While the notion of fraud may elude precise definition, it is a concept well-known to the law, and it must, in my view, import some aspect of impropriety, dishonesty or deceit ... Fraud is not mistake, error in interpreting a contract; fraud is 'something dishonest and morally wrong, and much mischief is ... done, as well as much unnecessary pain inflicted, by its use where "illegality" and "illegal" are the really appropriate expressions.' Cases where the demand on the letter of credit can be said to be 'clearly untrue or false', or 'utterly without justification', or where it is apparent there is 'no right to payment', all fall within the foregoing principles and must be read in the context of those 'fraud' principles.

If this can be taken as a summary or generalization of the Canadian position on the standard of fraud, the Canadian position is somewhat confusing or contradictory. As can be seen, the quoted passage, on one hand, is saying that fraud in Canada means something of 'dishonesty' or 'deceit,' or 'clearly untrue or false,' which is similar to common law fraud, requiring the intention of the fraudulent party. But on the other hand, it is saying that a call on the letter of credit that is 'utterly without justification' or 'where it is apparent there is "no right to payment"' can also mean fraud in Canada, which is similar to the American position, looking more to the sharpness of the fraudulent conduct. This may be the true reflection of the Canadian position, however: on one hand, being a country of English tradition, understandably the Canadian courts traditionally follow the approach of their English counterparts closely, adopting the standard of common law fraud; on the other hand, the influence of the US position in the area of letter of credit law, can be seen everywhere in the world, and at least some of the Canadian courts are also closely following the US approach on these issues.

The position in Australia

In Australia, in the small number of cases that have considered the fraud rule, two kinds of standard of fraud have been suggested: intentional fraud and gross equitable fraud.

A. INTENTIONAL FRAUD

The standard of intentional fraud was set forth in the case of *Contronic Distributors Pty Ltd v Bank of New South Wales*. When issuing the injunction, Justice Helsham said:

> It seems to me that the case could be decided on a simple basis of fraud. I think it is sufficient to enable ... Balfour ... in any event to get relief in these proceedings, to establish *an intention to obtain money by deceit* on the part of GEC at the time that the letter of credit is to be presented by it for payment. GEC would then be obtaining money by the use of documents it knew to be false and which were brought into being by it and with its connivance.

B. GROSS EQUITABLE FRAUD

The standard of gross equitable fraud was suggested in *Hortico (Australia) Pty Ltd v Energy Equip Co (Australia) Pty Ltd*, where Energy Australia had a contract with Hortico for the design, supply, and installation of a boiler. Hortico arranged for the issuance of a bank guarantee in favour of Energy Australia. Later the contract was terminated by both parties and Energy Australia made a demand on the guarantee for damages. Hortico brought the action to enjoin the payment under the guarantee, alleging, *inter alia*, that the guarantee was contemplated only to be security for the performance of the contract by the plaintiff and not also for damages, as the defendant claimed.

The plaintiff's argument was dismissed by Judge Young of the Supreme Court of New South Wales. The respected judge said in obiter, however:

> [W]ith commercial transactions such as the present, the courts have consistently taken a 'hands off' approach, and it does not seem to me that anything short of actual fraud would warrant this Court in intervening, though it may be in some cases (not this one), the *unconscionable conduct may be so gross* as to lead to exercise of the discretionary power.

The view that gross equitable fraud might invoke the fraud rule was restated some ten years later by the same justice in the case of *Inflatable Toy Co v State Bank of New South Wales*. In *Inflatable*, the plaintiff, the buyer, ordered from the seller inflatable plastic toys to be delivered in instalments and paid for by letters of credit. For one instalment, some discrepancies appeared between the documentation and the facts. The buyer accepted the discrepancies when the seller told it what had happened, but changed its mind later and brought an action to prevent the issuer from paying the accepted bill of exchange, alleging that the seller was guilty of fraud in presenting documents, which it knew to be untrue. Judge Young rejected the buyer's claim. But again as a passing dictum, after citing *Sztejn*, *Hortico* and other cases relating to the fraud rule, he stated, 'I should note, in case what I said is read later too widely, that it is still wise to keep open the possibility that *unconscionable conduct may be an exception.*'

The idea that gross equitable fraud may invoke the fraud rule was rejected by Judge Batt of the Supreme Court of Victoria in *Olex Focas Pty Ltd v Skodaexport Co*, however. In that case, Olex Focas entered into a contract with Skodaexport for the supply and installation of telecommunications, telesupervisory and instrumentation systems in connection with the construction of an oil pipeline in India. Skodaexport was the head-contractor for the project, and Olex was one of the subcontractors engaged by Skodaexport.

Skodaexport agreed to pay Olex what was termed mobilization/procurement advances for 15 percent of the contract price. As security for the repayment of the advances, Olex was required to provide independent guarantees to Skodaexport, termed mobilization/procurement guarantees (mobilization guarantees). In addition, Olex was required to provide another type of guarantee, termed performance guarantees, for 10 percent of the contract price, to secure the good performance of its obligations under the underlying contract. All the guarantees were payable 'at sight forthwith on first demand ... without protest or demur or proof.' Skodaexport was allowed to call upon part of the guarantees.

When disputes arose, Skodaexport allegedly threatened to call upon the full amount of the guarantees unless Olex would accept its terms for the settlement of the disputes. By this time, the advances secured by the mobilization guarantees had largely been repaid. The plaintiffs also claimed that collectively 95 percent of the equipment had been supplied and 78 percent of the design, construction, integration and commissioning services had been provided. Olex sought interlocutory injunctions to prevent the independent guarantees from being paid on two grounds: (1) that Skodaexport, by threatening to make demand on the guarantees, was acting fraudulently, without a belief that it was entitled to the sums secured by the guarantees; and (2) that Skodaexport, by threatening to call up the guarantees, was committing unconscionable conduct within the meaning of Section 51AA of the *Trade Practices Act 1974* (Cth).

Judge Batt, when considering the plaintiff's first basis, followed the traditional line of English cases requiring a high standard of proof and, at the beginning of his analysis, stated:

> Now in Victoria, as in England, the law is clear. The principle is clearly established that payment by a bank and a demand therefore by a beneficiary under an unconditional performance bond or guarantee, as under a confirmed irrevocable letter of credit, will not be restrained *except in a clear case of fraud,* of which the bank is clearly aware at the time of, probably, the proposed payment, or in the case of forgery of documents (which is probably applicable only to letters of credit) or, perhaps, in the case of illegality of the underlying contract.

Then the learned Judge Batt considered a number of English and Australian cases, cited long quotations from them to the effect that only clear fraud could activate the fraud rule, and rejected the plaintiffs' request for injunction on the basis of fraud. When considering the point espoused by Judge Young in *Hortico* that gross equitable fraud might invoke the fraud rule, Judge Batt said:

> In my view his Honour was speaking in very guarded terms, prefacing his mention of that concept by reference to the general 'hands-off' approach taken by courts with respect to commercial transactions ... *I would not* with respect, having regard to all the other cases I have cited, *treat gross unconscionability falling short of actual fraud as a ground for an injunction.*

Therefore, in Australia to date, while two kinds of misconduct that may invoke the fraud rule have been suggested, only 'intentional fraud' has been applied. As for gross equitable fraud, it has been mentioned twice by the same justice in obiter in the Supreme Court of New South Wales, but has not been applied in any case. Moreover, it has been rejected by the Supreme Court of Victoria. Whether the standard of gross equitable fraud can become a real ground for the application of the fraud rule in Australia remains to be seen.

... ...

4.4.2 The eUCP

With recent improvements in both the efficiency and safety of electronic commerce, the eUCP became operational in April 2002 to supplement the rules banks use to finance trade. While the drafters no doubt hoped (and likely anticipated) that the eUCP would become a routine part of financing international trade, to date this has not been the case. Use of the eUCP has been minimal, and for this reason the eUCP remains a supplement as opposed to being incorporated directly into the UCP 600.

Both the eUCP and the UCP 600 came into effect 1 July 2007. While the eUCP was updated to reflect the change from the UCP 500 to the UCP 600, its substance remains the same. The following extract, written prior to the update, more fully explores the justification for and content of the eUCP.

Roberto Bergami, 'eUCP: A Revolution in International Trade?' (2004) 8(1) *Vindobona Journal of International Commercial Law & Arbitration* 23–36

The world of commerce is continually seeking greater efficiency and returns from its processes and operations. Innovative solutions that will improve processing times, reduce errors and automate repetitive functions may well deliver such efficiencies, particularly if integrated systems can be built across organisations. In the past few years transport operators have been experimenting with the production of electronic transport documents with a view to developing seamless systems that will enable them to transfer data electronically in an acceptable format. This is not a small problem.

For shippers and forwarders, many of the electronic trade facilitation systems and initiatives sound complex, and it is too early to say whether they will have the critical mass to make any system an industry standard. The likelihood is that there will be several systems that will run alongside the current paper-based systems.

For many years, paper-based documents have enjoyed statutory recognition in matters such as negotiability, whereas generally the law has struggled to assign the same equivalence to electronic data purporting to represent a document. The traditional Bill of Lading provides a good example. It may be issued to order, so it can be negotiable and transferable from one party to another. It is produced in original form, physically on paper, with a definite number of originals issued and is arguably more difficult to alter. In most jurisdictions it enjoys its own legislation, giving it legality. The original bill is required to obtain discharge of the cargo at destination from the carrier or its agent.

Its electronic equivalent, by and large, does not enjoy the same status at law and is not something which can be seen or held (other than if on a physical media storage device), but may be displayed on a screen or printed as many times as one likes via a computer link. The ability to produce amounts of documents without control may bring its own set of potential problems, among which is the questionable use of original documents in this context.

An electronic 'document' can be copied many times over, with each copy being an original. Consequently eUCP refers to 'electronic records', and effectively consigns to history the notion of calling for 'original' documents in an electronic trade transaction.

Therefore trading parties must be willing to accept a 'new order of doing business' under the eUCP and this willingness is based on their degree of comfort, trust if you like, with the electronic 'wonder'.

Over the past 20 or so years the process of issuing L/C has been automated and 'electronicised', by the use of telegrams, cables and telexes (faxes are too easily manipulated so they were never accepted as operative instruments by the banks), but the documentary presentation required by the beneficiary to the banks under the L/C mechanism has not. Some promote the notion of an electronic-based, 'paperless' process as a far superior method of operation because it would increase efficiencies and decrease error rates. Error rates are a worldwide problem, with the ICC reporting error rates, on first presentation of documents from beneficiaries (sellers) to presenting banks (exporter's bank), of between 60% and 70%. Given that L/C provide a conditional guarantee of payment only if the documents are correct, this is an obvious point of concern.

THE eUCP

It is appropriate to consider the eUCP in some detail and to discuss these rules to understand their operation. The eUCP do not change the basic requirement for correctness of documents, rather they accept the use of electronic submission of documents.

The eUCP is issued in versions, according to Art e1—unlike the UCP that has a publication number. Actually the eUCP have been published already within (at least) three separate documents: 500/2, 500/3 and 500/4—the eUCP will therefore be issued and referred to by 'versions', currently being 1.0.

In accordance with Article e1, if a L/C allows the use of eUCP, then it should state the version and where this is not stated then either the current version is applicable, or the version in use at the time of acceptance of an amendment to the L/C will apply. The problem here is that a different version may apply during the life of the L/C and this could complicate rather than facilitate the transaction. Any beneficiary needs to be particularly careful about this provision and counsel involved in providing any advice should ensure this point is well understood.

When a L/C is issued subject to eUCP, the relevant portions of the UCP 500 apply, even without reference to the UCP 500, according to Art e2(a). The eUCP

> provisions shall prevail to the extent that they would produce a result different from the application of the UCP.

According to Art e2(c), where the L/C is issued subject to the eUCP and only paper documents are presented, the transaction is subject to the UCP 500 only. Where the L/C is issued subject to eUCP and only paper documents are permitted, then the transaction is subject to UCP 500. Although this seems a bit detailed and confusing, the basic message is one of consistency—that is, all electronic documents are subject to eUCP and all paper-based ones are subject to UCP 500 and this interpretation is based on what is actually done by the beneficiary, not, apparently, according to what is stated on the L/C—if an electronic record is presented, even from an external source, then the eUCP will apply.

To clarify the operations of these rules, Art e3 provides a set of definitions, or more accurately, statement of equivalence with UCP 500 ...

The submission and subsequent checking of data contents in an electronic record is an important consideration because it will affect the producers of the documents and the banks alike. In the producers of documents we include not only the sellers, but also the carriers (and/or their agents) who may be responsible for creating electronic transport documents. Whilst the banks have a requirement to check the data content to ascertain compliance with the terms of the L/C (eg integrity and genuineness), perhaps by reference to header and footer tags, depending on the program and system used, other required information may be suppressed from being displayed, making the task of data verification difficult, if not impossible. Therefore there needs to be agreement between the documentation producer and presenter and the banks on what is acceptable. This may raise issues of program specific requirements and systems compatibility, particularly when considering the issues of place of presentation and receipt of the electronic record. The place of presentation is an electronic address and the presumption is that information will be able to be sent to that address. One can only wonder about the repercussions of sending a message to an electronic address that is not being delivered due to a problem at the receiving end, eg a problem with the server or an outage in the receiver's system.

The eUCP allows for presentation of electronic documents at different stages, that is, separate messages, and will not regard the presentation of documents as complete until such a time as it receives a notice of completeness. In building in flexibility on presentation of electronic records, the rules have also had to impose on the document presenter an obligation to notify the bank of when the presentation is complete. The argument from the bank's point of view may be that they would not know whether all the records had been presented, and indeed it would not be their role to determine whether this is so—a fair point which appears to be consistent with the long established UCP 500 principles, that is that the bank's role is merely to check for compliance.

Until the bank receives notice of completeness, the time of presentation in a eUCP credit has not occurred.

Recent technology has probably advanced far enough for the security over the signatures to be acceptable with digital certificates and public key/private key infrastructure in place. Again, though, one has to come back to the point of integrated or compatible systems, so the format of the data is acceptable to all. This may mean having to reconfigure the current set-up or adopting a new one. Solutions can always be found, but at a cost.

An interesting point relevant to the format applicability of presented comments can be found in Art e4, whereby there is a requirement for a L/C under these rules to specify a format for electronic document presentation. Beware the unfortunate bank that fails to specify this, because under these rules, in the absence of preciseness, any electronic format will do, regardless of whether the bank can read it or not. Under these circumstances, the bank would not presumably be entitled to reject the electronic documents for the sole reason they could not be read. Of course if the documentation presenter was to deliberately try to make it impossible for the electronic record to be read, for example, by using a prototype program which was proprietary and was incompatible with most commercial programs, then the bank may well have right of recourse under local law. To the best of the present writer's knowledge, this is not yet known.

Article e5 deals with presentation of documents. This is an important article because it specifically allows for separate presentation of documents and not necessarily at the same time. Electronic records may be lodged by the beneficiary (or another party), as long as there is a reference to the L/C on the electronic record, as per sub-article (e).

The potential problem is with arranging for the lodgement of documents by a party other than the beneficiary ... the 'conditional' guarantee of payment is given from the issuing bank to the beneficiary. It can also be seen that ... the exporter (beneficiary) sends the goods out and the documentation is subsequently lodged with the bank ... The typical flow of documents under the traditional L/C is subject to UCP 500, where after despatch of the goods, only paper documents are lodged by the beneficiary to the bank. ...

Under the traditional UCP 500 system the beneficiary have control of all the documents before they are lodged with the advising bank and would therefore be in a position to potentially rectify any non-compliance issues with external document producers ...

In the course of a L/C transaction, it is common for most of the documents to be produced by the beneficiary, but some may not be able to be, eg a transport document. Under Article e5, the beneficiary could ask the carrier (as an example) to transmit the document (record) direct to the bank ...

Of course if the presentation of documents (record) was to be structured in this fashion, the beneficiary may no longer have the opportunity to check the data contents before the record reaches the bank. This would potentially weaken the position of the beneficiary if the bank was to discover discrepancies after receipt of the record.

Such an arrangement would give rise to a number of considerations, including:

(a) what would the ramifications be if the record submitted was found to be discrepant?

(b) what if the record was submitted late or not sent at all?

(c) how and when will the beneficiary know/be notified of the submission of the record?

The failure of an external party to submit the correct data, or even to submit the data at all, is no defence to the beneficiary and it must be remembered in any case that, the beneficiary is a party to the L/C, but that carriers and other service providers are not a part of that transaction. There would be a contract of carriage between the beneficiary and the carrier, but when dealing with the L/C operations banks cannot consider such contractual relationships.

The most immediate outcome in case of any problems with L/C compliance is likely to be that the beneficiary would lose the guarantee of payment and may well incur financial losses.

Subsequently, the beneficiary may be able to commence some recovery action from the carrier, but the outcome of this course of action may not be so certain. The beneficiary would have to receive some form of confirmation from the external submitter of the electronic record that indeed the record had been lodged, so the notice of completeness may be issued, pursuant to Art e5(c). If such arrangements are envisaged, counsel advising a client needs to ensure that there are adequate contractual arrangements in place to cover such eventualities.

The availability of examination of data of an electronic document is another aspect worthy of notice. Article e6 allows for electronic records to make reference to an external system via a hyperlink, but also warns, at (a):

> The failure of the indicated system to provide access to the required electronic record at the time of examination shall constitute a discrepancy.

Banks checking electronic records may be directed to access and examine data held externally. The bank's role will only be to check that the data contents on the external sources comply with the L/C requirements. Of course where the secure external data sources are utilised, the bank will need to be provided with the relevant means of access. This is a security issue the record presenter will need to consider. In any case the bank will need to be provided with accurate details so as to reach and access that source. For example, if an internet address is given, then it would be of utmost importance that the complete and accurate address be provided.

Of particular importance in this context is the syntax that one must use to reach a particular resource. Dots, underscores, and file extensions are all items that, if incorrect, will simply fail to reach the pinpointed electronic target. Under such circumstances the bank could not be reasonably expected to guess or attempt to 'blindly' find the correct address—a case of the proverbial needle in the internet haystack!

Therefore the issue of accessibility of electronic data that may be archived for retrieval is a very important consideration—if the system is not functioning properly this may give rise to a rejection of the documents and the risk of not being paid.

So far as the presentation of original documents is concerned, such a requirement would not be in harmony with the notion of electronic data—what would be an original document, if it is in an electronic format? By contrast, it would be relatively simple for a traditional paper-based document to have originality assigned to it. Consequently, Art e8 allows the presentation of one electronic record as being adequate to satisfy the presentation requirements of the L/C.

The time period for examination of documents under Art e7 begins the banking day following receipt of notice of completeness.

Dates have always been important in L/C transactions and particular date meanings have been given under Art e9. In the absence of a specific date on the electronic record, the date of issuance may either be the date the record was sent by the issuer, or if that date is not apparent, then the date the record was received would be applicable.

Article e10 specifically deals with transport documents. A transport document not bearing a date of shipment or despatch will be deemed issued when the electronic record is issued. But if this record has a notation evidencing a date of shipment or dispatch, then that will be regarded as the issue date. The notation does not have to be separately authenticated.

An important admission that the electronic world is less than perfect can be found in the Art e11, with reference to corruption of electronic records after they have been received. Rather than apportion blame, the rules specify that the record may be requested to be sent again, as a replacement. The rules only specifically address the corruption after the record has been received, as before receipt any corruption is the responsibility of the presenter. As corruption is not defined by the rules, presumably this is any distortion, or damage, or loss of data.

Article e12 carries a disclaimer exonerating the banks against the usual identification of the issuer, authenticity of the message and so on; these are consistent with the UCP 500.

A STEP FORWARD?

So are the eUCP a step forward? These rules are to enable the beneficiary to have an alternative presentation method to the traditional paper-based chase. But these rules go beyond the beneficiary as they also capture carriers and other documentations producers. In the weeks preceding the launch of the eUCP there was much talk about these rules being a revolution, and why not? In theory they could do away with paper-based transactions, leading to paperless trading, but in practice this may take some time to achieve.

Traders and documentation producers have a number of questions to answer including:

- Do I want to use electronic records?
- Does my current system allow me to do so?
- Do my current service providers, such as carriers, insurers, etc, want to generate electronic documents?
- Does my system interact with that of my service providers?
- If not, what is needed to make it work? Whose system should be changed to bring into a common integrated standard? If multiple providers are being used, can all reach consensus on a standard?
- What systems does the bank have in place? Will I still be able to use multiple banks, or will I need to be locked into one only, potentially losing any negotiations power? Will that make it more or less expensive?

Information technology (IT) solutions can take time and are expensive and they are particularly difficult for small enterprises with limited resources and perhaps a lower IT knowledge base. Banks have developed their own electronic software solutions that customers can use, but nothing is perfect.

For the beneficiary, particularly the small enterprise, it is also a case of a new work practice. People have been used to dealing with documents and are comfortable, it seems, with shuffling paper, because they can see it, but with an electronic file that was sent, are you sure it was sent? ... it may well be a perceptual case of *habeas corpus.*

This may be particularly so if the electronic submission of documents is arranged to take place directly from an external source to the bank. How do I know it has been done? Where is the evidence? Late presentation of an electronic record will still leave the beneficiary with a discrepancy and no defence under the L/C.

SOME COMMENTS FROM INDUSTRY

...

All of the Australian banks, several freight forwarders and shipping lines, debt insurers and international traders reported no activities or interest in the eUCP [in late-2002 and early 2003]. Similarly enquiries to banks in Thailand, Malaysia, China, New Zealand, the USA, Belgium and Slovenia revealed that they had not begun using eUCP. One bank in the UK went as far as advising that even though they were members of BOLERO (a well known electronic trading system).

> we do not foresee the use of electronic documents in general world trade for some years to come. I believe you will find that is the view of most of the UK banks.

Given the high importance and reputation of the UK in global financial terms, this is some statement.

My findings seem to correlate quite well with reports that banks in Germany, Singapore and Canada did not appear ready to embark on the eUCP 500. The general consensus there, was that a lot more education was needed about the rules and the banks had not yet completed an analysis of their infrastructure.

The realisation that eUCP will not be taken up as readily as some may have hoped was alluded to by Dan Taylor, a co-author of the eUCP and Vice Chairman of the ICC Banking Commission:

> the use of eUCP will develop slowly over time as technologies are adapted ... The new set of rules requires that users be educated, and the eUCP is no exception.
>
> Within banks, significant analyses concerning the impact of electronic presentation have to be completed to determine all of the procedural, risk and system changes that have to be made.

This is perhaps a lot more realistic than the initial excitement:

> The eUCP, 18 months in preparation, is expected to revolutionise the way documentary credits are used.

....

As the above extract makes clear, the eUCP has the potential to increase the productivity of document presentation while at the same time reducing the error rate so prevalent in the traditional method. On the other hand, the implementation of the eUCP has been and remains problematic for a number of reasons. From a business sense, traders must take steps to ensure that they have the resources needed to properly obtain and maintain the appropriate systems necessary for the submission of electronic documents and successful implementation of the eUCP. From a legal standpoint, legal representatives must ensure that they fully understand—and are able to communicate to their clients—the risks and potential consequences of electronic submission. It is also important that legal counsel ensure that contractual agreements are drafted in a manner so as to address these issues and events.

4.4.3 Other types of credit

Other types of credit may be utilised by the parties. A few of the more common other types of credit are now mentioned.

A *revolving credit* involves the buyer instructing the bank to open a standing credit that the seller can draw on for each transaction (subject to qualifications, such as a maximum drawing limit per transaction). A revolving credit is almost exclusively used between parties that are regular trading partners with a high level of familiarity and trust, with the benefit of the credit being that the buyer does not have to repeatedly open a new credit with each transaction.

A *packing credit* (also referred to as a *pre-shipment credit* or *anticipatory credit*) allows for the seller to get paid for the transaction against the production of certain specified documents before it actually ships the goods. In essence, the packing credit allows the beneficiary to borrow against the letter of credit prior to fulfilling all of the requirements of the credit. Generally used by traders unfamiliar with standard international trading practices, the packing credit normally allows for payment to be made following production of the documents showing the goods have been received for shipment (for example, a mate's receipt or forwarder's certificate).

A *red clause credit* (so called as it was originally written in red ink to draw attention to the unique nature of the credit) allows the seller (beneficiary) to obtain a pre-shipment advance from the advising/confirming bank (which takes responsibility for issuing the advance). Although use of this type of credit is no longer common, it is most often used when a beneficiary is unable to secure a packing credit advance from its own bank, or the beneficiary utilises the red clause credit to purchase raw materials to manufacture the goods, or to make cash payments for the goods purchased from another supplier or to purchase quota.

Under normal circumstances, the applicant decides to what extent and under what conditions the beneficiary will receive the advance and the 'red clause' must clearly specify the total value of the advance(s) (which may be given as a percentage of the total credit amount). Advances for this type of credit are unsecured and usually require the beneficiary to produce a bill of exchange drawn for the value of the advance and a letter of undertaking promising to effect shipment in accordance with the terms of the credit. The beneficiary may also be required to provide a statement as to the specific purpose for which the advanced money will be used.

In the event that the beneficiary fails to fulfil its obligations under the credit and a claim is made against the issuing bank, the applicant is immediately responsible for the repayment of the advances to the issuing bank and any interest due.[61]

A *transferable credit* is another common method of finance, and is specifically covered by Article 48 of the UCP 500. Article 48(a) of the UCP 500 describes a transferable credit as a:

> Credit under which the Beneficiary (First Beneficiary) may request the bank authorized to pay, incur a deferred payment undertaking, accept or negotiate (the 'Transferring Bank'), or in the case of a freely negotiable Credit, the bank specifically authorized in the Credit as a

---

61 See *Tukan Timber Ltd v Barclays Bank Plc* [1981] 1 Lloyd's Rep 171.

> Transferring Bank, to make the Credit available in whole or in part to one or more other Beneficiary(ies) (Second Beneficiary(ies)).

Once the bank has consented to the transfer, the second beneficiary can obtain payment by simply presenting the documents in its own name. Thus, in layperson's terms, a transferable credit essentially is a normal credit with an option attached allowing the intermediary (first beneficiary/transferor) to transfer its rights and obligations to another supplier (second beneficiary/transferee). If the transfer is effected, the second beneficiary is thus required to supply the goods under the terms and conditions set out by the buyer (applicant).

Importantly, a credit can be transferred only if it is expressly designated as 'transferable' by the issuing bank.[62]

Additionally, regardless of the designation of the credit, the transferring bank is not obliged to effect a transfer unless and until it expressly consents to the transfer.[63] As a default, Article 38(c) of the UCP 600 states that all of the charges in respect of transfers—including commissions, fees, costs or expenses owing to the transferring bank—are payable by the first beneficiary, unless otherwise agreed. Moreover, the transferring bank is under no obligation to effect the transfer until all such charges are paid. As a default, 'a transferable Credit can be transferred once only,'[64] and 'unless otherwise stated in the credit', 'the credit cannot be transferred at the request of the Second Beneficiary to any subsequent Third Beneficiary'.[65] However, and similarly with back-to-back credits, the seller must ensure that the credit allows for appropriate changes to be made in a transfer so as to effect multiple transfers and minimise the risk of being bypassed in any future transactions.

Interestingly, Article 38(d) of the UCP 600 does allow for fractions of a transferable credit (not exceeding in the aggregate the amount of the credit) to be transferred separately, provided partial shipment/drawings are not excluded by the credit, and the aggregate of such transfers will be considered as constituting only one transfer of the credit. This automatic default right of divisibility differs from the traditional common law viewpoint.

This type of credit is usually employed:

- When the intermediary is either unable to supply some or all of the merchandise called for in the sales contract and credit, and it thus wishes to transfer part, or all, of the credit to another party;

---

62 Under the UCP 500, Article 48(b) explicitly stated that: 'Terms such as "divisible", "fractionable", "assignable", and "transmissible" do not render the Credit transferable—if such terms were used they were to be disregarded.' It should also be noted that Article 49 of the UCP 500 provided for the assignment of proceeds, even if the credit was non-transferable. In such a case, the article provided that transferability of the credit 'shall not affect the Beneficiary's right to assign any proceeds to which he may be, or may become, entitled under such Credit, in accordance with the provisions of the applicable law'. As this article related only to the assignment of proceeds and not to the assignment of the right to perform under the credit itself, it is a much weaker form of providing security to another party. It also depended heavily upon the property law applicable to the transaction.

63 See UCP 600, Article 38(a). For judicial interpretation of the predecessor to this clause, Article 48(c) of the UCP 500, see *Bank Negara Indonesia 1946 v Lariza (Singapore) Pte Ltd* (PC) [1988] 1 MLJ 205.

64 Article 48(g) of the UCP 500 made this explicitly clear.

65 UCP 500, Article 48(g).

- When the party is unable to secure back-to-back credit (see below), but the ultimate supplier wishes to use a documentary credit facility; or
- Where the party acts as the sourcing agent and is responsible for distributing the portions of the credit to various suppliers.

As a transferable credit can only normally be transferred once, the *back-to-back credit* (also referred to as a *countervailing credit*) was devised to allow for the issuance of two (or more) letters of credit: one in favour of the buyer and one in favour of the seller. Predominantly used in external trade (where a buyer purchases goods in one overseas country and re-sells them in another country) or in string contracts (where the goods are sold and resold by several buyers (middlemen) before being purchased by the final buyer), a back-to-back credit is created when an exporter holding an irrevocable letter of credit has the buyer's bank (the advising bank) open a second credit in favour of the merchandise supplier. The two credits are identical in all respects, except that the supplier becomes the beneficiary of the back-to-back credit and the details relating to prices and invoicing will also differ depending upon each of the sales contracts. It is important to remember, however, that all transactions are legally separate—this means that two documentary credits have been issued.

To further illustrate, using a string contract (usually associated with trade in commodities): the final buyer will open a letter of credit in favour of the immediate seller (that is, the party who has sold the goods to the final buyer). The immediate

Figure 4.2: Letter of credit string contract

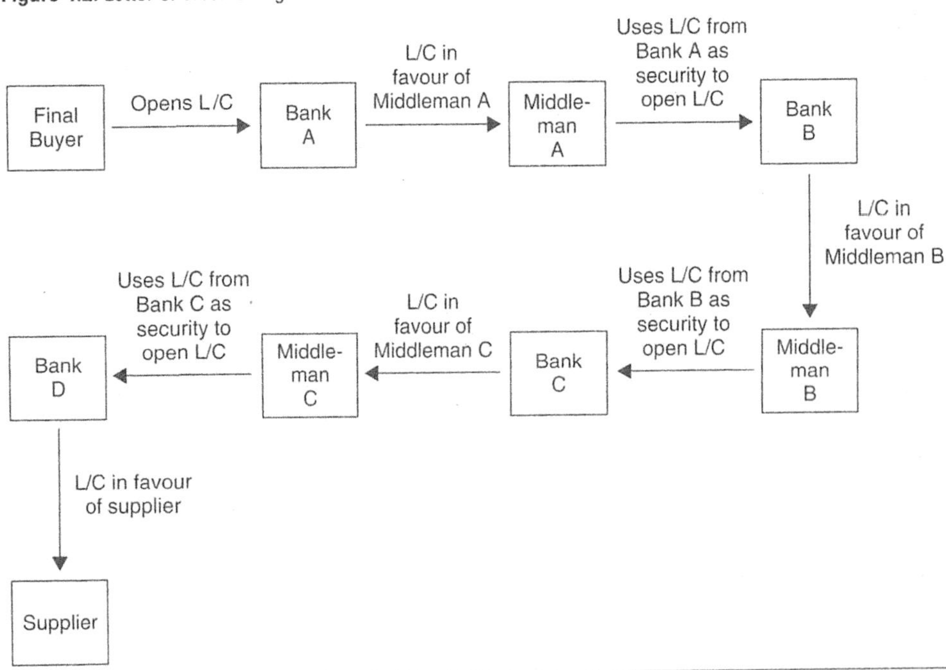

seller will then use the credit as security to open a letter of credit with the party that sold it the goods (that is, its supplier).[66] This process can be repeated for as many parties (middlemen) as are involved in the transaction, with each using the credit in its favour as security for the credit it must open for its predecessor in the 'string' of contracts. Each credit in the 'string' is identical, except of course in terms of prices and invoices. The initial credit is now referred to as the 'overriding credit'—it is the most important credit in the 'string', as it is the 'foundation on which the whole financial structure of the arrangement rests'.[67] It is important to note that a bank only has recourse against the preceding party in the transaction and, for this reason, some are hesitant (or refuse) to extend this particular credit.

4.5 Standby letters of credit and guarantees

4.5.1 Standby letters of credit

Similar to an ordinary letter of credit, a *standby letter of credit* is an undertaking by the bank to effect payment to the beneficiary upon the presentation of certain documents. However, while payment on an ordinary letter of credit is directed towards the seller (beneficiary) in fulfilment of the terms of the sales contract, a standby letter of credit aims to protect the beneficiary against a default by the other party to the underlying contract.

In essence, standby letters of credit are used as a guarantee of payment. They are utilised for a number of different reasons relating to non-performance or non-compliance of an agreement or contract. One example of such a situation is where the seller provides a standby letter of credit in favour of the buyer (as the beneficiary) to be activated if non-conforming or unsatisfactory goods are shipped. Another example could be where a builder opens a standby letter of credit in favour of the landowner or government in case it fails to complete the building on time or in a satisfactory manner.

It should be obvious at this point that a standby letter of credit protects the purchaser by providing an avenue for immediate recourse when that party has paid all of, or a portion of, the purchase price before it has inspected the completed product or received the goods. But standby letters of credit are also commonly used to allow one party to use its credit facility to guarantee a third party's credit facility, and this often occurs when a parent company opens the credit in favour of a lending bank to guarantee facilities granted to its subsidiary. Such usage enables the company to leverage the strength of one entity (such as its credit standing, track record, capital, etc) to support a weaker one.

The exact documents needed to activate the credit will be specified in the credit itself and will differ depending upon the circumstances of the underlying transaction. In many cases, the credit will be activated merely upon a simple written demand by

66 In practice, the same bank will often—but not always—control the various credits.

67 C Murphy, *Schmitthoff Export Trade: The Law and Practice of International Trade*, 11th edn, Thomson Sweet Maxwell, London, 2007, p 227.

the beneficiary accompanied by sight drafts for the amount claimed (the beneficiary may or may not have to make a written declaration that the applicant has not fulfilled its duties under the underlying contract, shipped unsatisfactory goods, or whatever the case may be). As long as the documents are compliant, the issuing bank will pay despite an allegation or claim by the applicant that the activation of the credit would breach the underlying commercial contract. Thus, it is often very easy for the beneficiary to secure immediate relief when it believes the other party (the applicant) has not fulfilled its obligations under the underlying contract. This also means that the money has already transferred to the beneficiary—any dispute over whether the credit was properly activated will be discussed, resolved or litigated after the transfer.

It is worth noting that, under both the UK and Australian approach, mere allegations of fraud are not enough to warrant non-payment. Instead, the bank will only refuse to pay if fraud is established or obvious. When there is some fraudulent agreement or understanding between the applicant and the beneficiary ('rotten at the root'), the courts may intervene.[68] For instance, in the Australian case of *Contronic Distributors Pty Ltd v Bank of NSW*, Judge Helsham in the Supreme Court of New South Wales concentrated on the knowledge of the seller, and found that a seller can be restrained from presenting a letter of credit for payment or having payment made against it when the seller knows the documents are fraudulent.[69] Article 19 of the UNCITRAL Convention on Independent Guarantees and Stand-by Letters of Credit permits a court to issue a provisional order blocking payment to the beneficiary if it can be shown that a document is not genuine, that the documents show no payment is due, or that 'the demand has no conceivable basis'. It then gives five illustrations and prohibits injunctions on any other basis. It is unclear whether 'fraud against the transaction' is covered in any of these situations.

Most standby letters of credit completed prior to 1 January 1999 incorporated the UCP 500; however at that time the ICC-developed International Standby Practices (ISP 98) came into force and, being compatible with the UNCITRAL Convention on Independent Guarantees and Stand-by Letters of Credit, has since garnered much use.

4.5.2 Guarantees

A guarantee is an undertaking by a third party that a contract or a legal act will be correctly carried out (for example, that money will be repaid). In international business law, a guarantee is an undertaking by a third party to pay the required amount to the creditor if the principal does not comply with its obligations and defaults.

In order to be properly established and enforceable, the guarantee must be in writing (or evidenced in writing) and signed by the guarantor. The potential liability of the guarantor depends upon the terms of the contract of guarantee, but the principle of coextensiveness applies, meaning the potential liability of the guarantor will only equal that of the principal debtor. Moreover, any action that discharges the debtor would automatically discharge the guarantor. Under normal circumstances,

68 See *Solo Industries UK Ltd v Canara Bank* (CA) [2001] 1 WLR 1800.

69 [1984] 3 NSWLR 110.

when a bank acts as a guarantor it will require a counter-indemnity from the customer (principal debtor), enabling it to recover in full any amounts it must pay, with interest.

Guarantees can take on numerous forms. For example, a *conditional guarantee* does not become payable until the guarantor verifies that the applicant is in breach of its contractual obligations, and that as a result of that breach the beneficiary has suffered or incurred loss or damage. In this regard, the guarantor can and often does become involved in any dispute regarding the underlying sales contract between the parties. For this reason, some banks are hesitant to issue conditional guarantees.

By contrast, when a *demand guarantee* has been given, the guarantor is under an obligation to pay upon demand by the beneficiary against the presentation of the specified documents. To illustrate, an importer of steel in Australia can ask a Japanese exporter for a demand guarantee. The exporter would then need to purchase a guarantee from a bank and send it to the Australian importer. From that point, the exporter's failure to fulfil the conditions of the contract could result in the importer going to the bank and presenting the demand guarantee. At that point, the bank is obligated to give the importer the predefined amount of money specified. The exporter would then be obligated to repay the money (plus expenses and interest) to the bank.

A demand guarantee is similar to a letter of credit, but actually provides more protection. Whereas the letter of credit only provides protection against non-payment, a demand guarantee can provide protection against non-performance, late performance and even defective performance.

Other forms of guarantees, such as a *performance bond* (a bond issued to one party as a guarantee against the failure of the other party to meet obligations specified in the underlying contract), or an *advance payment guarantee* (also referred to as a *repayment guarantee*—a guarantee enabling a buyer to recover an advance payment made under a contract or order if the other party fails to fulfil its contractual obligations), similarly provide a simple avenue for the beneficiary to recover money owing to it (or damages) under the underlying contract in the event of non-performance.

Several international efforts have attempted to develop standards and codify principles. For instance, the ICC has developed the Uniform Rules for Demand Guarantees (1992), which follows on from its 1978 Uniform Rules for Contract Guarantees. For either to apply, the parties would need to incorporate the rules in the contract. Moreover, as introduced in section 4.5.1, UNCITRAL has negotiated a Convention on Independent Guarantees and Standby Letters of Credit, which has been in force since 2000 but has only managed to garner minimal interest.

4.6 Conclusion

In this chapter we provided readers with a basic overview of the issues involved with the payment and financing of an international sale of goods. By this stage, readers should have some appreciation of the importance of documentary credits to international commerce. Readers should also have an understanding of the payment risks of conducting international business transactions, as well as be able to outline the main payment options utilised in international business.

The chapter principally dealt with payment using documentary credits. As a letter of credit is the most common form of payment in an international transaction, the chapter devoted significant attention to the procedural and substantive issues that may arise. Three fundamental principles of the letter of credit—the autonomy of the letter of credit, the doctrine of strict compliance and the fraud exception—were also reviewed at length. The importance of these principles, and how they operate in practice in the differing jurisdictions, cannot be understated. Legal counsel and business representatives should fully understand the intricacies of the principles and potential consequences resulting from any misuse. Readers should also have a basic understanding of the significance and operation of other types of credits, including standby letters of credit.

Questions

With regard to the case study at the beginning of this chapter:

1. Why have letters of credit been described as 'the life blood of international commerce'?
2. Would you advise BUY to use an advisory or confirming bank in its transaction with SELL Corp? Why, or why not?
3. What is the difference between a revocable letter of credit and an irrevocable letter of credit? Why will most banks not accept a revocable letter of credit?
4. Could BUY refuse payment if the sales contract mistakenly referred to it as 'BY Pty Ltd'? What about if it referred to it as 'BUY CORP'? What if the error was in the letter of credit, as opposed to the sales contract?
5. If following shipment but prior to receipt of the goods BUY refuses to pay for the steel, will SELL Corp be paid? Will BUY be liable? If so, who will hold it liable and how can they enforce their rights?
6. Can BUY stop payment if it confirms that SELL Corp has shipped steel that fails to conform to the terms of the sales contract? Does it make a difference whether SELL Corp acted in good faith or fraudulently?
7. If the bill of lading is forged and the steel is never sent, is BUY still liable for payment?
8. What are the differences in the fraud exception as applied in the USA, the UK, Canada and Australia?
9. What are some of the legal difficulties encountered with the use of the eUCP?
10. When would a standby letter of credit be used? What are the risks to the parties?
11. What effect do financial crises, or restrictions on the access to credit, have on traders? Is credit really the 'life blood' of trade?

PART III

Import and Export Regulations

CHAPTER 5

customs law

CHOCOLATE Pty Ltd is a Canberra-based company engaged in the importation, manufacture and distribution of chocolate and other confectionery products. CHOCOLATE has plans to market a new chocolate bar filled with a mixture of almonds and hazelnuts in the Australian market. CHOCOLATE is currently deciding whether it should:

1 Import the manufactured product;
2 Import the chocolate, almonds and hazelnuts separately and complete the manufacturing process in Australia;
3 Import the chocolate, import the almond and hazelnut mixture as a single item and complete the manufacturing process in Australia; or
4 Import the chocolate, use local almonds and hazelnuts and complete the manufacturing process in Australia.

CHOCOLATE is interested how Australian customs law will impact upon its decision.

5.1 Introduction

All imported goods must be properly identified, classified and valued before being allowed to enter into Australia in order for customs officials to determine, *inter alia*, the applicable tariff rate payable, whether the goods are allowed into or prohibited from being imported into Australia, and whether the applicable quota for the good imported from the exporting country has been reached for the particular good.[1]

The initial determination as to the classification of the goods is made by the Australian Customs Service ('Customs'). Section 167 of the *Customs Act 1901* (Cth) sets out that an importer dissatisfied with the classification of the goods can challenge the decision by paying the duty required under protest and bringing an action to recover the amount paid. In practice, however, the first step in reviewing the classification determination is by Customs through internal review. If the internal review fails to resolve the issue, tribunal review is available through the Administrative Appeals Tribunal (AAT). Appeals of an AAT decision can be made to the Federal Court of Australia.

1 See Chapter 6 for detailed information on import controls. Chapter 7 provides detailed information on export controls.

This chapter provides a comprehensive overview of Australian customs law, with the focus being on selected issues of importance to international traders. The chapter is divided into three parts:

- Product classification;
- Rules of origin; and
- Valuation of the goods.

The chapter first introduces the Harmonised System and describes how goods are identified and classified for tariff purposes when they cross borders. Contemporary—and often common—problems and concerns are raised through the use of case law. The chapter then introduces rules of origin; that is, the procedure used to determine where the goods are deemed to have originated. Finally, the chapter briefly reviews the rules relating to how imported goods are valued.

5.2 Part A: Product classification

5.2.1 The Harmonised System

In order to facilitate and simplify international trade, product classifications have been standardised internationally and are guided by the Harmonised Commodity Description and Coding System ('Harmonised System', or HS). The HS is an international product nomenclature convention developed by the World Customs Organization (WCO) to serve as a legal and logical structure for the establishment of national customs tariff systems around the world.

The HS separates goods into groups of items and identifies them by a six-digit code (for example, '6401.20'):

- The first two digits indicate the chapter under which the goods fall (for example, 64 refers to Chapter 64: 'Beverages, Spirits and Vinegar').
- The second two digits usually identify the category of the product (for example, '6401': beer; '6402': spirits). These first four digits are often referred to as a 'heading'.
- The next two digits (digits five and six), are known as 'subheadings' and identify a subcategory of the heading (for example, '6401.20': vodka; '6401.30': rum).

The HS is the 'core', standardised system and should be the same for the classification of any item in any customs territory. Thus, the above-mentioned first six-digit nomenclature must be used by contracting parties as the basis of their domestic import and export tariffs and statistical requirements. However, customs territories may subdivide according to their needs and vary their interpretation by determining their own definition of the item's classification.[2] Accordingly, digits seven and eight can be added, which further detail the subcategory of digits five and six, and are generally

2 For example, a state may conform with a definition of an item in order to align its interests with those of a customs union or free trade area (for example, Australia–New Zealand Closer Economic Relations, Australia–USA Free Trade Agreement, etc). This alignment of interests is set out in trade arrangements and will define the rate of duty applicable to the commercial transactions, and whether it will be a general or a preferential rate of duty.

specific to each customs territory. Customs territories are also allowed to classify items to a still greater degree of specificity (to the ten-digit level) if they deem it in their interests.

In Australia, the *Customs Tariff Act 1995* (Cth) (*Tariff Act*) is the legislation that gives effect to the HS and directs the classification and duty rates of imported goods:

- Schedule 1 of this act provides the country name and abbreviations to which special tariff rates apply.[3]
- Schedule 2 provides the General Rules for the Interpretation of Schedule 3 (GRI).
- Schedule 3 lists the tariff classification and applicable rates of duty. It is divided into sections and chapters containing Australia's classifications and duty rates for imported goods. The HS six digits are supplemented by a further four digits that define the rates of duty within each chapter of the *Tariff Act*.
- Schedule 4 sets out a number of concessional items that are subjected to a tariff concession order (TCO) or departmental by-laws.
- Schedules 5 and 6 present the classification and tariff rate for goods originating from two of Australia's free trade area partners (the USA and Thailand) that are not entitled to duty-free access to Australia.

Before providing an example of a product classification and applicable duty rate under the *Tariff Act*,[4] it is worthwhile to note that while most duties are charged at an '*ad valorem*' rate (that is, as a percentage of the value of the goods, such as 10 per cent of the value of the goods), the duty can also be charged as a 'specific' rate (that is, as a set rate per unit that does not change with the price of the goods; for example, $10 per kilogram), or a 'mixed' rate (for example, 10 per cent of the value of the goods plus $5 per tonne).

Customs Tariff, Schedule 3

Chapter 18: Cocoa and cocoa preparations

1801 Cocoa beans, whole or broken, raw or roasted

1802 Cocoa shells, husks, skins and other cocoa waste

1803 Cocoa paste, whether or not defatted

1804 Cocoa butter, fat and oil

1805 Cocoa powder, not containing added sugar or other sweetening matter

1806 Chocolate and other food preparations containing cocoa

NOTES:

1 This Chapter does not cover the preparations of 0403, 1901, 1904, 1905, 2105.00.00, 2202, 2208, 3003 or 3004.

2 1806 includes sugar confectionery containing cocoa and, subject to Note 1 to this Chapter, other food preparations containing cocoa.

---

3 Students are recommended to visit the Customs website and browse the schedules: see [www.customs.gov.au/site/page.cfm?u=5663#tariff488].

4 Note that the duty rates payable in this example have been slightly modified for illustrative purposes.

Reference	Number	Statistical Code/Unit	Goods	Rate #
1801.00.00	01	Kg	Cocoa beans, whole or broken, raw or roasted	Free
1802.00.00	02	Kg	Cocoa shells, husks, skins and other cocoa waste	Free
1803			Cocoa paste, whether or not defatted:	
1803.10.00	03	Kg	Not defatted	Free
1803.20.00	04	Kg	Wholly or partly defatted	Free
1804.00.00	05	Kg	Cocoa butter, fat and oil	Free
1805.00.00	06	Kg	Cocoa powder, not containing added sugar or other sweetening matter	Free
1806	07	Kg	Chocolate and other food preparations containing cocoa:	5%
1806.10.00	07	Kg	Cocoa powder, containing added sugar or other sweetening matter	5%
1806.20.00	19	Kg	Other preparations in blocks, slabs or bars weighing more than 2kg or in liquid, paste, powder, granular, or other bulk form in containers or immediate packings, of a content exceeding 2kg	
1806.3	11	Kg	Other, in blocks, slabs or bars:	
			filled chocolate confectionery	15%
1806.31.00	12	Kg	Other	
1806.32.00			Not filled	7%
	13	Kg	Chocolate confectionery	
	14	Kg	Other	
1806.90.00			Other	11%
	17	Kg	Chocolate confectionery	
	18	Kg	Other	

Unless otherwise indicated NS, PG FI, DC, LDC and SG rates are Free.
Unless otherwise indicated general rate applies for CA.
Unless indicated in Schedule 5, rates for US originating goods are Free.
Unless indicated in Schedule 6, rates for TH originating goods are Free.

DCS denotes the rate for countries and places listed in Part 4 of Schedule 1 to this Act.
DCT denotes the rate for HK, KR, SG and TW.
If no DCT rate shown, DCS rate applies. If no DCT or DCS rate shown general rate applies.

Chapter 8: Edible fruit and nuts; peel of citrus fruit or melons

0801 Coconuts, brazil nuts and cashew nuts, fresh or dried, whether or not shelled or peeled

0802 Other nuts, fresh or dried, whether or not shelled or peeled

0803 Bananas, including plantains, fresh or dried

0804 Dates, figs, pineapples, avocados, guavas, mangoes and mangosteens, fresh or dried

0805 Citrus fruit, fresh or dried

0806 Grapes, fresh or dried

0807 Melons (including watermelons) and pawpaws (papayas), fresh

0808 Apples, pears and quinces, fresh

0809 Apricots, cherries, peaches (including nectarines), plums and sloes, fresh

0810 Other fruit, fresh

0811 Fruit and nuts, uncooked or cooked by steaming or boiling in water, frozen, whether or not containing added sugar or other sweetening matter

0812 Fruit and nuts, provisionally preserved (for example, by sulphur dioxide gas, in brine, in sulphur water or in other preservative solutions), but unsuitable in that state for immediate consumption

0813 Fruit, dried, other than that of 0801 to 0806; mixtures of nuts or dried fruits of this Chapter

0814 Peel of citrus fruit or melons (including watermelons), fresh, frozen, dried or provisionally preserved in brine, in sulphur water or in other preservative solutions

NOTES:

1 This Chapter does not cover inedible nuts or fruits.

2 Chilled fruits and nuts are to be classified in the same headings as the corresponding fresh fruits and nuts.

3 Dried fruit or dried nuts of this Chapter may be partially rehydrated, or treated for the following purposes:

(a) For additional preservation or stabilisation (for exmaple, by moderate heat treatment, sulphuring, the addition of sorbic acid or potassium sorbate),

(b) To improve or maintain their appearance (for example, by the addition of vegetable oil or small quantities of glucose syrup), provided that they retain the character of dried fruit or dried nuts.

...

Unless otherwise indicated NZ, PG, FI, DC, LDC and SG rates are Free.
Unless otherwise indicated general rate applies for CA.
Unless indicated in Schedule 5, rates for US originating goods are Free.
Unless indicated in Schedule 6, rates for TH originating goods are Free.

Reference	Number/Statistical Code/Unit	Goods	Rate #
...			
0802		Other nuts, fresh or dried, whether or not shelled or peeled:	
0802.1		Almonds:	
0802.11.00	07 kg	In shell	5%
			DCS: 4%
			DCT: 5%
0802.12.00	08 kg	Shelled	8%
			DCS: 4%
			SCT: 5%
0802.2		Hazelnuts or filberts	
0802.21.00	09 kg	In shell	Free
0802.22.00	10 kg	Shelled	Free

DCS denotes the rate for countries and places listed in Part 4 of Schedule 1 to this Act.
DCT denotes the rate for HK, KR, SG and TW.
If no DCT rate shown, DCS rate applies. If no DCT or DCS rate shown, general rate applies

....

While at first glance the classification of goods may appear straightforward and uncontroversial, a more thorough inspection reveals the numerous issues and problems that may come up during product classifications. For instance, interpretative problems may arise in identifying the nature of the goods and determining which product classification is appropriate. This problem is compounded when the goods in question appear to fall within two or more items in the *Tariff Act*. In such a circumstance, recourse should be had to the GRI (Schedule 2 of the *Tariff Act*) and to the Interpretative Notes and Opinions provided by the WCO, as incorporated by the Australian legislation.

The remainder of this section is separated into two parts:

- Identification of the goods; and
- Classification of the goods.

5.2.2 Identification of the goods

In order to impose a duty on imported goods, the tariff item that corresponds to the goods must first be identified.[5] To identify under which tariff item the goods should be

5 See *Times Consultants Pty Ltd v Collector of Customs* (1978) 76 ALR 313. See also *Re Gissing and Collector of Customs* 1 ALD 144 at 145, where the tribunal stated: 'The question raised by the application is one of classification. In order to answer the question, it is necessary to identify the goods and by construing the tariff, to determine which provisions of the tariff includes the goods so identified.'

placed, an objective test has been formulated that requires the assessor to have regard to the form of the goods at the time of importation (such as the nature, condition, distinguishing characteristics or state of the goods) and not to the description of the goods.[6] The tribunal in *Re Sterns Playland Pty Ltd and Collector of Customs (No 2)* explained the task of identifying the goods as follows:

> As always in tariff classification matters, the first step is to identify the imported goods. Although the question of identification can often be resolved fairly readily by asking the question what is it?—anyone with knowledge of the Tariff will be aware that in addition to the answer produced in response to that question, other matters may also need to be considered before one turns to the next task, namely classification in accordance with the Tariff. All the characteristics which goods present on informed inspection or even, in some cases, on scientific analysis, may have a relevance to this frequently complex task ... As the Tariff recognizes, imported goods, because of their diverse characteristics or components and because of their capacity for being identified by informed minds in a variety of ways, may well 'fall' within two or more items in the Tariff. Indeed, most goods are capable of being identified specifically (as a particular article of commerce) or generically by reference to the materials or substances from which they are made. It is one of the important functions of the Rules for the Interpretation of Sch 1 (in Pt 1 of that Schedule to the Tariff) to provide mechanisms for resolving, in those circumstances, which of the various items etc into which the goods may 'fall' is the item etc that 'applies' to the imported goods.[7]

The following extract—often cited in classification cases—provides an outline of eight principles of interpretation to be used when identifying the goods.

Re Tridon Pty Ltd and Collector of Customs 4 ALD 615, No N81/123 Customs Tariff (17/6/1982)[8]

5. As the Tribunal has said on many previous occasions, the starting point in resolving questions of Tariff classification, is to identify the goods in their condition as imported (see *Re Gissing and Collector of Customs* (1977) 1 ALD 144). The principles with respect to identification of goods were recently restated by the Tribunal ... in *Re Sterns Playland Pty Ltd and Collector of Customs* (No N81/75). Those principles may be conveniently summarized (although not exhaustively stated) as follows:

(i) Identification must be objective, having regard to the characteristics which the goods, on informed inspection, present:

(ii) The identification of goods cannot be controlled by the descriptions of goods adopted in the nomenclature of the Tariff:

(iii) Nevertheless in identifying goods it is necessary to be aware of the structure of the nomenclature, the basis on which goods are classified and the characteristics of goods which may be relevant to the frequently complex task of classification:

(iv) In the identification of goods, knowledge of how those who trade in the goods describe them will usually be relevant, but not necessarily conclusive:

(v) All the descriptive terms, both specific and generic, by which the goods may fairly be identified may be relevant to the classification of the goods within the Tariff:

6 See *Re Gissing*, ibid at 146; *Re Sterns Playland Pty Ltd and Collector of Customs* (1982) 4 ALD 562.

7 (1982) 4 ALD 562 at 565–6 (citations omitted).

8 Citations omitted.

> (vi) Descriptive terms may be of varying degrees of specificity (eg windscreen wiper blade refills, parts for a windscreen wiper or parts for a motor vehicle). Generic descriptions may be by reference to the materials or substances from which the goods are manufactured:
>
> (vii) Identification will frequently extend to characterisation of goods by reference to their design features or by reference to their suitability for a particular use where those characteristics emerge from informed inspection of the goods as imported … The extent to which these characteristics may be relevant to the ultimate classification of the goods and whether evidence of the use to which goods are put after importation is relevant, will depend upon the language of the Tariff Nomenclature:
>
> (viii) Composite goods, notwithstanding that they have components which are separately identifiable, may nevertheless be identifiable in combination as a new entity if the identity of the separate units is subordinated to the identity of the combination:
>
> … …

Importantly, identification must also be undertaken in an impartial manner so as not to predetermine the question of classification. The Tribunal in *Re Toyworld Ltd and Collector of Customs (Vic)* stated:

> As always, there is a danger when one is involved in the process of identification of goods that the adoption of a particular linguistic form may prejudge the ultimate class of classification. To do this is to over emphasise the process of identification, the aim of which is to act as a light with which to guide the seeker after items of the tariff which may be candidates for consideration as items within which the goods in question may fall. It is not a correct approach to predetermine conclusively, by a fine choice of language in the identification process, whether an article of goods will in fact fall within a particular item.[9]

Identification and classification of goods is very often an uncomplicated and trouble-free exercise. However, as noted above, the identification and classification of goods is not always straightforward. For instance, trouble can arise when the identification of the good is unclear and does not reveal its true nature or function or the description of the good is ambiguous so that it seems to fall with two or more categories.[10] Despite this, a single classification must be found as all goods must be placed into a single classification in order to determine, *inter alia*, the appropriate duty rate to be paid. In such a circumstance, it may be necessary for Customs to make additional enquiries beyond the initial inspection in order to be able to make a fully informed classification decision.[11]

Moreover, when the goods cannot be identified through an informed inspection, principle (vii) of *Tridon's* case makes clear that the 'use' of the goods could be used in determining the proper identification of the goods:

> Identification will frequently extend to characterisation of goods by reference to their *design features*, or by reference to their suitability for a particular *use* where those characteristics emerge from informed inspection of the goods as imported.[12]

---

9 [1984] AATA 3 at para 11.

10 Importers must ensure that goods entering Australia are correctly labelled, and it is an offence to knowingly apply, or for imported goods to carry, false trade descriptions (including weight, origin, manufacturer, preparation, contents or copyright). See *Commerce (Trade Descriptions) Act 1905* (Cth), ss 3–4, 7 and 9.

11 See *Re Times Consultants Pty Limited v Collector of Customs (Queensland)* [1987] FCA 311 at 328; *Chemark Services Pty Ltd v Collector of Customs* (1991) 24 ALD 578.

12 Reference omitted, emphasis added.

The Full Federal Court in *Chinese Food and Wine Suppliers Pty Ltd v Collector of Customs* further explained the 'objective test' standard, elaborated upon the concept of an 'informed inspection' as well as further clarified the concept, and determinative factors, of 'use'. In the case, the applicant alleged that the two liquid products imported from China, one known as Wu Chia Pi Chiew and the other as Chu Yeh Ching Chiew, both contained in 500ml bottles, were medicaments and should be classified as such [Item 30.03 of Schedule 3] under the *Tariff Act*. The Customs Collector, on the other hand, concluded that the goods should be classified as spirits, liqueurs and other spirituous beverages and compound alcoholic preparations for the manufacture of beverages, containing not more than 57% by volume of alcohol [22.09.91] under the *Tariff Act*. The Tribunal agreed. The reason for the appeal was that if the goods fall within Item 30.03 as medicaments a far lower rate of duty is attracted than if they fall under paragraph 22.09.91.

Chinese Food and Wine Supplies Pty Ltd and Collector of Customs (1987) 72 ALR 591

5. Chapter 30 of Schedule 3 to the *Tariff Act* deals with Pharmaceutical Products. Item 30.03 relates to medicaments. Note 1 to Chapter 30 is in the following terms:

1(1) In 30.03, 'medicaments' means goods (other than dietetic, diabetic or fortified foods, tonic beverages, spa water or similar foods or beverages) that are—

- (a) goods comprising 2 or more constituents that have been mixed or compounded together for a therapeutic or prophylactic use; or
- (b) unmixed goods suitable for such a use that have been put up in measured doses or in forms or in packs of a kind sold by retail for therapeutic or prophylactic purposes, but does not include goods falling within 30.02 or 30.04.

(2) For the purposes of this note and paragraph 3(d)—

- (a) the following goods shall be deemed to comprise two or more constituents that have been mixed or compounded together:
  - (i) colloidal solutions and suspensions (other than colloidal sulphur);
  - (ii) vegetable extracts obtained by the treatment of mixtures of vegetable materials;
  - (iii) salts and concentrates obtained by evaporating natural mineral waters; and
- (b) the following goods shall be deemed to be unmixed goods:
  - (i) unmixed products dissolved in water;
  - (ii) goods falling within Chapter 28;
  - (iii) goods falling within Chapter 29; and
  - (iv) simple vegetable extracts that have not been prepared, or that have been standardized or dissolved in any solvent but not further prepared, being goods falling within 13.03.

...

8. The sole question argued on this appeal was whether the goods, which admittedly comprise two or more constituents that have been mixed or compounded together, attract the description 'for a therapeutic use'. If they do, then the appellant succeeds and the lower rate of duty relating to the importation of medicaments applies.

...

10. The critical findings of the Tribunal that led it to conclude that the goods with which this case is concerned were manufactured for export and sale as beverages were expressed by the Tribunal in these terms:

42. If, when the goods imported were prepared, their constituents were mixed or compounded together for a therapeutic purpose, they did not, in our view, lose their character as medicaments by being exported from China and imported into Australia. However, although much of the evidence was directed to showing that in China goods of the types of those which are the subject of review in these proceedings are prepared for a therapeutic purpose, there was other evidence before the Tribunal indicating that the goods imported were prepared, or manufactured, for another purpose, namely for the purpose of export from China as a beverage.

43. The evidence of that is, first, the sales catalogue issued by the manufacturer with the title 'Wines' on its cover and with both types of goods included in it. The display of goods of those types in the liquor department of the supermarket in Hong Kong is not of itself alone evidence of the manufacturer's purpose in preparing them; but, when viewed in combination with the sales catalogue, it has significance. Finally, there are the labels and the general presentation of the goods as imported into Australia. The bottles in which they are contained are not of the size or type generally used for medicinal products but rather such as are used for beverages, and particularly alcoholic beverages. The carton in which each Wu Chia Pi Chiew bottle is packed is of the type and appearance used for bottles of spirituous liquor; they are fairly attractive and in no way resemble the type of cartons in which bottles of medicinal products are generally packed. The statement on the Wu Chia Pi Chiew bottles that it is 'an excellent drink very relishable and refreshing' is appropriate to a beverage, not to a medicinal product.

44. We have come to the conclusion, therefore, that, although the goods which the applicant imported are of the same type as goods manufactured in China for therapeutic purposes, they themselves were manufactured for a different purpose, that is to say for export and sale as beverages. That being so, we find that they are not medicaments. They are both beverages containing respectively about 53% and 44% by volume of ethyl alcohol. That is their identity.

11. The two kinds of goods were imported into Australia in 500ml bottles each of which is similar in appearance to a wine bottle. The bottles of Wu Chia Pi Chiew were contained in cardboard cartons. Each carton bears the name of the product and two identical statements in Chinese script. Each carton also bears the following label in the English language which has been affixed to the carton:

WU CHIA PI CHIEW

Ingredients: Kao Liang Chiew, granulated sugar, red wine yeast, radix angelicae sinensis, rhizoma ligustici, root bark of Chinese silkvine, citrus peel, rhizome polygonati odorati.

Direction of use: Regular use recommended any quantity as desired.

Imported & distributed by: Chinese Wine & Food Supplies Pty Ltd, 206 Lt Bourke St, Melbourne, Australia.

Volume 500ml. B.

The bottle of Wu Chia Pi Chiew contained in each cardboard carton bears two labels. One label is brightly coloured in gold and green and is written in both Chinese script and the English language. At the bottom of the label is the following statement in the English language:

'Wu Chia Pi Chiew' red and transparent in colour, fragrant in flavour, slightly sweet and without stimulants is an excellent drink very relishable and refreshing.

12. The other label on the carton has a white background with black print, is written in the English language and states:

> WU CHIA PI CHIEW
>
> Ingredients: Kao Liang Chiew, granulated sugar, red wine yeast, radix angelicae sinensis, rhizoma ligustici, root bark of Chinese silkvine, citrus peel, rhizome polygonati odorati.
>
> Direction of use: Regular use recommended any quantity as desired.
>
> Imported & distributed by: Chinese Wine & Food Supplies Pty Ltd, 206 Lt Bourke St, Melbourne, Australia.
>
> Volume 500ml. B.'

13. The bottles of Chu Yeh Ching Chiew were not in individual cartons when imported. Each bottle bears two labels. One label is deep green in colour with a gold rim containing mainly Chinese script but with the name of the product in English as 'Chu Yeh Ching Chiew'. The Tribunal found that the second label on the bottle had clearly been put on to it for the purposes of its importation into Australia. This label is in the English language and reads as follows:

> CHU YEH CHING CHIEW
>
> Ingredients: Feng Chiew, sugar, bamboo leaf, citrus peel, radix angelicae sinensis, christin loosestrife, rhizome kaemferiae, flos caryophylli.
>
> Directions of use: To be taken any quantity as desired.
>
> Imported and distributed by: Chinese Wine & Food Supplies Pty Ltd, 206 Lt Bourke St, Melbourne, Australia.
>
> Volume 500 ml. B.'

14. The Tribunal was critical of certain statements on the labels of the bottles of Chu Yeh Ching Chiew and of the cartons. Some of the statements were described by it as 'seriously misleading'. The Tribunal said:

> It is totally incorrect to say the product is 'without stimulants', as the analysis made on 5 September 1985 shows that it contains 53.3% by volume of ethyl alcohol at 20 degrees C. It is doubtful whether, if the flavour is the same as the smell which comes from the product when the bottle is opened, many persons in Australia would regard the flavour as fragrant; however that is essentially a matter of taste. The combination of the recommendation on the carton label of regular use in 'any quantities as desired', the omission of any clear reference to alcohol from the list of ingredients and the statements that it is 'without stimulants' and that it 'is an excellent drink very relishable and refreshing' are misleading in the extreme. In the statement of the ingredients the reference to Kao Liang Chiew is to the alcoholic base but to a person not familiar with Chinese medicinal products that would not convey the information that there was an alcohol base and certainly not one of 53.3%. To a person unfamiliar with Chinese medicinal products, the impression given by the labelling would be that the product is an aromatic non-alcoholic drink without medicinal qualities.

15. The Tribunal was also critical of certain of the statements on the bottles of Chu Yeh Ching Chiew. It said:

there is no reference to alcohol among the ingredients, only a reference to Feng Chiew, and the directions for use in terms that it is to be taken in any quantity as desired might well lead a person not familiar with Chinese medicinal products to believe that the product was a non-alcoholic drink; the contents of the labels would certainly not alert such a person to the very high percentage of alcohol, 45% by analysis on 5 September 1985.

...

17. It was not disputed that in Chinese traditional medicine both types of preparation were regarded as having therapeutic value; but different views were expressed by various witnesses as to whether the preparations in suit had any therapeutic value. The Tribunal comprehensively stated and analysed the evidence of the witnesses and found that:

- the goods were probably manufactured in accordance with the methods provided for in the China Pharmacopeia for the preparation of medicinal products for use in Chinese traditional medicine;
- the names which they bear are those of products the ingredients and medicinal uses of which are set out in Chinese Tinctures;
- the goods comprise more than two constituents that have been mixed or compounded in China;
- goods of the same type are mixed or compounded in China for medicinal use;
- goods of the same type have a therapeutic use within the meaning of that phrase in the *Therapeutic Goods Act 1966* (Cth); and
- goods of the same type are standard preparations manufactured in accordance with the China Pharmacopeia and Chinese Tinctures.

...

21. Item 30.03 assigns a much lower rate of duty to medicaments than would otherwise be applicable to them under paragraph 22.09.91. To qualify for the lower rate the medicaments must be goods, other than certain specified foods or beverages, that are goods for a therapeutic or prophylactic use. Goods are treated as being of two kinds: mixed and unmixed. Mixed goods are goods comprising two or more constituents that have been mixed or compounded together. Certain deeming provisions determine whether some goods comprise two or more constituents that have been mixed or compounded together (see Note 1(2)(a) to Chapter 30) and whether other goods are unmixed goods (see Note 1(2)(b) to Chapter 30).

22. The requirement in the case of goods comprising two or more constituents that those constituents 'have been mixed or compounded together' plainly means that the mixing or compounding together shall have taken place before the importation of the goods. In the present case there is no dispute that the goods were mixed together in China before importation. In my opinion it is the goods resulting from the mixing or compounding process that must be for a therapeutic or prophylactic use in order that the goods answer the description of medicaments for the purposes of Item 30.03. The language of Note 1 to Chapter 30 is perhaps susceptible either of that construction or the construction that the two or more constituents, as distinct from the goods which result from the mixing or compounding together, have been mixed or compounded together for a therapeutic or prophylactic use; but any ambiguity is resolved when Note 1 is construed as a whole and in the light of the evident purpose of Item 30.03. If the relevant part of Note 1 were recast in an unambiguous form it might read as follows:

1(1) In 30.03 'medicaments' means goods ... that are—

(a) goods (comprising 2 or more constituents that have been mixed or compounded together) for a therapeutic or prophylactic use;

23. I cannot discern any convincing reason why the *Tariff Act* would fasten on the therapeutic or prophylactic use of constituents that have been mixed or compounded together to produce goods as determinative of the character of the goods as medicaments and therefore afford a far more favourable rate of customs duty. There is no sound reason why Item 30.03 in Schedule 3 of the *Tariff Act* would be concerned with therapeutic or prophylactic use of the constituents of goods as distinct from the goods themselves. The requirement that the constituents have been mixed or compounded together is descriptive of the resultant goods exigible to duty rather than determinative of the question of therapeutic or prophylactic use. It is the goods to which Item 30.03 is directed; not any goods, but goods for therapeutic or prophylactic use produced by the mixing or compounding together of two or more constituents. Of course, the goods are the sum of their components and are produced by the mixing or compounding together of two or more constituents. In one sense if the goods have a therapeutic or prophylactic use they merely reflect the like use of their constituents. If, contrary to my view of Chapter 30, the note is directed to the therapeutic or prophylactic use of the constituents as distinct from the goods produced then the anomalous result would follow that the goods could be manufactured outside Australia by mixing or compounding at least two constituents together for a therapeutic or prophylactic use, but the goods themselves exported to Australia for another use. For example, goods may be manufactured in the country of origin following a mixing or compounding together for a therapeutic use but exported to Australia for a quite different use because of perhaps some special feature or peculiarity of the local market. Item 30.03 was not intended to apply to goods answering that description.

24. Note 1(1)(b) gives some guidance to the interpretation of Note 1(1)(a). Note 1(1)(b) speaks of 'unmixed goods suitable for such a use that have been put up in measured doses or in forms or in packs of a kind sold by retail for therapeutic or prophylactic purposes'. It thus plainly is directed to the therapeutic or prophylactic use of the unmixed goods themselves. It would be odd if the two paragraphs ((a) and (b)) were speaking of different uses; in the case of paragraph (a) the use to which the constituents which produce mixed goods are to be put and in the case of paragraph (b) the use to which the unmixed goods themselves are to be put.

25. It is the goods themselves in the condition in which they are imported here to which it is generally necessary to look under the *Tariff Act* to determine the identification of goods for purposes of customs duty. Conformity with this general approach is achieved in the case of Chapter 30 if, on its proper interpretation, it is the therapeutic or prophylactic use to which the goods will be put in Australia to which the Chapter is directed.

26. Whether the goods in suit properly fall within Item 33.03 of the customs tariff is determined by an objective test not by the intentions of the manufacturer in China or of the exporter or the importer. The test is applied at the port of entry of the goods and at the time of entry. The characteristics of the goods, their get-up, colour, decoration, labelling and packaging are all relevant considerations. In some cases a visual inspection of the goods and their packaging will disclose characteristics of the goods and enable a judgement to be made as to whether they are for therapeutic or prophylactic use. But visual inspection will not necessarily provide the answer in each case. Tests may have to be carried out and enquiries made to ascertain the relevant characteristics of the goods. In the present case samples were taken and sent for chemical analysis. As the Tribunal noted, the paucity of the information contained in the labelling of the goods necessitated further enquiries being made in respect of them.

27. The critical elements upon which the Tribunal relied, namely, the labelling and the general presentation of the goods as imported into Australia, the analysis of the liquid contained in the

bottles, the contents of the sales catalogue issued with the title 'Wines' on its cover with both kinds of goods included in it and the display of goods of those kinds in the liquor section of a supermarket in Hong Kong are in my view all relevant matters which the Tribunal was entitled to consider whichever of the two interpretations of Note 1(1)(a) was applied by it.

28. There is abundant evidence to support the finding that the two kinds of goods were not for therapeutic use in Australia.

29. There is no precise evidence as to who manufactured or produced either class of goods; but there was ample evidence that a Chinese corporation, the China National Cereals, Oils and Foodstuffs Import and Export Corporation, was the exporter of the goods and that they were manufactured for it and under its authority. There was no evidence to the contrary and no evidence suggesting that anybody else was the manufacturer. In these circumstances, even if the correct question is (which I do not think it is) whether the mixing or compounding together of the constituents took place in China for a therapeutic purpose there is evidence sufficient to support the Tribunal's finding that the mixing and compounding was not for therapeutic use. The finding that the goods in suit were manufactured in China for the purpose of export and sale as beverages is supported by the evidence and should not be disturbed.

30. I would dismiss the appeal with costs.

... ...

A difficult interpretive issue that regularly arises is whether goods should be identified as 'individual goods' or as part of an 'unassembled entity'. The Tribunal in *Re Gissing and Collector of Customs* summarised the difficulty of the situation:

> Identification of goods to be classified is often a simple exercise. When goods are separate units, each identical with the others, and possessing no distinctive feature by reason of their association, each unit may be identified self-evidently as the relevant entity for classification.[13]

On the other hand, there is sometimes a relationship between or among various units of such a kind as to identify them as a combination rather than as separate units. The test to be applied is whether the identity of the units is subordinated to the identity of the combination. Courts in the USA have developed the 'doctrine of entireties' as an aid in ascertaining proper classification, the underlying principle corresponding with the test of subordinated identity:

> If what is imported as a unit is actually and commercially two or more individual entities, which, even though imported joined or assembled together, nevertheless, retain their individual identities and are not subordinated to the identity of the combination, duties will be imposed upon the individual entities in the combination as though they had been imported separately. Conversely, if there are imported in one importation separate entities, which by their nature are obviously intended to be used as a unit, or to be joined together by mere assembly, and in such use or joining the individual identities of the separate entities are subordinated to the identity of the combined entity, duty will be imposed upon the entity they represent.[14]

The test, though simply expressed, may prove difficult to apply with confidence in all factual situations, as the US Court of Customs and Patent Appeals noted:

---

13 (1977) 1 ALD 144 at 145.

14 *Donalds Ltd v United States* 32 Cust Ct 310 (1954) at 315.

> The difficulty which is experienced in this type of case is not so much the formulation of a workable rule as it is the application of the provisions thereof to a given factual situation. Where it is apparent that the components of an importation have no useful function until joined into a single entity, it is, of course, relatively easy to say that the result constitutes an entirety. Where, however, the several components of a unit are to any extent alone susceptible of a separate use, the question of whether their individual identities are subordinated to the newly created entity is not so readily answered.[15]

In *Re Cemac Associated and Collector of Customs*,[16] the tribunal considered whether goods imported were individual items or unassembled goods. In the case, the applicant imported four containers of components for access flooring, which included the following items:

- 4325 floor panels;
- 4145 steel pedestal heads;
- 675 steel pedestal heads;
- 675 neoprene gaskets;
- 4820 steel pedestal bases;
- 8060 steel stringers;
- 8060 neoprene gaskets; and
- Two panel lifters.

Upon importation, the applicant entered the subject goods under various sub-items appropriate to the individual components (sub-items 40.14.9, 44.23.9, 73.21.9, 73.21.3, and paragraph 39.02.520). The collector, however, considered that the imported components were an unassembled access floor and that the goods should therefore be classified as an entirety, rather than by reference to the individual components, as unassembled structure of steel (sub-item 73.21.9) at a rate of duty of 35 per cent. The applicant paid the additional duties under protest and sought review of the decision. The two classifications in contention were as follows:

> 44.23. Builders' carpentry and joinery (including prefabricated and sectional buildings and assembled parquet flooring panels)
>
> 73.21. Structures and parts of structures, (including hangars and other buildings, bridges and bridge-sections, lock-gates, towers, lattice masts, roofs, roofing, framework, door and window frames, shutters, balustrades, pillars and columns), of iron or steel; plates, strip, rods, angles, shapes, sections, tubes and the like, prepared for use in structures, of iron or steel.

It was not in dispute that the imported goods were not simply a random selection of components, but rather the precise number of components ordered by Cemac to enable it to fulfil a contract to install an access floor in a Western Australian building.

15 *Miniature Fashions Inc v United States* (1966) 54 CCPA 11 at 15, as cited in *Re Gissing and Collector of Customs* (1977) 1 ALD 144 at 145.

16 (1986) 7 ALD 411.

Re Cemac Associated and Collector of Customs (1986) 7 ALD 411[17]

27. There is a principle of Tariff classification which, in this country, finds secure statutory support in r 2(1)(b) of the Interpretative Rules, that where goods of a particular kind are referred to in an item etc of the Tariff, that reference includes goods imported in an unassembled or disassembled state which, if assembled, would be goods of that kind. Where this principle operates it is convenient to refer to the components as having been 'notionally' assembled, notwithstanding that, in their condition as imported, they were not so assembled. Before r 2(1)(b) can be applied, however, the question is—is there a Tariff item etc within which the imported components, if notionally assembled, fall?

28. This principle has much in common with that facet of the American doctrine of entireties which establishes that 'when two or more parts of an article are shipped together and are intended to be used together as one article, and by mere assembly they are made into one article, they shall be regarded as entireties for Tariff purposes'. This aspect of the entireties doctrine appears to run parallel with and be supported by rule 10(h) of the Rules for Interpretation of the Schedules to the US *Tariff Act* of 1930 which is not dissimilar to r 2(1) of the Australian Interpretative Rules. Rule 10(h) provides that:

> 10—For the purposes of these Schedules
>
> ...
>
> (h) unless the context requires otherwise, a tariff description for an article covers such article, whether assembled or not assembled, and whether finished or not finished.
>
> (see also r10(a) of the American Rules)

29. However, even in the United States, the doctrine does not apply automatically in every case where goods are imported in an unassembled state. As was said in *Donalds Ltd Inc v United States* 32 Cust Ct 310, CD 1619, at 315:

> As is the case with every rule of classification, where long-continued administrative practice, established judicial construction, or manifest contrary legislative intent can be shown, the rule must yield.

30. So far as the law of this country is concerned, it is true that in *Whitton v Falkiner* at 125–126, Isaacs J, in an obiter dictum, referred with approval to certain American cases on the doctrine of entireties. None of the other Judges found it necessary to address the point. His Honour was sounding a caveat as to whether the issue presented on the pleadings in an action under s167 of the *Customs Act* for recovery of duty paid under protest was necessarily correct. The headnote to the report of the decision in the Supreme Court of Victoria indicated that what was in fact imported in the one importation was a 'Miller patent petrol-electric railless road train' consisting of a series of eleven vehicles—an engine car of the petrol-electric type, described as a 'travelling power-house' and ten other cars or trailers of the electric type driven by power supplied by the engine car. They were evidently imported, however, in an unassembled or knocked-down condition. The dispute as to classification had arisen in

17 Citations omitted.

respect of the chassis of the engine car and trailers, evidently regarded by the parties as classifiable separately from the other imported components. At 125–126, his Honour said:

> Lest, however, the decision should be misunderstood, I think it right to say that, if it were necessary to decide the point, I should not be prepared to accept the plaintiff's right to separate the composite and complete article actually imported into its various constituent parts so as to secure piecemeal reductions on each of those several parts as if they were in fact imported separately.
>
> If parts are in fact and reality separately imported, so that they may not, according to circumstances, form when assembled with each other, or with other parts of a like character, a complete whole, the possibility of future combination is not a matter which the Customs can insist on. But, on the other hand, if in truth a complete machine is imported by the same person, at the same time, though its parts are disconnected for convenience of transport or otherwise, and need only unpacking and assembling to constitute the complete machine, I am disposed to the view that the Crown can properly regard the importation in its integrity as that of the one machine, and claim duty as upon that machine.
>
> If that principle be correct, and if it were to be applied here to each vehicle, the argument of separate integer, however applicable to cases of separate importation, would be inadmissible. Such a question has been considered in several American cases—notably *Isaacs v Jonas* 148 US, 648 and *United States v Citroen* 223 US, 407, at p 416. It must be added that both parties in the present instances have deliberately abstained from treating the whole importation, namely, the train, as a unit. What the result, therefore, of considering the whole train as a unit would be, I do not inquire.

31. As was said in the *Citroen* decision, the foundation for the American doctrine is that 'the dutiable classification of articles imported must be ascertained by an examination of the imported article itself, in the condition in which it is imported'. The Court went on to observe that:

> This, of course, does not mean that a prescribed rate of duty can be escaped by resort to disguise or artifice. When it is found that the article imported is in fact the article described in a particular paragraph of the tariff act, an effort to make it appear otherwise is simply a fraud on the revenue, and cannot be permitted to succeed.

32. Similar reasoning has been applied by this Tribunal in respect of unassembled components for goods of a particular kind imported on the one ship, but in ostensibly separate importations. In each of those cases, however, the unassembled components, if assembled, were goods of a kind described in an item of the Tariff to which r 2(1) of the Interpretative Rules applied.

33. At the time of the decision of the High Court in *Whitton v Falkiner* the *Customs Tariff 1908* was structured quite differently from either the *Customs Tariff Act 1966* or the present *Tariff Act* (*Customs Tariff Act 1982*). In particular, it did not include the present Interpretative Rules or any other provision comparable to the present r 2(1)(b). In the absence of any statutory guidance by Parliament, the American doctrine of entireties provided some judicial support for a principle of Tariff classification now expressly embodied in the *Tariff Act* itself.

34. In our view, r 2(1)(b) affirms the principle at the heart of the entireties doctrine, namely that where duty at a specified rate is imposed upon goods of a particular kind by an item of the Tariff, that duty cannot be avoided by importing such goods in an unassembled or disassembled state. Unless the terms of an item etc or of the notes to a Division or Chapter otherwise require (see r 1(2)), the unassembled components for goods of a particular kind are classified in the item appropriate to those components, if assembled, and duty at the same rate as for the assembled goods is payable accordingly.

35. Where components for goods are imported in an unassembled state, the question to be asked, in our view, is whether those components, if assembled, would be goods of a particular kind referred to in an item etc of the Tariff. It is by seeking the answer to that question that the proper classification of the goods in accordance with the will of Parliament as expressed in the Tariff will be resolved.

Unassembled structures of steel

36. Turning then to the Tariff, item 73.21 applies to 'Structures of ... steel' and, if r 2(1) applies, it is to be read as including unassembled structures of steel ... we are unable to agree that item 73.21 does not refer to 'goods of a particular kind'. In our view the words of the item, including the examples that the item provides of the types of structures that fall within it, serve to identify the characteristics of the goods that the item is intended to encompass. 'Goods of a particular kind', in the context of r 2(1)(b), means no more than goods that are described with particularity. To so describe goods, in order to differentiate one species of goods from another, is one of the prime functions of the Tariff nomenclature. We see no ground, therefore, for limiting the meaning of these words in the way submitted by Mr Dalton [for the applicant]. Serious anomalies in the construction of the Tariff could arise if r 2(1) was construed in such a narrow and restrictive way. It is difficult to imagine any major structure of steel of a kind to which the item applies being imported otherwise than in an unassembled or disassembled state. In our view, therefore, item 73.21 does refer to 'goods of a particular kind' within the meaning of r 2(1)(b) of the Interpretative Rules. Thus the item is to be read as including a reference to unassembled structures of steel.

37. If there was any doubt that this was the intended scope of r 2(1), that doubt is dispelled, in our view, by reference to the terms of the comparable r 2(a) in the Rules for the Interpretation of the Nomenclature annexed to the Brussels Convention on Nomenclature which this country has adopted as the basis of its Customs Tariff. That rule provides, so far as relevant, as follows:

> (a) Any reference in a heading [cf item] to an article ... shall ... be taken to include a reference to that article complete or finished ... imported unassembled or disassembled.

38. As Mason J said in *D & R Henderson* (at 135):

> The [Brussels] Convention was ratified by Australia on 18th April, 1973. By the Convention each contracting party undertook that it would compile its customs tariff in accordance with the Nomenclature which is defined in the Convention so as to include the headings and their relative numbers, the section and chapter notes and the general rules for the interpretation of the Nomenclature set out in the Annex to the Convention.
>
> Although the *Customs Tariff 1965* and the relevant amendments to it were enacted before Australia ratified the Convention, notwithstanding the absence in the Act of any reference to the Convention, it is evident that the Act adopted the Convention Nomenclature in anticipation of subsequent Australian ratification. If the language of a statute is ambiguous it is permissible to refer to the provisions of an international convention to which the statute is intended to give effect in order to assist in resolving an ambiguity, even if the statute is enacted before ratification of the convention.

39. Consistently with Australia's international obligations under this Convention, it is our view that r 2(1)(b) of the Australian Interpretative Rules should be construed so as to resolve any doubts as to the intended scope of that rule conformably with the language of the comparable r 2(a) in the Brussels Rules. (cf *Re Tridon* at 624).

40. The word 'article' as used in r 2(a) of the Brussels Rules is a word of the broadest import, capable of applying to any commodity or piece of goods. When r 2(1) of the Australian Interpretative Rules is contrasted with r 2(a) of the Brussels Rules, it becomes clearer, in our view, that the reference to 'goods of a particular kind' was not intended to limit the scope of the rule, as Mr Dalton submitted, to 'definite articles', but rather to ensure its application to any commodity or type of goods capable of being imported in an unassembled or disassembled state. We construe r 2(1)(b) accordingly.

41. The next question is whether the imported components, or at least some of them, fall to that item. A consideration of the types of structures, or parts of structures that are expressly referred to, indicate that the item is able to encompass buildings (eg hangars and other buildings) and sub-assemblies of iron and steel of a kind used in building work (eg roofs, roofing frameworks, door and window frames, shutters). As expanded by r (2)(1), the item extends to any such prefabricated buildings or sub-assemblies imported in an unassembled or disassembled state.

42. We agree with Mr Hegarty [for the Customs Collector] that the references in the item to particular types of structures are by way of example and are not intended to be exhaustive of the scope of the item. Thus, other sub-assemblies of iron or steel for use in building work that are of the same character as a roofing framework or a roof of steel are capable of falling within item 73.21. If such a sub-assembly is imported unassembled it also falls to that item.

43. In respect of a structure every component of which is of steel, there is no difficulty in finding that the structure in its entirety is classified within item 73.21. However, where the structure includes some components or materials not of steel more difficult questions may arise. The problem is more apparent when, as in the present case, components made of identifiably different materials are imported in an unassembled state.

44. In our view there is no doubt that the imported components include, at least in part, an unassembled structure of steel that falls to item 73.21, namely the pedestals, pedestal heads, base plates and stringers. Because they are merely incidental to this unassembled structure, it is our view that the neoprene gaskets should also be seen as forming an integral part of that structure and should therefore be classified as part of it. The panels, however, have caused us some concern as to whether they should be seen as forming part of a composite 'unassembled structure of steel' or whether, by reason of the mixture of substances from which they were made, of which steel is only one part, they should be seen as separate articles not forming part of a total unassembled structure of steel. In our view, this is the central issue in the case.

45. In terms of value, the panels represented approximately 80% of the total invoiced cost of the imported components. Whilst this fact is not relevant to how the goods should be classified, it indicates the significance of the panels and the importance to the applicant of the proper resolution of this question. If all the components are classified to item 73.21 they attract a rate of duty of 35%. However, if the panels are classified to item 44.23 as the applicant contends, the rate of duty on the panels is reduced to 15% (but see para 50).

46. There are some arguments that, in our view, point to the conclusion that the panels should not be seen as constituting part of a composite 'structure of steel', albeit unassembled. In the first place, whilst the structural framework upon which the panels are placed is itself readily identifiable (when assembled) as an integrated steel framework, of a kind similar to the roofing frameworks specifically mentioned in item 73.21, the panels are arguably not wholly integrated with that structure. Certainly, they are not designed so as to be physically attached to it otherwise than by their

own weight. They are readily removable and can be shifted or replaced as need be. In the second place, the panels are themselves composite goods consisting not only of steel, but also of particle board and carpet. Although, as earlier noted, the panels, if stripped of the carpet, would present as substantially covered in steel, the Collector did not demur at the claim by the applicant that panels, if imported separately, would be classified as articles of wood within item 44.23 because the particle board core gives to the goods their essential character as floor panels. The steel and carpet components were seen as of less importance.

47. On the other hand, the structures and part of structures exemplified in item 73.21 are, in some cases at least, more than just a framework of structural steel. The reference to 'hangars and other buildings' plainly contemplates more than just the structural framework for such buildings. The same is no doubt true of the reference to bridges. Furthermore, there is no doubt on the evidence before us that the imported components, including the panels, have been imported for the purpose of assembly, after importation, into a particular access floor of which the panels are an indispensable component.

48. A 'structure', within the ordinary meaning of that word, is something that has been built or constructed such as a building, a bridge or a framework. As Humphreys J said in *Hobday v Nicol* (1944) 1 All ER 302 at 303–4:

> Structure, as I understand it, is anything which is constructed; and it involves the notion of something which is put together, consisting of a number of different things which are so put together or built together, constructed as to make one whole which then is called a structure.

49. Having given the matter very careful consideration, we have concluded that the whole of the imported components are appropriately classified as an unassembled structure of steel falling to item 73.21. The critical consideration that, in our view, tips the scales in this direction is the fact that the panels have been designed and manufactured for the express purpose of being fitted to the steel understructure. The panels themselves have a covering of steel. However they may be classified if imported separately, they present, in our view, as steel covered panels to which a carpet covering has been added for aesthetic appearances. Viewed as such, it is logical to see the panels as an integral part of a composite structure of steel, all the components of which are classified within item 73.21.

50. If we were wrong in concluding that all the components should be seen as an unassembled structure of steel, it would follow, in our view, that all the components, except the panels, would be classifiable within item 73.21 whilst the panels would be classified separately according to which of the several components (steel, wood or carpet) gives to the panels their essential character as panels. The parties presented the case on the basis that the wood component did so and that the panels should be seen therefore as articles of builders carpentry and joinery falling to item 44.23. This question was not adequately addressed at the hearing and we do not wish, therefore, to express any concluded opinion on it. If it be the case, as we were told, that it is the wood component that gives the panels their essential character and if it be the fact that the wood component is particle board, we are at a loss to understand why item 44.18 would not need to be considered. That item applies to 'reconstituted wood' of which particle board, as we understand it, is a prime example. The prescribed rate of duty under that item is 30%. If it had been necessary for us to decide this question, we would have needed to hear further evidence and argument on the composition and essential characteristics of the panels.

> 51. Finally, if our approach to the classification of the goods was wrong and the issue originally posed by the parties was correct, the question is which component (the steel understructure falling to item 73.21 or the panels which we assume for this purpose fall to an item in Chapter 44) gives to the goods their essential character as an 'access floor'. Viewed as an entirety, it is our opinion that neither the steel understructure nor the flooring panels alone can be said to give to the goods their essential character as an access floor. Neither component has a dominant influence in stamping upon the assembled components their character as an access floor. We consider both the understructure and the panels contribute equally to that which constitutes the essence of access flooring, namely an elevated floor with readily accessible underfloor space. The understructure creates the space; the panels constitute the floor and allow access to the space.
>
> 52. In the circumstances, as the classification question cannot be resolved in accordance with r 3(1)(b) of the Interpretative Rules, it would fall to be determined under r 3(1)(c) which provides that:
>
> > (c) If the item, sub-item, paragraph or sub-paragraph that applies to the goods cannot be ascertained in accordance with paragraph (a) or paragraph (b) the item, sub-item, paragraph or sub-paragraph, as the case may be, that applies to the goods is that item, sub-item, paragraphs or sub-paragraphs that occurs last in Schedule 3 among those items, sub-items, paragraphs or sub-paragraphs, which equally merit consideration when determining the item, sub-item, paragraph or sub-paragraph, as the case may be, that applies to the goods.
>
> Of the items in Schedule 3 which equally merit consideration, item 73.21 is the item that last occurs and it would be the item that therefore applies to the whole of the imported components. The final outcome, in the circumstances of this case, would be no different so far as the applicant is concerned whether all the components fall to item 73.21 or only the components of the steel understructure.
>
> 53. In the result, as the Collector's classification of the goods within sub-item 73.21.9 was not otherwise challenged, the decision of the Collector will be affirmed.
>
> ....

Thus, where there is a direct numerical relationship between the number of the individual items and the number of entities that they would form if assembled, the tribunal will likely find the goods to be unassembled entities.[18] On the other hand, where the goods are found to simply be a 'random selection of components', the identity of the individual components has likely not been subsumed into the whole of an unassembled entity.[19]

Under certain circumstances, goods separately ordered, invoiced and packed, but shipped and imported on the same ship, can also be regarded as separate importations for customs purposes. For instance, the Tribunal in *Re Atlas Copco Australia Pty Ltd and Collector of Customs* stated:

18 See also *Re Progress Metals Pty Ltd and Collector of Customs* (1984) 6 ALD 171 (the goods were a set of components and parts for putting together a number of bicycles); *Re Landis & Gyr (Aust) Pty Ltd and Collector of Customs* (1984) 6 ALN N82 (the goods were supplied as a specific number of kits, each to be assembled together by the importer into the same number of time switches as there were kits).

19 See *Re Diasonics Pty Ltd and Collector of Customs* (1986) 9 ALN N100.

> In answering the question whether there was one importation of four discrete importations, we have taken the view that a broad overall approach should be adopted taking into account all the circumstances. We have not thought it correct to draw fine and subtle distinctions. While a legal question, it should be answered in a robust and common-sense way having regard to commercial and practical realities and in the light of the totality of the circumstances taken in combination.[20]

In resolving the issue, the tribunal found that as there was one supplier, one consignee, one ship, one port of destination, and as the goods all went together to comprise 15 unassembled portable air compressors, it would be unrealistic to hold that they were discrete importations.

The tribunal in *Technifex Inc v Chief Executive Officer of Customs*[21] also considered whether goods imported in separate shipments in different vessels as numerous items of machinery and prefabricated parts should be classified as one entity. In this case, however, the tribunal found the goods—which were to be assembled to form the 'Titanic Experience' located at Fox Studios in Sydney—were not subject to the doctrine of entireties and that the goods in each of the several shipments must separately be objectively identified then classified.[22] Thus, parts imported separately cannot be treated as an entirety.

Another important identification issue is whether goods whose identity is not subsumed into the whole as unassembled entities should be identified in their own right or as a parts and/or accessories of other goods. For instance, is a radio part of a car? Is film part of a camera? Is a bullet part of a gun? Is petrol part of a car?[23]

In general, goods that are built into other goods (through, say, a process of manufacture) will be considered parts of those goods. This is true even if the original goods are not essential to the functioning of the goods (for instance, a radio in a vehicle). For instance, in *Walterscheid Australia Pty Ltd v Collector of Customs*, Judge Davies, in holding that PTO shafts can be 'accessories' for tractors even though they do not assist in the hauling or pushing operation of a tractor, stated:

> It was simply necessary that the article should be a part for or an accessory for a tractor as defined and moreover, that the article should be used solely or principally as such a part or accessory. If a cigarette lighter is built into a tractor in the course of manufacture, that lighter will be part of the tractor and a replacement lighter will be a part for the tractor. It will be of no significance that the lighter is simply incorporated into the tractor for the convenience of the driver and in no way assists the hauling or pushing function of the tractor. Likewise, an accessory does not have to relate to the essential function of the tractor.[24]

---

20 (1984) 7 ALD 204 at 208.

21 [2001] AATA 536.

22 See also *Re Landis & Gyr (Australia) Pty Limited and Collector of Customs* [1984] 6 ALN N82 (stating 'Goods which have come in one ship may be examined to ascertain whether they form an entirety while goods which have been imported separately, in different vessels or in different aircraft, cannot be treated as a collective whole.'); *Re Progress Metal Works Pty Ltd and Collector of Customs* [1984] 6 ALD 171. These decisions followed US precedent on the issue: see *United States v Shoverling* 146 US 76 (1982); *Landis* at para 34; *Progress Metal* at para 34.

23 The High Court found in the negative in the latter three examples: see *Deputy Commissioner of Taxation v Polaroid Australia Pty Ltd* (1971) 46 ALJR 32 at 34.

24 *Walterscheid Australia Pty Ltd v Collector of Customs* [1987] 7 AAR 555 at 565; *Re National Panasonic (Australia) Pty Ltd and Collector of Customs* (1985) 7 ALD 647 at 657–59. However, the test is complicated, and the fact that certain goods are essential to the functioning of other goods is not determinative in

5.2.3 Classification of the goods

At its simplest, classification of goods simply involves applying the relevant provision of the *Tariff Act* to facts of a particular matter. Classification, however, can be much more complicated.

As should be clear from the extracts in the proceeding section, classification is to be guided by Schedule 2, rule 1 of the *Tariff Act*, which incorporates the General Rules for the Interpretation (GRI). The GRI provide the interpretive rules to be used for establishing the tariff classification of goods.[25] They contain six hierarchical rules, the first four of which are interrelated and must be applied in sequence. Rules five and six stand alone and are only applied as needed. There are two consequences resulting from the hierarchical structure of the GRI:

- First, the goods must first be classified in the HS under the four-digit heading whose terms most specifically describe the merchandise (unless otherwise required or directed by the GRIs); and
- Second, only four-digit headings are comparable (meaning consideration should not be given to the terms of any subheading within any four-digit heading when considering the proper classification of merchandise at the four-digit heading level).

To illustrate:

> an electric toothbrush could potentially be classified in heading 8509 as an electromechanical domestic appliance with self-contained motor and in heading 9603 as a brush. Within heading 9603, subheading 9603.21 provides for 'toothbrushes.' No consideration should be given to this subheading when comparing the terms of the headings to determine the appropriate heading for classification of the electric toothbrush (as merchandise must first be classified in the Harmonized System at the heading level by the terms of the headings).[26]

The interpretive rules, with explanation and examples, are detailed below.[27]

5.2.3a Rule 1 of the GRI

> The titles of Sections, Chapters and sub-Chapters are provided for ease of reference only; for legal purposes, classification shall be determined according to the terms of the headings

---

the matter. The High Court (ibid) stated: 'One thing does not become part of another simply because the latter thing cannot be put to proper use without the aid of the former, even if, in use, the two things are fixed together.' There is a substantial body of jurisprudence interpreting the term 'accessory': see *Air International Pty Ltd and Chief Executive Officer of Customs* [2000] AATA 1149; *Air International Pty Ltd v Chief Executive Officer of Customs* [2001] FCA 1386; *Pirelli Tyres Australia Pty Ltd v Collector of Customs* (1999) 58 ALD 517; *Diethelm Manufacturing Pty Ltd v Commissioner of Taxation* (1993) 44 FCR 450; *Thomson Australian Holdings Pty Ltd v Commissioner of Taxation* (1988) 20 FCR 85; *Hygienic Lily Ltd v Deputy Commissioner of Taxation* (1987) 13 FCR 396.

25 See for example *Rheem Australia Ltd v Collector of Customs* (1988) 78 ALR 285 at 300.

26 US Department of Homeland Security (US Customs and Border Protection), 'What Every Member of the Trade Community Should Know About: Tariff Classification', May 2004, p 13.

27 The following examples are largely drawn from and based on US Department of Homeland Security (US Customs and Border Protection), 'What Every Member of the Trade Community Should Know About: Tariff Classification', May 2004.

> and any relative Section or Chapter Notes and, provided such headings or Notes do not otherwise require, according to the following provisions [GRIs 2–6]

GRI 1 takes precedence over the other five rules and requires that classification be determined first according to the terms of the headings of the HS and any relative section or chapter notes. Thus, according to GRI 1, if a provision specifically and completely describes a product, then the product is to be classified in that provision. For instance, fresh mangoes are classified under heading 0804, which provides for 'Dates, Figs, Pineapples, Avocados, Guavas, Mangoes and Mangosteens, Fresh or Dried'.

Under GRI 1, products can also be classified by the terms of a section note. For instance, as Note 3 to Section XVI to the HS directs classification of composite machines described therein on the basis of the 'principal function' of the machines, GRI 1 requires such machines to be classified as so directed in that note.

Finally, GRI 1 states that if the texts of the headings and of the notes cannot, by themselves, determine the appropriate heading for classification of the goods, then classification is to be determined by the appropriate GRIs that follow GRI 1; that is, GRIs 2–6.

5.2.3b Rule 2 of the GRI

> (a) Any reference in a heading to an article shall be taken to include a reference to that article incomplete or unfinished, provided that, as presented, the incomplete or unfinished article has the essential character of the complete or finished article. It shall also include a reference to that article complete or finished (or falling to be classified as complete or finished by virtue of this Rule), entered unassembled or disassembled.
>
> (b) Any reference in a heading to a material or substance shall be taken to include a reference to mixtures or combinations of that material or substance with other materials or substances. Any reference to goods of a given material or substance shall be taken to include a reference to goods consisting wholly or partly of such material or substance. The classification of goods consisting of more than one material or substance shall be according to the principles of Rule 3.

Note that both sections of GRI 2 deal with the classification of goods that are imported as:

- Incomplete or unfinished;
- Unassembled or disassembled; or
- Composed of mixtures or combinations of materials or substances.

GRI 2(a)

GRI 2(a) has two parts. Part one pertains to incomplete or unfinished goods, and part two deals with unassembled or disassembled goods.

The first part of GRI 2(a) extends the scope of any heading that refers to a particular article to cover not only the complete article, but also an incomplete or unfinished version of that article, provided that, as presented, it has the 'essential character' of the complete or finished article. To illustrate, an unpainted ceramic statuette of the wallaby that will be painted after importation would still generally have the essential character of a ceramic statuette of heading 6913 ('Statuettes and Other Ornamental Ceramic

Articles'), in that it would still be recognised and identified as a ceramic statuette, and would therefore be classified pursuant to GRI 2(a) as the finished product in heading 6913.

The second part of GRI 2(a) provides that complete or finished articles that are imported in an unassembled or disassembled form (which may occur for reasons related to such things as packing, handling or transportation) are to be classified in the same heading as the assembled article. GRI 2(a) further provides that incomplete or unfinished articles imported in an unassembled or disassembled form are to be classified in the same heading as the complete or finished article, provided that as presented they have the essential character of the complete or finished article (as provided for in the first part of GRI 2(a)). To illustrate, the second part of GRI 2(a) would mean a shipment of an unassembled bicycle (containing all parts and components necessary to build a bicycle) would be classified in heading 8712 as an assembled, finished bicycle as if it were entered (or imported) as the assembled, finished bicycle.

GRI 2 (b)

GRI 2(b) provides for the classification of (1) mixtures and combinations of materials or substances and of (2) goods consisting of two or more materials or substances. Provided another heading does not refer to the goods in their mixed or composite state, the rule extends headings referring (1) to a material or substance to include mixtures or combinations of that material or substance with other materials or substances, and (2) to goods of a given material or substance to include goods consisting wholly or partly of that material or substance.

However, if the addition of another material or substance deprives the imported good of the character of the kind mentioned in the heading under consideration, then resort must be made to GRI 3 for classification of the merchandise. In other words, if (upon initial consideration) mixtures and combinations of materials or substances, and goods consisting of more than one material or substance, are potentially classifiable under two or more headings, they must be classified according to the principles of GRI 3. The US Customs Guide provides the following illustration:

> Under GRI 2(b), a stainless steel travel mug with a plastic handle would be classifiable in heading 7323 as a table, kitchen or other household article of steel despite the plastic handle (as it retains the character of a table, kitchen or other household article of steel as mentioned in heading 7323). If a travel mug, however, contained relatively equal amounts of stainless steel and plastic (eg, the outside or outer surface of the mug is made of plastic and the inside or inner surface (lining) of the mug is made of stainless steel), then the travel mug would be potentially classifiable under two headings: heading 3924 as tableware, kitchenware or other household article of plastic and heading 7323 as a table, kitchen or other household article of steel. (Or, contrasting this product with the initial one considered in this example, a travel mug consisting of relatively equal amounts of stainless steel and plastic does not have the character of a table, kitchen or other household article of steel as mentioned in heading 7323.) In this situation, pursuant to GRI 2(b), resort would need to be made to GRI 3 for classification of the product.[28]

28 Ibid, p 16.

5.2.3c Rule 3 of the GRI

When, by application of Rule 2(b) or for any other reason, goods are, prima facie, classifiable under two or more headings, classification shall be effected as follows:

(a) The heading which provides the most specific description shall be preferred to headings providing a more general description. However, when two or more headings each refer to part only of the materials or substances contained in mixed or composite goods or to part only of the items in a set put up for retail sale, those headings are to be regarded as equally specific in relation to those goods, even if one of them gives a more complete or precise description of the goods.
(b) Mixtures, composite goods consisting of different materials or made up of different components, and goods put up in sets for retail sale, which cannot be classified by reference to 3(a), shall be classified as if they consisted of the material or component which gives them their essential character, insofar as this criterion is applicable.
(c) When goods cannot be classified by reference to 3(a) or 3(b), they shall be classified under the heading which occurs last in numerical order among those which equally merit consideration.

GRI 3 provides for the classification of goods that are prima facie (or initially considered) classifiable under two or more headings.[29] In such a circumstance, classification shall be effected according to the rules set out in the three sub-parts. Operating sequentially, GRI 3 provides for:

(a) Most specific description;
(b) Essential character; and
(c) Last-occurring heading.

GRI 3(a)

GRI 3(a) initially provides that goods should be classified in the heading that provides the most specific description. Therefore, under this criterion, a description by name is generally more specific than a description by class and a description that more clearly identifies a product is generally more specific than one that is less complete.

EXAMPLE 1: An example of a description by name in one heading that is more specific than a description by class in another heading is as follow: 'shavers and hair clippers with self-contained electric motor' of heading 8510 is more specific than 'electro-mechanical tools for working in the hand with self-contained electric motor' of heading 8467 or 'electro-mechanical domestic appliances with self-contained electric motor' of heading 8509.

EXAMPLE 2: An example of a description in one heading that more clearly identifies a product than a description in another heading (and thus the first description is more specific than the second description) is as follows: A product identified as 'unframed safety glass made of toughened or laminated glass that is shaped and identifiable for use in airplanes' is more clearly described by

29 Goods are prima facie classifiable under two or more headings if the goods—as identified—meet the description in the heading and are not precluded from classification there by virtue of Section or Chapter Notes.

the article description 'safety glass' of heading 7007 than by the article description 'parts of goods of heading 8801 or 8802' (parts of aircraft and spacecraft) of heading 8803.[30]

GRI 3(a) further provides that when two or more headings each refer to only one of the materials or substances in mixed or composite goods, or to only some of the articles included in a set put up for retail sale, those headings are to be regarded as equally specific in relation to those goods, even if one of them gives a more complete or precise description of the goods. If such a situation exists, resort must be made to GRI 3(b).

GRI 3(b)

GRI 3(b) deals with mixed goods, composite goods, and goods put up in sets for retail sale as described in the second sentence to GRI 3(a)[31], which are potentially classifiable in 'more than' one heading because each good consists of two or more different ingredients, materials, components or articles and no heading provides for the goods as a whole. GRI 3(b) provides that classification of the goods should be made according to the ingredient, material, component or article that gives the mixtures, composite goods, or sets their 'essential character'.

MIXTURE EXAMPLE: An example of a 'mixture' coming within the purview of GRI 3(b) would be a mixture of barley of heading 1003 and oats of heading 1004 in equal amounts. In such an instance, there is a product consisting of two or more ingredients with each ingredient having a provision in which it could potentially be classified and no provision exists in the Harmonized System that provides for the mixture as a whole.

COMPOSITE GOOD EXAMPLE: An example of a 'composite good' coming within the purview of GRI 3(b) would be a combined flashlight of heading 8513 and radio of heading 8527 (ie, both are contained in the same housing). In such an instance, there is a product consisting of two or more different units or components that are located in the same housing with each component having a provision in which it could potentially be classified and no provision exists in the Harmonized System that provides for the composite good as a whole.

SET EXAMPLE: An example of a 'set' coming within the purview of GRI 3(b) would be a hairdressing kit consisting of a pair of electric hair clippers of heading 8510, a comb of heading 9615, a pair of scissors of heading 8213, and a brush of heading 9603. In such an instance, there is a product that consists of more than one item or article with each article having a provision in which it could potentially be classified and no provision exists in the Harmonized System that provides for the set as a whole. In the above-mentioned hairdressing kit, the articles are put up together to meet the particular need or carry out the specific activity of grooming hair.[32]

---

30 US Department of Homeland Security (US Customs and Border Protection), 'What Every Member of the Trade Community Should Know About: Tariff Classification', May 2004, p 18.

31 For the purposes of GRI 3(b), the term 'goods put up in sets for retail sale' means that the goods under consideration must (a) consist of at least two different articles of a different type or nature (for example, two table knives are not such a 'set' described in GRI 3(b)) which are, prima facie, classifiable in different headings; (b) consist of products or articles put up together to meet a particular need or carry out a specific activity; and (c) are put up in a manner suitable for sale directly to users without repacking.

32 US Department of Homeland Security (US Customs and Border Protection), 'What Every Member of the Trade Community Should Know About: Tariff Classification', May 2004, p 19.

It is important to note that the term 'essential character' is not defined in the HS. The Explanatory Notes to the HS, however, state that the factor which determines the 'essential character' of a good varies depending upon the type of goods at issue; in other words, the term 'essential character' cannot be clearly defined and instead must be determined on a case-by-case basis. Therefore, depending on the goods at issue, the essential character may be determined by the nature of the material or component (not the will of the importer or manufacturer), its bulk, quality, weight or value, by the role of a constituent material in relation to the use of the goods, or by any of a number of other factors.

In each of the above examples, the ingredient, material, component or article that imparts the *essential character* to the particular good would first need to be determined. The good would then be classified as if made from, or consisting entirely of, that ingredient, material, component or article. If no ingredient, material, component or article is found to impart the essential character to a particular good, then GRI 3(c) is used in order to classify the good.

The essential character test has been discussed and clarified in a number of disputes. For instance, in *Re Playcorp Pty Ltd v Collector of Customs*,[33] customs classified the imported goods at issue as lamps within Item 9405 of Schedule 3 of the *Customs Tariff Act 1987* (Cth). The applicant contended that the goods should have been classified as musical boxes under Item 9208 (arguing that the essential character is conferred by the musical mechanism, it being the principle purpose of the item), or alternatively, if the essential character of the goods is conferred by the light feature, the goods should be identified as an image projector and accordingly should be classified as image projectors under Item 9008. The respondent on the other hand argued the item should be classified as a night lamp under Item 9405. The the tribunal utilised the classification principles set out *Re Tridon*[34] and found the essential character of the items were 'toys', and thus instructed the good be classified under Item 9503. The tribunal's reasoning is set out below.

Playcorp Pty Ltd v Collector of Customs

(1992) 15 AAR 86

33. Thus, although [the *Re Tridon* classification] principle (ii) affirms that the identification of goods cannot be controlled by the description of goods adopted in the nomenclature of the Tariff, principle (iii) requires awareness of the structure of the Tariff in classification. Chapter 95 covers toys and includes heading 9503 which reads:

> Other toys; reduced-size ('scale') models and similar recreational models, working or not; puzzles of all kinds

To understand the reference to 'other toys' it is necessary to refer back to headings 9501 and 9502. They refer to 'wheeled toys designed to be ridden by children' and 'dolls representing human

33 (1992) 15 AAR 86.

34 *Re Tridon Pty Ltd and Collector of Customs* 4 ALD 615, No N81/123 Customs Tariff (17/6/1982).

beings' respectively. Thus 9503 is the heading covering toys which are not wheeled toys or dolls. We find that heading 9503 covers the subject goods. The Chapter Notes to Chapter 95 contain nothing which would exclude the subject goods from Chapter 95.

34. The Tribunal therefore must consider into which of the subheadings under 9503 the goods 'fall'. Subheading 9503.50.00 is 'Toy musical instruments and apparatus'. We consider that to be a specific description of the subject goods. We therefore find that they fall to subheading 9503.50.00. It seems relevant to note that a toy musical instrument or apparatus that did not play some form of music would not be much of a toy as children could neither play with it nor derive amusement from it.

35. Mr Slonim [for the applicant] submitted that the essential character of the goods was that of a musical box. He further submitted that it was apparent from a close examination of the goods that the major proportion of the cost of manufacture is represented by the mechanical components of the musical box and that the optical feature 'costs a few cents to replace'. We do not accept either of those submissions. We have already dealt with the first. As to the second, we cannot agree that close examination of the goods yields information as to the cost of manufacture of the different components. To rely on expert evidence as to those matters would be to enter into the area referred to by Morling and Wilcox JJ 'as entirely inappropriate' in *Times Consultants* at p 328.

36. We also consider it appropriate to state that in our view the effect of Mr Vallis' evidence, which was called by the respondent, was to confirm the essential differences between the subject goods and 'night lights' rather than to establish that the subject goods are night lights. Mr Vallis is responsible for overseeing the design, development and sourcing of products in the Click range and the marketing of those products. He said that the range includes a large number of night lights. He was asked to explain what he meant by the term 'night light' and he replied:

> A night light is a unit designed to produce a subdued level of lighting. The primary purpose is to provide comfort to a young child in a darkened room.

He explained that some young children are apprehensive in a dark room. He said that in designing night lights, one tries to design a product which an adult will conceive will have some appeal to a child and which will therefore sell in the market place. He said a night light may be decorated in some way.

37. Mr Corke [for the Collector of Customs] then produced four different night lights, each of which is marketed in Australia by Click Industries. They were received into evidence as exhibits. They were all similar in that they plug into a power point and are therefore run off mains electricity. They provide only a very subdued light, the source of which is plugged directly into the power point. The four exhibits included one which had two night lights in the small package. One of those two was decorated with a small drawing of a ringtail possum which was in no way enlarged when the light was on. In fact it was scarcely visible when the light was on. None of the others had any decorative feature whatsoever or anything which would provide any appeal to a child other than providing a very soft and weak source of light in a room.

38. These exhibits are dim lights and nothing more. They do not provide any amusement by music or pictures, or even any colour or interest either when turned on or off. They would run indefinitely when plugged in and therefore they provide a reliable light during the night. In contrast, the subject goods, being battery operated, would be likely to run out during the night, running the risk

> of a child waking up frightened in a darkened room. The fact that the goods are described on their box as a 'musical night light' is relevant but not necessarily conclusive of the issue. (See principle (iv) as set out in *Re Tridon*.) In this matter we are satisfied it is not a correct description.
>
> 39. The respondent, in the presentation of its case also entered into the 'entirely inappropriate area' referred to in *Times Consultants*. As set out in its statement of facts and contentions, it relied primarily on the fact that the Galaxy Trotter lamp mechanism which is powered by a battery lasts longer than the musical mechanism … It appears to us that *Times Consultants* precludes attention being given to such evidence. However the fact that the apparatus is battery powered rather than powered by mains electricity is apparent on inspection and it is common knowledge that simple batteries provide a less reliable source of electricity than mains power.
>
> 40. We accept Mr Slonim's submission that inspection reveals, first, that the music box can be operated in the absence of a power source or light source for the optical component, and secondly, that the projection feature of the unit does not function in the absence of the music box feature, as the dome will not rotate unless the musical component is turned on. We also accept his submission that it is apparent from an objective examination of the subject goods that they are 'more than lamps' and hence cannot be classified as lamps. That would ignore both the musical and projection characteristics of the goods.
>
> 41. Thus we accept Mr Slonim's submission that the most significant feature of the subject goods in terms of the amusement provided is the musical component. But the fact that all three features of music, images and light combine to provide amusement, in our view, determines the essential character of the goods as toys. However, even if we had not decided to classify the goods as toys rather than as musical boxes, the Chapter Notes to Chapter 92—'Musical Instruments' would compel such a classification as note 1(c) provides that the chapter does not cover:
>
> (c) Toy instruments or apparatus (9503)
>
> We have already made it clear that we find that the subject goods are a toy musical apparatus.
>
> 42. The decision under review will be set aside and the matter remitted to the respondent for reconsideration in accordance with the direction that the subject goods are to be classified under subheading 9503.50.00 in Schedule 3 to the *Customs Tariff Act 1987*.

… … …

The 'more than' principle has also been discussed in several Australian cases. The tribunal in *Avion Engineering Pty Ltd and Collector of Customs*[35] quoted the US customs court case of *Robert Bosch Corp v US*[36] to explain the principle:

> The court there held that if an article was more than the goods specified in the Customs Tariff, its identity was not the same as the identity of those goods, and that whether it was more than those goods, depended upon whether its essential character was retained or had been lost.[37]

The 'more than' principle was applied by the Administrative Appeal Tribunal in *Re Tridon Pty Ltd and Collector of Customs*.[38]

---

35 [1988] AATA 586.

36 63 Cus Ct 96 (1969).

37 Ibid at para 18.

38 The principle was also discussed, but its use rejected, in *Re Moore Le Messurier Pty Ltd and Australian Timber Importers Federation* (1985) 7 ALD 640; *Australian Greetings Pty Ltd and Collector of Customs* [1987] AATA 60.

Re Tridon Pty Ltd and Collector of Customs

No N81/123 Customs Tariff, Administrative Appeals Tribunal, 4 ALD 615 (1982)[39]

14. In our view, however, there is only one way of ascertaining what goods fall within an item, sub-item, paragraph or sub-paragraph and that is by application of the Rules for Interpretation of Schedule 1, rule 1(2) of which provides as follows:

> (2) For the purpose of ascertaining whether goods fall within an item, sub-item, paragraph or sub-paragraph or whether an item, sub-item, paragraph or sub-paragraph applies to goods, regard shall, subject to sub-rule (3) of this rule, be had to the terms of items (including sub-items, paragraphs and sub-paragraphs) and of notes to Divisions and Chapters and, except where those terms otherwise require, to rules 2, 3 and 4 of these Rules.

...

16. In the present case, the goods are identifiable as follows:

(i) specifically, as windscreen wiper blade refills;
(ii) by reference to use, as parts for electrical windscreen wipers;
(iii) less specifically, by reference to use, as parts for a motor vehicle;
(iv) by reference to composition, as goods partly of unhardened vulcanised rubber, partly of plastic and partly of metal.

The imported goods are not identifiable simply as articles of unhardened vulcanised rubber. As imported they are more than that. The rubber squeegee, plastic spine and metal clip in combination, produce a new article of commerce in which the identity of the individual components is subordinated to the identity of the combination.

Classification

17. In order to classify the goods, regard must be had to the descriptions employed in the Nomenclature of the Tariff (see, in particular, Interpretative Rule 1(2) paragraph 14 above). In the language of the Act (see s14) and the Rules for the Interpretation of Schedule 1, the question more precisely is to ascertain firstly, into which items, etc the goods 'fall' and, secondly, to determine which is the item that 'applies'. Normally goods will be classified within the item etc which most specifically describes the goods (cf Rule 3(1)(a)). That result can be controlled, however, by the Divisional or Chapter Notes.

18. There is no item in the Nomenclature of the Tariff in which windscreen wiper blade refills are described by that specific name. It is necessary, therefore, to consider the other forms of identification referred to above. The items in Schedule 1 of the Tariff to which goods as so identified may potentially fall are as follows:

(a) Item 85.09 as electrical windscreen wipers, by operation of Note 2 to Division XVI (provided Note 1(a) does not prevent that operation). The evidence establishes that the refills are parts of a kind used solely or principally with such wipers.

(b) Item 87.06 as 'parts and accessories for motor vehicles of a kind falling within item 87.01, 87.02 or 87.03'. By operation of Note 2(g) to Division XVII (which includes Chapter 87) however, a reference in that Division to 'parts or accessories for goods' is to be read as not including 'goods falling within an item in Chapter 85'. Thus if the goods fall to Chapter 85, they cannot fall to Chapter 87.

39 Citations omitted.

(c) Item 40.14 as 'other goods made of unhardened vulcanised rubber' by operation of Interpretative Rule 2(3) (see paragraph 9(v) above), the refills being partly of such rubber. For present purposes we accept, for the reasons given in the Collector's s 37 statement, that none of the preceding items in Chapter 40 referable to goods of unhardened vulcanised rubber (ie items 40.07 to 40.13 inclusive) are more appropriate. There is a Note to Chapter 40 (Note 3(c)) which excludes from that Chapter parts for electrical appliances that are of hardened rubber and fall within an item in Division XVI. But there is no similar exclusion of parts made of 'unhardened vulcanized rubber'.

(d) Item 39.07 as goods made of plastic also by operation of Interpretative Rule 2(3), the goods being partly of plastic. By operation of Note 1(i) to Chapter 39, however, the goods cannot fall to that Chapter if they are 'machinery and mechanical or electrical appliances and equipment falling within an item in Division XVI'. Similarly, they are excluded from Chapter 39 by Note 1(j) if they are 'parts for vehicles ... falling within an item in Division XVII'.

(e) Probably to item 73.40 as 'Other goods made of iron or steel' again by operation of Interpretative Rule 2(3). The precise nature of the metal clip and the item in the Tariff to which it would 'fall' were not identified at the hearing. Note 1(f) to Division XV (which includes Chapter 73) excludes from that Division 'goods falling within an item in Division XVI'.

19. A consideration of the various items to which the refills may potentially fall leaves no room for doubt that, amongst those potential classifications, classification within item 85.09 by operation of Note 2 to Division XVI would seem to be the most appropriate. It is the most specific description of the goods (cf Interpretative Rule 3(1)(a)) and as between that item and all the other possible items (except item 40.14) there are Divisional or Chapter Notes which would preclude classification otherwise than in Division XVI if the goods 'fall' to item 85.09. Indeed, were it not for Note 1(a) to Division XVI which makes the composition of the goods relevant, no serious consideration would need to be given to item 40.14, it providing a far less specific description of the goods than item 85.09.

20. The first question, therefore, (but not necessarily the only question) is whether Note 1(a) to Division XVI precludes the operation of rule 2 in relation to the subject goods. There being no dispute that the goods are goods of unhardened vulcanised rubber which by application of Interpretative Rule 2(3) are capable of classification (ie they fall) within item 40.14, the question which needs to be considered is whether, on the proper construction of that Note, the imported goods are of the kind referred to. Unfortunately, that question was not canvassed in any depth at the hearing.

Are the goods of the requisite kind?

21. It is not all goods which fall to item 40.14 that come within the ambit of Note 1(a) in Division XVI. It is only such of those goods 'that are of a kind used on machinery or mechanical or electrical appliances or for other industrial purposes'.

22. As a matter of first impression the words 'or for other industrial purposes' tend to colour the preceding words namely 'machinery or mechanical or electrical appliances'. Indeed, the opening words of Note 1(a), namely 'transmission, conveyor or elevator belts or belting ...' carry the connotation of parts for industrial equipment. Literally, the Note can be read as referring to two quite separate classes of goods—on the one hand, belts and belting and on the other, goods of rubber of the requisite kind. The two classes of goods referred to are linked by the words 'and goods'. If read disjunctively, the 'industrial' connotation in relation to the second group of goods may be weaker than if the paragraph is read as a whole. There is, in our view, some ambiguity in the language that has been used.

23. Given that the question as posed by the facts of this case depends entirely upon the proper construction of Divisional and Chapter Notes and Tariff items drawn from the Brussels Nomenclature, it is appropriate, in our view, to consult the provisions of the Annex to the Convention on Nomenclature for the Classification of Goods in Customs Tariffs ('the Brussels Convention') on which the Australian Tariff is based. As Mason J said in [*D & R Henderson (Manufacturing) Pty Ltd v Forbes (Collector of Customs)*]:

> If the language of a statute is ambiguous it is permissible to refer to the provisions of an international convention to which the statute is intended to give effect in order to assist in resolving an ambiguity, even if the statute is enacted before ratification of the convention.[40]

It is also appropriate to refer to the Explanatory Notes prepared by the Nomenclature Committee established by the Convention for such guidance as those Notes may properly give.

The Brussels Nomenclature

24. The Brussels Nomenclature is intended to set out in systematic form the goods handled in international trade. Section (cf our Divisional) Notes and Chapter Notes are part of the mechanism provided for resolving problems of competing classifications.

25. Comparison of Note 1(a) to Division XVI of the Australian Tariff with the equivalent Note 1(a) in Section XVI to the Brussels Annex is revealing. The Brussels Note is as follows:

> 1 This section does not cover:
>
> (a) Transmission, conveyor or elevator belts or belting, of artificial plastic material of Chapter 39, or of vulcanised rubber (heading No. 40.10); or other articles of a kind used in machinery or mechanical or electrical appliances or for other industrial purposes, of unhardened vulcanised rubber (heading No. 40.14);

26. The textual adaptations made pursuant to Article II of the Brussels Convention in order to give effect to this Note in the Australian Tariff are significant. By abandoning the words 'or other articles of a kind used in machinery etc' in favour of the words 'and goods ... of a kind used on machinery etc' the draftsman has, in our view, laid the ground for the ambiguity to which we referred. In addition the words 'in machinery' convey a different shade of meaning from the words 'on machinery'.

27. Comparison between the other sub-paragraphs in Note 1 to Division XVI of the Australian Tariff and in Note 1 to Section XVI of the Brussels Annex indicates that in the very similar Note (e) with respect to goods of textile, the adaptation of the Brussels Note into the Australian Tariff is much closer. The Australian Note excludes from Division XVI:

> (e) transmission, conveyor or elevator belts falling within item 59.16 or other goods of textile material of a kind commonly used in machinery or plant falling within item 59.17.

The comparable Note in the Brussels Annex reads as follows:

> (e) Transmission, conveyor or elevator belts of textile material (heading No. 59.16) or other articles of textile material of a kind commonly used in machinery or plant (heading No. 59.17);

Leaving aside Note 1(g) where the substance of the Australian Note remains the same as Brussels, but where some potentially misleading omissions have been made (see Note 2 to Division XV) the

40 (1974) 48 ALJR 132 at 135.

textual adaptations made in translating the rest of Brussels Note 1 into Australian law are of no apparent consequence.

28. Reference to the Explanatory Notes prepared by the Brussels Nomenclature Committee merely confirms what Note 2 to Division XVI makes obvious namely that 'In general, parts which are recognisable as specialized to or mainly for use with particular machines or apparatus ... are classified under the same heading as those machines or apparatus, subject, of course, to the exclusions mentioned in Part (I) above'. (See Volume 3 at p1156). The exclusions, of course, are those referred to in our Note 1 to Division XVII. With respect to goods of unhardened vulcanised rubber excluded by Note 1(a) the Explanatory Notes give as examples—'rubber tyres, tubes etc (heading 40.11) and washers etc (heading 40.14)'.

29. Having regard to the fact that Australia's international obligations under Article II of the Brussels Convention include an undertaking that 'it will make no changes in the chapter or section notes in a manner modifying the scope of the chapters, sections and headings as laid down in the Nomenclature' (see Article II(b)(ii)), we consider that we should construe Divisional Note 1(a) in such a way as to conform to that undertaking. When read in the light of the equivalent Brussels Note, the goods contemplated by Note 1(a) are, in our view, goods used in machinery or mechanical or electrical appliances for industrial purposes. So construed, Note 1(a) does not, in our view, apply to the imported goods. Windscreen wiper blade refills are not goods of that kind.

30. The view that Note 1(a) was not intended to apply to the imported goods is supported, we think, if one looks at the consequences of taking the goods out of Division XVI. For this purpose, we will assume that Note 1(a) achieves that result.

31. It was implicit in the arguments put to us by Mr Miller [for the Customs Collector] and as set out in the Collector's s 37 statement, that if the Note 1(a) operated to remove the goods from Division XVI, item 40.14 would not only be the item to which the goods 'fell' but would also be the item which 'applied' to the goods. In other words, the items to which the goods were potentially seen as 'falling' were simply item 40.14 or item 85.09. No other items appear to have been contemplated as relevant. If that had been the case the conclusion that item 40.14 applied to the goods would have followed logically, there being no other items in contention. But as we earlier observed, a number of other items become relevant if the goods are found incapable of falling to Chapter 85.

32. Because of the inconclusive state of the argument on this point, a further submission was invited from the respondent as to the item that 'applied' if the goods were taken out of Division XVI by Note 1(a). Unfortunately, no submission was received by us. We have therefore been left to resolve the ultimate classification of the goods as best we may on the evidence and material before us.

33. If Chapter 85 is excluded, the items remaining to be considered are items 39.06 (plastic), 40.14 (rubber), possibly 73.40 (metal) and 87.06 in Division XVII (parts for motor vehicles). Item 39.06 is incapable of applying if the goods are parts for vehicles falling within an item in Division XVII (see Note 1(j) to Chapter 39). Item 73.40 is similarly excluded by Note 1(g) to Division XV, if the goods fall within an item in Division XVII. Thus the only remaining items to which the goods fall and which need to be considered are item 40.14 and item 87.06. The question as to which of these items applies would have to be resolved in accordance with rule 3 of the Interpretative Rules. Rule 3(1)(a) says that if one item provides a 'more specific description' of the goods than the other, then the first mentioned item is the item that applies. In the present case, it is our view that 'parts for a motor vehicle' is a more specific description than 'goods of unhardened vulcanized rubber'. In the result, if

> Note 1(a) were applied to take the goods out of Division XVI, they would, in our view, be classifiable in Division XVII within item 87.06. Instead of being classified under the most appropriate description as 'parts for an electrical windscreen wiper' in item 85.09, they would be classified less appropriately as parts for a motor vehicle in Division XVII. Note 2 to Division XVII indicates, however, that Division XVII was not intended to apply if the parts were more specifically described and more appropriately classified in Chapter 85.
>
> 34. The question may well be asked why would parts specifically designed for use as parts for an electric windscreen wiper be taken out of Division XVI because they have a component of rubber if they are not ultimately classified as goods of unhardened vulcanised rubber but rather as parts for a motor vehicle? To our minds, the answer to that question lies in the fact that the imported goods are not goods of the kind referred to in Note 1(a) to Division XVI and were not intended to be taken out of Division XVI by that Note.
>
> **The appropriate classification**
>
> 35. In our view, therefore, the imported refills are not excluded from Division XVI by Note 1(a); they are goods to which Note 2 in that Division applies and they are properly classified as electrical windscreen wipers in item 85.09. The goods were correctly entered by the applicant by Warrant No. 07009551. We set aside the decision of the Collector to classify the goods within sub-item 40.14.9 and in substitution for that decision decide that the imported goods are correctly classified within sub-item 85.09.9. The Collector's demand for additional duty was incorrectly made and the Tribunal remits the matter to the Collector with the direction to implement the Tribunal's decision accordingly.

… … …

GRI 3(c)

GRI 3(c), which applies only if the goods cannot be classified using GRI 3(a) or (b), states that the goods should be classified under the heading that occurs last in numerical order among those that equally merit consideration.

EXAMPLE: In the above-mentioned example of the mixed good consisting of barley and oats in equal amounts, if neither the barley nor the oats is found to impart the essential character to the product, then by application of GRI 3 (c) the product would be classified in heading 1004 as if consisting solely of the oats. This is because the heading number for the oats found in the mixture occurs last in numerical order as between it and the barley (ie, 1003 for the barley and 1004 for the oats).[41]

5.2.3d Rule 4 of the GRI

Goods which cannot be classified in accordance with the above rules shall be classified under the heading appropriate to the goods to which they are most akin.

---

41 US Department of Homeland Security (US Customs and Border Protection), 'What Every Member of the Trade Community Should Know About: Tariff Classification', May 2004, p 20.

If goods cannot be classified according to GRIs 1–3, then GRI 4 requires that the goods 'be classified under the heading appropriate to the goods to which they are most akin'. In applying this rule, a determination regarding the 'kinship' of goods depends on such factors as description, character, composition, appearance, purpose or intended use, designation, production process and the nature of the goods.[42] As GRIs 1–3 will cover a substantial majority of all goods, GRI 4 is infrequently used.

5.2.3e Rule 5 of the GRI

> In addition to the foregoing provisions, the following rules shall apply in respect of the goods referred to therein:
>
> (a) Camera cases, musical instrument cases, gun cases, drawing instrument cases, necklace cases and similar containers, specially shaped or fitted to contain a specific article or set of articles, suitable for long-term use and entered with the articles for which they are intended, shall be classified with such articles when of a kind normally sold therewith. This rule does not, however, apply to containers which give the whole its essential character;
>
> (b) Subject to the provisions of rule 5(a) above, packing materials and packing containers entered with the goods therein shall be classified with the goods if they are of a kind normally used for packing such goods. However, this provision is not binding when such packing materials or packing containers are clearly suitable for repetitive use.The two sections of GRI 5 deal with various types of containers presented with the articles for which they are intended.

GRI 5(a)

GRI 5(a) states that long-term use cases, boxes and similar containers imported with the articles for which they are intended are to be classified with the articles if they are of a kind of container normally sold with such articles. GRI 5(a) specifically mentions camera cases, musical instrument cases, gun cases, drawing instrument cases and necklace cases as examples. Importantly, however, GRI 5(a) does not apply to containers that give the imported article its essential character (for example, a silver tray or dish containing tea, or a high-quality ornamental ceramic bowl containing candies or sweets). Such merchandise is to be classified under the heading for the container.

GRI 5(b)

GRI 5(b) states that packaging containers and materials not normally intended to be reused are classified with the articles in which they are presented or imported. For instance, cardboard boxes or containers containing food products would be classified as the food products. However, this rule does not apply to packaging materials or packing containers clearly suitable for repetitive use (such as certain metal drums or containers of iron or steel for compressed or liquefied gas). Under such circumstances, the packing materials or containers are to be classified separately from the materials that they hold.

---

42 See for example *Re Versatile Carpets Pty Ltd and Collector of Customs* (1985) 7 ALN N167.

5.2.3f Rule 6 of the GRI

> For legal purposes, the classification of goods in the subheadings of a heading shall be determined according to the terms of those subheadings and any related Subheading Notes and, *mutatis mutandis*, to the above Rules, on the understanding that only subheadings at the same level are comparable. For the purposes of this rule, the relative Section, Chapter Notes also apply, unless the context otherwise requires.

GRI 6 mandates that, for legal purposes, GRIs 1–5 govern, *mutatis mutandis*, classification at subheading levels within the same heading. Stated more clearly, GRI 6 states that GRIs 1–5 are to be reapplied to determine the classification of goods at the subheading level. Goods are to be classified at equal—that is, the same—subheading levels within the same heading under the subheading that most specifically describes or identifies them (or as otherwise required or directed under GRIs 1–5). Moreover, only subheadings at the same level within the same heading are comparable; therefore, consideration should not be given to the terms of any subheading within another subheading when considering the proper classification of merchandise at the higher level subheading.

GRI 6 EXAMPLES: [43]

EXAMPLE 1: A framed glass mirror is found to be classified in heading 7009. Thereafter, it would have to be classified within the subheading structure of that heading by application of GRIs 1 to 5 pursuant to GRI 6:

70.09—GLASS MIRRORS, WHETHER OR NOT FRAMED, INCLUDING REAR-VIEW MIRRORS.

7009.10—Rear-view mirrors for vehicles

—Other:

7009.91—Unframed

7009.92—Framed

Initially, a determination would need to be made as to whether the framed glass mirror is classified at the 5-digit (or 'one-dash') subheading level in 5-digit subheading 7009.1 ('rear-view mirrors for vehicles') or in 5-digit subheading 7009.9 ('other'). If the product is found to be classified in 5-digit subheading 7009.1 (as a rear-view mirror for a vehicle), then the classification analysis would end there and the product would be classified in subheading 7009.10 (as 5-digit subheading 7009.1 is not further subdivided). In the instant case, the framed glass mirror does not satisfy the article description for 5-digit subheading 7009.1. Therefore, the product would be classified at the 5-digit subheading level in 5-digit subheading 7009.9 (as a glass mirror other than a rear-view mirror for a vehicle). Next, a determination would have to be made as to whether the product is classified at the 6-digit (or 'two-dash') subheading level within 5-digit subheading 7009.9 in 6-digit subheading 7009.91 (as an *unframed* glass mirror other than a rear-view mirror for a vehicle) or in 6-digit

43 US Department of Homeland Security (US Customs and Border Protection), 'What Every Member of the Trade Community Should Know About: Tariff Classification', May 2004, pp 22–3.

subheading 7009.92 (as a *framed* glass mirror other than a rear-view mirror for a vehicle). The framed glass mirror would be classified in subheading 7009.92 by application of GRI 1 pursuant to GRI 6.

EXAMPLE 2: A set consisting of a shovel, fork, and pick for use in gardening would be classified in heading 8201 as each article is specifically provided for in the terms to that heading. Within heading 8201, shovels are provided for in subheading 8201.10, forks in subheading 8201.20, and picks in subheading 8201.30. Consequently, one would need to resort to GRI 3 pursuant to GRI 6 in order to classify the set at the subheading level within heading 8201. That is, one would need to determine which of the three articles imparts the essential character to the set pursuant to GRI 3(b). If no one article is found to impart the essential character to the set, then one would classify the set under subheading 8201.30 because the subheading number for that article occurs last in numerical order as provided for in GRI 3(c).

The examples above provide that under GRI 6 goods must first be classified by heading level, and only after the appropriate heading has been determined, then by equa subheading levels (first by five-digit and then by six-digit international levels) within tha heading. When considering the appropriate classification at a particular subheading level consideration should not be given to any of the terms of any lower-level subheading (as the analysis at each subheading level should be conducted without consideration of the terms of any lower-level subheading provision). This step-by-step analysis applies without exception throughout the HS (and throughout any national subheading levels a found in a particular country's HS-based tariff system).

5.3 Part B: Rules of origin

After identifying and classifying the goods, it is still necessary to ascertain the rate of duty applicable to the imported goods. As tariff rates are not applied on a uniform, most-favoured nation basis due to preferential trading arrangements (such as bilateral and regional free trade agreements, customs unions, and the Generalised System of Preferences offered to developing countries), it is necessary to determine the origin of the imported goods so that the proper tariff rate can then be applied. Moreover, origin determinations are also necessary to administer a number of trade laws, such as the administration of quotas and the applications of trade remedy laws.

While determining the origin of goods used to be fairly standard, increases in technology and the rise of multinational companies has transformed the manufacturing sector and made it much more difficult to determine the origin of certain goods. For instance, companies now not only source materials from multiple countries, but also perform different manufacturing stages in different countries. This problem has been exacerbated by the rapid increase in the number of preferential trade agreements since the mid-1990s, which have in turn increased the differences in rates and administrative burdens on traders and customs officials.

As free trade agreements and preferential trading schemes now account for a large percentage of world trade, companies should consider rules of origin regimes in any strategic planning. Legal representatives must ensure that companies understand the different rules of origin and provide them with enough detail and analysis to allow them to include them as an integral factor when determining in which countries to invest, where to purchase inputs or raw/intermediate materials, and where to assemble the final products.

The potential impact—and importance—of rules of origin to business cannot be overstated. All things being equal, firms will purchase from the cheapest supplier. However, as countries deviate from most-favoured nation treatment in the form of trade preferences and even trade restrictions, the national origin of inputs/materials/goods can become a determinative factor. For instance, if both a Chinese and a Thai producer can both supply an Australian importer with a certain number of goods for $100, but the tariff rate attached to the Chinese goods is 10 per cent *ad valorem* and Thai goods enter Australia duty free, the Thai goods are $10 cheaper than the Chinese goods.

Thus, prior to entering into a contract to purchase commercial goods from abroad, a business should determine the origin of the raw materials and/or intermediate parts of the goods it is considering purchasing and the impact on the origin of the final goods in order to ascertain whether any trade restrictions or preferences apply. If a raw material or intermediate part is restricted or subject to a quota or similar measure, further advice should be sought (from legal advisers as well as the government and customs) prior to proceeding with the contract. If the goods are subject to a tariff rate (above duty free), the additional costs resulting from the tariff rate must be factored into calculations to determine whether to source the product from abroad or (if feasible) locally.

It should be clear at this point that the origin of goods can be a determining factor of whether the goods are imported to a certain destination. Thus, any company considering various location sites for a new manufacturing or assembly plant should consider the origin of the final goods in each of its targeted export markets. A strategic decision to locate a manufacturing or assembly plant in a country that will receive the most beneficial treatment from the targeted export markets could minimise trade restrictions and maximise the trade preferences attached to the goods. Thus, potential trade preferences and restrictions are two of the many factors that companies should consider when determining where to locate manufacturing and assembly plants and where to source raw materials or intermediate parts.[44]

5.3.1 The international rules

Determining the origin of a product when it is wholly obtained and manufactured in a single country is often accomplished without any difficulties. When a product is made from materials originating in one or more countries and is manufactured, transformed or assembled in another country, however, rules of origin must be used to determine the origin of the product and, correspondingly, the rate of duty to be applied.

The following extract reviews the most prominent methods of determining origin, as well as briefly summarising the multilateral effort at harmonising the tests to determine rules of origin.

---

44 Other factors to consider would include the cost of capital, labour and transportation, potential economies of scale, tax rates and the level of education and/or skill of the labour force.

Joseph A LaNasa, III, 'Rules of Origin and the Uruguay Round's Effectiveness in Harmonizing and Regulating Them' (1996) 90 *American Journal of International Law* 625

[T]here are at least four different methods or criteria for determining origin:

(1) the rule of last substantial transformation;

(2) the ad valorem percentage test;

(3) a test involving specific manufacturing or processing operations that confer or do not confer origin upon the goods; and

(4) the requirement of a specified change in tariff classification.

All these methods of determining origin are designed to prevent simple assembly and packaging operations from conferring origin.

Last substantial transformation

The rule of last substantial transformation captures the heart of the meaning of rules of origin in a simple, concise way. For a product to be from a particular state or trading area, it must be substantially transformed there into a 'new and different article ... "having a distinctive name, character or use".' To prevent a product from having multiple countries of origin, the rule attributes the good to the country where it last underwent substantial transformation.

As countries increasingly treat similar imported goods differently according to where they originated and as the size of the preference or penalty increases, companies have more incentives to circumvent the spirit of the rules of origin. In other words, even though precisely defined rules of origin are generally desirable, as this precision increases, it becomes easier to circumvent the purpose of the law while formally complying with the language of the rules. The flexibility of the last substantial transformation rule enables customs authorities and courts to look beyond the form of the transaction to see if a substantial transformation actually occurred. In making their determinations, customs authorities and courts will consider a variety of factors, including whether the article was changed from a producer good to a consumer good, the amount of value added to the good, the complexity of the processing operation, and whether the good underwent a change in tariff classification.

This flexibility, however, is also the biggest drawback of the rule because it can lead to unpredictable, seemingly arbitrary results that undermine the certainty that firms require for strategic planning. Instead of refining the abstract concept of substantial transformation through repeated application to factual situations, the selective, inconsistent use of the criteria has led to increasing uncertainty and confusion.

...

In summary, the substantial transformation rule has many advantages, including its flexibility and development through application to specific facts in an adversarial situation. However, these advantages are also the root of its disadvantages: inconsistent applications, lack of certainty, discretionary nature, and high costs of the resulting origin determinations. While the last substantial transformation rule should not be used as a method of determining origin because more objective, predictable and easier-to-use regulations are needed, the last substantial transformation standard should be the motivating principle behind the development and continued refinement of more precise, defined rules of origin because it captures the purpose of origin determinations in a simple, concise manner.

Value-added percentage test

The value-added test defines the degree of transformation required to confer origin on the good in terms of the minimum percentage of its value that must come from the originating country or the maximum amount of its value that may come from the use of imported parts and materials. If the floor is not reached or the ceiling exceeded, the last production process will not confer origin. While the value-added method is often praised for its simplicity and precision, in practice it is unsatisfactory because it generates substantial compliance costs and uncertainty for companies.

The uncertainty derives from the fact that the test ignores exchange rate risk and fluctuations in the price of raw materials and intermediate goods. The status of goods can change daily as the currency values or the price of raw materials or intermediate goods fluctuates, unless the firm is able to obtain a binding advance ruling from the customs authorities. Additionally, the attribution of origin of identical goods may vary with each importing country, depending on the exchange rate between the importing country's currency and that of the processing country. Furthermore, because the value-added test is a bright-line test, it often results in seemingly arbitrary results for borderline cases. For example, if the rules require 50 percent local value added to confer origin, a good with 49 percent local value added will be denied origin, resulting in a difference of only 1 percent local value added between it and a good considered to originate there.

This test leads to inconsistent results for similar products because countries determine the amount of value added on the basis of different methods of calculation, different sales prices and the qualification of different costs as local value added.

Value-added rules of origin may be circumvented by the use of transfer pricing, which is especially prevalent when the parties to the transaction are related. For example, to increase the amount of local value added to ensure that the good qualifies as originating in the country of assembly, related parties could reduce the price of the imported materials used in the finished product. To limit or prevent this manipulation of 'value added', the rules of origin often require the related parties to show that their price is similar to prices reached in arm's-length transactions.

...

As with any defined test of origin, the value-added test is subject to industry capture during its formative stage. For example, American automobile manufacturers pressured the negotiators of the North American Free Trade Agreement into accepting special overly restrictive rules of origin for automobiles that require them to have higher regional value content than most other goods under the Agreement. Furthermore, purportedly to prevent roll-up, NAFTA requires the producer to improve the accuracy of the calculation by tracing the value of imported automotive parts throughout the production chain, which imposes substantial additional compliance costs and administrative burdens on the manufacturer. The combination of requiring higher regional value content and the tracing provisions forces automotive companies to manufacture the drive trains and engines within the free trade area if they want the vehicles to qualify for preferential treatment, or, if they want to limit the applicability of the rules of origin, to locate their assembly plant in the largest target market, ie, the United States.

Because it can be very costly and difficult to comply with the administrative requirements of value-added rules of origin, especially if they require tracing the value of specific parts and materials, firms will often find it cheaper not to observe such rules, forgoing the trade preferences and paying the most-favored-nation tariff, when the good is the product of complex manufacturing or does not otherwise face high tariff or nontariff barriers ...

In summary, owing to differences in methods of calculation, fluctuations in values, and the costs of compliance, the value-added test is not a satisfactory method of determining origin.

Specified processes

The specified process test of origin, also referred to as a technical test, prescribes certain production processes that may (positive test) or may not (negative test) confer originating status. The specified process test serves as a useful supplemental test of origin because it can easily be tailored to meet a specific situation in a clear, precise manner. However, it is not a satisfactory primary test of origin because it would be extremely difficult, if not impossible, to define a process test for each of the enormous array of products on the international market and to update these rules as new products and technological advances in production are made. In addition, a process test for defining origin would be highly susceptible to capture by industry lobbying groups; since the test would be framed in technical terms, its content would be hidden from public view, and the drafters and administrators of the rule would therefore have to rely on industry for information. For example, the European Commission's Regulation 288/89 stated that origin is conferred on an integrated circuit whenever it undergoes diffusion, even though diffusion is followed by assembly and testing, processes that are more labor-intensive and may add more value than diffusion. This product-specific technical rule allegedly was adopted because EC producers of integrated circuits performed the diffusion in Europe and then had the testing and assembly done in third countries, while Japanese producers of integrated circuits had them tested and assembled in Europe. Therefore, this regulation conferred EC origin on goods produced by EC manufacturers while denying EC origin to goods produced by Japanese manufacturers, thereby allowing the European companies to trade their integrated circuits on better terms than the Japanese. Because negative technical tests only delineate which processes do not confer origin, they are easily targeted at a particular foreign company. For example, Commission Regulation 2071/89, on determining the origin of photocopiers, stated that the incorporation of an optical system into a photocopying apparatus will not confer origin, but it did not explain which operations would confer origin. This regulation was allegedly designed to deny US origin to Ricoh copiers assembled in the United States by a Japanese corporation. These copiers contained imported Japanese optical systems and thus, according to the rules of origin, were 'Japanese'. As antidumping duties had been imposed on Ricoh copiers from Japan, these copiers, despite having been assembled in the United States, were also subject to those duties.

Change in tariff classification

This method specifies the change in tariff classification required to confer origin on a good under the Harmonized Commodity Description and Coding System (Harmonized System). The Harmonized System has been adopted for customs tariffs and trade statistical purposes by countries representing 90 percent of world trade, making it one of the most basic and widely applied laws in international trade. It provides a uniform, hierarchical nomenclature to be used in defining origin determinations for all products in international trade.

...

The hierarchical framework of the Harmonized System, its division by industry, and its systematic arrangement of headings by ascending degrees of technical sophistication and economic effort provide an easy-to-use underlying structure for origin determinations. This structure also gives drafters of rules of origin the flexibility to define classification changes precisely, including the incorporation of exceptions and special rules, without sacrificing objectivity, certainty or identity. Nevertheless, the Harmonized System is a means for tariff classification and was primarily designed for the dual purposes of categorizing commodities and compiling statistics. Since it was not designed to be used for origin determinations, changes in classification under the system are not always an appropriate or effective test of origin. An origin scheme based on change in tariff classification must therefore be supplemented by exceptions that describe when a sufficient transformation has occurred despite the lack of change in tariff classification, when a change in classification is not a sufficient transformation, and which processes are not sufficient to confer origin even though they lead to a change in classification. These exceptions often require the use of process and value-added tests of origin, which introduces the problems associated with those tests into the tariff classification system, albeit on a lesser scale than if they were the primary tests. As with any process system, both the required changes and the exceptions lists must be updated to reflect new products and technological advances.

The change-in-tariff-classification method of determining origin is conceptually simple and easy to apply and leads to consistent, predictable results once the product is classified. However, classification can give rise to problems, because products are not always categorized in a uniform manner, despite the substantial efforts of the Harmonized System Committee to ensure that they are.

Efforts at global harmonization of rules of origin

Beginning in the early twentieth century, rules of origin gradually emerged with the development of differentiated tariffs and other trade measures. Prior to the Uruguay Round of Multinational Trade Negotiations, the GATT [General Agreement on Tariffs and Trade] did not regulate or harmonize rules of origin; instead, it left each contracting party free to determine its own.

Attempts by the International Chamber of Commerce (ICC) to harmonize rules of origin in 1953 by establishing the abstract principle of substantial transformation as the guiding definition to be used in compiling lists of processes that confer origin on manufactured goods were rejected by the GATT. Some countries were skeptical of any kind of international definition of origin because they considered rules of origin to be 'inescapably bound up with national economic policies, which are unavoidably different in different countries.' This disagreement still exists between countries that view rules of origin as an instrument of commercial policy and those that view them as technical, objective, neutral instruments.

Annex D1 of the Kyoto Convention of 1973 represented a multilateral attempt to move toward the harmonization of preferential and nonpreferential rules of origin. The annex set forth guidelines based on the principles of wholly obtained goods and last substantial transformation that countries were to use in drafting their rules of origin. Because it was recognized in the Kyoto Convention that substantial transformation is a rather vague concept, the annex listed methods to be used in defining substantial transformation more precisely but left the parties with discretion to fashion the rules of origin as they deemed fit.

By the 1980s, the European Community's use of rules of origin to implement politically motivated, trade-restrictive and trade-distortive policies led to the latest attempt to regulate and harmonize the rules of origin: their inclusion as a topic for negotiation in the Uruguay Round. In recent years, the Community had engaged in result-oriented rule making. Under pressure from European industrial lobbies, the Commission or the Origin Committee would change rules of origin by adopting new interpretations that made their application stricter, reformulating them in more carefully tailored and stringent language, and enacting special rules for specific products so that goods produced by foreign companies that had initially been in compliance with the technical requirements of the applicable origin regulations were no longer in compliance with them and were therefore subject to higher tariff rates, restrictive quotas or antidumping duties.

The Origin Agreement

HARMONIZATION OF NONPREFERENTIAL RULES OF ORIGIN

The Origin Agreement concluded at the Uruguay Round seeks to harmonize the nonpreferential rules of origin used by signatory countries into a single set of international rules. While the Origin Agreement does not harmonize preferential rules of origin, it does seek to provide them with more transparency and foster the development of a rule of law regarding their application through suggested procedural reforms.

The Origin Agreement will harmonize nonpreferential rules of origin by means of a two-step process. First, it anticipates a three-year transitional period, during which the harmonized rules will be drafted and adopted by the Technical Committee on Rules of Origin; the Committee on Rules of Origin will periodically consider the results, 'with a view to endorsing such interpretations and opinions.' Since the rules were drafted in a multilateral, nearly global forum that will use them for all nonpreferential purposes, the ability of any one country to draw up its own rules in politically motivated ways will be limited. For example, if the United States tries to protect its domestic car industry with the unduly restrictive harmonized rule of origin, those very companies will be injured if they seek to export their automobiles abroad. Once the harmonization work program is completed, a GATT ministerial conference will adopt the results as an annex to the Origin Agreement, together with a time frame for its entry into force.

The Technical Committee will develop a detailed harmonized definition for determining when goods are wholly obtained in one country and a harmonized list of minimal operations or processes that do not by themselves confer origin on a good. Most important, the Technical Committee will define when the last substantial transformation of a good produced in more than one country occurs, primarily through application of the change-in-tariff-classification method at the heading or subheading level. The Technical Committee will use the Harmonized System as the underlying nomenclature, and, when supplemental tests are necessary, it may resort to the value-added and specified processing methods. The Origin Agreement states that origin will be conferred where the last substantial transformation occurred, not where the most significant one occurred. This rule increases certainty of application and simplifies the determination of origin because the customs authorities can disregard previous operations.

...

After the transitional period ends, the harmonized nonpreferential rules of origin will be applied for all nonpreferential purposes by the signatory countries. Because the harmonized rules will be defined primarily in terms of change in tariff classification and secondarily in terms of specified value-added requirements and specified technical processes, they will replace vague, discretionary concepts such as substantial transformation or last substantial process with more mechanical, clearer tests that will enhance the capacity of firms to plan their production, purchasing and investment strategies. These rules therefore represent a substantial advance over the existing system of multiple rules of origin that are applied differently for different purposes. Application of the harmonized rules, however, will not ensure harmonized origin determinations because the member countries may disagree over how to interpret and apply the rules or how to classify the goods. In addition, both during and after the transitional period, the member countries may apply their own preferential rules.

...

Procedural reforms

The Origin Agreement imposes a variety of procedural safeguards on the formulation and application of rules of origin, in hopes of creating a more transparent, lawlike system for applications of the preferential rules. These safeguards apply to preferential and nonpreferential rules of origin and enter into effect when a country signs the Origin Agreement.

The procedural safeguards require signatory countries to publish the rules of origin and any applications of them, and not to apply any changes in the rules retroactively. They allow any interested person to request an assessment of origin, which request may be made in advance of trading, and require the member country's customs administrators to respond by issuing and publishing, within 150 days of the request, a binding assessment of origin that clearly and precisely states what requirements must be met to confer origin. The assessment of origin will be binding in all comparable situations for three years. The administrative authorities' ruling on the origin assessment request will protect any confidential information, unless the person or government providing it specifically permits its disclosure or judicial proceedings require its disclosure.

Any administrative action taken with regard to the determination of origin for either preferential or nonpreferential purposes may be promptly reviewed by an independent judicial, administrative or arbitral tribunal, which has the authority to modify or reverse the determination. Prompt review by an independent body will lead to a system closer to one based on the rule of law. It will serve to increase the transparency, neutrality, consistency and legitimacy of origin determinations, because an independent body will decide the correctness of their application after hearing presentations by both sides. In addition, by making the determinations binding in all comparable situations for three years, requiring their publication, and subjecting them to review, the Origin Agreement exerts considerable pressure on customs authorities to explain their reasoning. The resulting increased transparency and consistency of the process will enable other interested parties to make more cogent arguments for favorable rulings using the prior assessments as precedents.

These procedural reforms, which improve on the American system of permitting advance rulings with judicial review, will engender more fact-specific origin determinations and place them in a context more akin to the common law. The fairer, more objective determinations that can be expected to emerge as the rules are explained through application to specific factual situations will give firms foreknowledge of the origin and corresponding treatment of the final good and thus facilitate the rational planning of their purchasing and production processes.

... ...

In most countries, the origin of a good is the country where the good was wholly obtained or, if more than one country is involved, the country where it was substantially transformed (the *rule of last substantial transformation*). Therefore, the site of the last substantial transformation is essentially the core test for determining the origin of goods originating in more than one country. The last substantial transformation rule is flexible and there are a number of different ways to determine whether a substantial transformation has occurred. But, as illustrated in the above extract, the rule of the substantial transformation does have its limits and there is often a need to impose another form of origin test.

The reason behind the rules of origin regime is to prevent goods from having multiple countries of origin and attribute their origin to the place where they underwent substantial transformation. For substantial transformation, it is understandable that the product must be substantially transformed into a new and different product, acquiring a distinctive name, character and functionality. For example, a substantial transformation may be found where fresh cocoa from Brazil is transformed into chocolate in Switzerland. The site of substantial transformation would be Switzerland because the cocoa was transformed into a new and distinctive product, with different functions and characteristics. If the chocolate were to be exported to Malaysia to be packaged before being exported to Australia for consumer purchase, the origin would remain Switzerland, as the packaging would not substantially transform the good.

Of course, determining the origin of the goods would be irrelevant if countries treated all trading partners equally; that is, if countries actually applied their most-favoured nation (MFN) rates to all nations. This is, of course, unlikely to happen in the near (or medium, or perhaps even long) term. Thus, as a second-best option, many commentators have called for real harmonisation of the rules of origin. The Origin Agreement is helpful in that it attempts to create a more transparent, technical, predictable process for all determinations of origin, but countries continue to apply different rules of origin, resulting in inconsistent determinations and accusations of political bias. Rules of origin are an integral component of trading relationships that can influence purchasing, manufacturing and investment decisions; accordingly transparent, predictable and harmonised rules evenly applied by all nations would be of great assistance to traders and would lower the cost of international business transactions.

5.3.2 Rules of origin in Australia

Rules of origin regimes usually make use of one or more of the determinative methods described in the extract above, and generally rely on a number of these methods, depending upon the good. This is particularly the case of a rules of origin system based on the change in tariff classification approach, which is normally combined with a value-added test or a manufacturing process test for certain products.

In Australia, the rules guiding determination of origin are set out in Part VIII, Division 1A of the *Customs Act 1901* (Cth). These provisions not only concern the rules for determining the origin of goods, they also cover the circumstances in which a reduced or free duty of rate may apply to in accordance with the World Trade Organization (WTO) Agreement on Rules of Origin.

The method applied is, in the main, the value-added method; however, the rules regarding origin can—and have been—amended by agreement between Australia and its trading partners, such as via free trade agreements (FTAs). Thus, while Australian FTAs with New Zealand and Singapore generally apply the value-added method to determine origin, the change in tariff classification (CTC) was adopted as the predominant rules of origin determination in the Australian FTAs with the USA and Thailand. It should also be noted that Australia is in discussions with New Zealand regarding amending the Australia New Zealand Closer Economic Relations Trade Agreement (ANZCERTA) to apply the CTC approach, and it is very likely that Australia will adopt the CTC approach in all of its prospective FTAs.

However, the CTC is not always an effective test for origin determinations—for example, when a product or material has not undergone a sufficient transformation to allow a change in its classification, or there is a 'transformation' but it does not result in a change in tariff classification. In such situations, the CTC test must be supplemented by additional requirements or tests, such as a specified process or value-added test of origin. Such supplements are seen, for instance, in Australia's FTAs with the USA and Thailand, where the CTC rules are supported by a regional value content (RVC) test, which requires that a certain percentage of the goods' value originates in one of the countries party to the FTA (for example, the FTA may specify that at least 45 per cent of the value of the goods must originate from the other FTA party in order to qualify for preferential treatment under the FTA).[45]

To some extent, Australia also relies on the most technical of origin tests—that which demands that non-originating goods undergo certain manufacturing processes before being exported. For instance, Australia's FTA with Thailand and the USA both require a specific manufacturing process be used in order for chemical and plastic products to qualify as originating from a FTA partner country. More specifically, these agreements states that if a chemical reaction results from the combination of materials produced in an FTA party with those imported from outside the FTA parties, the good produced is eligible for preferential rate of duty regardless of whether it would comply with a CTC test. However, if the product originated from a chemical reaction resulting from the combination of materials imported from areas outside the FTA parties, it must meet the CTC test in order to qualify for a preferential rate of duty.

The following case extract demonstrates some of the more important issues involved in determining origin when an FTA is at issue. The case relates to the importation into Australia by Gaylor Jewellery Sales Pty Limited (Gaylor) of a number of consignments of gold jewellery exported from New Zealand by Koalic Enterprises Limited (Koalic).

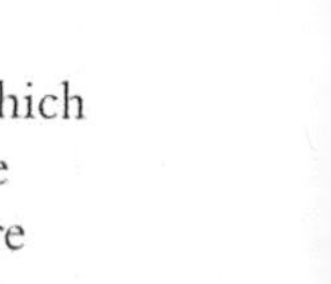

Re Gaylor Jewellery Sales Pty Limited and Collector of Customs

AAT No 5926, (1990) 12 AAR 86

3 The material adduced ... was not in dispute and showed:

(a) Koalic purchases in New Zealand fine (ie pure) gold of New Zealand origin and forwards that gold to a fabricator in Italy or in England for fabrication into gold chains. Uno A Erre Italia Srl performs about 85% of Koalic's fabrication.

45 It should be noted that an exception to the RVC method exists when the exporter or the producer is not able to qualify their goods as originating because the product cannot meet the HS requirements for change in tariff classification. The provisions are called *de minimis*, and are designed for general goods or textiles and apparel. For instance, the USA often negotiates for the *de minimis* exception for both general goods and (especially) for textiles and apparel in its FTAs.

(b) The fabricator converts the fine gold by the addition of other metals into a gold alloy suitable for manufacture into gold chains.

(c) The gold alloy is then fabricated into chains and necklaces, with an O-ring soldered onto each end thereof. The chains and necklaces, together with the necessary fasteners, are then sent from Italy or England to New Zealand, where a fastener is attached to one O-ring on each chain or necklace. They are then exported to Australia.

(d) The New Zealand gold provided by Koalic remains the property of that company throughout the fabrication process, and the fabricator accounts to Koalic for the actual quantity of gold used. Any surplus gold after an order has been completed is retained by the fabricator for use in future orders placed by Koalic.

(e) The value of the gold in the chains and necklaces is at least 70% of the total value thereof and the cost of fabrication is less than 30% of that total value.

4 The facts in this matter are similar to those that were before the Tribunal for consideration in *Re Rubis Investments Pty Limited and The Collector of Customs* (1984) 1 AAR 368. There it was held:

(a) the attaching of the clasp in New Zealand was the last process performed in bringing the goods to their completed state of manufacture;

(b) the assembly of the previously manufactured parts into completed goods was a process of manufacture; and

(c) the goods therefore qualified for preferential rates under s 151 of the *Customs Act 1901*, since they were partly manufactured in New Zealand, the process last performed in their manufacture was performed in that country, and not less than one-half of their cost was represented by the value of New Zealand materials.

5 In *Rubis*, it was common ground that the requirements of s 151(3)(c) of the *Customs Act 1901* were satisfied because 'not less than one-half of the factory or work costs of the gold chains was represented by the value of 'materials of New Zealand' (ie, the fine gold costing NZ $81 000). However, in the applications now under consideration, the respondent argues that the present requirements of s 151 are not met, so that the goods imported by Gaylor do not qualify for preferential treatment.

6 Thus at the time of the gold being shipped to Italy for fabrication into gold chain, the raw material was clearly material of New Zealand within the meaning of s 151(7) of the *Customs Act 1901*. In Italy, the gold was fabricated into various types of gold chain. The New Zealand gold remained the property of Koalic at all times. The gold ingredient of the chain represented a minimum of 70% of the cost of the jewellery, Koalic having been charged by the Italian company an amount representing the labour cost of crafting the gold into chains and handling charges. The chain was forwarded to New Zealand where there was attached a clasp. The finished product, the chain, was then packed into boxes and exported to Australia.

7 If the gold itself had, prior to fabrication into chains, been exported to Australia, the material would have been 'material of New Zealand'. Has the change wrought upon the gold by fabrication in Italy rendered it not then 'material of New Zealand', but rather one of a number of materials of mixed origin incorporated in a final product for export to Australia, and not then entitled to the preferential tariff treatment afforded pursuant to s 151 of the Act?

8 The respondent Collector of Customs answered this question in the affirmative …

…

11 The respondent Collector's argument can, as we see it, be reduced to two primary issues— first, that by reason of the addition by the fabricator of substances to the fine gold to produce an alloy, that alloy could not be properly regarded as being gold of New Zealand origin. Secondly, that even if it were gold of New Zealand origin, it was not now eligible for preferential treatment

because of changes in legislation subsequent to the decision of the Tribunal in *Re Rubis Investments Pty Limited* (supra).

12 Dealing with the first issue, it is our view that the gold does not cease to be gold of New Zealand origin merely because substances are added to render it, for example, more durable. Thus a gold watch does not cease to be a gold watch merely because its case is made of 22 carat or 18 carat gold and not pure gold. In *Young v Cook* (1877) 3 EX D 101, Cleasby B, in dealing with the meaning of the expression 'gold of the weight of two ounces' for the purposes of the *Revenue Act 1867*, stated at page 106:

> I think it (the above 'expression') undoubtedly signifies taken by itself, not pure gold which is commercially unknown, but gold with whatever alloy there is in 22, 18, 15 or 9-carat gold, or whatever it might be.

13 We are of the opinion that a purchaser of a chain or necklace would regard it as a gold chain or gold necklace, even though it be not made of pure gold. As the gold of which the chain or necklace is comprised is gold of New Zealand origin, we consider that the material of which they are comprised is 'material of New Zealand' within the meaning of the legislation. Support for this view is to be found in the Macquarie Dictionary (Rev Ed) definition of material as:

> 1 the substance or substances of which a thing is made or composed. 2 any constituent element of a thing.

Accordingly, the respondent's first argument fails.

14 Turning to the respondent's second issue, s 5(1) of the *Customs Tariff Act 1987* defines the expression 'Preference Country' as meaning, inter alia, New Zealand. Section 22 of that Act provides that subject to ss 23, 24, 25, 27 and 29, the duty in respect of goods shall be ascertained:

(a) ... (b) where the goods are the produce or manufacture of a Preference Country, other than Canada, by reference to:

(i) where a rate of duty that applies in relation to the Preference Country is set out in the third column of the tariff classification under which the goods are classified—that rate of duty; or

(ii) in any other case—Free; or

(c) ...

15 It was agreed between the parties that the goods in question would fall within the sub-heading 7113.19.00, Sub-Chapter III of Chapter 71 in the *Customs Tariff Act 1987*. That Sub-Chapter provides in part as follows:

JEWELLERY, GOLDSMITHS' AND SILVERSMITHS' WARES AND OTHER ARTICLES 7113 ARTICLES OF JEWELLERY AND PARTS THEREOF, OF PRECIOUS METAL OR OF METAL CLAD WITH PRECIOUS METAL:

- 7113.1—Of precious metal whether or not plated or clad with precious metal;
- 7113.11.00—Of silver, whether or not plated or 25% with other precious metal
- DC:20% CAN:15%
- 7113.19.00—Of other precious metal, whether or 25% not plated or clad with precious metal
- DC:20% CAN:15%
- 7113.20.00—Of base metal clad with precious metal 25%
- DC:20% CAN:15%

16 As that heading does not specify a rate of duty applicable in relation to New Zealand, the goods would be entitled to be admitted free of duty—s 22(b)(ii).

17 For this exemption to apply, the goods must be the produce or manufacture of New Zealand. Subsections (6), (7) and (13) of s 151 of the *Customs Act 1901* are as follows:

(6) For the purposes of this Act, goods are the manufacture of a country, being New Zealand, Papua New Guinea, Canada or a country that is not a Preference Country, if they were wholly manufactured in the country from one or more of:

(a) unmanufactured raw products;

(b) materials wholly manufactured in one or both of Australia and the country; and

(c) materials imported into the country that the comptroller has determined, by notice in writing published in the Gazette, to be manufactured raw materials of the country.

(7) For the purposes of this Act, goods are the manufacture of New Zealand if:

(a) the last process in their manufacture was performed in New Zealand; and

(b) not less than 50%, or, where the goods are in a class in respect of which the Comptroller has determined, by notice in writing published in the Gazette, that another percentage is appropriate, that other percentage, of their factory or works cost is represented by the value of labour or materials, or of labour and materials, of New Zealand or of Australia and New Zealand.

(13) For the purposes of this section, the Comptroller may, by notice in writing published in the Gazette.

(a) specify the manner in which the factory or works cost of goods is to be determined; and

(b) specify the manner in which the value of labour, the value of materials or the value of labour and materials is to be determined.

18 For the purposes of ss(7)(a), it was conceded on the basis of the decision in *Re Rubis Investments Pty Limited* (supra) that the last process in the manufacture of the chains and necklaces imported by Gaylor was performed in New Zealand. There has not been any relevant determination made pursuant to ss (7)(b).

19 Article 3 of ANZCERTA (deemed to have 'entered into force' on 1 January 1983) dealing with Rules of Origin, provides inter alia as follows:

1. Goods exported from the territory of a Member State directly into the territory of the other Member State or which, if not exported directly, were at the time of their export from the territory of a Member State destined for the territory of the other Member State and were subsequently imported into the territory of that other Member State, shall be treated as goods originating in the territory of the first Member State if those goods are:

(a) ...

(b) ...

(c) partly manufactured in the territory of that Member State, subject to the following conditions:

(i) the process last performed in the manufacture of the goods was performed in the territory of that Member State; and

(ii) the expenditure on one or more of the items set out below is not less than one-half of the factory or works cost of such goods in their finished state:

A material that originates in the territory of one or both Member States;

B labour and factory overheads incurred in the territory of one or both Member States;

C inner containers that originate in the territory of one or both Member States.

2. The factory or works cost referred to in paragraph 1(c)(ii) of this Article shall be the sum of costs of materials (excluding customs, excise or other duties), labour, factory overheads, and inner containers.'

20 Following upon the 1988 review of the operation of ANZCERTA, there was an exchange of letters between the then respective Ministers of Customs of Australia and New Zealand. The letter dated 16 August 1988 from the Minister of Customs of New Zealand (which embodied the letter of the same date from the Minister of Customs of Australia) is as follows [in relevant part]:

> The Explanatory Note concerning Article 3 of the Agreement contains an approach to the treatment of materials of mixed origin which constitutes a change of practice for both Customs agencies. In the event that any existing trade is disadvantaged by the change within the first six months of its operations, I understand the two Customs agencies will consult to see if special provisions are appropriate to preserve the benefits of preference for that trade.
>
> I understand that as part of the joint understanding the two Customs agencies will report to their respective Ministers by 1 September 1989 indicating areas where harmonisation has been achieved, outstanding areas where it is intended that harmonisation will take place and the time frame for achieving such harmonisation. I would be grateful if, in replying, you would confirm that this is your understanding.

[The New Zealand Minister for Customs confirmed the interpretation and understanding between the two Governments.]

21 The Joint Understanding attached to the letter dated 16 August 1988 from the Minister of Customs for Australia dealt with a number of matters, and under the heading 'Rules of Origin' stated:

> The two Customs agencies have a common view on the technical application of the rules of origin. A revised Explanatory Note is attached to this joint understanding. This note seeks to simplify arrangements for trans-Tasman traders and at the same time minimise economic distortions created by the existence of different tariff regimes on intermediate goods from third countries.

22 The revised Explanatory Note attached to the Joint Understanding read (in its relevant parts) as follows:

> The two Customs agencies have a common view on the technical application of the rules of origin and are working jointly to align legislation. The application of origin criteria will be monitored to identify any circumstances inconsistent with the objectives of the Agreement that need to be addressed. Any proposals to amend the substance or interpretive detail of the rules will be the subject of consultation with a view to maintaining a common approach.
>
> Investigations of origin status of imported goods by both Customs agencies are carried out without the necessity to consult or advise the other administration. This practice will continue unless the circumstances of a particular case are such that there might be a need for advice to be given to the other Customs agency.
>
> MATERIALS OF MIXED ORIGIN
>
> In terms of Article 3.1(c)(ii), in calculating the value of an imported component incorporated in a final product for export to the other Member State the value of that imported component will be taken as:
>
> - wholly of qualifying area content provided that in its imported form it qualified under the rules of origin on importation into the Member State which manufactured the final product.
> - totally without qualifying area content if in its imported form it did not qualify under the rules of origin on importation into the Member State which manufactured the final product.

23 As was stated in *Re Rubis* (supra) at p 375, ANZCERTA made no mention of the substantial transformation criterion adopted by the Kyoto Convention in April 1977, although the contracting parties could have adopted that criterion had they so desired. Further, as was stated by Dixon J as he then was in *Chow Hung Ching v The King* [1948] HCA 37; (1948) 77 CLR 449 at p 478:

> a treaty, at all events one which does not terminate a state of war, has no legal effect upon the rights and duties of the subjects of the Crown and speaking generally no power resides in the Crown to compel them to obey the provisions of a treaty.
>
> ...
>
> Accordingly, we have not taken the provisions of the Kyoto Convention into account for the purposes of our decision.

24 By Notice No 88/11 dated 18 August 1988 (which took effect from that date) published in the Commonwealth of Australia Gazette dated 7 September 1988, a delegate of the Comptroller-General of Customs, pursuant to s 151(13)(b) of the *Customs Act 1901*, specified that the manner in which the value of labour and materials was to be determined for the purposes of that paragraph in regard to New Zealand was the manner specified in the Schedule to the Notice. That Schedule read:

THE SCHEDULE

The value of labour and materials shall be determined by the sum of the following:

(a) (i) in the case of materials wholly produced or manufactured in New Zealand or in Australia or in New Zealand and in Australia but not including any duties or other taxes paid or payable in the country of manufacture of the goods in respect of such materials—the cost of those materials; or

(ii) in the case of materials partly manufactured and exported from Australia to New Zealand for incorporation in a final product for export to Australia from New Zealand, the cost of those imported materials into New Zealand will be:

A wholly of qualifying area content provided that in their imported form they qualified under the rules of origin on importation into New Zealand for incorporation in the final product;

B totally without qualifying area content if in their imported form they did not qualify under the rules of origin on importation into New Zealand and incorporated in the final product; or

(iii) in the case of materials partly manufactured in New Zealand, the value shall be the proportion of the cost of manufacture of those materials incurred in New Zealand or in New Zealand and Australia, but not including any duties or other taxes paid or payable in the country of manufacture of the goods in respect of such materials.

(b) manufacturing wages;

(c) factory overhead expenses; and

(d) the cost of inside containers of the manufacture of New Zealand or of Australia, or of New Zealand and Australia.

25 By Notice No 88/14 dated 18 November 1988 (which took effect from that date), published in the Commonwealth of Australia Gazette dated 30 November 1988, Notice No 88/11 was revoked and a fresh specification made of the manner in which the value of labour and materials was to be determined. The Schedule to this Notice was as follows:

THE SCHEDULE

The value of labour and materials shall be determined by the sum of the following:

(a) (i) in the case of materials wholly produced or manufactured in New Zealand or in Australia or in New Zealand and in Australia but not including any duties or other taxes paid or payable in the country of manufacture of the goods in respect of such materials—the cost of those materials; or

(ii) in the cases of materials partly manufactured and exported from Australia to New Zealand for incorporation in a final product for export to Australia from New Zealand, the cost of those imported materials into New Zealand will be:

(A) wholly of qualifying area content provided that in their imported form they qualified under the rules of origin on importation into New Zealand for incorporation in the final product;

(B) totally without qualifying area content if in their imported form they did not qualify under the rules of origin on importation into New Zealand and incorporation in the final product; or

(iii) in the case of materials partly manufactured in New Zealand, the value shall be the proportion of the cost of manufacture of those materials incurred in New Zealand or in New Zealand and Australia, but not including any duties or other taxes paid or payable in the country of manufacture of the goods in respect of such materials;

(b) manufacturing wages;

(c) factory overhead expenses; and

(d) the cost of inside containers of the manufacture of New Zealand or of Australia, or of New Zealand and Australia.

For the purpose of this notice 'materials' means those goods which, had they been exported from Australia and were later imported into Australia would have had at the time of such importation the same identity for the purposes of the *Customs Tariff Act 1987* as they had at the time of their prior exportation.

26 The applicant challenged the validity of the two Notices Nos 88/11 and 88/14 on the ground that they were outside the power conferred by ss 151(13)(b). The sub-section enables the Comptroller to 'specify the manner in which the value of labour, the value of materials or the value of labour and materials is to be determined' for the purposes of that section.

27 So far as Notice No 88/11 is concerned, it provided that the value of labour and materials was to be determined, in the case of materials partly manufactured in New Zealand, by the sum of four items—viz items (a)(iii), (b), (c) and (d). In our view, specification in this manner of the method by which the value of labour and materials was to be determined came squarely within s 151(13)(b) and consequently Notice No 88/11 was a valid exercise of the power to specify thereby conferred.

28 Different considerations apply in the case of Notice No 88/14. To the extent that the formula in Notice No 88/11 is repeated in Notice No 88/14, it is not, in our view, open to challenge on the ground that it is outside the power conferred by s 151(13)(b) upon the Comptroller. However, the formula concludes with a paragraph stating:

For the purposes of this notice 'materials' means those goods which, had they been exported from Australia and were later imported into Australia would have had at the time of such importation the same identity for the purposes of the *Customs Tariff Act 1987* as they had at the time of their prior exportation.

29 It was argued for the applicant that while s 151(13)(b) authorizes the Comptroller to specify the manner in which, *inter alia*, the value of labour and materials is to be determined, it does not authorize the Comptroller to exclude from that calculation a certain category of materials. If s 151(13)(b) were to be regarded as sufficiently wide to permit such an exclusion, this would permit the exclusion of materials of Australia or New Zealand, even though there is a clear intention in s 151(7) that these be taken into account.

30 In our view, the construction which the applicant contended should be placed upon s 151(13)(b) is the correct one. The final paragraph in Notice No 88/14 goes beyond specifying the manner in which the value of labour and materials is to be determined, inasmuch as it excludes altogether the value of certain materials, and is therefore, in our view, invalid. It would have been competent for the Comptroller to have made a specific determination under s 151(7)(b) of the Act of a percentage of factory or works cost which would have taken into account costs of manufacture incurred outside New Zealand.

31 Section 46 of the *Acts Interpretation Act 1901* provides as follows:

> Where an Act confers upon any authority power to make, grant or issue any instrument (including rules, regulations or by-laws), then:
>
> (a) unless the contrary intention appears, expressions used in any instrument so made, granted or issued shall have the same meanings as in the Act conferring the power, and this Act shall apply to any instrument so made, granted or issued as if it were an Act and as if each such rule, regulation or by-law were a section of an Act; and
>
> (b) any instrument so made, granted or issued shall be read and construed subject to the Act under which it was made, granted or issued, and so as not to exceed the power of that authority, to the intent that where any such instrument would, but for this section, have been construed as being in excess of the power conferred upon that authority, it shall nevertheless be a valid instrument to the extent to which it is not in excess of that power.

32 Having regard to the provisions of paragraph (b) of that Section, we consider that the invalidity of the final paragraph of Notice No 88/14 does not affect the validity of the remainder of the determination set out in that Notice, particularly as the remainder of that determination is identical with the manner of determination set out in Notice No 88/11.

33 Of the consignments of gold jewellery covered by these applications, three were entered for home consumption on 12 October 1988 (while Notice No 88/11 was in force) and the remainder were entered for home consumption subsequent to 18 November 1988 (when Notice No 88/14 came into force). Having regard to the view we have taken in relation to Notice No 88/14, we consider that all applications fall to be governed by the same requirements, and that as not less than 50% of the factory or works cost of the goods is represented by the value of labour and materials of New Zealand, the goods qualify for preferential rates under s 151.

34 In the circumstances, the decision under review is set aside and in lieu thereof, we decide that the imported jewellery was entitled to entry at the New Zealand preferential rate, viz, free. The applicant will therefore be entitled to a refund of the duty paid under protest.

... ...

5.4 Part C: Valuation of goods

After establishing the origin and classification of the goods, the next step is to determine the value of the goods for the purpose of imposing duty. Division 2 of Part VIII of the *Customs Act 1901* (Cth) regulates the practice of customs valuation pursuant to Art VII of the GATT and the WTO Agreement on Implementation of Article VI of the General Agreement on Tariffs and Trade (the Valuation Agreement).

Article VII of the GATT provides the principles for the valuation process and prohibits the use of arbitrary practices in the valuation field. It states that the customs valuation of goods should be based on the 'actual value' of the imported goods and expressly bans the use of unfair valuation systems, namely the use of market price of the goods in the exporting country, arbitrary or fictitious values, imposition of minimum values or use of the selling price in the country of importation.[46]

According to the GATT, the valuation regime should be driven by a precise method of valuation, which should be applied by a hierarchy order. These methods are discussed below.

5.4.1 Transaction value: the primary valuation method

Considered the primary method of customs valuation, the transaction value is to be used before the application of any other criterion of valuation. In Australia, 95 per cent of imported goods imported are valued by the transaction value method. Section 161(1) of the *Customs Act 1901* states that the transaction value of the goods is:

> the sum of their adjusted price in the import sales transaction and of their price related costs to the extent that those costs have not been taken into account in determining the price of the goods.

In other words, the transaction value is the price actually paid or payable for the goods when sold for export to the customs territory of the importing country. Basically, the transaction value is calculated by deducting from the price of the goods in the contract of sale certain prescribed matters, such as costs of overseas freight and insurance. Three methods of determining the adjusted price are: price actually paid or payable; transaction between related parties; and exclusive and inclusive costs.

5.4.1a Price actually paid or payable

The price is defined in s 154 of the *Customs Act* and attempts to embody every consideration passing from the purchaser, directly or indirectly, to the benefit of the vendor in respect of the import sales transaction. This may take the form not only of currency, but also the value of goods and services provided to the vendor or to the vendor's benefit.

5.4.1b Transaction between related parties

The fact that the purchaser and the vendor are related parties will not in itself prevent the transaction value from being valid. An analysis of all the surrounding circumstances should be undertaken by the customs authorities in order to determine the influence of the relationship on the price of the transaction. If a positive determination is found, the importer must still be given the opportunity to respond and prove that the value of the goods under the related sales closely approximate the value of the goods in an analogous situation.

46 For an example, see the United States of America Selling Price (ASP).

5.4.1c Exclusive and inclusive costs

The next stage in the valuation of the transaction process is to examine the costs that may be added or subtracted from the price actually paid or payable. The charges that must be added to the price are those that are not already included in the price, such as shipping costs, royalties and license fees, as well as advertising and warranty fees.

Excludable or deductable costs are those of the purchaser's account undertaken after importation, such as costs for construction, maintenance and technical assistance, finance and administration expenses, and Australian inland freight and insurance. In the case of a licence to reproduce the same imported goods in the importing country, the importer and the producer will not be liable for the payment of licence fees associated with the manufacture of the goods. Royalties and licensee fees that are to be added to the price for customs purposes are only those closely connected to the actual sale of the goods.

5.4.2 Identical goods value

Where the collector cannot determine the customs value by using the transaction value method, recourse should be made to the sale of identical goods exported into Australia at about the same time; that is, within approximately 45 days. Identical goods must be goods which are the same in all material respects—including physical characteristics, quality and reputation—as the imported goods. The sale of the identical merchandise must be preferably at the same commercial level and substantially in same quantities, but if such comparison is not possible, then adjustments are allowed.

5.4.3 Similar goods value

On the impossibility of finding identical goods for comparison purposes, the customs collector will use a method of valuation based on the likeness of the goods rather than on their declared value or identity. The similar goods method of valuation should be established by using similar goods exported to Australia at about the same time as the imported good. The similar goods used for reference must be sold to the buyer at the same or substantially the same commercial level, as well as with the same or substantially the same quantity.

5.4.4 Deductive value

If the customs value of the imported goods cannot be determined by using any of the methods above, the customs value of the goods is the deductive value of the imported goods. The deductive value is the unit price at which the imported goods—or identical or similar goods—are sold in the greatest aggregate quantity to non-related persons at the first commercial level after the importation. This means that if the prices vary depending on the quantity purchased, the operative price for valuation purposes will be determined according to the greatest number of units sold. The deductive value of the goods is a very attractive method of valuation for importers who not only sell big quantities to big purchasers at a lower price, but also sell small quantities to many purchasers to obtain a lower valuation.

5.4.5 Computed value

The computed value method has a restricted scope because it can be used only if the goods to be valued are the exporter's goods. This means that the goods must be directly exported by the producer or manufacturer, rather than through an intermediary. The essence of the restriction is to arrive at a value according to the producer's own record of the costs of production.

- The computed value criterion of valuation is the sum of the costs, charges and expenses, or the value, of the materials employed in the production of the imported goods;
- An amount for profit and general expenses, considered together as a whole, equal to that usually reflected in sales of goods of the same class or kind as the goods being valued which are made in the country of exportation; and
- Costs of insurance, handling and transportation.

The problem presented by the computed value method of valuation is that the customs authorities have to agree that the information contained in the documents concerning the production costs of the goods that are supplied by the producer are satisfactory. Further, in case the customs authorities do not accept the documentation, verification of the data has to be undertaken with the consent of the producer, as well as notice to and non-objection by the government. Once the information regarding the computed values is provided, the customs authority of the state concerned will assess two factors in order to accept the documentation:

- Whether the information supplied by the producer is consistent with the accounting principles of the country of production; and
- Whether the general expense and profit amount claimed is consistent with that reflected in sales of goods of the same class and kind.

5.4.6 Fall-back value

The fall-back value criterion of valuation will be applied when all the above methods have failed to arrive at a customs value. It requires the customs collector to go back and review all the preceding methods of valuation to arrive at an acceptable customs value.

For example, if the sale took place 47 days (rather than 45 days) away from the date of the importation of the goods, the identical value method could not be applied, even though the values used were reasonable. In this case, the sale could nevertheless be used to produce a value under the fall-back value criterion.

5.5 Conclusion

This chapter provided detailed information on Australian customs law, with the focus on the most relevant issues to international traders. The chapter first introduced the harmonised tariff system before covering three key areas: product classification, rules of origin, and valuation of the goods. It is necessary for readers to understand how goods are identified and classified for tariff purposes when they cross borders, as well as the rules of origin. It is also necessary for readers to have some understanding of how imported goods are valued by customs agencies.

The importance of customs law to the international trade of goods cannot be overstated. As this chapter demonstrates, several aspects of customs determinations and law can have significant financial and other consequences. In most cases, customs determinations and laws will determine whether the importation/exportation of goods is even financially viable. For this reason, all lawyers and business executives engaged in international business transactions should have a basic appreciation and understanding of the customs laws detailed in this chapter.

Questions[47]

With regard to the case study at the beginning of this chapter:

1 a Please advise CHOCOLATE Pty Ltd on the tariff rates for slabs of filled chocolate and unfilled chocolate.
  b Does the country of origin come into consideration when formulating your advice?
2 What is the purpose of the GRIs? How do they operate?
3 Would slabs of chocolate confectionery imported from the same source at the same time as the almond-and-hazelnut filling be identified as individual goods or unassembled entities?
4 How would the addition of a decorative, non-edible *faux* gold ornament into an slab of chocolate affect the identification of the goods for the purposes of customs law?
5 a How would the importation of chocolate slabs pre-filled with the almond-and-hazelnut filling be classified?
  b How would the importation of the slabs of chocolate be classified if they were not pre-filled?
6 a How would the almonds and hazelnuts be classified if imported separately?
  b How would the almonds and hazelnuts be classified if imported as a pre-ground mixture?
  c Would it matter if the mixture was comprised of 80 per cent almonds and 20 per cent hazelnuts?
7 a Why are rules of origins necessary? What purpose do they serve?
  b Can you explain the differences between the four different methods or criteria for determining origin?
8 How do the preferences offered to certain countries affect business decisions relating to the importation of goods?
9 Assuming that Switzerland and Ghana both supply chocolate of equal quality and price, would CHOCOLATE have a financial incentive to select the Ghanaian chocolate in preference to the Swiss chocolate?

47 Note, you may have to refer to Schedule 3 of the *Tariff Act* in order to answer some of the following questions.

10 Assuming that China, Korea and the USA all supply almonds and hazelnuts of equal quality and price, would CHOCOLATE have a financial incentive to select one country's product over the others?

11 Would CHOCOLATE have an incentive to import unshelled almonds over the shelled variety?

12 Assume that it would cost CHOCOLATE 7 per cent more to buy locally sourced almonds, hazelnuts or the pre-mixed almond or hazelnuts than to purchase them from China or Korea, and 4 per cent more than to import them from the USA. Should CHOCOLATE import the goods (and if so, from where) or source the products locally?

13 What would be the origin of the pre-mixed almond and hazelnut blend if a Chinese company ground the nuts after sourcing the almonds from the USA and the hazelnuts from Argentina?

14 Why did the tribunal in *Re Gaylor Jewellery Sales Pty Limited v Collector of Customs* decide that the goods at issue were entitled to entry at a preferential rate?

15 Why is the transaction value the preferred method of valuing the imported goods? Why can it not be used in every situation?

CHAPTER 6

import controls

Cool Breeze Ltd (CBL) is an Australian manufacturer of cotton clothing. CBL's products are of high quality and command relatively high prices.

CBL's business had been operating at a substantial profit until the last few years. More recently, CBL has experienced significant competition from overseas suppliers based in India, China and Bangladesh. CBL has seen its profits steadily erode, and last year it experienced a loss of revenue.

This year does not look any more promising. CBL suspects that its Chinese competitors may be receiving government subsidies. It believes that some of its Indian competition must be selling at a loss because their prices seem impossibly low. In addition, the competition from Bangladeshi companies has come completely out of nowhere; based on the tariffs Australia imposes on cotton clothing, CBL never anticipated such significant and serious Bangladeshi competition.

CBL wants to know what help it might be able to receive from the Australian Government. It contacts you, its lawyer, for advice.

6.1 Introduction

Any business that engages in international activity—be it importing, exporting or both—needs to be aware of the types of restrictions governments may impose upon products crossing national borders. Some of these restrictions will also be of interest to companies that conduct their business entirely domestically.

In this chapter, we discuss regulations that are imposed upon products entering into a country. These are referred to as *import controls*. The following chapter addresses *export controls*, which are regulations that affect products leaving a country.

While at first blush it might seem that import controls would be of relevance only to importers and export controls only to exporters, that is not the case. Both sets of regulations are important to importers and to exporters.

EXAMPLE: Let us consider an imaginary company, ABC Limited, which is an importer of chemicals for use in Australia, but which does not export anything. The Australian Government has the authority under certain circumstances to impose a variety of import controls on the chemicals imported by ABC Limited and its competitors. These include tariffs, complete prohibitions upon importation, and limitations placed on importation due to findings of dumping or other practices injurious to the domestic industry. ABC Limited will certainly want to be aware of these existing and potential import controls. In addition, however, ABC Limited should also be apprised of any applicable *export controls* imposed by governments of countries from which ABC Limited imports.

As will be discussed further in Chapter 7, there are numerous international agreements and conventions governing the importation and exportation of materials that may be hazardous or have military application; chemicals may fall into these categories. Export controls agreed to by Australia and other countries may therefore be relevant to ABC Limited. Similarly, if ABC Limited were an export-based business, it would need to be cognizant of Australia's export control regimes. In addition, for any country into which ABC Limited exports chemicals, it would want to know about any applicable import controls that country imposed upon the types of products ABC Limited exports. Finally, even companies with solely domestic operations may have reason to learn about import and export controls. Using the chemical company as an example again, if ABC Limited felt that foreign competition was causing it injury in the Australian market, it could consider petitioning the Australian Government to impose restrictions upon those foreign imports. Familiarity with a subset of Australia's import controls, known as trade remedies, will enable ABC Limited to make an informed decision as to whether to petition for relief, and, if so, pursuant to which of the available trade remedies. Similarly, even if ABC Limited is not exporting its chemicals, if any of the types of chemicals it produces are subject to Australia's export controls, it may have obligations to track its customers or otherwise to keep a record of who purchases its products and in what quantities.

Import and export controls are therefore something that will have relevance to a large number of businesses within any country.

In this chapter, as we focus on import controls, we will be keeping in mind that these regulations may be important for a wide range of companies.

Some of the most prevalent import controls are the *trade remedies*, alluded to in the above example. 'Trade remedies' is an umbrella term for three different potential measures a government may impose on imports. These are antidumping duties, countervailing duties and safeguard measures. In addition to trade remedies, however, there are other ways countries can restrict imports, including by imposing tariffs, quantitative restrictions and non-tariff barriers such as health and safety or technical requirements. By the end of this chapter you should have a better understanding of each of these types of import controls.

6.2 Tariffs

One way that countries have historically attempted to limit imports from other countries has been to impose import duties, more commonly referred to as tariffs, on imported products. A tariff is a tax on imports that is levied at the border. A government may wish to control the level of imports of a certain product in order to provide assistance or protection to the domestic manufacturers of like or similar products.

An additional motivation could be a desire to raise the cost for domestic consumers of purchasing 'undesirable' products, such as alcohol or cigarettes.[1]

For every business considering exporting its products, it will be important to identify any applicable tariffs that potential import markets impose on the type of product the business is selling. The level of applicable tariffs in different export markets can make the difference between an export being viable in an overseas market or not. A simple example will illustrate the point.

EXAMPLE: Assume that the Marshall Company produces ballpoint pens and manufactures them at a cost of $0.50 per pen. It then sells them in its home market of Australia for $0.55 per pen, or a 10 per cent profit.

Marshall is now considering expanding its operations into overseas markets. One potential destination for the Marshall pens is Fabercastellia, where ballpoint pens regularly sell for $0.57. Assuming Marshall can sell its pens in Fabercastellia for a cost of less than $0.57 per pen, it may make business sense to enter the Fabercastellia market. However, Marshall's cost of selling in Fabercastellia may exceed its home market cost of $0.50 due to tariffs imposed by Fabercastellia on imported pens

Let us assume that Fabercastellia imposes an *ad valorem* (assessed as a percentage of the product value) tariff on imported pens of 20 per cent. This means that the cost to Marshall (excluding transportation, shipping and other transit costs) of exporting a pen to Fabercastellia is not $0.50, but $0.60—the cost of manufacture plus the 20 per cent tariff. Unless Marshall believes it can sell its pens in Fabercastellia for more than $0.60 per pen, it will not be economically efficient to export to Fabercastellia.

Accordingly, it is imperative for an exporter of goods such as Marshall to be aware of the tariffs being levied by its potential export destinations on the types of goods—in this case, ballpoint pens—that it intends to export.

6.2.1 Determining the applicable tariff rate

As discussed in Chapter 5, the Harmonised Commodity Description and Coding System (Harmonised System, or HS) developed by the World Customs Organization (WCO) establishes classifications to the six-digit level that all countries should utilise in their tariff schedules. Individual countries may then elect to further classify items to a greater degree of specificity (for example, to the 10-digit level) to suit their own needs.[2]

While the coding to identify products subject to tariffs is therefore largely uniform, the tariffs that countries apply to given products vary widely. For example, developing countries often maintain high tariffs on a broad range of products. Developed countries on the other hand are more likely to have lower tariffs on industrial and manufactured goods, but many maintain higher tariffs on agricultural products. An exporter will need

1 Poorer countries may utilise tariffs primarily as a revenue-raising mechanism, rather than as an effort to limit imports or assist domestic producers.

2 See for example the Harmonized Tariff Schedule of the USA, which specifies tariffs at a 10-digit level of specificity.

to reference the tariff schedules for each of its would-be export markets to determine what tariff rates will apply to its goods.

One of the primary functions served by the predecessor to the World Trade Organization (WTO), the General Agreement on Tariffs and Trade (GATT),[3] was to persuade contracting parties to the agreement to convert non-tariff import barriers (such as quotas) into tariffs, and then to negotiate reciprocal commitments to lower those tariffs. Through a series of seven rounds of negotiations, the contracting parties to the GATT lowered their average industrial tariffs significantly. In addition, the GATT and now the WTO institutionalised the rule of most-favoured nation treatment (MFN), which requires WTO members to give other WTO members treatment no less favourable than that given to any other member.[4]

Accordingly, the general rule is that whatever tariff WTO member A applies on product X from WTO member B, it must apply that same rate on product X coming from other WTO members, such as C, D and E. However, there are a number of important exceptions to this general rule.

In practice, WTO members generally have several different categories of tariff rates that vary depending on the country of export.

6.2.2 Exceptions to the MFN rule

As noted above, the WTO permits members to deviate from the general principle of MFN in a number of instances. Perhaps the most important instance is where there is an applicable free trade agreement (FTA) or customs union (CU). Article XXIV of the GATT allows members to maintain customs unions or FTAs—which result in the removal of tariff barriers amongst the CU or FTA partners[5]—while maintaining external tariffs on products originating outside the CU or FTA.[6] Thus if Australia maintains an external tariff of 20 per cent on imports of leather footwear, for example, it does not

---

3 The GATT was entered into in 1947 (GATT 1947) and largely focused on, first, converting quotas and other non-tariff barriers to tariffs; second, committing to upper limits for those tariffs (referred to as *tariff bindings*); and, third, negotiating reciprocal commitments to reduce tariff levels. Over time, signatories determined that a new treaty should be entered into that would include all of the GATT commitments, but would additionally provide new disciplines on issues such as sanitary and phytosanitary measures, technical barriers to trade, trade in services and intellectual property, and would contain a new, strengthened dispute resolution process. The Uruguay Round of trade negotiations was devoted to creating and shaping this new treaty—the WTO. One of the integral parts of the WTO is GATT 1994, which comprises the provisions of GATT 1947 as amended, along with protocols, decisions and understandings relating to various provisions. Accordingly, the GATT articles remain applicable and are an important component of the WTO.

4 GATT, Article I.

5 Pursuant to Article XXIV: 8, internal barriers must be removed on 'substantially all the trade' between the CU or FTA partners. It is unclear what 'substantially all' means, however. In the only dispute to address this question, the Appellate Body merely stated that '"substantially all the trade" is not the same as all the trade, and also that "substantially all the trade" is something considerably more than merely some of the trade': see *Turkey—Restrictions on Imports of Textile and Clothing Products* (1999) WT/DS34/AB/R, AB-1999-5, para 48 (Report of the Appellate Body).

6 With the caveat that the 'duties and other regulations of commerce' applied by FTA and CU members to WTO members outside the CU or FTA 'shall not be higher or more restrictive' after the agreement takes effect than previously: GATT, Article XXIV: 5.

have to charge that tariff on leather footwear entering Australia from New Zealand, because Australia and New Zealand's trade between themselves is subject to an FTA—the Australia–New Zealand Closer Economic Relations Trade Agreement (ANZCERTA)—which provides for duty-free access for each other's products. Furthermore, pursuant to a provision known as the Enabling Clause, developed country WTO members are permitted to provide more favourable tariff treatment to developing countries than they provide to other developed countries, and to provide more favourable treatment still to least developed countries. Likewise, developing countries may reach trade agreements among themselves (subject to less stringent requirements than under Article XXIV) that result in lower tariffs being applied among the participating developing countries than are applied to other countries.[7]

Between applicable FTAs, CUs and preferential treatment given pursuant to the Enabling Clause, many developed countries give better than MFN treatment to the vast majority of their trading partners. For example, the European Communities (EC) give better than MFN treatment to incoming products from all WTO members except nine. Thus the EC only applies its MFN rates to Australia, Canada, Chinese Taipei (Taiwan), the Hong Kong Special Administrative Region of China, Japan, Korea, New Zealand, Singapore and the USA, with all other WTO members qualifying for a more favourable rate. It is for this reason that some commentators have expressed concern that MFN has become 'LFN'—the rate given to least-favoured nations.[8]

Because the applicable tariff rate may depend on the country of origin of the import, countries have national laws or regulations that establish how the customs authorities are to determine the origin of a product—in other words, from what country did the product come? This may seem like a simple process, but unfortunately for exporters it can be quite complicated. There is no single universally accepted method for determining the origin of a given product. Accordingly, rules of origin vary from country to country. It therefore can be very time-consuming and costly for exporters to satisfy the requirements of numerous different customs authorities with their different requirements.

Sometimes this process is straightforward. When the import is a primary product—for example, Australian passionfruit—or is a manufactured product that was made entirely within a given country—for example, a woollen rug made in New Zealand from New Zealand wool—the inquiry is simple. However, imagine a silk scarf shipped from Australia that was designed by an Australian designer, made from Chinese silk, loomed in India, dyed and cut in Italy, and had tassels added in Vietnam before being delivered to the Australian designer, who attaches a small designer logo. What is the origin of the scarf? Likewise some manufactured goods such as cars may contain inputs from numerous countries.

Complying with rules of origin requirements can be more expensive than it is worth. Thus some manufacturers choose to accept a higher tariff rate instead of taking the

---

7 'Differential and More Favourable Treatment Reciprocity and Fuller Participation of Developing Countries', Decision of 28 November 1979 (L/4903) ('Enabling Clause'), paras. 1 and 2.

8 'The Future of the WTO: Addressing Institutional Challenges in the New Millennium, Report of the Consultative Board to the Director-General Supachai Panitchpakdi', pp 19–21 [www.wto.org/english/thewto_e/10anniv_e/future_wto_e.pdf.].

time and effort to attempt to demonstrate their products qualify for a lower applicable rate by virtue of their country of origin.[9] What businesses engaged in exporting need to determine is:

- The applicable tariff rates their export destinations levy on the types of goods they export;
- Which category of tariff rate the exporting country falls under (for example, MFN rate, an FTA rate, etc); and
- The applicable rules of origin that the importing country applies, including what paperwork is required to demonstrate origin.

Rules of origin issues are discussed in more detail in Chapter 5.

6.3 Trade remedies

As mentioned in Section 6.1, there are three major types of trade remedies that countries employ in response to injurious competition from abroad: antidumping duties, countervailing duties and safeguards actions. Countries that are not members of the WTO may apply these remedies pursuant to their applicable domestic regulatory schemes, but WTO members are somewhat more limited in their ability to utilise trade remedies.

Because these types of measures are seen as being subject to potential protectionist abuse, there are three WTO agreements as well as various GATT articles that impose procedural and substantive disciplines on the use of antidumping duties, countervailing duties and safeguard measures. These are addressed respectively in:

- GATT, Article VI, and the Agreement on Implementation of Article VI of the General Agreement on Tariffs and Trade 1994 (the Anti-Dumping Agreement, or ADA);
- GATT, Articles VI and XVI, and the Agreement on Subsidies and Countervailing Measures (ASCM); and
- GATT, Article XIX, together with the Agreement on Safeguards.

Familiarity with the WTO rules is important because almost all of the world's major economies—including Australia and 152 other countries—are WTO members.

Antidumping duties, countervailing duties and safeguard measures are all *offensive* trade remedies; that is to say, they are measures that a government applies itself to certain imports. It is also possible to initiate *defensive* measures—by bringing a complaint before the WTO alleging the improper application of trade remedies by a fellow WTO member, or regarding a potential violation by any WTO member of the ADA, ASCM, or Agreement on Safeguards. Such challenges have constituted a significant percentage of WTO dispute settlement proceedings initiated to date.

It should also be noted that the relevant WTO agreements provide general parameters regarding the trade remedies WTO members may employ, such as notice requirements and the duration and nature of measures that may be imposed; but these

9 See for example O Cadot et al, 'Product-specific Rules of Origin in EU and US Preferential Trading Arrangements: an Assessment' (2006) 5 *World Trade Review* 199.

agreements do not mandate particular legislative provisions or terms. Therefore, each WTO member is entitled to maintain its own unique statutory provisions dictating how and when trade remedies will be applied. However, members are limited to applying the approved remedies, namely antidumping duties, countervailing duties and safeguard measures. Each of these trade remedies is discussed in turn below.

6.3.1 Antidumping duties

Dumping occurs when a company sells products abroad for less than 'normal value', which essentially means selling the product for lower prices abroad than it sells it for in its home market; or, if it does not make any sales in its home country, in a third-country market. This measure of dumping is sometimes referred to as *international price discrimination*. It is also considered dumping to sell at prices that are too low to cover the costs of producing the goods.

Dumping is treated by many countries as being 'unfair', and the WTO permits members to take measures to combat dumping where the dumping causes material injury to the domestic industry.[10] The measures that are permitted under the WTO are either to impose duties—akin to a tariff—on the imports of goods that have been found to have been dumped, or to accept a price undertaking, where an importer agrees its goods will be sold at or above certain prices.

Article 18.1 of the ADA provides: 'No specific action against dumping of exports from another Member can be taken except in accordance with the provisions of GATT 1994, as interpreted by this Agreement.' In dispute settlement proceedings, the WTO Appellate Body has confirmed that the GATT, Article VI, and the ADA, Article 18.1, preclude remedies other than those set forth in the ADA.[11]

The level of duties is not to exceed the degree of dumping, though it may be set at a lesser duty.[12] In other words, duties may be applied to offset dumping, but not to penalise it.

Although the WTO permits the imposition of antidumping duties to offset dumping, many countries would like to see antidumping laws abolished, or, barring that, significantly curtailed. Certain countries have imposed antidumping duties so frequently that this 'remedy' for dumping is seen by many as a protectionist tool that needs to be reined in.

Prior to the entry into force of the WTO, the major imposers of antidumping duties were the USA, the EC, Canada, and Australia. Since the creation of the WTO, India and South Africa have replaced Australia and Canada in the top four, with other developing countries such as Mexico, Argentina, Brazil and China also making increasing use of antidumping measures. Although there are many proposals to impose new disciplines on the use of antidumping measures, and improving antidumping disciplines

---

10 'The contracting parties recognize that dumping … is to be condemned if it causes or threatens material injury': GATT, Article VI(1).

11 *United States—Anti-Dumping Act 1916* (WT/DS136, 162/AB/R; Appellate Body report adopted 26 September 2000) (treble damages are an impermissible remedy); *United States—Continued Dumping and Subsidy Offset Act 2000* (WT/DS217, 234/AB/R; Appellate Body report adopted 27 January 2003) (paying the collected duties to the domestic industry is not permissible).

12 ADA, Article 9.1.

is an agenda item in the current round of WTO negotiations (commonly referred to as the 'Doha Round' after the place of inception of the negotiations), it is unlikely that the supporters of antidumping proceedings will agree to significant changes to the ADA.

From the standpoint of a business that has domestic and overseas markets, the regulation of dumping may seem counterintuitive, as it may be a perfectly rational economic decision to price in a manner that would be defined as dumping, particularly when there are different *elasticities of demand* in the home and overseas markets. Elasticity of demand refers to the degree to which the demand for a product will change in connection with a change in the product's price.

- When demand for a product changes significantly in response to a price change, we say that the demand for that product is *elastic*. Products for which demand might be elastic include non-essential items for which there are available substitutes. Examples could include cola drinks, which could be substituted for with other caffeinated beverages; beef, which could be substituted for with pork, lamb or chicken; or cotton clothing, which could be substituted for with synthetic materials.
- When demand remains relatively constant even when prices change, we say that demand is *inelastic*. Products for which demand might be inelastic include items that are considered staple food items, such as milk; petrol, tyres and other products necessary to keep a car running; and brand-name items with a high level of status or quality associated with the brand. For example, for customers that demand products from the exclusive jewellery store Tiffany's, it is unlikely that an increase in Tiffany's prices would lead many customers to shop elsewhere instead.

Now consider a situation where the demand for a product is high at home, but low abroad. It may be that in the home market, the producer can command a higher price because the product is more popular at home—in other words, the demand for the product is relatively inelastic. Likewise, the demand for the product is more sensitive to price changes overseas. In instances such as this, businesses may decide, reasonably, to charge different prices in different markets—charging a higher price in the market that attaches greater utility to the product (in other words, where the demand is less elastic) than it does in the market that attaches a lower utility to the product (where demand is more elastic).

EXAMPLE: In the case of New Zealand, it is easy to imagine situations where there are not many competitors in the domestic market, but there are overseas.

Consider the selling of whitegoods. In New Zealand, prices are quite high for washing machines, refrigerators and other whitegoods, compared to prices in larger developed markets such as the USA. Why is this so? Some of it is due to exchange rates, and the cost of transporting goods to New Zealand. But some of it is due to the level of competition. In the USA, there are many more brands competing in the market, leading to greater price competition. There are also higher sales volumes, which can lead to lower prices.

Assume that New Zealand has a high-end whitegoods manufacturer, Disher & Plate (D&P). D&P may be able to charge quite high prices in New Zealand; as it is the only brand manufactured in the country, consumers may be willing to pay more for that particular brand name. Moreover, because it is such a small market, many manufacturers may choose not to try to sell in New Zealand, because the costs of operating in a new country are high and the potential rewards in a small market are limited. Thus D&P may face little or no competition for the high-end whitegoods market in New Zealand. This means D&P probably experiences relatively inelastic demand in its home market, meaning it can charge relatively high prices without worrying too much about losing customers.

Now think about what it might be like when D&P sells in an overseas market such as the USA. The USA has a lot of consumers, but also a wide variety of product options. There are many brands of whitegoods available, both domestic and brands from Europe and Asia. So D&P would face more competition in the US market and may decide therefore to charge lower prices in the USA in order to compete. This would make complete sense as a business matter, and D&P might well be making a profit in both places—just a higher one in New Zealand. But if D&P actually did price its whitegoods at lower prices in the USA than New Zealand, it would be dumping.

Does the example above make any economic sense? Not really. Thus one of the most important things for businesses to realise with respect to the regulation of dumping is that the regulations do not exist out of a desire to enhance economic efficiency. Instead, dumping laws reflect national regulatory decisions to protect producers in certain circumstances, even though so doing arguably will be at the expense of consumers (who will be deprived of the lower prices foreign exporters might otherwise charge them).

On the other hand, consider the following scenario.

EXAMPLE: Imagine that a producer is able to charge high prices at home because its government has erected trade barriers to keep out foreign competition. Then imagine that the producer floods one or more overseas markets with sales made at heavily discounted prices—or even at a loss—in order to increase its share in foreign markets. The producer uses the monopoly profits from its home market sales to subsidise the losses overseas, with the goal of driving other producers out of the foreign markets, at which point it would then be able to raise prices substantially as it would be the monopoly supplier in its home and export markets.

Would this predatory pricing be fair? Most think not. Some commentators defend the necessity of antidumping laws to deter this sort of predatory conduct. Over the past several decades, Japan has been subject to intermittent criticism (much of it from the USA) for its regulatory practices, which some believe protect Japanese producers from foreign competition and do not sufficiently deter anticompetitive conduct. Economists, however, tend to believe the need for antidumping laws is significantly overstated.

There are few markets where predatory conduct could succeed long-term. In most cases, once the producer raised its prices to monopoly levels, new entrants would join the market selling at lower prices; and for the industries where predatory conduct could theoretically succeed—primarily those with very high barriers to entry—economists argue that antitrust or competition laws adequately regulate against this risk.

In addition to the price discrimination context discussed in the above example, dumping may also be found where sales are made at below the cost of production. At first blush it may seem reasonable to allow countries to impose duties on foreign sales that are sold at a loss. However, as an economic proposition this also proves to be problematic.

From the standpoint of a business, it is rational to sell where marginal revenue is equal to or greater than marginal cost of a given unit. This means the incremental amount of money made on a given sale is greater than or equal to the incremental cost of a given sale. An example may assist in understanding this concept.

EXAMPLE: Imagine a factory that produces television sets. There are fixed costs associated with running the factory such as rent, debt repayment, and other expenses that are incurred no matter how many or how few television sets are produced. There are also variable costs, which as the name implies, vary depending on the number of units produced. For example, the factory's costs for raw materials will increase as it produces more television sets, and decrease if it produces fewer. *Marginal costs* are the incremental costs of producing each additional television set. *Variable costs* are the sum of all the marginal costs.

As a long-term proposition, a business will need to earn enough money to cover all of its costs—enough to pay to keep the factory running, pay the workers, and make the televisions. However, in the short term, when the company is deciding prices, it is economic good sense to make any given sale so long as the marginal revenue for that television is higher than the marginal cost to make that unit. If it costs more to make a TV than one would get paid for it, the company will stop producing. But so long as *long-term* the company can cover all of its fixed and variable costs, it is rational to make *short-term* sales that do not cover all costs, so long as they cover marginal costs. Therefore, some sales at below cost—meaning below total cost, factoring in all fixed costs of production—would be rational for a business to make.

It might similarly be rational business practice to sell at a loss in other contexts. For example, a new company—or an existing one introducing a new product—might be willing to sell at a short-term loss to gain market entry. We see this in the domestic context quite frequently; businesses will offer low introductory prices and then raise them later once consumers have had the opportunity to try the product and become familiar with it.

Another context in which sales might rationally be made at a loss is that of perishable agricultural products.

EXAMPLE: Assume that, taking into account fixed and variable costs over the course of a growing season, the average cost of producing a box of tomatoes is $4, and the marginal cost of producing an additional box—that is, the costs incurred to pick and pack the tomatoes—is $2.

In general, to remain afloat over time the farm will need to sell its tomatoes for an average price in excess of $4 per box. However, at certain times of the season prices will be much higher than $4 due to high demand, while at other times, prices will be lower than $4 due to excess supply on the market. In the latter situation it is rational to sell at below $4 so long as the marginal costs are covered; that is, if a box is sold for $2 or more. However, if the farmer must pay $2 to get the tomatoes picked and packed, it is not worth it to pay that $2 for a return of less than $2. If the tomatoes could only be sold for $1.50 per box, for example, the farmer would incur a smaller loss by letting the tomatoes rot on the vine than by selling them. On the other hand, if the tomatoes can be sold for more than $2 but less than $4, it would be rational to make such sales because marginal costs are being covered. As a business matter this is preferable to letting the tomatoes rot and making no sales.

We have seen several examples of sales that are economically rational even though they are made at less than normal value or below cost. Yet each of these circumstances could be deemed to be dumping, and antidumping duties could be imposed if the sales caused material injury in the destination overseas market. Business instincts alone are thus insufficient to ensure a company will not become subject to an antidumping investigation. Instead, exporting companies need to be aware of what can constitute dumping so that they can set their prices with the common dumping rules in mind.

6.3.1a How is dumping regulated?

The WTO does not prohibit dumping, but does permit members to conduct antidumping investigations and to impose antidumping duties subject to certain elaborated parameters. Within the WTO, antidumping is regulated by the GATT, Article VI, and by the ADA. The WTO also imposes reporting obligations on members. In particular, members must notify the Committee on Anti-dumping Practices (ADP Committee)[13] of their laws and regulations pertaining to antidumping, and identify what agency or agencies have the authority to conduct antidumping investigations.[14]

Members must also notify the ADP Committee twice annually of any new antidumping measures imposed, as well as any already in force.[15] In terms of investigations, in general members must make three findings before dumping duties may be imposed:

- First, it must be established that the imported product is being dumped in the investigating country's market;
- Second, the domestic industry must demonstrate that it is suffering material injury or is likely about to suffer material injury (referred to as 'threat' of injury'); and
- Third, the domestic industry must show *causation*, meaning that the injury it is suffering is due to the imports rather than to another cause.

The term 'dumping' is, therefore, shorthand for the situation where a product is sold more cheaply overseas or for less than the cost of production, and these sales cause material injury to the domestic industry producing a like product.

In most countries, each of these determinations is made by government agencies or departments that report to an ultimate political authority. For example, in Australia the Australian Customs Service undertakes each analysis. The most notable exceptions to this practice are the USA, Canada and Argentina.[16] In the USA, for example, the determination of dumping (and, if relevant, causation) is made by the Department of Commerce, which is an agency that reports to the executive branch (the President). However, the injury determination is made by the International Trade Commission, which is an independent agency that does not report to the President. It is thought that decisions made by independent agencies may be less susceptible to political influence

13 ADA, Article. 18.5.

14 ADA, Article 16.5.

15 ADA, Article 16.4.

16 GN Horlick & PA Clarke, 'Standards for Panels Reviewing Antidumping Determinations under the GATT and WTO', in E-U Petersmann (ed), *The GATT/WTO Dispute Settlement System: International Law, International Organizations, and Dispute Settlement*, Kluwer, London & Boston, 1997, p 317.

than decisions made wholly by agencies or departments that fall under the jurisdiction of a political entity. That said, the US system is often criticised for the results it reaches, so partial independence alone is no guarantee that political considerations will not play, or be perceived to play, a role. In Australia there is an element of independent review available in the form of an appeal from certain decisions to the Trade Measures Review Officer (TMRO). The TMRO is an independent appeals body that is part of the Attorney-General's Department.

Businesses that export should take care to avoid becoming subject to antidumping investigations. Even if a company is not engaged in dumping and a negative determination is reached for that company, going through all the steps of an antidumping proceeding can be very costly and time-consuming:

- There are generally very tight deadlines within which to provide information to the investigating agency or agencies.
- The investigating authorities often require data to be presented in a format different from that used by companies in their ordinary course of business. Thus responding properly generally requires the generation of new documents, rather than merely copying existing files.
- The investigating authorities often elect to *verify* the information that the foreign respondent companies have submitted. The verification is usually in the form of an in-person audit, with one or more representatives from the investigating agency travelling to the respondent company to look at the company's sales and cost records. To prepare adequately for this process, companies frequently have legal counsel and/or international trade consultants assist them in collecting the data to support the information submitted to the authorities. There is thus often a period of multiple weeks during which preparations and the verification occur. Companies then have to make their key officers available to meet with the investigating officials. The entire process can be highly disruptive to the day-to-day operations of a business.

Even with best efforts, companies may nonetheless find themselves subject to an antidumping investigation. While there are guidelines within the ADA, and domestic statutes that require domestic industries to make certain showings before a dumping investigation will be initiated, these are not overly onerous thresholds. Investigations generally encapsulate all of the major producers of a given like product within a country (cases are generally styled as 'Product X from country Y'; for example, 'Canned peaches from South Africa') rather than being limited to a particular supplier. As a result, companies that are not engaging in dumping may still need to respond to investigations. Failure to respond can result in the investigating agency utilising facts supplied by the petitioning industry,[17] which almost always results in higher antidumping margins for a company than it would have achieved had it cooperated with the investigation.

---

17 ADA, Article 6.8 provides: 'In cases in which any interested party refuses access to, or otherwise does not provide, necessary information within a reasonable period or significantly impedes the investigation, preliminary and final determinations, affirmative or negative, may be made on the basis of the facts available.'

With these costly proceedings sometimes unavoidable, what can companies do to minimise their risk of having duties imposed?

- First, businesses should understand what 'dumping' means and how it is regulated in their export markets.
- Second, they should develop pricing policies with due regard to the possibility of antidumping investigations.
- Third, they should take care to keep meticulous accounting records and documentation relating to all sales. When investigating authorities determine that corporate records are inadequate to permit verification of data submitted, that data may be rejected, which can in turn lead to a finding of dumping and ultimately imposition of duties. Furthermore, some of this information can be useful in defending against a claim of injury. For example, if a company has correspondence from its customers that makes it clear the company's product was selected on the basis of unique, non-price-related features, this may help refute the domestic industry's argument that it has lost sales due to the low prices of foreign competition.

On the flip side, companies facing foreign competition should be aware of the existence of trade remedies provisions in their countries' domestic laws and their potential to invoke them. Complaints of dumping must be made 'by or on behalf of the domestic industry'[18] to remove the potential for a non-representative and/or small segment of the industry to initiate proceedings. When the producers of over half of the output of the like product have joined the petition, this standard is automatically met, and in no circumstances are investigations to be initiated where there is less than 25 per cent industry support.[19] The domestic producers will generally need to allege dumping of a like product, injury and causation in order to trigger the initiation of an investigation.[20]

6.3.2 Countervailing duties

Countervailing duties (CVDs) are imposed in much the same fashion as antidumping duties; in particular, the investigatory process requires an injury determination that is much the same as that made in antidumping investigations. However, instead of serving as a remedy to counteract dumping, CVDs are used to counteract the effect of government subsidies.

The concept is that when a government provides aid to a company, that company has been given an advantage that may favourably skew its ability to compete in overseas markets. Importing governments may therefore, if certain circumstances are satisfied, impose a CVD on products that have been subsidised. The idea is to impose a duty that will offset the amount of the subsidy received, thus negating its effect in the export market.

18 ADA, Article 5.4.

19 Ibid.

20 It is generally possible, though not common, for investigating authorities to initiate investigations of their own accord (that is, to self-initiate without a petition being filed).

Domestic CVD regulations must be consistent with the ASCM. Accordingly, we look to that agreement for some key definitions.

Article 1: Definition of a Subsidy

1.1 For the purpose of this Agreement, a subsidy shall be deemed to exist if:

(a) (1) there is a financial contribution by a government or any public body within the territory of a Member (referred to in this Agreement as 'government'), ie where:

- (i) a government practice involves a direct transfer of funds (eg grants, loans, and equity infusion), potential direct transfers of funds or liabilities (eg loan guarantees);
- (ii) government revenue that is otherwise due is foregone or not collected (eg fiscal incentives such as tax credits);[21]
- (iii) a government provides goods or services other than general infrastructure, or purchases goods;
- (iv) a government makes payments to a funding mechanism, or entrusts or directs a private body to carry out one or more of the type of functions illustrated in (i) to (iii) above which would normally be vested in the government and the practice, in no real sense, differs from practices normally followed by governments; or

(a) (2) there is any form of income or price support in the sense of Article XVI of GATT 1994; and

(b) a benefit is thereby conferred.

Thus a subsidy can come in the form of a payment or price support from the government, but it can also constitute the government forgoing a payment in a way that gives a benefit.

In theory, this could apply to quite a lot. Governments often apply tax credits or give financial incentives to businesses to operate in certain regions or for research and development. However, not all such actions are subject to the WTO's subsidies disciplines. Subsidies are only subject to discipline if they are sufficiently specific.[22] The idea is that subsidies which are targeted are more likely to benefit the recipients' ability to compete, and therefore have the potential to distort comparative advantage. In contrast, if a government confers a benefit on all citizens—perhaps in the form of a $100 tax credit to each individual—this would not be likely to alter trading patterns and thus is not of particular concern as being potentially 'unfair'. A subsidy such as the latter would not be classified as a specific subsidy because of its extremely broad application. The ASCM defines specificity as follows (internal references and footnotes omitted):

21 'In accordance with the provisions of Article XVI of GATT 1994 (Note to Article XVI) and the provisions of Annexes I through III of this Agreement, the exemption of an exported product from duties or taxes borne by the like product when destined for domestic consumption, or the remission of such duties or taxes in amounts not in excess of those which have accrued, shall not be deemed to be a subsidy.'

22 ASCM, Article 1.2.

Article 2: Specificity

2.1 In order to determine whether a subsidy, as defined in paragraph 1 of Article 1, is specific to an enterprise or industry or group of enterprises or industries (referred to in this Agreement as 'certain enterprises') within the jurisdiction of the granting authority, the following principles shall apply:

(a) Where the granting authority, or the legislation pursuant to which the granting authority operates, explicitly limits access to a subsidy to certain enterprises, such subsidy shall be specific.

(b) Where the granting authority, or the legislation pursuant to which the granting authority operates, establishes objective criteria or conditions governing the eligibility for, and the amount of, a subsidy, specificity shall not exist, provided that the eligibility is automatic and that such criteria and conditions are strictly adhered to. The criteria or conditions must be clearly spelled out in law, regulation, or other official document, so as to be capable of verification.

(c) If, notwithstanding any appearance of non-specificity resulting from the application of the principles laid down in subparagraphs (a) and (b), there are reasons to believe that the subsidy may in fact be specific, other factors may be considered. Such factors are: use of a subsidy programme by a limited number of certain enterprises, predominant use by certain enterprises, the granting of disproportionately large amounts of subsidy to certain enterprises, and the manner in which discretion has been exercised by the granting authority in the decision to grant a subsidy. In applying this subparagraph, account shall be taken of the extent of diversification of economic activities within the jurisdiction of the granting authority, as well as of the length of time during which the subsidy programme has been in operation.

2.2 A subsidy which is limited to certain enterprises located within a designated geographical region within the jurisdiction of the granting authority shall be specific. It is understood that the setting or change of generally applicable tax rates by all levels of government entitled to do so shall not be deemed to be a specific subsidy for the purposes of this Agreement.

2.3 Any subsidy falling under the provisions of Article 3 shall be deemed to be specific.[23]

2.4 Any determination of specificity under the provisions of this Article shall be clearly substantiated on the basis of positive evidence.

Thus we can see that the more targeted a subsidy is, the more likely it will be deemed 'specific' under the ASCM.

Within the category of specific subsidies, the ASCM goes on to further identify which subsidies may be subject to discipline. In particular, certain types of subsidies are called 'red light' subsidies and are prohibited, and others are identified as 'yellow light' subsidies, which while not prohibited are actionable. In addition, there used to be a 'green light' category of subsidies, which were explicitly identified as being permissible. Subsidies that fell into this category were[24]:

- Subsidies for certain types of R&D;
- Government assistance to promote regional development in areas with high unemployment or low income relative to the rest of the country; and
- One-time payments to help companies meet new environmental standards requirements.

23 Subsidies falling under Article 3 are the 'red light' category of prohibited subsidies, discussed below.

24 ASCM, Article 8.

The green light category of non-actionable subsidies lapsed, pursuant to Article 31 of the ASCM, five years after the WTO entered into force. However the red and yellow light categories remain in force, and are discussed in more detail below.

6.3.2a The red light category

The red light category of prohibited subsidies is quite narrow, only covering two types of subsidies:[25]

1 Subsidies contingent on export performance; and
2 Import substitution subsidies, which are conditioned upon the use of domestic content.

These two types of subsidies are prohibited because they are seen as being the most trade distorting and the least justifiable as a tool of domestic policy. It bears noting however that least developed countries are exempted from the first of these prohibitions and can still give export subsidies.[26]

Members are not permitted to grant red light subsidies[27] and the prohibition on subsidies contingent on export performance extends both to *de jure* and *de facto* contingencies.[28] If a WTO member believes another member is granting a prohibited subsidy, it can request consultations with that member.[29] Failing resolution via consultation, it can challenge a red light subsidy by bringing an expedited dispute settlement proceeding.[30] If the complaining member succeeds in demonstrating that a red light subsidy is being given, there is no need for the complaining party to demonstrate injury and the subsidy must be withdrawn 'without delay'.[31] Alternatively, the member could elect to respond to the subsidy through domestic action rather than through WTO dispute resolution. If it chooses this route it would conduct a domestic investigation, which requires findings of subsidisation, injury, and causation. If affirmative findings are made, the member can then impose a CVD on the subsidised product.

The Agreement on Agriculture provides somewhat different disciplines on agricultural subsidies. Some export subsidies on agricultural products are currently

---

25 ASCM, Article 3.1. It should be noted that pursuant to the provisions of the Agreement on Agriculture, agricultural export subsidies are not currently prohibited. If the Doha Round is concluded, however, it is anticipated that agricultural export subsidies will be phased out and ultimately eliminated. Member countries have already agreed in principle to this; but as long as the Doha Round remains a 'single undertaking' there will be no binding commitment to phase out export subsidies until the entire round is concluded.

26 ASCM, Article 27.2 and Annex VII. This exception also applies to certain developing countries so long as their GDPs remain under $1000 per annum, ibid. There was initially an exemption for other developing countries from the first category, and for least developed countries and developing countries from the second; however these exemptions were phased out pursuant to ASCM, Article 27.2(b) and 27.3.

27 ASCM, Article 3.2.

28 *Canada—Measures Affecting the Export of Civilian Aircraft*, WT/DS70/AB/R, para 167 (Appellate Body report, 23 July 1999).

29 ASCM, Article 4.1.

30 ASCM, Article 4.4.

31 The dispute settlement panel identifies the timeframe in which this is expected to happen: ASCM, Article 4.7.

permitted. However, agricultural export subsidies that are 'contingent upon export performance' violate Article 3.1(a) of the ASCM and are prohibited. Export subsidies that fall within the commitment levels established pursuant to the Agreement on Agriculture, however, are deemed not to violate the ASCM.[32]

6.3.2b The yellow light category

The yellow light category is less well-defined and is where most of the WTO dispute settlement cases involving subsidies arise. This category of subsidies is what is called 'actionable', meaning that the subsidies are not prohibited, but if certain circumstances are established, affected members may take actions against them. As will be explained in more detail below, the actions that may be taken are either bringing a WTO complaint or initiating domestic CVD proceedings.

In order for a subsidy to be considered 'actionable' it must be causing 'adverse effects to the interests of other members'. Adverse effects include[33]:

(a) injury to the domestic industry of another Member;
(b) nullification or impairment of benefits accruing directly or indirectly to other Members under GATT 1994 in particular the benefits of concessions bound under Article II of GATT 1994;
(c) serious prejudice to the interests of another Member.

The injury standard is the same as that applicable in antidumping investigations, namely whether the domestic industry has suffered material injury or if there is an imminent threat of material injury.

Nullification or impairment of benefits accruing under GATT 1994 refers, among other fact scenarios, to the situation whereby members have negotiated and agreed to lower their tariffs to certain rates, a situation that then gives members expected increased access into other markets; but the provision of a subsidy by one member alters another member's market penetration expectations.

'Serious prejudice' may arise where one or more of the following applies[34]:

(a) the effect of the subsidy is to displace or impede the imports of a like product of another Member into the market of the subsidizing Member;
(b) the effect of the subsidy is to displace or impede the exports of a like product of another Member from a third country market;
(c) the effect of the subsidy is a significant price undercutting by the subsidized product as compared with the price of a like product of another Member in the same market or significant price suppression, price depression or lost sales in the same market;
(d) the effect of the subsidy is an increase in the world market share of the subsidizing Member in a particular subsidized primary product or commodity as compared to the average share it had during the previous period of three years and this increase follows a consistent trend over a period when subsidies have been granted.

---

32 For further discussion on subsidies under the Agreement on Agriculture, see S Lester and B Mercurio, *World Trade Law: Text, Materials and Commentary*, Hart, Oxford & Portland, 2008, pp 450–2.

33 ASCM, Article 5.

34 ASCM, Article 6.3.

In the context of an actionable subsidy, the affected WTO member has the choice of undertaking a domestic investigation or obtaining a remedy through the WTO dispute settlement process. While both processes—domestic investigation and WTO dispute settlement proceeding—can be initiated, only one remedy may be implemented.[35] If a member elects to conduct a domestic investigation, upon an affirmative finding of subsidisation, injury and causation it is permitted to impose a CVD on the subsidised product. CVD investigations and the imposition of duties by WTO members must be in accordance with the provisions of the ASCM and the GATT, Article VI.[36] As with antidumping, these provisions set parameters within which domestic regulatory schemes must fall, but do not prescribe a single acceptable method for conducting investigations. Also similar to the antidumping framework, CVDs may only be imposed at a level no higher than the amount of the subsidy.[37]

It is also possible, following an affirmative preliminary finding of subsidisation and injury, to enter into an undertaking with the subsidising government that it will eliminate or curtail the subsidy, or with the exporter that it will raise its prices so as to eliminate the injurious effects of the subsidy it is receiving.[38]

In general, countries usually address actionable subsidies by doing nothing or by utilising their domestic investigation process, rather than by initiating WTO dispute settlement. There are a number of reasons why this may be the case:

- First, members might prefer to impose CVDs because it is more protectionist; it provides more direct protection from competition to impose a CVD—which will impede the ability of the subsidised imports to compete in the domestic market—than does having the subsidy removed.
- In addition, bringing WTO disputes is costly; and it can take upwards of a year or longer before a final decision is reached, and longer still before the offending country has to bring its measures into conformity. It is comparatively quick and inexpensive for a government to conduct a domestic investigation, most of the costs of which are borne by the private parties involved.
- Finally, domestic investigations are less politically visible and therefore do not involve as much of a potential strain on the relations between the governments involved.

On the flip side, however, there are reasons why in some circumstances members might prefer to initiate WTO proceedings. One potential motivation could be that, as a matter of principle, a member might prefer to respond to a protectionist measure by having that measure removed rather than by imposing a further protectionist measure. In addition, the WTO may be a better forum if a member wishes to raise the profile of the issue to apply pressure on the subsidising member. This was likely part of the motivation for the USA and the EC to bring to the WTO their claims against one another relating to airline subsidisation.[39] Furthermore, when member A's subsidy is affecting member B

---

35 ASCM, note 35.

36 ASCM, Article 10.

37 ASCM, Article 19.4.

38 ASCM, Article 18.

39 *European Communities—Measures Affecting Trade in Large Civil Aircraft* (DS316); *United States—Measures Affecting Trade in Large Civil Aircraft* (second complaint) (WT/DS316).

suppliers' ability to compete within member A suppliers in the third country market of member C, member B would not address the problem by imposing a CVD on imports into member B. Instead member B may seek to bring a WTO complaint with the goal of having the subsidy withdrawn or the adverse effects thereof removed.

In addition to the possibility of initiating WTO dispute settlement offensively, for purposes of having a prohibited or actionable subsidy removed, a member may also utilise the WTO dispute settlement system defensively. If member A conducts an investigation and imposes CVDs on products from member B, member B may initiate dispute settlement proceedings against member A if it believes member A's investigation and/or imposition of duties was inconsistent with provisions of the ASCM or other WTO obligations. As noted above, the green light category of subsidies ceased to be non-actionable on 31 December 1999. However, developing countries have sought to revisit the issue and the possibility of certain allowable subsidies (in effect revisiting the expired Article 8) is one of the agenda items in the current Doha Round of WTO negotiations.[40] In the interim, members have agreed to 'exercise due restraint' in challenging these types of subsidies.[41]

As with the imposition of antidumping duties, the use of CVDs to counteract subsidies is the subject of controversy. While subsidies to producers may give them a leg-up in a foreign market, this is not unambiguously a negative. To be sure, subsidies help foreign producers. But they also help domestic consumers—both end-users and domestic producers that use the subsidised imported product as an input. Thus it is sometimes said that governments should thank foreign countries for subsidising, not try to stop or counteract such activity.

The following extract critiques some of the rationales for CVD laws.

Michael J Trebilcock and Robert Howse, *The Regulation of International Trade*, 2nd ed, Routledge, London, 1999, pp 213–17

Efficiency rationales

The traditional argument for countervailing duties is that subsidies distort comparative advantage and hence lead to the inefficient allocation of global economic resources. While this may often be true, a plausible characterization of many subsidies is that they correct or compensate for market imperfections or externalities that would otherwise exist, and thus enhance efficient resource allocation. In many cases subsidies serve to produce 'a more efficient resource allocation, that is, resource allocation more consonant with the actual production possibilities and consumer preferences than that yielded by wholly private transactions'. The task of evaluating whether subsidies contribute to or derogate from efficient resource allocation is daunting. According to Schwartz and Harper, the exercise is at best highly indeterminate because of three factors: (a) the pervasiveness of externalities which subsidies help internalize; (b) what the authors rather opaquely call potential private-public intersectorial economies, which embrace the collective validation of

40 Implementation-related Issues and Concerns Decision of 14 November 2001, WT/MIN(01)/17 20 November 2001, para 10.2.

41 Ibid.

all kinds of preferences that may not be adequately captured in private market transactions (eg protection of national security, preserving the family farm and rural lifestyles, promoting regional development, etc); and (c) the possibility that a positive government benefit to a firm may be designed to offset some other burden that has been imposed by government (eg high minimum wage laws, stringent occupational health and safety requirements, plant closing or environmental obligations).

Even if subsidies are truly distortive of international trade, the question that remains is whether countervailing duty laws improve resource allocation ... it has now been convincingly demonstrated that in almost every conceivable set of circumstances, countervailing duties reduce domestic social welfare in the *importing* country, where social welfare is defined as the maximization of producer, consumer and government surplus. Gains to domestic producers from the higher prices induced by the duties are offset by losses to consumers who remain in the market and pay the higher prices, while some consumers who would have purchased the product are priced out of the market and suffer welfare losses. Even accounting for the increase in government surplus in terms of increased revenue from duties, consumer losses outweigh all gains, leaving total welfare lower. Thus however ambiguous the welfare effect of a subsidy either in the country providing it or globally, there is nothing ambiguous about the welfare effects of the subsidy in the importing country. This analysis suggests that rather than condemning foreign subsidies, importing countries should send expressions of their gratitude to the subsidizing country, noting only their regret that the subsidies are not larger and timeless.

A further efficiency argument that is sometimes directed against subsidies is that government support in the form of export subsidies is intended or at least serves to assist firms in practising predatory pricing. It is argued that subsidies may enable a firm to sell at a lower price in the foreign market in order to eliminate competition and thereafter reap monopoly profits. Predation nationally or internationally is a practice that unambiguously lowers economic welfare. However ... there is little theoretical or empirical basis for allegations of predation in international trade. Moreover, current countervailing duty laws do not consider factors that would support a claim of predation, such as industry concentration and barriers to entry. As in the case of antidumping, concerns over predation (potentially a valid reason for the prevention of some forms of subsidization) do not justify existing countervailing duty laws.

Fairness rationales

THE LEVEL PLAYING FIELD RATIONALE

Some advocates of countervailing duties argue that subsidies constitute unfair trade and disturb the 'level-playing field' in international trade. Professor Robert Hudec, a distinguished international trade scholar, provides a useful taxonomy of many of the unfair trade claims that presently enjoy wide currency. He draws a basic distinction between what he calls offensive 'unfairness' and defensive 'unfairness'. With respect to offensive unfairness, the claim is often made that domestic policies adopted by governments in exporters' countries of origin provide them with unfair advantages in competing in importing country markets or in third-country markets. With respect to defensive unfairness, the claim is often made that a country has adopted domestic policies that unfairly favour its own products and unfairly penalize foreign producers who wish to sell into this country's market.

In the case of countervailing duty laws, the complaint of offensive unfairness focuses on the fact that foreign firms are able to out-compete domestic firms in the latter's market as a result of some artificial advantage that the foreign firms enjoy by virtue of government subsidies or other benefits conferred on them in their country of origin. This unfairness claim is difficult both to unravel and to contain. At one level, even in the case of an explicit export subsidy, one can reasonably argue that, as suggested above, consumers in the export market are better off as a result of the foreign subsidy and that it should be viewed as a form of foreign aid that on balance increases the welfare of citizens in the importing country. At another level, the claim of unfairness relating to foreign governments' actions has no natural limits to it. Unless one is prepared to adopt a *laissez-faire* baseline as one's normative reference point, and to view every government deviation from this baseline as a form of unfairness where it has some impact on the pattern of international trade, one is quickly forced to accept that almost everything that modern governments do is likely, either directly or indirectly, to affect the pattern of economic activities within a country and therefore, by extension, the pattern of international trade flows to which that country contributes. For example, such basic activities of governments as investments in physical infrastructure, eg roads and communications systems, investments in public education and basic research, investments in health care systems, etc all shape in one way or another a country's comparative advantages or disadvantages in international trade.

According to liberal trade theory, only if differing productive conditions exist across countries can gains be derived from international trade; countries will specialize in the production of the goods that they can produce relatively cheaply, and purchase from abroad, at lower cost, goods in which they have a comparative disadvantage. If all countries were to have identical productive conditions, then no country would have a comparative advantage in the production of any good and there would be no gains from trade. Thus, if subsidies disturb the 'level playing field' they serve to increase potential gains from trade. It is at least arguable that differing subsidization policies across countries, like different education levels or different tax structures, are simply one of the factors that contribute to different productive conditions across countries. Moreover, it is to point out the obvious that, given an assumption of scarce resources, a country that chooses to subsidize one set of activities cannot subsidize another set of activities, which some of its trading partners may, as a matter of domestic policy priorities, choose to subsidize instead.

In recent debates where these kinds of claims of offensive unfairness are made, three new areas have emerged. First, it is sometimes argued that the quiescent state of Japanese competition/antitrust law permits Japanese firms, through acquisition of dominant market positions or through collusive arrangements in Japan, to garner supra-national profits in the Japanese market and to use these to fund subsequent aggressive export initiatives. Second, it is widely claimed that lax environmental laws in many countries constitute a form of implicit subsidy that confer on firms originating in these countries an artificial advantage in export markets. Third, it is often argued that weak labour laws pertaining to such matters as minimum wages, hours of work, child labour, workplace safety conditions, again operate as implicit subsidies to firms located in countries with such policies and confer on them an artificial advantage in export markets. In all three cases, the policy choices for governments in importing countries are either to attempt to persuade or induce the country of origin to harmonize its laws up to the standards of those prevailing in the exporting country; or to harmonize to some agreed intermediate solution; or to impose unilaterally some border measure, like a countervailing duty, designed to neutralize whatever artificial advantages are claimed to be associated with these domestic policy differences.

As Bhagwati points out, fairness arguments can be pushed to almost any lengths:

> If Bangladesh has a current comparative advantage in textiles, due to lower wages, we no longer need to worry about being scolded as protectionists when we reject imports of Bangladeshi textiles as unfair trade caused by her 'pauper labour'. After all, the low Bangladeshi wages are a result of

> inadequate population control *policies* and of inefficient economic policies that inhibit investment and growth and hence a rise in real wages. In like manner, if the United States continues to produce textiles, which rely heavily on immigrant labor, often illegal, this is unfair trade since American immigration *policy* encourages this outcome, and therefore a Structural Impediments Initiative demand for changed immigration policy needs to be made against the United States to ensure level playing fields.

This is not to argue that claims of unfairness have no role at all in international trade law. Debates within the European Union over a Social Protocol and the negotiation of side accords to the North American Free Trade Agreement (NAFTA) on labour and environmental standards highlight the importance that these issues have assumed.

...

Unfair impact rationales

Even if there were no efficiency or fair trade rationales that justify countervailing duty laws, there are possible arguments for countervailing duty laws that take account of the disruptive impact of imports on vulnerable members of society. In particular, it may be that distributive justice or communitarian values can be vindicated through the use of this form of protectionism. On distributive justice grounds, countervailing duty laws might be justifiable to the extent that they improve the lot of the least-advantaged members of society. However, countervailing duty laws are not designed to address these concerns ... the application of countervailing duties focuses on factors ill-suited to uncovering any injury suffered by an industry as a result of foreign subsidies and factors even less well-suited to discovering the impact on the least-advantaged stakeholders in these industries. In addition ... it is clear that in practice distributive justice concerns have not been addressed through antidumping cases; it is unlikely that the evidence is any different for countervailing duty cases. Moreover, there is no principled reason to treat some of the least advantaged as more deserving of protection because the threat to their welfare derives from subsidized imports rather than unsubsidized imports, domestic competition, or other internal factors.

Similarly, the vindication of communitarian values would require that policies be adopted that prevent the disruption of long-standing communities. However, countervailing duty laws are also poorly suited to the achievement of this end. Current formulations of the injury test inquire into the adverse effects on the domestic industry without investigating whether these impacts are being sustained by dependent communities. Finally, it must be emphasized that, in general, protectionist trade remedies such as countervailing duties are not the most appropriate policy instruments for vindicating these values. Instead ... labour adjustment assistance programmes, or short-term safeguard relief where appropriate, more directly and effectively address transition costs suffered by workers.

... ...

Whatever one thinks about the desirability of countervailing duty laws, it is important for businesses to be aware of the general practice of countervailing subsidies. Businesses that are considering seeking government aid should keep in mind that certain types of assistance could constitute a subsidy under the SCM Agreement. A company that is receiving such aid could therefore find its exports being the subject of domestic countervailing duty investigations and perhaps have countervailing duties imposed on the exports. Alternatively, the importing country or countries might initiate a WTO dispute settlement proceeding. If the complainants prevailed, the subsidy would have to be removed. On the flip side, businesses that face foreign competition in their domestic markets should know about countervailing measures as well. If foreign competitors are receiving government subsidies and the domestic industry believes it is being injured as a result, it may wish to petition the government to initiate a countervailing duty investigation. Finally, if a company is subject to a countervailing duty proceeding in another country, it should notify its government if it believes the foreign investigation has been conducted in any way inconsistent with the provisions of the SCM Agreement.

6.3.3 Safeguard measures

The third and final type of trade remedy that WTO members can employ is safeguard measures. As we have seen, both dumping and countervailable subsidies are viewed by some as being unfair. In the case of dumping, it is argued that products that are sold too cheaply in an overseas market are harming the manufacturers in that overseas market, and that this way of selling is unfair. Likewise, the rationale for allowing CVDs to be imposed is that it is unfair to give a subsidy if that subsidy is specific and thereby, by being sold in an overseas market, causes harm to the industry selling the like product in the overseas market. Antidumping duties and CVDs are accordingly often referred to as 'unfair trade remedies'.

Safeguard measures are different because there is no allegation that the imports at issue are in any way unfair. With safeguards, there is no attempt to justify their use on the basis that the imports coming in have been sold too cheaply, or have been unfairly subsidised, or have in any other way been introduced into the market in an improper way. Yet it is nonetheless possible for a country to apply a safeguard measure to protect an industry against competition from imports. Because safeguard measures are applied in situations everyone agrees entail only 'fair' trade, they are permitted only in narrow circumstances, with higher thresholds having to be satisfied than is the case for antidumping or countervailing measures.

In the GATT era, countries utilised informal arrangements among themselves from time to time to limit imports. These were referred to variously as orderly marketing arrangements (OMAs), voluntary restraint agreements (VRAs) or voluntary export restraints (VERs). The agreements were often between the government of the importing country and the exporting companies from the exporting country, and generally were not memorialised in formal agreements. Instead, they were notionally a 'voluntary' decision of the exporters to limit the quantities they would export to the importing country and/or to increase prices. As one might imagine, 'voluntary' actions such as these tended to be the result of intense political pressure at the governmental level to reduce trade frictions. The WTO Agreement on Safeguards makes clear that WTO members are no longer permitted to seek, take or maintain these types of informal measures.[42] Instead, in the absence of dumping or countervailable subsidisation, the only trade remedy that may be used is a safeguard measure that accords with the WTO rules.

---

42 Agreement on Safeguards, Article 11.

6.3.3a What are safeguard measures?

Safeguard measures provide an opportunity for a country to provide temporary relief to a domestic industry from unexpected surges in imports. The concept is to give the affected domestic industry some breathing room in which to make adjustments necessary to enable it to compete in the newly configured trading environment. The temporary protection may be provided either in the form of higher tariffs or by imposing a quota or tariff-rate quota.[43]

As with the other trade remedies, an industry that wishes to have a safeguard measure imposed needs to petition the relevant government agency, which will then conduct an investigation. The investigating authority will determine whether there has been an increase (either absolute or relative) in imports, whether the domestic producers of the like products are suffering or at imminent threat of suffering serious injury, and whether there is causation linking the imports to the injury. It is important to note that the injury standard is 'serious injury', whereas for dumping and CVDs it is 'material injury'. 'Serious injury' is a higher threshold; because safeguards are applied without any allegations of unfairness, the rules surrounding their application are more stringent than for the other trade remedies. Domestic agencies must conduct their investigations pursuant to the parameters set forth in the GATT, Article XIX, and the Agreement on Safeguards. Similar to the other trade remedies, the GATT/WTO rules do not mandate one particular methodology that must be used in conducting safeguards investigations. Instead they provide parameters within which those investigations may be conducted and safeguards imposed.

If an investigating authority recommends the imposition of a safeguard, any safeguard imposed shall only apply to the extent necessary to prevent or remedy the serious injury and to facilitate adjustment. The purpose of safeguards is supposed to be to give companies a window of time within which to react and adjust to new market dynamics. They are not supposed to be an opportunity to continue to employ practices and behaviours that have proven to be inefficient. Safeguard measures are not to exceed four years in the first instance, though there is the possibility of renewing the measure once, meaning that eight years is the total possible time period.[44]

Interestingly, in contrast to the situation with dumping or CVDs, if safeguard relief is provided to a domestic industry, the government is supposed to adjust the level of concessions it is otherwise providing to affected exporting members.[45] If possible, the member imposing the safeguard and the affected members are to negotiate to attempt to agree upon acceptable adjustments to concessions and other obligations.[46] If no agreement can be reached, the exporting country can decide on its own to suspend substantially equivalent concessions.[47] However, the Agreement on Safeguards contains a significant loophole which provides that if the safeguard measure conforms with the

---

43 With a tariff-rate quota, a certain tariff rate applies up to a set level of imports, after which point a different, higher tariff applies to any further imports.

44 Agreement on Safeguards, Article 7.1 and 7.2.

45 Agreement on Safeguards, Article 8.1.

46 Ibid.

47 Agreement on Safeguards, Article 8.2.

Agreement and was taken as a result of increased imports, the exporting country cannot suspend concessions for the first three years of the safeguard measure.[48] Thus as a practical matter there is no necessity to provide compensation until three years after a safeguard measure takes effect. This is somewhat problematic, given that safeguard measures are applied to trade that is acknowledged by all to be 'fair'.

In addition, when WTO members have brought dispute settlement actions challenging safeguard actions applied by other members as being inconsistent with the Agreement on Safeguards, such claims have been almost uniformly successful. Yet the victories do not result in much relief to the exporting industry as the safeguards have been in place for a significant period (challenges often take close to three years to proceed through the entire dispute settlement process), yet no compensating concessions have been due nor become due by virtue of the successful dispute settlement action.

EXAMPLE: New Zealand and Australia experienced this phenomenon when they initiated a WTO dispute against the USA in which they complained that a US safeguard measure levied against fresh, frozen and chilled lamb meat was inconsistent with the Agreement on Safeguards. The complainants were successful before the panel, and the panel's findings were upheld by the Appellate Body. However, this victory did not result in much of a benefit for the affected New Zealand and Australian industries. The safeguard measure was intended to be in place for a period of three years. By the time the dispute had wound its way through the panel and Appellate Body process and the USA ultimately removed the safeguard, there were only a few months remaining before the safeguard measure would have expired.[49]

Nonetheless, cases successfully challenging the imposition of safeguard measures may forestall the renewal of measures that have been imposed, and may have systemic benefits for the complainant, such as dissuading members from imposing safeguard measures in the future.

Thus even if a safeguard is highly vulnerable to challenge, it may be worthwhile for an industry to petition its government for relief in the form of a safeguard. It must be remembered though that because the injury standard is more stringent than that used in antidumping and CVD investigations, it is more difficult to successfully petition for safeguard relief.

Unlike countervailing measures and antidumping duties, there is little controversy over whether some form of safeguard remedy should be available. Most believe that the ability to impose safeguards should be kept limited, as it entails imposing restrictions on trade that is in no way unfair. However, it is also commonly thought that it is important for WTO members to have some form of safety valve that permits them to provide limited relief to industries to allow them to adjust to the changes in market competition that inevitably result from trade liberalisation measures. There are thus some concerns that the Appellate Body's narrow interpretations of the Agreement on Safeguards—which make it very difficult to impose a safeguard consistent with the Agreement—will

48 Agreement on Safeguards, Article 8.3.

49 *United States—Safeguard Measures on Imports of Fresh, Chilled or Frozen Lamb Meat from New Zealand and Australia*, WT/DS177/178/AB/R (adopted 16 May 2001).

lead to problems, as members may find themselves unable to provide their industries with the temporary adjustment room they feel is needed.

6.3.4 Australia's trade remedies procedures

As previously indicated, the WTO agreements governing trade remedies provide parameters within which domestic activities must fit, but leave enough room for individual members to maintain their own differing regulations pursuant to which domestic investigations are conducted. In this section we briefly describe the trade remedies process in Australia.

6.3.4a Antidumping and Countervailing Duty Investigations

The Australian Customs Service (Customs) is the agency responsible for conducting antidumping and CVD investigations. The requirements and processes for these two types of investigations are similar in many respects.[50]

In the first instance, a domestic industry lodges an application seeking the imposition of antidumping duties and/or countervailing measures with Customs. The application should allege that imports of goods like those produced by the domestic industry are being dumped and/or subsidised, and that their sale in Australia is causing or threatening to cause material injury to the Australian industry. The application must be submitted on behalf of a sufficient segment of the domestic industry, and therefore cannot be lodged by a single small player in the market.

Following the lodging of an application, the CEO of Customs has 20 days to determine whether the application meets the mandatory procedural requirements. If it does, Customs will then issue a public notice setting forth the applicants' claims and explaining the investigation process. The investigation process is undertaken by the Trade Measures Branch, which has up to 155 days to conduct its investigation and report its findings to the Minister for Justice and Customs (the Minister).[51]

Pursuant to the public notice, Customs seeks submissions from all interested parties, including the respondent foreign companies and any other parties not already known to have an interest in the proceedings. These submissions are due within 40 days of the commencement of the investigation. Customs then reviews the submissions and, in some cases, will seek to verify the information submitted, including by conducting onsite visits to respondent companies.

Once the data has been analysed, the CEO of Customs decides whether or not to make a Preliminary Affirmative Determination (PAD). The CEO may make a PAD as early as day 60 of the investigation, and is only permitted to do so if three criteria are met:

- First, that there is sufficient evidence of dumping and/or subsidisation;
- Second, that the domestic industry is being materially injured or is in imminent threat of such an injury; and

---

50 This summary is drawn in large part from Australian Customs Service materials. More detailed information may be found on the Customs website [www.customs.gov.au].

51 The Minister has the authority to approve extensions of time on a case-by-case basis, where warranted.

- Third that there is causation—that the dumping or subsidisation is what is causing the injury.

Once a PAD is made, Customs may impose provisional measures by which it levies temporary additional duties designed to prevent material injury while the investigation is being conducted.

By day 110 of the investigation, Customs must place on public record a Statement of Essential Facts (SEF) in which it sets out the key information upon which it will base its recommendations to the Minister. There is then a 20-day period during which interested parties may submit comments in response to the SEF. Customs then has 25 days remaining in which to consider any new submissions and prepare a report and recommendations for the Minister. The Minister then decides whether to publish a notice that antidumping and/or CVD measures will be imposed.

Subsequently, interested parties have 30 days in which to appeal to the Trade Measures Review Officer (TMRO), which provides an independent appeal mechanism for certain decisions. The TMRO has the authority to review decisions by the Minister to publish or not to publish a dumping or CVD notice, and decisions by the CEO to terminate an investigation, or where a negative prima facie decision or negative preliminary decision has been reached. The TMRO review is limited to the record that was before the CEO and/or Minister, and the TMRO must provide an opportunity for interested parties to make submissions with respect to the appeals issues. The TMRO has the authority to overturn a decision of the CEO to reject an application, but it does not have the authority to overturn a decision of the Minister. However, it may recommend that the Minister remit certain issues back to Customs for further investigation. Some decisions of the Minister are not reviewable at all, including decisions to accept an undertaking with respect to a dumping or subsidy matter, and decisions to continue or decline to continue dumping or countervailing measures.[52]

The following is an excerpt from a TMRO decision:

Pineapple prepared or preserved in containers exported from the People's Republic of China and the Philippines—Review of Ministerial decision to impose dumping duties—21 February 2007

Review of publication decision—Canned pineapples from the Philippines

By notice dated 7 November 2006, published in Commonwealth of Australia Gazette (Gazette) on 13 November 2006, the Minister for Justice and Customs made a declaration that section 8 of the *Customs Tariff Anti Dumping Act 1975* (the *Dumping Duty Act*) applied in relation to food service and industrial (FSI) pineapple imported to Australia from the Philippines after 11 August 2006. Farlier, on 28 September 2006, the Minister by notice declared section 8 of the *Dumping Duty Act* applicable to both FSI and consumer pineapple imported from the Philippines after 11 August 2006. This notice was published in Gazette S185 of 10 October 2006. In the 7 November notice, the Minister specified that his earlier declaration in relation to FSI pineapple was of no effect, although the declaration remained on foot with respect to consumer pineapple.

52 A list of decisions the Review Officer may and may not review may be accessed at [www.ag.gov.au/www/agd/agd.nsf/Page/Tradelaw_Trademeasuresreview_ReviewableDecisions].

I received five applications for review of the Minister's decision, two from SPC Ardmona Operations Ltd (SPCA) dated 8 November and 12 December 2006, two from Del Monte Philippines Inc (Del Monte) and GTL Limited (GTL) and the other from HJ Heinz Company Australia Ltd (Heinz). Del Monte, GTL and SPCA were represented by Corrs Chambers Westgarth Solicitors and Heinz by Rodda Coburn and Co, Trade Consultants of Sydney. SPCA, Del Monte, GTL and Heinz are all interested parties entitled to make an application as they are all persons who are likely to be concerned with the importation or exportation to Australia of goods or like goods the subject of the decision to impose dumping duties, in terms of the definition in section 269ZX of the *Customs Act 1901* (the Act).

On 22 December 2006, pursuant to section 269ZZI of the Act, I published a notice in the *Australian Financial Review* indicating that I would be conducting a review of the decision. I subsequently received a submission from Golden Circle Ltd (GCL), as the Australian industry participant.

Claim by Heinz

Heinz is an importer of consumer pineapple from the Philippines into Australia. It purchases its pineapple from GTL. The pineapple is sold to Grocery Holdings Pty Ltd who sells at retail level through Coles and BiLo stores. Imports began in July 2005, following Heinz's decision to begin selling a range of canned fruit products including peaches, pears, apricots and fruit salad.

Heinz seeks review of the finding by Customs in relation to ascertained export prices for Heinz branded consumer pineapple. The application notes that the ascertained export price determined by Customs in relation to consumer pineapple imported from the Philippines by Del Monte (0.70 USD/kg) is *lower* than the export price paid by Heinz for consumer pineapple from the Philippines (total weighted average price FOB 0.93 USD/kg). If this were true, the consumer pineapple being exported from the Philippines by Del Monte and purchased by Heinz was not being imported at dumped prices.

Heinz' submission is straightforward: the export price ascertained by Customs in relation to consumer pineapple imported from the Philippines is simply not reflective of the export price paid under Heinz's pricing arrangements with Del Monte.

In section 6.3 of Trade Measures Report No 112 (TMR112), Customs notes that export prices in relation to pineapple exported from the Philippines could not, except in relation to one exporter, Dole Philippines Inc (Dole), be determined from the information provided by the exporters (notably Del Monte and GTL). Accordingly, export price was ascertained by reference to subsection 269TAB(3) of the Act. That section provides that:

> *Where the Minister is satisfied that sufficient information has not been furnished, or is not available, to enable the export price of goods to be ascertained under the preceding subsections, the export price of those goods shall be such amount as is determined by the Minister having regard to all relevant information.*

In accordance with this subsection, Customs proceeded to determine export prices for all exporters based on the verified information provided by Dole and Castle and Cooke Worldwide Ltd (CCWW), an affiliated company of Dole. In fact, the ascertained export prices for pineapples exported by Del Monte mirrored that for Dole and that of GTL mirrored CCWW.

In order to determine whether this was a reasonable approach for Customs to take, it is necessary to review the information provided by the other exporters and importers in relation to pineapple exported from the Philippines.

Heinz provided a significant amount of information to Customs before publication of the Statement of Essential Facts (SEF). An Importer Visit Report was completed by Customs in relation to Heinz and Customs was furnished with detailed evidence of prices paid by Heinz on exported pineapple. The information provided by Heinz included two relevant confidential attachments which provided full details of export prices paid by Heinz during the investigation period. Those confidential attachments show export price by shipment in 2005 as well as the weighted average export price paid by Heinz. Those documents reveal the weighted average export price to be well above both the ascertained export price and the non-injurious price determined by Customs in relation to consumer pineapple exported from the Philippines.

There is nothing in the SEF to suggest that the information provided by Heinz was considered by Customs to be either insufficient or unreliable. However, the SEF does state that 'Customs does not have sufficient information to satisfactorily establish the roles and responsibilities of all parties involved in the manufacture and sale of consumer and FSI pineapple to Australia [from the Philippines].'

Heinz did not make any submission to Customs in response to the SEF. However, other interested parties (GTL and RD2 International) responded to the SEF arguing that export prices in relation to Del Monte and GTL should not be determined in accordance with subsection 269TAB(3). Those submissions suggested that the ascertained export prices were not an accurate reflection of those paid to Del Monte and GTL. Both further submissions invited Customs to verify further information. It is very clear that Customs was alerted to the fact, at that stage, that the export prices ascertained in relation to Del Monte and GTL under subsection 269TAB(3) were not considered accurate by either the exporters or the importers.

Notwithstanding these submissions in response to the SEF, Customs continued to maintain in the publication of TMR112 that the information provided by Heinz and others was considered not to contain 'sufficient information or evidence in order to establish export prices' under subsection 269TAB(1). However, I cannot see that it follows that the information should therefore be excluded from consideration under subsection 269TAB(3), which requires Customs to consider all 'relevant information' for the purposes of ascertaining export prices. It is clear from the divergence between the information provided by Heinz and the export price ascertained by Customs that Customs disregarded that information for the purposes of determining export prices.

From Customs' statements it appears that the reason for discounting the information provided rests in Customs' inability to identify the precise relationship between Del Monte and GTL. I agree that it is not clear on the face of the information provided what that relationship is, although it is clear that GTL is a wholly owned subsidiary of Del Monte. However, the fact that Customs had been alerted to the inaccuracy of the ascertained export price should have given Customs pause to consider attempting to verify the information with which they had been provided. This may have required specifically requesting information from either GTL or Del Monte on the relationship between those companies. Indeed, it is likely that Heinz could have provided that information.

Moreover, subsection 269TAB(4) enables the Minister to disregard information that he or she considers to be unreliable. Customs considered that because more than one party was involved in the supply chain before the goods entered Australia, and the relationship of these parties could not be verified, the information about export prices was unreliable and for that reason considered that the Dole information should be used as it had been verified. However, Customs did have verified information that showed certain Australian customers, such as Heinz, were paying much higher prices for the pineapple product than the ascertained normal values.

> Part XVB of the Act is intended to give effect to Australia's obligations under the Agreement on the Implementation of Article VI of the General Agreement on Tariffs and Trade, known as the Anti Dumping Agreement. Article 6.2 of the Agreement requires that during an anti dumping investigation all interested parties shall have a full opportunity for the defence of their interests. I consider that a better opportunity should have been accorded to Heinz in this case to defend its interests. It is clear that Del Monte and GTL laboured under certain misconceptions about the anti dumping process in Australia and the rigour with which investigations are carried out. One of the over arching reasons for having the anti dumping agreement is to ensure that arbitrary decisions are not made about dumping matters and that imposition of duties occurs only where there is a clear linkage between imports that are actually at dumped prices and material injury to domestic injury. It is ironic that in this matter dumping duties have been recommended when there are reasonable grounds for doubting whether the products in question were sold at dumped prices into the Australian market by Del Monte or GTL.
>
> In my opinion, Customs should be directed to reconsider ascertained export prices for Heinz-branded consumer pineapple, taking into account the 'relevant information' provided by Heinz and others in the course of the review.

... ...

In addition to the TMRO process, legal challenges can be brought with respect to many aspects of the process. Such actions are brought before the Federal Court of Australia, principally under the *Administrative Decisions (Judicial Review) Act 1977* (Cth).

6.3.4b Safeguards investigations

Pursuant to Article 12.6 of the Agreement on Safeguards, all WTO members must notify the Committee on Safeguards as to their applicable laws and procedures pertaining to the investigation and imposition of safeguards, and any modifications thereto. Upon the establishment of the Productivity Commission in 1998, Australia duly notified its updated procedures to the Committee on Safeguards.[53]

Safeguards investigations in Australia are initiated by the Treasurer through a reference to the Productivity Commission, which in 1998 assumed the functions previously undertaken by the Industry Commission.[54] The Productivity Commission is the investigating authority for requested safeguard measures. Australia does not maintain specific legislation relating to imposing safeguard measures. Instead, safeguards in the form of quotas would be imposed under the *Customs Act 1901* (Cth) and safeguards in the form of increased tariffs would be imposed through a Tariff Bill or Notice of a Tariff Bill.

---

53 Notification of Laws and Administrative Procedures Relating to Safeguard Measures—Communication from Australia, G/SG/N/1/AUS/2 (2 July 1998).

54 The Productivity Commission is an independent statutory body and advises the government on a wide variety of macroeconomic issues. It also undertakes public inquiries into matters such as productivity and industry development.

6.4 Other non-tariff barriers to imports

In addition to the trade remedies discussed above, businesses may find themselves subject to other forms of trade barriers that do not involve the imposition of elevated tariffs. Such barriers are therefore referred to as non-tariff barriers (also referred to as NTBs). In this section we identify barriers that are generally prohibited; exceptions to those general rules; and other types of measures that can act as non-tariff barriers.[55]

6.4.1 Generally prohibited barriers

It is generally not permissible under WTO rules to impose bans or other quantitative restrictions on imports.[56] A major aim of the GATT was to get signatory countries to convert quotas and other non-tariff barriers to tariffs, and then to lower the tariffs over time. Thus most quotas have been phased out in favour of tariffs. That said, there are some limited circumstances under which quantitative restrictions are permitted.

When quantitative restrictions are allowed they must be administered on a non-discriminatory basis.[57] Thus if an import quota is imposed, the administering country will not be able to allocate the entire quota to its favoured allies, and will instead need to develop a non-discriminatory method for allocating the quota rights, such as basing shares upon historical levels of market penetration. However, it is usually the case that even when an exception may apply, an outright ban will only be appropriate if it is the least trade restrictive option available to achieve the applicable policy goal. Accordingly, if an exporter learns that a would-be destination for its product has imposed a ban on the importation of the like product, the exporter should attempt to determine whether there would be a way the destination country could achieve the same policy goal (for example, health or safety) through regulations other than banning imports.

In addition, as is discussed in section 6.3.3 above, voluntary restraint agreements, voluntary export restraints and orderly marketing arrangements are no longer permitted under WTO rules.

6.4.2 Exceptions pursuant to the WTO agreements

There are a number of exceptions to the general prohibitions on quantitative restrictions. For example, as was discussed in section 6.3.3 above, safeguard measures may take the

---

55 Additional non-tariff barriers not discussed here include government procurement practices, and customs formalities and procedures. For a discussion of these barriers, see for example P Van den Bossche, *The Law and Policy of the World Trade Organization*, Cambridge University Press, Cambridge & New York, 2005, p 457.

56 GATT, Article XI.

57 GATT, Article XIII.

form of quotas or tariff-rate quotas in addition to tariffs. In the event that an exception applies to permit a WTO member to impose a quantitative restriction on imports, it generally must do so in accordance with the GATT, Article XIII, which requires that quantitative restrictions be imposed in a non-discriminatory manner.[58] Space precludes discussing each possible exception, so we focus here on the major exceptions provisions of the WTO, namely Articles XX and XXI of the GATT.[59]

6.4.2a GATT, Article XX: general exceptions

Article XX of the GATT is the 'General Exceptions' article applicable to GATT obligations, including the most-favoured nation principle (GATT, Article I) and the prohibition on quantitative restrictions (GATT Article XI). The article contains an introductory paragraph known as the *chapeau*, and several enumerated provisions as follows:

Article XX: General Exceptions

Subject to the requirement that such measures are not applied in a manner which would constitute a means of arbitrary or unjustifiable discrimination between countries where the same conditions prevail, or a disguised restriction on international trade, nothing in this Agreement shall be construed to prevent the adoption or enforcement by any contracting party of measures:

(a) necessary to protect public morals;
(b) necessary to protect human, animal or plant life or health;
(c) relating to the importations or exportations of gold or silver;
(d) necessary to secure compliance with laws or regulations which are not inconsistent with the provisions of this Agreement, including those relating to customs enforcement, the enforcement of monopolies operated under paragraph 4 of Article II and Article XVII, the protection of patents, trade marks and copyrights, and the prevention of deceptive practices;
(e) relating to the products of prison labour;
(f) imposed for the protection of national treasures of artistic, historic or archaeological value;
(g) relating to the conservation of exhaustible natural resources if such measures are made effective in conjunction with restrictions on domestic production or consumption;
(h) undertaken in pursuance of obligations under any intergovernmental commodity agreement

58 Exceptions to this are set forth in the GATT, Article XIV: Exceptions to Rule of Non-Discrimination. Article XIV permits governments to discriminate in applying balance-of-payments quantitative restrictions, when so doing will increase trade without harming the country which is being discriminated against. This provision was used heavily by European countries against the USA in the 1950s, but has not been used since the end of that decade: see R E Hudec, 'Tiger, Tiger, in the House: A Critical Appraisal of the Case Against Discriminatory Trade Measures' (1988), in R E Hudec, *Essays on the Nature of International Trade Law*, Cameron May, London, 1999, pp 299–300.

59 Other exceptions include the ability to safeguard balance of payments (GATT, Article XII) and for developing countries to impose quantitative restrictions to protect infant industries (GATT, Article XVIII, Section C). Notwithstanding the potential to protect infant industries through the imposition of quantitative restrictions, developing countries have not done so in recent years: see PC Mavroidis, *Trade in Goods: The GATT and Other Agreements Regulating Trade in Goods*, Oxford University Press, Oxford, 2007, p 63.

> which conforms to criteria submitted to the CONTRACTING PARTIES and not disapproved by them or which is itself so submitted and not so disapproved;
>
> (i) involving restrictions on exports of domestic materials necessary to ensure essential quantities of such materials to a domestic processing industry during periods when the domestic price of such materials is held below the world price as part of a governmental stabilization plan; Provided that such restrictions shall not operate to increase the exports of or the protection afforded to such domestic industry, and shall not depart from the provisions of this Agreement relating to non-discrimination;
>
> (j) essential to the acquisition or distribution of products in general or local short supply; Provided that any such measures shall be consistent with the principle that all contracting parties are entitled to an equitable share of the international supply of such products, and that any such measures, which are inconsistent with the other provisions of the Agreement shall be discontinued as soon as the conditions giving rise to them have ceased to exist. The CONTRACTING PARTIES shall review the need for this sub-paragraph not later than 30 June 1960.

... ...

To fall within one of the Article XX exceptions, an import control would need to both meet the criteria set forth in one of the elaborated paragraphs, and satisfy the conditions set forth in the *chapeau* (the introductory paragraph). Countries often maintain import and export controls that would likely satisfy the conditions of one of these paragraphs. (Export controls are discussed in the next chapter and many of the examples provided there are also relevant to import controls.) It is more common however for Article XX to be invoked to justify import restrictions rather than export controls.

The context in which Article XX applies is when there is a breach of a GATT obligation—for example, a ban on imports in violation of the GATT, Article XI—and a member seeks to argue that its ban is nonetheless justified because it falls within one of the enumerated exceptions. There are numerous contexts in which Article XX could be invoked. For example, Article XX(a), the public morals exception, could be used to justify restrictions on the importation of pornography, or of alcohol into certain Muslim countries. Article XX(b) and (g) have been invoked in numerous WTO disputes relating to the protection of human, animal or plant life or health, or the environment (respectively).[60]

Businesses that are involved in the importation or exportation of materials that can cause environmental damage may well run up against import restrictions domestically or overseas. Many import restrictions are imposed pursuant to commitments under multilateral environmental agreements (MEAs) or other international treaties, but others simply reflect domestic policy choices of the nation imposing the measures.

---

60 For example *United States—Standards for Reformulated and Conventional Gasoline*, WT/DS/2/AB/R (Appellate Body report adopted 20 May 1996); *European Communities—Measures Affecting Asbestos and Asbestos-Containing Products*, WT/DS/135/AB/R (Appellate Body report adopted 5 April 2001); *United States—Import Prohibition of Certain Shrimp and Shrimp Products*, WT/DS/58/AB/R (Appellate Body report adopted 6 November 1998).

To complicate matters, there is a potential for a clash between the trade restrictive measures required by the major MEAs and the non-discrimination principles of the WTO. The following extract describes the potential for conflict.

Duncan Brack, 'Multilateral Environmental Agreements: An Overview', in Halina Ward and Duncan Brack (eds) *Trade, Investment and the Environment*, The Royal Institute of International Affairs/Earthscan Publications Ltd, London, 2000, pp 122, 125–9[61]

In the first place, GATT Articles I ('Most Favoured Nation' Treatment) and III (National Treatment) outlaw discrimination in trade: WTO Members are not permitted to discriminate between traded 'like products' produced by other WTO members, or between domestic and international 'like products'. Yet all three major MEAs [CITES, the Montreal Protocol and the Basel Convention] discriminate against countries on the basis of their environmental performance, requiring parties to restrict trade to a greater extent with non-parties than they do with parties; indeed, such discrimination is one of the points of these MEAs, since they are aimed to promote sustainable activities while punishing unsustainable behaviour.

Second, GATT Article XI (Elimination of Quantitative Restrictions) forbids any restrictions other than duties, taxes or other charges on imports from and exports to other WTO members; yet each of the three MEAs requires precisely such quantitative restrictions.

Third, Article III requires imported and domestic 'like products' to be treated identically. The meaning of the term 'like product' has become one of the most difficult issues in the trade-environment arena. Originally incorporated into the GATT in order to prevent discrimination on the grounds of national origin, GATT and WTO dispute panels have interpreted the term more broadly to prevent discrimination in cases where process methods, rather than product characteristics, have been the distinguishing characteristic of the product and the justification for trade measures—for example the US embargo on imports of shrimp caught by methods that kill sea turtles. Yet the Montreal Protocol envisages restrictions on trade in products made with but not containing ozone-depleting substances (originating from non-parties), while domestic products produced in this way are not subject to such regulation—although so far this provision has not been put into practice.

It is possible, however, that an MEA trade measure could be 'saved' by the General Exceptions clause of the GATT, Article XX ...

Unlike many MEAs, where terms tend to be defined in the treaty or in subsequent decisions of conferences of the parties, interpretation of the MTS [Multilateral Trading System] usually proceeds through a case-law-type approach, relying on the findings of dispute panels in particular cases. Since there has never been a dispute brought before a GATT or WTO panel involving an MEA trade measure, it is impossible to say for certain whether it would be found to be incompatible with the MTS.

It is possible, however, to extrapolate from the arguments and findings in a series of trade-environment disputes that were brought before panels—involving, in this case, unilaterally imposed trade measures. In each of these cases the panel found the environmental measures in question not to be justifiable, because either:

61 The chapter has also been reprinted in T Cottier and M Oesch, *International Trade Regulation: Law and Policy in the WTO, the European Union, and Switzerland*, Cameron May, London, 2005, with this excerpt appearing at pp 680–2.

- the measures were not 'necessary' (Article XX(b)) to the achievement of the environmental goal, because the panel believed that there were less trade-restrictive or GATT-inconsistent measures also available; or
- the measures did not 'relate to the conservation of exhaustible natural resources' (Article XX(g)), because the policies in question were extra-jurisdictional: they attempted to modify the behaviour of other WTO members and could not therefore be considered to be primarily aimed at conserving the natural resources of the country applying the trade measures; or
- the measures represented 'arbitrary or unjustifiable discrimination' (Article XX headnote), in that there were less discriminatory methods available that could have been employed.

It is of course dangerous to extrapolate from arguments used in cases of trade measures imposed unilaterally to those involving the application of trade measures mandated by or in pursuance of the requirements of multilateral agreements ...

Furthermore, WTO dispute panels, and the WTO Appellate Body, have become steadily more sophisticated in their arguments, and more conscious of the environmental debate. The recent Appellate Body decision in the *Shrimp/Turtle* dispute, for example, used the reference in the Preamble to the Marrakesh Agreement establishing the WTO—'allowing for the optimal use of the world's resources in accordance with the objective of sustainable development, seeking both to protect and preserve the environment and to enhance the means for doing so ...'—to dispose of the argument that species protection was not a legitimate objective for trade measures. It also stressed, as have several panels before it, the desirability of multilateral agreements as opposed to unilateral measures.

Unsurprisingly, however, neither panels nor the Appellate Body have ever speculated as to the acceptability of trade measures taken under such agreements under the MTS. It is therefore still not clear as to how panels would rule. Even some of the arguments used in the *Shrimp/Turtle* Appellate Body finding suggest that they might rule against an MEA trade measure: 'Perhaps the most conspicuous flaw in this measure's application relates to its intended and actual coercive effect on the specific policy decisions made by foreign governments ...'

However, it is not acceptable, in international trade relations, for one WTO Member to use an economic embargo to require other Members to adopt essentially the same comprehensive regulatory program, to achieve a certain policy goal, as that in force within that Member's territory.

Trade measures employed under the three main MEAs cited above are now unlikely to be challenged in the WTO because of the wide international acceptability they enjoy—though this perhaps less true of the Basel Convention, where the amendment banning trade in waste between OECD and non-OECD countries ... has aroused hostility among some of the industries involved. The possible MTS incompatibility of the amendment has been raised explicitly by those opposed to the principle as an argument against adopting or ratifying it ...

The continuation of this potential conflict between the MTS and MEAs is undesirable for a number of reasons including the following:

- the fact that it is not known for certain how a dispute panel would rule on an MEA trade measure creates an unstable and uncertain situation ...
- it creates the spectre of a potential challenge to an existing MEA, bringing the two international regimes of trade liberalization and environmental protection directly into conflict;

- it increases the likelihood of conflict over the negotiation of future MEAs with trade measures, potentially weakening their effectiveness—the 'political chill' argument;
- finally, the perception that the WTO threatens environmental sustainability, already widespread in some quarters, assists neither the growth of the MTS nor the further spread of trade liberalization, even where this would have environmental benefit.

Resolution of the problem is therefore required.

... ...

6.4.2b National security

In addition to the general exceptions described above, the WTO has provision for members to be permitted to take actions—which would include trade restrictive measures—in certain national security contexts. The GATT, Article XXI, is the security exceptions article, and it provides:

> (1) Nothing in this Agreement shall be construed:
> (a) to require any contracting party to furnish any information the disclosure of which it considers contrary to its essential security interests; or
> (b) to prevent any contracting party from taking any action which it considers necessary for the protection of its essential security interests
> (i) relating to fissionable materials or the materials from which they are derived;
> (ii) relating to the traffic in arms, ammunition and implements of war and to such traffic in other goods and materials as is carried on directly or indirectly for the purpose of supplying a military establishment;
> (iii) taken in time of war or other emergency in international relations; or
> (c) to prevent any contracting party from taking any action in pursuance of its obligations under the United Nations Charter for the maintenance of international peace and security.

There has been almost no invocation of Article XXI in GATT/WTO dispute settlement. This is likely because members are hesitant to challenge the defence-related actions of another sovereign state. In one of the only disputes to have arisen, Nicaragua brought a complaint against the USA in response to its import and export embargo of Nicaragua. Nicaragua claimed the embargo violated the GATT, Article XI, and the USA responded that its measures fell under Article XXI and that such measures are not justiciable. Terms of reference for the panel were extremely limited and precluded the panel from determining whether the US measure was justified under Article XXI. As such, this case is of limited utility in determining the scope of Article XXI.[62] While case law on the scope of Article XXI is limited, and the article has not been invoked except rarely, it is nonetheless an important provision. While disputes have not, in the main, implicated Article XXI, this should not be taken to mean that members have not taken trade-restrictive actions pursuant to this article. Instead we can conclude, as noted above, that members are loath to challenge each other's national-security-related activities.

62 See United States—Trade Measures Affecting Nicaragua, L/6053 (GATT, October 13, 1986). See also discussion in PC Mavroidis, *Trade in Goods: The GATT and Other Agreements Regulating Trade in Goods*, Oxford University Press, Oxford & New York, 2007.

A business engaged in the production of military or dual-use technology will find that import controls (and export controls) relating to such products are quite common. As is canvassed in more detail in Chapter 7, import restrictions often relate to weapons, nuclear material and other items of potential military application.

6.4.3 Regulations as non-tariff barriers

Many non-tariff barriers arise as a result of the food-health-and-safety-related regulations and standards that countries impose. For example, if a country requires that meat imports have undergone rigorous testing and quality assurance measures, such regulations may effectively exclude some would-be exporters from participating in the market of the country imposing the regulations. Regardless of whether such regulations are justified under national laws or WTO rules, they can serve as trade barriers to businesses. In some instances, a business may be faced with regulatory requirements that violate domestic law or WTO rules; and that its government could therefore challenge in a WTO dispute settlement proceeding. Businesses need to be aware of any applicable restrictions imposed by their would-be export markets, but should also be aware of the disciplines the WTO imposes on such restrictions.

The WTO agreements on Technical Barriers to Trade (TBT Agreement) and Sanitary and Phytosanitary Measures (SPS Agreement) provide parameters within which WTO members can establish technical regulations and standards or labelling requirements (TBT measures), including a special category of such regulations relating to sanitary and phytosanitary measures to protect human, animal or plant life or health (SPS measures). If a business feels it is being subjected to a regulation that does not conform to the TBT Agreement or, if applicable, the SPS Agreement, it should notify the appropriate government authorities.

6.4.3a TBT measures

Countries may impose a number of restrictions on imports in the form of technical regulations, standards and labelling requirements. Such measures have the potential to be burdensome and expensive to comply with, particularly for exporters shipping to multiple countries that may each have their own different regulations. The TBT Agreement exists in order to impose disciplines to minimise the protectionist potential that technical barriers to trade might otherwise pose.

The TBT Agreement sets forth a number of limitations on WTO members' ability to impose technical regulations, standards and conformity assessment procedures. Of these the most important are the requirements that such regulations, standards and procedures be applied to imported products on an MFN and national treatment basis.[63] In addition, where international standards exist, members must use those standards as a basis for their technical regulations.[64] This requirement of harmonisation is designed to prevent the problem of exporters having to satisfy multitudes of different, perhaps conflicting, standards

---

63 TBT Agreement, Article 2.1 (technical regulations); Article 5.1.1 (conformity assessment procedures) and Annex 3D (standards).

64 TBT Agreement, Article 2.4.

and regulations in its destination markets. Further, regulations should not be more trade restrictive than necessary to fulfil their objectives, which must in turn be legitimate.[65]

Sanitary and phytosanitary (SPS) measures are a type of TBT measure. Pursuant to the TBT Agreement, measures that fall within the definition of the SPS Agreement are deemed SPS measures and only the SPS Agreement will apply, not the TBT Agreement.[66]

6.4.3b SPS measures

The SPS Agreement provides a framework within which members may impose measures relating to the protection of health and safety. In particular, it applies to measures to protect animal or plant life or health from the entry, establishment or spread of pests or diseases,[67] from risks arising from additives, contaminants, or other toxins in foods or beverages,[68] and from risks arising from the introduction or spread of pests or from plant or animal diseases.[69] It is essentially an elaboration of the principle in the GATT, Article XX(b), discussed above. However, the SPS Agreement imposes affirmative obligations on members, whereas Article XX serves as an exception to other affirmative obligations. Thus, while there is an overlap between the SPS Agreement and the GATT, Article XX(b), there are measures that would only fall under the SPS Agreement (for example, an SPS measure that does not breach any GATT obligation) and others that would only fall under XX(b) (for example, a ban that does not meet the definition of an SPS measure). To the extent there is an overlap, measures that are consistent with the SPS Agreement are deemed consistent with the GATT, Article XX(b).[70]

The SPS Agreement permits WTO members to reach their own decisions as to their desired level of health and safety protection,[71] but when measures are imposed that restrict imports they must be supported by scientific findings and be based upon a risk assessment.[72] Measures cannot be more trade restrictive than necessary to achieve the level of protection the member wishes to establish.[73]

Countries frequently initiate consultations with other WTO members with respect to the appropriateness of SPS measures that have been imposed. Many of these are resolved through consultations, but others have progressed to the panel, and in some cases Appellate Body stage, resulting in published reports.

Australia has been the subject of a relatively large number of such complaints (only the EC has been subject to as many consultations requests on SPS issues as Australia).[74]

---

65 TBT Agreement, Article 2.3.

66 TBT Agreement, Articles 1.4 and 1.5.

67 SPS Agreement, Annex A(1)(a).

68 SPS Agreement, Annex A(1)(b).

69 SPS Agreement, Annex A(1)(c) and (d).

70 SPS Agreement, Article 2.4. The converse is not true, however.

71 SPS Agreement, Article 2.1.

72 SPS Agreement, Articles 2.2 and 5.1.

73 SPS Agreement, Article 5.6.

74 A listing of Australia's involvement in current WTO disputes is available at [www.dfat.gov.au/trade/negotiations/disputes/index.html]. A complete list of all WTO complaints, including agreements implicated, may be accessed at [www.worldtradelaw.net].

One case that progressed through the full WTO dispute settlement process was *Australia–Salmon*, in which Canada complained that Australian quarantine measures on imports of fresh, frozen and chilled salmon were inconsistent with its WTO obligations under the SPS Agreement. The panel and Appellate Body determined that certain of Australia's quarantine measures were not in conformity with Australia's WTO obligations.[75] Excerpts from the Appellate Body report follow.

Australia—Measures Affecting Importation of Salmon (WT/DS18/AB/R. 20 October 1998) (Report of the Appellate Body)[76]

I. Introduction

1. Australia and Canada appeal from certain issues of law and legal interpretations in the Panel Report, *Australia—Measures Affecting Importation of Salmon.* The Panel was established to consider a complaint by Canada regarding Australia's prohibition on the importation of fresh, chilled or frozen salmon from Canada under Quarantine Proclamation 86A ('QP86A'), dated 19 February 1975 and any amendments or modifications thereto.

2. Before the promulgation of QP86A on 30 June 1975, Australia imposed no restrictions on the importation of salmonid products. QP86A 'prohibit[s] the importation into Australia of dead fish of the sub-order Salmonidae, or any parts (other than semen or ova) of fish of that sub-order, in any form unless: ... prior to importation into Australia the fish or parts of fish have been subject to such treatment as in the opinion of the Director of Quarantine is likely to prevent the introduction of any infectious or contagious disease, or disease or pest affecting persons, animals or plants'. Pursuant to QP86A and in accordance with the authority delegated therein, the Director of Quarantine has permitted the entry of commercial imports of heat-treated salmon products for human consumption as well as non-commercial quantities of other salmon (primarily for scientific purposes) subject to prescribed conditions. Canada requested access to the Australian market for fresh, chilled or frozen, ie, uncooked, salmon. Australia conducted an import risk analysis for uncooked, wild, adult, ocean-caught Pacific salmonid product ('ocean-caught Pacific salmon'). This category of salmon is to be distinguished from the other categories of salmon for which Canada seeks access to the Australian market ('other Canadian salmon'). The risk analysis on ocean-caught Pacific salmon was first set forth in the 1995 Draft Report, revised in May 1996 and finalized in December of 1996 (the '1996 Final Report'). The 1996 Final Report concluded that:

> it is recommended that the present quarantine policies for uncooked salmon products remain in place.

The Director of Quarantine, on the basis of the 1996 Final Report, decided on 13 December 1996 that:

75 *Australia—Measures Affecting Importation of Salmon* (WT/DS18/AB/R, 20 October 1998). Canada subsequently brought additional proceedings against Australia claiming that Australia had not complied properly with the Appellate Body's decision. The panel again sided with Canada in these compliance proceedings: see WT/DS18/RW, 18 February 2000.

76 Internal citations and references omitted.

having regard to Australian Government policy on quarantine and after taking account of Australia's international obligations, importation of uncooked, wild, adult, ocean-caught Pacific salmonid product from the Pacific rim of North America should not be permitted on quarantine grounds.

...

Article 5.1 of the SPS Agreement

112. We first address the question of whether the Panel erred in finding that the measure at issue, as it applies to ocean-caught Pacific salmon, is not based on a risk assessment and that Australia, therefore, has acted inconsistently with Article 5.1 and, by implication, Article 2.2 of the SPS Agreement.

113. The Panel first addressed the issue of whether the 1996 Final Report is a risk assessment within the meaning of Article 5.1 of the SPS Agreement. It did not make a *finding* on this issue but *assumed*, for the purpose of its further examination, that the 1996 Final Report meets the requirements of a risk assessment. It subsequently examined whether the SPS measure at issue, which, in its view, is the heat-treatment requirement, is based on the 1996 Final Report, 'the only risk assessment forwarded by Australia'. In paragraph 8.99 of its Report, the Panel came to the conclusion that 'the measure at issue—in so far as it applies to ocean-caught Pacific salmon—is not "based on" a risk assessment,' and that, therefore, Australia has acted inconsistently with Article 5.1 and, by implication, Article 2.2 of the SPS Agreement.

114. Australia appeals from the Panel's finding that the measure in dispute was not based on a risk assessment. In the view of Australia, this finding is vitiated by the Panel's conclusion that the SPS measure in dispute is the heat-treatment requirement rather than the import prohibition.

115. We recall that we have found that the SPS measure at issue is the import prohibition on fresh, chilled or frozen salmon, not the heat-treatment requirement. The import prohibition is, therefore, the measure which must be examined under the SPS Agreement. More particularly, under Article 5.1, the Panel should have determined whether the import prohibition on fresh, chilled or frozen salmon was based on a risk assessment, instead of examining whether the heat-treatment requirement was based on a risk assessment. We believe this to be an error of law and we therefore reverse the Panel's finding in paragraph 8.99 that the SPS measure, as it applies to ocean-caught Pacific salmon, is not based on a risk assessment, and that Australia has acted inconsistently with Article 5.1 and, by implication, Article 2.2 of the SPS Agreement.

116. The Panel did not examine whether the import prohibition on fresh, chilled or frozen salmon, the proper SPS measure at issue in this dispute, is based on a risk assessment, and there is no finding on this question in the Panel Report.

117. We are cognizant of the provisions of Article 17 of the DSU that state our jurisdiction and our mandate. Article 17.6 of the DSU provides: 'An appeal shall be limited to issues of law covered in the panel report and legal interpretations developed by the panel.' Article 17.13 of the DSU states: 'The Appellate Body may uphold, modify or reverse the legal findings and conclusions of the panel.' In certain appeals, when we reverse a panel's finding on a legal issue, we may examine and decide an issue that was not specifically addressed by the panel, in order to complete the legal analysis and resolve the dispute between the parties. This occurred, for example, in the appeals in *United States—Gasoline, Canada—Certain Measures Concerning Periodicals, European Communities—Measures Affecting the Importation of Certain Poultry Products ('European Communities—Poultry')*, and *United States—Import Prohibition of Certain Shrimp and Shrimp Products.*

118. As we have reversed the Panel's finding that the SPS measure at issue, erroneously identified as the heat-treatment requirement, is not based on a risk assessment, we believe that—to the extent possible on the basis of the factual findings of the Panel and/or of undisputed facts in the Panel record—we should complete the legal analysis and determine whether the actual SPS measure at issue, ie, Australia's *import prohibition* on fresh, chilled or frozen ocean-caught Pacific salmon, is based on a risk assessment.

119. In examining whether Australia's import prohibition is consistent with Article 5.1, we first have to address whether the 1996 Final Report is, indeed, as Australia contends, a risk assessment within the meaning of Article 5.1 of the SPS Agreement. After a detailed analysis of the requirements of the SPS Agreement relating to risk assessments, and a detailed analysis on whether the 1996 Final Report fulfils these requirements, the Panel *assumed*—without making a finding on this issue—'that the 1996 Final Report meets the requirements of a risk assessment set out in Articles 5.1 and 5.2'. We do not believe it appropriate to base our examination of Article 5.1 on this *assumption* made by the Panel that the 1996 Final Report is a proper risk assessment. We must, therefore, address this question ourselves. This is possible, because the Panel made all the factual findings necessary to enable us to examine whether the 1996 Final Report meets the requirements of a risk assessment under Article 5.1 of the SPS Agreement.

120. Paragraph 4 of Annex A of the SPS Agreement defines two types of 'risk assessment'. We agree with the Panel that the type of risk assessment which is required in this case is the type defined in the first part of paragraph 4 of Annex A, which reads as follows:

> *Risk Assessment*—The evaluation of the likelihood of entry, establishment or spread of a pest or disease within the territory of an importing Member according to the sanitary or phytosanitary measures which might be applied, and of the associated potential biological and economic consequences;

121. On the basis of this definition, we consider that, in this case, a risk assessment within the meaning of Article 5.1 must:

(1) *identify* the diseases whose entry, establishment or spread a Member wants to prevent within its territory, as well as the potential biological and economic consequences associated with the entry, establishment or spread of these diseases;
(2) *evaluate the likelihood* of entry, establishment or spread of these diseases, as well as the associated potential biological and economic consequences; and
(3) evaluate the likelihood of entry, establishment or spread of these diseases *according to the SPS measures which might be applied.*

122. We note that the Panel identified the same three requirements for a risk assessment, within the meaning of Article 5.1 and the first part of paragraph 4 of Annex A of the SPS Agreement.

123. Before taking up the question of whether the 1996 Final Report satisfies these requirements, we note that the first definition in paragraph 4 of Annex A speaks about the evaluation of 'likelihood.' In our report in *European Communities—Hormones*, we referred to the dictionary meaning of 'probability' as 'degrees of likelihood' and 'a thing that is judged likely to be true', for the purpose of distinguishing the terms 'potential' and 'probability'. For the present purpose, we refer in the same manner to the ordinary meaning of 'likelihood', and we consider that it has the same meaning as 'probability'. On this basis, as well as on the basis of the definition of 'risk' and 'risk assessment' developed by the Office international des épizooties ('OIE')

and the OIE *Guidelines for Risk Assessment,* we maintain that for a risk assessment to fall within the meaning of Article 5.1 and the first definition in paragraph 4 of Annex A, it is not sufficient that a risk assessment conclude that there is a *possibility* of entry, establishment or spread of diseases and associated biological and economic consequences. A proper risk assessment of this type must evaluate the 'likelihood', ie, the 'probability', of entry, establishment or spread of diseases and associated biological and economic consequences as well as the 'likelihood', ie, 'probability', of entry, establishment or spread of diseases *according to the SPS measures which might be applied.*

124. We note that, although the Panel stated that the definition of a risk assessment for this type of measure requires an 'evaluation of the likelihood', for the purpose of satisfying the second and third requirements, it subsequently was hesitant in applying these requirements, by stating or suggesting in paragraphs 8.80, 8.83, 8.89 and 8.91, that *some* evaluation of the likelihood or probability would suffice. We consider this hesitation unfortunate. We do not agree with the Panel that a risk assessment of this type needs only *some* evaluation of the likelihood or probability. The definition of this type of risk assessment in paragraph 4 of Annex A refers to 'the evaluation of the likelihood' and not to *some* evaluation of the likelihood. We agree, however, with the Panel's statements in paragraph 8.80 that the SPS Agreement does not require that the evaluation of the likelihood needs to be done quantitatively. The likelihood may be expressed either quantitatively or qualitatively. Furthermore, we recall, as does the Panel, that we stated in *European Communities—Hormones* that there is no requirement for a risk assessment to establish a certain magnitude or threshold level of degree of risk.

125. The Panel adds to these considerations, the following statement:

> we consider that a risk assessment, on which to base an import prohibition in accordance with Article 5.1, 6remised on the concept of 'zero risk'. Otherwise, all import prohibitions would be based on a risk assessment since there is a risk (ie, a *possibility* of an adverse event occurring), however remote, associated with most (if not all) imports.

In its third participant's submission, the European Communities states that it finds this statement perplexing. The European Communities is concerned that what the Panel affirmed might be misconstrued to mean that 'zero risk' as an appropriate level of protection is not a choice open to Members under the SPS Agreement. The statement by the Panel quoted above is not appealed, and we merely note that it is important to distinguish—perhaps more carefully than the Panel did—between the evaluation of 'risk' in a risk assessment and the determination of the appropriate level of protection. As stated in our Report in *European Communities—Hormones*, the 'risk' evaluated in a risk assessment must be an ascertainable risk; theoretical uncertainty is 'not the kind of risk which, under Article 5.1, is to be assessed.' This does not mean, however, that a Member cannot determine its own appropriate level of protection to be 'zero risk'.

126. Applying our three-pronged test set out in paragraph 128 [sic: paragraph 121] above, to the 1996 Final Report in order to determine whether that Report meets the requirements of a risk assessment within the meaning of Article 5.1 and the first definition in paragraph 4 of Annex A, we note that the Panel found that the 1996 Final Report identifies the diseases whose entry, establishment or spread Australia wants to prevent as well as the potential biological and economic

consequences associated with the entry, establishment or spread of such diseases. The Panel, therefore, concluded that 'the 1996 Final Report meets the first requirement of a risk assessment'. We agree with the Panel.

127. With regard to the second requirement for a risk assessment of the type applicable in this case, namely, the *evaluation of the likelihood* of entry, establishment or spread of the diseases of concern *and* of the associated potential biological and economic consequences, we note that the Panel stated in paragraph 8.82 of its Report:

> the 1996 Final Report uses the words probability, possibility and likelihood on different occasions and evaluates elements of probability for *some* of the diseases of concern. (emphasis added)
>
> At the meeting with experts advising the Panel Australia stated that 'we contend we have conducted a probability risk assessment' and implied that assessing risk as low or small is a statement of probability (Transcript, para 155).

After citing some passages from the 1996 Final Report which evaluate elements of probability, the Panel concluded:

> Considering the evidence before us, we note that the 1996 Final Report addresses *some* elements of both probability and possibility. We shall, therefore, assume—without making a finding on this issue—that it meets the requirement set out above. (emphasis added)

128. We believe, however, that on the basis of the facts found by the Panel, it could, and should, have come to the conclusion that the 1996 Final Report does not contain the 'evaluation of the likelihood of entry, establishment or spread' of the diseases of concern 'and of the associated potential biological and economic consequences' as required by paragraph 4 of Annex A of the SPS Agreement. As we have already emphasized, *some* evaluation of the likelihood is not enough.

129. In arriving at our conclusion that the 1996 Final Report does *not* meet the second requirement of a risk assessment of the type applicable in this case, we rely, in particular, on the Panel's factual findings in paragraph 8.83 of its Report:

> that the 1996 Final Report (as stated by several of the experts advising the Panel) lends more weight to the unknown and uncertain elements of the assessment than the 1995 Draft Report (on which the 1996 Final Report is based). This, on occasions, results in general and vague statements of mere possibility of adverse effects occurring; statements which constitute neither a quantitative nor a qualitative assessment of probability.
>
> Wooldridge answers, p 6, quoted in para 8. and Rodgers answers, p 1 ('As such, the 1995 report is a more useful document, in the sense of an internal risk assessment exercise, since it "evaluates" the data to conclude that a negligible risk exists, while at the same time recognising that the overall risk of disease introduction cannot be quantified. The final report seems to lend more weight to the unknown elements of the assessment and as such is more cautious, which results in an outcome closer to the "unacceptable" rather than the "negligible but acceptable" end of the scale').
>
> This led the experts advising the Panel on this issue to the conclusion that the 1996 Final Report does *not* appropriately assess probability as is required in their view. See Burmaster's answer to Panel Question 1, Burmaster answers, p 1; Rodgers, Transcript, para 26 ('[The 1996 Final Report] assesses risks on a disease-by-disease basis but in a textural form and does not assign any probabilities that would be needed to reach a conclusion. In this respect, therefore, I think, it possibly does fall short of determining any probability based on the information

available') and Wooldridge, Transcript, para 55 ('since [the 1996 Final Report] looks only at the possibility of the unwanted outcomes of infection and disease importation, rather than the probability, in my opinion, it does not in any event fulfil the essential requirements of a risk assessment').

130. We might add that the existence of unknown and uncertain elements does not justify a departure from the requirements of Articles 5.1, 5.2 and 5.3, read together with paragraph 4 of Annex A, for a risk assessment. We recall that Article 5.2 requires that 'in the assessment of risk, Members shall take into account available scientific evidence'. We further recall that Article 2, entitled 'Basic Rights and Obligations', requires in paragraph 2 that 'Members shall ensure that any sanitary … measure … is based on scientific principles and is not maintained without sufficient scientific evidence, except as provided for in paragraph 7 of Article 5.' As we stated in *European Communities—Hormones*, 'Articles 2.2 and 5.1 should constantly be read together. Article 2.2 informs Article 5.1: the elements that define the basic obligation set out in Article 2.2 impart meaning to Article 5.1.'

131. We, therefore, come to the conclusion that the 1996 Final Report does *not* meet the second requirement of the type of risk assessment applicable in this case, ie, the evaluation of the likelihood of entry, establishment or spread of the diseases of concern and of the potential associated biological and economic consequences.

132. We turn now to the third requirement of a risk assessment within the meaning of Article 5.1 and the first definition in paragraph 4 of Annex A of the SPS Agreement, namely, the evaluation of the likelihood of entry, establishment or spread of a disease *according to the SPS measures which might be applied.* We agree with the Panel that the measures which might be applied are those which reduce the risks of concern, and are referred to in the 1996 Final Report as risk reduction factors. We note that the Panel observed that the 1996 Final Report examines a large number of different risk reduction factors for each of the 24 diseases of concern, and we note that the Panel came to the following factual finding:

> For most of these risk reduction factors, the 1996 Final Report provides *some* evaluation of the extent to which these factors could reduce risk. (emphasis added)

133. With regard to the quarantine policy options considered to reduce the *total* risk associated with all diseases of concern, the Panel, arrived at these factual findings:

> that the 1996 Final Report does not substantively *evaluate* the relative risks associated with these different options. Even though the definition of risk assessment requires an 'evaluation ... according to the sanitary ... measures which might be applied', *the 1996 Final Report identifies such measures but does not, in any substantial way, evaluate or assess their relative effectiveness in reducing the overall disease risk.* (emphasis added)

Thereafter, the Panel stated:

> Considering the evidence before us, we recall that the 1996 Final Report addresses and *to some extent evaluates* a series of risk reduction factors, in particular, on a disease-by-disease basis. We shall, therefore, assume—without making a finding on this issue—that the 1996 Final Report ... does make such evaluation according to and taking into account the sanitary measures or options—considered to reduce the alleged risk—which might be applied. (emphasis added)

134. We believe that the above assumption is not justified by the Panel's factual findings in paragraphs 8.89 and 8.90 of its Report. On the basis of its factual findings, the Panel should have

> come to the conclusion that the 1996 Final Report does not fulfil the third requirement for the type of risk assessment applicable in this case, ie, it does not contain the required evaluation of the likelihood of entry, establishment or spread of the diseases of concern according to the SPS measures which might be applied. We recall that, contrary to the Panel, we consider that *some* evaluation of the likelihood is not enough.
>
> 135. We conclude, on the basis of the factual findings made by the Panel and the requirements for a risk assessment as set forth above, that the 1996 Final Report meets neither the second nor the third requirement for the type of risk assessment applicable in this case, and, therefore, that the 1996 Final Report is *not* a proper risk assessment within the meaning of Article 5.1 and the first definition in paragraph 4 of Annex A.
>
> 136. Inasmuch as we have found that the 1996 Final Report is not a proper risk assessment, and since it was the only risk assessment put forward by Australia, we conclude that the measure at issue, ie, the import prohibition on fresh, chilled or frozen salmon, is not based on a risk assessment as required by Article 5.1 of the SPS Agreement, and, therefore, that Australia has acted inconsistently with Article 5.1 of the SPS Agreement.

… … …

Other disagreements regarding Australia's quarantine measures have reached the level of a WTO dispute being initiated, but have not progressed much further. One such dispute was brought by the Philippines regarding Australian quarantine measures on fresh pineapples.[77] The Philippines' request for consultations was received on 18 October 2002, and consultations were held in November 2002. However, the Philippines has not moved to the next procedural stage, which would be to request the establishment of a panel. The Philippines also initiated another dispute against Australia, again with respect to quarantine measures, this time applying more broadly to fresh fruit and vegetables. In that dispute the Philippines did request the establishment of a panel, and one was duly established on 29 August 2003. However, the proceeding has not progressed to the next procedural stage of appointing panellists.[78] The EC additionally requested consultations with Australia regarding its quarantine regime for imports in April 2003. A dispute settlement panel was established in November 2003, but was not composed. The parties notified a settlement of the dispute to the WTO on 9 March 2007.[79]

More recently, New Zealand initiated a dispute settlement proceeding complaining that Australia Quarantine Inspection Service (AQIS) measures with respect to apples cannot be justified under the SPS Agreement. Australia maintained a ban on apples from New Zealand for more than 80 years on the basis that apple imports from New Zealand could lead to the establishment of fire blight and introduce other plant pests into Australia. After repeated requests from New Zealand to lift the ban, AQIS conducted a risk assessment in which it concluded that New Zealand apples could be imported, but only subject to stringent restrictions. New Zealand did not feel that these restrictions

77 *Australia—Certain Measures Affecting the Importation of Fresh Pineapple Fruit* (WT/DS/271).

78 *Australia—Certain Measures Affecting the Importation of Fresh Fruit and Vegetables* (WT/DS270).

79 *Australia—Quarantine Regime for Imports* (WT/DS287).

were defensible under the SPS Agreement, and accordingly brought a challenge. As of the time of writing, the panel has yet to issue its decision.[80]

Businesses should be aware of the potential for abuse of SPS and TBT measures, and should notify their governments if they believe measures are being imposed inappropriately on their exports. Likewise, it is important to understand that there are limitations on what measures governments may impose. In addition, businesses should be aware of whether their trading partners are WTO members or not. In the trade remedies context this is not a major issue as the main users of trade remedies are all WTO members. However, all countries impose some restrictions on imports in the form of health and safety regulations and other standards. If an exporter is shipping to a WTO member, that importer's regulations will need to be consistent with the WTO agreements. But if the importing country is not a WTO member, it is not under the same obligations and the exporting business may not have attractive remedies available if arbitrary measures are imposed. Companies would thus do well to consider not only the regulatory schemes in place in their destination markets, but also whether the destination country is a WTO member. If the country is not a WTO member, the business may wish to obtain particular assurances with respect to regulatory procedures and requirements before entering into agreements to supply that market.

6.5 Conclusion

In this chapter we have examined a number of methods by which governments may impose restrictions upon imports entering the country. Non-tariff barriers such as the trade remedies and other import controls discussed here can significantly impact companies' ability to compete—for the better or the worse. While the current scope of permissible trade remedies (particularly with respect to antidumping duties and countervailing measures) is subject to criticism by many, the fact remains that these measures are available, and they are used. Accordingly, businesses need to be aware of the trade remedies and other import controls that could be applied to their exports, as well as the range of measures they could seek to have their governments impose on imports with which they compete. In addition, businesses that become subject to import controls should consult with legal counsel if they have concerns that measures being applied to them are—in procedure or substance—inconsistent with any of the relevant WTO agreements.

80 *Australia—Measures Affecting the Importation of Apples from New Zealand* (WT/DS367).

Questions

With regard to the case study at the beginning of this chapter:

1 a If the Chinese manufacturers competing with CBL in the Australian market are receiving government subsidies, what options might CBL discuss with the Australian government? What department(s) would it contact?

b For what types of subsidies could Australia initiate a WTO dispute against China?

2 a What options might CBL discuss with the government with respect to imported clothing from India? What department(s) would it contact?

b If the Indian manufacturers are in fact making money in the Australian market, is there nonetheless government action that can be taken?

3 a What measures could the Australian Government take with respect to the competition CBL is facing from Bangladesh? What department(s) would CBL contact?

b Assume the Bangladeshi imports were, in addition to the description provided, also being sold at low prices. Assess the pros and cons of an antidumping investigation versus a safeguards investigation.

4 Why is dumping treated as an unfair trade practice?

a Do you think this is a good idea?

b How else could predatory conduct be controlled?

c Why do you think the WTO permits the imposition of antidumping duties?

5 In the TMRO review excerpt provided in Section 6.3.4a, why was it significant that Heinz had paid more than normal value for the pineapple product under investigation?

6 Why is subsidisation treated as an unfair trade practice?

a Do you think this is a good idea?

b Identify advantages and disadvantages of imposing CVDs to offset subsidies.

c Who benefits and who is disadvantaged?

7 Assume developing country Alvidia does not require employers to provide workers with paid holiday leave, health insurance coverage or other benefits common in developed countries.

a Is Alvidia effectively subsidising its companies?

b Could this constitute a countervailable subsidy?

8 a In what ways is it more controversial for countries to provide relief from competition in the form of safeguard measures than antidumping duties or countervailing measures?

b In what ways is it less controversial?

9 a Assume the country Biglandia is subsidising its textiles industry, and that this results in textiles being exported to Newlandia in increased numbers and sold for very low prices. Make the best case you can for the position that it is not in Newlandia's interests to seek to impose CVDs on the subsidised imports.

b Assume now that Biglandia's largest textiles producer, Clothco, is selling off last year's unsold merchandise at rock-bottom prices in the Newlandia market. Make the best case you can for the position that it is not in Newlandia's interests to seek to impose antidumping duties on the imported items.

10 If an industry is receiving a yellow light subsidy, what are the different actions that may be taken by the country into which the industry's products are exported? What are the pros and cons of each choice?

11 Explain how SPS measures and technical standards can act as non-tariff barriers.
 a If there is a legitimate reason to impose such measures, does it matter that their imposition may impede trade flows?
 b What do you think constitutes a legitimate reason? Should countries have a say into whether the policy decisions of other sovereign states are legitimate?

12 Explain the potential clash between WTO obligations and import restraints imposed pursuant to MEAs.

CHAPTER 7

export controls and national security

A recently established Australian business, Aussie Traders International (ATI), intends to import and export various chemicals and to trade with customers in as many countries as possible. One of the business units ATI intends to establish will handle the exportation of chemical waste products for disposal in overseas markets, where the cost of disposal is low. Another unit is slated to provide chemicals to overseas companies that in turn supply their local militaries and defence agencies.

ATI has not yet established any internal procedures to ensure its compliance with applicable export control regulations. In fact, ATI's management knows little about the existence or scope of Australia's export controls. However, ATI's management does realise this is an area about which it needs to become more informed, and it is therefore seeking the advice of legal counsel.

7.1 Introduction

In the previous chapter, we discussed many of the ways in which a country can impose restrictions on imports and why a country might choose to impose such limits. In this chapter, we examine the inverse phenomenon: when countries limit what may leave—rather than come across—national borders. Such restrictions are broadly known as export controls. Export controls are often, though not always, imposed for national security reasons. Thus the terms 'export controls' and 'national security' are often seen used together, and it is for this reason we include both in the chapter title. However, as is canvassed below, governments impose controls over exports in furtherance of a variety of objectives, not solely for security purposes. In this chapter we reference a wide range of Australian export controls as examples. After reading this chapter, you should be able to give thoughtful consideration to what advice a company such as ATI (in the above case study) should be given to ensure its practices are in conformity with applicable national law. In addition, you should be able to identify some internal mechanisms ATI should put into place with respect to monitoring its export control compliance.

Export controls are, as the name suggests, controls placed over exports. While the meaning of 'export' may seem relatively straightforward, it is important to keep in mind that exports include not only the physical transfer of goods across a country's borders, but can also encompass the electronic transfer or transmittal of technology or other data to an international source. 'Controls' covers a number of potential measures. Export controls can take the form of a comprehensive prohibition on the export of a given product or type of products, or may be in the narrower form of a restriction on exports, where exporting may be possible if certain procedures such as licensing requirements are first satisfied. Australia maintains both types of export controls.

The most stringent type of export control is an outright ban on exports. In some limited instances, governments do impose bans on the exportation of certain types of products. More commonly however, if a country wishes to regulate the exportation of an item, it does so by imposing restrictions or limitations on the export, rather than a complete prohibition upon the exportation.

Restrictions can take a variety of forms, but at a minimum an export licence or certificate is generally required from the relevant government department or ministry. As a general matter, most export controls do not restrict trade per se, but rather make specific types of trade more visible and transparent by requiring that licensing procedures be followed. As a result, trade in materials and technologies that have civilian as well as military uses (so-called dual-use products) is less likely to end up leading to further proliferation of weapons of mass destruction such as nuclear, chemical and biological weapons. Similarly, certain trade in wildlife, hazardous waste, and culturally significant items is regulated to ensure that prohibited forms of trade do not occur. In some cases, obtaining an export licence is a pro forma exercise, but for a wide array of products, exporters will have to meet certain criteria before they are granted their export licences.

Sometimes there are domestic policy reasons for keeping certain types of goods from leaving the country, such as a desire to prevent depletion of scarce resources, or a wish to mitigate inflationary pressures. Foreign policy motivations also often underlie export controls. Countries may elect to restrict exports to a country whose policies are disfavoured, as in the case of the widespread boycotts of South Africa during the apartheid era. In addition, a country may decide that for national security reasons it does not wish to permit the export of items that could be put to military or other strategic use by unfriendly countries. Many export controls are put into place pursuant to obligations arising under international treaties or non-binding commitments made under more informal international arrangements. Various examples of export controls are discussed below.

As noted above, a significant subset of the export controls imposed by many countries comprise restrictions on the exportation of weapons of mass destruction (WMD) and the technology and components that would assist a nation in developing WMD. Conventions and agreements to limit trade in the materials of war have been in existence since before the First World War. The Versailles Treaty of 1919 restated the pre-war prohibition on the use of poisonous gases. The Geneva Protocol of 1925 affirmed this prohibition and also added a ban on the use of bacterial warfare.[1] Over the past 80 years or more, many such agreements have been entered into. With the advent of ever more sophisticated means of communication and the increase in terrorist activity on a large scale, numerous countries are concerned that more needs to be done

1 Protocol for the Prohibition of the Use of Asphyxiating, Poisonous or Other Gases, and of Bacteriological Methods of Warfare. Geneva, 17 June 1925. The text of the Geneva Protocol may be accessed at [www.icrc.org/ihl.nsf/FULL/280?OpenDocument].

to ensure that WMD do not fall into the hands of rogue states, terrorist organisations, or other perceived threats to national and international peace and stability. On the one hand it would be fairly difficult to obtain a nuclear warhead and transfer it across national borders. However, transferring parts, technology, know-how, and dual-use items is much harder to detect. Similarly, some chemical and biological WMD may involve the use of relatively small amounts of chemicals or biological agents. Tracking the location and transfer of these products poses serious challenges. Accordingly, a number of agreements, conventions and protocols have developed in the more recent past as countries—particularly the developed world—have decided that working together is essential in order to prevent deadly weapons from falling into the hands of dangerous entities.

Exporters thus need to maintain a high level of awareness regarding national export control regulations. While individuals may generally take items with them when leaving the country without triggering export control concerns, this is not always the case. For goods upon which there is a ban on exportation, it is simply prohibited to remove such items from the country, whether for non-commercial use or any other purpose. More commonly, however, export controls will be of primary concern to businesses that export items for commercial purposes, rather than to individuals transporting items for non-commercial use.

A wide variety of items can be the subject of export controls. These items fall under a range of competent agencies or ministries. For example, in the case of Australia, export procedures are managed by the Australian Customs Service (ACS); however, the ACS procedures cover export controls imposed by numerous other departments including:

- The Attorney-General's Department;
- The Department of Agriculture, Fisheries and Forestry;
- The Department of Resources, Energy and Tourism;
- The Department of Health and Ageing;
- Medicare Australia;
- The Department of Defence;
- The Department of Foreign Affairs and Trade;
- The Department of the Environment and Water Resources;
- The Department of Employment and Workplace Relations; and
- The Australian Federal Police.[2]

While centralised information will likely be available through a nation's customs authorities, it is nonetheless important for exporting businesses to be cognisant of the relevant government ministries, agencies, or departments that have jurisdiction over the types of products the businesses are exporting.

7.2 Export controls and the WTO

Before delving into more detail regarding specific types of export control, it is important to recognise that nations may be constrained to some degree in the export controls

2 For detailed information on Australia's customs regime for export controls, see the Australian Customs Service Manual, Volume 12: *Export Control*, accessible electronically at [www.customs.gov.au/webdata/resources/files/ACSmanual_vol12.pdf].

they may impose. Countries that are members of the World Trade Organization (WTO) must ensure that their export controls are consistent with WTO rules. To be sure, export controls are not a major focus of the WTO; instead the emphasis is generally on limiting and monitoring import restrictions. Most members want to increase exports, not limit them. Nonetheless, there are circumstances when members do seek to limit exports, and these restrictions must be imposed in accordance with relevant WTO provisions. Although the WTO does not regulate exports to a significant degree, there are some limitations. Many export controls would fall foul of WTO rules but for the existence of a number of applicable exceptions. However, to the extent the WTO rules apply, most common export controls would seem to fall comfortably within one of the exceptions. This section sets out the applicable WTO rules and exceptions applicable to export controls.

7.2.1 Export controls based on country of destination

In general, the most-favoured-nation principle (MFN) prohibits discrimination in connection with, *inter alia*, exportation of products. The General Agreement on Tariffs and Trade (GATT), Article I:1 provides in relevant part:

> ... with respect to all rules and formalities in connection with ... exportation ... any advantage, favour, privilege or immunity granted by any contracting party to any product ... destined for any other country shall be accorded immediately and unconditionally to the like product ... destined for the territories of all other contracting parties.

Thus as a general matter, a WTO member cannot permit exports of a product to another country but prohibit exports of that same or like product to another WTO member.

This rule is not absolute, however.

- First, the MFN obligation only applies when the like product is destined for the territory of another WTO member. It therefore is not a WTO violation for WTO members to restrict exports to non-WTO members. This is an important distinction. While most major economies in the world are members of the WTO, a number of politically unstable countries are not, including Afghanistan, Iraq and North Korea. Therefore if a WTO member bans exports of arms or other sensitive items to North Korea while permitting such exports to WTO members, Article I is not implicated.
- In addition, it may be possible for a WTO member to restrict exports based on country of destination, notwithstanding the GATT, Article 1, if the circumstances fall within one of the exceptions to the general GATT principles. These exceptions are discussed in Sections 7.2.1d and 7.2.1e below.

7.2.1a GATT, Article XI: no export restrictions other than duties, taxes or other charges

Article XI of the GATT sets forth a general provision relevant to export controls:

> Article XI: General Elimination of Quantitative Restrictions

> 1. No prohibitions or restrictions other than duties, taxes or other charges, whether made effective through quotas, import or export licences or other measures, shall be instituted or maintained by any contracting party on the importation of any product of the territory of any other contracting party or on the exportation or sale for export of any product destined for the territory of any other contracting party …

The general rules therefore are that the only types of limitations on exports should be in the form of 'duties, taxes or other charges', and that bans, quotas and export licence requirements are generally prohibited.

It should be noted that Article XI:1 does not prohibit export taxes per se, but any such taxes must be non-discriminatory and transparent pursuant to the GATT, Articles I and X respectively. It is also permissible, although uncommon, to impose export tariffs.[3]

7.2.1b Voluntary restrictions on exports

The types of export restraints mentioned thus far have involved laws or regulations imposing restrictions on exporting. In other words, the government has in some way established criteria that limit or prohibit the export of a given product or products. In addition to governmentally imposed restrictions, it is also possible for companies themselves to reach an agreement with foreign companies or a foreign nation to limit export volumes. In practice, however, such agreements generally violate national laws or international rules and thus do not occur often. This is not to say that they never occur; in fact they used to be far more prevalent.

In the GATT era, it was not infrequent for contracting parties to negotiate these so-called 'grey area' measures. Pursuant to these measures, the companies in a given country's industry agreed to limit their exports into another country. The USA reached numerous such agreements with Japanese companies—often in the field of electronics or cars—particularly in the 1980s. These arrangements were variously referred to as voluntary restraints on exports (VERs), orderly marketing arrangements (OMAs) or voluntary restraint agreements (VRAs).[4] Grey area measures were the subject of a great deal of criticism because they were not transparent; such deals were not recorded in writing and were not the result of state–state negotiations.[5]

During the Uruguay Round of multilateral trade negotiations, which culminated in the formation of the WTO, it was agreed that grey area measures should no longer be permitted. Accordingly, this issue is addressed in the WTO Agreement on Safeguards. Article 11.1(b) of that agreement makes clear that members may not enter into arrangements whereby businesses agree to limit their exports to a member country:

> Furthermore, a Member shall not seek, take or maintain any voluntary export restraints, orderly marketing arrangements or any other similar measures on the export or the

---

3 See generally S Lester & B Mercurio, *World Trade Law: Text, Materials and Commentary*, Hart Publishing, Oxford & Portland, Oregon, 2008, p 271.

4 For ease of reference, VERs, OMAs and VRAs are referred to in this chapter as VERs.

5 See generally EM Hizon, 'The Safeguard Measure/VER Dilemma: The Jekyll and Hyde of Trade Protection' (1994) 15 *Nw J Int'l L and Bus* 105.

> import side.[6] These include actions taken by a single Member as well as actions under agreements, arrangements and understandings entered into by two or more Members. Any such measure in effect on the date of entry into force of the WTO Agreement shall be brought into conformity with this Agreement or phased out in accordance with paragraph 2.

The only protective measures that WTO members may enter into are the trade remedies discussed in Chapter 6.

While VERs are no longer permitted under the WTO, it is likely that they are still used from time to time. As noted above, these arrangements are often not transparent and may not be reduced to writing; as such, they may be difficult to detect. In addition, there is the question of who would initiate a WTO dispute settlement proceeding if a VER were entered into. The recent Softwood Lumber Agreement entered into between the USA and Canada provides a useful example.

EXAMPLE: The USA and Canada have been engaged in trade disputes for decades over Canada's exports of softwood lumber to the USA. The USA has imposed antidumping duties and countervailing duties on Canadian softwood lumber on numerous occasions, and Canada has challenged the US measures in national, NAFTA and WTO dispute settlement proceedings.

In 2006, Canada and the USA entered into an agreement relating to softwood lumber exports from Canada to the USA, pursuant to which the parties agreed to terminate much of the litigation between them relating to softwood lumber. For its part, Canada additionally agreed that in soft markets for softwood lumber, its exporting provinces would either collect export taxes or collect lower export taxes in combination with limiting export volumes.[7]

One could interpret this agreement as constituting a VER, yet who would bring a WTO complaint over it? Clearly not the USA or Canada. It is unclear what—if any—other member would have standing to complain. And if another member did wish to bring a complaint, it is unclear how that member would or could demonstrate it had suffered nullification or impairment as a result of the Softwood Lumber Agreement.

Thus, while VERs are technically prohibited, it is likely that they are still in use, albeit less frequently than before.

7.2.1c Exceptions: when are export controls permitted?

As explained above, the general WTO rule is that export controls are not permitted. However, that rule is subject to limited exceptions set forth in the GATT, Article XI:2(a) and (b):

---

6 Note 4 to this provision clarifies that: 'Examples of similar measures include export moderation, export-price or import-price monitoring systems, export or import surveillance, compulsory import cartels and discretionary export or import licensing schemes, any of which afford protection.'

7 Softwood Lumber Agreement between the Government of the USA and the Government of Canada, as amended, entry into force on 12 October 2006. The agreement is accessible electronically at [www.ustr.gov/assets/World_Regions/Americas/Canada/asset_upload_file847_9896.pdf], and the amendments (the agreement was amended only one month after its original conclusion) at [www.ustr.gov/assets/World_Regions/Americas/Canada/asset_upload_file667_9897.pdf].

> Article XI: General Elimination of Quantitative Restrictions
>
> 2. The provisions of paragraph 1 of this Article shall not extend to the following:
>
> (a) Export prohibitions or restrictions temporarily applied to prevent or relieve critical shortages of foodstuffs or other products essential to the exporting contracting party;
>
> (b) Import and export prohibitions or restrictions necessary to the application of standards or regulations for the classification, grading or marketing of commodities in international trade.

In addition, broader exceptions to the general rule are to be found in the GATT, Articles XX and XXI, which were briefly discussed in Chapter 6. The types of export controls most commonly used tend to be ones that could fall within the Article XX or XXI exceptions.[8]

7.2.1d GATT, Article XX

The GATT, Article XX, is the 'General Exceptions' article applicable to GATT obligations, including Articles I and XI. It provides as follows:

> Article XX: General Exceptions
>
> Subject to the requirement that such measures are not applied in a manner which would constitute a means of arbitrary or unjustifiable discrimination between countries where the same conditions prevail, or a disguised restriction on international trade, nothing in this Agreement shall be construed to prevent the adoption or enforcement by any contracting party of measures:
>
> (a) necessary to protect public morals;
>
> (b) necessary to protect human, animal or plant life or health;
>
> (c) relating to the importations or exportations of gold or silver;
>
> (d) necessary to secure compliance with laws or regulations which are not inconsistent with the provisions of this Agreement, including those relating to customs enforcement, the enforcement of monopolies operated under paragraph 4 of Article II and Article XVII, the protection of patents, trade marks and copyrights, and the prevention of deceptive practices;
>
> (e) relating to the products of prison labour;
>
> (f) imposed for the protection of national treasures of artistic, historic or archaeological value;
>
> (g) relating to the conservation of exhaustible natural resources if such measures are made effective in conjunction with restrictions on domestic production or consumption;
>
> (h) undertaken in pursuance of obligations under any intergovernmental commodity agreement which conforms to criteria submitted to the CONTRACTING PARTIES and not disapproved by them or which is itself so submitted and not so disapproved;
>
> (i) involving restrictions on exports of domestic materials necessary to ensure essential quantities of such materials to a domestic processing industry during periods when the domestic price of such materials is held below the world price as part of a governmental stabilization plan; *Provided* that such restrictions shall not operate to increase the exports of or the protection afforded to such domestic industry, and shall not depart from the provisions of this Agreement relating to non-discrimination;

---

8 Occasionally issues also arise as to whether certain export restrictions violate the Agreement on Subsidies and Countervailing Measures or otherwise violate WTO other obligations.

(j) essential to the acquisition or distribution of products in general or local short supply; *Provided* that any such measures shall be consistent with the principle that all contracting parties are entitled to an equitable share of the international supply of such products, and that any such measures, which are inconsistent with the other provisions of the Agreement shall be discontinued as soon as the conditions giving rise to them have ceased to exist. The CONTRACTING PARTIES shall review the need for this sub-paragraph not later than 30 June 1960.

To fall within one of the Article XX exceptions, an export control would need to both meet the criteria set forth in one of the elaborated paragraphs, and satisfy the conditions set forth in the *chapeau* (the introductory paragraph). Countries often maintain export controls that would likely satisfy the conditions of one of these paragraphs. For example, obligations pursuant to the Convention on International Trade in Endangered Species would likely fall within the scope of Article XX(b); measures pursuant to conventions such as the Basel Convention that address the exportation of pollutants would likely fall within the scope of Article XX(g); and export controls relating to cultural and national heritage treasures would likely fit within Article XX(f).

7.2.1e GATT, Article XXI

In addition to the exceptions available under the GATT, Article XX, the WTO additionally provides exceptions relevant to members' essential security interests in the GATT Article XXI:

Article XXI: Security Exceptions

Nothing in this Agreement shall be construed

(a) to require any contracting party to furnish any information the disclosure of which it considers contrary to its essential security interests; or
(b) to prevent any contracting party from taking any action which it considers necessary for the protection of its essential security interests
  (i) relating to fissionable materials or the materials from which they are derived;
  (ii) relating to the traffic in arms, ammunition and implements of war and to such traffic in other goods and materials as is carried on directly or indirectly for the purpose of supplying a military establishment;
  (iii) taken in time of war or other emergency in international relations; or
(c) to prevent any contracting party from taking any action in pursuance of its obligations under the United Nations Charter for the maintenance of international peace and security.

There has been much academic discussion regarding the scope of Article XXI in general, and what is meant by 'essential security interests' and by 'emergency in international relations'.[9] However, there is general agreement that Article XXI(c)

9 See for example WA Cann Jr, 'Creating Standards of Accountability for the Use of the WTO Security Exception: Reducing the Role of Power Based Relations and Establishing a New Balance Between Sovereignty and Multilaterialism' (2001) 26 *Yale Journal of International Law* 413; D Akande & S Williams, 'International Adjudication on National Security Issues: What Role for the WTO?' (2002–03) 43 *Virginia Journal of International Law* 365; A Emmerson, 'Conceptualizing Security Exceptions: Legal Doctrine or Political Excuse?' (2008) 11 *J Int'l Econ L* 135; DT Shapiro, 'Be Careful What You Wish For: US Politics and the Future of the National Security Exception to the GATT' (1997) 31 *George Washington Journal of International Law & Economics* 97.

includes at a minimum measures authorised by the United Nations (UN) Security Council under Chapter VI of the UN Charter in order to maintain peace and security. Many forms of export control are domestic measures taken pursuant to Security Council resolutions, and would therefore seem to fall squarely within Article XXI(c). For measures that do not fit this description, WTO members may assert that one of the subsections of Article XXI(b) is applicable. Any such measure would have to be both necessary for the protection of essential security interests and fit into one of the three subsections.

Article XX(b)(i) is reasonably straightforward and would appear to permit members to impose export restrictions on fissionable materials—either for purposes of nuclear non-proliferation or safety of disposal. Restrictions on the export of dual-use technology as well as military items would seem to fit within the scope of Article XXI(b)(ii). The most controversial provision is Article XXI(b)(iii), which includes the undefined term 'emergency in international relations'. The USA has argued that the meaning of this and other terms in Article XXI are to be determined by a given member in its given circumstances—in other words, that the article is self-judging. Others strongly disagree with this view. However, the exact meaning of this provision has yet to be explored fully in GATT or WTO jurisprudence.[10]

In 1996, the USA enacted the *Cuban Liberty and Democratic Solidarity (LIBERTAD) Act* of 1996, popularly referred to as the *Helms-Burton Act* (after the two principal sponsors of the legislation).[11] The European Communities initiated a WTO dispute settlement proceeding challenging the WTO-compatibility of this act, and Article XXI was poised to play a central role in the dispute. However, the dispute was ultimately settled and no panel report was ever issued. The following commentary highlights the sensitivities associated with Article XXI.[12]

John H Jackson and Andreas F Lowenfeld, 'ASIL Insights: Helms-Burton, the US, and the WTO' (March 1997)

Rarely has a move by the US government to impose its political views on other countries' economies aroused as much anger as has the *Cuban Liberty and Democratic Solidarity (Libertad) Act* of 1996, widely known as the *Helms-Burton Act*.

...

Helms-Burton does several things. It freezes the 35 year-old US embargo against trade with and investment in Cuba, which applies not only to US firms but also to overseas firms owned or controlled by 'US persons'. It opens third country companies 'trafficking' in Cuban property once owned by Americans to suits in the United States by the former owners, suits that could result in damages equal not to the value of trade being conducted by the defendants, but to the value of the property

10 For a discussion of the scope of Article XXI, see M Matsushita, TJ Schoenbaum & P C Mavroidis, *The World Trade Organization: Law, Practice, and Policy*, 2nd edn, Oxford University Press, Oxford & New York, 2006, pp 220–4.

11 22 USC §§ 6021–6091.

12 Accessible at [www.asil.org/insight7.cfm].

once owned by the American plaintiffs, and possibly even to three times that value. And it requires exclusion from the United States, even for visits, of officers or controlling shareholders—and their families—of companies that 'traffic' in property formerly owned or claimed to be owned by American nationals.

Even before the bill was passed, European, Canadian, and Mexican officials asserted that the United States was unlawfully exercising its jurisdiction extraterritorially, in that it was threatening to punish lawful activity—trade, investment, and tourism—carried out by residents of, say, Canada or Great Britain with an independent country, Cuba.

. . .

The EU has now taken its case to the World Trade Organization and its new dispute settlement procedures.

The WTO complaint against the US raises a list of possible inconsistencies with various parts of the WTO treaty texts. Although the arguments to be made about these are not yet clear, at least to the public, the US may have valid defenses to the substance of some of the complaint.

One subject of this complex case is particularly perplexing and cuts across the many specific complaints and arguments. This is the subject of the 'national security exceptions' in the WTO treaty texts, both GATT Article 21 applying to trade in goods, and GATS [General Agreement on Trade in Services] Article 14 applying to trade in services. Some argue these would provide a defense for the US to many if not all of the US *Helms-Burton* measures, even if some of these measures would otherwise be considered to be inconsistent with US treaty obligations. These exceptions, however, if given a broad interpretation could undermine the whole WTO treaty and impair the security and stability of the world trading system for which the WTO has been created.

On the other hand, national security is obviously extremely important to all nations, and for an international organization to disregard the importance of this subject and to easily override national concerns and policy conclusions relating to it, could lead powerful trading nations to ignore or disregard the rules of such organization. A key interpretation question for the national security exception is whether this exception permits a WTO member to decide for itself, to 'auto-determine', whether the criteria for invoking the exception exist. If the answer is yes, then arguably a government need only invoke the exception to end a proceeding against it, no matter what the underlying facts of the case are.

The critical language of the national security exception reads:

Nothing in this Agreement shall be construed ...

(b) to prevent any contracting party from taking any action which it considers necessary for the protection of its essential security interests
  (i) relating to fissionable materials ...
  (ii) relating to the traffic of arms ...
  (iii) taken in time of war or other emergency in international relations ...

Is this a free-floating mandate to any member nation to decide when it may take a trade-restrictive action notwithstanding what is written in GATT or GATS? Or is there some implied requirement that a WTO member invoking the national security exception have a good faith rationale for avoiding the restraints of the trade treaties? After all, any product can be linked to national security: Premier Khrushchev, mocking US export controls, once suggested an embargo on buttons, because they can be used to hold up soldiers' trousers. It has seriously been argued that a shoe industry deserved protection from imports because an army must have shoes.

Cases in the GATT prior to the WTO are 'guidance' for the WTO, but very few GATT cases (and so far, no WTO cases) have addressed the meaning of Article XXI. There is some GATT practice supporting 'auto-determination', but the only time a GATT panel has favored this approach, its view was constrained by particular 'terms of reference' to the panel, which are not today present in the case.

It was the United States, more than any other participant in the Uruguay Round, that urged adoption of a dispute settlement system that could not be frustrated by a prospective defendant. Now that system has been invoked by the European Union to require creation of a three-person panel to hear the complaint against *Helms-Burton*. On the merits, the United States might well have a number of defenses. And on the question of auto-determination, the US case is at least plausible—more plausible than a contention that Cuba in 1997 poses a security [threat] to the United States giving rise to an emergency in international relations. But some reports suggest that the United States is not prepared to take its chances in court. It is walking away from the arena, just as it did in the Nicaragua case before the World Court a decade ago. It seems to us that the greatest threat is not to the EU from *Helms-Burton* or to the United States from Cuba, but to the world trading system and its firm but still fragile system for compulsory adjudication and enforcement of trade disputes.

...

But even with full participation of the US before a panel, there are still tough policy decisions. It would not be in the interest of the US to develop a complete auto-determination interpretation of the national security exception, allowing governments to protect shoe or bubble-gum industries merely by invoking the exception with not even a threshold or 'reasonableness' criterion. Governments could also be tempted to invoke the exception to justify discriminatory trade actions to favor a particular nation whose friendship is needed for military and political policy concerns, or to justify certain regional trade arrangements that do not fulfill the normal GATT/WTO criteria for approval. A panel (and an appellate body panel if an appeal occurred) would need to consider judiciously and with great care competing policy objectives of the national security language. It is even conceivable that a line could be drawn that would prevent such abuse mentioned above, yet defer to the US in the *Helms-Burton* case. In any event, the careful consideration of this subject would take some time under the WTO procedures, and might give additional breathing space to the parties to reach a settlement. After all, it is likely not to be in the interests of the European Community to create a precedent that intruded too far on national determinations about 'essential security interests'.

... ...|...

7.3 Controlling proliferation of weapons and other military items

Perhaps the most familiar association of export controls is with weapons and other items of potential military application. Exporters of materials that may have military applications, even if such materials also have civilian uses, should have complete familiarity with the export control regimes their governments maintain, and should regularly monitor those regimes for any changes or additional limitations.

The risk of proliferation of WMD is well recognised as a threat to international peace and security. There is a strong international interest in assuring that additional countries do not develop nuclear weapons capability and that countries not develop new capabilities to use chemical or biological agents as weapons. It is therefore of paramount importance that countries that do have such capacity or technology ensure that their nationals do not transfer this expertise to undesirable recipients. Controlling, limiting and monitoring the transfer of weapons or dual-use items is the basic aim of most export control regimes. The excerpt below explores some of the past problems with export control regimes and signal the steps needed to impose effective export controls.

Institute for Science and International Security (ISIS), 'Roadmap to Responsible Export Controls: Learning from the Past' (2003)[13]

Illicit exports have contributed to many countries' secret nuclear weapons programs and continue to be critical to secret weapons programs in Iraq, Iran, North Korea, and other countries. Illegal exports could also allow terrorists to obtain items needed to make nuclear weapons.

Underdeveloped or unenforced export controls lead to the illicit export of sensitive nuclear or nuclear-related equipment, materials, or technology. To prevent nuclear proliferation, states must maintain effective and ever improving export controls.

The purpose of export controls is to limit the ability of unauthorized users to obtain unlawful commodities. To minimize exploitation of the system, loopholes in laws and regulations need to be eliminated, corporate internal compliance systems must be improved, and vigilance and political support has to be sustained.

A failure to recognize the possibility or consequences of illicit sales is dangerous. Past cases of nuclear proliferation have depended heavily on illicit foreign assistance. Proliferant states and terrorist groups are adept at identifying and exploiting weak or poorly enforced export controls in supplier states. Therefore, establishing and implementing effective export controls is imperative to stopping the proliferation of nuclear weapons.

Creating an adequate export control system is complicated, with significant problems to overcome. Often there is an overemphasis on 'landing the deal' without adequately weighing the security risks posed by a sensitive export. Too often sales are viewed as essential to the survival of a company and too little attention is paid to the effort to prevent illicit procurement. However, the long-term viability of companies can be threatened if they are found responsible for conducting illegal exports. The goal, therefore, is to create a sustainable system of effective controls without unduly hampering legitimate trade.

...

13 Available at [www.exportcontrols.org].

Key elements of an effective export control system[14]

...

The purpose of nuclear export controls is not to deny the export of every nuclear weapon-related commodity, but to create obstacles and bottlenecks in secret nuclear programs by recognizing key items and blocking their transfer.

The German Peace Research Institute has identified several functions of export controls:

Delaying and Increasing costs. Export controls can delay the acquisition of nuclear weapons and increase the costs of success.

Deterrence. The threat to punish violations of foreign trade restrictions is a deterrent against those who would illegally export and import items. Two conditions, however, must be met. First, a significant probability of detection must exist. Second, the severity of the punishment must outweigh the potential benefits.

Detecting and preventing proliferation. Export controls increase the probability that illicit procurement is uncovered and the sinister intentions of would-be proliferants discovered. If a country is detected trying to import items illicitly, an effective export control system can increase scrutiny of that country and improve the chance of preventing future illicit efforts.

Intelligence gathering. The process of operating an effective export control system provides governments with opportunities to identify and analyze clandestine nuclear programs.

Confidence-building. An effective export control system, particularly in conjunction with international safeguards and national intelligence activities, can create confidence within the international community that a state is abiding by its international obligations. If no violations of export control regulations are registered, states can more credibly believe that these countries are not engaged in clandestine nuclear activities.

Triggering safeguards or broadened declarations. Export controls provide the mechanism to define items subject to international safeguards. Internationally agreed lists of controlled items serve to define what a state must declare or report to the International Atomic Energy Agency (IAEA) under advanced safeguards agreements.

Supplier's treaty compliance. By controlling the foreign trade activities of their citizens and of firms under their jurisdiction, states fulfill their obligations under Article III of the Nuclear Non-Proliferation Treaty (NPT) and the Nuclear Suppliers Group.

For export controls to be effective, governments and companies need to work together. In the United States, the Department of Energy has initiated the International Nuclear Export Control Program (INECP) that aims to strengthen international export control practices. Although written mainly from the perspective of the government, the INECP has summarized the roles of companies and governments regarding effective export control:

- Export controls rest on an interlocking set of national and international laws, regulations, and agreements. These laws require a transparent and standardized national licensing system and competent technical review of proposed transfers of nuclear-related materials, equipment, and technologies. These reviews must take into account national laws, international

14 Available at {www.exportcontrols.org/key_elements.htm#key}.

obligations, and proliferation risks associated with a particular item or technology, as well as the reliability of the end-user and intermediate consignees.

- Industry awareness and compliance are the prerequisites for the success of any nation's system of nuclear export controls. Key goals are promoting communication between government and industry and establishing procedures for industry to regulate the export of controlled commodities. The government should promote industry use of internal compliance programs and other tools-of-the-trade to reinforce export control 'best practices' at facilities that produce nuclear related commodities.
- The last line of defense in export controls is a government's ability to prevent illicit shipments while facilitating legitimate commerce. Weaknesses in this area are a leading proliferation risk today. This risk is particularly acute for states engaging in significant transshipment trade. In collaboration with other agencies, the governments should provide tools that enable customs personnel, border guards, and other officials in partnering countries to enforce their national nuclear export control requirements.

...

Ensuring end-user verification

If corporations are to play a major role in thwarting would-be proliferators, they require reliable, current information about the end-users of sensitive items. This type of information is vital in deciding whether to refuse sales or reject contractual commitments, especially in cases where the export is in fact legal, but the end-use of the export remains in question.

Companies often depend on governments for this kind of information. Unfortunately, despite the existence of many databases, key information about certain companies is unavailable or kept secret by governments.

In addition, many companies and governments do not have the resources or expertise to create a system to thoroughly examine end-users. One Russian export control expert, for example, said that more than 90 percent of all Russian enterprises do not have books or other resources with which to research the companies buying their items. Thus, a seller in Russia has a difficult time verifying whether the information the customer provides is reliable and accurate. There is no international centralized database of known front companies or otherwise denied persons. Many countries possess such lists, but often times access to the lists from outside organizations proves difficult. In some cases, the language barrier cannot be overcome, foreign companies are denied access to other country's established lists, or lists are classified and restricted to cleared national officials only.

There remains a need for an open international database on end-users that can be accessed by all companies. To create this database, countries must be more willing to share information on end users.

... ...

As the above excerpt illustrates, it is essential that businesses take active steps to ensure their operations are consistent with applicable export control laws. These include having internal compliance mechanisms as well as regularly reviewing the content of the applicable regulations.[15]

15 Detailed, useful advice on establishing such internal procedures is available at [www.exportcontrols.org].

Efforts to control weapons proliferation are focused not only on nuclear weapons technology, but also chemical, biological and other toxic elements that have the potential to be used as weapons. Some of these efforts take the form of binding international obligations (see Section 7.3.1 below), while others are managed via more informal international relationships (see Section 7.3.2 below).

7.3.1 International obligations

Export prohibitions or restrictions are sometimes mandated pursuant to a country's obligations arising under its international commitments. These obligations can arise in a number of different contexts, including security, protection of the environment and protection of endangered species.

Such commitments can arise out of binding multilateral treaties or as a result of UN resolutions. The former category includes the 1968 Nuclear Nonproliferation Treaty,[16] the 1972 Biological Weapons Convention[17] and the 1993 Chemical Weapons Convention.[18] A further example is the 1925 Protocol for the Prohibition of the Use in War of Asphyxiating, Poisonous or Other Gases, and of Bacteriological Methods of Warfare (the Geneva Protocol).[19] The Geneva Protocol was originally conceived of by the USA as an agreement to prohibit the export of gases for wartime use. In the drafting process, France suggested a protocol prohibiting the use of poisonous gases, and this was then extended to include bacteriological agents at Poland's suggestion.[20]

7.3.1a UN Security Council resolutions

The UN Security Council has, on numerous occasions, passed resolutions that embargo specific nations from receiving imports of weapons, weapon-grade material and certain products, such as chemicals that may have military applications, or other items that may have military uses. Such embargoes sometimes lead to complete prohibitions on the export of certain materials and to restrictions on exports of others.

---

16 Treaty on the Non-Proliferation of Nuclear Weapons, opened for signature 1 July 1968, 21 UST 483, TIAS No 6839, 729 UNTS 161.

17 Convention on the Prohibition of the Development, Production and Stockpiling of Bacteriological (Biological) and Toxin Weapons and on Their Destruction, opened for signature 10 April 1972, 26 UST 583, TIAS No 8062, 1015 UNTS 163. This convention is also sometimes called the Biological and Toxin Weapons Convention.

18 Convention on the Prohibition of the Development, Production and Stockpiling and Use of Chemical Weapons and on Their Destruction, opened for signature 13 January 1993, entered into force 29 April 1997, 32 *ILM* 800.

19 Signed at Geneva 17 June 1925; entered into force 8 February 1928.

20 The prohibition on poisonous gases had previously been set forth in the Versailles and Washington Treaties. See generally United States Department of State: Current Treaties and Agreements: Protocol for the Prohibition of the Use in War of Asphyxiating, Poisonous or Other Gases, and of Bacteriological Methods of Warfare (Geneva Protocol) accessible at [www.state.gov/t/ac/trt/4784.htm]. The Geneva Protocol entered into force in 1928. While most major powers ratified this Protocol before the Second World War, Japan did not do so until 1970 and the USA until 1975. For further information about the Geneva Protocol, see [www.fas.org/nuke/control/geneva/index.html].

EXAMPLE: At present, Afghanistan is subject to a series of UN resolutions[21] that require states to prevent the export of a variety of military items and technical assistance of a military nature. Australia has implemented this resolution by maintaining a prohibition on the export of acetic anhydride in any circumstance where Afghanistan would be the intermediate or final destination for the product. It additionally restricts exports of arms and other military materiel to Afghanistan, requiring would-be exporters to obtain permits from the Department of Foreign Affairs and Trade (DFAT).[22]

As of December 2008, Australia maintains export controls pursuant to a number of other UN resolutions, including controls relating to Liberia and Sierra Leone:

- Liberia is at present an embargoed country; permits from DFAT are required to export any military equipment where Liberia is the final or intermediate destination.[23]
- Sierra Leone is also at present an embargoed country; permits from DFAT are required for exports of paramilitary equipment such as batons, whips, body armour, restraining devices, and riot protection shields where Sierra Leone is the final or intermediate destination.[24]

Not all UN resolutions affecting export controls come from the Security Council. For example, in the case of the resolution to control trade in diamonds, the relevant resolution came from the General Assembly.

7.3.1b Trade in rough diamonds: the Kimberley Process

The process by which certain diamond trade is managed is called the Kimberley Process.[25] In contrast to the UN resolutions discussed above, which entailed direct

---

21 Including UN Security Council Resolutions 1735 (2006), 1390 (2002) and 1267 (1999) (all relating to military materiel and assistance), and Resolution 1267 (which also relates to asset freeze obligations).

22 Each country has its own procedures for implementing trade sanctions it is required to take pursuant to UN action. Australia implements territorial aspects of trade sanctions via regulations pursuant to the Customs (Prohibited Imports) Regulations 1956, the Customs (Prohibited Exports) Regulations 1958, and the Customs Regulations 1926, each of which is administered by the ACS. The Australian regulations pertaining to Afghanistan are the Charter of the United Nations (Sanctions—Afghanistan) Regulations 2008.

23 Pursuant to Resolution 1521 (2003) concerning Liberia. The sanctions regime and the mandate of the Security Council Committee established pursuant to Resolution 1521 have been modified by subsequent resolutions, in particular Security Council Resolutions 1532 (2004) and 1683 (2006). The regime was extended by Resolution 1792 in December 2007. The sanctions currently in effect may be viewed at [www.un.org/sc/committees/1521/index.shtml].

24 Pursuant to Resolution 1132 (1997) concerning Sierra Leone. The sanctions regime and the mandate of the Security Council Committee established pursuant to Resolution 1132 have been modified by subsequent resolutions, in particular Security Council Resolution 1171 (1998). The sanctions currently in effect may be viewed at [www.un.org/sc/committees/1132/index.shtml].

25 See generally [www.kimberleyprocess.com]. Current participants in the Kimberley Process are Angola, Armenia, Australia, Bangladesh, Belarus, Botswana, Brazil, Canada, Central African Republic, People's Republic of China, Democratic Republic of Congo, Cote d'Ivoire, Croatia, European Community, Ghana, Guinea, Guyana, Indian, Indonesia, Israel, Japan, Republic of Korea, Democratic Republic of Laos, Lebanon, Lesotho, Liberia, Malaysia, Mauritius, Namibia, New Zealand, Norway, Republic of Congo, Russian Federation, Sierra Leone, Singapore, South Africa, Sri Lanka, Switzerland, Tanzania, Thailand, Togo, Turkey, Ukraine, United Arab Emirates, USA, Venezuela, Vietnam, and Zimbabwe.

limitations on exporting military items to embargoed countries, the Kimberley Process uses an indirect method to affect the ability of African warlords to obtain weapons. In particular, the Process seeks to cut out trade in the diamonds that fund certain armed conflicts—so-called 'blood diamonds' or 'conflict diamonds'.

The following excerpt explains the history and general parameters of the Kimberley Process.

The Kimberley Process[26]

The Kimberley Process started when Southern African diamond-producing states met in Kimberley, South Africa, in May 2000, to discuss ways to stop the trade in 'conflict diamonds' and ensure that diamond purchases were not funding violence.

In December 2000, the United Nations General Assembly adopted a landmark resolution supporting the creation of an international certification scheme for rough diamonds. By November 2002, negotiations between governments, the international diamond industry and civil society organisations resulted in the creation of the Kimberley Process Certification Scheme (KPCS). The KPCS document sets out the requirements for controlling rough diamond production and trade. The KPCS entered into force in 2003, when participating countries started to implement its rules.

Who is involved?

The Kimberley Process (KP) is open to all countries that are willing and able to implement its requirements. As of September 2007, the KP has 48 members, representing 74 countries, with the European Community and its Member States counting as an individual participant. KP members account for approximately 99.8% of the global production of rough diamonds.

...

How does the Kimberley Process work?

The Kimberley Process Certification Scheme (KPCS) imposes extensive requirements on its members to enable them to certify shipments of rough diamonds as 'conflict-free' and prevent conflict diamonds from entering the legitimate trade. Under the terms of the KPCS, participating states must meet 'minimum requirements' and must put in place national legislation and institutions; export, import and internal controls; and also commit to transparency and the exchange of statistical data. Participants can only legally trade with other participants who have also met the minimum requirements of the scheme, and international shipments of rough diamonds must be accompanied by a KP certificate guaranteeing that they are conflict-free.

...

The Kimberley Process: unique and effective

The Kimberley Process Certification Scheme (KPCS) has evolved into an effective mechanism for stemming the trade in conflict diamonds and is recognized as a unique conflict-prevention instrument to promote peace and security. The joint efforts of governments, industry leaders and

26 See [www.kimberleyprocess.com].

civil society representatives have enabled the Kimberley Process (KP) to curb successfully the flow of conflict diamonds in a very short period of time. Diamond experts estimate that conflict diamonds now represent a fraction of one percent of the international trade in diamonds, compared to estimates of up to 15% in the 1990s.

...

Companies need a Kimberley Process (KP) certificate when they plan to export rough diamonds from a participant country if the diamonds fall under the relevant customs tariff (subheadings 7102.10, 7102.21 or 7102.31) in the schedule to the Customs Tariff. The exporting authorities in both country of export and the destination country require this certificate to verify that the exporter is meeting all KP requirements.

...

Since its inception, the Kimberley Process has been backed by the United Nations, both the General Assembly and the Security Council. Every year, the KP Chair is requested to report to the General Assembly on the work of the KP, and each year since 2000, the General Assembly has adopted a resolution on the role of diamonds in fuelling conflict, backing the KP by consensus. The Security Council also endorsed the KP in its resolution 1459 (2003) and has worked with the Kimberley Process, most recently on the cases of Liberia and Cote d'Ivoire.

... ...

In order to fulfil its Kimberley Process obligations, Australia has deemed rough diamonds to be restricted exports. They may only be exported if accompanied by a permit from the Minister for Industry, Tourism and Resources, and an Australian Kimberley Process Certificate, and if the destination is a country that is participating in the Kimberley Process Certification Scheme.

Although the Security Council has endorsed the Kimberley Process, the scheme itself is found in a political document that does not contain legally binding commitments. As such, the scheme itself is not subject to WTO scrutiny. Instead, the issue arises at the level of national implementation of the Kimberley Process.

There is some uncertainty as to whether domestic measures taken to implement the Process would fall under Article XXI(b) or Article XXI(c) of the GATT. A number of countries were concerned that complying with the Kimberley Process could be perceived as a violation of WTO obligations and might not fit into an applicable exception.[27] Accordingly, these countries sought a waiver from WTO obligations, and the General Council agreed to this in order to provide legal certainty, but without passing judgment one way or another over the WTO-consistency of measures taken to implement the Kimberley Process.[28]

27 See Chairman of the Kimberley Process, Non-Paper, Kimberley Process: Workshop on WTO Conformity, 15–17 February 2002 (revised version 14 March 2002), available at [www.kimberleyprocess.com/download/getfile/42].

28 The original waiver was granted by Decision of 15 May 2003, WT/L/518. That waiver expired at the end of 2006 and was extended until 31 December 2012 by Decision of 15 December 2006, WT/L/676. For a critique of this process and discussion of the legal issues, see J Pauwelyn, 'WTO Compassion or Superiority Complex? What to Make of the WTO Waiver for "Conflict Diamonds"' (2003) 24 *Mich J Int'l L* 1177.

7.3.2 Informal international non-proliferation arrangements

In addition to commitments arising out of multilateral treaties and UN resolutions, many countries additionally have security-related export control systems in place that are based on voluntary, non-binding agreements among interested countries. Such agreements are informal political arrangements and operate on a consensus basis. These arrangements include the Nuclear Suppliers Group, The Australia Group, the Missile Technology Control Regime and the Wassenaar Arrangement.

These regimes have been established primarily as a result of the increasing proliferation of WMD. The regimes each maintain a control list, which comprises both items of single (solely military) use and of dual (that is, both military and civil) use that members' national export control regimes should monitor and regulate via licensing procedures.[29]

7.3.2a The Nuclear Suppliers Group

The Nuclear Suppliers Group (NSG) consists of various nuclear supplier countries, including the USA, Australia, New Zealand and Japan,[30] which have established a set of agreed-upon Guidelines. The Guidelines are designed to encourage the non-proliferation of nuclear weapons via nuclear and nuclear-related exports. Each government participating in the NSG implements the Guidelines in accordance with its individual laws and regulatory practices.

In general, exports of nuclear or nuclear-related material are only permitted if a valid export licence is granted. Applications for such licences are made and decided upon at the national level in accordance with national requirements.[31]

7.3.2b The Australia Group

The Australia Group comprises 40 countries, plus the European Commission, which work together to prevent chemical and biological weapons (CBW) proliferation.[32] It is an informal undertaking that does not impose any legally binding obligations on its participants. Australia has been the permanent Chair of the Australia Group since it was first established in 1985.

Participants in the Australia Group strive to fight CBW proliferation by strengthening export controls and harmonising national export licensing measures

---

29 See for example D H Joyner, 'Restructuring the Multilateral Export Control Regime' (2004) 9 *J Conflict & Security L* 181 at 183–5.

30 As of September 2008, the NSG comprised Argentina, Australia, Austria, Belarus, Belgium, Brazil, Bulgaria, Canada, China, Croatia, Cyprus, Czech Republic, Denmark, Estonia, Finland, France, Germany, Greece, Hungary, Ireland, Italy, Japan, Kazakhstan, Republic of Korea, Latvia, Lithuania, Luxembourg, Malta, Netherlands, New Zealand, Norway, Poland, Portugal, Romania, Russian Federation, Slovakia, Slovenia, South Africa, Spain, Sweden, Switzerland, Turkey, Ukraine, UK and USA.

31 See generally [www.nuclearsuppliersgroup.org].

32 As of September 2008, the Australia Group comprised Argentina, Australia, Austria, Belgium, Bulgaria, Canada, Croatia, Republic of Cyprus, Czech Republic, Denmark, Estonia, European Commission, Finland, France, Germany, Greece, Hungary, Iceland, Ireland, Italy, Japan, Republic of Korea, Latvia, Lithuania, Luxembourg, Malta, Netherlands, New Zealand, Norway, Poland, Portugal, Romania, Slovak Republic, Slovenia, Spain, Sweden, Switzerland, Republic of Turkey, Ukraine, UK and USA.

on items that may have application in the CBW context. In this way, Australia Group participants seek to fully meet their obligations pursuant to the Chemical Weapons Convention and the Biological Weapons Convention. Australia Group members also promote the Group standards internationally as the benchmark for controlling chemical and biological exports with potential CBW use.[33] The following excerpt provides more detail on the Australia Group.

The Australia Group[34]

The origins of the Australia Group

In early 1984, a United Nations investigation team found that Iraq had used chemical weapons (CW) in the Iran-Iraq war in violation of the 1925 Geneva Protocol, and that at least some of the precursor chemicals and materials for its CW program had been sourced through legitimate trade channels. In response, several countries introduced export controls on certain chemicals that could be used to manufacture CW.

These controls suffered from a lack of uniformity, and it soon became apparent that attempts were being made to circumvent them. This led Australia to propose a meeting of the countries with export controls with the aim of harmonising their national licensing measures and enhancing cooperation. The first meeting of what subsequently became known as the Australia Group took place in Brussels in June 1985. At that meeting, the 15 participating countries and the European Commission agreed that there was value in exploring how existing export controls might be made more effective to prevent the spread of CW.

The Group has met regularly since then, and annual meetings are now held in Paris. The scope of the export controls discussed by the Group has evolved to address emerging threats and challenges. Evidence of the diversion of dual-use materials to biological weapons programs in the early 1990s led to participants' adoption of export controls on specific biological agents. The control lists developed by the Group have also expanded to include technologies and equipment which can be used in the manufacturing or disposal of chemical and biological weapons.

...

Activities

The Australia Group is an informal arrangement. The purpose of Australia Group meetings is to explore the scope for increasing the effectiveness of existing controls, including through information exchange, the harmonisation of national measures and, where necessary, the consideration of the introduction of additional measures.

All participants have licensing measures over 63 chemical weapons precursors. Participants also require licences for the export of specific:

- Dual-use chemical manufacturing facilities, equipment and related technology;
- Plant pathogens;

33 See generally [www.australiagroup.net/en/index.html].

34 Ibid.

- Animal pathogens;
- Biological agents; and
- Dual-use biological equipment and related technology.

The above items form the basis for the Group's 'common control lists', which have been developed during Australia Group consultations and are adjusted from time to time to ensure their continued effectiveness. Measures agreed by meetings of the Group are applied on a national basis, although all participants agree they will be more effective if similar measures are introduced by all potential exporters of relevant chemicals, biological agents and equipment and by countries of possible transhipment. Under these measures, exports are denied only if there is a well founded concern about potential diversion for CBW purposes.

...

Objectives of the group

...

The principal objective of Australia Group participants is to use licensing measures to ensure that exports of certain chemicals, biological agents, and dual-use chemical and biological manufacturing facilities and equipment, do not contribute to the spread of CBW. The Group achieves this by harmonising participating countries' national export licensing measures. The Group's activities are especially important given that the international chemical and biotechnology industries are a target for proliferators as a source of materials for CBW programs.

...

As to the nature of the export licensing measures taken by participating countries, important considerations are:

- the measures should be effective in impeding the production of chemical and biological weapons;
- they should be reasonably easy and economical to implement, and should be practical;
- they should not impede the normal trade of materials and equipment used for legitimate purposes;
- they are a licensing requirement on exports and not automatic bans on the export of such items. In practice they constitute monitoring and licensing control arrangements for exports: an export is denied only if there is particular concern about potential diversion for CBW purposes.

Measures agreed by meetings of the Group are applied on a national basis, although all participants agree they will be more effective if similar measures are introduced by all potential exporters of relevant chemicals, biological agents and equipment and by countries of possible transhipment.

Export licensing measures also serve to demonstrate the determination of participating countries to avoid not only direct but also inadvertent involvement in the spread of chemical and biological weapons, and to express their opposition to the use of these weapons. It is also in the interest of commercial firms and research institutes and of their governments to ensure that such firms and institutes are not inadvertently supplying chemicals, chemical equipment, biological agents or biological equipment for use in the manufacture of chemical or biological weapons. This principle has been firmly supported by industry.

> Participating countries recognise from the outset that export licensing measures are not a substitute for the strict and universal observance of the 1925 Protocol and the 1972 Biological and Toxin Weapons Convention (BWC) and the early implementation of and universal adherence to the Chemical Weapons Convention (CWC), which entered into force on 29 April 1997. All members of the Australia Group are States Parties to the BWC and are original States Parties to the CWC. Support for these regimes and their objectives remains the overriding objective of the countries participating in the Australia Group.
>
> **Outline of the Australia Group export licensing system**
>
> Each participant in the Australia Group has introduced licensing measures on the export of certain chemicals, biological agents, and dual-use chemical and biological manufacturing facilities and equipment with a view to ensuring that exports of these items from their countries do not contribute to the spread of chemical and biological weapons.
>
> All participating countries have licensing measures over 54 chemical weapons precursor chemicals. Participating countries also require licences for the export of dual-use facilities and equipment related to the manufacture of chemical weapons.
>
> All participating countries operate controls based on lists of human, animal and plant agents as well as BW dual-use equipment developed during Australia Group consultations. Participating countries require licences for exports of such items.
>
> … … …

7.3.2c The Missile Technology Control Regime

The Missile Technology Control Regime (MTCR) was established in 1987 by Canada, France, Germany, Italy, Japan, the UK and the USA. At present the MTCR comprises 34 partner countries, each of which has equal standing within the Regime.[35] Similar to the NSG and the Australia Group, the MTCR is a voluntary arrangement, and decisions are made on a consensus basis. Partner countries have agreed to work together to further their common goal of non-proliferation of unmanned delivery systems that are capable of delivering WMD. Non-proliferation efforts are targeted at rockets, other unmanned air vehicle delivery systems, and associated equipment, material and technology. Via the MTCR, partner countries coordinate their national export licensing schemes targeted at preventing the proliferation of such delivery systems.

Complementary to the NSG and the Australia Group, the MTCR was also created in the face of increasing proliferation of WMD. In the initial years, the MTCR focused primarily on state actors. However, since the terrorist attacks in the USA carried out on 11 September 2001, efforts have additionally focused on decreasing the likelihood that terrorist organisations or individuals would be able to obtain WMD delivery systems. In this regard, the MTCR seeks, via common export control policy guidelines (the MTCR Guidelines), to keep a close guard over the transfer of materials, equipment and

35 As of September 2008 the 34 MTCR partners were as follows: Argentina, Australia, Austria, Belgium, Bulgaria, Brazil, Canada, Czech Republic, Denmark, Finland, France, Germany, Greece, Hungary, Iceland, Ireland, Italy, Japan, Luxembourg, Netherlands, New Zealand, Norway, Poland, Portugal, Republic of Korea, Russian Federation, South Africa, Spain, Sweden, Switzerland, Turkey, Ukraine, UK and USA.

technologies that may be used to create WMD delivery systems. The MTCR Guidelines are applied by partner countries to an agreed, shared list of controlled items (the MTCR Equipment, Software and Technology Annex). Partners keep each other abreast of any relevant export licensing issues that arise nationally.[36]

7.3.2d The Wassenaar Arrangement

The Wassenaar Arrangement represents an effort by participating states[37] to promote transparency and responsibility for the export of conventional arms and dual-use goods and technologies. This Arrangement replaced the Coordinating Committees on Multilateral Export Controls (COCOM), which had been created in 1949 by 17 countries to agree to and enforce export controls limiting the transfer of sensitive items to communist countries.[38] When COCOM was disbanded in 1994, the Wassenaar Arrangement took its place, becoming operational in 1996. It is administered from Vienna, Austria.

Wassenaar Arrangement members agree to export control lists, which each country then implements according to its own national processes. The Arrangement therefore does not mandate that participating states take a certain action in any particular instance; the decision to permit or forbid the exportation of any given item is left entirely to each sovereign state to determine in accordance with national legislation and policy.[39] The Wassenaar Arrangement has established best practices to prevent transfers of certain types of weapons, guidelines for the export of small arms and light weapons, and other procedures to guide participating countries in establishing export controls over conventional arms and dual-use goods and technologies.

The excerpt below provides additional details regarding the Wassenaar Arrangement.

Institute for Science and International Security (ISIS), 'Key Elements of an Effective Export Control System'[40]

...

Governments have met for over two decades to work out satisfactory arrangements for exporting dual-use items. The results of such meetings can be seen in agreements such as the Wassenaar

36 See generally [www.mtcr.info/english/index.html].

37 States currently participating in the Wassenaar Arrangement are: Argentina, Australia, Austria, Belgium, Bulgaria, Canada, Croatia, Czech Republic, Denmark, Estonia, Finland, France, Germany, Greece, Hungary, Ireland, Italy, Japan, Latvia, Lithuania, Luxembourg, Malta, Netherlands, New Zealand, Norway, Poland, Portugal, Republic of Korea, Romania, Russian Federation, Slovakia, Slovenia, South Africa, Spain, Sweden, Switzerland, Turkey, Ukraine, UK and USA.

38 See for example PL Fitzgerald, 'Pierre Goes Online: Blacklisting and Secondary Boycotts in US Trade Policy' (1998) 31 *Vand J Transnat'l L* 1 at n.10.

39 See generally [www.wassenaar.org/index.html]. This decentralising of export control measures has been subject to criticism: see PL Fitzgerald, above note 38.

40 [www.exportcontrols.org/key_elements.htm].

Arrangement on Export Controls for Conventional Arms and Dual-Use Goods and Technologies (WA) [which] was established to promote transparency and greater responsibility in transfers of conventional arms and dual-use goods and technologies. Participating states seek, through their respective national policies, to ensure that transfers of these items do not contribute to the development or enhancement of military capabilities, which undermine nonproliferation goals. Towards this aim, WA obtained from its member states a collection of the 'best practices' for effective export control policies, including:

- Consultations occur among relevant government agencies within the exporting country with respect to license applications to export very sensitive list (VSL) items. During these consultations, the appropriateness of the quantity and technological level of the item to the stated end-use, and bona fides of the end-user are among the criteria considered;
- In order to determine, *inter alia*, the risk of diversion or unauthorized use, additional information on end-users may be gathered, as necessary, using appropriate means ranging from documentation to visitation (with consent of the visiting country) prior to the licensing decision;
- As necessary, post-shipment verification may be carried out through appropriate means by the exporter, supplier or officials of the exporting country.

While these examples are specifically for items considered most sensitive, the same careful procedures would be required for other, less sensitive items, as well.

. . .

[A strong enforcement mechanism is essential to effective export controls. The Wassenaar Arrangement has been identified as having identified practices important to an effective enforcement scheme. Some of these recommended practices include:]

- Using threat assessment techniques and procedures for evaluating parties involved in a proposed export transaction, paying particular attention to those considered to be suspicious, unreliable, or presenting a high risk of diversion;
- Maintaining a list of problem end-users to identify license applications deserving closer inspection;
- Obtaining assurances regarding end-use and non re-export of licensed items, as appropriate;
- As necessary, confirming that exported goods have reached their intended destinations using appropriate means, ranging from documentation to on-site verification;
- Seeking voluntary compliance by industry. As appropriate, encourage development by industry of internal compliance programs;
- Providing adequate resources and training for enforcement officers;
- Ensuring that national laws and regulations have statutes of limitations sufficiently long to permit the detection and prosecution of export control violators; and
- Establishing effective penalties (including, as appropriate, criminal sanctions, civil fines, publicity and restriction or denial of export privileges) sufficient to punish and deter violations of export controls.

... ...

Companies involved in exporting computers, computer equipment, source code, software, or other items that may be considered dual-use, as well as those exporting military items, should consult the current Wassenaar Arrangement Munitions and Dual-Use Lists to determine whether any of their potential exports are listed. If any of a company's potential exports are present on a Wassenaar list the company needs to be cognisant of the national regulations its country has in place to control such exports.

7.3.3 Domestic national security policies

In addition to international obligations and more informal international commitments, countries may also have domestic laws that dictate export controls aimed at stemming the proliferation of WMD. For example, Australia's *Weapons of Mass Destruction (Prevention of Proliferation) Act 1995* prohibits supplying tangible or intangible goods or services that may contribute to any WMD program.

In addition, permits are required from the Australian Minister for Defence to export any type of defence or strategic goods, equipment, technology or material. This includes items such as explosives, nuclear material, all forms of military transport, and stealth materials. Restricted items include equipment, facilities, technologies, and materials that have a valid civil application but which may be diverted for use in WMD programs.

With respect to biological agents, Australia maintains a list of controlled agents and equipment which is available from the Department of Defence website. Permits for export of these items are issued by the Department of Defence. This export control covers biological agents and equipment that have the potential to be used in WMD programs. These agents include items that have a civil application, but also have the potential to be diverted for use in connection with WMD. Australia maintains a similar export control for chemical compounds that could be used in WMD programs, including mixtures or finished products that contain 25 per cent or more of a controlled chemical.

7.4 Economic boycotts and anti-boycott legislation

We have seen a number of examples of export controls that aim to keep weapons out of the wrong hands. A different type of export control is the economic boycott. This is where a country prohibits its nationals from importing to, and/or exporting from, a country—in other words, a country attempts to influence behaviour by withholding commerce rather than arms. In recent history there have been a number of notable economic boycotts, including the boycott by many countries of South Africa under apartheid pursuant to UN resolution;[41] the US embargo of grain to the Soviet Union in the early 1980s; the ongoing Arab boycotts of Israel and the US embargo of Cuba.

41 Following 25 years of UN Security Council resolutions condemning South Africa's apartheid system, in Resolution 5 of 1989 the UN added to the condemnation a call for a sweeping economic embargo on transactions with the South African Government. See UN Doc S/RES/569 (1985); PL Fitzgerald, above note 38 at 17 note 71.

Some economic boycotts are undertaken on a multilateral basis pursuant to UN procedures as regulated by Chapter VII of the UN Charter.[42] In other cases, however, individual countries may determine that it is in their security or other interests to boycott another country; these types of economic boycotts are more controversial. An example of this is the USA's continued economic embargo of Cuba, and in particular the *Cuban Liberty and Democratic Solidarity (LIBERTAD) Act* of 1996 (the *Helms-Burton Act*), discussed in Section 7.2.1e above.

Additionally controversial are efforts to impose or enforce economic boycotts extraterritorially. Such efforts often take the form of what is sometimes referred to as a 'secondary boycott', whereby it is prohibited to do business with entities in third countries that in turn do business in or with the subject of the primary boycott. One such effort occurred in the early 1980s.

EXAMPLE: When the Soviet Union endorsed the imposition of martial law in Poland in December 1981, the USA took steps to prevent foreign subsidiaries of US corporations from selling pipeline equipment to the Soviet Union. The US regulations additionally extended to European companies not controlled by US corporations, to the extent such companies would be re-exporting products manufactured pursuant to licences granted by US nationals or products originally imported from the USA.[43]

Further examples of secondary boycotts include provisions in US legislation pertaining to Canadians engaging in trade with Cuba, and provisions in the Arab League's boycott against Israel that reached US firms doing business with Israel.[44]

Affected third countries often react negatively to the imposition of secondary boycotts. Upon the introduction of the Soviet pipeline secondary boycott, the European Communities Commission complained to the US State Department that the extraterritorial nature of the regulations went beyond the scope of US jurisdiction. Affected European companies fulfilled their obligations under their contracts with Soviet entities, in all cases with government approval and in some cases by government mandate.

The latter situation arose due to the introduction of anti-boycott measures by some European governments.[45] Anti-boycott legislation essentially requires local companies to disregard the requirements of a boycott—most commonly, a secondary boycott. The USA introduced anti-boycott legislation in the late 1970s that prohibited US entities from cooperating with the Arab–Israeli boycott or related secondary boycott blacklist. The legislation did not question the Arab League's right to impose a primary boycott on

42 UN Charter, Article 41.

43 Amendment of Oil and Gas Controls to the USSR, 22 June 1982, 47 Fed Reg 27250. For discussions of the pipeline dispute, see KM Meessen (ed), *International Law of Export Control: Jurisdictional Issues*, Graham & Trotman/Martinus Nijhoff, London & Boston, 1992, pp 4–5; and entries appearing in (1984) 27 *German Yearbook of International Law* at 28–141.

44 Fitzgerald above note 38 at 49–50 and notes 209–14.

45 The initial US response was to blacklist these companies, though it ultimately relaxed the sanctions and the regulations. See Meessen above note 43, pp 4–5.

its own dealings with Israel, but rather addressed the effects of the secondary boycott on US actors.[46] In addition, Canada responded to the US secondary boycott with respect to Cuba by requiring Canadian nationals and businesses to refuse to cooperate with the US embargo.[47]

Exporters need to be aware of what international and national restrictions are in place, not only with respect to the items that may be exported, but also the permissible recipients. Where economic boycotts are in place, it is important to determine whether there are any secondary boycotts that could affect an exporter based outside the target of the primary boycott. Likewise, if there is a secondary boycott, a would-be exporter needs to determine whether its government has enacted any anti-boycott legislation or otherwise requires the exporter to disregard the terms of the secondary boycott.

7.5 Environmental and endangered species protection

As awareness has grown regarding the harmful effects of various pollutants, a number of international agreements or conventions have been entered into that seek to minimise the release into the atmosphere of substances that can cause environmental damage. Multilateral environmental agreements tend to focus on different types of pollutants, but share common goals of coordination, transparency, and agreeing upon lists of substances that should be controlled. The conventions generally impose some obligations with respect to imports, but also relate to exports, which is why they are discussed here.[48] In addition, the Convention on International Trade in Endangered Species (CITES) shares similar methods and goals in its efforts to protect endangered species from extinction.

7.5.1 Hazardous waste: the Basel Convention

The Basel Convention on the Control of Transboundary Movements of Hazardous Wastes and their Disposal (Basel Convention) is an international environmental agreement with 170 parties. It was formed to address the indiscriminate dumping of hazardous (toxic, poisonous, explosive, corrosive, flammable, ecotoxic and infectious) waste, including the illegal dumping of such items by developed country entities into developing nations. Hazardous waste, when not disposed of properly, can render water and soil unusable for decades and can cause significant health problems.[49] Key aspects of the Convention are as follows:

---

46 Fitzgerald above note 45 at 49–60.

47 *Canada Foreign Extraterritorial Measures Act 1985*, 24 *ILM* 794; Fitzgerald above note 45 at 61.

48 There are myriad international agreements pertaining to environmental protection. Only a selection of the major ones is canvassed here.

49 Basel Convention on the Control of Transboundary Movements of Hazardous Wastes and their Disposal, 22 March 1989, 1673 *UNTS* 125; 28 *ILM* 657 (1989). See generally |www.basel.int/|.

The Basel Convention on the Control of Transboundary Movements of Hazardous Wastes and their Disposal[50]

Origins of the Convention

In the late 1980s, a tightening of environmental regulations in industrialized countries led to a dramatic rise in the cost of hazardous waste disposal. Searching for cheaper ways to get rid of the wastes, 'toxic traders' began shipping hazardous waste to developing countries and to Eastern Europe. When this activity was revealed, international outrage led to the drafting and adoption of the Basel Convention.

During its first Decade (1989–1999), the Convention was principally devoted to setting up a framework for controlling the 'transboundary' movements of hazardous wastes, that is, the movement of hazardous wastes across international frontiers. It also developed the criteria for 'environmentally sound management'. A Control System, based on prior written notification, was also put into place.

About the Present Decade

During The Present Decade (2000–2010), the Convention will build on this framework by emphasizing full implementation and enforcement of treaty commitments. The other area of focus will be the minimization of hazardous waste generation.

...

The goal of minimizing hazardous wastes

A central goal of the Basel Convention is 'environmentally sound management' (ESM), the aim of which is to protect human health and the environment by minimizing hazardous waste production whenever possible. ESM means addressing the issue through an 'integrated life-cycle approach', which involves strong controls from the generation of a hazardous waste to its storage, transport, treatment, reuse, recycling, recovery and final disposal.

...

An overview of compliance and enforcement

The Basel Convention contains specific provisions for the monitoring of implementation and compliance. A number of articles in the Convention oblige Parties (national governments which have acceded to the Convention) to take appropriate measures to implement and enforce its provisions, including measures to prevent and punish conduct in contravention of the Convention.

The system that controls the movement of hazardous waste

Because hazardous wastes pose such a potential threat to human health and the environment, one of the guiding principles of the Basel Convention is that, in order to minimize the threat, hazardous wastes should be dealt with as close to where they are produced as possible. Therefore, under the Convention, transboundary movements of hazardous wastes or other wastes can take place

50 [www.basel.int/convention/basics.html].

only upon prior written notification by the State of export to the competent authorities of the States of import and transit (if appropriate). Each shipment of hazardous waste or other waste must be accompanied by a movement document from the point at which a transboundary movement begins to the point of disposal. Hazardous waste shipments made without such documents are illegal. In addition, there are outright bans on the export of these wastes to certain countries. Transboundary movements can take place, however, if the state of export does not have the capability of managing or disposing of the hazardous waste in an environmentally sound manner.

... ...

In Australia, exporters must obtain permits from the Minister for the Environment and Heritage in order to export hazardous waste. This includes waste that is explosive, flammable, poisonous or toxic; infectious substances; clinical waste; waste oils; and waste residue from manufacture or household waste as defined by the Basel Convention. Australia implements the Basel Convention through the *Hazardous Waste (Regulation of Exports and Imports) Act 1989* (Cth) as amended.

7.5.2 The Stockholm Convention on Persistent Organic Pollutants

The Stockholm Convention on Persistent Organic Pollutants (POPs) is a relatively new agreement; it was adopted in 2001 and entered into force in 2004.[51] This Convention is administered by the UN Environment Programme and is based in Geneva.

The Stockholm Convention requires parties to undertake steps to eliminate or reduce their release into the environment of POPs. POPs are chemicals that take a very long time to degrade and, as such, remain intact in the environment for a significant time period. These chemicals disperse across wide geographic areas and end up accumulating in the fatty tissues of people and animals.[52] This exposure can lead to serious health problems. However, because of the long distances POPs can travel, a single country cannot, on its own, take sufficient measures to protect its citizens from the effects of POPs; thus the impetus for this treaty.

The Convention requires parties to prohibit the export (and import) of an established list of chemicals and to restrict the use and production of a separate list of chemicals.[53] The identified chemicals may only be exported under limited conditions. If there is a specific exemption or acceptable use in effect, the chemicals may be exported for the purpose of environmentally sound disposal or to countries that are permitted to use the chemicals as per their acceptable use, or to non-parties that certify the intended use and that appropriate protective measures will be taken. If there is no specified exemption or

---

51 Stockholm Convention on Persistent Organic Pollutants, 22 May 2001, 40 *ILM* 532 (2001); [http://chm.pops.int/].

52 [http://chm.pops.int/Convention/tabid/54/language/en-US/Default.aspx]. Under the Convention there are 12 identified POPs: Aldrin, Chlordane, DDT, Dieldrin, dioxins, Endrin, Furans, Heptachlor, Hexachlorobenzene (HCB), Mirex, Polychlorinated Biphenyls (PCBs), and Toxaphene (also called camphechlor): [http://chm.pops.int/Convention/12POPs/tabid/296/language/en-US/Default.aspx].

53 Stockholm Convention, Article 3.1(a) (ii); 3.1(b).

acceptable use, then exports are prohibited except for the purpose of environmentally sound disposal.[54]

7.5.3 The Rotterdam Convention

The Rotterdam Convention on the Prior Informed Consent Procedure for Certain Hazardous Chemicals and Pesticides in International Trade (the Rotterdam Convention, or PIC Convention)[55] entered into force on 24 February 2004. Some of the core elements of this convention are as follows:

The Rotterdam Convention on the Prior Informed Consent Procedure for Certain Hazardous Chemicals and Pesticides in International Trade[56]

The objectives of the Convention are:

- to promote shared responsibility and cooperative efforts among Parties in the international trade of certain hazardous chemicals in order to protect human health and the environment from potential harm;
- to contribute to the environmentally sound use of those hazardous chemicals, by facilitating information exchange about their characteristics, by providing for a national decision-making process on their import and export and by disseminating these decisions to Parties.

The Convention creates legally binding obligations for the implementation of the Prior Informed Consent (PIC) procedure. It built on the voluntary PIC procedure, initiated by UNEP and FAO in 1989 and ceased on 24 February 2006.

...

Major provisions

The Convention covers pesticides and industrial chemicals that have been banned or severely restricted for health or environmental reasons by Parties and which have been notified by Parties for inclusion in the PIC procedure. One notification from each of two specified regions triggers consideration of addition of a chemical to Annex III of the Convention. Severely hazardous pesticide formulations that present a hazard under conditions of use in developing countries or countries with economies in transition may also be nominated for inclusion in Annex III.

...

Once a chemical is included in Annex III, a 'decision guidance document' (DGD) containing information concerning the chemical and the regulatory decisions to ban or severely restrict the chemical for health or environmental reasons, is circulated to all Parties.

Parties have nine months to prepare a response concerning the future import of the chemical. The response can consist of either a final decision (to allow import of the chemical, not to allow

54 Stockholm Convention, Article 3.2(b) and (c).

55 (1999) 38 *ILM* 1. See generally [www.pic.int/home.php?type=t&id=5&sid=16].

56 [www.pic.int/home.php?type=t&id=5&sid=16].

import, or to allow import subject to specified conditions) or an interim response. Decisions by an importing country must be trade neutral (ie, apply equally to domestic production for domestic use as well as to imports from any source).

The import decisions are circulated and exporting country Parties are obligated under the Convention to take appropriate measure to ensure that exporters within its jurisdiction comply with the decisions.

The Convention promotes the exchange of information on a very broad range of chemicals. It does so through:

…

- the requirement for a Party that plans to export a chemical that is banned or severely restricted for use within its territory, to inform the importing Party that such export will take place, before the first shipment and annually thereafter;
- the requirement for an exporting Party, when exporting chemicals that are to be used for occupational purposes, to ensure that an up-to-date safety data sheet is sent to the importer; and
- labeling requirements for exports of chemicals included in the PIC procedure, as well as for other chemicals that are banned or severely restricted in the exporting country.

…

Export notification

Article 12 and Annex V of the Convention sets out the provisions and information requirements related to export notification. Where a chemical banned or severely restricted by a Party is exported, that Party shall provide an export notification to the importing Party. The importing Party has the obligation to acknowledge receipt of the export notification within 30 days.

At the request of the third meeting of the Conference of the Parties the Secretariat has developed this standard form for export notification in order to facilitate Parties in meeting their obligations under the Convention.

……

As the above sections illustrate, there are aspects of the aims and procedures of the Basel Convention, Stockholm Convention and Rotterdam Convention that overlap. In order to take advantage of potential synergies, the Ad Hoc Joint Working Group on enhancing cooperation and coordination among the Basel, Rotterdam and Stockholm Conventions was established by the Conference of Parties of each of the Conventions. The group is composed of 15 representatives of parties of each Convention, for a total of 45 members. The mandate of the group is to prepare joint recommendations on enhancing cooperation and coordination among the three Conventions for consideration by the Conferences of the Parties of each.[57] The recommendations will be considered at the meetings of the upcoming Conferences of the Parties.[58]

57 [http://chm.pops.int/Convention/tabid/54/language/en-US/Default.aspx].

58 Documents and other information about the group are available at the joint website: [http://ahjwg.chem.unep.ch/].

7.5.4 Endangered species

The Convention on International Trade in Endangered Species of Wild Fauna and Flora (CITES)[59] is an international agreement between governments that aims to ensure that the survival of endangered plants and animals is not threatened as a result of international trade of these items.

Trade in plant and animal wildlife is big business, accounting for billions of dollars annually. This trade includes both the international sale of live plants and animals, but also a multitude of products derived from live specimens, including foods, medicines, tourist souvenirs, and wood and leather items.

The CITES text was agreed to at a meeting of 80 countries in Washington DC on 3 March 1973, and entered into force on 1 July 1975. CITES has since expanded to comprise 173 states that have agreed to be bound by the Convention. Parties to CITES adopt their own domestic legislation to implement the Convention at the national level.

The Convention lists in its appendices animal and plant species (and products manufactured therefrom) which are given differing levels of protection:

- Appendix I is species that are threatened with extinction; trade in these species is only permitted under exceptional circumstances.
- Appendix II includes species that, while not necessarily on the verge of extinction, require managed trade to ensure their continued survival does not become compromised.
- Finally, Appendix III contains species protected in one or more countries, where at least one country has asked the other CITES parties for assistance in controlling the trade in a particular species.

Species listed in the CITES appendices may only be exported (or imported) pursuant to the CITES procedures, as well as any stricter national laws. In general, however, import and export permits are required. Export permits are not to be issued unless the specimen was obtained legally, the trade will not undermine the survival of the species, and an import permit has already been issued.[60]

7.5.5 Montreal Protocol on Substances that Deplete the Ozone Layer

The Montreal Protocol on Substances that Deplete the Ozone Layer (Montreal Protocol) sets out obligations for each state party to phase out the use of ozone-depleting substances. As of December 2007, 191 countries were party to the Montreal Protocol.

In Australia, the legislation implementing Australia's obligations pursuant to the Protocol is the *Ozone Protection and Synthetic Greenhouse Gas Management Act 1989* (Cth). Pursuant to that Act, Australia maintains an absolute prohibition on

---

59 Convention on International Trade in Endangered Species of Wild Fauna and Flora, 3 March 1973, (1973) 993 *UNTS* 243; 12 *ILM* 1085.

60 See 'How CITES Works' at [www.cites.org/eng/disc/how.shtml].

the export of hydrobromofluorocarbons (HBFCs). Licences to export are required from the Minister for the Environment and Heritage to export a number of other chemicals, including chlorfluorocarbons (CFCs), hydrochlorofluorocarbons (HCFCs), hydrofluorocarbons (HFCs), perfluorocarbons (PFCs), bromochloromethane (BCMs) and methyl bromide.

7.6 Cultural and heritage goods

Many countries, particularly those with a rich archaeological endowment and those with indigenous communities, impose export controls limiting the flow of cultural and heritage goods from the country. As noted in Section 7.2.1d above, these export controls will fall within the GATT, Article XX(f), so long as the restricted items can be considered 'national treasures of artistic, historic or archaeological value'.

There are two international conventions that recognise the right of nations to maintain possession of their cultural treasures:

- The 1970 UNESCO Convention on the Means of Prohibiting and Preventing the Illicit Import, Export and Transfer of Ownership of Cultural Property (1970); and
- The UNIDROIT Convention on Stolen or Illegally Exported Cultural Objects (Rome, 24 June 1995).

The UNESCO Convention requires signatories to create their own export controls to prevent their own cultural property from being illicitly exported. There is therefore no standard international export control. The UNIDROIT Convention is intended to be complementary to the UNESCO Convention. Unlike the UNESCO Convention, it is self-executing and provides private rights of action with respect to stolen or illicitly exported cultural property.

EXAMPLE: Australia has a number of objects that it has designated as cultural or heritage goods by listing them on a National Cultural Heritage Control List.[61] Items can be designated as either Class A or Class B.

Class A items are prohibited exports and may not be exported under any condition. Examples of Class A objects include Victoria Cross medals awarded to Australian service personnel; metal armour worn by Ned Kelly at the siege of Glenrowan in Victoria in 1880; and certain Aboriginal and Torres Strait Islander objects including human remains, rock art, and bark and log coffins used as traditional burial objects.

Class B items are restricted exports of cultural significance to Australia and may be exported if granted a permit by the Minister for the Environment and Heritage pursuant to the *Movable Cultural Heritage Act 1986* (Cth). Examples of Class B objects include some items of Australian Aboriginal or Torres Strait Islander heritage, as well as items falling into one or more of several

61 See [www.arts.gov.au/movable/exporting_cultural_heritage_objects/the_national_cultural_heritage_control_list].

categories, including archaeology, fossils and meteorites, fine or decorative arts, and items of historical significance.[62]

7.7 Public morals and other domestic policies

As we have seen, export controls can apply to a wide range of potential goods and transactions. In this section we briefly discuss public morals as a motivation for certain export controls and identify as examples an additional range of export controls imposed by Australia.

7.7.1 Public morals

As noted above (Section 7.2.1d), one of the GATT Article XX exceptions to the general WTO rules pertains to measures 'necessary to protect public morals'.[63] What might fall under the scope of this exception? In the WTO context, the analogous provision under the General Agreement on Trade in Services (GATS) was found to include gambling services.[64] In the *US–Gambling* dispute, the Panel determined that the term encompassed 'standards of right and wrong conduct maintained by or on behalf of a community or nation'.[65]

Different WTO members may have different standards of right or wrong conduct, which may lead to different policy choices regarding import or export restrictions.

> EXAMPLE: Looking at Australia's export controls, there are a few restrictions that may have their roots in public morals-type concerns. These include 'pornography and other objectionable material' and 'suicide devices'. For the former, permits are required from the Director of the Classification Board to export electronic, film and print items that describe, depict, or otherwise deal with sex, drug misuse or addiction, crime, cruelty, violence, terrorist acts, or revolting or abhorrent phenomena in a way that offends against the standards of morality, decency and propriety generally accepted by reasonable adults. In the case of devices designed or customised to be used by a person to commit suicide, or to assist another person to commit suicide, these have been designated as prohibited exports and may not be exported under any circumstances.

---

62 The complete lists of Class A and Class B items can be accessed electronically at the website identified in note 61 above.

63 GATT, Article XX(a).

64 *United States—Measures Affecting the Cross-Border Supply of Gambling and Betting Services ('US—Gambling')*, Report of the Panel, WT/DS285/R; *US—Gambling*, Report of the Appellate Body, WT/DS285/AB/R, 7 April 2005. The relevant provision of the GATS is Article XIV(a). The GATS was negotiated and agreed to during the Uruguay Round of GATT negotiations and came into force on 1 January 2005 as a part of the newly created WTO. The GATT only covers trade in goods; the GATS provides additional coverage for trade in services. The GATT, the GATS and the Agreement on Trade-related Aspects of Intellectual Property (the TRIPS Agreement) comprise the three main pillars under the WTO umbrella.

65 *US—Gambling*, Report of the Panel, WT/DS285/R, para 6.465.

7.7.2 Other export controls

Finally, we provide as examples other Australian export controls that reflect a wide range of domestic policy choices. As you will see, many of these mirror the concerns addressed through international fora such as arms control, law enforcement, conservation, and health and safety. Consider for each of these why Australia might maintain such an export control and whether you can identify a WTO exception that seems applicable.

Australia restricts the export of:

- Cetaceans (whales, dolphins, and porpoises): permits are required from the Department of the Environment and Heritage to import or export cetaceans, parts of cetaceans and products derived from cetaceans.
- Counterfeit credit, debit, or charge cards: permits are required from the Minister for Home Affairs.
- Drugs, in particular narcotic drugs and psychotropic substances, including plants, parts of plants, chemicals and chemical compounds: permits are required from the Secretary to the Department of Health and Ageing for any exports via post or air cargo. Passengers on aircraft or ships may be exempt from permits for certain drugs carried in their accompanied luggage if such drugs are for their own medical treatment (or that of a person or animal in their care) and certain other conditions are satisfied.
- Domestic cat or dog fur: permits are required from the Minister for Home Affairs.
- Firearms, parts, accessories and ammunition: permits are required from the Minister of Defence. For personal firearms, limited quantities of items such as parts, magazines, sights and ammunition can be exported subject to permits issued by Delegates of the Minster of Defence and can be applied for at any Customs Office.
- Human blood and tissue: permits are required from the Department of Health and Ageing.
- Precursor goods: permits from the Secretary to the Department of Health are required for items that can be converted into other substances that have the potential to be abused and are therefore a public health concern.
- Prescription medicines that are subsidised by the Australian Government under the Pharmaceutical Benefits Scheme (PBS):[66] exporters can export a reasonable amount of PBS drugs for their own use or for a person accompanying the exporter, such as a child or elderly relative. Persons intending to use PBS drugs outside of Australia need to complete a PBS Medicine Export Declaration (available from the Health Insurance Commission or Customs Information and Support Centres).
- Radioactive substances: permits are issued by the Minister for Industry, Tourism and Resources for uranium, thorium and fissionable materials, including plutonium.
- Radioactive waste: permits from the Minister for Industry, Tourism and Resources are required to export radioactive waste to Pacific Island developing countries.
- Toothfish: permits from the Minister for Fisheries, Forestry and Conservation are required to export Antarctic toothfish and Patagonian toothfish found in

66 The PBS can only be accessed by Australian residents and others eligible to receive Medicare benefits.

sub-Antarctic waters. This restriction applies to all fish and fish parts of these species, whether fresh, frozen, smoked, preserved, or in any other form.

Wine and brandy: permits from the Australian Wine and Brandy Corporation are required for bulk consignments of wine, brandy, grape spirit, and wine-derived products exceeding 100 litres.

7.8 Conclusion

This chapter has exposed you to a broad sampling of different types of export control measures. Export controls exist to further a wide range of policy aims in addition to the frequently invoked national security objectives. Thus, companies that import or export should be aware of the scope of export controls that could be applicable to their business activities.

Complying with export control measures requires dedicated effort as measures may differ from country to country, and indeed certain types of measures may exist in some countries but not in others. This is particularly important for companies that trade in goods that have potential civil as well as military uses, as the 'dual-use' nature of a product might not always be obvious. In addition, companies should educate themselves with respect to international treaties that seek to monitor and/or control trade in the products they import or export. As we have seen, the product coverage of such treaties is quite broad, ranging from chemical, nuclear and biological weapons, to hazardous waste, to conflict diamonds, to endangered species. Businesses therefore would do well to have internal procedures in place to ensure that they comply with relevant documentation, certification, notification, and other requirements that may be imposed by their own governments or those of countries to which they export.

Questions

With regard to the case study at the beginning of this chapter:

1 ATI wishes to export chemical waste from industrial chemicals for disposal overseas. In what ways might export controls limit or otherwise affect ATI's ability to export as planned?
2 ATI is also interested in commencing exports of chemicals to defence contractors and other military suppliers. What export controls may apply to these transactions?
3 What advice would you give ATI with respect to how it should ensure its own compliance with applicable export control laws?
4 Agraria, a WTO member, is suffering from drought and its primary crop, corn, is in short supply. It accordingly imposes a temporary ban on the exportation of corn in order to keep food shortages to a minimum. May Agraria maintain this export control consistent with its WTO obligations?
5 In 2009, a national export control restricts the export of certain chemicals to Libya, Iraq and North Korea, but the export is unregulated if destined for any other country. Explain whether or not this violates any WTO rules.

6 A trading company wishes to export exotic animals to overseas destinations. What export controls may apply to these transactions?
7 Why might WTO members wish to avoid litigating the scope of Article XXI of the GATT?
8 Other than those discussed, what export controls can you think of that might fall under the GATT, Article XX(a), (b) or (g)?
9 What steps should an exporter of dual-use technology take to make sure it is compliant with any applicable export controls?
10 What do you think is the rationale for Australia's export control on drugs subsidised by the PBS?
11 ABC, an Australian company, is exporting large volumes of surfboards to customers in the country of Surfland, a WTO member. ABC learns that Surfland companies have asked their government for relief from the foreign surfboard competition. ABC is worried that if an antidumping investigation takes place, it may be unable to continue profitably supplying the Surfland market. May ABC instead agree to voluntarily cap its exports to Surfland?

PART IV

Intellectual Property and the Transfer of Technology

CHAPTER 8

protection of intellectual property

Successful Software is a high-tech company based in Brisbane, Australia, which is particularly known for its user-friendly, virus-resistant word-processing software. The software is sold for $250 in Australia, $150 in other developed countries and at a discounted rate of $65 in developing countries. The software accounts for the majority of the company's revenue.

The software is available online as a download, as well as in the tangible form of a set of installation disks. Successful Software does not actually manufacture the install disks, but rather engages a Chinese company to produce the disks and package the product. The final product is then shipped from China to every country where the software is sold.

Successful Software has recently been alerted that a large number of unauthorised copies of the software are appearing in markets and street stalls all over Asia and North America. Furthermore, Successful Software has recently discovered a store in Pitt Street Mall, Sydney, selling versions of the software meant to be sold only in Malaysia and New Zealand, at a significantly lower price than the retail rate.

8.1 Introduction

In order to exploit the opportunities created by expanding a business abroad (that is, beyond the mere exportation of goods or a one-off cross border transaction), those involved in commerce must understand how intellectual properly (IP) law relates to international trade. It is the role of the lawyer advising the business to fully understand not only the principles of IP and how they relate to international trade, but also to provide explanations, analysis and recommendations, so that the client may take decisions with full knowledge of the risks and potential rewards.

This chapter does not set out to explain the complete law of IP, but instead aims to provide several examples of how IP relates to international trade. The chapter also provides useful examples of real-world situations, risks and recommendations.

The chapter begins with a review of the basic principles of IP law, including both the international framework and an overview of Australian law. The chapter then discusses three contemporary—and contentious—IP-related issues relevant to industry and lawyers: namely pirated and counterfeit goods, parallel imported goods, and compulsory licences. By the end of the chapter, students should have some understanding of the complexity of these issues, the interplay of the political, economic and legal interests at the heart of all of these issues, and the role of the lawyer in protecting, challenging or enforcing IP rights.

8.2 IP law: the basics

The Convention Establishing the World Intellectual Property Organization (1967) (WIPO Convention) defines 'intellectual property' as including rights relating to:

- literary, artistic and scientific works,
- performances of performing artists, phonograms, and broadcasts,
- inventions in all fields of human endeavour,
- scientific discoveries,
- industrial designs,
- trademarks, service marks, and commercial names and designations,
- protection against unfair competition,

and all other rights resulting from intellectual activity in the industrial, scientific, literary or artistic fields.[1]

WIPO further clarifies the term 'intellectual property' as simply 'creations of the mind: inventions, literary and artistic works, and symbols, names, images, and designs used in commerce'.[2] Intellectual property rights (IPRs) are thus the legal rights resulting from intellectual activity in the industrial, scientific, literary and artistic fields.

Countries provide protection for creative efforts for one of two reasons:

1 The moral and economic rights of creators in their creations and the rights of the public in access to those creations; or
2 To promote creativity and the dissemination of information to the community in order to promote social development.

Civil law countries, such as France, have historically granted protection based upon the first option (so-called 'moral rights'), whereas common law countries, including Australia, base protection on the second model (the so-called 'utilitarian model').

The following extract illustrates the key aspects of the utilitarian balance between the creator and the public.

Intellectual Property and Competition Review Committee, Review of Intellectual Property Legislation under the Competition Principles Agreement (Ergas Committee) (2000), pp 22–24[3]

The general objective of the system of intellectual property law in Australia is utilitarian, and more specifically economic, rather than moral in character. It serves to (and, in the Committee's view, should

1 WIPO Convention, Article 2(viii). It is important to note at the outset that not all of the rights mentioned as relating to intellectual property are specifically protected under Australian laws.

2 See [www.wipo.int/about-ip/en/].

3 Available at [www.ipaustralia.gov.au/about/ipcr.shtml].

aim to) maximise the difference between the social value of intellectual property created and used, and the social cost of its creation, including the cost of administering the system. More specifically, the intellectual property laws ought to provide incentives for efficient investment in innovation.

The creation of intellectual property involves considerable effort and can entail substantial resource outlays. Private producers will not have an incentive to make these outlays unless they receive an appropriate return. This is only attainable if producers can appropriate at least some of the value that users place on the outputs of the creative process. The characteristics of intellectual property mean that in many instances the results of investment in creative effort can be reproduced at little or no cost.

Put slightly differently, without a system of intellectual property rights it is difficult to prevent free riding by those who did not contribute to the original investment. Creators could therefore find it difficult to recoup the cost of their investment, let alone its economic value. Under these circumstances, economic incentives for intellectual property investment would likely be deficient, leading to under investment in creative effort. To varying extents, and in varying ways, the intellectual property laws help redress this problem.

While seeking to redress the problems associated with free riding, the intellectual property laws must also seek to address the adverse economic effects that the grant of protection may itself create. For example, given that patents are granted to the first person to register an invention, the race to win patents could result in a higher than efficient investment of resources. The inefficiency occurs because the private reward from accruing monopoly profits outweighs the social gain from accelerating the invention process. Encouraging patent applications at an early stage of the innovation process can help address this issue.

Similarly, where innovation is cumulative, the incentive to develop subsequent inventions may depend on the price that second-generation innovators must pay for first-generation technology. A number of provisions of intellectual property law help address this issue by lowering the costs of subsequent innovations. For example, patent registration requires inventors to fully describe and disclose their invention, thus helping subsequent innovators to build on the advances made in existing inventions.

Last, but by no means least, conferring intellectual property rights, while encouraging investment in creative effort, can allow the owners of the rights to unduly restrict the diffusion and use of the results of these efforts. In an ideal world, purchasers of ideas, whose cost of reproduction is virtually zero, would at the margin of consumption face a price that was itself close to zero. However, in practice, IP rights ensure that owners of ideas can, and almost always do, charge some positive price at that margin. As a result, the consumption of the existing output of investment in creative effort falls below that which, in the short term, would maximise social income. In addition, while most intellectual property rights do not confer monopoly power, some do, and when this occurs, the owner of these rights is likely to further restrict diffusion below the level that maximizes society's gain from the stock of knowledge.

Consequently, there is a cost associated with granting intellectual property rights. Intellectual property laws must therefore involve some balancing between the incentives to invest in creative effort and the incentives for disseminating material that is the subject of intellectual property protection. This balance turns on determining the appropriate scope and strength of protection, in terms of the conditions under which protection is granted, the scope and effectiveness of the exclusive privileges protection provides, and the duration of the protection given.

Balancing between providing incentives to invest in innovation on one hand and for efficient diffusion of innovation on the other is a central and perhaps the crucial element in the design of intellectual property laws.

… … …

Two longstanding WIPO-administered treaties—the Paris Convention for the Protection of Industrial Property (1883) (Paris Convention) and the Berne Convention for the Protection of Literary and Artistic Works (1886) (Berne Convention) provide the basis for modern-day IP protection. Since the advent of the World Trade Organization (WTO) in 1995, the Agreement on Trade Related Aspects of Intellectual Property (TRIPS Agreement) has become the most important international agreement relating to intellectual property.[4] The TRIPS Agreement, which incorporates substantial parts of both the Paris and Berne Conventions, mandates minimum protection in seven areas of IP:

- Copyright and related rights;
- Trademarks;
- Geographical indications;
- Industrial designs;
- Patents;
- Layout designs of integrated circuits; and
- Protection of undisclosed information.

The TRIPS Agreement also provides for minimum standards of enforcement and other related procedures. Perhaps as importantly as providing minimum standards, the TRIPS Agreement also provides for binding and enforceable dispute settlement through the WTO dispute settlement mechanism.

The TRIPS Agreement remains controversial, as it is the first international treaty directly linking IPRs to the international trade regime.

Some of the most significant elements contained in the TRIPS Agreement are the following:

- The minimum patent term, which is set at 20 years; and the minimum copyright protection term for sound recordings and performances, which is set at 50 years (from the date of recording) for recordings and 20 years for performances;
- The requirement that computer programs and databases be protected by copyright, and in the case of computer programs, that they receive the level of copyright protection accorded to literary works;
- The requirement to provide for the registration of service marks;
- An extension and strengthening of the provisions of the Paris Convention regarding the registration/use of well-known marks and geographical indications;
- The inability of a country to force the use of a local mark in combination with a foreign trademark, and the prohibition on compulsory licensing of marks;
- The requirement to protect integrated circuit layout designs for a term of at least 10 years;
- The requirement to protect artificially developed new varieties of micro-organisms through patents;
- The requirement that no areas of technology are excluded from patent protection, with the optional exceptions of medical methods for the treatment of humans, and of new life forms above the micro-organism level;
- The requirement to protect new plant varieties, within the patent system, or with a separate system of breeder's rights, or both;

4 The importance of the TRIPS Agreement to IP protection and enforcement is due to the fact that every member of the WTO must abide by its terms and conditions. The WTO currently has 153 members, with Russia and Saudi Arabia the most economically significant non-members.

- The requirement to develop a legal system for protecting trade secrets from unfair disclosure in accordance with principles of fair competition and the requirement to protect test data;
- The imposition of limitations to the application of compulsory licensing and government use of patents, and the requirement for adequate compensation;
- Limitations on exceptions to exclusive intellectual property rights where the interests of rights holders may be prejudiced;
- Acknowledgment of the possibility of anticompetitive abuse of IP rights and affirmation of the right to take action against abusive practices; and
- Reversal of the burden of proof for process patents, and prohibition of any distinction in patent rights based on whether goods are locally produced or imported.[5]

As noted above, the TRIPS Agreement establishes minimum standards of IP protection that each WTO member must accord to nationals of other members.[6] Such a regulatory, harmonised approach is different from the approaches of the other covered agreements of the WTO, and might have prevented further developments outside of the multilateral forum. However, Article 1.1 of the TRIPS Agreement specifically permits members to apply higher levels of protection, so long as the principles of most-favoured nation (MFN) and national treatment are respected. Thus unlike Article XXIV of the GATT, Article 4 of the TRIPS Agreement does not exempt free trade agreements (FTAs) from the operation of MFN—any member which grants 'any advantage, favour, privilege or immunity' to the nationals of *any* other country (whether a WTO member or not) must accord the same treatment to the nationals of other WTO members.

Such higher standards of IP protection than those mandated by the TRIPS Agreement are often called 'TRIPS-Plus' provisions. Members may negotiate FTAs which provide for TRIPS-Plus provisions that require, *inter alia*, the inclusion of:

- Additional protectable subject matter;
- Broader and more extensive standards of protection;
- Stronger enforcement mechanisms; and
- A weakening of 'flexibilities' and 'special and differential treatment' granted to developing and least developed countries in the TRIPS Agreement.

For example, commonly included in FTAs negotiated by the USA is a provision requiring signatories to extend copyright protection from the TRIPS minimum standard of life of the author plus 50 years to life of the author plus 70 years.[7]

5 See Intellectual Property and Competition Review Committee, 'Review of Intellectual Property Legislation under the Competition Principles Agreement' (Ergas Committee), pp 28–9; available at [www.ipaustralia.gov.au/about/ipcr.shtml].

6 TRIPS Agreement, Article 1.3. The Agreement also requires that members comply with certain provisions of other international IP agreements, most notably the Paris Convention (TRIPS Agreement, Article 2.1) and the Berne Convention (excluding Article 6) (TRIPS Agreement, Article 9.1).

7 This TRIPS-Plus requirement first appeared in the US-Singapore FTA (Article 16.4.4(a)) and was followed in FTAs with Chile (Article 17.5.4(a)), Australia (Article 17.4.4(a)), Morocco (Article 15.5.5(a)), CAFTA-DR (Article 15.5.4(a)), Bahrain (Article 14.4.4(a)), Oman (Article 15.4.4(a)) and Korea (Article 18.4.4(a)), and in trade promotion agreements (TPAs) with Peru (Article 16.5.5(a)), Colombia (Article 16.5.5(a)) and Panama (Article 15.5.4(a)). The exception to this trend is the US-Jordan FTA, which does not address the issue. As a result of its FTA with the USA, Australia amended legislation dealing with several aspects of intellectual property, including several controversial amendments relating to patents.

The effect of these provisions may be to 'ratchet up' international IP standards, as the more FTAs are negotiated, the more far-reaching the implications of the FTA provisions could become. In such a circumstance, if enough FTAs are negotiated containing TRIPS-Plus provisions, these provisions will essentially become the new minimum standard from which any future WTO trade round will proceed.[8] For some industries, such as pharmaceuticals, this will result in increased earnings and growth, but the trade-off could be higher consumer prices and less access to information for the public and for generic producers.

8.3 Selected areas of concern to international business

The remaining part of this chapter will discuss three IP-related issues of contemporary relevance to business and lawyers:

- The first issue, pirated and counterfeit goods, has over the past decade emerged as one of the most worrying issues for the global business community.
- The second issue, parallel importation of legitimate products, remains a controversial issue both at the international and domestic level, despite years of discussion.
- Finally, the chapter will discuss the recent controversies surrounding the legality and compatibility of compulsory licences in relation to the pharmaceutical industry, global public health and the international trading system.

8.3.1 Pirated and counterfeit goods

Although the terms 'piracy' and 'counterfeiting' are often used interchangeably, counterfeiting refers to the 'unauthorized copying of a trademark owned by another for use on an identical or similar product and passing off the unauthorized copy as the genuine product', while piracy can refer to copyright (that is, unauthorised copying of books and CDs), patent infringement (that is, the unauthorised use of an invention that is the subject of a patent), and theft of trade secrets, know-how and proprietary business information.[9] Of course, the terms 'counterfeit' and 'piracy' are not mutually exclusive, as a pirated article may be deceptively labelled and therefore be counterfeit.[10]

Due to a host of factors—most notably technological advances that have allowed for the dramatic rise in the availability of copying technologies, the speed at which counterfeits can be produced and the widespread distribution of such materials—trade

8 See B Mercurio, 'TRIPS-Plus Provisions in FTAs: Recent Trends', in L Bartels & F Ortino (eds), *Regional Trade Agreements and the WTO Legal System*, Oxford University Press, Oxford, 2006, p 223.

9 DCK Chow, 'Why China Does Not Take Commercial Piracy Seriously' (2006) 32 *Ohio Northern University Law Review* 203 at notes 1 and 2.

10 Intellectual Property and Competition Review Committee, 'Review of Intellectual Property Legislation under the Competition Principles Agreement' (Ergas Committee), pp 42 (available at [www.ipaustralia.gov.au/about/ipcr.shtml]): 'the production, importation, distribution and sale of pirated copies of copyright material may also involve breaches of trade mark laws, other intellectual property laws (such as those protecting designs) and various consumer protection laws'.

in pirated and counterfeit goods is growing worldwide at an alarming rate[11] and now makes up an estimated 5–7 per cent of the total world trade.[12] Such scale of piracy and counterfeiting could not have been imagined just a short time ago, as within the space of not much more than a decade, counterfeiting and piracy has evolved from:

> [a] localized cottage industry concentrating on the copying of high-end designer goods into a sophisticated black-market industry involving the manufacturing and sale of counterfeit versions of an unimaginable number of products.[13]

Today, counterfeiting and piracy affects almost every industry, 'from apparel and footwear, high-tech industrial goods, medicines, automotive, food and beverages, and cosmetics to copyrighted works, including entertainment and business software, movies, music, and books'.[14] Among the industries most notoriously affected are automobile parts, industrial machinery, agriculture-related products and parts, textiles and clothing, luxury goods and pharmaceuticals.[15] The counterfeiting of pharmaceuticals is particularly serious, as counterfeit medicines often do not meet safety and efficacy standards, and this can result in death or large-scale resistance to proven drugs.[16] To illustrate the scope of the problem, the World Health Organization (WHO) recently found 50–90 per cent of the antimalarial drugs on the market and more than half of the sampled anti-retroviral drugs used to treat HIV/AIDS failed to meet international standards.[17]

The negative effect of piracy and counterfeiting on the business community is obvious, but the harm extends far beyond those entities and also impacts upon government, tax revenue, security and consumers.[18] Consumers are, of course, both victims and accomplices in the process, as they both unwittingly buy counterfeit or pirated products thinking that they have purchased genuine items, and also sometimes knowingly buy lower-priced counterfeit or pirated items. The Organisation for Economic Co-operation and Development (OECD) states:

> The degree to which consumers knowingly buy counterfeit or pirated products depends on the characteristics of the products concerned. For example, consumers who would

11 See Office of the US Trade Representative (USTR), 'Special 301 Report', (2006) available at [www.ustr.gov/assets/Document_Library/Reports_Publications/2006/2006_Special_301_Review/asset_upload_file473_9336.pdf].

12 US Chamber of Commerce, 'What are Counterfeiting and Piracy Costing the American Economy?' 1 (2005), available at [http://uschambercounterfeitingandpiracy.notlong.com] (citing estimates from the World Customs Organization).

13 BJ Olson, MR Graham, J Maltbie & R Epperson, 'The 10 Things Every Practitioner should Know about Anti-Counterfeiting and Anti-Piracy Protection' (2007) 7 *Journal of High Technology Law* 106 at 107.

14 Ibid at 108.

15 See US Chamber of Commerce above note 12, pp 8–10.

16 See World Health Organization, 'Counterfeit Medicines', (14 November 2006): [www.who.int/mediacentre/factsheets/fs275/en/].

17 WHO, 'WHO Medicines Strategy 2004–2007: Countries at the Core', p 3. China, India and Russia are believed to manufacture the majority of counterfeit medicines. See USTR Special 301 Report above note 11.

18 See for example Organisation for Economic Co-operation and Development (OECD), 'The Economic Impact of Counterfeiting' (1998), p 22, available at [www.oecd.org/dataoecd/11/11/2090589.pdf].

knowingly purchase counterfeit garments without any hesitation may have no interest in purchasing counterfeit pharmaceutical products.[19]

An OECD report released in 2007 summarises the growing scope and wide-ranging nature of the problem of counterfeiting and piracy as follows:

> Counterfeiting and piracy are longstanding problems which are growing in scope and magnitude. They are of concern to governments because of (i) the negative impact that they can have on innovation, (ii) the threat they pose to the welfare of consumers and (iii) the substantial resources that they channel to criminal networks, organised crime and other groups that disrupt and corrupt society. They are of concern to business because of the impact that they have on (i) sales and licensing, (ii) brand value and firm reputation, and (iii) the ability of firms to benefit from the breakthroughs they make in developing new products. They are of concern to consumers because of the significant health and safety risks that substandard counterfeit and pirated products could pose to those who consume the items.[20]

The same OECD report concludes that trade in counterfeit and pirated products amounts to approximately US$200 billion (the report also notes that this amount is larger than the national GDPs of about 150 economies around the world).[21] This figure is conservative, and does not include the large volume of counterfeit and pirated products that never enter into international trade (products that are produced and consumed domestically); nor does it include the large quantities of pirated digital products distributed via the internet (for example, music and movies). When these other factors are added to the total, the cost of piracy is much higher.

Another estimate calculates worldwide losses due to counterfeiting and piracy at US$600 billion per year,[22] while the US Chamber of Commerce estimates that counterfeiting and piracy costs the USA alone US$200–250 billion in lost revenues annually, resulting in a loss of 750 000 US jobs.[23] In Australia, a report conducted by the Allen Consulting Group found that counterfeiting resulted in AUS$677 million of lost sales in the Australian toy, software and video games industries ($445.7 million lost sales in the business software industry; $100 million lost sales in the computer and

---

19 Ibid, p 9.

20 Ibid, p 8.

21 Ibid, p 16.

22 See Business Action to Stop Counterfeiting and Piracy (BASCAP): [www.uscib.org/index.asp?DocumentID=3492]. The BASCAP total is calculated using figures from the World Customs Organization and Interpol.

23 US Chamber of Commerce above note 12, p 1. For information on the methodology used to calculate figures, see K Olsen, 'Counterfeiting and Piracy: Measurement Issues', Background report for the WIPO/OECD Expert Meeting on Measurement and Statistical Issues Geneva, 17–18 October 2005. The Business Software Alliance estimates that a 10 per cent reduction in computer piracy would result in US$400 billion worth of additional revenue, which then would lead to job creation and increased tax revenue. See Business Software Alliance, 'Expanding the Frontiers of Our Digital Future: Reducing Software Piracy to Accelerate Global Benefits' (2005) at 6, available at [www.bsa.org/idcstudy/pdfs/WhitePaper.pdf]. See also US Chamber of Commerce, p 10.

video games industry; and $131.7 million lost sales in the toy industry).[24] The report found that lost sales resulting from the counterfeiting represented $200 million in lost profits. The report additionally found that a one-third reduction in counterfeiting (achieved over a five-year period) would increase real GDP (that is, national income) by $41.0 million per year and noted that in net present value terms, these gains represented a $466.3 million benefit to the Australian economy.[25] As a result, the report considered that government tax revenue would increase by $34.4 million per year (in net present value terms, the report claimed these gains represented a $487.2 million benefit to Australian governments).[26] Finally, the report concluded by stating that the 'financial and business services' sector and 'other manufacturing' sector could increase employment of up to 403 jobs and increase in output of up to $59.5 million per year.[27]

Most governments and industry representatives believe that China is the most significant source of pirated and counterfeit goods. The following extract details the scope of the problem in China, including its economic consequences, as well as positing reasons why, despite China now having fairly rigorous IP laws and regulations, it remains a serious concern to governments and industry.

Congressional-Executive Commission on China, Dirksen Senate Office Building, 16 May 2005, Statement of Professor Daniel CK Chow, 'Counterfeiting in China'[28]

I. Introduction

In terms of size, scope, and magnitude, counterfeiting in China is considered by many to [be] the most serious counterfeiting problem in world history. (As used here, counterfeiting refers to the unauthorized use of trademarks owned by another on identical or similar goods.) A recent study by the PRC [People's Republic of China] State Council Research and Development Center reported that in 2001 the PRC economy was flooded with between $19–$24 billion worth of counterfeit goods. Brand owners in China estimate that 15 to 20% of all well-known brands in China are counterfeit and estimate their losses to be in the tens of billions of dollars. Counterfeiting is estimated to now account for approximately 8% of China's gross domestic product.

China is also a leading exporter of counterfeit products to other countries in Asia, Europe, and the United States. In 2003, China accounted for 66% or over $62 million of the $94 million

24 The Allen Consulting Group, 'Counterfeiting of Toys, Business Software, and Computer and Video Games' (November 2003), Report to the Australian Toy Association, the Business Software Association of Australia and the Interactive Entertainment Association of Australia, p vii available at [www.allenconsult.com.au/resources/MCS2_Counterfeit_finalFinal.pdf]. For information on the methodology used to calculate figures, see pp 13–15.

25 Ibid, p 36.

26 Ibid.

27 Ibid.

28 Available at [www.cecc.gov/pages/roundtables/051605/Chow.php]. See also Chow above note 8.

of all counterfeit and infringing goods seized by the US Customs Service at ports of entry into the United States. Mid-year figures in 2004 indicate that seizures are sharply higher with $64 million seized in the first half of 2004 alone. An ominous development is that beginning in 2004, exports of counterfeits from China to the United States and other parts of the world may begin to increase significantly for the foreseeable future.

II. Origins and causes of counterfeiting

There are several explanations for the unprecedented size and scope of counterfeiting in China:

(1) *Foreign Direct Investment and Advanced Technology.* China's economic growth through the decade of the 1990s has been fueled in large part by foreign direct investment (FDI) from multi-national enterprises (MNEs). In the 1990s, China emerged as the world's second largest recipient of foreign direct investment behind only the United States and in 2002, China surpassed the United States to become the world's largest recipient of foreign direct investment with $50 billion of foreign capital inflows. FDI is the best means in the world today for the transfer of advanced technology, intellectual property, and other forms of valuable information. In many cases today the intellectual property component of a FDI in the form of patents, copyrights, and trademarks is the most important component of the foreign investment. For example, the value of the Coca-Cola trademark in China is worth more many more times to that company than the millions of dollars in capital that it has invested in China. The same is true for the patents and copyrights owned by pharmaceutical companies and software companies doing business in China today. However, while MNEs are creating a transfer of technology through FDI that is being absorbed into China's legitimate economy through joint ventures and wholly foreign owned enterprises some of this intellectual property is also being diverted into China's illegitimate economy as pirates steal this technology to engage in counterfeiting and other forms of commercial piracy. It is no coincidence that China, the world's largest recipient of FDI, advanced technology, and intellectual property also has the world's most serious commercial piracy problem.

(2) *State Support of Counterfeiting and Local Protectionism.* No problem of this size and scope could exist without the direct or indirect involvement of the state. In China, the national government in Beijing appears to be sincere in its recognition of the importance of protecting intellectual property rights, but national level authorities are policy and law-making bodies whereas enforcement occurs on the ground at the local level. At this level, local governments are either directly or indirectly involved in supporting the trade in counterfeit goods and are often reluctant to punish counterfeiters.

(3) *Ineffective Legal Enforcement and Lack of Deterrence.* China has a developing legal system that is weak in many respects by comparison to legal systems in advanced industrialized countries such as the United States. While China's intellectual property laws are now considered by most observers to be in compliance with the standards set by TRIPS, enforcement of these laws remains inadequate and fails to create sufficient deterrence of counterfeiting.

The combination of these factors—the world's largest influx of foreign direct investment and widespread access to advanced technology, direct or indirect government involvement and support of the counterfeit trade, and a weak legal system that does not create sufficient deterrence for counterfeiters in a very lucrative trade—has resulted in a counterfeiting and commercial piracy problem that is unprecedented in world history.

III. Overview of counterfeiting in China

The illegal trade in counterfeit goods in China can be divided into two components: manufacture and distribution:

(1) *Manufacture:* The manufacture of counterfeit products tends to be concentrated in China's southeast region in coastal areas near Taiwan and Hong Kong. Criminal organizations in Hong Kong and Taiwan involved in smuggling, prostitution, and narcotics have now branched out into counterfeiting because of its lucrative nature. These criminal organizations supply the capital and start up costs and use the borders between China and their headquarters in Taiwan and Hong Kong to frustrate and elude law enforcement.

(2) *Distribution:* Distribution of counterfeit products occurs through a series of large open air or partially enclosed wholesale markets. These wholesale markets are found in strategic locations around the country and are positioned to serve large densely populated urban areas. These wholesale markets are established and regulated by the local Administration of Industry and Commerce (AIC), a branch of the local government responsible for promoting, regulating, and policing commercial activity. Based on the experience of the author, every wholesale market in China traffics in counterfeit goods. As AICs are also one of the primary government entities in China charged with enforcement against counterfeiting, AICs are faced with a conflict of interest as they are charged with policing and enforcing the very markets in which AICs and the local government have a substantial investment and financial interest. Shutting down these wholesale markets would not only result in a direct loss of revenue to the AIC but would also have many [repercussions] as many retail businesses, hotels, restaurants, and nightclubs are all supported by the trade in counterfeit goods.

IV. Barriers to effective enforcement against counterfeiting

(1) *Local Protectionism:* While it appears that central level leaders understand the importance of protecting intellectual property for promoting China's long-term economic development, central level authorities are legislative and policy-making bodies. Actual implementation and enforcement of the law occurs at the local level where there continue to be questionable commitments to suppressing counterfeiting, copyright piracy, and other forms of economic crimes. Local areas benefit directly and indirectly from counterfeiting. In some areas, counterfeiting provides jobs and generates revenue that are essential to support the local economy. In some cases, counterfeiters voluntarily pay substantial taxes to local authorities. In other cases, legitimate businesses such as hotels, restaurants, nightclubs, storage and transportation companies have been created to support the trade in counterfeit goods. The payment of taxes and the creation of lawful supporting businesses has integrated counterfeiting into the legitimate local economy. It is no exaggeration to say that some local areas in China are entirely supported by the trade in counterfeit goods and that local residents are ready to use any means necessary to protect their illegal trade. A crackdown on counterfeiting would result in shutdown of the local economy with all of the attendant costs of unemployment, dislocation, social turmoil, and chaos. Because the costs of a crackdown at the local level can be so severe, counterfeiting is heavily defended at local levels.

(2) *Inadequate Punishment:* Local protectionism and a weak legal system contribute to the lack of adequate enforcement against counterfeiting. The result is that the Chinese enforcement system does not create deterrence. To be sure there is no lack of enforcement activity. To the contrary, it is relatively easy to obtain an administrative action in the form of a raid and seizure action against suspected counterfeiters. The problem is that once the enforcement action is completed the level of fines and criminal prosecutions are so low that whatever sanctions are meted out do not create deterrence. For example, the average fine imposed on the counterfeiter or infringer in 2000 was $794, a figure that is so low as to be considered a cost of doing business in a very lucrative trade. The amount of compensation awarded to brand owners in 2000 stands at $19, a negligible amount. Damages awarded by AICs seek to award the brand owner the profits earned by the counterfeiter after deducting all expenses (as represented by the counterfeiter) and are not based upon economic losses suffered. As for criminal prosecutions, in 2000 only about 1 in 500 cases were referred to judicial authorities for criminal prosecutions. Enforcement in China does not create fear in counterfeiters or deterrence.

V. Exports from China

Recent changes indicate an ominous development: exports from China are likely to increase dramatically beginning in 2004.

(1) *Exports to the United States:* In 2003, US Customs seized a total of $94 million of counterfeit and infringing goods in ports of entry at the United States. Of this total, products originating in China accounted for 66% of the total and $62 million of the total. The 2003 figures for China represent a significant increase over comparable 2002 figures when China [accounted] for 49% of all counterfeiting and infringing products and $48 million of the total $98 million of illegal product seized by US Customs. Counterfeits from China and Hong Kong (through which many counterfeits produced in China are transshipped) accounted for $80 million or 75% of the total. No other country accounted for more than 3% of counterfeit products. As many counterfeit products, such as auto parts, that originate in China are transshipped through other countries, such as those in South America and through Canada, before ultimately entering the United States, China likely accounts for a significantly higher percentage than the 66% set forth [in] the 2003 US Customs statistics. It is possible that China accounts for as much as 80% or more of the counterfeit goods that enter the United States. Note that the $94 million figure represents only the value of the products that are seized by US Customs in 2003, which can only be a tiny fraction of what enters the US market. If the total value of the products seized represents 1% of the counterfeiting and infringing product that enters the US market then the total value of counterfeits that entered the US market in 2003 is approximately $10 billion with China accounting for between $6 and $8 billion of that total. It is possible that the actual figures are much higher.

(2) *WTO Commitments:* There is likely to be a significant increase in the amount of counterfeit products exported from China to the United States beginning in 2004 and for the foreseeable future for several reasons. In accordance with its WTO obligations, China has amended its foreign trade laws in December 2003 to eliminate the monopoly on export rights that had been limited to state trading companies. Under prior law, only certain designated state trading companies were permitted to lawfully export products from China to other countries. This restriction meant that counterfeiters had to find a compliant state trading company that

was willing to work together with the counterfeiter in exporting the illegal goods overseas. To be sure, there was no shortage of export companies willing to work with counterfeiters in exporting counterfeit and infringing products, but this requirement nevertheless created an additional obstacle and costs that have now been removed. The effect of the elimination of the monopoly on exports rights means that anyone can now lawfully export products from China. As counterfeiters are likely to take full advantage of the elimination of this restriction, exports of counterfeits from China to the United States are likely to surge for the foreseeable future. US Customs mid-year seizure figures for 2004 indicate that there is a sharp increase in seizure activity: $64 million in counterfeit goods were seized by mid-year 2004 compared to $38 million by mid-year 2003.

(3) *Lack of Criminal Laws:* China does not appear to have any current criminal laws that specifically apply to the export of counterfeit products. As the earlier discussion indicated, China has criminal laws against commercial scale counterfeiting within China, although the effective enforcement of these laws is impeded by various obstacles. In the area of exports, however, it is arguable that there are no applicable criminal laws at all, and that counterfeiters can export with impunity from both civil and criminal liability. As pressure mounts on China to obtain better enforcement results within China, it is likely that counterfeiters will turn increasingly to exports as a source of revenue.

… … …

As the above extract demonstrates, the scope of counterfeiting and piracy problem is far reaching and multi-faceted. For this reason, attempts to combat piracy and counterfeiting occur at both the governmental and private levels. Each will be addressed in turn.

8.3.1a Combating piracy and counterfeiting: governmental level

The WTO TRIPS Agreement, in combination with the various WIPO agreements, mandates a high level of protection for IPRs by which all signatory countries must abide. The enforcement provisions in TRIPS require:

- effective action against infringements, including expeditious remedies to prevent infringements and remedies which constitute a deterrent to further infringements (Article 41.1);
- procedures that are fair and equitable, are not unnecessarily complicated or costly, and do not entail any unreasonable time limits or unwarranted delays (Article 41.2);
- transparency in the form of written decisions on the merits, made available to the parties to a proceeding without undue delay (Article 41.3);
- adequate civil or administrative procedures and remedies, including the availability of civil injunctions (Article 44);
- disposal or destruction of pirated goods (Article 46) and the disposal or destruction of materials and implements the predominant use of which has been in the creation of the infringing goods (Article 46);
- provisional measures, including the availability of *ex parte* civil search orders (Article 50);
- adequate border measures, such as applications to 'suspend' the release of infringing goods at the border (Articles 51 and 52) and the disposal or destruction of infringing goods (Article 59);
- adequate criminal procedures, including deterrent penalties (Article 61); and

- availability of seizure, forfeiture and destruction of infringing goods, materials and implements the predominant use of which has been in the commission of the offence (Article 61).[29]

Of course, as we will see in greater detail below, countries differ on their level of enforcement of IPRs from extremely vigilant to almost non-existent enforcement. Developed countries are generally the leaders in promoting and protecting IPRs, while developing countries tend to be lax, if not recalcitrant, in their treatment of IPRs. Thus, even though most developing countries are signatories to the WTO (and therefore the TRIPS Agreement), enforcement of IPRs remains problematic.

Governments can use a variety of laws and measures to enforce IPRs:

- As noted above, governments have laws that can both seize goods which infringe IP and exclude them from entering the country, as well as seize goods already within the jurisdiction, with criminal and civil penalties potentially applying in both cases.
- Governments can attempt to enforce their IPRs by persuasion at a host of international institutions, including the WIPO and the WTO.
- Countries that are members of the WTO can also make use of the dispute settlement mechanism of the WTO by filing a complaint against another member for violations of the TRIPS Agreement.
- Finally, governments can issue their own reports and threaten action if the conduct is not remedied.

The USA utilises this last strategy with regularity, and in fact US law requires the Office of the US Trade Representative (USTR) to identify countries that deny adequate and effective protection for IPRs, or deny fair and equitable market access for persons that rely on intellectual property protection and, among other things, to publish a detailed examination and evaluation regarding the adequacy and effectiveness of IPRs in the identified countries.[30] The current list includes a number of countries, divided into three categories:

- Priority Watch List (the worst offenders—current countries include China, Russia, Argentina, Belize, Brazil, Egypt, India, Indonesia, Israel, Lebanon, Turkey, Ukraine and Venezuela);
- Watch List (35 countries, including Canada and the EU); and
- Section 306 Monitoring (Paraguay is the only country in this list).

Australia does not currently appear on any list.

There is no set formula for persuading nations to adopt stricter IP enforcement standards, and developed countries employ both carrots and sticks in an attempt to have these countries improve IP protection and enforcement. For instance, developed countries have delicately negotiated with Russia and other Eastern European and Eurasian countries in an attempt to persuade them to adopt new intellectual property laws that increase protection as well as aid protection and enforcement. On the other

---

29 See further International Intellectual Property Alliance, 'Copyright Enforcement under the TRIPS Agreement' (2004), available at [www.iipa.com/rbi/2004_Oct19_TRIPS.pdf].

30 See s 182 of the *Trade Act 1974*, as amended by the *Omnibus Trade and Competitiveness Act 1988* and the *Uruguay Round Agreements Act 1994* ('Special 301').

hand, a firmer stance has now been taken with regards to China. This is not surprising, given the scope of the counterfeiting problem in China is unequalled (as detailed in the above extract). China has long been criticised for its lax attitude, laws and enforcement of IPRs, and although (at least in part) as a result of its admittance to the WTO, China has altered its laws in order to comply with the TRIPS Agreement, enforcement remains a problem.[31]

Although efforts at combating piracy and counterfeiting have improved at the governmental level over the past decade through the strengthening of legal frameworks, increased enforcement efforts and large-scale awareness campaigns, rates of piracy and counterfeiting remain high. An OECD report released in 2007 identifies eight key areas requiring the attention of policymakers in order to further combat piracy and counterfeiting.

OECD, 'The Economic Impact of Counterfeiting and Piracy' (OECD, 2007), pp 25–8[32]

Governments have been working with each other through trade agreements and multilateral organisations to strengthen IP protection.

Intergovernmental initiatives have included the establishment of a comprehensive multilateral legal framework within the World Trade Organisation (WTO), as well as co-operation in a number of specific fields. On the enforcement front, the World Intellectual Property Organisation (WIPO), Interpol and the World Customs Organisation have all developed specific programmes to improve enforcement of IPRs. In the area of health, the World Health Organisation (WHO) is supporting specific initiatives to undermine the counterfeiting of medicines. Issues have also been addressed in the G8, and as part of a Global Congress that several multilateral institutions have organised with industry support.

There may be scope for strengthening multilateral disciplines.

As indicated, the basic multilateral rules governing IPR are established in the WTO's TRIPS Agreement. Under that Agreement governments are obliged to ensure that intellectual property rights can be enforced under their laws and that penalties for infringement are sufficient to deter violations.

31 See generally WP Alford, *To Steal a Book is an Elegant Offense: Intellectual Property Law in Chinese Civilization*, Stanford University Press, Stanford, 1995; RC Bird, 'Defending Intellectual Property Rights in the BRIC Economies' (2006) 43 *American Business Law Journal* 317; P Yu, 'From Pirates to Partners: Protecting Intellectual Property in China in the Twenty-first Century' (2000) 50 *Am U L Rev* 131; J Tao, 'Problems and New Developments in the Enforcement of Intellectual Property Rights in China', in P Torremans, H Shan, J Erauw (eds), *Intellectual Property and TRIPS Compliance in China: Chinese and European Perspectives*, Edward Elgar Publishing, 2007, pp 107–24; Special 301 Report above note 11 at 21. It should be noted that the National Working Group for intellectual property protection headed by Vice Premier Wu Yi recently produced a report outlining ways to improve IP protection and enforcement, in part by conducting a province-by-province review of the problem and a review of judicial enforcement of anti-counterfeiting laws: National Working Group for IPR Protection, China's Action Plan on IPR Protection 2007: [http://english.ipr.gov.cn/ipr/en/info/Article.jsp?a_no=67391&col_no=102&dir=200704].

32 [www.oecd.org/dataoecd/13/12/38707619.pdf].

In addition to the TRIPS Agreement, many regional and bilateral agreements contain provisions on IPR. In a number of cases, the obligations contained in these agreements go beyond those contained in TRIPS. The actions that have been taken suggest that there may be scope for enhancing disciplines. Consideration could be given by governments, for example, to: (i) strengthening civil and criminal remedies to more effectively redress the harm caused to IPR holders; (ii) expanding the scope of border measures to cover exports as well as goods in transit or transhipment; and (iii) requiring that certain types of information related to counterfeiting and piracy be made available to the public.

At the national level, two of the principal challenges in combating counterfeiting and piracy are to (i) find ways to enhance enforcement and (ii) raise awareness of counterfeiting and piracy issues. More may need to be done to undermine counterfeiting and piracy at the point where infringement originates; once goods enter domestic or international trade, the task becomes far more difficult.

Most economies appear to have the legal and regulatory mechanisms in place to adequately combat counterfeiting and piracy. Enforcement, however, is viewed by many as weak; a common criticism is that the resources devoted to IPR enforcement are insufficient and that those who engage in counterfeiting and piracy are not sufficiently penalised for their actions when they are caught.

As resource challenges are likely to persist, governments may need to consider focusing enforcement activities on operations which will have the greatest impact, such as disruption of counterfeiting and piracy activities at the points where infringement originates (place of manufacture, point of importation). Once items move into domestic or international trade, the chances for detecting illicit items are greatly reduced. Stopping infringing activities at the source is however not always possible; this is why efficient border enforcement procedures are also essential.

Raising awareness is an important aspect of combating counterfeiting and piracy and needs to be pursued vigorously. Consumers should be adequately informed about the growing threat that substandard counterfeit and pirated products pose to their health and safety, and consumers and counterfeiters and pirates should be aware about the legal consequences of infringing IPRs or knowingly purchasing infringing products. Raising awareness could also have beneficial effects on consumer attitudes and behaviour towards counterfeiting and piracy.

A review of the situation in a number of OECD Member and non-Member economies has identified eight key areas requiring the attention of policymakers.

- *Co-ordination.* A number of ministries and related government bodies are generally involved in administering and enforcing IPRs. Effective coordination appears to be the key to strengthening planning and enforcement. Most economies surveyed in the report have promoted co-ordination, either by designating lead agencies, or by setting up special interagency working groups on IP protection.
- *Policy.* A clear policy on IP enforcement that contains concrete elements can provide the impetus needed to improve outcomes. However, only a few of the economies surveyed in the report have established detailed, measurable plans.
- *Legal and regulatory framework.* The legal and regulatory framework provides the parameters within which enforcement can be pursued. While the frameworks used by economies resemble

each other in key respects, there are some important differences. In some countries, the consumer of infringing products can be charged with a criminal offence; also, in one economy, the proceeds from IP crime can be recovered and used to finance additional enforcement activities.

- *Enforcement.* A good legal and regulatory framework is essential for combating counterfeiting and piracy, but it is not sufficient. Enforcement is critical. Most of the economies surveyed have increased the resources devoted to enforcement in recent years. Some have created specialised IP units and IP courts to enhance effectiveness. To increase impact, some have launched well publicised domestic campaigns aimed at disrupting counterfeiting and piracy activities. A number of countries allow customs authorities to check infringing goods destined for export, transit and transhipment, or to act upon their own initiative (*ex officio*).
- *International co-operation.* Counterfeiting and piracy is a global problem which needs be addressed on a co-operative basis for best results. Most economies participate in international forums such as WTO, WIPO or WCO. Some economies surveyed have been active at the bilateral or regional level, providing training and engaging in joint enforcement activities.
- *Awareness.* It is important for consumers, rights holders and government officials (i) to be aware of the counterfeiting and piracy problem, (ii) to understand what the effects are economy-wide as well as on individual stakeholders, and (iii) to know what concerned parties can do to combat counterfeiting and piracy activities. A number of economies have developed far-reaching training and education programmes. Increasing awareness has also included the development of information through surveys. Finally, some economies have conducted media campaigns and prepared exhibitions to heighten awareness.
- *Programme evaluation and measurement.* To help monitor progress and respond to the changing nature of counterfeiting and piracy, policies and programmes need to be reviewed regularly. A number of governments have developed regular monitoring or reporting schemes and have published findings; many regularly collect and disseminate statistical information providing insights into the situation.
- *Industry co-operation.* Government co-operation with industry is essential, as (i) right holders have the technical expertise to distinguish counterfeits from original products, and (ii) industry may have additional information regarding the functioning of distribution channels. Efforts to step up co-operation are underway, although they could benefit from being further increased.

… … …

8.3.1b Combating piracy and counterfeiting: private level

A number of legal avenues also exist to enable private companies to combat piracy, but their effectiveness is far from certain. The most effective way of combating piracy and protecting IPRs is enforcement at the border via seizure and exclusion orders enforced through customs laws or, in some countries, through special legislation (such as s 337 of the *Tariff Act 1930* in the USA). Blocking pirated items from entering through the border is difficult, however, as customs agencies simply do not have the resources to inspect every incoming shipment (customs generally inspect 1–2 per cent of imports); nor would international commerce want customs to inspect every shipment, as this would significantly increase the time and costs of trade. Moreover, even if customs agencies did inspect every incoming shipment, they would have a difficult time deciphering which goods were legitimate and which were counterfeit (the task is even tougher when parallel imported goods are permitted).

Thus, the reality is that the vast majority of seizures and exclusions occur when the IP owner (or other interested party) notifies customs of an impending shipment of counterfeit goods. Companies can also, *inter alia*:

- Actively monitor shops and online sales;
- Work with law enforcement to seize infringing material in the domestic market
- Develop technological innovations to prevent piracy (most applicable to software and similar products); and
- Engage in public awareness campaigns.

The following panel discussion is an exchange between four people engaged in the business of preventing piracy in the USA. It provides insight into the methods used, and the frustrations involved, in attempting to enforce IPRs. The issues discussed are equally applicable in Australia.

'The New Campaign Against Counterfeiting and Piracy' (2004) 14 *Fordham Intellectual Property, Media & Entertainment Law Journal* 955

Moderator: Bernard Korman, Former General Counsel, American Society of Composers, Authors & Publishers; Panelists: Barbara Kolsun, General Counsel, Kate Spade; Heather McDonald, Partner, Gibney, Anthony & Flaherty, LLP; Darren Pogoda, Legal Counsel, International Anti-Counterfeiting Coalition.

MR POGODA: ... the problem [with counterfeiting and piracy] has dramatically increased over the past twenty years ... because of access to better technology, access to computers and printers that can make perfect labels, and access to technology that can allow people to distribute the products a lot quicker.

I'll give a few more concrete examples of how large the problem can be—and all three of them are from right here in New York. In May 2001, there was a seizure of $125 million in fake goods from a house that contained secret tunnels, vaults, and trap doors, where they hid some of the more valuable fake goods. In July 2002, there was a seizure from a residential home of 5,000 fake Rolexes and Montblanc pens as well as a million dollars in cold, hard cash. The prosecutor stated at the time that they were using the sale of the fake goods to launder money from drug sales. More recently, in February 2003, six men were charged with importing thirty-five million fake cigarettes into the United States over a year-and-a-half period into ports in New York and New Jersey. They would hide them in kitchen pots and then sell the cigarettes through a tax-free business located in upstate New York on an Indian reservation. In addition to the fake cigarettes, two of those six men were also charged with importing counterfeit batteries.

These are just a few of the examples of how big the problem is ... It is organized, sophisticated criminal activity on a truly global scale ...

MS MCDONALD: My firm is the general counsel to the Rolex watch company. I went on my first seizure of counterfeit Rolex watches in 1986, so this is a problem that we have been fighting for a long time. As for the basic tools for enforcement, companies that are the victim of counterfeiters can rely on the criminal laws and the civil laws, which operate in parallel universes in this area.

Regarding criminal laws, there is a federal law, which was enacted originally in 1984. It says that if you traffic in counterfeit goods, you can go to jail for up to ten years now. It has been amended since its original version. And damages can be awarded in civil cases for up to millions of dollars. Under the criminal laws, you can go to jail for up to ten years and you have big fines payable to the government. There are also state criminal laws. Right now there are, I think, approximately thirty-five states that have their own criminal laws, making the sale of counterfeit goods a criminal action under the state law. This is particularly valuable because the federal government doesn't typically get involved in these criminal investigations unless there are huge, huge organized outfits that are selling counterfeit goods. So, if you can go to the state governments, if you can go to the local police departments, or if there is a law under which you can prosecute, it will give you a tremendous, additional remedy.

The state laws vary in terms of what their penalties are … Then there are the civil laws. The federal civil law that allows you to go after counterfeiters is a great remedy because it provides that as long as you can prove a pretty significant laundry list of things to a federal judge, you can proceed ex parte. This is almost unheard of in civil litigation these days. Usually, civil litigation is based on notice—a party doesn't get to do anything without everybody else knowing exactly what is coming. With ex parte, you can tell a judge that you have found somebody who is selling counterfeit goods and avoid the notice requirement. You have to prove that the goods are in fact counterfeit. You have to prove where they are going to be; you have to prove that it is the defendant who has them. I mean, you have to prove all the things you would have to prove to get a temporary restraining order ('TRO'), plus some. You have to notify the Office of the US Attorney General, in case they want to prosecute.

When you file, it's filed under seal. That is designed to protect the defendant in case you are wrong. If you sue somebody for selling counterfeit goods and file it in the Southern District of New York, this information will go into the press box and will appear on the front page of the *New York Post* the next day. And if you are wrong, you will have significantly damaged somebody's business reputation. So, it is filed under seal, ironically, to protect the defendants, but it is actually a huge protection for the plaintiffs as well, because if counterfeiters have any idea you are coming, by the time you get to their location there is not going to be anything there except some sweet little old lady selling yo-yos, and there won't be any records.

MS KOLSUN: You also have to post a bond. That similarly protects the counterfeiter in case you are wrong.

MS MCDONALD: If you get to go in ex parte, if you prove all of these things, in addition to getting a court to enter a TRO, you get the incredible remedy of a seizure order, which is also a very, very dramatic remedy. Once again, it is all ex parte.

It allows you to go with the US marshals or other law enforcement officers to the premises of the counterfeiter, which can be a business location or somebody's home. You basically get to knock on the door and say, 'Hi, I'm here with these seventeen US marshals, and we're going to look through your house and take all of your counterfeit goods and all of your business records related to that. You can come to court next Thursday and discuss this with the judge because that's what he decided is the return date.' This is a tremendous remedy.

When you can't get law enforcement interested in going after one of [Ms Kolsun's] favorite targets, you can go after one of these women who throws purse parties on the weekends and sells counterfeit handbags to all of the local ladies in the area. It is quite dramatic when you show up with a seizure order during the course of one of these purse parties, and all of these women are mortified and cry, 'Oh my God, I thought it was real.' Uh huh. And you get to take all of the stuff. It's a very dramatic remedy.

After you have seized the goods—obviously to hold them for safekeeping so that the defendants can't destroy them—you have to prove your case just like you do in any other litigation. You can get damages of millions of dollars.

It is very hard to prove what your losses are in a lot of instances because you can't necessarily make the argument that if this person sold 10 000 fake Rolex watches, and that if all of those watches were unavailable, then the same 10 000 people who bought the counterfeits would have gone out and bought the genuine ones. You can't argue that because a counterfeit might sell for $50 and a genuine might sell for $30 000. So, you cannot make the argument that it is a one-for-one lost sale.

The legislature has recognized this, and now you can seek statutory damages of between $500 and $100,000 per infringement. It is designed specifically for cases where there are no records and actual damage cannot be proved. So, that is a great remedy available as well.

...

Under the trademark law—and under the copyright law, but we've found it more useful under the trademark law—there is the concept of contributory liability. This has been very, very useful with regard to flea market owner–operators and mall operators because you can notify them that there is illegal activity going on, and if they fail to take any action to stop this, then they can be held liable for the illegal actions that are taking place on their premises. A variety of circuit courts have decided this in a variety of cases ... Flea markets, absolutely [this has happened]. I don't think there has been a litigation with a mall operator.

MS KOLSUN: No, but there are some very good cases, including the *Fonovisa Inc v Cherry Auction, Inc* case and the *Polo Ralph Lauren Corp v Chinatown Gift Shop* case, cases against the landlords in Chinatown. We use that case law against landlords in more formal settings.

For example, we're actually negotiating leases in malls. We're going to be opening Kate Spade stores in malls in various parts of the country ... We have had a tremendous problem with those malls that also lease space to little kiosks in the middle of the malls. If you've ever walked through a mall, you have seen those little kiosks, which were meant to recapture some of that space for purposes of collecting rent, but also were originally supposed to be for selling crafts and things like that. They have become a huge source of counterfeit goods.

There are at least a hundred malls that I am dealing with now where there is a store—a Neiman Marcus or a Nordstrom—that sells authentic Kate Spade merchandise and also a kiosk that sells counterfeit merchandise in the same mall. In those cases, we have dealt directly with the malls ... It is not just flea markets. It's stores, it's all sorts of places ...

MS MCDONALD: … [Chinatown] is actually the single largest retail center of counterfeit goods in the country. And most of the counterfeit goods that are sold everyplace else in the country come from vendors down in Chinatown or the organizations that they represent.

On a weekly basis, I drive around the city with a bunch of investigators and police officers in vans that have been painted with graffiti or have funny little signs on them so that they look different every time. When we drive up to a couple of stores down on Canal Street and come flying out of the van, everybody on the street goes nuts and runs around. People are carrying the bags and the watches everywhere, and we run out and seize the goods from these vendors …The second we hit three or four stores, all of the roll-down gates of the other stores come slamming down, often with customers inside them, who are then locked inside the locations. A number of times some of the customers inside actually have been our undercover agents, so we have an interesting window on what is going on inside there. And they won't let the customers out because if they let them out, then the door must be opened again and then we could come in and take the counterfeit goods.

But every time we do one of these seizures we notify the landlord of what is happening on the premises. And then if the landlord doesn't do something about it, then we go after the landlord. We actually have sued a number of landlords civilly. We never have had to go to a final judgment, although there are some published decisions that basically uphold the provision that the landlord can be liable if they know about this and don't take any appropriate action.

So, there is a lot of turnover because landlords will kick out one tenant, and then another tenant will rent the premises again. It's like a revolving door, but it helps to keep the landlords on their toes. It becomes a very expensive proposition for them if they refuse to take any action about the sale of counterfeit goods on their premises.

The federal standard is willful blindness. One is not allowed to be willfully blind. One cannot own a flea market where there are stalls that have open sales of counterfeit goods going on and say, 'Really, I didn't see anything. I just kind of walked down and collected my money, but I didn't see anything that was going on in there. How could I have known?'

…

MS KOLSUN: Truthfully, we have very good luck with the existing state laws because many of our private investigators are former state law enforcement people, either former cops, former sheriffs, or detectives. They have those relationships with the local law enforcement.

Also, there are all sorts of other laws that practitioners can use in the battle against counterfeiters, like tax laws—I mean, calling the Internal Revenue Service ('IRS')—counterfeiters don't pay taxes. The IRS and state tax authorities like these cases very much. We don't always know how they come out, but they appreciate the information and will do something. Also, there is asset seizure …

MS MCDONALD: Barbara, why don't you talk a little bit from the in-house counsel's perspective about how you find out about a problem and then what you do about it?

MS KOLSUN: First, I want to say particularly to the students in the room that intellectual property theft is an issue that is going to be a big part of your future, whether you have had any contact with counterfeiting or not. In case you haven't noticed, we don't make anything in this country anymore, and most of our assets are intellectual property. Think about every business that [Mr Pogoda] mentioned as members of our coalition. Pharmaceuticals, what is their asset? It's the intellectual property of patents by the people inventing the drugs and, of course, their trademarks—Pfizer, whatever. Similarly, Microsoft's product is intellectual property. And there are also companies like ours. If Kate Spade closed down tomorrow, and if somebody bought our company, he or she would be buying our assets such as our name, our trademark, our copyrights, a few computers, and maybe a few people whom they probably would let go after the merger …

Intellectual property is the most important thing in the world now … Especially with the birth of the Internet, it doesn't take much to have a business anymore. Think about eBay or other Web sites. Nobody even has to have a store anymore. Somebody basically can run something out of his or her apartment with a computer. One of our biggest problems both in the luxury brand area with consumer goods and the pharmaceuticals industry is counterfeiting online … There are people who make huge livings selling knockoff handbags and other goods. Fortunately, eBay has a very good system. It took many years to get there, by threatening to sue them under the doctrines of contributory and vicarious infringement. They have a system, called the Verified Rights Owner program, in which trademark owners can register with eBay and have the right to close down the auction site before or after the sale of counterfeit goods is made just on the basis of swearing that the item is counterfeit and that they are the rightful owners of the trademark. So, eBay has been very helpful. But that is only one tiny piece of the picture. There are Web sites everywhere. There is Yahoo!, Craigslist, and lots of other problems …

People contact us constantly wanting to return a handbag that they bought in Chinatown or somewhere else because the quality of it is so poor—can we fix it, can we return it? Of course we can't, we didn't make it.

Our goods don't have health and safety concerns, but consider pharmaceuticals … I remember years ago hearing a lecture at one of our IACC meetings by a law professor named Arthur Best from the University of Denver. He spoke about the fact that some day a wily lawyer was going to sue a pharmaceutical company for an injury caused by counterfeit goods. Think about that. When I heard that ten years ago, I thought that it would never happen. Pfizer didn't make the fake product. Why should they be held responsible? Well, you know what? The product has Pfizer's name on it.

MR POGODA: And this is another part of the problem that companies face. With regard to what [Ms Kolsun] was saying, a pharmaceutical company could be sued. I think the basis of the lawsuit would be not necessarily that the company made this counterfeit product—obviously it didn't—but that perhaps it didn't do enough to warn its customers that there were substandard products out there. That might be the basis of a lawsuit.

It's a difficult position for a company to be in, no matter what the product is. The question it must ask itself is: do I alert my customers to the fact I have a problem and then scare them all off and have them go to my competitors who are not admitting that they may have a similar problem? So, it's a very difficult position for a company to find itself in.

To their credit, the pharmaceutical industry responded very quickly to this Lipitor scare and notified their customers … In that situation, it was fortunate that nobody was hurt. But the next person who makes counterfeit pharmaceuticals might intend to hurt people and may put some kind of poison or biotoxin in the medicine. What is a company going to do at that point? How does it track back medicine that might have fake lot numbers or fake labels on it? In addition to having to come up with the resources to go after everybody that does this, these companies may find themselves in a position in which they are actually being sued for these misdeeds.

MS MCDONALD: It's not just with drugs and somebody who might intend to hurt people. There are also repercussions that come from what people don't necessarily think of. There have been instances in which counterfeit baby formula was sold. Now, it didn't have any horrifying effects that killed a child, but it did also not have the nutritional value that the label said it had. So, parents thought that they were feeding their children baby formula with the appropriate level of nutrition. It is a pretty horrifying situation …

MR POGODA: … most of the time, and especially in America, the supply chain from the manufacturer to the person who actually distributes the supply is pretty secure. The reason it is usually pretty secure is because it goes straight from the manufacturer to the distributor and that's it—there is nothing in between. It doesn't go anywhere else, doesn't get diverted, and doesn't get shipped anywhere.

But as people are beginning to turn to alternative sources for medicine—for instance, from Canada or the Internet where anybody could be sending stuff by mail ... It's estimated that thirty-five percent of the pharmaceuticals [in Mexico] are counterfeit, and they are brought into America. Or if an area in the country isn't served by one of the three or four major distributors of pharmaceuticals in America, they go to what is called the secondary wholesale market, which only accounts for about five percent of all the drugs. This is significant, but not a lot obviously, and that market is largely unchecked by federal and state regulators.

Take, for instance, somebody looking to slip something into the supply chain. Let's say the correct dosage for a particular drug is 200 milliliters. This person takes the label off, relabels it 400 milliliters, and sells it for twice the price. Then the consumer is getting only half of what he or she needs …

MS KOLSUN: By the way, this topic of talking to the press and broadcasting the counterfeiting problem in terms of pharmaceuticals versus luxury goods is a very contentious one within our trade association, as one can hear from the different points of view …

A big problem, little money. And so how do we divvy up that money? Wherever possible, we work with law enforcement because criminal actions give the most bang for the buck. It sends a message. People often don't do this again once they have been arrested, when they see a search warrant for their home, or when a policeman or even a private investigator has shown up. So, that has been very successful. We send a lot of cease-and-desist letters, which often have a good effect. A lot of people reply, 'I just didn't know' …

We don't sue people. The only civil action that we're involved in is one that [Ms McDonald's] firm handles—the Chinatown seizures. That is because Chinatown is such an enormous problem for us that we just can't count on pure criminal actions down there to solve the problem because the police just can't be there all the time. I don't know why Chinatown is such a huge problem.

…

MS KOLSUN: … I do a lot of interviews and I get asked all the time by reporters this question: 'Well, you know, Kate Spade bags are so expensive, why shouldn't we buy a knockoff?' The answer is that it's stealing, number one; it's no different than walking into the Kate Spade store in SoHo and stealing a bag right off of the shelves. How is it any different?

... I think education is key. I mean, yes, there definitely has to be some thought, and the music industry is certainly doing a lot of soul searching in terms of the price of a CD. But what makes something cost what it does? It's a fact that a legitimate business pays taxes, contributes to workers' compensation, and contributes to the health and safety of workers. People really don't understand that counterfeit goods, be they Kate Spade purses, Rolex watches, or knockoff pharmaceuticals, are not made under the conditions that genuine goods are. We have rules about how to make things so that they don't hurt people, so that the quality is of a certain level.

I don't know how to spread that message. It's truly the biggest challenge that we all face. In the last ten years we have joined together in organizations like the IACC so that we are sending a message that this isn't just about a knockoff Rolex watch. This is about a much bigger picture. This is about really the whole basis of our society.

...

MR POGODA: ... I hate to say it, but the generation of people ages five to about fifteen is kind of lost, but they certainly have the mentality that if it's on their computer screen, it's theirs for the taking. Obviously, at some point that mentality is going to have to be changed.

You can change it, like [Ms Kolsun] said, by telling people to look at the bigger picture. Depending on the product involved, there could be some severe consumer-health and safety risks to the public; a lot of governments will lose tax dollars; and companies will lose money because they're selling less product, which means they might lay off people.

Ask people to think about where their money is going. The US government has established links between counterfeit goods and terrorists looking to counterfeit goods as a means of funding. When people start looking at the fact that the September 11th attacks cost about $500 000 to put together and the fact that 1500 pirated copies of Microsoft Office 2000 easily could be sold for above that, maybe then people will think about where their money is going. They might begin to question why all twenty people on this corner in Chinatown have the exact same purse and whom is it coming from? Someone must be supplying them ...

QUESTIONER: Counterfeiting supporting terrorism is a little bit different.

MS MCDONALD: You would think so. The FBI has proven conclusively that most of the funding for the first World Trade Center bombing in 1993 came from the sale of counterfeit tee-shirts on Fifth Avenue in New York City. So, one has to ask, 'Where did the money for the one that killed a lot more people come from? Did it come from the sale of counterfeit goods?'

It's a big problem. Counterfeiting is not perceived as a crime on the same level as a lot of other crimes. So, some really big criminal people are getting involved in it. Why? Because the government doesn't take it as seriously, they are not going to go to jail for as long, and it is less likely that they are going to get caught.

QUESTIONER: ... My office is right near Bloomingdale's. Every day on that block—they are there morning and night. A lot of visitors come there. When people see them every single day, they come away and say, 'What could be so terrible? They are here.'

MR KORMAN: The inference must be that it is lawful … When the same people are displaying the same watches at the same place day after day after day, why does that continue? Wouldn't it seem sensible that persuasive people such as you three could arrange to have a sweep and just pick up all these things one day after a brief interview with the Police Commissioner?

…

QUESTIONER: … For certain purposes, as I understand it, landlords and property owners in New York City are responsible for what goes on—for example, on the sidewalk when it snows. I take it for this purpose Bloomingdale's is not responsible for what occurs on their sidewalk.

MS MCDONALD: Well, that's correct. In fact, there was one case on point in which it was determined that the activities by independent people on the sidewalk was not the property owner's responsibility. That is something that we tried to push for at the same time …

MS KOLSUN: … One of our greatest allies is US Customs. In addition to the registration of trademarks with the US Patent and Trademark Office, there is another system of recordation of trademarks with US Customs, which is very inexpensive and can be done by trademark holders in-house. I did all of ours.

Recording the trademarks with US Customs is only step one. Then the trademark holders have to go to ports and train. The IACC has a very good system involving a series of training sessions. We have an excellent relationship with US Customs. We do regular training almost every month at certain ports.

Now, think about how people come into the United States from a foreign country with their passports. Not every container is opened nor is every piece of luggage searched. To the extent that US Customs opens a container, it's very easy for them to determine counterfeit merchandise because they are given copies of our registered trademarks (or references to our registered trademarks) that tell them where our goods are supposed to come from.

For example, our goods are manufactured in certain factories in China and in Italy. If goods with the Kate Spade trademark come in from Taiwan, the Philippines, or another country that they are not manufactured in, then if US Customs stops that shipment and opens it, it will seize those products and give notice to the importer of record. If the importer doesn't raise his hands and say, 'Those are authentic,' then the goods are destroyed. This is an incredibly terrific mechanism for getting rid of goods, but it doesn't touch half of them.

MR KORMAN: I doubt that it's even five percent. But if it were five percent, I would think that is high.

MS KOLSUN: In addition, counterfeiters do all sorts of other clever things. For example, 'Louis Vuitton' bags come into the country covered in a little sheet … So, US Customs wouldn't see the Louis Vuitton pattern when the container came through and the container were opened …

Similarly, if you have ever seen a Kate Spade purse, we have little labels on the outside of our bags that say 'Kate Spade New York,' like this one. That is one of our distinctive little signs. Counterfeiters make those tags in the United States, import bags from China that have nothing on them, and then stick the tags on. You probably can peel off the 'Kate Spade New York' label with your thumb from any bag in Chinatown.

> MS MCDONALD: One of the biggest problems now is that they only can be arrested if the goods actually say 'Kate Spade.' So, they make bags that look just like all of the Kate Spade bags—same dimension, same colors, same handle length—but with no marking on them. And then the police can't do anything. Meanwhile, in the guy has a hundred little, teeny, tiny, peel-off stickers that say 'Kate Spade' in his pocket. Then he sticks the sticker on when he sells buyers the bag.
>
> ... ...

The above extract identifies a number of challenges in protecting and enforcing IPRs. It also provides an account of enforcement techniques industries use in an attempt at protecting their IPRs. The leading software company (and likely the world's largest victim of piracy), Microsoft, is a good example of a company struggling to enforce its IPRs in an increasingly globalised and technologically advanced world. Microsoft attempts to combat piracy in a number of ways, including:

- Hosting a website dedicated to facts, questions and answers, and informational links regarding software piracy;
- Spending monetary and human resources in an attempt to protect its software through technological advancement and security measures (such as 'key coding');
- Participating in industry trade groups (such as the Business Software Alliance) which allows the company to influence policy against infringers and counterfeiters; and
- Investing in high piracy regions in the hopes of at least gaining market share (or pirated products), so that eventually when the countries grow and demand their own IPRs protection, the market for legitimate Microsoft products will be strong.[33]

Despite these efforts, piracy in the software industry is rampant and accounts for perhaps the greatest amount of loss to the industry (it is estimated that 36 per cent of software installed on computers is counterfeit,[34] while 90 per cent of software installed in China is counterfeit[35]). Interestingly, Microsoft released a report in 2002 which even questions whether the continued enforcement efforts are financially worthwhile:

> Microsoft diligently defends its intellectual property rights, but unlicensed copying and use of software represents a loss of revenue to the Company. While this adversely affects US revenue, revenue loss is even more significant outside the United States, particularly in countries where laws are less protective of intellectual property rights. Throughout the world, Microsoft actively educates consumers on the benefits of licensing genuine products and educates lawmakers on the advantages of a business climate where intellectual property rights are protected. However, continued efforts may not affeçt revenue positively and further deterioration in compliance with existing legal protections or reductions in

33 See JM Sellers, 'The Black Market and Intellectual Property: A Potential Sherman Act Section Two Antitrust Defense?' (2004) 14 *Alb LJ Sci & Tech* 583 at 613.

34 See Business Software Alliance (BSA), 'First Annual BSA & IDC Global Software Piracy Study' (2004), available at [www.bsa.or.jp/file/PiracyStudy_E.pdf].

35 See J Melnitzer, 'Role Reversal' (30 May 2006) Inside Counsel, available at [www.insidecounsel.com/section/ip/488]; US Department of Commerce, 'Protecting Your Intellectual Property Rights (IPRs) in China: A Practical Guide for U.S. Companies', available at [www.mac.doc.gov/China/Docs/BusinessGuides/IntellectualPropertyRights.htm].

the legal protection for intellectual property rights of software developers could adversely affect revenue.[36]

Such a statement is worrying for a number of reasons, not least because it questions whether expending resources on combating piracy and counterfeiting is an efficient use of resources. Many companies face the same dilemma: spend increasing amounts of money to protect IPRs, or accept some amount of loss (perhaps in return for legitimate market share in the future). For this reason, many companies only prosecute large-scale infringers (and preferably registered companies, as they have assets and perhaps even shareholders).

Industry has also recently found it useful to improve cooperative efforts at the sector, cross-sector, national and international level in an attempt to improve its protection and enforcement efforts. Such cooperation can be demonstrated by the Verified Rights Owner system operated by eBay to stop counterfeit and otherwise infringing items being sold on its online auction site, through the formation of industry associations aimed at influencing policy (for example, the Business Alliance to Stop Counterfeiting and Piracy), and through enhancing public awareness of the illegality and consequences of piracy and counterfeiting. Private industry has also begun developing and refining technological solutions to stem the trade in pirated and counterfeit goods.

As with governmental efforts, however, there is room for increased industry efforts. The OECD report extracted above also offers five areas where industry could increase its attention and efforts.

OECD, 'The Economic Impact of Counterfeiting and Piracy' (OECD, 2007), pp 28–29[37]

Industry efforts to combat counterfeiting and piracy include (i) supporting research and analysis of issues related to counterfeiting and piracy, (ii) promoting awareness; (iii) pursuing IPR violators in courts; (iv) supporting government efforts to combat counterfeiting and piracy; and (v) taking action to make it harder for pirates and counterfeiters to copy and market their products (ie through technology, etc)

Efforts being taken by industry to combat counterfeiting and piracy are being pursued at the firm and sector levels, as well as across sectors. A number of cross-sector initiatives have an important international dimension [including] … The Business Alliance to Stop Counterfeiting and Piracy, which was launched in early 2005 under the auspices of the International Chamber of Commerce … [The BASCAP] is one of the more recent and comprehensive global initiatives launched by industry. It seeks to bring firms together to pursue a more unified approach to combating counterfeiting and piracy. Its efforts include the creation of platforms for exchanging information on the counterfeiting and piracy situation in different economies and sectors, and for sharing information on effective brand protection techniques. It also seeks to provide stakeholders with improved information on the efforts being taken to address

36 Microsoft Corp, 2002 10-K Report, Part II at 18, available at [www.microsoft.com/msft/reports/ar02/financials/item7.htm].

37 [www.oecd.org/dataoecd/13/12/38707619.pdf].

issues, with a view towards enhancing co-ordination. At the same time, research projects are being carried out to provide more effective methods for evaluating the counterfeiting and piracy situation in different economies. On the public policy front, efforts are being made to more effectively communicate the economic and social costs of counterfeiting and piracy to governments and the general public.

A 2007 BASCAP Global survey on Counterfeiting and Piracy revealed that industry efforts have mainly focused on initiatives to develop technologies to combat infringement. Resources have also been directed to aiding enforcement and improvising awareness, but to a lesser extent.

Collaboration and co-operation

Many industry groups and associations have developed specific activities to assist in uncovering and dealing with counterfeiting and piracy. Such groups provide central reference points that allow the industry sectors to share resources, information and experience, as well as providing a focus for interaction with government and enforcement authorities. Additionally, some of these industry groups also carry out surveillance, investigation and prosecution of producers and sellers of counterfeited and pirated goods.

Firms have recognized the importance of co-operation with government and with each other to strengthen enforcement efforts. In areas where counterfeit and pirated goods are being produced, this co-operation extends to supporting the activities of police in locating facilities and carrying out raids. With respect to imported items, industries are co-operating with customs and other enforcement authorities to identify and intercept counterfeited and pirated goods. In both cases, most industry sectors take an active interest in subsequent civil action and prosecution.

Training and awareness

Increased education of public officials, customs and law enforcement officers and consumers is an important aspect of industry efforts to combat counterfeiting and piracy. This kind of education is designed to increase the effectiveness of investigative efforts and prosecutions, and discourage consumers from buying counterfeited and pirated goods.

Authentication technologies

It has become easier for counterfeiters and pirates to deceive consumers through high quality packaging and/or through fake products that are virtually impossible to distinguish from authentic merchandise. In the case of trademark infringement, brand owners are constantly looking for cost-effective ways to provide retailers and end-users with a means to determine whether the products they have purchased are authentic. A number of companies are developing technologies to facilitate authentication and/or detection of genuine vs fake products. The technologies generally take two basic forms—those that are used to authenticate products and those that are used to track and trace the movement of products through supply chains. While a range of these technologies have been introduced in the last several years, their broad use and success has been limited by a variety of factors, including the ability of counterfeiters and pirates to adapt or copy the technologies.

Improving supply chain management should be an integral part of industry initiatives to combat counterfeiting and piracy.

One of the key challenges that counterfeiters and pirates face is distribution of their products. Rights holders can help to limit the extent to which this occurs by vigorously overseeing the movement of their products from production centres to retail sites. There is a related need to work actively with suppliers, distributors, retailers and consumers to encourage them to be vigilant in acquiring items.

... ...

It is unrealistic to expect that any industry efforts will eliminate piracy and counterfeiting. Improved efforts, however, can send a message to infringers that industry is serious about protecting its IPRs and branding and severely curtail trade in pirated and counterfeit goods. Cooperative efforts, targeted training and educational programs, improved technologies and supply-chain management can all play a role in reducing infringing activity.

8.3.2 Parallel importation

IP provisions can be used to prevent importation of legitimate goods which have been distributed in the market of another country by, or with the authorisation of, the owner of the IPRs. The term 'parallel importation' is often used to describe such provisions. Parallel imported products (also called 'grey market' goods) are not counterfeit or pirated goods; rather they are genuine goods sold in the country of export with the authorisation of the rights holder, but imported by a reseller without the authority of the rights holder in the country of importation.[38]

There are a number of reasons why authorised distributors in the importing country seek to prohibit parallel importation, most notably that parallel imported goods are often sold at a cheaper price than those sold by the authorised distributors.[39] Allowing the importation of parallel imports, therefore, would undercut the total sales and profits of the authorised distributor. A common example of parallel importation is where a manufacturer assigns or licenses its trademark rights to an exclusive distributor in one region (Region A), while a third party obtains the manufacturer's products from a different region (Region B), but imports and distributes them into the exclusive distributor's designated region (Region A) without the latter's consent. One only has to walk down Pitt Street in Sydney to see how the loosening of restrictions on parallel importation affects price. Once Australia relaxed its prohibition on parallel imported books and CDs, a plethora of stores opened up selling products authorised to be distributed in a foreign market (such as Malaysia or Indonesia), but diverted to Australia and sold at a lower price than the same product authorised to be sold in Australia. On the other hand, restraining the importation and marketing of parallel imported goods could raise issues involving restraint of trade and competition law.

Due to the complexity of these issues, as well as the divergence among national practice across the globe, the legality of parallel importation is determined by whether a country adopts the principle of international, national or regional exhaustion of IPRs:

38 Intellectual Property and Competition Review Committee, 'Review of Intellectual Property Legislation under the Competition Principles Agreement' (Ergas Committee), p 42.

39 Certain factors (fluctuating currencies, level of development, etc) allow goods to be discounted in some markets but not others (price discrimination).

- With international exhaustion, IP owners lose control over their goods once the goods are released into the stream of commerce; that is, IPRs are exhausted with the first legitimate sale regardless of where it occurs (international exhaustion is also sometimes referred to as the 'doctrine of first sale').
- With national exhaustion, the first sale of the goods in the domestic market does not 'exhaust' the mark owner's rights in foreign markets; that is, IPRs are not exhausted with the first sale and the unauthorised importation and sale of the goods in a foreign market infringes the owner's IPRs.
- With regional exhaustion, the first consensual sale of the IP-protected product by the rights holder exhausts any IPRs over products not only domestically, but within the entire region, and parallel imports within the region can no longer be opposed based on the IPRs. However, the system of regional exhaustion can be used to prevent the parallel importation of goods sold outside of the region; that is, it can prevent the parallel importation of goods into the region, but cannot prevent the parallel importation of goods once they are in the region.

The TRIPS Agreement does not offer any assistance on the issue of parallel importation. Instead, due to lack of consensus among the negotiating parties, Article 6 of the TRIPS Agreement merely states that 'nothing in this Agreement shall be used to address the issue of the exhaustion of intellectual property rights'. Members are therefore free to adopt whichever exhaustion model they believe is in the national interest.[40] Some countries, including Australia, operate a mixed system based on national exhaustion for some products and international or regional exhaustion for other products. Additionally, exhaustion regimes often differ depending upon the IPRs at issue.

8.3.2a Copyright

The Australian *Copyright Act 1968* remains based on a system of national exhaustion, meaning that exhaustion of rights only apply to legitimate sales within Australia and the rights owner can prevent parallel importation of the relevant product from a foreign country.[41] Thus, for most products, the system continues to allow IP owners (or licensees) to 'separate the world market into self-contained segments to secure the greatest return on the protected subject matter' by allowing IP owners (or licensees) to control the importation into Australia of copyright material via a system of national exhaustion, even if the products have been lawfully acquired overseas.[42]

Recent amendments to the Act, however, have relaxed the prohibition against certain categories of parallel imports. For instance, separate regimes resembling a system of international exhaustion now govern the importation of books and sound recordings.[43]

---

40 Likewise, neither the Berne Convention, Paris Convention or any other recent agreement, such as the 1996 WIPO 'internet treaties', explicitly determine the issue.

41 Sections 37 and 102.

42 Intellectual Property and Competition Review Committee, 'Review of Intellectual Property Legislation under the Competition Principles Agreement' (Ergas Committee), p 46.

43 This legislative amendment thus renders the lead case in the area redundant: *Interstate Parcel Express Co Pty Ltd v Time-Life International (Nederlands) BV* (1977) 138 CLR 534 'The Time-Life case'.

In terms of books, amendments introduced in 1990 allow books first published in a foreign country to be imported into Australia without restriction.[44] The Act, however, distinguishes books first published in Australia (that is, 'simultaneously' published in Australia and in a foreign country, which in practical terms means published in Australia within 30 days of first being published in a foreign country) and only allows importation into Australia under three limited circumstances:

1 To provide a single copy for a customer (subject to an undertaking that they will not enter into commercial dealings with that book);
2 To provide one or more copies for a non-profit library; and
3 To satisfy local orders that have been unfilled for more than 90 days.[45]

In terms of sound recordings, the Act now allows the importation of sound recordings when:

- The copy is non-infringing;
- The copy is made with the consent of the copyright owner; and
- The copy country is a party to the Berne Convention, a member of the WTO, and complies with the TRIPS Agreement in respect to copyright in literary, dramatic and musical works.[46]

Works and other subject matter that are 'accessories' are also no longer subject to a strict system of national exhaustion.

These amendments more closely align Australia with nations such as New Zealand, Canada, Japan, Singapore, Malaysia and South Korea, which all base their systems on international exhaustion. On the other hand, the USA still operates a system of national exhaustion which prohibits parallel imports of copyrighted material. Even in the USA, however, the system may be changing, as the Supreme Court in *Quality King Distributors Inc v L'Anza Research International Inc*[47] distinguished copyright associated with the goods (such as labels and packages) from those of the goods themselves (such as CDs or books). Meanwhile, the EU allows parallel importation between member countries but continues to prevent parallel importation from non-members to members of the EU. In other words, within the EU operates a system of regional exhaustion, but the EU retains a system of national exhaustion that applies to non-members.

Taking into consideration the fact that prices are likely to be higher in Australia (especially for books and software products) as a result of the restrictions on parallel importation and the nature of the Australian economic conditions, the Ergas Committee recommended repealing parallel importation provisions as a way of integrating Australia into larger, more competitive world markets and ensuring that Australian consumers do not pay more for copyrighted works than overseas consumers.[48]

---

44 These amendments were based on the recommendations of the Prices Surveillance Authority (PSA), as it was then known, made in 1999 to repeal the restrictions on parallel importation for books.

45 See *Copyright Act 1968* (Cth), ss 44A and 112A.

46 Section 10AA of the *Copyright Act 1968* (Cth). It is worth noting that s 130A shifts the burden of proof and requires the defendant (importer) to prove that the imported sound is non-infringing.

47 118 S Ct 1125 (1998).

48 Intellectual Property and Competition Review Committee, 'Review of Intellectual Property Legislation under the Competition Principles Agreement' (Ergas Committee), p 73.

While the government first introduced legislation designed to implement the Ergas Committee recommendations in early 2001 (and again in early 2002 following the re-election of the conservative Howard Government in October 2001), the legislation did not become law until 2003. In that year, the *Copyright Amendment (Parallel Importation) Act 2003* (Cth) amended Australian copyright laws to pass a watered-down version of the Committee recommendations. Although the government sought to permit parallel importation of books, periodical publications, printed music and computer software (together with electronic versions of books, periodical publications and printed music), amendments demanded by the Australian Democrats (who held the balance of power in the Senate) to remove those provisions permitting parallel importation of books, periodical publications and printed music (but not the electronic versions of those items) were included in the legislation. The Australian Democrats also ensured that restrictions against parallel importation of films made for direct distribution to the public (including DVDs) remained in place.

Thus, national exhaustion continues to apply to literary works (other than certain books), dramatic, printed musical and artistic works, periodical publications, broadcasts and cinematograph films. Australia therefore continues to operate a mixed system, whereby one set of rules based on the system of international exhaustion applies to books, a different set of rules based on international exhaustion applies to sound recordings, while all other IP goods are subject to national exhaustion and thus not allowed to be parallel imported into the country.

8.3.2b Trademarks

The Australian *Trade Marks Act 1995* adopts the principle of 'international exhaustion', in that the rights owners' ability to control the use of the trademark are exhausted when the goods are voluntarily placed on the market.[49] This principle is well entrenched in Australian legislation and jurisprudence.[50] However, the Australian position is less certain where goods are imported from abroad after an Australian trademark is assigned to the Australian distributor. The following extract from the Ergas Committee explains the situation and recommends amendment to the *Trade Mark Act*.

Intellectual Property and Competition Review Committee, Review of Intellectual Property Legislation under the Competition Principles Agreement (Ergas Committee) (2000),[51] pp 188–91

The Committee received submissions on parallel importation and the *Trade Marks Act 1995* which pointed to the uncertainty created when an overseas owner of a trade mark conditionally assigns

---

49 *Trade Marks Act* 1995 (Cth), s123: 'a person who uses a registered trade mark in relation to goods that are similar to goods in respect of which the trade mark is registered does not infringe the trade mark if the trade mark has been applied to, or in relation to, the goods by, or with the consent of, the registered owner of the trade mark.'

50 See *Transport Tyres v Montana Tyres, Rims & Tubes Ltd* (1999) AIPC 9–467 (Full Court of the Federal Court of Australia).

51 Available at [www.ipaustralia.gov.au/about/ipcr.shtml].

the trade mark to an Australian distributor. The assignment is made on the condition that the Australian trade mark must be reassigned to the overseas owner if the distributorship arrangement between the overseas owner of the trade mark and the Australian trade mark comes to an end. The purpose of such an arrangement is to permit the Australian distributor to prevent the parallel importation of trade marked goods from overseas that would compete with the Australian distributor.

In addition to questions about the legality of these arrangements, there may be substantial anti-competitive effects created by these assignments that are plainly aimed at giving the distributor the right to control the flow of the trade marked goods. If the overseas trade mark owner retained the Australian ownership of the trade mark and retained the Australian distributor merely as an authorised user, neither the Australian distributor nor the overseas trade mark owner could prevent parallel importing. This is due to the impact of s 123 of the *Trade Marks Act* and the various case law concerning parallel importation that was decided pursuant to the *Trademarks Act 1955* (Commonwealth).

Section 123(1) of the *Trade Marks Act 1995* provides that a mark applied to the same or similar goods 'with the consent of' the registered owner does not infringe. There are doubts as to what 'consent' means in this context, although it is presumed that the section is meant to introduce into trade mark legislation the concept of exhaustion of rights. However, before the introduction of s 123, arrangements preventing parallel importation of trade marked goods were effected through the mechanism of foreign companies assigning their Australian trade marks to local distributors in order to assist the local distributor to prevent parallel importation.

In the *Fender Guitar case*, *Fender Australia v Bevk*, Justice Burchett held that a local distributor, to whom the foreign owner had assigned its trade mark in Australia, was entitled to prevent the parallel importation of goods bearing the trade mark. On the facts before him, the Judge found that the local company had developed an independent reputation in the trade mark through the selection of the goods it imported and the after sales service it provided to the public. There was no challenge to the validity of the assignment of the trade mark from the foreign company to the local company. Following this case it became common for foreign companies to assign their Australian trade marks to local distributors in order to assist the local distributor to prevent parallel importation.

The recent *Montana case* (*Transport Tyre Sales Pty Ltd v Montana Tyres Rims and Tubes Pty Ltd* (1999) 43 IPR 481) has cast doubts on the *Fender Guitar* arrangements. An international manufacturer assigned its Australian trade marks to a local distributor, in order to use trade mark rights to challenge parallel importation. This case consolidates the consistent approach in Australian courts in rejecting the rights of an international trade mark owner to control the distribution channels of its goods through trade mark rights, affirming the 'exhaustion of rights doctrine'. However, the appeal judgment leaves unanswered some of the most important issues arising out of the facts in the *Montana case.* The Court did not consider the issue of 'sham' transactions in relation to the recording of assignments. There remains a question whether in some circumstances involving '*Fender*' assignments, where the assignment document does not on its face reflect the real agreement between the partics, the lodgement of the document could amount to a false suggestion thereby invalidating the assignment.

A submission by [Australian academic Prof] Mark Davison states that there are difficulties and inefficiencies associated with the present position, including:

- the situation is uncertain. Neither authorised Australian distributors nor the parallel importer are certain of the legality of the parallel importer's activity;
- trade mark owners and their Australian distributors will be entering into assignments and related agreements purely for the purpose of preventing parallel importing. There are

transactional costs incurred in these activities such as liability for capital gains tax and legal fees every time the trade mark is assigned and re-assigned; and

- parallel importers can have their trading activities ended by the stroke of a pen although there is no real change in the trade activities of the overseas owner, the Australian distributor or the parallel importer. The appropriateness of parallel importing from the policy perspective is not altered in any way by the mere conditional assignment of Australian ownership to an Australian distributor but the legality of parallel importing may hinge on it.

Davison therefore concludes: 'What is clear is that the type of artificial arrangements that have lead to the *Montana case* and *Fender v Bevk* should not impact on the legality of parallel importing of trade marked goods. Whatever policy position is taken on the issue of parallel importing, that position should not be capable of being altered by the formation of artificial arrangements in which an Australian distributor which was previously acting as an authorised user becomes the owner of the Australian trade mark in circumstances which demonstrate that it will simply continue to perform its role as an authorised user. Section 123 of the Act needs to be amended or a new sub-section introduced to clarify that issue of what is included within the concept of 'consent' by the trade mark owner to the application of the trade mark to goods. Such an amendment should make it clear that a registered owner who is, in effect, the authorised user of the overseas owner of the same trade mark is consenting to the application of the trade mark to goods made by or under the control of that overseas owner.

... ...

The Ergas Committee accepted that the current laws and regulations impose costs and uncertainties on all parties—including rights owners, importers and distributors. Thus, while recognising that exclusive dealing arrangements (such as the contractual assignment of trademarks) should be acceptable, and should only be prohibited when the arrangements substantially lessen competition in a market, the Committee did not believe that such arrangements should automatically trigger statutory provisions that protect a supplier from import competition. With this in mind, the Committee recommended legislative amendments to ensure that the assignment provisions are not used to circumvent the intent of the system of international exhaustion to allow the parallel importation of legitimately trademarked goods.

The government agreed to implement the Committee recommendation; however legislation to amend the *Trade Marks Act 1995* (Cth) was introduced in 2006 and the relevant section (s 123) was not included in the amending legislation. This area thus remains the subject of controversy and confusion.[52]

8.3.3 Compulsory licences

A compulsory licence has been defined as 'an authorisation given by a national authority, without or against the consent of the patent holder, for the exploitation of a particular

52 See *Brother Industries Ltd v Dynamic Supplies Pty Ltd* [2007] FCA 1490.

patented product or process, or other intellectual property right'.[53] The Australian Law Reform Commission (ALRC) explains:

> The concept of a compulsory licence over patents arose from the historical requirement that a patent holder must 'locally work' a patented product or process. This meant that the patent holder was required to use or produce the patented invention within the country in which the patent was registered. Where a patent holder failed to 'work' the invention locally, the patent was subject to forfeiture. Compulsory licences were developed as a less drastic means to ensure a patent was exploited.[54]

The historical justification for compulsory licences—for the promotion of the domestic industry—is no longer appropriate in an age of liberalised trade, international business and globalisation.[55] Today, compulsory licences are granted for a variety of reasons, such as:

- To ensure adequate supply of a product to the local population;
- Where the working of another patented invention is being prevented or hindered by a refusal to work a patent;
- To remedy anti-competitive conduct;
- To facilitate government use;
- To improve access to medicines; or
- Where the issuance of a licence is in the public interest.

As compulsory licensing provisions allow for the exploitation of a patented invention without the consent of the patent holder, the issue of compulsory licences is often contentious, both at the international and domestic level. The TRIPS Agreement provides the framework for regulating compulsory licences at the international level. Domestic compulsory licensing provisions generally track the international framework. This is the case in Australia, where the *Patents Act 1990* (Cth) is, on its face, TRIPS-compliant.

This section will first outline the relevant provisions in the TRIPS Agreement, including the resulting controversies and action involving the issue of access to medicines, before turning to Australian-specific issues and problems resulting from domestic legislation.

8.3.3a The international framework

While the TRIPS Agreement provides for a number of exceptions to the exclusive rights granted to IP owners, the most important of these exclusions are perhaps the general

53 ALRC, 'Genes and Ingenuity: Gene Patenting and Human Health', ALRC 99 (1999), p 711 (citing C Correa, *Intellectual Property Rights and the Use of Compulsory Licenses: Options for Developing Countries*, TRADE Working Papers 5, South Centre, 1999, p 3, available at [www.netamericas.net/Researchpapers/Documents/Ccorrea/Ccorrea3.doc]. The report is available at [www.austlii.edu.au/au/other/alrc/publications/reports/99/].

54 ALRC, p 712. For application in Australia, see *Fastening Supplies Proprietary Limited v Olin Mathieson Chemical Corp* (1969) 119 CLR 572 at 575.

55 See for example Intellectual Property and Competition Review Committee, *Review of Intellectual Property Legislation under the Competition Principles Agreement* (2000), p 162.

exceptions provided by Article 30[56] and the compulsory licensing provision of Article 31.

Article 31 permits members to grant compulsory licences for patented products and processes under limited circumstances and upon satisfying certain conditions. Under a compulsory licence, a government is forced to allow the production of a patented product without the necessary permission from the patent holder. In terms of pharmaceutical products, the aim of the practice is to allow countries to produce low-cost generic equivalents of the patented product in certain circumstances and under certain guidelines.

To avoid abuse, Article 31 conditions the granting of a compulsory licence on the following preconditions:

(a) authorization of such use shall be considered on its individual merits;

(b) such use may only be permitted if, prior to such use, the proposed user has made efforts to obtain authorization from the right holder on reasonable commercial terms and conditions and that such efforts have not been successful within a reasonable period of time. This requirement may be waived by a Member in the case of a national emergency or other circumstances of extreme urgency or in cases of public non-commercial use. In situations of national emergency or other circumstances of extreme urgency, the right holder shall, nevertheless, be notified as soon as reasonably practicable. In the case of public non-commercial use, where the government or contractor, without making a patent search, knows or has demonstrable grounds to know that a valid patent is or will be used by or for the government, the right holder shall be informed promptly;

(c) the scope and duration of such use shall be limited to the purpose for which it was authorized, and in the case of semi-conductor technology shall only be for public non-commercial use or to remedy a practice determined after judicial or administrative process to be anti-competitive;

(d) such use shall be non-exclusive;

(e) such use shall be non-assignable, except with that part of the enterprise or goodwill which enjoys such use;

(f) any such use shall be authorized predominantly for the supply of the domestic market of the Member authorizing such use;

(g) authorization for such use shall be liable, subject to adequate protection of the legitimate interests of the persons so authorized, to be terminated if and when the circumstances which led to it cease to exist and are unlikely to recur. The competent authority shall have the authority to review, upon motivated request, the continued existence of these circumstances;

(h) the right holder shall be paid adequate remuneration in the circumstances of each case, taking into account the economic value of the authorization;

(i) the legal validity of any decision relating to the authorization of such use shall be subject to judicial review or other independent review by a distinct higher authority in that Member;

(j) any decision relating to the remuneration provided in respect of such use shall be subject to judicial review or other independent review by a distinct higher authority in that Member; [and]

---

56 Article 30 grants members the right to legislate for limited exceptions to the exclusive rights conferred by a patent, provided that such exceptions do not unreasonably conflict with a normal exploitation of the patent and do not unreasonably prejudice the legitimate interests of the patent owner, taking account of the legitimate interests of third parties.

(k) Members are not obliged to apply the conditions set forth in subparagraphs (b) and (f) where such use is permitted to remedy a practice determined after judicial or administrative process to be anti-competitive. The need to correct anti-competitive practices may be taken into account in determining the amount of remuneration in such cases. Competent authorities shall have the authority to refuse termination of authorization if and when the conditions which led to such authorization are likely to recur[.]

One of the most important of these conditions is subsection (b), which permits the granting of a compulsory licence only if 'the proposed user has made efforts to obtain authorization from the right holder on reasonable commercial terms and conditions and that such efforts have not been successful within a reasonable period of time'. Importantly, 'This requirement may be waived in the case of national emergency or other circumstances of extreme urgency or in cases of public non-commercial use'. However, 'In situations of national emergency or other circumstances of extreme urgency, the right holder shall, nevertheless, be notified as soon as reasonably practicable'.

Subsection (f) also plays an important part in the current controversy surrounding patent protection and access to medicines in the developing world. Subsection (f) restricts the issuance of a compulsory licence unless it is used 'predominantly for the supply of the domestic market of the Member authorizing such use', meaning that a country must have the means to produce the product itself or it cannot get the benefit of the compulsory licensing provision. By requiring foreign compulsory licensees to supply a predominant part of their production to their domestic market, subparagraph (f) limits the licensee's ability to export medicines to countries with public health needs, and countries that have insufficient or no manufacturing capabilities thus cannot take advantage of the provision. When read with subparagraph (k), which provides that 'members are not obliged to apply the conditions set forth in subparagraph ... (f) where such use is permitted to remedy a practice determined after judicial or administrative process to be anti-competitive', the text appears to expressly limit a government's use of compulsory licensing to predominantly supply its domestic market, except when necessary to remedy anticompetitive practices.

Subsection (h) is also important to the current debate, and its wording has proven to be highly controversial. Subsection (h) requires the payment of 'adequate remuneration' based on the 'economic value of the authorization', but in practice members can neither agree on the meaning of 'adequate remuneration' or that of the 'economic value of the authorization'.

Thus, although Article 31 grants members the right to issue a compulsory licence, it severely limits the circumstances under which such a licence can be issued and requires that adequate remuneration be paid for the licence. While it is argued that such limitations and conditions guard against abuse, the practical effect of the limitations and conditions is that countries with manufacturing capabilities could make only very limited use of the provision, and those countries with insufficient or no manufacturing capabilities could not make use of the provision at all.

The controversy surrounding the issue of exceptions to the exclusive rights granted to the rights holder by the TRIPS Agreement has been intense. The following extract details the most notable controversy, that involving the issue of the compulsory licence provision of Article 31 as it relates to access to medicines and pharmaceutical products. It also introduces the WTO's response, in the form of the Doha Declaration on Public Health, and the 'Implementation Agreement', which further defines WTO-compliant compulsory licensing procedures.

Bryan Mercurio, 'TRIPs, Patents and Access to Life-Saving Drugs in the Developing World' (2004) 8 *Marquette Intellectual Property Law Review* 211 at 224–35

III. The Doha Declaration

A. POLITICAL CLIMATE LEADING TO DOHA

The issue of access to patented medicines gained worldwide attention in 2000, when several drug companies challenged the legality of the South African *Medical and Related Substances Control Act* of 1997, which allowed for compulsory licensing of patented pharmaceuticals. The lawsuit, filed in the domestic courts of South Africa, evoked a significant amount of sympathy, strong reactions, and unfavorable publicity for the pharmaceutical companies. At the same time, the US, one of the pharmaceutical companies' biggest supporters in the South African litigation, requested WTO consultations and the establishment of a panel against Brazil over the compulsory licensing provisions in Brazilian industrial property law.

As the negative publicity mounted, the US reversed its position on the South African compulsory licensing laws and negotiated a settlement to its WTO dispute settlement claim against Brazil whereby that country agreed to consult with the US before invoking any domestic compulsory licensing provisions. In April 2001, the pharmaceutical companies also relented and dropped their challenge to the South African legislation.

Then, in September 2001, the US position regarding compulsory licensing became untenable, as in the wake of the terrorist attacks of September 11 and the subsequent anthrax scares, the US government threatened to issue a compulsory license order against Bayer AG Corporation's antibiotic Cipro (ciprofloxacin) unless the company lowered its selling price so that it could make Cipro available to victims of anthrax attacks. The US position with regards to its own threat of issuing a compulsory license placed itself in a difficult position, as it was now hard-pressed to remain credible in its requests that developing countries resist overriding patents in favor of making the drug available to the masses. Many countries immediately noted the inconsistency and apparent double standard of the American position.

B. WHAT DOES THE DECLARATION DO FOR PATENT PROTECTION?

Heading into the Doha Round, the time was ripe for developing countries to push for a shift in stance from developed countries towards access to medicines. Not only did the highly visible plight of many poor and ravaged countries place a significant amount of pressure on developed nations to be sympathetic to the demands of the developing countries and the LDCs, but the US and Canada faced the possibility of looking extremely hypocritical in the wake of its post-September 2001 threats. In such a political climate, the US and other developed countries could not have possibly objected to the needs of the developing world.

While both developing and developed countries submitted proposals to clarify certain ambiguous terms and phrases in TRIPs, the developing countries secured much of what they sought in the final

Declaration. The final text of the Doha Declaration sought to 'clarify' the interpretation of TRIPs and emphasized the 'flexibilities' already written into the agreement, including the right of Members to invoke those provisions when needed. Paragraphs 1 through 5 acknowledge the importance of TRIPs to public health and recognize the flexibilities already existing in the Agreement. In this regard, these paragraphs contain the Declaration's most significant conclusions.

Paragraphs 1 through 3 outline the concerns of both developing and developed countries by providing context to the issue of intellectual property protection for medicines while recognizing the need to balance private property and public welfare interests. These paragraphs form the framework for understanding the rest of the Declaration. The Declaration begins by 'recogniz[ing] the gravity of the public health problems afflicting many developing and least-developed countries, especially those resulting from HIV/AIDS, tuberculosis, malaria and other epidemics.' Paragraphs 2 and 3 reiterate the concern over health epidemics and the high cost of medicines in developing countries. However, the first sentence of Paragraph 3 underlines the importance of intellectual property protection by reminding Members of the role that strong intellectual property protection plays in the development of new medicines. Paragraph 2 reiterates that relaxing protections will not completely eliminate the health problems in the developing world.

Paragraph 4 strongly affirms the principle that protecting public health and promoting access to medicines is a valid basis for Members to enact exceptions to patent protection in their domestic legislation. Specifically, Paragraph 4 provides that TRIPs 'does not and should not prevent Members from taking measures to protect public health' and 'affirm[s] that the Agreement can and should be interpreted and implemented in a manner supportive of WTO Members' right to protect public health and, in particular, to promote access to medicines for all.' The affirmation in Paragraph 4 reinforces the plain meaning interpretation of TRIPs Article 8, which permits Members to 'adopt measures necessary to protect public health.'

Paragraph 5 contains the most controversial provisions of the Doha Declaration, those that provide Members with flexibilities in implementing TRIPs. Paragraph 5 reaffirms the right of WTO Members to use the provisions in TRIPs for the purposes of Paragraph 4 and sets out the 'provisions,' which may be used for this purpose. The 'provisions' are as follows:

(a) In applying the customary rules of interpretation of public international law, each provision of the TRIPs Agreement shall be read in the light of the object and purpose of the Agreement as expressed, in particular, in its objectives and principles.

(b) Each member has the right to grant compulsory licenses and the freedom to determine the grounds upon which such licenses are granted.

(c) Each member has the right to determine what constitutes a national emergency or other circumstances of extreme urgency, it being understood that public health crises, including those relating to HIV/AIDS, tuberculosis, malaria and other epidemics, can represent a national emergency or other circumstances of extreme urgency.

(d) The effect of the provisions in the TRIPs Agreement that are relevant to the exhaustion of intellectual property rights is to leave each member free to establish its own regime for such exhaustion without challenge, subject to the most-favored nation and national treatment provisions of Articles 3 and 4.

Paragraph 6 'recognize[s] that WTO with insufficient or no manufacturing capacities in the pharmaceutical sector could face difficulties in making effective use of compulsory licensing under the TRIPS Agreement,' but the paragraph leaves the issue unresolved, instead instructing the Council for TRIPs to find an 'expeditious solution' to the problem and to report to the General Council before the end of 2002. It is regretful that this issue could not be resolved during the Doha Round, as extending the timeframe for negotiation simply delayed negotiation on this highly contentious issue.

Paragraph 7 extends the grace period for LDCs, delaying implementation of Sections 5 (patents) and 7 (confidential information) in relation to pharmaceutical products until January 1, 2016, for those countries.

It is also important to note that the Doha Declaration does not restrict Members' rights to use the dispute settlement procedure, with the exception of barring Members from challenging other Members' schemes dealing with the exhaustion of intellectual property rights. Consequently, developed countries can still use the Dispute Settlement Body (DSB) to enforce their intellectual property rights and while there is no doubt about the meaning of the statements in the Declaration, which clearly allow developing counties to use a number of different means to acquire necessary medicines, the legal effect of the Declaration is unclear. Ministerial Declarations are not binding on Members or the dispute settlement system, and the agreements negotiated by Members (WTO Agreement) would certainly prevail over the Doha Declaration, but the Declaration was careful to recognize this fact and the commitments in TRIPs do not seem to be contradictory to those commitments. Instead, the Declaration could be seen as being interpretive of the imprecise obligations and commitments spelled out in TRIPs; therefore, the Declaration would have persuasive authority in the dispute settlement process.

C. DOHA'S UNANSWERED QUESTIONS

The Doha Declaration provided developing countries with much of what they sought and certainly allows for much broader interpretation of the TRIPs Agreement with respect to a number of issues, including compulsory licensing and parallel importation of patented pharmaceutical products. The Declaration gave developing countries considerable leeway to provide for the health of its citizens by undercutting the profits that patent holders can otherwise earn from medical products, but developing countries did not achieve all their goals at Doha.

The key issue left unresolved by the Doha Round was how to ensure that a country with insufficient or no manufacturing capability in the pharmaceutical sector can receive needed drugs from a third country that has acquired a compulsory license for the purpose of exporting to that troubled nation. As TRIPs Article 31(f) limits compulsory licensing to situations 'predominantly for the supply of the domestic market,' clarification was needed to ensure that countries with insufficient or no manufacturing capabilities can take advantage of the provisions designed to assist them.

Although developing countries attempted to add to the Doha Declaration that '[n]othing in the TRIPs Agreement prevents Members from granting compulsory licenses to foreign suppliers to provide medicines in the domestic market' and 'nothing in the TRIPs Agreement will prevent Members to grant compulsory licenses to supply foreign markets,' they were unable to persuade developed countries to agree to such language. Therefore, the Doha Declaration simply recognized that Members with insufficient or no manufacturing capacities in the pharmaceutical sector could face difficulties in making effective use of compulsory licensing under TRIPs and instructs Members to resolve the issue by the end of 2002. Unfortunately, despite the best efforts of the Chairperson of the TRIPs Council and all Members, consensus could not be reached as to how best to resolve the problem until August 30, 2003.

The failure of developing countries to resolve the issue during or immediately following the Doha Round was of great importance and highly worrying, as Article 31(f) is predicated on the capacity of a nation to produce. As most LDCs and developing countries, and particularly those countries most needing the drugs, do not have sufficient manufacturing capabilities, the compulsory licensing provision in TRIPs was of no assistance. The issue was even more pressing when one considers that the implementation deadline for many developing countries is growing nearer. Under TRIPs, needy countries can procure medicines from other developing countries or LDCs that produce generic versions of the drugs and do not currently have patent protection for pharmaceutical products. However, this option will be unavailable once suppliers are required to become TRIPs-compliant in the coming years. Therefore, it was imperative that an agreement be reached; not only to assist countries so deeply enthralled in public health crises, but also so the WTO could look responsive to the needs of its less fortunate Members …

IV. The implementation agreement

A. THE AGREEMENT'S APPROACH

The debate over the Paragraph 6 Mandate lasted nearly two years, with both developed and developing countries presenting their positions and compromising in order to reach an agreement. While several WTO Members and NGOs produced draft resolutions throughout the negotiating process attempting to resolve the dilemma, the proposals were firmly divided along a north/south line. Developing countries suggested creating a new exception under Article 30 of TRIPs (entitled 'Exceptions' to [Patent] Rights Conferred') authorizing the manufacture and export of generic pharmaceuticals from producer to importing countries in a public health crisis, notwithstanding that the pharmaceutical is patented in the producer country. Developed countries also advocated amending TRIPs Article 31(f) to create a new exception to the rule that forbids producer countries from exporting more than a small amount of any generic pharmaceutical they make under a compulsory license.

In the end, and perhaps in exchange for developed countries dropping their demands for an exhaustive list of eligible countries, diseases, and pharmaceutical products, all Members agreed to use Article 31 to implement the Paragraph 6 Mandate in the Doha Declaration. Because Article 31 already establishes agreed terms and conditions for compulsory licensing to ensure a balance in situations in which use is permitted without authorization of the patent owner, most Members believe the solution will be effective in providing for the needs of developing countries and LDCs while also protecting intellectual property rights as best as practically possible.

On the other hand, several NGOs criticized the Article 31 solution as being too bureaucratic and slow and viewed the Article 30 solution as more practical due to the political nature of the world trading system. 'Unlike the Article 31(f) amendment, an Article 30 exception [would have] allow[ed] the producer country to manufacture and export without issuing a compulsory license.' This seemingly subtle difference is significant because 'compulsory licensing is … an extraordinary remedy' that has the potential to alienate and offend many developed countries and large multinational companies; as such, the producer country's government is unlikely to make that effort just to help a poor country wanting to import pharmaceuticals. Moreover, governments are often slow to act on their own health needs, so the likelihood that they will come to the aid of a foreign government needing assistance is remote. Further, and perhaps most importantly, only one country (Canada) has ever issued a compulsory license for pharmaceuticals since TRIPs entered into force. Instead, in every other case where a country has threatened to issue a compulsory license, the interested parties negotiated mutually satisfactory agreements and ended the threat of unilateral action. Thus, some commentators argue that even with the Article 31(f) solution implemented, compulsory licensing of pharmaceuticals for export to needy developing countries will rarely, if ever, occur. Instead, those commentators assert that it would have been more feasible to have exporting countries make the one-off amendments to their domestic patent laws to enable the implementation of an Article 30 exception.

Developed countries, however, successfully argued that any approach using Article 30 would 'permit otherwise infringing acts, [such as] supply[ing] a patented pharmaceutical for purposes of export[, and] seriously prejudice the rights and obligations of Members under the TRIPS Agreement.' For example, it is not immediately apparent how an Article 30 exception, consistently invoked with respect to pharmaceuticals, is to be reconciled with the Article 27.1 requirement that 'patents shall be available and patent rights enjoyable without discrimination as to ... the field of technology' of the invention. Similarly, it is not apparent how an exception created in the domestic patent law of a producer country, which provides domestic legal force to the Article 30 approach by authorizing the manufacture and export of generic pharmaceuticals for nationals of poor countries, but not for nationals of developed countries, could be reconciled with the Article 4 Most-Favoured-Nation (MFN) requirement. It is unfortunate that none of the proposals from developing countries or NGOs explained how these conflicts were to be addressed.

Textual uncertainties also plagued the proposed Article 30 approach. For instance, the NGO proposal recommended that the Article 30 exemption include language stating that the exception should be 'broader than medicines, and does not raise concerns regarding Article 27.1 restrictions on discrimination by field of technology.' However, such language was unlikely to sufficiently meet WTO standards because even such a facially neutral exception may discriminate in violation of Article 27.1 if in practice it is invoked repeatedly in respect of a single technology, such as pharmaceuticals.

Moreover, the Article 30 proposals would have had to contend with the current interpretations of WTO law as promulgated by the DSB, and the only WTO panel to have seriously considered Article 30 interpreted it narrowly, ruling it is illegal to manufacture and stockpile a patented product, even if that product is never sold while the patent remains in force. If such stockpiling cannot be authorized under Article 30, it seems impossible to authorize the manufacture for export and sale of a product while the patent remains in force. If this ruling is continued to be applied, it would mean that any TRIPs amendment or declaration that would have authorized the Article 30 approach would have had to create an exception for the latter situation, while maintaining the illegality of the former situation, or accept that the exemption would have effectively overturned existing case law, creating legal uncertainty with regards to the previously decided stockpiling issue.

Finally, it was never really understood how Members would put a new 'interpretation' of Article 30 into operation, and none of the proposals offered much explanation as to how to operationalize the approach. Instead, they asserted only that the WTO could operationalize the agreement by putting forward a new 'interpretation' of Article 30. However, the basis for this proposition is highly questionable. The procedure for adopting official interpretations is found in Article IX:2 of the WTO Agreement, which states that an interpretation 'shall not be used in a manner that would undermine the amendment provisions' that exist in the formal structural agreements. In other words, Members cannot side step the formal amendment process by declaring an 'interpretation.' It is this side stepping that may have been the undoing of an implementation exemption through 'interpretation,' as the Article 30 interpretation also appears to be inconsistent with Article 27.1 (non-discrimination) and Article 4 (MFN). Therefore, it is doubtful that the WTO would have been agreeable to adopting an official

> 'interpretation' of Article 30 that, while not violating Articles 27.1 and 4 on their face, would have in fact violated these Articles once it was relied on and used. This implicit overruling of Articles 27.1 and 4 would have appeared to make the 'interpretation' a covert (and prohibited) amendment.
>
> By contrast, Article 31 was the only possible solution that guaranteed legal and economic certainty for all parties. Resolving the problem through Article 31 will, by virtue of a formal guarantee provided by the government in question, supply generic manufacturers a high level of certainty to manufacture under a compulsory license without fear that they will be infringing patent laws. Thus, instead of merely obtaining an open-ended exception that would not even have guaranteed that they would be the only company to manufacture the product, manufacturers under an Article 31 exception will be certain that they are legally manufacturing the patented drug. Further, as the Chairperson's Draft pointed out, procedures in Article 31 are 'minimal and flexible' and have a fast-track provision in situations of extreme urgency or national emergency. While importing countries making use of these provisions must have strong and effective national legislation, the Article 31 approach does not require them to seek WTO approval before implementing the emergency provisions. Instead, for transparency's sake, importing countries making use of the provisions are simply required to notify the WTO of their use of the system.
>
> … … …

The Implementation Agreement provides an interim waiver allowing countries producing generic copies of patented products under compulsory licences to export the products to eligible importing countries. The waiver will remain in force until an amendment to TRIPS comes into force.

Assuming that both the requesting and providing nations protect pharmaceutical patents, the waiver requires two compulsory licences to be issued—one in the country requesting the drugs and the other by the country that will be supplying the drugs. Adequate remuneration is to be paid to the patent holder by the company producing the generic drug, not by the requesting country.

EXAMPLE: In the first, and thus far only, compulsory licence issued under the waiver, the requesting country—Rwanda—first had to ensure that its own laws allowed for the importation of generic versions of patented drugs. It then had to select a suitable supplier for the drugs. A Canadian firm was selected to supply the generic version of the needed drugs, and that company could only manufacture and export the drug to Rwanda (while paying a royalty to the patent holder) because of Canadian legislation implementing the provisions of the 2003 WTO Implementation Agreement. Shamefully, most countries have failed to provide the necessary legislation to enable the exportation of drugs under compulsory licence. Australia is one such country.

Countries electing to make use of the waiver must simply provide an eligibility notification to the WTO, which should include information on the manner in which a country determined it had no or insufficient manufacturing capability. Eligibility to make use of the waiver is through self-determination. All WTO members are eligible to import under this decision; however 23 developed countries have announced they will not use the system. In addition, several other high-income countries have announced they would use the system only for emergencies or extremely urgent situations (these include Hong Kong, Israel, Korea, Kuwait, Macao, Mexico, Qatar, Singapore, Taiwan, Turkey and the UAE).

Controversially, the Implementation Agreement contains provisions designed to ensure that drugs provided under compulsory licence actually reach their intended destination. The safeguards to prevent diversion include mandating that drugs supplied under compulsory licence be specially marketed or packaged with identifiable characteristics, such as distinguishable colours or shapes. Realising that such measures may raise the cost of the generic drugs, para 2(b)(ii) of the Agreement qualifies the requirement by stating: 'provided that such distinction is feasible and does not have a significant impact on price'. Other safeguards against diversion include the requirement that special packaging be used to distinguish from the patented drug, and an obligation on importing countries to take measures 'within their means' to prevent trade diversion and/or re-exportation of products imported into their countries.

8.3.3b Compulsory licensing in Australia

In Australia, Chapter 12 of the *Patents Act 1990* (Cth) regulates compulsory licences.[57] More specifically, s 133(1) of the *Patents Act* provides that a person may apply to a prescribed court for a compulsory licence to work a patent after a period of three years has elapsed following the granting of the patent. The court may make the order if it is satisfied that the 'reasonable requirements of the public' with respect to the patented invention have not been satisfied; and the patent holder has not given a satisfactory reason for failing to exploit the patent.[58]

Section 135 then provides the circumstances in which the 'reasonable requirements of the public' will be deemed not to have been satisfied:

- A new or existing trade or industry in Australia is unfairly prejudiced, or the demand in Australia for the patented product (or a product resulting from a patented process) is not reasonably met, because of the patent holder's failure to:
  - Manufacture sufficient quantities of the patented product and supply it on reasonable terms;
  - Carry on a patented process to a reasonable extent; or
  - Grant licences on reasonable terms.
- A trade or industry in Australia is unfairly prejudiced by the conditions the patent holder has attached to the purchase, hire or use of a patented product, or to the use or working of a patented process.
- The patented invention is not being worked in Australia on a commercial scale, but is capable of being worked in Australia.[59]

---

57 Compulsory licensing provisions have always been included in Australian patents legislation. See for example *Patents Act 1903* (Cth), s 87.

58 *Patents Act 1903* (Cth), s 133(2); Patents Regulations 1991 (Cth), r 12.1. However, a person cannot apply for a compulsory licence in respect of an innovation patent that has not been certified: s 133(1A).

59 *Patents Act 1990* (Cth), s 135(1). However, if it appears that the patent is not being worked on a commercial scale in Australia, the patent is capable of being worked in Australia, and the reason for non-working is due to the nature of the invention or some other cause, the court may adjourn the hearing of an application for a compulsory licence for a period sufficient to permit working on a commercial scale: s 135(2).

Finally, s 133(3B) sets out additional provisions that apply where the patent in question is an invention that cannot be worked without infringing another patent (referred to as a 'dependent patent').

The Australian law, on its face, complies with the provisions of Article 31 of the TRIPS Agreement. For instance, under the *Patents Act*, a compulsory licence must not be in the nature of an exclusive licence (s 133(3)(a)) and the patent holder is entitled to remuneration (s 133(5) provides that, failing an agreed rate, the rate shall be set by a prescribed court to be 'just and reasonable having regard to the economic value of the licence').

To date, there have not been any compulsory licences granted in Australia[60] and the issue has received scant judicial consideration,[61] although Judge Finkelstein in *Bristol-Myers Squibb Co v FH Faulding & Co Ltd* commented that the provisions 'may be cumbersome and expensive to apply'.[62]

8.4 Conclusion

This chapter has attempted to show the importance of understanding IP law as it relates to international trade. Beyond a mere understanding of the basic principles of IP (for example, copyright, patents, trademarks, etc) and the operation of IP regimes (that is, IP is granted by jurisdiction), it is important to lawyers and traders to appreciate how and why IP is relevant to their particular industries (or clients industries, as the case may be). In order to provide useful examples of the types of situations lawyers and traders will face, this chapter detailed three contemporary and contentious IP issues.

We first discussed piracy and counterfeit goods, a problem faced by every industry in every country. While there is no magic solution for preventing piracy and counterfeiting, the chapter detailed several techniques utilised by governments, industry and their legal representatives to curtail the infringements. The second issue discussed was parallel importation of goods. Without international guidelines or uniformity among nations, the issue of parallel importation of goods confuses many traders and lawyers alike. Complicating the situation is the fact that the legality of parallel imported products depends upon the IPRs at issue. To demonstrate, Australia's treatment of parallel imported products differs when copyright and trademark are at issue. The third issue discussed in the chapter was compulsory licences. Potentially relevant to all industries, the pharmaceutical industry has been most affected by compulsory licences. For that reason, the chapter detailed the recent controversy at the WTO surrounding compulsory licensing of pharmaceuticals. The chapter also briefly introduced compulsory licensing in Australia.

Intellectual property issues are complex for a number of reasons. Not only are they sometimes difficult to fully understand from a legal perspective, but the interplay of the

60 See House of Representatives Standing Committee on Industry Science and Technology, *Genetic Manipulation: The Threat or the Glory?* (1992), p 227; ALRC, 'Genes and Ingenuity: Gene Patenting and Human Health', ALRC 99 (1999), p 716.

61 See *Fastening Supplies Proprietary Limited v Olin Mathieson Chemical Corp* (1969) 119 CLR 572; *Wissen Pty Ltd v Lown* (1987) AIPC 90; *Bristol-Myers Squibb Co v FH Faulding & Co Ltd* (2000) 170 ALR 439.

62 *Bristol-Myers Squibb Co v FH Faulding & Co Ltd* (2000) 170 ALR 439 at 480; ALRC, 'Genes and Ingenuity: Gene Patenting and Human Health', ALRC 99 (1999), p 716 note 28.

political, economic and legal interests at the heart of all of these issues adds even more intricacy to the issues. This chapter attempted to provide useful examples, while at the same time demonstrating how a lawyer can be involved in protecting, challenging or enforcing IPRs.

Questions

With regard to the case study at the beginning of this chapter:

1 What advice would you give to Successful Software to allow them to better protect and enforce their IPRs?

2 Are there any circumstances, situations or countries/markets where Successful Software may be interested in wilfully ignoring infringement of their software?

3 What are the benefits and costs of Successful Software instigating legal action against infringement of its IPRs?

4 a Would you advise Successful Software to take up the issue of counterfeit copies of its software with the Australian Government?
  b Would the government be interested?
  c Would your advice differ if the infringing copies were in North America rather than Asia?

5 What are the advantages and disadvantages of:
  a A system of national exhaustion of IPRs;
  b A system of international exhaustion of IPRs?

6 Why does Australia operate a mixed system of applying international exhaustion to the importation of some copyrighted works and national exhaustion to the importation of other copyrighted works?

7 Are there any differences in the treatment of parallel imported copyright works and trademarked products?

8 Why did the Ergas Committee recommend that Australia's current laws regarding the parallel importation of trademarked products be amended? Do you agree?

9 a Is it possible for Australia to allow parallel imported software from New Zealand but not from other nations, including Malaysia?
  b Would it make any difference to your advice if Successful Software had licensed its copyright and/or trademark to another company in Malaysia? In New Zealand? In Australia?

CHAPTER 9

agency, distributorships and licensing

True Blue Pty Ltd has created a small, handheld device which is capable of allowing the user to simultaneously read an e-book, watch a movie and play a video game (the ALLBERRY). True Blue manufactures some of the hardware and data chips used in the device, and it has been granted patents for some of these products. It has also been granted a patent for the process by which the ALLBERRY processes data.

True Blue is a small Australian company with no sales experience abroad. Its only previous invention, a toaster with a built-in television screen and internet access, failed to generate interest and was abandoned before production. True Blue has only manufactured 200 ALLBERRY units but believes the ALLBERRY is destined to become a 'must have' item for both teenagers and working professionals. However, it isn't sure how it should proceed. A large number of companies from Asia, North America, Europe and Latin America have expressed interest in the product, several of which have the capacity to manufacture and distribute it on a large scale. True Blue is unsure whether it should manufacture and distribute the ALLBERRY, whether it should manufacture the ALLBERRY but partner with a foreign company to distribute the product abroad, or whether it should allow a foreign company to manufacture and distribute the ALLBERRY.

9.1 Introduction

Once a company establishes an exporting presence beyond the occasional sale abroad, or it sees growth potential, it may seek to deepen its presence abroad through the establishment of a representative office in the targeted foreign market. As opportunities further develop, the company may wish to expand its presence even further through the use of an agent or distributor to further develop the business. Establishing a more visible presence in a foreign market has several obvious benefits, including the potential for greater and faster growth, increased marketing opportunities and brand exposure, and improved local knowledge. On the other hand, such steps are complicated, risky and not guaranteed to be successful. Some companies are therefore understandably hesitant to take such steps and expose themselves to the associated risks. Another strategy to profit from a product/invention without the associated risks involved with agency or distributorships is through licensing (that is, a company granting another company a licence to produce and/or distribute its goods). Companies often make use of licensing to substantially raise revenue with very minimal effort. Of course, licensing carries its own risks and pitfalls.

This chapter seeks to introduce and explain all of the above concepts, with a particular focus on the legal issues that may arise in each case. The first part of the chapter will assess agency and distributorships (while also briefly mentioning the representative office). The second part of the chapter will assess licensing, with a particular focus on the licensing of technology.

9.2 Agency and distributorships

The importance of selecting the appropriate business structure of a company's overseas operations can be crucial to the success (or failure) of the venture. As with any business decision, the selection of a structure should come only after a careful weighing of the costs, benefits, risks and level of control to the company. The decision to select a representative office, agent or distributor (over the others) all have certain benefits, detriments and risks (both legal and economic). This section will introduce all three concepts, but primarily seeks to identify issues unique to relationships with foreign agents and distributors that legal practitioners and their clients should take into consideration.

9.2.1 Representative office

A company establishes a representative office in a foreign market to promote its products/services and to provide information; for example, regarding government and industry requirements, technical advice, and support to local importers and distributors. The office does not take orders, sell the products/services or accept payments. In essence, a representative office is the first step towards establishing a presence—or a deeper presence—in a foreign country. It is a contact point for locals and can provide information, advice and support, but it does not engage in any commercial activities. For this reason, the expected benefits of a representative office are less than those of an agent or distributor, as are the legal and economic risks. However, a representative office may assume the function of agent or distributor, such as after the parties have established a viable relationship and the representative has demonstrated its capacity to satisfy this further function.

9.2.2 Agency and distributorship

The decision to enter into an agency or distributorship agreement is an important step that merits serious consideration. Utilising the wrong form, or entering into an agreement without carefully doing due diligence, can have several negative unintended consequences. It should also be mentioned at this stage that, although the exporting company usually is free to select the format of its expansion, the choice may be taken out of its control and mandated by the domestic law of the target market.

The primary role of an agent usually is to identify potential customers for the supplier, handle or assist with marketing on the supplier's behalf, and obtain orders for the supplier's goods or services on terms established by the supplier. The supplier then fills the orders. Thus, the agent does not take title to the goods.[1] Instead, the sales agreement remains between the seller (located in the exporting country) and the buyer (located in the importing country). The agent, normally located in the buyer's country, serves primarily as an intermediary by which the agreement is concluded.[2] The agent, therefore, does not bear the risk that the buyer will not pay. The risk remains entirely with the seller. Likewise, the buyer's recourse for faulty, defective or otherwise inappropriate goods remains solely with the seller. Correspondingly, the supplier has the right to accept or reject orders, and is not ordinarily contractually bound by the agent's actions (although local law may intervene to bind the supplier). In most instances, the agent simply forwards a purchase order to the seller when it receives it from the buyer and never actually possesses the goods (in the physical as well as the legal sense). The agent usually does not possess or control a warehouse, does not coordinate transport arrangements and has no control over the price or terms of the sales contract. Simply put, the seller agrees to the terms of sale and the agent cannot choose to deviate from those terms.[3] However, in some agency agreements, the agent also acts as collection agent for the supplier and may even provide after-sales warranty service to customers. An agent is compensated on a commission basis and usually is subject to significant control by the supplier.

By contrast, a distributor is essentially a customer of the supplier, with the supplier providing goods to the distributor under the term of the agreements. The distributor takes title to and possession of the goods and is responsible for finding buyers and selling the goods (for their own account) within a defined geographic territory. Such an arrangement avoids the need for the exporting seller to locate and contract with multiple buyers in a foreign location, while also shifting the risks associated with selling in a foreign market. Thus, the distributor normally bears the risk of being able to sell and deliver the goods and to obtain payment from the final customer. The distributor's compensation is in the form of the resale margin over the price paid to the supplier. The supplier generally retains little control over the distributor, although this may vary from case to case.

---

1 When the agent has authority to enter into contractual arrangements with a buyer, a contractual relationship is entered into between the agent and the buyer, but the arrangements generally bind the seller. The seller must therefore trust its agent to enter into commercially sensible contracts with trustworthy buyers. In certain circumstances, the seller can require the agent to guarantee payment of the contractual purchase price (the agent is then referred to as a *del credere agent*). It is rare for the seller (principal) to enter into a relationship with the agent whereby the agent can bind the seller (principal), and for good reason. Such relationships can raise a host of legal issues, including jurisdiction and standing to sue (and be sued). In an attempt to provide international certainty, the International Institute for the Unification of Private Law (UNIDROIT) drafted the Convention on Agency in the International Sale of Goods, Geneva (17 February 1983). The Convention has not been widely adopted and is yet to come into force.

2 In the vast majority of instances, the seller engages the agent to find it buyers in the targeted market, although the agent can also be engaged by the buyer to find it prospective sellers.

3 In most countries, agents do not even have the power to bind the seller; however it is important to ensure this is the case in the host jurisdiction when considering an agency relationship. In some countries, agents are deemed to have the power to enter into contracts on behalf of the seller, despite contractual language between the seller and agent to the contrary.

9.2.2a Agent and distributor: the relationship

When negotiating an agency or distributor agreement, it is essential to obtain advice from qualified local counsel in the host nation. Owing to varying intricacies and protections in certain jurisdictions, the intent to create one form of agreement may be defeated due to the inclusion (or exclusion) of certain words or phrases. Thus, while a particular contract may aim to set up an agency agreement, it may in fact create an agency-distributorship hybrid, or may even be deemed to be some other alternative (such as a special niche agreement created and regulated by the laws of the host country).

It is therefore important to remember—regardless of the legal form intended by the parties—that local law may deem the relationship to be something different than was intended or understood by the foreign investor. This could have severe consequences, and potentially produce unexpected liability for the client.[4]

9.2.2b Retaining an agent or distributor

It is important for any supplier not only to select an appropriate, qualified agent or distributor, but also to ensure that both the supplier and the agent/distributor have the same expectations and goals. In an agency relationship or a distributorship, both the manufacturer and the distributor are responsible for maintaining the reputation of the foreign company and representing its interests in an appropriate manner. Thus, prior to completing negotiations and signing a binding contract, the supplier should complete a thorough due diligence investigation to determine whether the agent/distributor individual is not only reliable, honest and effective, but also that the goals and ambitions for all concerned parties match.[5] Likewise, it is also in the interests of the prospective agent/distributor to complete a due diligence investigation of the supplier to ensure that its needs and expectations can be met.

9.2.2c Contractual issues

Once the supplier selects a suitable agent or distributor, the appropriate contractual arrangement must be drafted. The supplier's local counsel, together with counsel qualified in the host country, should jointly be involved in the negotiating and drafting process. The following issues, at a minimum, should be considered.

Local law

The importance of local laws cannot be overlooked or underestimated in any agency or distributorship agreement. Local law may be procedurally cumbersome or even provide substantive difficulties to achieving the aims and objectives of the arrangement. For instance, a local law may require that any contractual arrangements with a local

---

4 While this often occurs in jurisdictions with less developed legal frameworks or highly protectionist tendencies, it can also occur in open and advanced countries. For instance, a 'distributor' under foreign law may be considered an agent for the purposes of the US *Foreign Corrupt Practices Act 1977*. See 15 USC § 78m and 78dd-1 to 78dd-3.

5 Due diligence is also important to compliance under certain statutes (such as, for US suppliers, the US *Foreign Corrupt Practices Act 1977*).

agent or distributor be registered with a government office. In some cases, the contracts must be translated into the official language of the host country prior to registration. Where applicable, the parties should clearly state in the contracts which version of the contract controls in case of any conflicting language between the two versions. In some cases, the choice of which language controls is not left with the parties with local law requiring the local language version to be the official, controlling version of the contract. Local law may also permit or require the involvement of a government agency in the negotiation process, even when both parties already are in agreement as to terms of the arrangement.

Another important matter relating to local laws is import restrictions or compliance issues. The issue of import restrictions is discussed at length in Chapter 6, but it should be noted here that both the supplier and agent or distributor should ensure that they are aware of and in compliance with all applicable importation and distribution laws and regulations. As the local agent or distributor will likely be more familiar with such issues than the foreign supplier, it may be prudent to allocate the responsibility to the agent or distributor in the contractual agreement.

Independent contractor status

Must countries allow agents and distributors to be deemed independent contractors, rather than employees of the supplier. Government interference, however, could lead to an agent or distributor being deemed to be an employee, instead of merely an independent contractor. This is likely to occur when the agent or distributor is under the direct authority of the supplier (particularly in an exclusive arrangement), or if the agent or distributor receives a salary in addition to sales commissions. If the agent is deemed to be an employee, the situation becomes more complicated as the 'employee' and the supplier will be subject to local labour laws (including being subject to mandatory benefits and protection from termination). Likewise, the classification of the agent or distributor as an employee can also have negative consequences on the agent or distributor. For instance, while an independent agent or distributor will normally not be subject to income tax in the supplier's country, they may have such tax liabilities if classified as an employee. It is therefore crucial that any business investigating whether to use an agent or distributor in a foreign market fully investigate all potentially relevant laws in the host country.

Export compliance

Export compliance issues are the subject of Chapter 7, but it should be mentioned at this point that the supplier must comply with all relevant export laws, including possible licensing requirements. The exportation of certain goods may be regulated or prohibited, and exports of goods may also be prohibited from being sent to certain individuals, groups or nations. Failure to comply with such laws, which are normally based on national security and foreign policy concerns, could be costly.

Intellectual property licensing

The second part of this chapter provides detailed insight into licensing, but it is worth noting here that the licensing of intellectual property rights (IPRs) to a foreign agent or distributor may raise issues in the host jurisdiction. If local licensing laws are deemed applicable, the agreement may be subject to certain burdens and restrictions, including exclusivity, royalty payments, taxes, updating requirements and termination. Moreover, in some countries licensing agreements must be approved by the relevant government agencies prior to their taking effect.

It is also important for any supplier licensing its IPRs in another market to ensure that it has properly registered them in the targeted market. In addition, the contractual arrangement between the supplier and agent or distributor should prohibit that party from registering any of the supplier's IPRs in its own name. As mentioned in Chapter 9, the supplier also should consider including grant-back provisions in the licence agreement that allow the supplier to benefit from any translations, modifications and improvements created by the agent or distributor (to the extent permitted by local law).

Force majeure

The contract between the supplier and the agent or distributor should contain a *force majeure* clause describing the situations in which the parties will not be responsible for a failure to perform in accordance with the contract provisions because of unforeseen events arising beyond their control. This should specifically include the possibility of changes in government relations and policies between the relevant governments.

Governing law

As with any contract, the parties should select the law governing the contract and the appropriate forum, should a dispute arise. However, in many jurisdictions—particularly in the case of agency relationships—the choice of law will be unenforceable and the law of the host nation must be applied. Moreover, even if the host country permits the law of the supplier's home country (or any other law) to apply, it will likely still have mandatory laws that continue to apply and cannot be avoided by contract.

Competition law

Several provisions common in an agency or distributorship relationship have the potential to raise competition law concerns of the host nations. These issues include the use of exclusive licenses, the establishment of exclusive sales territory, non-compete clauses and restrictions on a distributor's resale pricing. Local law may prohibit certain provisions or require clearance from the relevant governmental agencies in advance.

9.2.3 Agents

Agency laws differ between countries, and the typical freedom-to-contract regime common to Australia and other common law countries is unlike the more regulatory model used in civil law countries and much of the developing world. In the latter cases, agency is more extensively regulated and the distinction between an agent and a distributor is sometimes blurred in a manner not anticipated or contemplated by the seller. For this reason, knowledge and understanding of the local host nation's law is critical to any decision regarding whether or not to enter into an agency relationship.

Several issues typically arise that are unique to a supplier's relationship with a foreign agent. This section will briefly discuss such issues.

9.2.3a Regulation of agents

Most jurisdictions have laws regulating agents. For instance, in some jurisdictions agents are required to be citizens of the country in which they act as representatives. Some jurisdictions have registration requirements, whereby all agents must register with a government office. Other jurisdictions have more complicated regulations dividing agents by type, with different requirements and restrictions applicable to each type of agent. Importantly, in the vast majority of countries the agency relationship can be exclusive without raising any competition law issues.

The laws regulating agents differ widely among nations, with some countries having special labour laws specifically providing for an agency relationship (thus either avoiding the agent being deemed an employee if certain steps are taken and others avoided, or specifically providing protections for the agent), while others do not distinguish between employee agents and independent agents (thus likely providing more protection to the agent/employee than the seller intends). For instance, European Union Council Directive 86/653/EEC (18 December 1986) is designed to protect the agent—and thereby restrict the parties' freedom to contract—through specific provisions on the rights and obligations of the parties, remuneration and termination of the relationship.[6]

In countries that do not have a special provision governing the agency relationship, it is wise to specifically (and repeatedly) use the terms and language normally associated with independent contractors. This also includes avoiding certain items, such as specifying working hours. Other potentially troublesome issues include the nationality of the agent, with some countries requiring any agent to be a national of the host country.

9.2.3b Termination of agents

Almost all jurisdictions regulate the ability of the principal to terminate the arrangement and the compensation that must be paid to the agent on termination. Most jurisdictions impose mandatory notice periods prior to termination, with serious consequences resulting from failure to abide by the notice provisions (including reinstatement and fines). Most also impose obligations on the principal to compensate an agent whose contract is terminated, and base their compensation provisions on the length of the term for which the agent represented the principal, the amount of money the agent invested in developing the business, and the goodwill created by the agent. In most jurisdictions, notice and compensation provisions are mandatory law and cannot be avoided by contract.

---

6 This Council Directive has been held to apply even where the contract between the seller (principal) and the agent was governed by foreign law and despite the fact that the Directive does not contain a clause restricting choice of a non-EU member country law to the detriment of the agent. In the case, the seller (principal) was held to be liable for compensation upon the termination of the agency relationship even though the contract did not provide for payment and local law (State of California, USA) did not mandate compensatory payment: see *Ingmar GB v Eaton Leonard Technologies Inc* (Case C-381/98) [2001] *All ER (EC)* 57. See also EU Council Directive 86/643, which requires member countries to adopt legislation that strictly regulates commercial agents (including the duties of the agent to the principal and of the principal to the agent, default remuneration provisions, notice requirements for termination and compensation for the agent after termination): OJ (L 382), 17–21 (31 December 1986).

9.2.3c Non-competition following termination

Most jurisdictions limit the scope and length of non-compete covenants that survive termination of the agency relationship as to geographical scope, duration and the universe of products covered by the covenant. Limits to non-compete covenants are mandatory law and cannot be avoided by contract.

9.2.3d Scope of authority

Even if it is clear to all parties involved that the agent should not have the authority to bind the supplier by executing sales contracts or order forms, the contract should explicitly address the issue. The contract should also address whether the agent's representations to customers constitute warranties by the supplier. Despite such language, however, some jurisdictions allow the agent to bind its principal to agreements with third parties, notwithstanding clear contractual limitations. The supplier should also ascertain whether the local law allows for the agent's representations to customers to constitute warranties by the principal.

9.2.3e Harmonisation

In 2002, the International Chamber of Commerce (ICC) revised its Model Commercial Agency Contract in an attempt at harmonising state practice.[7] The ICC attempts to accomplish this largely by incorporating standard practice and generally recognised principles on such issues as the function of agents, responsibilities of the parties, acceptance of orders by the principal, exclusivity, undertakings not to compete, sales targets, sub-agents, commissions and termination. It is useful for students to read through the Model Commercial Agency Contract to familiarise themselves with the contractual issues associated with the agency relationship. It is important to remember, however, that national law should be consulted prior to formalising any relationship, as it may differ substantially from the Model Contract.

9.2.4 Distributors

The use of a distributor can bring great benefits to the supplier, but there are risks and cautions that must be acknowledged and understood. For instance, the manufacturer loses a large amount of control over the goods and, depending upon the country at issue, may even lose the ability to set or influence the resale price. These types of issues must be fully explored before deciding whether to use a distributor in a given location. Distribution agreements generally have fewer legal requirements than agency agreements, but some nations do impose procedural and substantive requirements.[8] This section will briefly discuss several legal issues that can arise in a supplier's relationship with a foreign distributor.

---

7 Publication No 644, Paris, 2002.

8 Through careful planning, however, it may be possible to arrange the distribution agreement in such a manner as to avoid the most onerous conditions (for instance, the exporting company may take partial ownership of the local distributor). But not all issues can be avoided, nor should be avoided.

9.2.4a Creating the relationship

One of the most fundamental concepts of a distributorship is that the distributor cannot bind the seller: the distributor enters into sales contracts only in its own right. Therefore, in contradistinction to an agent, a distributor buys the exporting company's goods and resells them through its own networks. In doing so, the distributor takes title to the goods and therefore bears the associated risks, such as buyer non-payment, or being unable to re-sell the goods. The commercial risks are therefore shifted to the distributor, as opposed to remaining with the exporting seller in an agency relationship. In most cases, the distributor not only takes legal title to the goods, but also takes physical possession of the goods for a period of time prior to their resale. In such a circumstance, the distributor must warehouse the goods and pay all associated costs.

When a distribution agreement is sought, the contractual agreement must clearly state the intention of the parties so there can be no doubt that a distributorship, not an agency relationship, is intended to be created. In doing so, the contract must reflect the characteristics of a distribution agreement. Similarly to other contractual provisions, if the arrangement has the characteristics of an agency relationship, it may be deemed as such by the courts or administratively.

Another less obvious issue which often causes complications is whether the distributor has the authority to use sub-distributors. If so, issues such as whether the manufacturer approves each sub-distributor, whether the manufacturer is a party to the arrangement and under what circumstances a sub-distributor can be employed or terminated need to be addressed.

9.2.4b Exclusivity

The majority of distribution agreements are either exclusive or sole distribution agreements:

- In an exclusive agreement, the supplier grants the distributor the exclusive rights to buy and sell the goods within a certain territorial restriction (for example, within Australia). The supplier can therefore neither appoint another distributor nor directly sell the goods in the territory during the duration of the agreement.
- In a sole distributor agreement, the supplier promises not to appoint another distributor during the duration of the agreement, but retains the right to directly sell the goods in the territory.

The majority of agreements are exclusive (although the terms are often mistakenly used interchangeably). In both cases, the supplier will normally insist that its distributor sells only its products, rather than acting as distributor for a number of competitive suppliers.

Unsurprisingly, exclusive distributor arrangements may trigger the competition policies and laws in the host nations. Similarly to agency, the enforceability of restrictive distributor arrangements may depend upon whether the host nation is a common law country (freedom to contract) or civil law country (restrictive on termination clauses especially). The restrictions most likely to raise the ire of local authorities are a prohibition on the distributor from selling competitors goods and a territorial restriction only allowing sales within a defined geographical territory. Other laws governing distribution arrangements could also be clearly designed to favour the national (local distributors), with restrictions mandating local (or locally owned) distributors and the application of domestic labour laws and other mandatory laws favouring local nationals and business interests. Local counsel should be consulted to determine the acceptable parameters of any exclusivity or other restrictive clause under the laws of the host country.[9]

In Australia, s 47 of the *Trade Practices Act 1974* (Cth) prohibits 'exclusive dealing', but s 93 allows parties to seek an exemption from the operation of s 47 by simply notifying the Australian Competition and Consumer Commission (ACCC). Once notification occurs, the parties may engage (or continue to engage) in the exclusive dealing (that is, the exclusive distributorship) unless the ACCC issues a notice stating that there is no public benefit, or that any benefit is outweighed by anticompetitive detriment.

Similarly, while s 45 prohibits contracts, arrangements or understandings that restrict dealings or affect competition, s 88(1)(a) allows the ACCC to grant an authorisation to:

> make a contract or arrangement, or arrive at an understanding, where a provision of the proposed contract, arrangement or understanding would be, or might be, an exclusionary provision or would have the purpose, or would have or might have the effect, of substantially lessening competition within the meaning of section 45.[10]

9.2.4c Payment methods and currency conversion

As with any trade in goods, the contractual arrangement between the parties should address the currency of payment (and allocate the currency exchange risk). However, in some jurisdictions governmental regulations may not allow payment to be made in a currency other than that of the host jurisdiction. If payment in another currency is allowed at the time the contract is signed, the supplier should be aware that unforeseen events (such as a liquidity or monetary crisis in the distributor's home country) could interrupt or even prohibit payment in foreign currencies. It is therefore crucial for an emergency plan to be incorporated into the contract (such as payment in the local currency or the convertible currency of a third party). Other corresponding issues, such as the accrual of interest to compensate the supplier until payments can be received (and at what interest rate), should also be addressed.

9.2.4d Duration and termination

The termination of a distributorship is often the source of frustration (and costs) to the supplier. Naturally, all countries allow for termination with cause, but difficulties generally arise in defining and interpreting 'cause'.[11] For this reason, parties are advised to define the term in the contract. For instance, the contract could explicitly state termination triggers such as not meeting defined sales figures, gross misconduct, *force*

---

9 In the EU, exclusivity between a supplier and a distributor is regulated by a complicated Commission Regulation 2790/1999 that establishes a block exemption for certain provisions and prohibits others: OJ (L 336) 21–25 (29 December 1999).

10 For more on the effect of the *Trade Practices Act* on distribution agreements, see *Melway Publishing Pty Ltd v Robert Hicks Pty Ltd (t/as Auto Fashions Australia)* (2001) 205 CLR 1.

11 Depending upon the jurisdiction, it may be required that the distributor be given the opportunity to correct the defect.

majeure, insolvency, etc.[12] Of course, as one cannot possibly think of all ways in which 'cause' could occur, it is just as important to ensure the list is not exhaustive. Importantly, the local law should also be consulted, as it may provide a definition of 'cause'.

Termination is difficult, but not impossible, when the distributor's performance is deemed unsatisfactory or if the relationship between the seller (principal) and distributor becomes unworkable.[13] In most if not all jurisdictions, notice must be given to the distributor (and sometimes the government) prior to termination.[14] The contractual agreement between the seller (principal) and distributor should provide for the manner and form of the notice (for example, sent by registered mail).[15] If ineffective notice is given, the notice may be deemed invalid and local law may equate termination with inappropriate notice to termination without just cause. If the agreement is terminated without just cause, the distributor's rights may be extensive and may include monetary settlement, damages or even the reinstatement of their position as distributor.[16]

The consequences of even being accused of wrongful termination could be severe. In some jurisdictions, the seller (principal) could be denied the right to import into the country while the legality of the termination is being determined (that is, the exporting company may not change distributors or otherwise sell the product in the host country until the outcome is known), or the imported goods could be stopped at customs and attached as collateral.

One would also think that a distribution agreement can automatically be terminated upon its expiration, but in some jurisdictions the law does not immediately allow termination (these laws are aimed at protecting local jobs). Finally, if the parties continue to perform a fixed-term distribution contract beyond its stated term, it may be treated by local law as having indefinite duration. Subsequent termination could result in an accusation of wrongful termination with all resulting consequences.

9.2.4e Statutory warranties

In many jurisdictions, warranty provisions are imposed by statute and are mandatory laws that cannot be avoided, waived or limited. As a result, suppliers may find it useful to contractually require distributors to maintain product liability insurance issued by a carrier approved by the supplier in a specified amount, naming the supplier as an additional insured. The distributor also may be contractually required to indemnify the supplier for liabilities arising from its sale or use of the supplier's products.

---

12 The distribution agreement should state what should be done with inventory and materials if termination occurs.

13 In such circumstances, the seller (principal) may be forced to pay a termination fee to the distributor in order to end the relationship.

14 The same is true for agency agreements.

15 In some jurisdictions, waiver of termination rights may not be allowed for public policy reasons (in that the government may wish to more equally allocate the bargaining power of the parties and to protect the rights of the domestic national).

16 If the agreement is terminated with just cause, the rights granted are usually limited.

9.2.4f Harmonisation

In 2002, the ICC published the ICC Model Distributorship Contract, in an attempt at creating uniform state practice.[17] It is useful for students to read through the Model Distributorship Contract to familiarise themselves with the contractual issues associated with distributorships. It is important to remember, however, that national law should be consulted prior to formalising any relationship as it may differ substantially from the Model Contract.

9.3 Licensing of IPRs

The licensing of IPRs is an alternative path a company may take to enter into a foreign market. Licensing is the process of an IPRs owner (the licensor) granting another person or company (the licensee) the right to utilise the IPRs in return for payment (such as set fee, royalties or sale of product back to the licensor). The licensor does not transfer any legal interest to the licensee when it enters into a licensing agreement—the licence agreement simply makes lawful something that would otherwise be unlawful (that is, the non-rights holder using, manufacturing or distributing the product subject to the IPRs). The licensee is then responsible for exploiting the IPRs in a certain territory; the licensee bears the responsibility of and carries the financial risks for such exploitation.

Any form of intellectual property (IP) is capable of being licensed. For example, a book publisher may license another publisher to print and distribute its copyrighted book list within a defined territory; a fast-food restaurant may license its trademark rights when entering into a franchise agreement with a franchisee (for more detailed information on franchising, see Chapter 10); and an automobile manufacturer may license its patented technology and know-how, enabling the recipient to manufacture and distribute certain cars within its territory. In this chapter, we shall for the most part focus on technology and patents to illustrate the issues involved with licensing.[18]

The licensing of technology is an attractive option for a number of reasons. For instance, it may be that tariff and other barriers and/or costs (such as manufacturing and transport costs) make it financially unfeasible to locally manufacture the product subject to the technology and export it to another country. It may also be the case that the company with the technology does not have the monetary backing, business and legal connections, or the appetite for risk (such as exchange rate, regulatory, tax, expropriation, etc) to attempt to produce the product in a foreign country. Alternatively, the company may simply want to focus on, for instance, keeping its technological edge instead of diverting executive and management talent into distributing its product abroad (or even domestically). In such circumstances, licensing is extremely attractive as it can produce sizeable returns in the form of royalties without the capital investment, effort and risks associated with more direct forms of foreign investment. Licensing is also necessary for use with subsidiaries and joint ventures (which both need the technological assistance

17 ICC Publication No 646, Paris, 2002.

18 Issues involving trademark licensing are discussed in Chapter 10.

and know-how of the parent/partner company), and is sometimes used a first step or test case for foreign direct investment (FDI).[19]

Licensing can also offer immense benefits for the licensee, which usually acquires access to technology it could not produce on its own without the need to invest in the research and development of the technology. The licensee can also usually maximise its position in the host nation due to several factors, including local knowledge and connections, labour costs and geographic location.

Licensing does, of course, carry some risk for the licensor:

- First, an appropriate and trustworthy licensee must be found.
- Second, the licensor loses a considerable amount of control over the product.
- Third, the licensor must ensure that the licensee can both carry itself appropriately and effectively produce and sell the product. Depending upon the structure of the licensing agreement, the licensor's options for directly entering the target market in the future could be substantially curtailed and, at the conclusion of the licensing agreement, the licensee may be in a position to be a direct competitor to the licensor.
- Fourth, the laws, regulations and policies of the targeted nation may impact upon the choice of whether or not licensing is right for the business.

A licensing agreement can essentially be viewed as a partnership. If the licensee succeeds, the licensor's royalties will increase and both parties will be pleased with the result. The arrangement can then be extended in time and through future generations of technology. If the arrangement is not successful (for financial or other reasons), there are opportunities for withdrawal and the partnership ceases to exist.

The remaining parts of this chapter will first outline the basic types of licensing agreements, before listing several factors that businesses should consider and address when negotiating and deciding to enter into a licensing agreement. The chapter then provides a more detailed account of some risks when dealing with foreign licensees and government regulations and policy; and goes on to provide extracts that analyse the potential conflict between licensing agreements and competition law. The chapter concludes with a sample licensing agreement.

9.4 Licensing: the basics

9.4.1 Types of licences

There are many different types of licensing agreements. Most licensing agreements involve one or more forms of IPRs. For instance, it is very common for a licensing agreement to involve patents, copyright and know-how; this is commonly referred to as a 'hybrid licence'. There are also several categories of licensing agreements. The broad categories of licensing agreements include:

19 In such circumstances, the licensing agreement will be included as part of the investment or joint venture agreement. Licensing can also be used for more nefarious reasons, such as to avoid royalty limitations imposed on joint ventures or for the minimisation of tax liabilities.

- *Use licences:* this type of licensing agreement allows the licensee to use the subject matter of the license, but does not allow for any copying, modification, selling or distributing of the licensed matter. An example is an end-use licence which is typically granted to users of computer software.
- *Manufacturing licences:*[20] this type of licence grants the specific right to manufacture the technology covered in the licensing agreement, manufacture products that include the licensed technology, or to manufacture products through the use of the licensed technology.
- *Distribution licences:* while a manufacturing licence grants the licensee a right to manufacture the licensed technology, the distribution licence extends the manufacturing licence to allow the licensee to distribute the manufactured product. Most often, the rights granted by a distribution licence will include the right to market and sell the manufactured products in a specific geographic territory or demographic market. Occasionally, however, the licence could require that the product must only be sold to the licensor.
- *Sub-licences:* depending upon the terms of the 'use' licence, the licensee may be granted the right to sub-licence all or part of its legal rights (as granted in the original license) to a third party. Sub-licences are often helpful when the licensee wishes to engage the services of an agent or distributor to assist in the distribution of the licensed product within its geographic territory.

Before entering into a licensing agreement, both parties must clearly identify and clarify every feature of the agreement in order to ascertain whether the strategy is appropriate for their respective needs. Key considerations include:

- What type of technology and IPRs does the licensor possess?
- Does the licensor have the exclusive rights to the technology and IPRs?
- What technology and IPRs are being licensed? Does the 'licensor' instead really want/desire to transfer its rights to the 'licensee'?
- What legal regimes will be implicated and what are the consequences?
- Will any government authorisations be needed to effectuate the licence?

Depending upon the industry and technology at issue, licensing agreements can become highly specialised, detailed, complex and rather lengthy contracts. Negotiations are both time-consuming and costly, and the importance of legal representation at an early stage in the process cannot be overstated. Legal representation can assist in the negotiations, and draft the licensing agreement to ensure that the description of rights and limitations are adequately and accurately defined. Lawyers for both parties should ensure their respective clients understand the precise extent to which the IPRs and know-how are being licensed, as well as the contractual restrictions and limitations placed on the licensee (or sub-licensee).

We do not attempt to cover or even note every potential point or issue that may arise during a negotiation; that said, in negotiating and drafting a licensing agreement,

---

20 If copyright is licensed, the licensee will have the right to 'copy', as opposed to 'manufacture'.

several critical areas must be addressed in a clear manner, lest both parties run the risk of litigation, unanticipated consequences or other similar costly and unwelcome interruptions and intrusions. Key considerations include:

- What controls will the licensor maintain over the technology and IPRs?
- What type of exploitation is being licensed (use, manufacture, or manufacturing and/or distribution)?
- Has the term 'know-how' been clearly described and detailed so as to avoid any misunderstandings?
- Will the licensee be allowed to sub-license?
- Will the licence be exclusive or non-exclusive?
- Will there be any geographic or territorial restrictions? Will the volume of goods manufactured be limited in any way? Will the use of the IPRs subject to the licence be tied to any specific areas (such as where the licensor has expertise)?
- Will any geographical, territorial or any other limitations or restrictions potentially clash with any domestic competition law policies?
- Will any training, expert assistance and maintenance be provided by the licensor? If so, which party will be responsible for the costs? What will be covered (salaries, travel expenses, cost of living, accommodation, etc)?
- Will any technical and marketing assistance be provided? If so, how and at which party's expense?
- Will the licensor be required to provide updated technology to the licensee at any time during the licensing agreement (when relevant, at regular intervals, etc)?
- Will the licensing agreement contain a grant-back provision for improvements made to the technology by the licensee? Is such a provision consistent with all relevant local laws?
- How will the licensor be compensated (that is, how will the royalty rate be set)?
- Will infringements be defined in the licensing agreement? How will they be managed?
- How will performance benchmarks, quality control and other similar issues be managed by the licensing agreement?
- How will the commencement and termination clauses be drafted?
- Will the agreement be subject to litigation or arbitration? In what jurisdiction and/or subject to what rules?

We will now review some of the more important categories that should be negotiated and included in a technology licensing agreement.

9.4.2 Scope of the licence

Determining the precise scope of the patent rights to be granted under the technology licence is a key aspect of any licence. As licences can include multiple patents covering the technology, a licence should be drafted to ensure that all the patents necessary to practise the technology are included in the scope of the licence. The licensing agreement should also state whether all statutory patent rights or only a subsection of such patent rights are being licensed (that is, making, using, offering to sell, selling or importing).[21] The agreement should also state whether the licence is exclusive or non-exclusive, and whether any territorial limits are imposed.[22] When a licensee acquires an exclusive license, it has the exclusive rights to utilise the licensed patent rights in the specified geographic territory and field of use, to the exclusion of others. The licensor cannot therefore grant subsequent licences for the same territory for the duration of the original licence. Licences may contain field-of-use restrictions that limit the licensee's utilisation of the technology within certain defined fields of use or applications.[23] For example, a licensor may grant the licensee an exclusive licence to make, practise, use, sell, distribute and advertise the licensed patent rights throughout the world; or it could grant an exclusive licence to use plastic compound XYZ, as claimed in Australian Patent 1234 to make, use and sell plastic photo frames within Australia. The licensor will also want to reserve all rights in the technology not explicitly granted to the licensee.

The licence should also include the information or knowledge that the licensor controls and which is essential for the licensee to fully and effectively utilise the whole technology that is the subject of the technology-licensing agreement, but which is not covered by the licensed patent(s). This knowledge and information is often termed 'know-how'.[24] The licensee will normally want to acquire as much know-how as it possibly can (and have it throughout the entire period of the licence), while the licensor may wish to limit both the time period and extent of the licensee's access to information external to the licensed patents for a variety of reasons (such as cost, expenditure of time and competitive edge). Licensors, for instance, very rarely wish to have the licensee benefit from any improvements on the technology made during the lifetime of the licence. Of course, the licensee could also potentially make improvements on the technology during the lifetime of the licence, and the licensing agreement should include a provision regarding the licensor's right to access the know-how improvement information of the licensee. Licensors must also ensure that, if any fee must be paid to a third-party in order to disseminate the information to the licensee, the licensing

---

21 While some licensing agreements use these words verbatim, most others use a variety of terms to describe various patent rights, including research, design, practice, develop, improve, modify, distribute, market, advertise, export, have made, utilise, dispose and exploit.

22 The licence should describe the physical/geographic territories in which the licensee may utilise the rights granted in the licence. So as to protect each party, it is also wise to include a warranty of availability, in which the licensor warrants that patents covering the technology are issued in the territories covered by the licence (or, if a worldwide grant is used, to territories in which the licensor owns the patent).

23 A licensor may, for instance, wish to more fully exploit the technology by using a field-of-use restriction in order to grant additional licences to third parties to use the technology in the same geographic territory but in other fields of use.

24 The following can all be used to encapsulate the term know-how: trade secrets, proprietary or confidential information, technical information, design models, information known to personnel involved in the development of the technology, testing programs, testing data, assembly/packaging technology and proprietary tools. Licensors should also insist on confidentiality restrictions on the licensee's use and disclosure of any know-how disclosed or otherwise made accessible to the licensee (subject to carve outs; that is, information that is or becomes publicly available other than through a breach of the licensee's confidentiality obligations under the licensing agreement).

agreement specifically allocates the cost to one of the parties. Licensing agreements should, therefore, be drafted to identify specifically what the licensor must produce and who pays the fees.

If the licensing agreement includes some form of training of the licensee's employees by the licensor, the licence should include specific provisions regarding the number of employees to be trained, the extent of the training, and who bears the cost of training.

9.4.3 Improvements in the technology

Improvements to the technology often are developed during the course of a licensing agreement by the licensor, licensee (or sub-licensee) or any unrelated third party, some of which may render the licensed technology obsolete. The licensing agreement should define each party's rights to improvements made during the course of the agreement, and also deal with compensatory issues thus resulting. Failure of the licensing agreement to provide for such issues will result in only the party that developed the improvements having any rights in the improvements, or the ability to demand compensation/royalties for the improvements. This also means that the licensing agreement should not only define what is meant by the term 'improvement', but also address which, if any, improvements are encompassed by the licence. Compare the following two examples:

1 '"Improvements" shall mean findings, improvements, enhancements, discoveries, inventions, additions, modifications, formulations, derivative works, or changes (whether or not patented or patentable) with respect to the Licensed Technology developed after execution of this Agreement.'
2 '"Improvements" shall mean any invention, idea, trade secret, know-how, or derivative work that is in some manner dependent upon or that includes any portion or uses any portion of Licensed Technology, whether or not patentable, copyrightable, or otherwise protectable as intellectual property that is subsequently acquired or developed by Licensee during the term of this Agreement.'[25]

The licensee will generally want the licence to provide that the licensee has rights to any patentable improvements made by the licensor at the previously agreed-upon royalty rate, while the licensor will normally want to keep such patentable improvements separate from the original agreement so that it can exploit the improvements by, for instance, charging the licensee a higher royalty rate. Either way, the licensing agreement can require the licensor to notify the licensee upon developing a patentable improvement, which could either guarantee that the licensee is aware of the improvement or even simply provide the licensee a right of first negotiation regarding the terms and conditions of a new licensing agreement.

When any improvements to the technology are made by the licensee, the licensor will want to ensure that such improvements are encompassed in the licence so that the licensee must assign any and all rights to patentable improvements to the licensor: a grant-back

25 E Horwitz, 'Patent and Technology Licencing' (2007) 24(10) *The Computer and Internet Lawyer* 28 at 31.

provision. Conversely, the licensee will want to separate the improvements from the licence.

The importance of negotiating for improvements to the technology cannot be overemphasised, not only to avoid disputes between licensors and licensees, but also so as to ensure that technological advancement is not stifled.

9.4.4 Duration

The licensing agreement should address the duration of the licence. Technology licences are, for the most part, limited to the life of the licensed patent(s) or other IPRs; but even then there are some important considerations, including whether patent term extensions and reissues extend the licence, and whether patents relating to the technology granted during the licence extend the licence. The issue is even more complex when the licensor has granted worldwide patent rights or patent rights in a number of countries. In such circumstances, a definite time period term is often used in lieu of the patent expiration date. In these cases, the parties may want to negotiate the terms of renewal for each territory in the original licensing agreement.

Depending upon the technology at issue, it may be wise for the licensor to license not only IPRs, but also to specifically license know-how, trade secrets, or other non-patented subject matter. The reason for this is that in some countries, including the USA, licensors are prohibited from charging royalties for the licence of a patent beyond the life of the patent.

9.4.5 Best-efforts clause

When an exclusive licence has been granted, the licensee has the ability to effectively 'kill' the technology by not using or commercialising it. The licensee may want to 'kill' the technology for a number of reasons, but most prevalent are either that the technology has become obsolete or non-competitive, or that the licensee has developed its own competing technology that it wishes to market.

The licensor can protect against its technology being 'killed' by including a best-efforts clause into the licensing agreement. The clause could require the licensee to use 'reasonable efforts' to commercialise the technology and/or provide for minimum performance standards provisions. If the best-efforts clause is breached, the licensor can generally either convert the exclusive licence to a non-exclusive licence, or terminate the licence.

9.4.6 Savings clause

If an exclusive licence has been granted, the agreement should include a savings clause to prevent the licensor from losing all rights in the licence in the event that the government voids the exclusive licence. Governments have been known to void exclusive licences for a number of reasons, including public policy, competition or public emergency reasons. The savings clause should be drafted so as to ensure that the licence granted shall not terminate upon its exclusivity being voided, but instead that the licence shall remain exclusive to the extent permitted by such government action and shall become non-exclusive to the extent necessary to conform with applicable laws and regulations.

9.4.7 Sub-licences

The licensing agreement should also clearly state whether and to what extent the licensee will be allowed to sub-license the licensed technology. There are several advantages to allowing the licensee to sub-license; for instance, a licensee with its main base of operations and sales team in one geographic location (say, the USA) can sub-license the technology to a non-US entity in order to make use of local knowledge and contacts, as well as to expand distribution, sales and royalties. In this example, other geographic markets are penetrated quicker, more cheaply, and probably more effectively using a sub-licence than if the US licensee had to develop its own sales and distribution network in the target territory.

Some licensors are, however, hesitant to allow sub-licences as they involve another layer between themselves and their technology. In other words, there is a sense of loss of control over the licensed technology. This hesitation can be overcome in the licensing agreement by providing the licensor with a measure of control over who can become a sub-licensee, the quality of their product, marketing procedures, royalty rates payable, collection procedures, and duration and termination clauses.[26] Thus, it is crucial that the licensing agreement clearly sets out whether the licensor or licensee has the final authority to authorise and approve each sub-licence and, if that party is the licensor, on what grounds authorisation and approval can be withheld.

9.4.8 Ownership, validity, and infringement actions brought by third parties

As IPRs are the key to a technology licence, the licensee should attempt to negotiate for the licensor to make non-infringement representations and/or provide indemnification for losses incurred by the licensee for claims that the technology infringes on third-party rights. A simple clause in the contract indicating that the licensor, to the best of its knowledge, believes each patent listed in licensing agreement was validly issued under the laws of the country that issued it, and is not aware of any patents or any other prior act that would invalidate any of the patents subject to the licence should suffice. An additional clause stating that the licensor has not received any notice of any potential or threatened claim of infringement of any third-party patents and is not aware of any facts that could give rise to any claim of infringement relating to licensee use and practice of the licensed technology can also help to fully protect the licensee.

9.4.9 Representations and warranties

Since the licensor's ownership of the technology is the key to the entire licensing agreement, licensees should obtain a representation and warranty respecting the licensor's ownership of the patents covering the licensed technology. If the licensor did not invent the licensed patents, the licensor should represent and warrant that it has been validly

---

26 It is normal for the licensing agreement to include terms such that the licensee will step into the roles of the sub-licensee in the event that party defaults on its royalty payments. Clauses are also often inserted that protect the licensor from assuming unexpected and unfavourable sub-licences.

and permanently assigned all rights in the patents. The licensee should also consider having the licensor represent that the patents are not encumbered as collateral, liens, judgments, third-party agreements or understandings or in any other way. Finally, if the licence is exclusive, the licensor should represent that the licensor has not and is under no obligation to grant a licence to any third party.

9.4.10 Indemnification

A licensee should also seek to have the licensor indemnify it (as well as sub-licensees) and hold it harmless against and in respect of any and all infringement claims arising from use of the licensed technology. The indemnification should continue beyond the termination of the licence and the timing of indemnification payments. Licensees should also seek to have indemnification arising or resulting from or related to any breach or inaccuracy of any representation and warranty of licensor, or the failure of licensor to perform any of its obligations or covenants. However, the licensor should negotiate for an exclusion from the indemnity for any claims based on the licensee's wilful infringement of a third party's patent.

9.4.11 Litigation provisions

If an exclusive licence has been granted, the licensing agreement must select one of the parties to be the principal in enforcing the IPRs in the licensed technology via litigation. The licence should also provide that the other party has the authority to maintain such actions should the designated party fail to defend or initiate an infringement action (usually defined as within a certain number of days after becoming aware of the infringement). Most licensing agreements also include provisions that provide for payment of litigation costs and division of recovery.

9.4.12 Record-keeping and audit clauses

As the payment of royalties to the licensor are usually based upon the production or sales of the licensed technology, the licensing agreement should require the licensee (and any sub-licensees) to maintain adequate records in order to substantiate the basis of the royalty payments to the licensor (such as invoices, manufacturing records, sales figures and tax filings). The records must be subject to verification through an independent audit, and should be kept safe and verifiable for at least a determinate period of time. The parties may also want to negotiate who should bear the costs of the audits and storage.

9.5 Technology licensing: risks

The introduction of this chapter stated that the risks of licensing technology are normally less than those of proceeding to directly invest in a target nation; however, and while this is true, the risks of licensing technology are not insubstantial. For instance, the technology subject to the licence can be stolen by the licensee, an employee of the licensee or any other involved party. Licensing involves giving up some control of the technology, and before entering into any licensing agreement the licensor should be fully informed of the risks and consequences of the technology being stolen. The licensor's lawyers should also brief the licensor on any possible remedies and enforcement plans in the event of stolen technology.

Other potential burdens of licensing technology include:

- Double taxation could be imposed (if no treaty exists between governments);
- The host nation's laws may favour the domestic party to the detriment of the licensor (for example, requiring the training of local personnel, or the transfer of new, updated technology as it becomes available, etc);
- Sections of the licensing agreement could be held to be invalid (for example, for being too restrictive on home users) by legislative,[27] executive or judicial action in the host nation:
- A change in government could result in difficulties for the licensor (such as renegotiation of royalties, foreign exchange controls, expropriation, etc);
- Parallel imported goods could enter the domestic market of the licensor and begin to compete for sales;
- The licensee could become a competitor at the expiration of the patent.

The risks for the licensee are also substantial. For instance, if the technology transferred is older, outdated technology, it will be cheaper for the licensee to obtain; but depending upon the structure and business model of the licensee, this could be problematic if the licensee wishes to export the product. Other potential risks include the potential for an unevenly drafted licensing agreement favouring the licensor (as it will be the party with significantly more bargaining power), and the possibility that high royalties could threaten the viability of the enterprise (while at the same time sending currency reserves from the host nation to the licensor's nation).

Developing countries have, for the most part, historically relied upon the developing world for technological advancement, and for this reason, of all the licensed technologies, patent and know-how licensing are the most important to the developing world. For the most part, licensors have encountered problems licensing technologies to developing country licensees due to large-scale government involvement and invasive regulations and policies promulgated in an effort to rebalance the power and negotiating strength between the licensor and the licensee, as well as to promote its own form of 'development'. Developing countries as a whole have largely taken an economic-regulation-oriented approach to licensing agreements, which has focused on attempting to prohibit certain clauses in technology licensing agreements which they believe either take advantage of the weaker bargaining position of the licensee, or which they see as inimical to the development process.

On the other hand, developed countries have generally seen the issue from a competition point of view, and accordingly believed that only those clauses that could unreasonably restrict the freedom of the recipient to compete, or that placed an

27 Limitations on the levels of royalties, prohibitions on certain clauses or actions (export restraints, resale price maintenance (setting minimum price levels), mandatory grant-back) and the inclusion of certain clauses or actions (ie updated technology) are common features of the law in many developing countries. The laws of several developing countries, such as many European nations as well as Canada, have also contained such restrictions and clauses in the recent past.

unreasonable restraint on the competitive freedom of third parties, should be regulated. It is not difficult to see how these two approaches may lead to opposing viewpoints on a number of issues (for example, a tie-in clause might be acceptable on a competition-based approach, but may be seen as a barrier to the development of local supply chains in the developing country approach).[28]

The advent of the Trade-related Aspects of Intellectual Property Rights (TRIPS) Agreement, along with the resurgence in bilateral investment agreements (BITs) and comprehensive free trade agreements (FTAs), has largely settled the debate in favour of the developed country position and made many instruments used in the past rather difficult to apply today. The following extract dating from the late 1980s provides an overview of the development of these government laws and regulations, as well as showing the kind of restrictions typically seen in licensing agreements involving developing countries during that period. While most developing countries have shifted their 'development' approach and significantly loosened regulations over the 20 years since the extract was written, in order to encourage technology transfers and investment, others have resisted change, and the ideas and policies detailed in the extract remain valid. For this reason, those countries with a more favourable climate (Singapore, Hong Kong and now Mexico) will receive more technology transfers (both in sheer number and technological sophistication) than those with a less favourable or even hostile climate (Algeria, Bolivia, Ecuador and Venezuela).[29]

Guo Qingjiang, 'Barriers to Technology Transfer' (1987) 1987 *Colum Bus L Rev* 117 at 127–31

A. North America: Mexico

In an effort to alleviate a severe balance of payments problem immediately following World War II, Mexico implemented an import substitution program from 1940 to 1970 which encouraged foreign investment in the form of factories. Instead of building new facilities for the production of goods to be exported from Mexico, foreign investors, who were primarily interested in selling to the Mexican market, simply purchased domestic factories. Consequently, foreign-owned enterprises came to dominate the manufacturing and service sectors of the economy. Moreover, investment was centered in urban areas, increasing over-urbanization of the population. In response to these unwelcome developments, the government sought to regulate the transfer of technology by legislation. In 1972, Mexico enacted the Law on the Registration of Contracts and Agreements Regarding the Transfer of Technology. Acknowledging that restrictive business practices 'hinder the healthy development of industry ... place an undue burden on the balance of payments, and make the country's industry

28 See UNCTAD, 'Transfer of Technology', *IIA Issues Paper Series* (Geneva, 2001), pp 22–3, available at [www.unctad.org/en/docs//psiteiitd28.en.pdf].

29 UNCTAD drafted a 'Draft International Code of Conduct on the Transfer of Technology', and while some developing countries would like to see it as a mandatory code, most other countries want it to remain as merely unenforceable guidelines. It has now been abandoned. The Code is available at [http://stdev.unctad.org/compendium/documents/totcode%20.html]. For more information, see UNCTAD, 'Transfer of Technology', *IIA Issues Paper Series* (Geneva, 2001), available at [www.unctad.org/en/docs//psiteiitd28.en.pdf].

subservient to technology suppliers,' Article 7 of the law prohibited the registration of agreements or contracts containing provisions detrimental to the national economy. Grant-backs, restrictions on licensee research, tying, export restrictions, exclusive sales, restrictions on personnel, price and production fixing, and contracts longer than ten years are specifically prohibited.

In 1982, the Mexican government amended this law and enacted the Law on Control and Registration of Transfer of Technology and the Use and Exploitation of Patents and Trademarks. Under Chapter III of the law—Denial of Registration—any attempt to impose an obligation on the licensee to keep the technology secret beyond the duration of the agreement, was prohibited along with other previously sanctioned activities. At the same time, regulations pursuant to the law were enacted. In the regulations, 'restrictive business practices' were more clearly defined and detailed to provide industries with guidelines as to what kind of arrangements should be rejected.

Mexican legislation on transfer of technology is typical of the legislation in this field implemented by other developing countries. It has been the model after which most other developing countries have patterned their own laws.

B. South America: The Andean countries

Another approach to legislation in this field followed by developing countries is that of the Andean Common Market ('ANCOM'). In the 1970's, Latin American countries actively acquired technology from developed countries. For example, in 1978, Latin America's share of payments made to United States based firms for royalties and fees amounted to 43 percent of all payments from developing countries. Foreign technology is the basis for the establishment of new industries in Latin America.

In 1962, Brazil enacted Law 4,131 on foreign investment, which was the first general regulation in Latin America to systematically deal with technology transfer. Five years later, Colombia and Chile set up new agencies to deal with technology transfer.

With these efforts as background, the Andean countries formulated a transfer of technology policy in Decision 24 (1970). This well-known Decision declared the need to improve the bargaining position of domestic enterprises in the transfer of technology. In article 20, the following set of restrictive business practices were identified: tying, permanent restrictions on use of personnel, price fixing, restrictions on production volume, restrictions on dealing with competing technology, sale arrangements in favor of the licensor, grant-backs, and payment requirements for non-use technology. Member countries are not permitted to authorize technology transfer agreements containing such clauses. Export restrictions and similar restrictive business practices are dealt with under other articles. As in the Mexican legislation, the control of restrictive business practices is a major objective of Latin American regulations governing the transfer of technology.

C. Asia: People's Republic of China and India

Asia has recently emerged as an important recipient of business and investment. Since the People's Republic of China ('PRC') declared its new open policy in 1977, much attention has been attracted by the so-called 'one-billion market.' The Chinese government is aware of the importance of technology and, since 1977, has made strong efforts to facilitate technology transfer from abroad.

From 1977 to 1980, Chinese importation of technology was mainly in the form of turn-key projects. During that period, many billion-dollar petro-chemical projects were imported from other countries, primarily Japan and West Germany. This 'foreign leap forward' program could not continue, because, by late 1979 the value of the contracts signed greatly exceeded China's ability to pay. As a result, the Chinese government suspended or cancelled many contracts. A new policy encouraging licensing, rather than turn-key projects, was subsequently adopted. The Chinese government viewed this as 'buying hens to lay eggs,' in the hope that imported technology could be used to generate new technology.

As with any developing country in the course of acquiring technology, China has experienced restrictive business practices. After almost a decade of experimentation, the Chinese government promulgated the Regulations on Administration of Technology Import Contracts on May 24, 1985. The regulation sought to expand economic and technical cooperation with foreign countries and to promote national economic development. In addition, the following restrictive business practices were deemed illegal:

1) tying raw materials, equipment and parts; 2) patent pooling, tying unnecessary technology; 3) restrictions on transferee's own research; 4) transferee restrictions on dealing in competing technology; 5) non-reciprocal terms for exchanging future improvements; 6) restrictions on volume and sale price of the products produced by the technology; 7) restrictions on export; and 8) obligations after expiration of arrangement.

After painful experience with foreign intervention between the mid-19th and mid-20th centuries, China has for the past thirty years pursued a policy of self-reliance in technology development. However, despite progress in technology and economic development, the Chinese felt that self-development alone was not enough to match the pace of world technological development. The present policy encourages cooperation with foreign companies in the field of technology development. However, no less emphasis is put on ultimate independence from technology suppliers. To avoid foreign domination and the effects of restrictive business practices, licensing agreements are preferred. Chinese concern about restrictive business practices dates from the very beginning of its new open policy. An example of this is the PRC's Law Concerning Transfer of Technology to Joint Ventures Using Chinese and Foreign Investment. Some restrictive business practices such as non-reciprocal grant-back clauses, export restrictions and tying arrangements are regulated. Since a large amount of foreign technology is expected to enter the Chinese market in the coming twenty years, the elimination of restrictive business practices is an issue of high priority in China.

Like China, India's policy toward technology transfer stresses rapid domestic assimilation of technology with a view to achieving technological self-reliance through adaptation of imported technology. Realizing the imperfect conditions in the market of international transfer of technology because of restrictive business practices, the Indian Government has taken a very selective approach to the importation of technology. Royalty payments exceeding five percent of ex-factory value of production are rarely permitted. However, instead of publishing laws and regulations that specifically govern technology transfers, as most developing countries have done, the Indian Government has preferred an administrative approach. The Foreign Investment Board has been created to make final decisions on the approval of technology transfer agreements. Even before an agreement reaches the Foreign Investment Board, however, it must first be submitted to the Minister of Industry. The Minister gathers views and opinions from various technical authorities and administrative bodies concerned with the product. Only those proposed agreements that contain appropriate technology and only a limited number of restrictive business practice clauses are forwarded to the Foreign Investment Board.

In addition to preliminary administrative screening, guidelines have been established to protect entrepreneurs from entering into unfavorable agreements. Among other things, 'arrangements or clauses which in any manner bind the Indian party with regard to procurement of capital goods, components, spares, raw materials, pricing policy, or selling arrangements should be avoided.'

In 1969, India enacted the *Monopolies and Restrictive Trade Practice Act*. Though the Act is primarily directed toward preventing foreign investors from accumulating economic power, the provisions which outlaw territorial and use restrictions have direct application to the transfer of technology.

... ...

9.6 Technology transfers: competition law

Countries have now largely moved away from using defensive, restrictive laws and regulations to contain and limit the power of international companies using licensing agreements, and today the common view among both developed and developing countries seems to be that market imperfections are best addressed by measures aimed at improving the contestability of such markets.[30] For this reason, competition policy has now acquired a greater significance in modulating the conditions under which technology transfer takes place.[31] The following extract from economist Keith Maskus details how IPRs may lead to abuse of competitive conditions.

Keith E Maskus, 'Intellectual Property Rights and Economic Development' (2000) 32 *Case Western Reserve Journal of International Law* 471 at 499–502

Because intellectual property rights create market power, their use is potentially subject to anticompetitive abuses. Such concerns are often overstated. Intellectual property rights define the boundaries within which an inventor or creator has exclusive use rights. Such rights rarely create strong monopoly positions unless they are combined with restrictions on competitive entry by other firms. Indeed, IPRS are critical for promoting R&D that generates dynamic competition.

Nonetheless, the scope of IPRs is limited in order to promote access, dissemination, and competition. Attempts by rights holders to extend their use of IPRs beyond permitted limits are abuses of the competitive system. It is useful to review the forms in which such abuse may occur. For example, monopoly pricing represents one potential abuse, although in competitive markets there are usually market substitutes that discipline the ability of IPRs to support monopoly prices. Therefore, pricing decisions are rarely regulated by public authorities in industrial countries except for purposes of limiting the costs of maintaining public health and nutrition.

Perceived abuses of IPRs typically relate to strategic business decisions, including selling practices and licensing restrictions. There is a large literature on the competitive effects of market

30 UNCTAD, 'Transfer of Technology', *IIA Issues Paper Series* (Geneva, 2001), p 22, available at [www.unctad.org/en/docs//psiteiitd28.en.pdf].

31 Ibid. See also Y Zhan & X Zhu, 'Intellectual Property Right Abuses in the Patent Licensing of Technology Standards from Developed Countries to Developing Countries: A Study of Some Typical Cases from China' (2007) 10 *The Journal of World Intellectual Property* 187–200.

power created by patents, trademarks, and protected know-how. There are few concrete guidelines in the area because of the complex nature of markets for information and technology. Vertical licensing agreements, for example, could serve the purpose of ensuring downstream product quality, which improves competition. However, tie-in sales of unrelated products to technology purchasers may represent an attempt to extend the scope of a property right, which damages competition.

Potential competitive problems raised by the exploitation of IPRs include the following. First, horizontal cartels of competing firms may occur through licensing agreements that fix prices, limit output, or divide markets. Actual and potential competitors could be both licensees and licensors, either in the market for the product or technology itself or in extended markets. For example, patent-pooling and cross-licensing agreements between competing licensors may reduce competition in downstream product markets that use the licensed technologies as key inputs, particularly where the agreements set prices or restrict territories, customers, and fields of use.

In industrial countries competition authorities have found it difficult to set general rules covering such licensing contracts. Instead, investigations are undertaken to determine whether an agreement presents the potential for cartelization of a significant share of a particular market. Concerns also arise over agreements requiring resale price maintenance of distributors' prices, which could result in vertical price-fixing unrelated to the need to monitor and enforce quality assurance. Clearly such risks are greater the more regulated is entry into distribution contracts, a common problem in developing countries.

Second, licensing agreements for intellectual property could anti-competitively exclude rival firms from competing in particular markets by raising barriers to entry. This could be the case with tie-in sales, in which a licensor gains a dominant position for the tied good. Potential competitors would be forced to enter in both the markets for the protected technology and the tied good, raising costs. Similar problems exist if licensees are required only to use the licensor's technology, which may also require use of future technologies. Such restrictions could result in a dominant position for licensors in secondary markets and limit competitive entry by rival firms. A related difficulty arises when licensors block the development of competing new technologies through exclusive grant-back provisions and exclusivity arrangements in future technology purchases. Competition policy must try to assess the potential anticompetitive impacts of licensing arrangements before deciding whether and how to regulate them. Note that such impacts depend crucially on the structure of the markets in which licensing contracts operate, the share of markets they cover, and the difficulty of entry for rival enterprises.

A third general class of problems relates to attempts to acquire excessive market power by purchasing exclusive rights to competing technologies and products, with the intention of preventing their commercial use. Such efforts effectively are horizontal mergers, which must be analyzed in terms of their impact on market concentration. A final problem is non-price predation, in which IPRs may be used to bring bad-faith litigation and opposition proceedings in order to exclude and harass competitors. This may be particularly damaging in cases where potential rivals are small and new and therefore lack the resources needed to defend themselves in court. In turn, this problem could stifle the development and introduction of competing technologies and products. The task for competition authorities is to distinguish predatory behavior from legitimate enforcement of IPRs. For example, firms may refuse to license technologies in particular markets or to particular firms, which could be interpreted either as legitimate business practice or unfair competition.

The message is that there are complex relationships between IPRs and their potential abuse. Property rights support market power, the exercise of which does not necessarily constitute an abuse. Competition policy makers need to distinguish various forms of behavior in terms of potential impacts on competition and consumer welfare. In this view, it is likely advisable for countries developing competition rules to follow some form of the American 'rule of reason' approach, rather than attempting to codify rules covering specific actions, which is the EU approach. More specifically, a rule of per se illegality might apply to attempts to monopolize horizontal production and distribution channels, while the rule-of-reason standard might apply to vertical arrangements and tied sales. Patent licensing and pooling arrangements, while not necessarily anticompetitive, might warrant some scrutiny. Note further that the TRIPS Agreement permits use of non-exclusive compulsory licenses under prescribed circumstances to overcome abusive practices, so long as adequate compensation is paid.

Thus, there is scope for nations to promote competition in the operation of patent and trademark licensing. In this context, however, note that many foreign enterprises remain frustrated by the intrusive examination procedures employed by licensing authorities in approving technology contracts. Thus, some balance must be struck between encouraging competition and discouraging entry.

… … …

It is clear that the granting of IPRs and their concurrent limited-time monopolies serve to encourage creativity and further investment in artistic and industrial endeavours. Likewise, the need to balance the incentive to create with society's interests is also clear. In this regard, the interaction between IP law and competition policy is often closely scrutinised, as IPRs can have the effect of restricting competition.

Article 40 of the TRIPS Agreement recognises the competing interests by allowing members to prevent or control anticompetitive activity. Article 40 states, in the relevant part:

> 1. Members agree that some licensing practices or conditions pertaining to intellectual property rights which restrain competition may have adverse effects on trade and may impede the transfer and dissemination of technology.
>
> 2. Nothing in this Agreement shall prevent Members from specifying in their legislation licensing practices or conditions that may in particular cases constitute an abuse of intellectual property rights having an adverse effect on competition in the relevant market. As provided above, a Member may adopt, consistently with the other provisions of this Agreement, appropriate measures to prevent or control such practices, which may include for example, exclusive grantback conditions, conditions preventing challenges to validity and coercive package licensing, in the light of relevant laws and regulations of that Member.

The overarching concern is that IPRs will result in an increased level of market power to the detriment of competition within the marketplace and consumer interests. For this reason, laws exist to prevent parties from using IPRs as a pretext for entering into agreements to fix prices, to divide markets, or to otherwise monopolise supply. On the other hand, licensing IPRs can be pro-competition and serve the interests of the consumer, in that they can result in increased production and distribution far beyond the capabilities of the rights owner. Undue restrictions on licensing arrangements could prevent the efficient use and deployment of IPRs, thus reducing both return on investment, incentive to further creation and impacting consumer interests. Thus, competition policy seeks to balance these competing interests by sanctioning licensing arrangements that increase market efficiency, while preventing arrangements that would negatively affect competition and social welfare.

Striking the right balance between the protection of IPRs and competition policy is complex and often opaque. In most countries, the relevant authorities now realise that the protection of IPRs is important, and that IPRs can coexist with competition policy; that is, that all IPRs are not per se anticompetitive. It is also understood that the licensing of IP is often an efficient, pro-competitive and consumer-friendly manner of utilising IPRs. Thus, one of the key issues relevant authorities face when balancing IPRs with competition policy is the extent of market power the rights owner yields in the relevant territory. Oftentimes, subjective decisions become determinative. In many instances, the balance struck by the authorities seems capricious, as in almost every country some companies are relentlessly prosecuted by the relevant authorities (for example, Microsoft in the EU), while other companies that engage in similar behaviour escape diligent and sustained review (for example, Gazprom in the EU). Such inconsistent enforcement leads to unpredictable markets and an unfavourable investment climate.

As mentioned in the above extract, countries take different approaches in regulating IPRs and competition law. For instance, Professor Maskus refers to the differing approaches taken by the USA and the EU. The USA takes a 'rule by reason' approach, formulated through the *Antitrust Guidelines for the Licensing of Intellectual Property*. Issued by the US Department of Justice and the Federal Trade Commission (FTC) in 1995 to assist parties in understanding when the Department of Justice or FTC will normally challenge a practice as being anticompetitive, the Guidelines (which include licensing of copyright, patent, trade secret and know-how) state general enforcement policy. The Guidelines embody three general principles:

- For the purposes of antitrust analysis, intellectual property is comparable to other forms of property;
- There is no presumption that intellectual property creates market power in the antitrust context; and
- Intellectual property licensing allows firms to combine complementary factors of production and is generally pro-competitive.[32]

Realising that licensing arrangements often promote innovation and enhance competition, the Guidelines create an antitrust 'safety zone' in order to provide some degree of certainty and thus to encourage such activity. Thus, absent extraordinary circumstances, a condition in an IP licensing arrangement will not be challenged if (1) the restraint is not facially anticompetitive and (2) the licensor and licensee collectively account for no more than 20 per cent of each relevant market significantly affected by the restraint.[33]

In addition, a restraint in an IP licensing arrangement that may affect competition in a technology or innovation market will not be challenged if (1) the restraint is not facially anticompetitive and (2) four or more independently controlled entities in addition to the parties to the licensing arrangement possess assets, characteristics and incentive to engage in research and development that is a close substitute for that in the IP arrangement.[34]

---

32 *Antitrust Guidelines for the Licensing of Intellectual Property* (1995), para 2.

33 *Antitrust Guidelines for the Licensing of Intellectual Property* (1995), para 4.3.

34 Ibid.

Licensing arrangements falling outside of the 'safety zone' are not presumed to be anticompetitive, but will be evaluated based on the considerations set out in detail in the *Guidelines* (and indeed, most will be lawful and pro-competitive).

In contrast, the EU takes a more formalistic approach to evaluating when the licensing of IP may result in anticompetitive conduct. In 2004, the European Commission enacted a Block Exemption Regulation on IP licensing agreements, whereby agreements covered by the block exemption benefit from a safe harbour as regards the application of the EU competition rules. Therefore, the EU attempts to add certainty to licensing arrangements through the exemption of certain categories from the prohibitions on anticompetitive practices. Under the group exemption, licensing arrangements are deemed to be in the public interest, and therefore exempted from the prohibitions on anticompetitive practices, if they fall within the terms of one of the eight group exemptions.

The exemption covers technology transfer agreements, and includes agreements for the licensing of patents, know-how, software copyrights or any combination thereof, whereby a licensor allows a licensee to use a licensed technology for the manufacture of products or the provision of services. Mere licences to sell a product are not covered by the block exemption (there are other block exemptions that cover certain restrictions in sales licences).

In order to qualify for the block exemption, the market share of the companies involved must have:

- Combined market share of less than 20 per cent on the relevant technology and product market if the parties to the agreement are competitors; or
- Individual market shares of less than 30 per cent on the relevant technology and product market if the parties to the agreement are non-competitors.

Agreements will also fail to qualify under the safe harbour exemption if they contain any 'black-listed' restrictions. The list and type of such restrictions vary depending on whether or not the parties are competitors. When the parties are competitors, the 'black-listed' restrictions are (subject to some exceptions):

- The restriction of a party's ability to determine its prices when selling products to third parties;
- The limitation of output except when imposed in a non-reciprocal agreement or only on one of the licensees in a reciprocal agreement;
- The allocation of markets or customers with some exceptions, in particular regarding field-of-use restrictions or restrictions of active and certain passive sales in non-reciprocal agreements and under specific conditions;
- The restriction of the licensee's ability to exploit its own technology; and
- The restriction of the parties' ability to carry out research and development, unless the restriction is indispensable to prevent the disclosure of the licensed know-how.

When the parties are not competitors, the 'black-listed' restrictions are (subject to some exceptions):

- The restriction of a party's ability to determine its prices when selling products to third parties, with the exception of maximum or recommended prices;

- The restriction of the territory into which, or of the customers to whom, the licensee may passively sell the contract products; this is subject to some exceptions—in particular, licensees can be restricted from passively selling:
  - Into an exclusive territory or to an exclusive customer group that the licensor allocates to itself; and
  - During the first two years into an exclusive territory or to an exclusive customer group that the licensor allocates to another licensee;
- The restriction of active or passive sales to end-users by a licensee that is a member of a selective distribution system at the retail level; however, the licensor may prohibit the licensee from operating out of an unauthorised place of establishment.

While the 'black listed' restrictions are essentially per se illegal, the exemption further excludes other restrictions from the block exemption, meaning they must be assessed on a case-by-case basis to weigh their pro- and anticompetitive effects, including:

- Exclusive grant-back clauses on the licensee's severable improvements;
- Licensee's obligation to assign to the licensor severable improvements;
- No-challenge clauses;
- When the parties are not competitors, limitation on the licensee's ability to exploit its own technology, or limitation on any party's ability to carry out research and development unless the restriction is indispensable to prevent the disclosure of the licensed know-how (if the parties are competitors, this becomes a 'black-listed' restriction).

In Australia, s 51(3) of the *Trade Practices Act 1974* (Cth) exempts IP licences and assignments from competition law. More specifically, the section exempts the imposing of, or giving effect to, a condition of a licence and assignment from certain sections of the *Trade Practices Act* concerning restrictive trade practices, to the extent that those conditions *relate to* the subject matter of the relevant IPR.[35] The sections subject to the exemption deal with collusive conduct (s 45), contracts, arrangements or understanding in relation to price (s 45A), exclusive dealing (s 47), acquisitions (s 50), and acquisitions outside of Australia (s 50A). The sections to which the exemption does not apply are those dealing with abuse of market power (s 46), misuse of market power in the trans-Tasman market (s 46A), and retail price maintenance (s 48).

The s 51 exemptions are controversial, and some believe they should be repealed in the interests of competition. Critics claim that removing the exemption would subject exclusive licences, territorial restrictions, best endeavours clauses, price and quantity restrictions, and horizontal arrangements (such as cross-licences or other arrangements or understandings between competitors) to the Act; however, the critics also claim that this would not adversely affect the use of licensing and assignment of IPRs because such arrangements rarely have the effect of substantially lessening competition or breach

35 In the case of trademarks, the exception applies to the extent that it relates to the kinds, qualities or standards of goods bearing the mark that may be produced or supplied, or the giving effect to the provision to that extent: see s 51(3)(c)(ii).

the per se provisions of Part IV of the Act.[36] In contradistinction, proponents claim the exemption is an essential incentive for research, innovation and the development of new technologies. Therefore, proponents assert, repealing the exemption 'would be likely to result in increases in cost and uncertainty without leading to a more efficient operation of markets or the fuller achievement of the objectives of intellectual property laws'.[37] In this regard, the increased uncertainty could lead to industry exiting Australia for jurisdictions with clearer, more certain regulations. Moreover, proponents claim that the exemptions have not created 'any hardship or undesirable economic effect'.[38]

The final report of the Ergas Committee is one of Australia's most important developments in the area of IP and competition policy. The Ergas Committee recognised that certain IPRs and IP licensing arrangements can be pro-competition, but also recognised the need to balance the incentive to create and society's interests. In this regard, the Committee did not agree that simply repealing the exemptions was warranted, but neither did it believe that the current exemptions remained the most efficient and effective way to balance all of the competing interests involved with IPRs and competition law.

Final Report by the Intellectual Property and Competition Review Committee (Ergas Committee), September 2000, pp 209–14

Overall, although the broad design of Part IV dates back to the early 1970s, the approach it sets out has performed remarkably well in the test of time. Relying on prohibitions for conduct that is likely to lessen competition, with scope in most, though not all, instances for authorisation on grounds of public benefit, Part IV has provided a flexible framework in which to accommodate change both in the operation of the economy and in the intellectual understanding of the competitive process. Great confidence can consequently be placed in this framework and in its ability to handle the diverse and complex types of rights the system of Intellectual Property laws involves.

Having said that, it is important to note that the content of the Part IV prohibitions is to some degree shaped by the period in which it was enacted. More specifically, at the time of the passing of the Act, the Australian economy was heavily regulated; many markets were protected from international competition by a combination of explicit protective measures and by the high costs of transport and communications; and there was a well-established tradition of cartelisation, as well as of other arrangements that dampened competition. As a result, it was reasonable to presume that many forms of conduct were harmful, leaving scope for those that had an efficiency justification to demonstrate that justification through a public inquisitorial process.

The intellectual climate also played a part. In the early 1970s, most participants in the policy debate would have reasonably assumed that many practices that involved tying, bundling, price

36 See for example National Competition Council, *1999 Review of Sections 51(2) and 51(3) of the Trade Practices Act 1974*, p 221.

37 *Final Report by the Intellectual Property and Competition Review Committee (Ergas Committee)*, September 2000, p 208; available at [www.ipaustralia.gov.au/about/ipcr.shtml].

38 Ibid. A third group believes the exemptions are ambiguous and therefore the scope of the provision is uncertain and subject to a range of interpretations: see for example ibid, p 207 (citing the Australian Government Solicitor).

discrimination or resale price maintenance, were primarily means of lessening competition and exploiting consumers. Today it would be recognised that while these practices can lessen competition in some circumstances, there are many instances in which they enhance efficiency and make for more vigorous rivalry. The presumption of harm would therefore require far more nuance than appears in the prohibitions as they stand.

This is not to deny that significant change has occurred in respect of the relevant provisions. For instance, the repeal in 1995 of s 49 of the Act highlights the adjustments that have been made in the face of changed circumstances and understanding. Nonetheless, it remains the case that the Act establishes a presumption that seems adverse to a range of conduct that may be more uncertain in its effects.

It is not the Committee's remit to comment on, or seek amendment to, the overall provisions of the Act. We do not claim to be in a position to do so, since the matters at issue are complex and deserve close and detailed examination. However, we do note that our views have been reached on the basis of analyzing the Act as it stands, and of considering the effects that (given the Act as it stands) would flow from different approaches to the coverage by the Act of conduct relating to the exercise of IP rights.

As a general matter, the Committee recognises that intellectual property has important features that differentiate it, to a greater or lesser extent, from other property or assets. It is well known that intellectual property is typically non-excludable: that is, preventing others from using IP in the absence of an effective system of IP rights is difficult and at times impossible. Intellectual property is also typically non-rivalrous, in the sense that greater consumption by one party does not reduce the scope for consumption by others.

Partly reflecting these factors, and of great importance to the issue at hand, contracts and licenses and assignments have a pivotal role in securing efficient use of intellectual property. This is for three reasons:

1 The initial owners of IP rights are often not the parties best placed to exploit the output of their creative efforts. This is most plainly the case with specialised inventors, who remain responsible for some of the most important innovations in industrial use; it also applies to small, research-intensive arms. In these circumstances, licenses and assignments are needed to ensure that control over the rights is allocated to the parties that can exploit them most effectively.

2 In many, if not most, areas of technology, rights do not map simply into products. Commercial products often embody technology covered by claims in tens or even hundreds of patents. And the inter-dependence between rights is even greater in the innovation process itself, which frequently involves combining technological inputs owned by multiple rights owners. Complex webs of cross-licenses are required if these accumulated technical capabilities are to be put to productive use.

3 Even independent of the factors set out above, the costs of impeding efficient licensing of IP can be especially high. As noted above, knowledge is non-rivalrous: increased access to it by one party does not reduce the stock available to others. As a result, when parties are forced to 'invent around' existing knowledge, there is a risk that the resources consumed in the process will, in social terms, be largely wasted. Even when the result of inventing around is greater immediate competition, and hence a lower allocative efficiency loss, the benefits can readily be swamped by the productive inefficiency the duplication of outlays entails.

All of this means that it is essential that firms have the scope to enter into efficient contracts that involve intellectual property rights, free of onerous and ultimately counter-productive regulatory burdens. Great caution is therefore needed in imposing on transactions in IP rights constraints that may be less costly when applied in other areas of property.

However, this should not involve an open slather for owners of IP rights to act as they please, without regard to the community's interest in competitive markets.

The Committee recognises that the IP legislation confers upon the intellectual property right holder a series of exclusive privileges designed to promote innovation. Given that these rights are conferred by legislation, they should be able to be effectively exercised even when this involves (as it generally must) the exclusion of others. However, these rights should not be capable of being used to *go beyond* the market power those rights directly confer. That is, the right holder should not be allowed to extend the statutory right into a wider right of exclusion with the effect of substantially lessening competition (SLC).

Put in slightly different terms, the system of IP rights acts to provide to those who invest in creative effort a claim on the differential efficiency associated with the results of their Investment—that is, of the social gain consequent on that investment's outcomes. Those rights should not be used to secure a gain that goes beyond that differential efficiency through the exercise of market power. Thus, it is an inherent element in the IP right that the owner of a patent on an invention can secure an income dependent on the unique efficiency that invention allows; but it ought not to be acceptable for the owner of that patent to, say through the formation of a patent pool with owners of competing patents, effect a horizontal cartel, raise prices and secure monopoly rents. The grant of IP rights seeks to provide for creators a return on their investment in creation—the rights should not be used to secure returns that do not come from the social contribution that creation makes.

The importance of ensuring that IP rights are not used in ways that go beyond the scope of the grant is especially great in a system in which IP rights are relatively strong—as is, and should remain, the case in Australia. (Indeed, several of the Committee's recommendations make these rights clearer and more certain, and hence ultimately add to their strength). Such strong rights are necessarily more likely to confer a degree of market power; and they can more readily be used in ways that go beyond their policy purpose. For example, where rights are well-defined and readily tradeable, it may be easier for firms to rely on licence arrangements involving these rights to effect horizontal price agreements, than they could in a regime where the rights were uncertain. Or, it may be easier for an incumbent firm to enter into licence arrangements with potential competitors who own technology that could be used to challenge the incumbent's market position, therefore making it advantageous for those potential competitors not themselves to compete in the incumbent's market. In other words, the strength of IP rights, precisely because it facilitates agreements involving those rights, can make the anti-competitive use of the rights more likely.

The central question then is whether the current s 51(3) strikes an appropriate balance in allowing the exercise of the rights but not their use in ways that go beyond the purposes underlying the rights.

As is evident from the advice provided by the AGS [Australian Government Solicitor], there are flaws in the drafting of s 51(3) that under any scenario would require amendment. Leaving aside drafting considerations, the Committee believes that the uncertainty surrounding the scope of the section, and the possibility that it may exempt virtually all agreements which touch on IP from relevant sections of the *Trade Practices Act*, make the current section inappropriate. At the same time, the Committee does not see a clear policy rationale for the uneven coverage of the section; for instance, the exclusion of the provisions dealing with resale price maintenance.

As a result, we do not believe that the section properly defines the interaction between IP laws and Part IV prohibitions. The issue is what reforms would best meet the public interest.

The Committee does not believe that simple repeal of the section would be desirable. Any assessment of repealing the section must take account of the effect repeal would have on licensing and assignment decisions. More specifically, it seems reasonable to suppose that the per se prohibitions embodied in the Act, and the potentially burdensome requirements for administrative review, would catch many license conditions that are usually socially beneficial—for example, tying and exclusive dealing arrangements in patent licenses. Over the longer term, this could both reduce innovation and distort competition between those (typically smaller and more specialised) firms that depended on licenses and assignments and those that did not.

Having ruled out simple repeal, the Committee does not believe that the proposals adopted by the NCC [National Competition Council] fully address its concerns. We are not clear what content would be left in the section if (in line with the NCC's recommendations) all horizontal arrangements and all price and quantity restrictions were removed from its scope.

As the vast majority of intellectual property licences could be said to fall within these categories, we believe that adoption of the NCC's proposals would amount to a repeal of the section. By eliminating the protection the Committee believes is desirable, such a move would impose unnecessary costs on the innovation process.

Rather, it is our view that achieving an appropriate balance between the needs of the IP system and the wider goals of competition policy requires a careful reframing of the section. More specifically, we believe this balance can best be addressed through the following changes:

- repealing s 51(3) and related provisions from the TPA;
- amending s 51(1)(a)(i) of TPA to list all the relevant IP statutes [patents, trade marks, designs, copyright, circuit layouts and plant breeder's rights]; and
- including amendments in the TPA to ensure that a contravention of Part IV of the TPA, or of s 4D of that Act, shall not be taken to have been committed by reason of the imposing of conditions in a licence, or the inclusion of conditions in a contract, arrangement or understanding, that relate to the subject matter of that intellectual property statute, so long as those conditions do not result, or are not likely to result, in a substantial lessening of competition. The term 'substantial lessening of competition' is to be interpreted in a manner consistent with the case law under the TPA more generally.

The Committee also notes that the imposing of conditions in a licence, or the inclusion of conditions in a contract, arrangement or understanding, should also clearly mean the refusal by the owner of an IP right to enter into a licence, contract, arrangement or understanding. This means that the intellectual property owner still has the benefit of the relevant provisions even in the absence of a contract. However, this will not over-ride separate provisions made in the IP legislation that bear on compulsory licensing.

To assist users of the IP system to better understand the proposed changes, the Committee considers it appropriate that the ACCC be required to issue guidelines on how it will implement enforcement activities related to the provisions. These should provide sufficient guidance to owners of intellectual property rights as to the types of behaviour likely to result in a substantial lessening of competition. The guidelines should also make provisions for potential contractors to seek written clearance from the ACCC on whether the proposed behaviour is likely to result in a substantial lessening of competition. This written clarification should be quick and simple and operate in a similar fashion to the 'letters of Comfort' provision included in the ACCC Merger Guidelines. Furthermore, the Committee believes the guidelines should be drafted in close consultation with the public and, in particular, with intellectual property owners, users, licensees and facilitators. The Committee also believes that the ACCC should be required to undertake a public education and or awareness program, in conjunction with other relevant bodies, on the effects of the changes to the TPA.

These changes would ensure that conduct relating to the subject matter of IP rights, which does not result in a substantial lessening of competition, would be exempt from the relevant provisions of the TPA. It would accept [sic] that conduct from the Act's *per se* prohibitions, thus minimising the range of instances in which administrative procedures such as authorization or notification were required.

The Committee notes that in the normal course of trade there are almost always alternative or suitably equivalent products or processes in the market place; as a result, instances in which contractual arrangements relating to intellectual property could or would potentially result in a substantial lessening of competition are likely to be rare. In most instances, it will be apparent to practitioners whether serious competition issue arises—much as it is in the other contexts in which Part IV applies. The Committee therefore believes that the proposed system will ensure the efficient development and use of intellectual property rights and ensure that these rights are not exploited to extend market power beyond the scope of the right initially granted.

… … …

The recommendations of the Committee were not acted upon.

The following sample patent licensing agreement will not only help you become familiar with the content of such an agreement, but will also assist with identifying potentially troubling issues.

Sample Licensing Agreement[39]

This agreement is made and entered into between ____________________ a for-profit corporation organised under the laws of ____________________ (hereinafter called Licensor) having its principal office at ____________________,

and

____________________ a for-profit corporation organised under the laws of ____________________ (hereinafter called Licensee), having its principal office at ____________________ ____________________.

Witnesseth that:

1. whereas, Licensor has the right to grant licences under the licensed patent rights (as hereinafter defined), and wishes to have the inventions covered by the licensed patent rights in the public interest; and
2. whereas Licensee wishes to obtain a licence under the licensed patent rights upon the terms and conditions hereinafter set forth:

Now, therefore, in consideration of the premises and the faithful performance of the covenants herein contained it is agreed as follows:

39 The sample licensing agreement has been adopted mainly from a sample prepared by Dr Frederic Erbisch, Director (retired), Office of Intellectual Property, Michigan State University (USA). See [www.1000ventures.com/doc/legal/agr_sample_license_exclusive_byum.html]. The authors have also supplemented the draft with knowledge gained in practice.

Article I—Definitions

For the purpose of this agreement, the following definitions shall apply:

1. **Licensed Patent Rights:** Shall mean:
   a. Patent Application Serial No______________ filed ___________________________by ____________________.
   b. Any and all improvements developed by **Licensor**, whether patentable or not, relating to the **Licensed Patent Rights**, which **Licensor** may now or may hereafter develop, own or control.
   c. Any or all patents, which may issue on patent rights and improvements thereof, developed by **Licensor** and any and all divisions, continuations, continuations-in-part, reissues and extensions of such patents.
2. **Product(s):** Shall mean any materials including plants and/or seeds, compositions, techniques, devices, methods or inventions relating to or based on the **Licensed Patent Rights**, developed on the date of this agreement or in the future.
3. **Gross Sales:** Shall mean total ____________________ (Currency Unit) value(s) of Product(s) FOB manufactured based on the **Licensed Patent Rights**.
4. **Confidential Proprietary Information:** Shall mean with respect to any Party all scientific, business or financial information relating to such Party, its subsidiaries or affiliates or their respective businesses, except when such information:
   a. Becomes known to the other Party prior to receipt from such first Party;
   b. Becomes publicly known through sources other than such first Party;
   c. Is lawfully received by such other Party from a party other than the first Party; or
   d. Is approved for release by written authorisation from such first Party.
5. **Exclusive Licence:** Shall mean a licence, including the right to sub-licence, whereby **Licensee's** rights are sole and entire and operate to exclude all others, including **Licensor** and its affiliates except as otherwise expressly provided herein.
6. **Know-how:** Shall mean any and all technical data, information, materials, trade secrets, technology, formulas, processes, and ideas, including any improvements thereto, in any form in which the foregoing may exist, now owned or co-owned by or exclusively, semi-exclusively or non-exclusively licensed to any party prior to the date of this Agreement or hereafter acquired by any party during the term of this agreement.
7. **Intellectual Property Rights:** Shall mean any and all inventions, materials, **Know-how**, trade secrets, technology, formulas, processes, ideas or other discoveries conceived or reduced to practices, whether patentable or not.
8. **Royalty(ies):** Shall mean revenues received in the form of cash and/or equity from holdings from **Licensees** as a result of licensing and using, selling, making, having made, sublicensing or leasing of **Licensed Patent Rights**.

Article II—Grant of exclusive licence

1. **Licensor** hereby grants to **Licensee** the exclusive [worldwide, option] licence with the right to sub-licence others, to make, have made, use, sell and lease the **Products** described in the **Licensed Patent Rights**.

2. **Licensor** retains the right to continue to use **Licensed Patent Rights** in any way for non-commercial purposes.
3. It is understood by **Licensee** that the **Licensed Patent Rights** were developed under ______ Grant No ________. The _________ Government has a non-exclusive royalty-free licence for governmental purposes.

Article III—Licence payments

1. **Initial payment and royalty rate.** For the licensed herein granted:
   a. **Licensee** agrees to pay a sign-up fee of __________ ( ).
   b. **Licensee** shall pay an earned royalty of _____ per cent (%) of **Licensee's Gross Sales** of **Products** and fifty per cent (50%) of the sub-licensing receipts.
   c. **Licensee** shall pay an annual royalty of _________ ( ) for each leased **Product**.
2. **Sub-licences.** The granting and terms of all sub-licences is entirely at **Licensee's** discretion provided that all sub-licences shall be subjected to the terms and conditions of this agreement.
3. **Minimum royalty: Licensee** will pay **Licensor**, when submitting their royalty report a minimum royalty of ___________ (______) annually.
4. **When a sale is made:** A sale of **Licensed Patent Rights** shall be regarded as being made upon payment for **Products** made using **Licensed Patent Rights**.
5. **Payments:** All sums payable by **Licensee** hereunder shall be paid to **Licensor** in ___________ [name of country] and in the currency of US dollars.
6. **Interest:** In the event any royalties are not paid as specified herein, a compound interest of eighteen per cent (18%) shall be due in addition to the royalties accrued for the default period.

Article IV—Reports, books and records

1. **Reports.** Within thirty (30) days after the end of the calendar quarter annual period during which this agreement shall be executed and delivered within thirty (30) days after the end of each following quarter annual period, **Licensee** shall make a written report to **Licensor** setting forth the **Gross Sales** of **Licensed Patent Rights** sold, leased or used by **Licensee** and total sub-licensing receipts during the quarter annual period. If there are no **Gross Sales** or sub-licensing receipts, a statement to that effect shall be made by **Licensee** to **Licensor**. At the time each report is made, **Licensee** shall pay to **Licensor** the royalties or other payments shown by such report to the payable hereunder.
2. **Books and records. Licensee** shall keep books and records in such reasonable detail as will permit the reports provided for in Paragraph 1. to be determined. **Licensee** further agrees to permit such books and reports to be inspected and audited by a representative or representatives of **Licensor** to the extent necessary to verify the reports provided for in paragraph 1; provided, however, that such representative or representatives shall indicate to **Licensor** only whether the reports and royalty paid are correct, if not, the reasons why not.

Article V—Marking

Licensee agrees to mark or have marked all **Products** made, used or leased by it or its sub-licensees under the **Licensed Patent Rights**, if and to the extent such markings shall be practical, with such patent markings as shall be desirable or required by applicable patent laws.

Article VI—Diligence

1. **Licensee** shall use its best efforts to bring **Licensed Patent Rights** to market through a thorough, vigorous and diligent program and to continue active, diligent marketing efforts throughout the life of this agreement.
2. **Licensee** shall deliver to **Licensor** on or before _______, a business plan for development of **Licensed Patent Rights**, which includes number and kind of personnel involved, time budgeted and planned for each phase of development and other items as appropriate for the development of the **Licensed Patent Rights.** Quarterly reports describing progress toward meeting the objectives of the business plan shall be provided.
3. **Licensee** shall permit an in-house inspection of **Licensee** facilities by **Licensor** on an annual basis beginning at _______________ .
4. **Licensee** failure to perform in accordance with either paragraph 1, 2 or 3 of this ARTICLE VI shall be grounds for **Licensor** to terminate this agreement.

Article VII—Irrevocable judgment with respect to validity of patents

If a judgment or decree shall be entered in any proceeding in which the validity or infringement of any claim of any patent under which the Licence is granted hereunder shall be in issue, which judgment or decree shall become not further reviewable though the exhaustion of all permissible applications for rehearing or review by a superior tribunal, or through the expiration of the time permitted for such application, (such a judgment or decree being hereinafter referred to as an irrevocable judgment) the construction placed on any such claim by such irrevocable judgment shall thereafter be followed not only as to such claim, but also as to all claims to which such instruction applies, with respect to acts occurring thereafter and if an irrevocable judgment shall hold any claim invalid, **Licensee** shall be relived thereafter from including in its reports hereunder that portion of the royalties due under ARTICLE III payable only because of such claim or any broader claim to which such irrevocable judgment shall be applicable, and from the performance of any other acts required by this agreement only because of any such claims.

Article VIII—Termination or conversion to non-exclusive licence

1. TERMINATION BY LICENSEE

Option of Licensee: Licensee may terminate the licence granted by this agreement, provided **Licensee** shall not be in default hereunder, by giving **Licensor** ninety (90) days notice to its intention to do so. If such notice shall be given, then upon the expiration of such ninety (90) days the termination shall become effective; but such termination shall not operate to relieve **Licensee** from its obligation to pay royalties or to satisfy any other obligations, accrued hereunder prior to the date of such termination.

2. TERMINATION BY LICENSOR

Option of Licensor: Licensor may, at its option, terminate this agreement by written notice to **Licensee** in case of:

a. Default in the payment of any royalties required to be paid by **Licensee** to **Licensor** hereunder.
b. Default in the making of any reports required hereunder and such default shall continue for a period of thirty (30) days after **Licensor** shall have given to **Licensee** a written notice of such default.

c. Default in the performance of any other material obligation contained in this agreement on the part of **Licensee** to be performed and such default shall continue for a period of thirty (30) days after **Licensor** shall have given to **Licensee** written notice of such default.

d. Adjudication that **Licensee** is bankrupt or insolvent.

e. The filing by **Licensee** of a petition of bankruptcy, or a petition or answer seeking reorganisation, readjustment or rearrangement of its business or affairs under any law or governmental regulation relating to bankruptcy or insolvency.

f. The appointment of a receiver of the business or for all or substantially all of the property of **Licensee**; or the making by **Licensee** of assignment or an attempted assignment for the benefit of its creditors; or the institution by **Licensee** of any proceedings for the liquidation or winding-up of its business or affairs.

3. EFFECT OF TERMINATION

Termination of this agreement shall not in any way operate to impair or destroy any of **Licensee's** or **Licensor's** rights or remedies, either at law or in equity, or to relieve **Licensee** of any of its obligations to pay royalties or to comply with any other of the obligations hereunder, accrued prior to the effective date of termination.

4. EFFECT OF DELAY, ETC

Failure or delay by **Licensor** to exercise its rights of termination hereunder by reason of any default by **Licensee** in carrying out any obligation imposed upon it by this agreement shall not operate to prejudice **Licensor's** right of termination for any other subsequent default by **Licensee**.

5. OPTION OF LICENSEE TO CONVERT TO NON-EXCLUSIVE LICENCE

Licensee shall have the right to convert this licence at the same royalty rate as for the exclusive Licensee, without right to sub-license and minimum royalties under ARTICLE III, Paragraph 3. shall not be due thereafter.

6. RETURN OF LICENSED PATENT RIGHTS

Upon termination of this agreement, all of the **Licensed Patent Rights** shall be returned to **Licensor**. In the event of termination of the agreement by **Licensee** or said conversion of the agreement by **Licensee**, **Licensee** shall grant to **Licensor** a non-exclusive, royalty-free Licence, with right to sub-licence, to manufacture, use and sell improvements including all known-how to **Licensed Patent Rights** made by **Licensee** during the period of this agreement prior to the termination or conversion, to the extent that such improvements are dominated by or derived from the **Licensed Patent Rights**.

Article IX—Term

Unless terminated as provided above, the term of this Agreement shall be from and after the date hereof until the expiration of the last to expire of the licensed issued patents or patents to issue under the **Licensed Patent Rights** under ARTICLE I. **Licensee** shall not be required to pay royalties due only by reason of its use, sale, licensing, lease or sub-licensing under issued patents licensed by this Agreement that have expired or been held to be invalid by an Irrevocable Judgment, where there are no other of such issued patents valid and unexpired covering the **Licensee's** use, sale, licensing, lease or sub-licensing; provided, however, that such non-payment of royalties shall not extend to royalty payments already made to **Licensor** more than six (6) months prior to **Licensee's** discovery of expiration or an Irrevocable Judgment.

Article X—Patent litigation

1. **Initiation.** In the event that **Licensor** advises **Licensee** in writing of a substantial infringement of the patents/copyrights included in the **Licensed Patent Rights, Licensee** may, but is not obligated to, bring suit or suits through attorneys of **Licensee's** selection with respect to such infringement. In the event **Licensee** fails to defend any declaratory judgment action brought against any patent or patents of the **Licensed Patent Rights, Licensor** on written notice to **Licensee** may terminate the Licence as to the particular patent or patents involved in such declaratory judgment action.
2. **Expenses and proceeds of litigation.** Where a suit or suits have been brought by **Licensee, Licensee** shall maintain the litigation at its own expense and shall keep any judgments and awards arising from these suits expecting that portion of the judgments attributable to royalties from the infringer shall be divided equally between **Licensor** and **Licensee** after deducting any and all expenses of such suits; provided, however, **Licensor** shall not be entitled to receive more under this provision than if the infringer had been licensed by **Licensee.**
3. **Licensor's right to sue.** If **Licensee** shall fail to commence suit on an infringement hereunder within one (1) year after the receipt of **Licensor's** written request to do so, **Licensor** in protection of its reversionary rights shall have the right to bring and prosecute such suits at its cost and expense through attorneys of its selection, in its own name, and all sums received or recovered by **Licensor** in or by reason of such suits shall be retained by **Licensor**; however, no more than one lawsuit at a time shall commence in any country.

Article XI—Patent filings and prosecuting

1. **Licensee** shall pay future costs of the prosecution of the patent applications pending as set forth in ARTICLE I, Paragraph 2, which are reasonably necessary to obtain a patent. Furthermore, **Licensee** will pay for the costs of filling, prosecuting and maintaining foreign counterpart applications to such pending patent applications, such foreign applications to be filed within ten (10) months prior to the filing date of the corresponding ___________ (Country) patent application.
2. **Licensor** shall own improvements by the inventors. **Licensee** shall pay future costs of preparation, filing, prosecuting and maintenance of patents and applications on patentable improvements made by inventors, however, in the event that **Licensee** refuses to file patent applications on such patentable improvements in ___________ [country] and selected foreign countries when requested by **Licensor**, the rights to such patentable improvements for said countries shall be returned to **Licensor.**
3. **Preparation** and maintenance of patent applications and patents undertaken at **Licensee's** cost shall be performed by patent attorneys selected by **Licensor**; due diligence and care shall be used in preparing, filling, prosecuting, and maintaining such applications on patentable subject matter. Both parties shall approve any and all patent related documents.
4. **Licensee** shall have the right to, on thirty (30) days written notice to **Licensor**, discontinue payment of its share of the prosecution and/or maintenance costs of any of said patents and/

or patent applications. Upon receipt of such written notice, **Licensor** shall have the right to continue such prosecution and/or maintenance on its own name at its own expense in which event the Licence shall be automatically terminated as to the subject matter claimed in said patents and/or applications.

5. **Notwithstanding** the aforegoing paragraph of this ARTICLE XI, **Licensee's** obligations under such paragraphs shall continue only so long as Licensee continues to have an Exclusive Licence under the Licensed Patent Rights and, in the event of conversion of the Licence to non-exclusive in accordance with ARTICLE VIII, Paragraph 1(b), after the date of such conversion:
   a. The costs of such thereafter preparation, filing, prosecuting and maintaining of said Licensed patents and patent applications shall be the responsibility of **Licensor**, provided such payments are at the sole discretion of the **Licensor**; and
   b. **Licensee** shall have a non-exclusive Licence without right to sub-license under those of such patents and applications under which **Licensee** had an **Exclusive Licence** prior to the conversion.

Article XII—Notices, assignees

1. **Notices.** Notices and payments required hereunder shall be deemed properly given if duly sent by first class mail and addressed to the parties at the addresses set forth above. The parties hereto will keep each other advised of address changes.
2. **Assignees, etc.** This Agreement shall be binding upon and shall inure to the benefit of the assigns of **Licensor** and upon and to the benefit of the successors of the entire business of **Licensor**, but neither this agreement nor any of the benefits thereof nor any rights thereunder shall, directly or indirectly, without the prior written consent of **Licensor**, be assigned, divided, or shared by **Licensor** to or with any other party or parties (except a successor of the entire business of **Licensor**).

Article XIII—Miscellaneous

1. **This agreement** is executed and delivered in ______________ [country] and shall be constructed in accordance with the laws of the Government of New South Wales, Australia.
2. **No other understanding.** This agreement sets forth the entire agreement and understanding between the parties as to the subject matter thereof and merges all prior discussions between them.
3. **No representations** or warranties regarding patents of third parties. No representations or warranty are made by **Licensor** that the **Licensed Patent Rights** manufactured, used, sold or leased under the **Exclusive Licence** granted herein is or will be free of claims of infringement of patent rights of any other person or persons. The **Licensor** warrants that it has title to the **Licensed Patent Rights** from the inventors.
4. **Indemnity. Licensee** shall indemnify, hold harmless, and defend **Licensor** and its trustees, officers, employees and agents against any and all allegations and actions for death, illness, personal injury, property damage, and improper business practices arising out of the use of the **Licensed Patent Rights**.

5. **Insurance.** During the term of this agreement, **Licensee** shall, maintain the following insurance coverage:
   a. Commercial general liability with a limit of no less than one million US dollars (US$1 000 000.00, option) each occurrence. Such insurance shall be written on a standard ISO occurrence form or substitute form providing equivalent coverage.
   b. Professional liability of no less than one million US dollars (US$1 000 000.00, option) each occurrence.
   c. Workers' compensation consistent with statutory requirements. Certificates of insurance shall be provided to **Licensor** upon request and shall include the provision for 30-day notification to the certificate holder of any cancellation or material alteration in the coverage.
6. **Advertising. Licensee** agrees that **Licensee** may not use in any way the name of **Licensor** or any logotypes or symbols associated with **Licensor** or the names of any researchers without the express written permission of **Licensor**.
7. **Confidentiality**. The parties agree to maintain discussions and proprietary information revealed pursuant to this agreement in confidence, to disclose them only to persons within their respective organisations having a need to know, and to furnish assurances to the other party that such persons understand this duty on confidentiality.
8. Disclaimer of Warranty. Licensed Patent Rights is experimental in nature and provided WITHOUT WARRANTY OR REPRESENTATIONS OF ANY SORT, EXPRESS OR IMPLIED, INCLUDING WITHOUT LIMITATION WARRANTIES OF MERCHANTABILITY AND FITNESS FOR A PARTICULAR PURPOSE OF NON INFRINGEMENT. Licensor makes no representations and provides no warranty that the use of the Licensed Patent Rights will not infringe any patent or proprietary rights of third parties.

In witness whereof, the parties hereto have caused this agreement to be executed by their duly authorised representatives.

The effective date of this agreement is ______________, 20___.

Licensor ______________________________

Name: ______________________________

Title: ______________________________

Licensee ______________________________

Name: ______________________________

Title: ______________________________

... ...

9.7 Conclusion

For many businesses, manufacturing and distributing a product from the place of manufacture is not suitable for a number of reasons. For instance, a seller may not have expertise marketing and distributing a product in a certain region. Or the seller may not be comfortable operating in a different cultural and linguistic setting. It could be that the business could grow much faster if it could be produced in another location, or even in multiple locations, due to the costs associated with manufacture or due to the proximity of the targeted sales markets. It could be that the inventor or company does not have the manufacturing capacity to meet expected demand, or that the inventor or company believes that the resulting product could be better manufactured, marketed and distributed by others, due to existing expertise and experience. These are just a few reasons why companies sometimes willingly give up control over the manufacture, marketing and distribution of their product.

This chapter provided an overview of several different relationships that can develop between the original seller and a third party. The first type of arrangement is where the seller continues to manufacture the product itself but entrusts the third party to market and promote the product. Agencies and distributorships—the main types of this arrangement—have been discussed in some detail. It is important not only to understand the differences between these two types of arrangements, but also to appreciate the legal consequences that can result through the use (or misuse) of the terms and arrangements. The chapter also focused on licensing arrangements; that is, when a seller contracts the use, manufacture or distribution of its product to a third party. This is an extremely common arrangement between international entities, and for this reason the chapter went into some detail regarding the risks and particulars of licensing contracts. In addition, the chapter also highlighted the potential for licensing arrangements to breach competition laws in certain jurisdictions.

When speaking generally, it could never be stated that certain types of arrangements were 'better' or 'worse' than others. Instead, it is the role of the legal representative to inform their clients of the potential advantages and disadvantages of a particular arrangement when contrasted with others. The ultimate choice of one arrangement over all others will necessarily depend upon the interests and situation of the client, product and marketplace.

Questions

With regard to the case study at the beginning of this chapter:

1 a Why does the local law of the host nation play such an important role in regulating agents and distributorships?

  b What effect can this regulation have on the supplier?

2 What are the some of the benefits of selecting an agent instead of a distributor, and vice versa?

3 a What are the advantages and disadvantages of True Blue licensing the ALLBERRY?
  b What are the risks that remain outside of the control of True Blue?

4 What types of licence agreement could True Blue negotiate with licensees, and what are the pros and cons of each approach?

5 Would you advise True Blue to license the technology to one manufacturer and distributor, or would you advise the company to negotiate separate licensing agreements with manufacturers/distributors in Asia, North America, Europe and Latin America? What are the benefits and burdens of each approach?

6 How best can True Blue guarantee the legality of its licensing agreements with companies in Asia, North America, Europe and Latin America, respectively?

7 a How can licensing agreements infringe upon competition law?
  b Why do countries take different approaches to the regulation of licensing under competition law?

8 Does Australia's regulation of licensing agreements resemble the USA's 'rule of reason' or the EU's codification of rules covering specific action (to use Professor Maskus' language)?

9 Why did the Ergas Committee recommend changes to the *Trade Practices Act* as it involves licences? Do you agree with the recommendations?

10 How could True Blue best prevent its technology from being stolen by the licensee or an employee of the licensee?

11 Will True Blue's licensing agreement with another company remain in force upon the expiration or revocation of its patent on the technology?

12 a Would you advise True Blue to use the sample licensing agreement extracted in the previous section?
   b Explain to True Blue the relevance and effect of each clause?

CHAPTER 10

franchising

Chicken Bar Pty Ltd is a gourmet chicken burger restaurant with two Sydney locations. The owner wishes to expand, but does not want to over-commit herself to multiple locations and is worried about the start-up and operating costs of more restaurants. She seeks advice on how to go about franchising her restaurants throughout Australia. She also wishes to know if it is worthwhile attempting to franchise Chicken Bar overseas, and, if so, what (if any) additional considerations she should be aware of when selecting locations and franchisees. Finally, she mentions that a letter has recently arrived from Chick'n'Bar, a New Zealand-based restaurant that has recently entered into the Australian market, claiming that Chicken Bar has violated the trademark of Chick'n'Bar.

10.1 Introduction

One of the most effective ways of expanding a 'brand' name and selling a product or service is by franchising. A business is usually suitable for franchising when it has built a strong 'brand' profile and wishes to expand by showing another business how to market and sell the product or service at issue. A plethora of businesses selling a wide variety of products and services can be franchised. These include fast food (such as McDonald's), automotive/muffler (such as Midas), juice bars (such as Boost Juice), bars/hotels/restaurants (such as Sizzler Steakhouse), bakeries (such as Michel's Patisserie), coffee shops (such as Starbucks), ice-cream (such as New Zealand Natural), hotel chains (such as Accor Hotels), tax services (such as H & R Block), mortgage brokers (such as Mortgage Choice) and many more.

One advantages of buying into a franchise is the advantage of selling a product with a proven business model and recognisable brand or logo. This saves the time and expense of building up a brand name and gaining customer loyalty. The franchisee may also gain the benefit of the franchisor's experience on matters such as site selection, operating manuals and building plans. Of course, the franchisee must pay for the privilege of operating under the franchisor's name, normally by both an upfront payment and through ongoing royalties. In this regard, the franchisee is essentially operating under a licence to use the franchisor's name—that is, part of the success of franchising depends upon the franchisor licensing its trademark and other intellectual property rights to the franchisee. In most circumstances, the franchisor sets out a strict regime by which the franchisee must market the product/service according to its instructions. The franchisee must also make use of the franchisor's technology and services in almost every step of the business. While the franchisee must expend some capital in starting to operate the franchise, both parties normally expend capital and carry risk.

The franchisor also benefits from the concept, as it avoids having to find the capital required to establish its multiple outlets and the risks associated with, *inter alia*, foreign laws on such matters as workplace relations and investment. Once successful, the franchisor can have an income stream with little downside.

In this chapter, we first set out the basic and broad principles of franchising, before providing two extracts; the first of these illustrates some general legal and commercial pitfalls regarding franchising, and the second illustrates the importance of trademarks to franchising by describing the troubles one franchisor had in entering the Australian market. The chapter then provides a detailed overview of the current Australian regulations, before concluding with a summary of how some other nations regulate franchising.

10.2 Franchising: the basics

There are three types of franchising agreements—services, production and distribution:

- A services agreement allows a franchisee to market and sell a service, such as the provision of tax services, and generally allows the franchisee to use the franchisor's trade name, trademark and brand name.
- In a production agreement, the franchisee manufactures a product according to the franchisor's instructions before selling it under its own name. Production agreements are common in the pre-packaged food product industry. An example of a production agreement would be a franchised bakery, such as Bakers Delight. A slight variation, called a business format system, involves the franchisee making or obtaining the product from an authorised source prior to selling it in its own premises under the franchisor's name. An example of this method is Michel's Patisserie.
- In a distribution agreement, the franchisee makes and/or sells products in a prescribed fashion on its own premises (which may be laid out according to the franchisor's instructions) but carrying the franchisor's name.

There are also four different variations of franchise agreements. It is important to stress at the outset that there is no 'perfect' or 'correct' format to use. Instead, the format that is chosen depends upon the level of economic and political risk that both parties feel comfortable undertaking.

- The first type of franchise agreement is a simple franchisor-to-franchisee agreement, whereby the prospective franchisee negotiates and deals directly with the franchisor.
- The second is the master franchise agreement, where the franchisor negotiates with one sub-franchisor in a target geographical area, which then negotiates with all other potential franchisees in that geographical area.

- The third is the area agreement, which occurs when the franchisor allows a franchisee to open numerous outlets within a certain geographical area.
- The fourth is a joint venture between the franchisor and local participants.

The governing law of franchise agreements is that of the host state, and every country regulates franchise agreements slightly differently, so it is important for any potential franchisor or franchisee to know the local rules. In fact, due to some countries requiring the prospective franchisor to maintain a business presence in the targeted country, none of the above four options may be available without the use of a subsidiary company. In addition, some countries also regulate the conduct of their franchisors regardless of where they are franchising. Moreover, if the franchisor undertakes to locate and invest in suitable premises for the franchisee, it must understand a number of local laws and regulations prior to granting and investing in the franchise (such as town planning laws and regulations, health and safety requirements, laws relating to the sale of goods, employment law, competition policy, intellectual property and enforcement provisions, tax legislation, monetary policy relating to exchange rate controls and profit repatriation and so on).

It is also important for the franchisor to ensure that its franchisees are independent contracting parties to the agreements, not agents, employees or partners, so as not to expose itself to third party liability. Simply stating this in the contract is not enough, and a relationship can be deemed to exist despite contractual language. For instance, an agency relationship can be deemed to exist where the franchisor places orders on behalf of the franchisee, or the franchisee delivers goods on behalf of the franchisor. Similar issues occur with licensing; but the franchisor has a brand standard to maintain and many franchisees are new to the business of franchising and unaccustomed to its unique peculiarities.

Generally speaking, laws regulating franchise agreements are drafted so as to provide protection for the franchisee given the unbalanced bargaining relationship between the parties. This imbalance occurs due to the fact that the franchisor is privy to all of the relevant information about the franchise (such as its financial position), while the franchisee is privy to no such information. Accordingly, regulations usually mandate certain disclosures, cooling-off periods and provisions providing for independent legal advice. In addition, the franchisor must avoid misrepresentation at every step of the negotiating process.[1]

In the following extract, prominent Australian franchising lawyer and academic Warren Pengilley expands upon the basic principles of franchising before embarking on an interesting analysis of various pitfalls to international franchising. The importance of this extract lies not so much in the current status of the information provided on the law and other peculiarities in each jurisdiction (no doubt some of it is dated), but more in the areas of interest and concern to lawyers and business in deciding to enter, negotiate and operate under franchise agreements.

---

1 In order to assist to lawmakers, potential franchisors and franchisees, the International Chamber of Commerce (ICC) has drafted a Model International Franchising Agreement. The International Institute for the Unification of Private Law (UNIDROIT) has also drafted a Guide to International Master Franchising Arrangements.

Warren Pengilley, 'International Franchising Arrangements and Problems in Their Negotiation' (1985) 7 *Northwestern Journal of International Law and Business* 185 at 185–207

[F]ranchising is little understood in legal circles. This is demonstrated by the various legislative approaches which have been adopted. In many countries, there is simply no law directly applicable to franchising ...

Almost certainly the reason for the lack of any common jurisprudential approach to franchising is that franchising relationships simply do not fit neatly into any of the common law moulds with which we are all familiar. Franchising typically partakes of a number of these relationships while not totally embracing any of them. For example, it partakes of, but does not totally embrace, the concepts of (1) employer and employee; (2) distributorship; (3) licensor and licensee; (4) agency; or (5) vendor and purchaser, to varying degrees, depending upon individual transactions. As one learned American author on franchising has put it:

> only since World War II and increasingly in the past ten years has franchising achieved recognition as a distinct method of marketing ... [but] there is no generally accepted definition of franchising in court decisions, regulation or legislation. Further, any definition would fail to include the many functions inherent in the system, as well as its potential for abuse ...

Given this lack of a legal definition, it is difficult to speak in terms of the law of any particular country. To study in this paper the laws of any one country rather than those of others would be an arbitrary, and unjustifiable, decision. To study the laws of all countries would be a feat beyond a paper of this length. The author has chosen, therefore, to speak in terms of broad principle because, despite the absence of a uniform legal approach to franchising, the broad economic and marketing parameters are similar in all countries in which franchising takes place.

Because of the scope of franchising, and particularly of international franchising, the basic problems involved in negotiation of franchising agreements are most frequently not inherently legal in nature. They are more likely to be problems of business, psychology, politics, and culture or problems of a technical and scientific kind. Above all, they are likely to be problems of tact, diplomacy, strategy, and tactics. Lawyers may or may not be good at solving these problems. But if the lawyer cannot look beyond the law, the lawyer will be a far greater hindrance than a help in any franchising negotiations. Unfortunately, lawyers do not necessarily receive basic training in the arts mentioned and many in the field of commerce argue that lawyers are not skilled in such arts.

II. What is franchising?

Franchising is a relationship which is very difficult to define in black letter terms—a factor which, of course, makes it so hard for legislators to write any laws about it.

It seems to be common ground that the franchising concept involves at least the following basics:

1 The use by a franchisee of a trade or quality mark or logo held by the franchisor;
2 The grant of a right by a franchisor to a franchisee to sell or use a developed system, product, or service;
3 The payment by the franchisee to the franchisor of consideration (usually an 'up front' fee or a 'royalty on sales' or some combination of the two).

That these basic concepts express generality is, however, readily apparent when one considers case law in the United States. In that country, economic issues have been extensively examined in the context of franchise restraints and in the application of the antitrust laws. When a trademark indicates the *source of a product,* the restraints allowed under United States antitrust laws have been markedly different to those allowed where the trademark indicates the quality of a product.

In the usual case, a franchisor, under United States antitrust law, cannot 'tie' the franchisee to purchase subsidiary or secondary products (in a fast food franchise, products such as napkins and table cloths for example). Nevertheless, quite extensive franchise ties have been permitted under such laws where the item being franchised is a whole system which, in the words of the court in *Principe v McDonald's:*

> offers its franchisees a complete method of doing business [in which] ... its regime pervades all facets of the business from the design of the menu board down to the amount of catsup on the hamburgers nothing [being] left to chance ...

In such a case there is, according to the United States courts, simply no subsidiary product to 'tie.' The whole system, complete with its totality of purchase requirements is one 'product.' The question of whether subsidiary product purchase requirements are illegal does not arise.

... The fact, however, that United States courts have been able to develop totally different economic rationales for arrangements which we would all typecast as 'franchises' should make us wary of too readily placing all franchise arrangements into one common mould. Within the generality of the franchising concept, there are considerable individual differences.

While franchising initially began as a method of manufacturing or distributing products, increasing sophistication in franchising has given rise to an ever increasing growth of 'systems franchises.' It is in this area that the greatest current expansion in franchising is taking place. The 'systems franchise' trend causes considerable frustration for lawyers. Necessarily if the 'system' works successfully, the parameters for negotiation of variations are narrow. It is no use, for example, attempting to negotiate with McDonald's to install a pay phone in their franchised fast food outlets. They will not negotiate on this point. It is simply not part of the 'system' so loudly and judicially praised for its success in *Principe.* The negotiating lawyer, therefore, needs to know more than just the law. The lawyer has to have marketing and commercial expertise to understand the reasons for the often apparently intransigent negotiating posture of franchisors. The lawyer must be able to explain the 'systems' logic to the client. Above all, the lawyer must have the capacity to distinguish that which is commercially important from that which is not and that which is of negotiating importance from that which is trivial.

...

IV. Why franchise internationally?

In addition to the reasons for franchising domestically (which are applicable to a greater or lesser degree internationally) the following reasons may be given for franchising internationally:

1 To utilize local management personnel and thus overcome problems of language and culture;

2 To overcome problems of detailed supervision often otherwise insuperable because of distance;

3 To leave compliance with local laws to those familiar with such laws and thus be able to market a product in a target country without incurring liability under the laws of such country;

4 To avoid laws which may inhibit or control foreign direct investment in particular countries. Franchising enables a product to be marketed in a country with restrictive direct investment laws without a direct investment being made by the franchisor in that country;

5 To overcome political difficulties such as the possibility of expropriation of overseas investment. The franchisee will normally be a resident of the target country and probably less vulnerable to such threats. In any event, if the property is expropriated, it is the franchisee's and not the franchisor's loss;

6 To take advantage of revenue, tax planning and similar financial considerations too complex to be discussed here. One of the more common reasons for franchising is to avoid the tariff imposts which, notwithstanding a veritable barrage of international agreements, still inhibit world trade. A franchise operation can avoid such tariffs.

V. The contents of international franchising agreements and lawyer involvement in their negotiation

The most important point of negotiation in international franchising agreements is the negotiation of the first document—usually a Master Franchise Agreement or the first of a number of direct franchise agreements. After this agreement has been negotiated the die is cast and the basic rules are established. Subsequent agreements will depend upon the initial document. If the first agreement is not properly negotiated, disaster will almost certainly follow in subsequent arrangements. The first agreement is thus often far more important for its 'follow up' effects than for its *inter partes* effect. It is imperative that the first agreement be properly drafted. Some deceptively elementary questions have to be decided initially. These questions are so elementary that they are not infrequently overlooked or given proper consideration.

A. NATURE OF THE TYPE OF DESIRED ARRANGEMENT

The most fundamental issue to be considered involves a consideration of the general nature of the franchising arrangement.

1. DIRECT FRANCHISING

The franchisor franchises individual outlets direct from the home country to the target country. Generally, this system only operates between proximate countries with similar societies and legal systems. There is, for example, a good deal of direct franchising from the United States into Canada and from Australia into New Zealand, and vice versa in each case.

2. ESTABLISHMENT OF A BRANCH OFFICE OR A SUBSIDIARY IN THE TARGET COUNTRY

Often decisions as to the actual method of conducting business (branch or subsidiary) will be based on financial and taxation considerations. The advantage of establishing a physical presence in the target country is that the franchisor can directly control the franchisees in the target country. The major obstacle is that the franchisor becomes committed in a number of countries around the world in which it would prefer not to have a direct presence. To some extent, the franchisor may believe it is losing the benefits of the franchising concept by having to establish subsidiaries in a wide variety of overseas countries.

3. JOINT VENTURE ARRANGEMENTS

A decision to operate by joint venture necessarily involves physical presence in the target country. Many of the advantages of international franchising (stated above) may not be realized for this reason. The chief advantage to a joint venture is that there is a sharing of risk. But the corporate problems of the franchisor are all too often overlooked. Not infrequently equal representation on boards and equal shareholdings may lead to inefficient decisionmaking. There are also complex problems which may be caused by foreign investment legislation in the target country if the franchisor is required to increase its investment there. Above all, it should be recognized that a joint venture involves a very active and continuing participation in the project by the franchisor.

4. MASTER OR AREA FRANCHISE

The franchisor gives the franchisee a specific area (usually a particular country or a significant part of it) to exploit, usually with the right to subfranchise. The advantage of such a system is less franchisor involvement. Master franchising particularly suits franchisors who are without substantial financial or managerial expertise. Moreover, it is a particularly useful form of franchising in situations involving long distances or different cultural and legal systems. For example, there are many 'Master' franchises into and out of Australia for reasons of distance.

These issues should never be considered without thinking of alternative methods of conducting business. Frequently it is assumed that franchising is the best business method although the point may not have been fully debated. Often the best business decision is not to do business at all. Some 'cross-examination' questions by the lawyer for a franchisee may be valuable in focusing the franchisee's thoughts on the difficulties and advantages in doing business in various organizational forms.

B. IMPORTANT POINTS IN THE AGREEMENT

Assuming a franchise arrangement of some sort is desired, the next point is the negotiation of the actual agreement. International franchising agreements, like domestic franchising agreements, have a certain number of matters which *must* be considered. It is essential that broad agreement be reached on these issues before any attempt is made to 'fine tune' the franchising arrangements. The most basic questions are:

- What is being franchised?
- What are the franchisor's obligations?
- What are the franchisee's obligations?
- What marks, including logos and patents, are involved and what is their legal status?
- What is the length of the franchise?
- What exclusivity provisions (product, territorial, or customer) are applicable? Of prime importance will be the question of territorial exclusivity as such security is often the basis upon which the franchisee makes a commitment.
- What are to be the payment arrangements? Is payment:
  - 'up front,' based upon a royalty, or a combination of both?
  - subject to minimum royalties?
  - to be made in the franchisor's currency, the franchisee's currency, or a third currency?

  - to be subject to agreed limitations on exchange rate variations?
  - to be made exclusive, inclusive or otherwise of certain taxes and imposts of the target country?
  - to be made monthly, quarterly, semi-annually, or at other designated times?
- Are royalties to be scaled up or down with the age of the franchise?
- Are there minimum performance provisions?
- What competition restraints (during the agreement and after termination) will exist?
- Are there to be any 'buy out' or 'buy back' options?
- What provisions apply relating to choice of law?

C. LAWYER INVOLVEMENT IN NEGOTIATIONS

When should lawyers become involved in franchise negotiations? Lawyer involvement in negotiation is desirable at an early stage. Lawyers must recognize, however, the needs of the commercial community. Lawyer involvement in franchising negotiations requires the lawyer to give immediate advice so that the negotiations can head down the right track. Although they are brought into negotiations early, lawyers should not think that they can or should run the negotiations or control the commercial direction of the proposed deal. Regrettably, this occurs all too often and there is thus a real client reluctance to involve lawyers until a later, often too late, stage.

D. ONE WHO CONTROLS THE DRAFT, CONTROLS THE NEGOTIATION

A basic rule of thumb which has been demonstrated on numerous occasions is that: 'One who controls the draft controls the negotiation.' It is tempting for a client to agree to allow the other party's lawyer to draft the agreement. This decision saves money. Nonetheless, this is often a short-sighted view. As a lawyer, it is easy to draft provisions favorable to your client and include clauses which are never deleted from the final agreement. Often such clauses are not even discussed as they are viewed as subsidiary items.

Often, however, the ability to control drafting is limited by the comparative power of the parties involved. A well-established franchisor will frequently have a Master Franchise arrangement which will be offered on a 'take-it-or-leave-it' basis. Similarly, traditional etiquette will often be important. Commonly, the party which conveys rights will present the first draft.

VI. Potential franchising pitfalls

Set out below is a limited selection of potential franchising difficulties; most are of a commercial nature. Commercial factors are the most obvious pitfalls and a lawyer should be aware of the more common ones. Some pitfalls are legal. These primarily involve delay, obfuscation, and annoyance at the administration of laws by government bureaucrats. One can normally ascertain prior to the conclusion of a franchising arrangement the existing state of the law. But how long it may take governments to act is completely unpredictable.

A. COMMERCIAL PITFALLS

1. SELECTION OF THE WRONG TARGET COUNTRY

The fundamental motivation of the franchisor in entering into a franchise is to make a profit. Most worldwide franchises are based in the United States. Why should a franchisor incur the difficulties of a franchising deal with its ongoing commitments unless there is an assurance of being adequately compensated?

...

Factors which are of chief importance in a target country include minimal government interference with the provisions agreed to by the parties and the capacity to remit profits back to the franchisor. Political stability of the target country is also a prime consideration ... For the franchisor, the ability to reach an agreement, withdraw funds, and deal with a politically stable country is quite fundamental. Selection of a target country which does not share these characteristics may be disaster for a franchisor and it is frequently a reason for the commercial failure of franchises.

2. NOT RECOGNISING LOCAL DIFFERENCES

Some countries might appear to have identical characteristics to those of the franchisor's home country but, in fact, have quite basic differences. An exclusive territory of two-thirds of Australia may look impressive when the area is circled on a map in New York, but that area may well have a population less than that of a reasonably sized United States city. It is surprising, but such elementary errors occur. Franchisees, in particular, should be careful in looking at impressive figures or systems from a country other than their own. Even countries similar on their face may be different enough to make it impractical to franchise the product or systems of one to the other.

3. NOT KNOWING WHAT IS BEING FRANCHISED OR WHAT THE PARTIES ARE REQUIRED TO DO

The first question raised in the basics of a franchising agreement is: 'What is being franchised?' This is not meant in jest. Many arrangements fail simply because the parties (franchisees in particular) never really seek to answer this question. Franchising literature is full of cases where there has been inadequate definition of the product being franchised or what the parties are to do.

4. INADEQUATE MARKET RESEARCH AND OTHER COMMERCIAL FAILURES

Some common commercial causes of franchising failures are:

- Inadequate market analysis;
- Product defects;
- Higher costs than expected;
- Inadequate definition of exclusivity arrangements, particularly in relation to territorial exclusivity;
- Poor timing;
- Prohibitively high franchise fees;
- Inadequate support from franchisor;
- The 'tyranny of distance' which may result in adequate information flow and lack of communication;
- Lack of appreciation of local customs;
- Personality clashes between franchisor and franchisee;
- Franchisee dissatisfaction with a franchise after working for a period of time. The remedies for the prevention and solution of these problems are obvious. They include: Better screening and research;
- Reorganised responsibilities;

- Improved communication facilities. There is nothing improper, for example, in the requirement that a franchisee maintain a telex link.
- Better support, especially in the start-up period. Such support should be specified in detail in the agreement negotiated between the parties. In particular, the agreement should state where and how much support is to be given and at whose cost;
- Avoiding franchisee dissatisfaction. Frequently this can be done by the franchisor requiring the franchisee to work for the franchisor for a reasonable period of time (with an option out available if dissatisfied) thus giving the franchisee the 'lay of the land.' It is fundamental to any franchise operation that the franchisee know the extent of all obligations. Some franchisors object to such an arrangement, arguing that it costs them money. Often this may be true. But allowing a franchisee to opt out on a basis previously agreed to will generally be far cheaper to the franchisor than establishing the franchise, only to find the franchisee disgruntled within six to twelve months.

5. TOO MUCH, TOO SOON

Franchises always take much longer to put into place than parties initially anticipate. If this fact is not realized and taken into account in planning, there will be cash flow problems.

Commercially speaking, there are other timing problems. Frequently a commercial marketer will fail to see why a trademark cannot be franchised even if an application for registration has not been filed or, if filed, not considered. To explain that government bureaucracies can take two to five years to deal with trademark registrations is not easy. The marketer may simply fail to understand why bureaucrats can take so long to decide something as simple as a trademark registration. Similarly, although the marketer will defend the uniqueness of the trademark, its value in the marketplace and its importance as the basis of a franchise operation, the marketer will, nonetheless, often want to push on with an arrangement notwithstanding the fact that the franchisee may ultimately receive no tradename protection. Doubts of the franchisee, and the lawyers, in relation to tradenames are dismissed as unfounded.

Franchisors should not even think of negotiating a franchise overseas prior to the registration of relevant tradenames, logos, and marks in the target country. In many countries, 'stealing' a trademark is not only not unethical, but an approved business practice. It can place franchisees in difficulty and can be both embarrassing and expensive if a franchisor has to 'buy back' a trademark from a local registrant should it be 'stolen' and, therefore, impossible to franchise in the target country.

A problem similar to 'too much too soon' occurs in relation to Master Franchise Agreements. The Master Franchisee may have to make a considerable up-front payment to the franchisor and may have to fund this payment by subfranchising. The problem which occurs is that the Master Franchisee may not have been a franchisee in the target country prior to signing up the Master Franchise Agreement. The franchisee may be having problems while, at the same time, subfranchising to franchisees who need guidance with their difficulties. The problem is one of overoptimism and greed. The combination can lead to all sorts of miscalculations.

A Master Franchisee should be required to run a franchise for some extended period before being permitted to subfranchise. Only in this way may the necessary experience be gained. Of course, such a requirement often goes against entrepreneurial spirit and cash-flow desires. But it does ensure a commitment by the Master Franchisee to deliver to subfranchisees what they expect.

Perhaps the greatest disaster in a Master Franchise arrangement is the nonperformance of the Master Franchisee. Ensuring that this does not occur is quite basic to the operation of the system. Frequently the reason for such nonperformance is the desire to subfranchise too quickly in circumstances where the Master Franchisee is both unaware of franchisee problems and is unable to service the proliferating outlets which have been established.

Franchisors generally are people with expansive ideas which, more often than not, need moderation. They believe in the explosive capacity of their creations. At a conference run by the International Franchising Association in Atlanta, Georgia on November 9–10, 1983, franchisors were asked their expansion plans for the next two years. An average figure revealed that participants expected an 81% growth in their franchise businesses in this period. The nub of many franchise problems is that many franchisors feel a sense of urgency. Some say: 'We have a great idea and we must make up for lost time.' Commercial mistakes often occur because of this attitude. Lawyers, by making probing inquiries, can often assist clients in avoiding such mistakes.

B. LEGAL PITFALLS

While the lawyer must be aware of the commercial pitfalls in international franchising in order to be a competent advisor, it is critical that the lawyer also be aware of the legal pitfalls which can occur in these arrangements. It is fundamental that competent local legal advice be obtained and that the correct questions are asked. In order to demonstrate this point, set out below are examples of a few of the potential pitfalls which are likely to be encountered.

1. ASSUMING THE GENERAL SIMILARITIES OF LEGAL SYSTEMS

Many Australian businesses have assumed the similarities of legal systems in entering the United States market. Australia and the United States are akin in many ways in relation to competition laws. But the Australian franchisor entering the United States market may be harassed by legal tactics which were not anticipated and are not understood. Treble damages under the antitrust law, the innovative actions brought by United States attorneys, and that an action successfully defended gives no right to costs, are but a few of the unexpected aspects of the United States legal system. Frequently the only way to avoid such problems is to opt for a Master Franchising Arrangement and avoid direct franchising or the establishment of a presence in the target country. The client, especially if a franchisor, should have an outline of the whole legal system explained by a competent target country lawyer. It is well worth the franchisor travelling to the target country purely for a conference of a few hours on this subject if the franchisor is unable to obtain competent advice in the home country.

2. NOT BELIEVING THAT THE POSITION IS AS DIFFERENT AS ONE HAS BEEN TOLD

Franchisors and their lawyers, coming generally from developed countries, are likely not to believe some situations even when meticulously explained. Sometimes the situation in the target country is so different that it is simply incredible to lawyers trained in a different legal environment. The advice to all lawyers when told of systems operating quite differently to their own—especially in relation to industrial property protection, competition laws, and bureaucratic consents—is: 'Believe it if it comes from a credible source.' Never judge the systems of other countries by preconceptions based upon a legal system with which you are familiar.

3. FAILING TO UNDERSTAND THE DIFFICULTIES IN ANTITRUST AND SIMILAR TYPES OF LAWS

Local competition laws create special problems for many franchise arrangements. On this issue, advice from target country lawyers is absolutely imperative. In some instances, local registration will be required. It is impossible to encapsulate world antitrust laws in this paper, nonetheless, their parameters are broad. In many countries (such as the United States, Canada, and Australia) a wide variety of restraints (primarily price fixing and resale price maintenance) are banned *per se*, but no specific government examination of agreements is required. In others (such as the Andean Pact countries), individual arrangements are examined by government agencies and approval must be obtained. Among other things, competition will be considered in granting consent. Chief among these are tying practices, time periods involved, resale price maintenance, export restrictions, and territorial restraints.

4. FAILURE TO APPRECIATE THE IMPACT OF LAWS SPECIFICALLY RELATING TO FRANCHISING

... The chief point concerning laws specifically applicable to franchises is not that they pose too many problems for reputable franchisors, but that they pose problems of delay in timing the launch of a franchise. Such delays must be anticipated. If such laws are ignored, dire results may follow. Even if one believes that conviction will not occur, the inevitable investigation, delays, and executive time involved in battling governmental authorities can mean that one may have no option but to comply with bureaucratic directives, rather than to take the risk on the point.

5. FAILURE TO COMPREHEND THE IMPORTANCE OF OTHER RELEVANT LAWS

There is a whole host of individual laws which, on their face, have nothing to do with franchising, but which can result in significant problems. Local advice on these types of laws is also of basic importance.

a. State laws in federal systems

All too frequently franchisors from unitary government countries do not appreciate the problems caused by state or provincial laws in federal systems such as Australia, the United States, or Canada. These laws are often crucial. Some simple examples from these countries illustrate how vital this point can be.

In Australia, nearly all packaging and labelling laws are state or territory laws. A Report by the Australian Trade Practices Commission concluded that such laws were administered by a host of different ministers and state bodies. While there was some uniformity, manufacturers selling nationally often were unable to obtain the benefits of common labelling. In some cases, labelling legal in one state was illegal in others. Such diverse laws at the state level must have an impact upon any 'system franchise.'

In the United States, one of the most significant pieces of legislation is the so-called 'franchise tax' of various states, the most well known of which is that of California. This state law taxes the profits of a company doing business in California on the basis of its worldwide profits regardless of whether it made a profit in California. Similarly, the California authorities claim to have the right to inspect records wherever they are placed in the world, thus causing not inconsiderable administrative problems. Double tax treaties with the United States are simply irrelevant when state laws can have such effect. The California law, which has been upheld by the United States Supreme Court precludes a foreigner establishing some type of permanent presence in California by way of subsidiary or joint venture and effectively compels either direct franchising (very difficult from a distance) or a Master Franchise Arrangement …

In Canada, one is likely to run afoul of the Charter of the French Language legislation in Quebec, if franchising there. The Charter is drafted in less than precise language and, of course, ruins the English language franchise precedent which the franchisor probably uses elsewhere in the world … One of the provisions of the legislation is that every person who has the right to have firms doing business in Quebec communicate in French. Some firms require certificates which stipulate that only French be used. Catalogues, brochures, and folders must be in French. Clearly such a provision has enormous impact upon any 'system franchise' and the costs of franchising in Quebec—particularly when the Quebec operation is small.

b. Other laws

Licensing controls and production regulations abound in various forms in all countries. Revenue laws are of fundamental importance. What one wants is to make everything tax deductible to the franchisee and nonassessable to the franchisor. Of course, it is rarely that simple. Stamp duties, sales tax, customs duties, receipt duties, often both at the state and federal level, are also fundamental to the viability of franchising arrangements. Foreign investment laws are quite significant.

Also important, but frequently overlooked, are immigration laws. The franchisor may promise to assist the franchisee by placing staff in the target country, only to find that an appropriate work permit will not be granted. This can work in reverse, too. If the franchisee is to work for or to be trained by the franchisor, immigration authorities in the home country may resolutely refuse to allow entry. Similarly, some countries have quite stringent laws relating to ethnic origins and job reservation.

6. PROBLEMS OF JURISDICTION AND APPLICABLE LAW

There is never a satisfactory resolution to the choice of law problem unless the franchisor and franchisee are geographically proximate. In the case of franchises into or out of the remote antipodes of Australia and New Zealand, there is difficulty in making the jurisdiction of the country of either the franchisor or franchisee exclusive. This author has never seen a reasoned approach to the issue in negotiations. Usually, the franchisor wins the day because of superior bargaining power although, generally speaking, the laws of the target country have the better claim to jurisdiction. It is in that country that the relevant activity is being conducted. In patent, trademark, and antitrust matters, the target country's laws will be applicable regardless of what the agreement says. Furthermore, one cannot opt out of the target company's bureaucracies by simply declaring the agreement subject to the laws of another jurisdiction.

The choice of law problem cannot, however, be simply ignored. To leave the question to the courts is to invite further litigation. In practice what seems to happen is that the franchisor wins or a compromise is reached whereby the party initiating litigation is required to litigate in the courts of the other party. This at least does have the benefit of discouraging litigation.

The lawyer in this field can do little but advise. It is the negotiating strength and skills of the parties which will determine the issue. Clients are, regrettably, too willing to accept the law of unknown jurisdictions. This tendency of commercial parties must be anticipated. Similarly, clients should be warned that target country laws must generally be obeyed regardless of what the agreement may say.

Some countries will not approve agreements unless there is a submission to the jurisdiction of the courts of the franchisee. While generally speaking, specific governmental interference in the terms of *inter partes* negotiated agreements is somewhat deplorable, one admirable aspect of such control can be the resolution of the choice of law problem. Andean Pact countries simply will not approve agreements which take away the jurisdiction of the courts of the relevant Andean Pact country. If the agreement is not approved, then no royalties can be remitted. Similar authoritarianism on this issue in other countries might solve many jurisdictional problems. The present position is that franchisees rarely obtain a reasonable arrangement of this issue by the processes of *inter partes* bargaining.

Jurisdiction clauses are always a potential pitfall, particularly in long-distance arrangements. They are not negotiated on their merits by commercial negotiators, but are regarded as trivial by the parties. Should a dispute arise, however, this often-overlooked provision of the agreement may take on a new significance.

VII. Concluding comments

Franchising is never short of its share of problems in either domestic or international agreements. But it is a fascinating subject for lawyer involvement. The lawyer is part negotiator and part marketing adviser, in addition to fulfilling the traditional role of legal advisor.

For a franchisor to consider operations in a target country, that country must be politically stable, with an appropriate market, where funds can be remitted, and where there is a minimum of governmental interference with the parties' franchising agreements. Most governments, for various reasons, have laws which both harass and tax franchise arrangements. This comment applies to the developed countries as much as to lesser-developed countries. Various examples given in this paper illustrate this point.

Lesser-developed countries merit sympathy in the franchising game. The many laws controlling most overseas arrangements in such nations certainly deter franchisors from considering franchising operations in those countries. Such laws frequently prevent them from receiving technology and business systems which would enhance their development. However, there is a significant danger of exploitation of lesser-developed nations through unscrupulous business practices. One must be sympathetic to the necessity to create various roadblocks to control such activities. Unfortunately, these roadblocks, when erected, also have the effect of hindering honest businesses attempting to set up arrangements beneficial to all.

The message to lawyers advising on international franchising arrangements is:

- Understand what franchising is about commercially because only then can one advise competently. If necessary, confer with marketers and reputable franchising consultants to sharpen these skills.
- Make inquiries in all matters and take local advice. Despite exhaustive inquiry, nearly every international franchise arrangement overlooks some important legal or commercial consideration.

- Above all, the cardinal rules in any evaluation of international franchising transactions are these:
  - Take the maximum time possible for negotiation.
  - Take the maximum time possible to comply with government requirements.
  - Assess the maximum possible legal and other costs which will be payable.

……………

The extract above provides a comprehensive introduction to franchising law and its potential benefits and detriments. Since the article was published, franchisors have continued rapidly expanding from their host nations to foreign markets. While US franchisors initially expanded to markets with cultural and economic similarities to the USA, such as Australia, Canada and the UK, growth potential is increasingly being sought in less developed, culturally different and even politically unstable countries. These differing environments challenged the notion that a franchisor could simply set up a successful franchise using the same model which proved successful in the home (or even similar) market. Thus, franchisors often have to change their product/service mix, delivery system, advertising, contractual arrangements and/or method of operation. Slogans, branding and other logos may also have to be changed to meet local expectations or appeal to the local market. Some countries manage these changes well, while others learn from experience. Although not directly related to franchising, legend has it that automobile manufacturer Chevrolet pulled out of the Latin American market following the failure of its marketing campaign for its small car, the Chevy Nova. In Spanish, *no va* literally translates to 'it doesn't go'.[2] On the other hand, in order to avoid having its automobile resemble a vulgar Spanish term, Mitsubishi marketed its 'Pajero' as the 'Montero' in Latin America.[3] In franchising, fast food franchises are the leaders in allowing local tastes and preferences to dictate menu items and even in-store configuration (such as McDonald's with the McCafe concept of upmarket stores starting in Australia before being exported to other markets, and localised cuisine such as the McOz burger in Australia and Grilled Pork Twisty Pasta on the breakfast menu in Hong Kong).

Such 'localisation' can be at odds with the franchising model—that is, cooperation and control by the franchisor and standardised characteristics between stores/outlets/markets—but is seemingly necessary in order to expand to some foreign markets. For this reason, franchising experts and academics have developed models which attempt to evaluate the likely success (or failure) of a franchise in certain foreign markets. Most models rely on four variables:

1 Economic;
2 Demographic;

---

2 Some doubt the accuracy of the anecdote: see G Erichsen, 'The Chevy Nova that Didn't Go: Commonly Told Tale is Just an Urban Legend', available at [http://spanish.about.com/cs/culture/a/chevy_nova.htm].

3 Ibid.

3 Distance; and
4 Political.[4]

Such models are also utilised to evaluate which type of franchise agreement should be used in each market.[5]

Franchising inevitably involves an evaluation not only of the potential of a foreign market, but also of the franchise itself. A franchise must assess its own readiness to enter into a foreign market; this would include its financial and human resources, knowledge, product and strategies. A franchise must also have firmly decided the level of risk and control it wishes to maintain in the foreign market. Large franchisors with a well-known brand name, international experience and a high level of sophistication are more likely to use a company-owned model of international franchising expansion in order to maintain a higher level of control of the product and brand. On the other hand, smaller franchisors with no brand presence or international experience are more likely to relinquish more control over foreign development to locals via a master franchising agreement. As more small and medium-sized businesses are now using the franchising model to expand abroad (and progressively more to countries which significantly differ culturally, economically and politically), the master franchising agreement is becoming an increasingly popular contractual choice.

10.3 The interaction between franchising and trademarks

As mentioned in the extract above, trademarks are of the utmost importance to franchising. For many companies, the value of their brand far exceeds the value of their physical assets. Securing a brand is based upon the legal recognition and protection granted by a trade mark. Like other forms of intellectual property, trademark protection is territorially based, meaning protection in one country does not automatically provide protection in another country.[6] In Australia, trademarks can be registered or unregistered,[7] but registration of trademarks is the most secure form of protection.

4 See for example I Alon & D McKee, 'How Do Franchisors Evaluate Foreign Markets?', in I Alon (ed), *Service Franchising: A Global Perspective* Springer, New York, 2006, pp 93–102.

5 Ibid.

6 International agreements have standardised trademark laws and have attempted to provide for mutual recognition of marks, but technicalities remain and registered marks in one country are still denied registration in other countries for a variety of reasons, including lack of distinctiveness or because of the existence of prior use or registration.

7 The core concepts of the action for passing off are reputation, misrepresentation and damage. Enforcement of an unregistered mark can be made under the tort of passing off (and the statutory misleading or deceptive conduct action) under the *Trade Practices Act 1974* (Cth)). In practice, the plaintiff must: (1) establish goodwill or a reputation attached to the goods or services; (2) demonstrate a misrepresentation by the defendant to the public (whether or not intentional) leading or likely to lead the public to believe that the goods or services offered by the defendant are the goods or services of the plaintiff; and (3) demonstrate that the misrepresentation has caused or threatened damage to the plaintiff's reputation or goodwill.

In Australia, the first person to use a trademark with respect to particular goods or services within Australia is the person entitled to registration.

Any business seeking to franchise its operations should seek to protect its trademarks—and other intellectual property rights—long before a final decision is taken regarding whether to expand into certain markets. At the very least, trademark issues should be addressed prior to entering into negotiations with a potential franchisee.

In some instances, this may mean simply registering a trademark in the foreign jurisdiction at issue. But even there, it can take up to or even beyond two years in some jurisdictions before the trademark application is even examined by the relevant authorities. Furthermore, acquiring trademark protection may not be as simple as registering trademarks in the foreign jurisdiction, as others may have already obtained (whether in good or bad faith) protection for a similar or identical trademark in that market. This may mean that the franchisor cannot use its preferred trademarks in the jurisdiction, or it may mean that negotiation or court action is required prior to obtaining the trademark.

The evaluative process begins with a search of the local trademark registry in order to ascertain whether its marks are already registered by another individual/business. If the marks are registered, the costs of any action to obtain the transfer of the marks as well as the likelihood of obtaining the marks must be factored into any decision to proceed.

If the marks have not been registered, the franchisor will either register the marks itself or contractually obligate the potential franchisee to register the marks (and thus provide no contractual warranty concerning the availability of the marks). The latter course of action is risky for a number of reasons, including the fact that eventualities resulting from the inability to register marks must be taken into consideration and contractually agreed (for example, what mark will be used, which party will pay for the change in signage, stationery, products, etc?). Perhaps more importantly, the strategy is hazardous and potentially costly in the event of a failed franchisor–franchisee relationship.[8] The safer course of action would be for the franchisor to register the trademarks in its own name before licensing their use to the franchisee.

Trademarks can become a major impediment to entering a market, with loss of brand identity, negative publicity and costs all potentially undermining a successful franchise. This can be illustrated by detailing the experience of multinational fast food chain Burger King and its experience in expanding to Australia.

EXAMPLE: Burger King's problems began on entering the Australian market in the early 1970s, when it discovered that a small takeaway food outlet in Adelaide had already registered the 'Burger King' mark in good faith. Having failed to acquire the trademark through negotiation, Burger King decided to use the name Hungry Jack's along with its existing marks and logos. The Australian rights were then acquired by John James (Jack) Cowin through Hungry Jacks Pty Ltd (HJPL). The relationship soured in the early 1990s, and Burger King announced plans to open

8 It should be noted that some countries require trademarks to be registered prior to their being licensed in a franchise agreement.

several 'Burger King'-branded restaurants throughout Australia, as well as terminate its agreement with HJPL in order to prevent further expansion of HJPL's Hungry Jack's.

The Supreme Court of New South Wales—in a judgment based upon claims regarding contractual interpretation, encroachment, and fiduciary duty—found Burger King had pursued a policy of disrupting, confining and thwarting HJPL's activities, and awarded compensation of AU$71 million (including $43.5 million for delays in opening company-owned restaurants and AU$24 million for loss of opportunity in introducing third party franchisees). The root of the Burger King's problems, however, was that it had allowed HJPL to acquire local trademark rights, and HJPL could thereby marginalise the franchisor in the market.[9]

10.4 Regulation of franchising agreements in Australia

When franchising first came to Australia in the early 1970s, the authorities took a rather laissez-faire approach to regulating the industry. In response to complaints regarding the imbalance of bargaining relationship of the parties, a voluntary code was introduced in the mid-1980s, but proved unsuccessful at instituting any meaningful reform. By the mid-1990s, it was clear that the industry needed legal regulation and in 1998—at a time when the Australian market consisted of 693 franchisors employing approximately 500 000 people and operating over 50 000 outlets with an annual turnover of $76.5 billion—the Franchising Code of Conduct was enacted as the Trade Practices (Industry Codes—Franchising) Regulations 1998 (Cth) and incorporated in Part IVB of the *Trade Practices Act 1974* (Cth).[10] According to a 2006 survey conducted by the Franchise Council of Australia and Griffith University, there are now 960 franchisors in Australia, operating approximately 62 000 outlets turning over $128 billion annually and employing 426 500 people.[11] The franchising sector is also estimated to have contributed 14 per cent to Australia's GDP in 2005.[12]

The Franchising Code of Conduct is a mandatory code that aims to ensure that franchisees are sufficiently informed about a franchise prior to entering into an agreement. More specifically, the Code defines key terms, provides for disclosure requirements, regulates conditions between the franchisor and franchisee, and provides for dispute settlement procedures between the parties. The Code applies to franchise

9 See *Hungry Jack's v Burger King* [1999] NSWSC 1029. See also A Terry & H Forrest, 'Where's the Beef? Why Burger King is Hungry Jack's in Australia and Other Complications in Building a Global Franchise Brand' (2008) 28 *Northwestern Journal of International Law and Business* 171–212.

10 See L Frazer, S Weaven & O Wright, 'Franchising Australia 2006 Survey' (2006), report prepared for the Franchise Council of Australia, available at [www.franchise.org.au/content/?action=getfile&id=450]. See generally [www.franchise.org.au].

11 Ibid.

12 Ibid.

agreements hosted in Australia;[13] however until recent amendments that took effect on 1 March 2008,[14] it did not apply to agreements between a foreign franchisor and only one franchisee or a master franchise. The Code has always applied to agreements between master franchisors and sub-franchisees, and where a foreign franchisor has granted multiple franchisees.

The Australian Competition and Consumer Commission (ACCC) is responsible for ensuring compliance with the Code. Failure to comply with the Code could render the franchisor liable to an action by the ACCC arising from a contravention of the *Trade Practices Act*, as well as a civil claim for damages and/or a declaration that the provisions of the franchise agreement are unenforceable.

Since the advent of the Code, there is been some difficulty in distinguishing a franchise agreement from other commercial agreements. For this reason, clause 4(3) of the Code provides that the following do not in themselves constitute a franchise agreement:

- An employer and employee relationship;
- A partnership relationship;
- A landlord and tenant relationship;
- A mortgagor and mortgagee relationship;
- A lender and borrower relationship;
- The relationship between the members of a registered cooperative.

The following case extract reviews Clause 4 of the Code, which provides the definition of what kind of agreement qualifies as a 'franchise agreement' under the Code. In the extract, the applicant is attempting to claim a breach of the Code while the respondent is denying that the arrangement between the parties qualifies as a 'franchise agreement'. The sources of information reviewed by the court are the respondent's Managing Director, Mr Dennis Dorval and the Managing Director of the applicant, Mr Richard Selwood.

Agro Holdings Ltd v Flexi-Coil (Australia) Pty Ltd

[1999] FCA 1658

27. The pleaded allegation is that the Termination Letters breached the terms of the Code in that they failed to give reasonable notice as required by clause 22(3) of the Code, the applicant not having consented to the terminations and failed to provide reasons for the terminations as required by the same paragraph.

13 Clause 2(2) was deleted in the recent amendments, meaning that the Code no longer operates concurrently with the *Petroleum Retail Marketing Franchise Act 1980* (Cth) (Oilcode).

14 The new Regulations took effect from 1 March 2008 not only for new franchise agreements, but also for existing franchise agreements. For instance, as a result of clause 6(2) requiring a disclosure document comply with Annexure 1 or 2 of the Code, franchisors needed to use an amended disclosure document from 1 March 2008. Franchisors also had to abide by clause 6(1) of the Code and produce a further disclosure document within four months of the end of the 2007/08 financial year.

28. A 'franchise agreement' is defined by clause 4 of the Code as follows:

(1) A 'franchise agreement' is an agreement:
 (a) that takes the form, in whole or part, of any of the following:
  (i) a written agreement;
  (ii) an oral agreement;
  (iii) an implied agreement; and
 (b) in which a person ('the franchisor') grants to another person ('the franchisee') the right to carry on the business of offering, supplying or distributing goods or services in Australia under a system or marketing plan substantially determined, controlled or suggested by the franchisor or an associate of the franchisor; and
 (c) under which the operation of the business will be substantially or materially associated with a trade mark, advertising or a commercial symbol:
  (i) owned, used or licensed by the franchisor or an associate of the franchisor; or
  (ii) specified by the franchisor or an associate or the franchisor; and
 (d) under which, before starting business or continuing the business, the franchisee must pay or agree to pay to the franchisor or an associate of the franchisor an amount including, for example:
  (i) an initial capital investment fee; or
  (ii) a payment for goods or services; or
  (iii) a fee based on a percentage of gross or net income whether or not called a royalty or franchise service fee; or
  (iv) a training fee or training school fee;

Then follow certain exclusions and inclusions none of which is contended as being relevant:

29. The requirement of clause 4(1)(a) for a written agreement is partly satisfied by the Dealer Agreement. For the applicant it is contended further elements of the Franchise Agreement may be implied.

30. Clause 4(1)(b) requires that there be a grant in the agreement of the right to carry on a business under 'a system or marketing plan substantially determined, controlled or suggested by the franchisor ...' Mr Selwood's evidence is that from the outset at each outlet advertising material was provided including large wall posters and editorial material (for newspapers) written by the respondent's advertising and promotions manager. I place no reliance on his evidence that such was in addition to the marketing plans also provided from the outset, of which no substantiation is provided. The evidence for the respondent is that there is no system or marketing plan stipulated in the Dealer Agreements (as is apparent from those agreements). It is deposed by Mr Dorval that the usual practice between the respondent and its dealers is that once a year the respondent's representative for a particular territory meets with each dealer and does a forecast of anticipated sales for the next year. This forecast is utilised to enable forward planning in factory production.

31. Mr Dorval's evidence was that on commencing business each dealer received a kit including parts, manuals, sales manuals, spare parts, a CD Rom, price books and service operator manuals the cost of which was approximately $600.

32. Mr Selwood referred to documents relating to merchandise and wearables issued by the respondent. Examination of that shows that it speaks of the relationship between the applicant and the respondent as 'partners in promotion' and does not in evidence any system or plan of the requisite type.

> 33. Clause 4(1)(c) is directed to the association with a trade mark, advertising or commercial symbol. Mr. Selwood's evidence was that he was told about the respondent's signage, corporate clothing, brochures and other advertising material. The applicant purchased from the respondent neon signs showing the respondent's name and in its colours at a cost of more than $600 each. Souvenirs and promotional items given away to customers were supplied by the respondent and charged to and paid by the applicant. The applicant was also supplied with and paid for the respondent's corporate clothing and hats with its logo. The evidence of Mr Dorval in response was that none of the respondent's trade marks, advertising or commercial symbols were owned, used, licensed or specified by the respondent or any of its associates. He said there was no requirement to display any signs, hats or flags nor was the dealer or its staff required to wear any special uniform or endorsed clothing.
>
> 34. Clause 4(1)(d) refers to the circumstances pertaining before the commencement of the business. There is evidence of denial by Mr Dorval of the requirement of any of the payments referred to in sub-clauses 4(1)(d)(i–iii). Mr.Selwood gave evidence of the respondent's training requirements and of his attendance at a training school. However Mr Dorval denies there was a training fee or training school fee received by dealers.
>
> 35. In my opinion the evidence does not show that the applicant has a strong case to make out its claim that the Code applies because the arrangements between the applicant and the respondent were a 'franchise agreement'. It is more probable than not that the applicant will not be able, on the present state of the evidence, to make out this claim.
>
> 36. In reaching that view I take into account that the requirements of clause 4 are cumulative. I also take into account that clause 4(1)(a) permits the franchise agreement to be in part written, oral and implied. My opinion is that there is no basis for implication of the requirements in pars 4(1)(b), (c) or (d).
>
> ... ...

Thus, Section 4 provides three key elements in defining a franchise agreement:

1 There is a common system or marketing plan for carrying out the business, supplying or distributing goods/services substantially controlled, determined or suggested by the franchisor;
2 The business operation is reliant on intellectual property which is owned by the franchisor; and
3 The franchisee must pay the franchisor an initial or ongoing fee.

Importantly, these conditions are cumulative, meaning the Code does not govern the contract unless all three conditions are satisfied.[15]

10.4.1 Disclosure requirements

One of the most important aspects of the Code of Conduct is the requirement that the franchisor (or master franchisee (also called sub-franchisee)) table key documents, called

15 See also *Clark Rubber Franchising Pty Ltd v Greatbay Pty Ltd* [2002] VSC 465; *Apple Computer (Aust) Pty Ltd v Mekrizis* (2003) ACSR 518; *Subway Systems Australia P/L v Thorpe* [2000] QSC 99; *Enviro Systems Renewable Resources v ASIC* [2001] SASC 11.

disclosure documents, to the franchisee enabling that party to make a reasonable decision as to whether to enter into the contract.[16] The Code requires the franchisor to issue a 'long-form' disclosure document when the franchisee is expected to have an annual turnover of more than $50 000 at any time during the franchise agreement, while the disclosure documents for a franchise which is expected to have an annual turnover of less than $50 000 per annum during the franchise agreement may be in either the 'long form' or 'short form'. However, it should be noted that where the franchisor has given the franchisee a short-form disclosure document and the franchisee requests additional information that is included in a long-form disclosure document, the franchisor is obliged to provide the requested information.

The Code specifies the specified format of the disclosure documents for both the long-form and short-form disclosures (in Annex 1 and Annex 2, respectively). In general, the purpose of the disclosure document is to provide current information relevant to, *inter alia*, operations, earnings information, operational requirements (such as what products and services the franchisee must buy from the franchisor), payments, criminal records and litigation, etc. Where a master franchise agreement is involved, both the franchisor and sub-franchisor must provide separate or joint disclosure documents to the sub-franchisee.

The franchisor (or master franchisee) must provide the potential franchisee with the disclosure document, along with a copy of the Code and a copy of the franchise agreement in the form it is to be executed,[17] at least 14 days before the franchisee enters into, renews or extends the term or scope of a franchise agreement (or pays a non-refundable deposit in relation to a proposed franchise agreement).[18] Furthermore, franchisors are also required to provide franchisees that are entitled to a long-form disclosure document with a copy of any agreement that they are required to enter into under the franchise agreement (such as leases, security, intellectual property licences and confidentiality agreements) at least 14 days before the signing of the franchise agreement, or, if they are not available at that time, as soon as they become available (franchisees provided with a the short-form disclosure document can request this information be provided).

Additional disclosure requirements include a signed statement from a company director saying whether the franchisor is able to pay its debts as and when they fall due, information about the history of the proposed franchisee site (including the circumstances under which a previous franchisee at the site ceased to operate)[19] and notification of materially relevant facts relating to the franchise within 14 days of the franchisor becoming aware of them (such as court proceedings).

---

16 It also appears the Code now requires the foreign franchisor and master franchisee to give to potential sub-franchisees either (1) a joint disclosure document (which may attach joint liability to the foreign franchisor for errors in detailing the obligations the foreign franchisor has to the master franchisee); or (2) a separate disclosure document for potential sub-franchisees (in which case the franchisee would receive two disclosure documents, one from the foreign franchisor and one from the Australian master franchisee). See clause 6B of the Code.

17 The 'in the form in which it is to be executed' language is potentially troublesome, as, taken literally, it does not allow for minor negotiated changes, correction of typographical errors or even the insertion of the franchisee's company name. Such an interpretation would be overly burdensome and it is not thought that such stringency would be enforced. Material changes, on the other hand, would certainly be caught under the provision.

18 Clause 6B(1) of the Code.

19 Long form only.

Additionally, a franchisor must update its disclosure document within four months after the end of each financial year and must provide a copy of a current disclosure statement within 14 days of the franchisee making such a request, as long as only one request has been made within the preceding 12 months (excluding requests made during contract renewal).

Moreover, a franchisor must also inform a franchisee (or prospective franchisee) of any materially relevant fact within a reasonable time (deemed to be not more than 14 days after the franchisor becomes aware of it) if the disclosure document does not already include the information. Clause 18(2) lists materially relevant facts as:

(a) change in majority ownership or control of the franchisor;
(b) proceedings by a public agency, a judgment in criminal or civil proceedings or an award in an arbitration against the franchisor or a franchisor director in Australia alleging:
  (i) breach of a franchise agreement; or
  (ii) contravention of trade practices law; or
  (iii) contravention of the *Corporations Act 2001*; or
  (iv) unconscionable conduct; or
  (v) misconduct; or
  (vi) an offence of dishonesty;
(c) a judgment against the franchisor, other than for unfair dismissal of an employee, under:
  (i) section 127A or 127B of the *Workplace Relations Act 1996*; or
  (ii) section 106 of the *Industrial Relations Act 1996* of New South Wales; or
  (iii) section 276 of the *Industrial Relations Act 1999* of Queensland;
(d) civil proceedings in Australia against the franchisor or a franchisor director by at least 10%, or 10, of the franchisees in Australia of the franchisor (whichever is the lower);
(e) any judgment that is entered against the franchisor in Australia, and is not discharged within 28 days, for at least:
  (i) for a small proprietary company—$100 000; or
  (ii) for any other company—$1 000 000;
(f) any judgment that is entered against the franchisor in a matter mentioned in item 4.2 of Annexure 1 or item 3.2 of Annexure 2;
(g) the franchisor becoming an externally-administered body corporate;
(h) a change in the intellectual property, or ownership or control of the intellectual property, that is material to the franchise system;
(i) the existence and content of any undertaking or order under section 87B of the Act.

Finally, it should also be noted that under Clause 6.1, when the franchisor requires franchisees to contribute to a marketing or other cooperative fund that it controls or administers, it must expressly state the following:

(a) the kinds of persons who contribute to the fund (for example, franchisee, franchisor, outside supplier);
(b) whether the franchisor must contribute to the fund in relation to businesses owned or operated by the franchisor that are substantially the same as the franchised business and, if so, whether the contribution is worked out in the same way as for a franchisee;
(c) how much the franchisee must contribute to the fund and whether other franchisees must contribute at a different rate;
(d) who controls or administers the fund;

(e) whether the fund is audited and, if so, by whom and when;
(f) whether the fund's financial statements can be inspected by, or will be given to, franchisees;
(g) the kinds of expense for which the fund may be used;
(h) the fund's expenses for the last financial year, including the percentage spent on production, advertising, administration and other stated expenses;
(i) whether the franchisor or its associates supply goods or services for which the fund pays and, if so, details of the goods or services;
(j) whether the franchisor must spend part of the fund on marketing, advertising or promoting the franchisee's business.

Moreover, where a franchise agreement requires the franchisee to contribute to a marketing or other cooperative fund, the franchisor must within four months of the end of the financial year (1) prepare a financial statement detailing all the fund's financial receipts and expenses for the last financial year; and (2) have the statement audited by a registered company auditor unless 75 per cent of the franchisor's franchisees in Australia have voted to exempt the franchisor from this requirement. This decision to forgo the audit requirement must be revisited every three years. The franchisor is also required to give the franchisee a copy of the statement within 30 days of preparing the statement and a copy of the auditor's report, if required, within 30 days of preparing the report.

10.4.2 Legal advice

Legal advisers for both the franchisor and franchisee must ensure that the contractual arrangement between the parties covers a variety of issues, such as care of goods, defective goods, service requirements, performance criteria, technical training and assistance, product supply and pricing arrangements. Legal advisers for the franchisor must ensure that the disclosure documents comply with the Code. In order to fulfil this requirement, lawyers for the franchisor will usually be required to draft the required summary of franchisee obligations and other required information. It should be noted again that the disclosure documents may need to be revised throughout negotiations if the circumstances relating to the disclosures change. Finally, the prospective franchisee must provide the franchisor with a signed statement indicating that it has been given independent advice by a legal adviser, business adviser or accountant regarding the agreement (or that it has been informed of its right to seek such advice but it has declined to do so), and that it has received, read and understand the disclosure documents and Code.

10.4.3 Cooling off

The Code requires that the franchise agreement contain a seven-day cooling-off period, meaning the franchisee has seven days following the signing of the contract or paying a non-refundable deposit, whichever is earlier, to back out of the deal and be given a refund (less reasonable expenses incurred by the franchisor) within 14 days.

10.4.4 Association of franchisees and prospective franchisees

Clause 15 of the Code prohibits the franchisor from inducing a franchisee or prospective franchisee not to form an association or not to associate with other franchisees or prospective franchisees for a lawful purpose.

10.4.5 Prohibition on release from liability

A franchise agreement entered into on or after 1 October 1998 must not contain, or require a franchisee to sign, a general release of the franchisor from liability towards the franchisee or a waiver of any verbal or written representation made by the franchisor.[20]

10.4.6 Acquisition of premises

If the franchisor purchases the premises and a lease of those premises to the franchisee is included in the franchise agreement, it is subject to the Code and the franchisor is required to provide the franchisee a copy of any lease, sublease, licence or other occupancy agreement that the franchisee is required to enter into under the franchise agreement at least 14 days before the franchise agreement is entered into if it is available at that time (or, if it is not, when it becomes available).

If the franchisee is entering into a retail lease along with the franchise, the lease agreement will likely be organised in one of three ways:

1 The franchisee leases the premises directly from the landlord;
2 The franchisor takes out a lease with the landlord, and subleases the premises to the franchisee; or
3 The franchisor takes out a lease with the landlord, and the franchisee is given the right to occupy the premises without any direct involvement in the lease agreement.

The first type of lease, where the franchisee leases the premises directly from the landlord, consists of an independent contract between the franchisee and the landlord. The franchisor is not directly involved in the contract, but could add valuable assistance in, for instance, selecting a suitable location for the business and negotiating the terms and conditions of the lease. Of course, as the franchisee is ultimately responsible for negotiating the lease, that party is responsible for ensuring that the terms of the lease correspond with the terms of the franchise agreement. It is also wise for the franchisee to discuss the details of the location and premises and terms of the lease with the franchisor to ensure that these correspond to the specifications set out by the franchisor.

The second type of lease—where the franchisor takes out a lease with the landlord and then subleases the premises to the franchisee—is sometimes referred to as a 'head lease', and involves two separate agreements. The first agreement is a lease between the franchisor and the landlord, while the second agreement is a sublease between the

20 The fact that this provision applies as from October 1998 and not 1 March 2008 is potentially troubling as, until March 2008, releases from liability were not prohibited. Most experts believe the October 1998 date written into the revised Code was in error.

franchisor and the franchisee. In this arrangement, the franchisor essentially becomes the landlord of the franchisee and, as such, can exert a large amount of control over the terms and conditions of the agreement. The benefits of such an arrangement include the utilisation of the franchisor's experience and bargaining power in locating and securing a lease with the landlord. However, such an arrangement can constrict the ability of the franchisee to make full use of the premises. In this arrangement, the Code obligates the franchisor to provide the franchisee with a copy of the lease within one month of it being signed.

In the third type of arrangement—where the franchisor takes out a lease with the landlord and the franchisee is only given the right to occupy the premises without any direct involvement in the lease agreement—the franchisor has the greatest control over the lease agreement, while the franchisee has little or no input into the terms and conditions of the lease. For this reason, the franchisee should ensure that the terms and length of occupancy meet its needs. In this arrangement, the Code obligates the franchisor to provide the franchisee with a copy of the document that gives the franchisee the right to occupy the premises within one month of the documents being signed, or a copy of the conditions of occupation within one month of occupation.

In both options two and three—that is, where the franchisor includes a lease as part of the franchising agreement—the franchisor will want to include a clause in the contract stating that a breach of the sublease is a breach of the franchising agreement, which could trigger termination. The franchisor will also want some sort of 'up-front' security covering several months rent to ensure default and subsequent liability. In addition, the franchisor should ensure that rent renewals and rental review are covered in the contract.

10.4.7 Duration and termination

Issues relating to the renewal, transfer, termination (including trigger events) should be addressed in the contract.

If a franchisee wishes to transfer the business, it must make a written request for the franchisor's consent (Clause 20 of the Code). The franchisor cannot unreasonably withhold consent. Clause 20(3) of the Code lists the following circumstances as reasonable reasons for a franchisor to withhold consent (the list does not appear to be exhaustive):

- (a) the proposed transferee is unlikely to be able to meet the financial obligations that the proposed transferee would have under the franchise agreement; or
- (b) the proposed transferee does not meet a reasonable requirement of the franchise agreement for the transfer of a franchise; or
- (c) the proposed transferee has not met the selection criteria of the franchisor; or
- (d) agreement to the transfer will have a significantly adverse effect on the franchise system; or
- (f) the proposed transferee does not agree in writing to comply with the obligations of the franchisee under the franchise agreement; or
- (g) the franchisee has not paid or made reasonable provision to pay an amount owing to the franchisor; or
- (h) the franchisee has breached the franchise agreement and has not remedied the breach.

In denying a request for transfer, the franchisor must provide a statement, in writing, indicating that consent is withheld and setting out why consent is withheld. If the franchisor fails to respond within 42 days after receiving the request, the franchisor is taken to have given consent to the transfer.

Clause 21 applies where a franchisor seeks to terminate a franchise agreement due to a breach of the agreement by the franchisee. In such a circumstance, the franchisor must tell the franchisee what the franchisor requires to be done to remedy the alleged breach and give the franchisee a reasonable opportunity to do so (not more than 30 days). If the breach is remedied in that time, the franchisor must not terminate the agreement as a result of that breach. Importantly, when drafting a termination clause into a master franchise agreement, the franchisor must ensure that termination of the master franchise agreement with the sub-franchisor does not terminate every agreement with all franchisees. Instead, it would be prudent to draft the agreement so that the franchisor would step into the place of sub-franchisor.

In some circumstances, however, the franchisor is not required to provide the franchisee with an opportunity to remedy the breach before terminating the agreement (Clause 23). These include where the franchisee:

(a) no longer holds a licence that the franchisee must hold to carry on the franchised business; or
(b) becomes bankrupt, insolvent under administration or an externally-administered body corporate; or
(c) voluntarily abandons the franchised business or the franchise relationship; or
(d) is convicted of a serious offence; or
(e) operates the franchised business in a way that endangers public health or safety; or
(f) is fraudulent in connection with operation of the franchised business; or
(g) agrees to termination of the franchise agreement.

In addition, Clause 22 of the Code provides for circumstances where the franchisor may have a right under the terms of the franchise agreement to terminate the agreement prior to the expiration of the agreement, even though the franchisee has neither breached the agreement nor consented to the termination. When a franchisor terminates a franchise agreement in these circumstances, it must provide the franchisee with reasonable notice of the proposed termination and the reasons for the termination.

10.4.8 Dispute settlement

The Code of Conduct provides for the franchise agreement to include a complaint-handling procedure that complies with the Code, and further provides the framework of a mandatory dispute resolution scheme for parties to a franchise agreement.[21]

The first step in the procedure for instigating a complaint against the other party is that the complainant must inform the other party in writing of the nature of the dispute, the outcome it is seeking and what action it believes will settle the dispute (Clause 29(1)

21 However, the ACCC may take immediate action if there is a blatant disregard of the law and/or immediate action is required. Likewise, an injunction may also be sought if immediate action is required.

of the Code). The parties to a franchise agreement must then attempt to resolve the dispute between themselves using the complaint-handling procedure (Clause 29(2)). If this mechanism fails to satisfactorily resolve the dispute within three weeks, either party can refer the matter to a mediator in an attempt to resolve the dispute (Clause 29(3)). The Office of the Mediation Adviser (OMA) can assist the parties in selecting and appointing a mediator, but if the parties cannot agree on who should be the mediator, either party may ask the mediation adviser to appoint a mediator (Clause 29(3)).[22] The OMA must appoint a mediator to the dispute within 14 days of receiving such a request (Clause 30(1)). After mediation has begun, the mediator must advise the OMA of this within 28 days.

The mediator may decide the time and place for the mediation (Clause 29(5)), but the mediation must be conducted in Australia (Clause 29(5A)). The parties must attend the mediation and try to resolve the dispute (Clause 29(6)).[23] Unless otherwise agreed, each party will be equally liable for costs associated with mediation or help to resolve the dispute. Parties still are liable, of course, for their own expenses involved in any preparatory material or services, such as legal or financial advice. If one party would like the mediation conducted in a particular location (such as its home city), it is common that the requesting party would pay for half the other party's travelling expenses. If the parties cannot agree on a location for the mediation, the appointed mediator will decide on a location that is central to both parties and the parties are liable for their own travel expenses.

If the mediation does not resolve the dispute within 30 days, either party may ask the mediator to terminate the mediation. The mediator must terminate the mediation if it receives such a request. The mediator may also terminate the mediation without receiving such a request at any time unless it is satisfied that a resolution of the dispute is imminent. If the mediator terminates the mediation under this clause, the mediator must issue a certificate stating the following: (a) the names of the parties; (b) the nature of the dispute; (c) that the mediation has finished; and (d) that the dispute has not been resolved.[24] The mediator must supply a copy of the certificate to the mediation adviser and to each of the parties to the dispute.[25]

The mediation procedures outlined in the Code do not affect the right of a party to a franchise agreement to take legal proceedings under the franchise agreement. Thus, if mediation fails to resolve the dispute, either party may proceed with other forms of dispute resolution (such as arbitration or litigation). Unlike mediation, these other forms of dispute settlement can be conducted outside of Australia.

10.4.9 Competition law

The relationship between a franchise agreement and the *Trade Practices Act 1974* (Cth) (TPA, competition law) must be fully understood by any franchisor operating in

22 The OMA website is available at [www.mediationadviser.com.au].

23 Clause 29(7) states that a party is taken to attend mediation if the party is represented at the mediation by a person who has the authority to enter an agreement to settle the dispute on behalf of the party.

24 Clause 30A(4) of the Code.

25 Clause 30A(5) of the Code.

Australia. For instance, failure to comply with the provisions regarding disclosure could be deemed misleading and deceptive conduct under the TPA.[26] Franchisors could run afoul of the *Trade Practices Act* for misleading and deceptive conduct or unconscionable conduct at any stage following the negotiation of the franchise agreement. A franchisor could also violate the *Trade Practices Act* in a number of other ways, such as requiring the franchisee to source purchases from certain suppliers, resale price maintenance and pyramid selling.[27] Importantly, the ACCC has made it clear that it will not allow companies to avoid the Code by simply by describing a franchise relationship as a licence.[28]

A recent example of the ACCC successfully prosecuting a company for breaching the TPA was that of *ACCC v Ewing*[29] (commonly referred to as *Synergy*).

EXAMPLE: The defendant, acting through its directors, entered into 'Licence Deeds' with 31 individuals whereby it would provide a business training and development program known as the 'Best Practice Program'. Under the terms of the Licence Deed, the 'licensee' acknowledged that it was merely entering into a 'licence' agreement and not a franchise relationship. The 'licensees' also provided a general release of liability to Synergy.

In return for a substantial fee, the 'licensees' would receive a five-day program training them how to approach and train prospective customers and conduct the business, as well as a workshop kit consisting of stationery, marketing materials, testimonials and similar items.[30] In promoting the value of its Best Practice Program, the defendant, Synergy, claimed that participants receiving the training would become accredited business development specialists and would earn $100 per hour in their first year of operation. It also implied that participants could potentially earn a six-figure income even if they had no previous consulting or other relevant background.

The court, however, was satisfied that the 'licence' agreements were 'franchise agreements' as that term is defined in clause 4 of the Code. It further held that Synergy had breached the Code (and therefore s 51AD of the TPA) and that the directors were also liable under subsection

26 See *ACCC v Ewing* [2004] FCA 5

27 For more detailed information, see C Cecere, 'Australia—Section 51AC of the *Trade Practices Act* Impact on Franchising Sector' (2003) 1(1) *International Journal of Franchising Law* 8–24.

28 For 'an overwhelming case of unreasonable, unfair, bullying, and thuggish behaviour in relation to each franchisee that amounts to unconscionable conduct by SNK for the purposes of s 51AC(1)', see *Simply No-Knead* (2000) 104 FCR 253 at 270 (Sundberg J). In this case, the franchisees complained that the franchisor, *inter alia*, pressured franchisees to comply with its demands by withholding orders of supplies, refusing to meet and discuss franchisee concerns, actively operating in competition with the franchisees, refusing to provide the franchisees with a 'disclosure document', and distributing promotional materials that omitted the franchisees' names. One notable aspect of this case is that Sundberg J found that conduct occurring after the formation of the conduct can nevertheless breach s 51AC. The case demonstrates how the threshold of conduct contravening s 51AC is not confined to traditional procedural unconscionability. In this case, all of the misconduct occurred after the formation of the contract. However, on the facts, Sundberg J was satisfied that the conduct of the defendant attracted the application of s 51AC. Ibid at 260–3, 270.

29 [2004] FCA 5.

30 See Freehills, 'Franchise follies: Lessons in licensing from the ACCC' (February 2004), available at [www.findlaw.com.au/article/11312.htm].

75B(1) of the TPA for being knowingly involved in the contraventions. The court made the following determinations and orders:

- A restraint on all of the respondents from repeating the above breaches;
- A restraint on all of the respondents from requiring a general release of liability in franchise agreements for a period of three years;
- A requirement on all of the respondents to provide a 14-day cooling-off period to all those who had signed agreements, and to refund in full any payments made by parties wishing to terminate;
- A requirement that the directors disclose the existence of the proceedings and the orders made in any franchise sale in which they were involved;
- A requirement that the directors implement an appropriate compliance program if the directors were involved in such business; and
- A requirement that the directors pay the ACCC's costs of $35 000.[31]

10.5 The regulation of franchise agreements in other jurisdictions and internationally

The regulation of franchising differs widely between various jurisdictions, and even within jurisdictions. For instance, in the USA franchising is regulated both at the federal and state level. At the federal level, pre-contract disclosure is required and enforceable by the Federal Trade Commission. Federal antitrust (competition) laws also are applicable to franchise agreements. At the state level, many (but not all) states require compliance with the Uniform Franchise Offering Circular, and some require registration with a state regulatory authority.

In New Zealand and the UK, by contrast, there is no federal regulatory regime. Instead, franchisors may comply with voluntary association codes. Likewise, in Canada, the Canadian Franchise Association Code of Ethics is voluntary; however two provinces (Alberta and Ontario) have legislation mandating pre-sale disclosure and fair dealing requirements.

Even more complicated is the situation in the EU, where franchise agreements are dealt with under the competition provision in Article 81 of the European Community Treaty pertaining to vertical agreements. The so-called Block Exemption Regulation exempts certain types of vertical agreements, including (by virtue of the Regulation and Commission Guidelines issued by the European Commission) franchise agreements. Under certain conditions, such as when market share exceeds 30 per cent, the

31 *ACCC v Ewing* [2004] FCA 5; Freehills, ibid.

exemption will cease to apply. For our purposes, it is sufficient to merely state that the European regime is complicated and multifaceted. It should also be noted that national laws relating to commercial contracts—which could include such provisions as pre-contract disclosure statements—continue to apply. Thus, one needs to look not only at the Block Exemption Regulation, but also the relevant domestic law to fully understand the law regarding franchising in the EU.

Internationally, the International Chamber of Commerce (ICC) Model International Franchising Contract (2000) creates a model franchising agreement based upon clauses found in international franchising agreements. The Model International Franchising Contract is comprehensive, in that it covers the spectrum of issues such as rights and obligations of the parties, territorial exclusivity, restraints, terms and renewal, good faith, know-how, improvements, intellectual property, assistance, supply of products, transfers and terminations. But the agreement is also controversial. For instance, the US Council for International Business disassociated itself from the agreement because it did not believe the model contract represented current international franchising practice, and because of concerns about the suitability of a model contract in this area.[32] The US reservation over the terms, as well as the suitability, of an international model contract serves as a reminder that all model agreements should be regarded with caution. Clients seek legal representation to serve their needs and interests, and sometimes international model contracts can counter those needs and interests. For this reason, lawyers must fully understand the effect of each provision of a model agreement (or any agreement!) on their client before recommending its adoption.

The ICC approach is in contrast to the International Institute for the Unification of Private Law (UNIDROIT)-drafted Guide to International Master Franchise Arrangements (2007), which takes a more traditional approach in merely offering a comprehensive examination of the master franchise arrangements, including fundamental concepts and elements, terms and renewal, rights, obligations and roles of the parties, controls, intellectual property and transfers.[33] The Guide is not intended to be used as model law, but is more designed to assist parties in negotiating and drafting international master franchise agreements.

More recently, UNIDROIT produced the Model Franchise Disclosure Law in 2002 to remedy, or at least lessen, the burden of franchisors having to understand and meet a variety of differing disclosure laws.[34] As many jurisdictions throughout both the developed and developing world now legislate for some form of pre-contract disclosure, there may in fact be a need for a model law; however, the usefulness and importance of the model law remains in doubt, as it depends entirely upon a large number of nations adopting it verbatim.

32 See ICC Model International Franchising Contract (2000), ICC Publication No 557, p 1, note 1. The Contract can be purchased at: [www.iccbooks.com/Product/ProductInfo.aspx?id=281].

33 The Guide (2nd edn) can be purchased at: [www.unidroit.org/english/guides/2007franchising/publication/main.htm].

34 The Model Law can be downloaded or purchased at: [www.unidroit.org/english/modellaws/2002franchise/main.htm].

10.6 Conclusion

Franchising is a very popular business method which can provide significant benefits to both the franchisor and franchisee. For the franchisee, doing business under an established name with a known brand image attracts an immediate customer base. For the franchisor, having others own and operate individual stores provides a steady stream of royalties with minimal effort and risk. Franchising is complicated, however, from both a business and a legal standpoint. These issues are compounded when a franchise seeks to expand internationally.

From a business perspective, many franchises fail when attempting to expand internationally. The reasons for the failures are numerous, but several fail due to lack of or incomplete research on the target market, selecting the wrong target market, a failure to account for local tastes and preferences, or attempting to expand quickly in a short period of time. From a legal perspective, franchising internationally is complex due to a host of reasons, including the importance of intellectual property rights (especially trademarks) to the franchise, the selection of the appropriate type of franchise agreement and differing legal systems (including competition and employment laws). For these reasons, it is important that lawyers from both the franchisor's home market as well as from the potential host market be involved in the negotiating process at an early stage.

This chapter provided an overview of these important issues before going into the law governing franchising in Australia in some detail. Examples of the regulation of franchising in other jurisdictions were also briefly covered. By using Australia and the other jurisdictions as examples, readers should be able to appreciate the wide and varied requirements and obligations needed before entering into a franchising agreement.

Questions

With regard to the case study at the beginning of this chapter:

1. What are the most important considerations when looking to become a franchisor or a franchisee?
2. How do the four forms of franchise arrangements differ?
3. What additional considerations are involved in franchising internationally?
4. What are the legal considerations and obligations which Chicken Bar should be made aware of and comply with if it decides to franchise the operation in Australia?
5. a. Which law applies to franchise agreements?
   b. Does Australian law apply to an Australian franchise seeking franchisees outside of Australia?
   c. What about to a foreign franchisor seeking franchisees in Australia?
6. a. What questions would you ask the owner of Chicken Bar in relation to the letter sent by Chick'n'Bar claiming infringement?
   b. What additional information do you require in order to offer advice in the matter?

7 Do franchising laws favour the franchisor or franchisee? Why?

8 How does competition law affect franchising?

9 a What are the similarities between the regulation of franchising in Australia and in the other jurisdictions mentioned in the chapter?

b What are the main points of departure?

10 a Based upon your understanding of the foreign law, would you advice Chicken Bar to expand to foreign jurisdictions?

b What other laws and issues should Chicken Bar consider?

PART V

Foreign Direct Investment

CHAPTER 11

FDI: issues, benefits and risks

FISHCO, a company based in Newcastle, Australia, provides technological, architectural, safety and commercial advice primarily on the construction of equipment used in the farming of salmon. In 2006, FISHCO entered into a joint venture with FARMCO, a US company engaged in the farming and supply of farmed salmon across California and throughout the USA. According to that agreement, FISHCO undertook to provide advice on the construction and development of fish farms for FARMCO at its premises on the Pacific Coast and along the rivers of California. In return for its services, FISHCO was given a 30 per cent stake in FARMCO in addition to a percentage of future sales. At the time of concluding the contract, FISHCO's investment was valued at US$50 million.

At the time the original investment was made, the Government of California supported the project and even promised future tax breaks if certain conditions were met, such as employing 65 per cent local workers, using 50 per cent US-made content in the construction of the farms, and exporting at least 75 per cent of the farmed salmon (so as not to compete with existing domestic supply). However, recent elections led to a change in government and the new state government opposes the development plans. In fact, the new government recently announced that it intended to expropriate fish farming facilities across the state in the public interest (at the time of the announcement, construction had begun on the fish farms but they were not yet operational). The government cited the 'unduly invasive' fish-farming methods currently in use in California, which allowed 'farmed salmon to escape from farms and negatively affect wild salmon as well as the salmon fishing industry generally, and that the farming of salmon was causing environmental damage' as the reason for the intended expropriations.

11.1 Introduction

A significant purpose of investment treaties is to provide legitimacy, predictability and security to foreign investors, while also protecting the interests of host countries. The perceived enemy is arbitrary state action and unfair treatment accorded to foreign investors. The ends sought are clear rules to both guide and govern foreign investment while also protecting the public interest of the countries in which foreign companies invest. Additional threats are the fear of a lack of clarity in the rules governing foreign investor practice, the flight of investor capital away from the application of arbitrary laws, and the risk that states might treat investors unfairly, and unequally compared to local investors. One way forward is to level the playing field in the international community: to establish internationally recognised rules governing foreign investments that are transparent in operation, that render states accountable for their actions, and that require foreign investors to comply with coherent standards of investment practice. The goal is to arrive at a predictable international investment regime that recognises differences in the interests and propensities of states without becoming supplicants of those differences.

This chapter traces the history and development of foreign direct investment in international investment law and analyses the investor protections that are currently available. Given that there are a number of multilateral and regional instruments regulating investment and close to 3000 bilateral trade and investment agreements, the analysis will be selective. Primacy will be given to those instruments that are most relevant to Australia, its nationals, and its corporations, in light of its role in the international community, including its primary and prospective investment partners. Emphasis will also be given to international investment agreements such as Chapter 11 of the North American Free Trade Agreement (NAFTA). While not directly applicable to Australia, Chapter 11 of the NAFTA is important in investment relations with any NAFTA party, notably the USA. In addition, the decisions on investment by NAFTA panels are influential internationally and have significantly impacted on the development of modern international investment law.

The chapter will also focus on the various standards of protection that are accorded to international investors under multilateral, regional and bilateral treaties, as well as under traditional principles of international law. Particular emphasis will be given to the protection of investors against expropriation, the standards with which states must comply in engaging in such expropriation, and how investors can make reasonably informed investment decisions in light of these standards. Further consideration will be given to a growing body of international arbitration law that has developed as a consequence of these international investment agreements, notably under the NAFTA, the International Centre for Settlement of Investment Disputes (ICSID) and the United Nations Commission on International Trade Law (UNCITRAL).

The specific intention is to provide a sound grasp of the issues Australian investors must consider before engaging in trans-border investment, including variations in the substantive laws governing such investments, the procedures by which they are applied to investors, and the legal consequences arising from their application. Importance will be placed on the need to appreciate salient differences in different investment treaty protocols, the distinctive manner in which arbitrators have construed them in particular contexts, and how such construction may influence investment practice in the future. Given the fluidity of investment law, it is not possible to provide wholly certain and predictable legal responses to investment conduct. What can be provided is an understanding of key issues faced in investment planning (including dispute resolution), underlying similarities and differences arising out of resort to different investment treaties, and the probability of arbitral tribunals protecting particular investors' practices.

The chapter will commence with an introduction to international investment law, including its meaning, as well as the perceived benefits and drawbacks of foreign investment to both the investor and the host nation. The chapter next discusses the regulation of foreign investment, both from an Australian and an international perspective. The chapter then examines the settlement of investment disputes, before analysing in some detail the provisions of the investment chapter in the NAFTA. In so doing, the section will analyse the principles, standards and rules that have evolved through that history, as well as their impact on current international investment law and practice.

11.2 Foreign direct investment: the basics

Foreign direct investment (FDI) plays an important role in international business and, more generally, the global economy.[1] For the company, FDI allows for expansion to new markets, shifting production facilities across borders, and accessing new or more advanced technology, products, skills and financing. For the host country or the foreign firm receiving the investment, FDI can provide new or updated technologies, much-needed capital infusion, innovation, updated and more efficient processes, organisational technologies and management skills, increased marketing networks, more highly skilled jobs, more competitive products, job creation and an impetus to economic development.[2]

A World Trade Organization (WTO) report on trade and investment provides a basic definition of FDI:

> Foreign direct investment (FDI) occurs when an investor based in one country (the home country) acquires an asset in another country (the host country) *with the intent to manage that asset.* The management dimension is what distinguishes FDI from portfolio investment in foreign stocks, bonds and other financial instruments. In most instances, both the investor and the asset it manages abroad are business firms. In such cases, the investor is typically referred to as the 'parent firm' and the asset as the 'affiliate' or 'subsidiary'.

There are three main categories of FDI:

1 *Equity capital* is the value of the multinational corporation's (MNC) investment in shares of an enterprise in a foreign country. An equity capital stake of 10 per cent or more of the ordinary shares or voting power in an incorporated enterprise, or its equivalent in an unincorporated enterprise, is normally considered as a threshold for the control of assets. This category includes both *mergers and acquisitions* and *Greenfield investments* (the creation of new facilities). Mergers and acquisitions are an important source of FDI for developed countries, although the relative importance varies considerably.

2 *Reinvested earnings* are the MNC's share of affiliate earnings not distributed as dividends or remitted to the MNC. Such retained profits by affiliates are assumed to

1 Useful websites include: [www.unctad.org]; [www.oecd.org]; [www.columbia.edu/cu/libraries/indiv/business/guides/fordinv.html]; [www.doc.gov]; [www.ita.gov]; [www.worldbank.org]; [www.opic.gov].

2 See [www.going-global.com/articles/understanding_foreign_direct_investment.htm].

be reinvested in the affiliate. This can represent up to 60 per cent of outward FDI in countries such as the USA and the UK.

3 *Other capital* refers to short- or long-term borrowing and lending of funds between the MNC and the affiliate.[3]

FDI could therefore involve a company from one country making a physical investment or taking a management interest in another country. The purchase from a company located in one country of a factory, machinery or equipment in a neighbouring country would certainly qualify as FDI, as would the building of a factory where none previously existed. On the other hand, the acquisition of stocks/shares as portfolio investment would ordinarily not be considered as FDI unless some element of management control attached to the purchase.

FDI can be classified by direction or by target. When classifying by direction, inward FDI is when foreign capital is invested in local resources; outward FDI (sometimes referred to as 'direct investment abroad'), is when local capital is invested in foreign resources. When classified by target, FDI can be accomplished either through a Greenfield investment or a merger or acquisition. If the FDI is in new facilities or the expansion of existing facilities, it is referred to as a Greenfield investment (also called 'insourcing'). Host nations usually target Greenfield investments because they are capital investments that directly create new jobs (often at higher rates than local firms) and production capacity, usually involve the transfer of technology and know-how, often involve investments in research and development, and can lead to increased linkages to the global market. However, Greenfield investments can lead to a reduction in market share for competing domestic firms if they are not as efficient or cannot produce to the same standards. Greenfield investments are also often criticised because profits are perceived to bypass the local economies and instead flow entirely back to the home economy of the MNC.

The primary type of FDI is through mergers and acquisitions. Mergers and acquisitions occur through the transfer of existing assets from local firms to foreign firms. Thus, a cross-border merger would occur when the assets and operation of firms from different countries are combined to establish a new legal entity. A cross-border acquisition occurs when the control of assets and operations is transferred from a local to a foreign company, with the local company becoming an affiliate of the foreign company.

A significant form of FDI today includes joint ventures; that is, when parties based in different home states engage in joint enterprises in one or the other home states and/ or in third jurisdictions. Joint ventures are frequently employed to capitalise investments and to acquire know-how in conducting the venture (such as specialized skills and products), as well as to gain access to foreign markets. Joint ventures may include a combination of investment options discussed above, such as Greenfield investments, as well as through mergers and acquisitions. Joint ventures are extremely prevalent in developing countries, where the government seeks to avoid majority foreign ownership (and control) by encouraging or requiring (whether officially or unofficially) foreign industry to take on a local partner prior to investing in the market.

---

3 WTO, 'Trade and Foreign Direct Investment', 9 October 1996, available at [www.wto.org/english/news_e/pres96_e/pr057_e.htm].

Jeffrey P Graham and R Barry Spaulding, 'Understanding Foreign Direct Investment' (2004)[4]

Proponents of foreign investment point out that the exchange of investment flows benefits both the home country (the country from which the investment originates) and the host country (the destination of the investment). Opponents of FDI note that multinational conglomerates are able to wield great power over smaller and weaker economies and can drive out much local competition. The truth lies somewhere in the middle.

For small and medium sized companies, FDI represents an opportunity to become more actively involved in international business activities. In the past 15 years, the classic definition of FDI ... has changed considerably. This notion of a change in the classic definition, however, must be kept in the proper context. Very clearly, over 2/3 of direct foreign investment is still made in the form of fixtures, machinery, equipment and buildings. Moreover, larger multinational corporations and conglomerates still make the overwhelming percentage of FDI. But, with the advent of the Internet, the increasing role of technology, loosening of direct investment restrictions in many markets and decreasing communication costs means that newer, non-traditional forms of investment will play an important role in the future. Many governments, especially in industrialized and developed nations, pay very close attention to foreign direct investment because the investment flows into and out of their economies can and does have a significant impact. In the United States, the Bureau of Economic Analysis, a section of the US Department of Commerce, is responsible for collecting economic data about the economy, including information about foreign direct investment flows. Monitoring this data is very helpful in trying to determine the impact of such investments on the overall economy, but is especially helpful in evaluating industry segments. State and local governments watch closely because they want to track their foreign investment attraction programs for successful outcomes.

How has FDI changed in the past decade?

As mentioned above, the overwhelming majority of foreign direct investment is made in the form of fixtures, machinery, equipment and buildings. This investment is achieved or accomplished mostly via mergers & acquisitions. In the case of traditional manufacturing, this has been the primary mechanism for investment and it has been heretofore very efficient. Within the past decade, however, there has been a dramatic increase in the number of technology startups and this, together with the rise in prominence of Internet usage, has fostered increasing changes in foreign investment patterns. Many of these high tech startups are very small companies that have grown out of research & development projects often affiliated with major universities and with some government sponsorship. Unlike traditional manufacturers, many of these companies do not require huge manufacturing plants and immense warehouses to store inventory. Another factor to consider is the number of companies whose primary product is an intellectual property right such as a software program or a software-based technology or process. Companies such as these can be housed almost anywhere and therefore making a capital investment in them does not require huge outlays for fixtures, machinery and plants.

In many cases, large companies still play a dominant role in investment activities in small, high tech oriented companies. However, unlike in the past, these larger companies are not

4 Available at [www.going-global.com/articles/understanding_foreign_direct_investment.htm].

necessarily acquiring smaller companies outright. There are several reasons for this, but the most important one is most likely the risk associated with such high tech ventures. In the case of mature industries, the products are well defined. The manufacturer usually wants to get closer to its foreign market or wants to circumvent some trade barrier by making a direct foreign investment. The major risk here is that you do not sell enough of the product that you manufactured. However, you have added additional capacity and in the case of multinational corporations this capacity can be used in a variety of ways.

High tech ventures tend to have longer incubation periods. That is, the product tends to require significant development time. In the case of software and other intellectual property type products, the product is constantly changing, even before it hits the marketplace. This makes the investment decision more complicated. When you invest in fixtures and machinery, you know what the real and book value of your investment will be. When you invest in a high tech venture, there is always an element of uncertainty. Unfortunately, the ... spate of dot.com failures [in the early 2000s] is quite illustrative of this point.

Therefore, the expanded role of technology and intellectual property has changed the foreign direct investment playing field. Companies are still motivated to make foreign investments, but because of the vagaries of technology investments, they are now finding new vehicles to accomplish their goals. Consider the following:

- Licensing and technology transfer. Licensing and technology transfer have been essential in promoting collaboration between the academic and business communities. Ever since legal hurdles were removed that allowed universities to hold title to research and development done in their labs, licensing agreements have helped turned raw technology into finished products that are viable in competitive marketplaces. With some help from a variety of government agencies in the form of grants for R&D as well as other financial assistance for such things as incubator programs, once timid college researchers are now stepping out and becoming cutting edge entrepreneurs. These strategic alliances have had a serious impact in several high tech industries, including but not limited to: medical and agricultural biotechnology, computer software engineering, telecommunications, advanced materials processing, ceramics, thin materials processing, photonics, digital multimedia production and publishing, optics and imaging and robotics and automation. Industry clusters are now growing up around the university labs where their derivative technologies were first discovered and nurtured. Licensing agreements allow companies to take full advantage of new and exciting technologies, while limiting their overall risk to royalty payments until a particular technology is fully developed and thus ready to put new products into the manufacturing pipeline.
- Reciprocal distribution agreements. Actually, this type of strategic alliance is more trade-based, but in a very real sense it does in fact represent a type of direct investment. Basically, two companies, usually within the same or affiliated industries, agree to act as a national distributor for each other's products. The classical example is to be found in the furniture industry. A US-based manufacturer of tables signs a reciprocal distribution agreement with a Spanish-based manufacturer of chairs. Both companies gain direct access to the other's distribution network without having to pay distributor support payments and other related expenses found within the distribution channel and neither company can hurt the other's market for its products. Without such an agreement in place, the Spanish manufacturer might very well have to invest

in a national sales office to coordinate its distributor network, manage warehousing, inventory and shipping as well as to handle administrative tasks such as accounting, public relations and advertising.

- Joint venture and other hybrid strategic alliances. The more traditional joint venture is bilateral, that is it involves two parties who are within the same industry who are partnering for some strategic advantage. Typical reasons might include a need for access to proprietary technology that might tip the competitive edge in another competitor's favor, desire to gain access to intellectual capital in the form of ultra-expensive human resources, access to heretofore closed channels of distribution in key regions of the world. One very good reason why many joint ventures only involve two parties is the difficulty in integrating different corporate cultures. With two domestic companies from the same country, it would still be very difficult. However, with two companies from different cultures, it is almost impossible at times. This is probably why pure joint ventures have a fairly high failure rate only five years after inception. Joint ventures involving three or more parties are usually called syndicates and are most often formed for specific projects such as large construction or public works projects that might involve a wide variety of expertise and resources for successful completion. In some cases, syndicates are actually easier to manage because the project itself sets certain limits on each party and close cooperation is not always a prerequisite for ultimate success of the endeavor.
- Portfolio investment. Yes, we know that you're paying attention and no we're not trying to trip you up here. Remember our definition of foreign direct investment as it pertains to controlling interest. For most of the latter part of the 20th century when FDI became an issue, a company's portfolio investments were not considered a direct investment if the amount of stock and/or capital was not enough to garner a significant voting interest amongst shareholders or owners. However, two or three companies with 'soft' investments in another company could find some mutual interests and use their shareholder power effectively for management control. This is another form of strategic alliance, sometimes called 'shadow alliances'. So, while most company portfolio investments do not strictly qualify as a direct foreign investment, there are instances within a certain context that they are in fact a real direct investment.

Why is FDI important for any consideration of going global?

The simple answer is that making a direct foreign investment allows companies to accomplish several tasks:

- Avoiding foreign government pressure for local production.
- Circumventing trade barriers, hidden and otherwise.
- Making the move from domestic export sales to a locally-based national sales office.
- Capability to increase total production capacity.
- Opportunities for co-production, joint ventures with local partners, joint marketing arrangements, licensing, etc.

A more complete response might address the issue of global business partnering in very general terms. While it is nice that many business writers like the expression, 'think globally, act locally', this often used cliché does not really mean very much to the average business executive in a small and medium sized company. The phrase does have significant connotations for multinational corporations. But for executives in SME's [small and medium enterprises], it is still just another buzzword. The simple explanation for this is the difference in perspective between executives of multinational corporations and small and medium sized companies. Multinational corporations are almost always concerned with worldwide manufacturing capacity and proximity to major markets. Small and medium sized companies tend to be more concerned with selling their products in overseas markets. The advent of the Internet has ushered in a new and very different mindset that tends to focus more on access issues. SME's in particular are now focusing on access to markets, access to expertise and most of all access to technology.

What would be some of the basic requirements for companies considering a foreign investment?

Depending on the industry sector and type of business, a foreign direct investment may be an attractive and viable option. With rapid globalization of many industries and vertical integration rapidly taking place on a global level, at a minimum a firm needs to keep abreast of global trends in their industry. From a competitive standpoint, it is important to be aware of whether a company's competitors are expanding into a foreign market and how they are doing that. At the same time, it also becomes important to monitor how globalization is affecting domestic clients. Often, it becomes imperative to follow the expansion of key clients overseas if an active business relationship is to be maintained.

New market access is also another major reason to invest in a foreign country. At some stage, export of product or service reaches a critical mass of amount and cost where foreign production or location begins to be more cost effective. Any decision on investing is thus a combination of a number of key factors including:

- assessment of internal resources
- competitiveness
- market analysis
- market expectations.

From an internal resources standpoint, does the firm have senior management support for the investment and the internal management and system capabilities to support the set up time, as well as ongoing management of a foreign subsidiary? Has the company conducted extensive market research involving both the industry, product and local regulations governing foreign investment which will set the broad market parameters for any investment decision? Is there a realistic assessment in place of what resource utilization the investment will entail? Has information on local industry and foreign investment regulations, incentives, profit retention, financing, distribution, and other factors been completely analyzed to determine the most viable vehicle for entering the market (greenfield, acquisition, merger, joint venture, etc)? Has a plan been drawn up with reasonable expectations for expansion into the market through that local vehicle? If the foreign economy, industry or foreign investment climate is characterized by government regulation, have the relevant government agencies been contacted and concurred? Have political risk and foreign exchange risks been factored into the business plan?

Outside of the analysis of internal resources, a vast amount of information is needed to assess the viability and ultimate method of foreign investment as outlined above.

... ...

Readers of this chapter should have already formed the conclusion that there are many positive and negative factors to take into account when a company is considering investing abroad. Likewise, there is a host of positive and negative factors that a host country must consider when formulating its investment policy.

On the investor side, the benefits of foreign investment include expanding the business to new markets, as well as shifting production facilities in order to make use of cheaper land, labour, tax laws, employment opportunities, lower transportation costs, and a multitude of other related benefits. However, there are many political and economic risks to foreign investment. These risks, or perceived obstacles to doing business abroad, involve the existence and interrelation of various factors such as:

- Corruption;
- Policy instability or uncertainty;
- Crime, theft, kidnapping, or social disorder;
- Presence of organised crime or localised mafia;
- Reintroduction of inflation;
- Problems securing financing;
- Exchange rate difficulties;
- Anticompetitive practices;
- Infrastructure deficiencies;
- Unclear systems of taxation and unclear tax regulations;
- Unreliable judiciary and differences in the legal system; and
- Property seizures, such as confiscation, expropriation, and nationalisation.

For the host nation, positive impacts of foreign investment include:

- Increased domestic capital formation;
- Innovation and advanced technology transfer;
- Management skill transfer;
- Increased marketing networks;
- Targeted regional and sectoral development;
- Fostering internal competition and entrepreneurship;
- Favourable effect on balance of payments;
- Increased domestic employment; and
- Increased economic development.

Potential negative impacts of foreign investment include:

- Industrial sector dominance in the domestic market;
- Technological dependence on foreign technology sources;
- Disturbance of domestic economic plans in favour of FDI-directed projects;
- Cultural change created by the infusion of foreign culture and foreign business practices;
- Corruption of local officials by unethical foreign investors; and
- Potential interference in domestic economic and political decision making in the host country by the home government of the multinational corporation.

Whatever the perceived threats and risks of FDI, the scale of FDI has risen quite dramatically over the past few decades, with a significant increase occurring between 1985 and 1995, when the total annual global flow of FDI rose from US$60 billion to US$315 billion.[5] In 2007, the total flow of FDI grew to an estimated US$1.5 trillion.[6] Encouragingly, FDI flows increased from 2006 levels in developed countries, developing countries and countries in transition.[7] Moreover, it has been suggested that the sales of foreign affiliates of MNCs now exceed the value of world trade in goods and services, that intra-firm trade among MNCs accounts for approximately one-third of world trade and that MNC exports to non-affiliates account for another third of world trade, with the remaining one-third accounted for by trade among national (non-MNC) firms.[8] Such high levels of FDI and intra-firm trade could not have been possible without the reduction of tariffs and other barriers accomplished by the General Agreement on Trade and Tariffs (GATT)/WTO, advances in communication, information systems and shipping technologies, and the willingness of nations to allow foreign investment in order to further economic development.

The financial and credit crisis that began in late 2007 and worsened in 2008, however, will almost certainly affect total volumes of FDI into the future as companies issue profit warnings, worry about demand, and struggle to raise capital and secure credit. In fact, preliminary data suggests a reduction in total FDI of more than 20 per cent in 2008 with European countries being particularly vulnerable.[9] FDI is forecast to drop even further in 2009.[10]

11.3 The regulation of FDI

Investment is regulated in some form by all countries, but the extent of the regulation varies widely. In the main, developed countries have been historically more welcoming of foreign investment than developing countries. Of course, some developed countries have occasionally enacted provisions that restrict or otherwise curtail investment, while some developing countries welcome foreign investment.

---

5 [www.wto.org/english/news_e/pres96_e/pr057_e.htm]. FDI flows into developing countries have increased from a yearly average of US$10 billion in the 1970s and less than US$20 billion in the 1980s to US$26.7 billion in 1990, US$179 billion in 1998 and US$208 billion in 1999.

6 United Nations Conference on Trade and Development (UNCTAD), 'Foreign Direct Investment Reached New Record in 2007', Press Release, 8 January 2008, available at [www.unctad.org/Templates/webflyer.asp?docid=9439&intItemID=1528&lang=1].

7 Ibid.

8 WTO, 'Trade and Foreign Direct Investment', 9 October 1996, available at [www.wto.org/english/news_e/pres96_e/pr057_e.htm].

9 Reduction in Europe includes the UK down 51 per cent, Germany down 49 per cent and Italy down 94 per cent. FDI in Singapore dropped 57 per cent, while the USA dropped only 6 per cent. Russia (18 per cent), China (11 per cent) and Brazil (21 per cent) all gained. See UNCTAD, 'Global Foreign Direct Investment Now in Decline—and Estimated to have Fallen during 2008', Press Release, 19 January 2009, available at [www.unctad.org/Templates/webflyer.asp?docid=10930&intItemID=1528&lang=1].

10 Ibid.

This section first provides a brief sketch of Australia's regulation of foreign investment before discussing investment regulations at the international level. While reading this section, it is important to think about the reasons why both the foreign investors as well as the host nation would want to conclude comprehensive bilateral or multilateral agreements on investment. What does the investor gain? What do the host countries gain? What do they lose?

11.3.1 Regulation of foreign investment in Australia

Like many of its trading partners, Australia has actively encouraged foreign investment while at the same time remaining interested in regulating the nature and extent of foreign ownership of Australian assets. In this regard, Australia retains the right to examine significant foreign investment proposals in all sectors to ensure they do not raise issues contrary to the national interest. Australia accomplishes this primarily through the *Foreign Acquisitions and Takeovers Act 1975* (Cth) (FATA), together with associated regulations and policy, and certain sector- or company-specific legislation.[11] The Foreign Investment Review Board (FIRB) administers the FATA and advises the Treasurer on foreign investment policy. The FIRB generally receives between 4500 and 6000 proposals for foreign investment approval annually.[12]

The FATA applies to share and asset acquisitions, investment in urban land, and agreements relating to the operation or control of Australian businesses. In every case, the FATA sets out a number of qualifications and procedures relating to foreign investment in Australia. For example, proposals from foreigners to make a Greenfield investment where the value of the company's assets is $10 million or more are not covered by the FATA; however they still must be notified to the Treasurer. The FATA also requires that foreign investors notify the Treasurer, through the FIRB, of certain acquisitions of interests in Australian corporations and land. In addition, the FATA empowers the Treasurer to make orders in regard to investment proposals which the Treasurer deems contrary to Australia's national interests. This more onerous requirement relates to, *inter alia*, certain share acquisitions whereby proposals to acquire Australian businesses must be notified to and receive the explicit approval of the Treasurer. For instance, proposals seeking to acquire interests of 15 per cent or more (by a single foreign entity or person) and 40 per cent or more (by two or more foreign entities or persons) in Australian businesses, or prescribed corporations whose assets are valued over $50 million, must be notified to the Treasurer and can be rejected if considered to be contrary to the 'national interest'. In the alternative, the Treasurer can approve the proposal subject to conditions that address national interest concerns.

The vagueness of the 'national interest' criterion is worrisome for many investors, who see it as arbitrary and subjective. This is especially the case during economic downturns. During such periods, economic nationalism increases and potential takeovers and mergers are more closely scrutinised. A recent example of this is

11 See for example the *Qantas Sale Act 1992* (Cth); the *Telstra Corporation Act 1991* (Cth); and the *Broadcasting Services Act 1992* (Cth).

12 For more information and statistics, see the website of the FIRB at [www.firb.gov.au/content/default.asp].

Chinalco's (a Chinese state-owned enterprise) US$19.5 billion investment in Australian mining company Rio Tinto. At the time of writing, the Treasurer (Wayne Swan) was considering whether to scuttle the deal on grounds of 'national interest';[13] since writing Rio has withdrawn from the deal in favour of a joint venture with BHP. Nevertheless, it is important to note that international transactions involving major Australian companies that impact upon the national interest are subject to governmental scrutiny and approval. The provision was last invoked in 2001, when the then Treasurer (Peter Costello) blocked the proposed bid by Royal Dutch Shell for Woodside Petroleum.

Australia also maintains certain restrictions, including limits on equity participation, in a few areas where foreign investment is thought to generate community concern. For example, Australia maintains equity restrictions that virtually exclude foreign ownership of Telstra, CSL, Qantas and other Australian international airlines, federal leased airports and shipping. Australia also requires that all FDI and all portfolio foreign investment of 5 per cent or more in the media sector require prior approval. These restrictions are not affected by Australian bilateral investment treaties (BITs) and free trade agreements (FTAs), including the much-discussed Australia–USA Free Trade Agreement (AUSFTA).

11.3.2 International regulation

The significance and regulation of foreign investment in Australia, or foreign investment by Australians abroad, is best understood by reflecting on the international environment in which such investment takes place. It is also important to appreciate the regulation of FDI that arises from multilateral, regional and bilateral agreements, not limited to those to which Australia is a party. As a practical matter, an Australian investing abroad must also be cognisant of the domestic law of the 'host' country, including the prospective impact of its law upon investments there.

This section will begin with an historical discussion of the global investment environment, notably the GATT and the WTO. Subsequent sections will consider the impact of global, regional and domestic laws upon foreign investment.

11.3.2a GATT/WTO

Following the Second World War, a new era of liberalisation of trade and investment began. The purpose was to reduce protectionist barriers to trade and investment that had preceded the War, and to oversee the development of institutional vehicles to guide the process of liberalisation. The liberalisation of trade was heralded by the adoption of the GATT in 1947. Investment, however, was excluded from its ambit.[14]

---

13 It should be noted that the investment is also awaiting approval from the governments of China, the UK and the USA, as well as regulatory and competition approvals in Australia and Germany and Rio Tinto's shareholders.

14 This is despite the fact that investment was included in the Havana Charter, which was designed to create an International Trade Organization (ITO) in the mid-1940s. However, due to resistance from the US Congress, the ITO never formed and the Havana Charter was abandoned. See S Lester & B Mercurio, *World Trade Law: Text, Materials and Commentary*, Hart, Oxford & Portland, 2008, pp 633–4.

Despite the fact that the GATT did not deal with the issue of investment, the contracting parties of the GATT adopted a resolution in 1955 on International Investment for Economic Development in which they 'urged' countries to conclude BITs as a way to encourage greater trade.[15] Moreover, the issue was directly addressed in the GATT panel decision of *Canada—Administration of the Foreign Investment Review Act (FIRA)*.[16] In that case, the USA complained that Canada's requirement that foreign investors provide undertakings pertaining to the purchase of certain products from domestic sources (local content requirements) and to the export of a certain amount or percentage of output (export performance requirements) as a condition for the approval of investment projects were inconsistent with Canada's GATT obligations. The Panel concluded that the local content requirements were inconsistent with the 'national treatment' obligation of Article III:4 of the GATT, but that the export performance requirements were not inconsistent with GATT obligations. It is important to remember that Canada's right to regulate foreign investment was not the issue; the issue was only whether Canada's trade-related measures under its foreign investment regulations were consistent with the GATT as it relates to trade obligations.

The WTO website emphasises the importance of this decision by stating:

> The panel decision in the *FIRA* case was significant in that it confirmed that existing obligations under the GATT were applicable to performance requirements imposed by governments in an investment context in so far as such requirements involve trade-distorting measures. At the same time, the panel's conclusion that export performance requirements were not covered by the GATT also underscored the limited scope of existing GATT disciplines with respect to such trade-related performance requirements.[17]

Investment was discussed further as part of the Uruguay Round of trade talks, which led to the creation of the WTO. The result was a very limited agreement, the Agreement on Trade-Related Investment Measures (the TRIMs Agreement), which essentially merely interprets and clarifies the GATT provisions on 'national treatment' for imported goods (Article III) and on quantitative restrictions on imports or exports of goods (Article XI) as they relate to investment measures. In other words, the TRIMs Agreement merely prohibits specific trade-distorting performance requirements on foreign investments, but does not directly regulate nor harmonise the regulation of foreign investment. The Agreement, therefore, has a limited focus, which relates merely to existing GATT disciplines on trade in goods; it does not regulate foreign investment per se, and it does not address measures such as local equity requirements, technology transfer and licensing requirements, local manufacturing requirements, personnel entry restrictions or local employment requirements.

---

15 International Investment for Economic Development Resolution, 4 March 1955, GATT BISD (3rd Supp), pp 49–50.

16 BISD 30S/140, 1984.

17 Technical Information on Trade and Investment, available at [www.wto.org/English/tratop_e/invest_e/invest_info_e.htm].

11.3.2b BITs and FTAs

Efforts to liberalise, or at least add certainty to, foreign investment began in earnest in the 1950s and 1960s. These efforts were lead by the USA, which concluded a series of trade treaties designed to encourage foreign investment. These treaties are known as Friendship, Commerce and Navigation Treaties (FCNTs).

The earmark of the FCNTs was the provision of both national treatment and most-favoured nation status to foreign investors. The FCNTs also provided for dispute resolution. Ordinarily, investors were required to first exhaust local remedies in the affected state. However, after they had done so, provision was made for submission of a dispute to the International Court of Justice with the consent of the affected state.

The FCNTs embodied the power of developed states to engage in FDI and offended certain developing countries; they were also resisted by the Soviet Union and its allies as illustrations of exploitive capitalism. As a result, they had a comparatively short span of influence and were offset by barriers built by states to protect themselves from FDI. They were also increasingly under siege as developing states gained power within the multilateral community, and as a plethora of developing states asserted their economic rights over resources once dominated by the empowered few. This movement culminated with the General Assembly of the United Nations adoption in 1974 of the Declaration of the New International Economic Order, which recognised state sovereignty over natural resources and other economic activities.

A countervailing movement, led by the Soviet Union, but including many developing states, sought international recognition for the right of states to expropriate foreign investment, without having to pay compensation of fair market value. The result was that, while the United Nation's Charter of Economic Rights and Duties of States recognised the right of states to expropriate foreign investment, it did not compel the payment of compensation and, arguably, it subjected expropriation to the vagaries of national laws as distinct from international standards of due process and compensation.[18]

The reincarnation of the FCNT is the modern BIT. UNCTAD provides the following definition of BITs:

> Bilateral investment treaties (BITs) are agreements between two countries for the reciprocal encouragement, promotion and protection of investments in each other's territories by companies based in either country. Treaties typically cover the following areas: scope and definition of investment, admission and establishment, national treatment, most-favoured-nation treatment, fair and equitable treatment, compensation in the event of expropriation or damage to the investment, guarantees of free transfers of funds, and dispute settlement mechanisms, both state–state and investor–state.[19]

Starting with Western European states in the 1960s, nations began to conclude a series of BITs to preserve FDI in the face of a multilateral treaty process that offered

---

18 United Nations General Assembly, Charter of Economic Rights and Duties of States, GA Res 3281 (XXIX), UN GAOR, 29th Session 2315th Plen Mtg, UN Doc A/RES/3281 (XXIX) (12 Dec 1974), reprinted in 14 *ILM* 251 (1975). See also CN Brower & J Tepe, Jr, 'The Charter of Economic Rights and Duties of States: A Reflection or a Rejection of International Law?' (1975) 9 *Int'l Law* 295; B Weston, 'The Charter of Economic Rights and Duties of States and the Deprivation of Foreign Owned Wealth' (1981) 75 *Am J Int'l L* 437.

19 UNCTAD, 'What are BITs?', available at [www.unctadxi.org/templates/Page_1006.aspx].

investors scant protection in the face of the combined voting force of the Eastern Bloc and developing states in the United Nations. Of note, the USA was initially reluctant to conclude BITs, preferring instead to concentrate on building free markets for US investment; however, it began to conclude BITs more actively in 1998.[20]

The primary features of BITs have always been to undermine discriminatory practices of states in relation to foreign investment. The subsidiary goal was to carve principles, standards and rules by which to regulate foreign investment consistent with these features. Key features usually include:

- Applying either national or most-favoured nation treatment to foreign investment, depending on which better protected the investor;
- Making provision for standards to govern the expropriation of investments and the payment of prompt, fair and reasonable compensation;
- Making provision for the transfer of funds for investment purposes at reasonable exchange rates;
- Limiting states in the 'performance requirements' they can impose on foreign investors;
- Prohibiting states from imposing requirements that investors hire local nationals; and
- Prohibiting foreign investors from submitting disputes to arbitration, as distinct from domestic courts of law, in the pursuit of fair and equitable treatment.

The inclusion of commercial arbitration is noteworthy, and is a shift from the general treaties of friendship grounded in diplomacy (which often included the submission of disputes to the International Court of Justice) to investment agreements that provide both distinct processes for government investment and applicable remedies.[21]

BITs are sometimes negotiated between developed countries and developing country partners, and have generally been regarded as adhesive in nature. Developed states present them as a *fait accompli* to developing states, which sign off on them for fear of otherwise being excluded from the BIT process. While developed states traditionally used BITs primarily to protect their FDI, developing states used them to protect their nationals and local markets. This is not to say that developed states were not protectionist; it merely acknowledges that they had less reason to protect their developed local markets and more sophisticated nationals than developing countries seeking foreign markets for their products.

Understandably, the process of concluding BITs has not been without controversy. The USA, notably, seeks to rely on customary international law to ensure that foreign states provide prompt, adequate and reasonable compensation in the event of an expropriation. Prospective investment partners sometimes blanch at the prospective impact of such customs and withdraw.

---

20 See US Bilateral Investment Treaty Program, State Department, Fact Sheet, 16 March 2005, available at [www.state.gov/e/eb/rls/fs/22422.htm].

21 See for example LE Trakman, 'Arbitrating Options: Turning a Morass into a Panacea' (2008) 31 *UNSW Law Journal* 292; LE Trakman, 'The Proliferation of Free Trade Agreements: Bane or Beauty?' (2008) 42 *Journal of International Trade Law* 367 ; C Schreuer, 'Fair and Equitable Treatment in Arbitral Practice' (2005) 6 *Journal of World Investment & Trade* 357.

Despite these controversies, BITs have grown in recent decades, with close to 3000 concluded, along with a number of FTAs that provide for investment.[22] Australia has negotiated 21 BITs, and has also negotiated FTAs with New Zealand (1983), Singapore (2003), Thailand (2005), the USA (2005) and Chile (2008). At the time of writing, Australia is also negotiating with the Association of Southeast Asian Nations (ASEAN) (together with New Zealand), China, the Gulf Cooperation Council, Malaysia and the Trans-Pacific Strategic Economic Partnership Agreement (Brunei, Dar es Salaam, Chile, New Zealand and Singapore), as well as considering negotiating with India, Korea and Indonesia. The majority of these FTAs will contain substantive investment obligations.

In developing domestic foreign investment policy, Australia has generally been receptive to foreign investment on the assumption that foreign investment enhances the economy and stimulates growth. However, as we will see from the extract in Section 11.4.2, Australia is interested in regulating the nature and extent of foreign ownership of Australian assets. Australian BITs and investment provisions in FTAs are fairly representative of most agreements negotiated by other nations. Of note, most BITs and FTAs include investment provisions providing for the resolution of disputes between the state parties to such agreements, and provide that a private investor from a partner state can proceed through arbitration against a host state that has allegedly violated the BIT in regard to that investor. However, Australia and some of its primary trade partners notably the USA, have avoided establishing a distinctive regime for resolving investment disputes (such as through a special arbitral regime set up under Chapter 11 of the NAFTA between the USA, Canada and Mexico).

11.3.3 Investment provisions in focus

As should be apparent from the above discussion, the scope of the modern BITs and FTAs are quite extensive (providing for, *inter alia*, national treatment, most-favoured nation treatment, fair and equitable treatment, restrictions on TRIMs (such as limitations or a prohibition on performance requirements), severe limitations on expropriations and some form of dispute settlement (either state–state or investor–state)). In addition, a small number of BITs contain provisions on the movement of certain employees. In general, most BITs and FTAs covering investment apply to all sectors, with any exempted sectors expressly stated in the agreement. It should also be apparent, or at least unsurprising, that these agreements have been the subject of much criticism for potentially overreaching into domestic public policy making.

There now follows an overview first of the investment provisions in the NAFTA, and second of the investment provisions of the AUSFTA. The NAFTA is discussed as it is the first FTA to provide a comprehensive chapter on investment; accordingly, it continues to be relied upon as a model for many other investment agreements and its dispute settlement mechanism has been frequently invoked. We discuss the AUSFTA

22 Vandevelde writes that in 1969 there were only 75 BITs. During the 1970s, nine BITs were negotiated per year; that rate doubled in the 1980s and has been increasingly exponentially ever since: see KJ Vandevelde, 'Of Politics and Markets: The Shifting Ideology of the BITs' (1993) 11 *Int'l Tax & Bus Law* 159 at 172. See also *Research Note: Recent Developments in International Investment Agreements*, United Nations Conference on Trade and Development (30 Aug 2005) (UNCTAD), available at [www.unctad.org].

as it is not only Australia's most important FTA to date, but it also represents the most comprehensive investment chapter in an Australian agreement and will no doubt be used as an at least partial template in further Australian FTA negotiations.

11.4 Investment provisions: BITs, FTAs and multilateral agreements

11.4.1 The NAFTA, Chapter 11

The NAFTA, a treaty between the USA, Mexico and Canada was the first modern agreement that protected investor 'rights' of nationals of one country while simultaneously circumscribing government behaviour in relation to investors from partner countries. In so doing, the NAFTA brought together parties with significantly different investment philosophies:

- The USA adhered to the model of a large-scale global superpower. Its interest was as a capital-intensive exporter seeking full compensation for its nationals engaged in exporting to NAFTA parties, including full and fair compensation for expropriation.
- A proponent of the Calvo Principle adopted by developing countries generally,[23] Mexico favoured preferential treatment for nationals, protective investment legislation, less-than-full compensation for foreign nationals and resistance to international treaties that varied from its national self-interest.[24]
- Canada represented the balance between these two philosophies: general support for the liberalisation of investment law, a fear of US investment expansionism, and a strong interest in protecting Canada's traditions and distinctiveness.[25]

The addition of Chapter 11 into the NAFTA has proven to be controversial, with criticism coming from sources as diverse as the US Congress[26] and antiglobalisation groups on the fringe.

However much the intention of the USA and Canadian negotiators may have been to blunt Mexico's history of confiscation,[27] the history of Chapter 11 of the NAFTA to

23 The Calvo Principle is a construct of an Argentine politician which requires foreign investor disputes to be resolved before local courts rather than through international tribunals. For comments on the Principle, somewhat from a US perspective, see B Cremades, 'Disputes Arising Out Of Foreign Direct Investment in Latin America: A New Look at the Calvo Doctrine and Jurisdictional Issues' (2004) 59 *Disp Resol J* 78.

24 See for example LE Trakman, 'Arbitrating under Chapter 11 of the NAFTA: A Mexican Investor vs the US', in *Doing Business in Mexico*, Transnational Leg Pub, New York, 2002.

25 For Canadian perspectives on Chapter 11, see for example L Ritchie Dawson (ed), *Whose Rights?: The NAFTA Chapter 11 Debate* (The Centre for Trade Law and Policy, Carleton University, Ottawa, 2002).

26 See for example 107 Cong Rec S4594 (21 May 2002).

27 The nationalisation of the Mexican oil industry is the best known example of Mexican expropriation. Other expropriations revolve around a series of devaluations of the Mexican peso, giving rise to litigation. See *Callejo v Bancomer*, 764 F2d 101(5th Cir) (1985).

date has done more to challenge the USA and Canada's resort to protective measures against foreign investors. As a result, the USA—previously the staunch protector of the foreign investor—has shifted away from such protection and liberalisation of investment. Typifying this attitudinal shift is the attempt by the USA to 'renegotiate' aspects of Chapter 11 of the NAFTA through 'clarification' of its most controversial provisions on the nature and limits of expropriation, national treatment, fair and equitable treatment, and consultation between NAFTA parties on its application in the future.[28] Moreover, the USA has also proposed that US courts be empowered to review Chapter 11 awards and that arbitral decisions be vacated for conflicting with US law.[29] These shifts from investment expansionism to protectionism are best understood in light of the mechanisms contained in Chapter 11, particularly those relating to the resolution of investment disputes.

11.4.1a NAFTA obligations

Chapter 11 is divided into two parts: Section A includes a list of rights to investment protection; Section B sets out the safeguard measures which investors may use to protect those rights. Each will be addressed in turn.

Section A

Substantive rights

The substantive provisions of Chapter 11, contained in Section A, are extensive, providing protection to NAFTA investors on an almost inexhaustible range of investments.[30] Despite the breadth of the list, however, Section A also includes reservations, exceptions, limitations and exclusions. Furthermore, it exempts NAFTA parties from certain non-conforming measures, including but not limited to national security, culturally sensitive areas, and industries such as telecommunications and Mexico's petroleum industry and sector-specific national programs.[31] Certain economic activities, such as selected financial and social services, are also reserved to the parties.[32] Finally, inconsistencies between Chapter 11 and any other Chapter will result in the other Chapter prevailing.[33]

NAFTA investors are protected against discrimination by standards of national treatment and most-favoured nation treatment (MFN).[34] Provision is also made for minimum standards of treatment, prohibiting NAFTA parties from imposing certain

---

28 Some Canadians have echoed this sentiment: see 'Canadian Memo on Investor–State Provisions', 13 November 1998, available at [www.insidetrade.com/sec-i/as_web.exe?SEC_IT1999+D+1750780].

29 For the proposal that Chapter 11 arbitral awards be subject to review by the Court of International Trade in the USA, see S3216 106th Cong (2000).

30 See NAFTA, Article 1139.

31 See NAFTA, Chapter 11, Articles 1101, 1108, 1112. See also the NAFTA, Annexes I–VI.

32 See NAFTA, Article 1101(2), (4).

33 See NAFTA, Articles 1112, 1138.

34 See NAFTA, Articles 1102, 1103.

performance requirements on foreign investors and compensating them for specific kinds of expropriation.[35]

Under national treatment, each party is required to treat investors and investments, of another NAFTA party no less favourably than it treats its own investors and their investments.[36] Compliance involves a comparison of relative treatment received and the justification for differentiation in treatment. If a prima facie case of discrimination is established, the onus shifts onto the other NAFTA party to justify the dissimilarity in treatment.[37]

Under MFN treatment, each party is obligated to provide NAFTA investors and investments with treatment no less favourable than it gives to investors and investments of any other party or non-party in comparable circumstances. These circumstances include establishing, acquiring, expanding, managing, conducting, operating, selling or otherwise disposing of investments. The application of the MFN standard also involves a comparison between the treatment accorded to a local compared to an investor of another NAFTA party. While the MFN standard is subject to reservations, contained in Annex IV, it is more expansive than national treatment. In particular, Article 1104 requires that NAFTA parties accord NAFTA investors with no less favourable treatment than that promised under any other treaty concluded after the NAFTA.

Standard of treatment

NAFTA investors and investments are guaranteed the optimal level of protection. Article 1104, dealing with standard of treatment, provides:

> Each Party shall accord to investors of another Party and to investments of investors of another Party the better of the treatment required by Articles 1102 and 1103.

Article 1104 includes a mechanism that grants NAFTA investors and investments the best available protection. It establishes a standard of treatment in cases where it is not clear whether national treatment or MFN treatment would accord NAFTA investors the best treatment. It obligates each party to accord treatment to investors and investments of the other parties which is the better of the treatment required by national treatment and MFN treatment.

Chapter 11 of the NAFTA also provides that NAFTA investors receive minimum standards of treatment under international law (see Article 1105). This ensures that, if a NAFTA party provides its nationals with a standard of treatment below such international standards, that party will still comply with minimum international standards in respect of the NAFTA investors of other parties, such as in the event of armed

35 The four standards of treatment under Chapter 11 are set out in Article 1102 (national treatment); Article 1103 (MFN treatment); Article 1104 (standard of treatment); and Article 1105 (minimum standard of treatment). For further information, see T Weiler, 'The Potential For Overlap in NAFTA Chapter 11 Obligations', in K Kennedy (ed), *The First Decade of NAFTA: The Future of Free Trade in North America*, Transnational Publishers, New York, 2004.

36 See NAFTA, Article 1102(4).

37 See for example *Pope & Talbot, Inc v Canada*, NAFTA/UNCITRAL Tribunal, Final Merits Awards, 10 April 2001 at 35–6; available at [www.naftalaw.org].

conflict. These standards, in combination, are construed as standards of fair and equitable treatment.[38]

Chapter 11 imposes performance requirements on NAFTA parties under Article 1106 that might otherwise diminish the value of the investment. Article 1106(1)(a)–(g) lists enumerated performance requirements that prohibit NAFTA parties from:

- Tying sales to foreign exchange earnings;
- Insisting that investors buy local products and services;
- Requiring a minimum of local content;
- Requesting foreign exchange inflows;
- Demanding technology transfers other than corrective anticompetitive measures;
- Demanding technology transfers to local companies in particular;
- Requiring specific levels of goods or services; and
- Requiring that foreign markets be supplied from local production.

Article 1109 also requires NAFTA parties to permit the free and uninterrupted transfer of investments at prevailing market rates of exchange.

These performance requirements are subject to the right of a NAFTA party to impose special formal and information requirements on investors, so long as they do not materially impair requisite protections and requirements under Chapter 11, including the equitable and good faith application of its law.[39] Specific prohibitions include not imposing national requirements on investors of other NAFTA parties,[40] although a NAFTA party may impose on boards of directors requirements that they do not materially impede the investor from exercising control over its investment.[41] Similarly, NAFTA parties are required not to place transfer restrictions on investors, subject to specific exceptions, so long as these are equitable, non-discriminatory and constitute good faith compliance with their law.[42] As we will see later, arbitral tribunals have construed these requirements restrictively to situations in which requirements are mandatory and compel the investor's behaviour.

Finally, Chapter 11 controversially limits the right of NAFTA parties to expropriate investments. On the one hand is the argument that the NAFTA's provisions on expropriation ought to be extended beyond the pre-existing international law on the subject.[43] On the other is the assertion that expropriation ought to be limited to

---

38 See generally N Rubins & NS Kinsella, *International Investment, Political Risk and Dispute Resolution: A Practitioner's Guide,* Oceana Publications, New York, 2005, p 212. See also C Schreuer, 'Fair and Equitable Treatment in Arbitral Practice' (2005) 6 *J World Trade & Inv* 357; B Choudhury, 'Evolution or Devolution? Defining Fair and Equitable Treatment in International Investment Law' (2005) 6 *J World Inv & Trade* 297 (2005).

39 See NAFTA, Article 1110(1–2).

40 See NAFTA, Article 1107(1).

41 See NAFTA, Article 1107(2).

42 See NAFTA, Article 1109.

43 See JM Wagner, 'International Investment, Expropriation and Environmental Protection' (1999) 29 *Golden Gate UL Rev* 465; WT Warren, 'Paying to Regulate: Guide to *Methanex v United States* and the NAFTA Investor Rights' (2001) 31 *Env't Rep* 10986.

governmental regulations that are clearly discriminatory and unreasonable in nature and effect.[44]

Section B

A primary characteristic of the NAFTA is that it provides for both the private and the public resolution of investment disputes. Article 2022 in the umbrella Chapter 20 provides that NAFTA parties shall encourage and facilitate the use of private international commercial arbitration to resolve disputes.[45] Chapter 11, in turn, provides investors with a choice: to proceed under its banner, or to resort to domestic courts. It includes within its standards protection for the environment, while enabling the parties to adopt environmental measures outside the framework of Chapter 11, such as under the North American Agreement on Environmental Cooperation (NAAEC).[46]

Procedural mechanisms

Section B of Chapter 11 established procedural mechanisms by which to assert substantive rights, including in particular the process of commercial arbitration by which investors can challenge NAFTA parties rather than having to rely on their domestic courts. The assumption is that the process of commercial arbitration operates independently of the party, is not tainted by national self-interest, and provides equal treatment and due process of law in accordance with principles governing international commercial arbitration.[47] An investor can only submit a claim to arbitration in respect of an alleged breach by a NAFTA party;[48] both the investor and the NAFTA party must consent to the application of NAFTA procedures;[49] and the investor must waive its rights to litigate in any other administrative tribunal or court.[50] A limitation period of three years applies to a claim.[51]

Before submitting to arbitration, Article 1118 provides for informal dispute resolution, notably through consultation and negotiation, along with a mandated cooling-off period. Articles 1119 and 1120 also subject the investor to formal requirements, including providing written notice to the NAFTA party of its intention to submit a claim to arbitration at least 90 days before submitting the claim, and not before six months have elapsed since the events giving rise to the claim. Following this

---

44 See J Gudofski, 'Shedding Light on Article 1110 of the NAFTA Concerning Expropriations: An Environmental Case Study' (2000) 21 *NWJ Int'l L & B* 243; JA Van Duzer, 'NAFTA Chapter 11 to Date: The Progress of a Work in Progress', in LR Dawson (ed), *Whose Rights? The NAFTA Chapter 11 Debate*, The Centre for Trade Law and Policy, Ottawa, 2002.

45 Article 2022 of the NAFTA provides: '1 Each Party, shall to the maximum extent possible, encourage and facilitate the use of arbitration and other means of alternative dispute resolution for the settlement of international commercial disputes between private parties in the free trade area.'

46 See North American Agreement on Environmental Cooperation, US Can Mex, 321 *ILM* 1482.

47 See NAFTA, Article 1115.

48 See NAFTA, Articles 1116–7.

49 See NAFTA, Artcles 1122.

50 See NAFTA, Article 1121.

51 See NAFTA, Articles 1116(2), 1117(2).

waiting period, Chapter 11 provides investors with three options: the ICSID; the ICSID Additional Facility; and the UNCITRAL.

The NAFTA also provides for the number of arbitrators as three, unless the parties agree otherwise. Each party selects one arbitrator and the third, who will act as the presiding arbitrator, is selected by agreement of the parties. Unlike under Chapter 19 (antidumping and countervailing measures) and Chapter 20 (consultations between NAFTA Parties), the arbitrators need not be nationals of the disputing NAFTA party, nor of any NAFTA party.

While the NAFTA does not create special procedures to govern panel hearings under Chapter 11, it does provide for the publication of the arbitral award. It also provides for expert reports and interim measures of protection to preserve the rights of a disputing party. In addition, it limits the types of awards a tribunal may reach. For example, unlike under US antitrust law, only monetary damages, interest, restitution, and costs may be awarded. Punitive damages are explicitly prohibited.[52] Unless the disputing parties agree otherwise, the arbitration shall be held in a country which is a signatory to the New York Convention. There are also time restrictions on a successful party's right to enforce the final award, such as precluding enforcement under the ICSID until 120 days have elapsed since the award.[53] Chapter 11 also requires each party to enforce the award in its territory. If a party fails to comply with the award, provision is made for establishing a panel under Article 2008, which shall determine the consequences of that failure to comply.[54] Finally, provision is made for the binding force of the award.[55]

Review of investment awards under the NAFTA

Chapter 11 effectively excludes courts from resolving investment disputes, expressly rejecting an appeal process. The parties have a limited right to seek review of an award, including to correct errors. In practice, investor requests for judicial review to date have been extensive. Domestic courts have applied the law of the place of arbitration, the *lex loci arbitri*. However, they have diverged over the applicable standards of review, the discretion accorded to arbitrators and the permissible reasons for modifying or nullifying an award. Such differences in both the process and results of a judicial review have given rise to investors shopping among the domestic courts of NAFTA parties for a sympathetic forum. The alternative, a second level of review or a Chapter 11 appellate process, has not evolved and is not likely to do so.

11.4.1b NAFTA jurisprudence

A number of Chapter 11 cases have been filed over the course of the Chapter's history, dealing not simply with 'investments', but also goods and services encompassed within other treaties, or arising under other parts of the NAFTA.

---

52 NAFTA, Article 1135(3).

53 NAFTA, Article 1136(3)(b).

54 NAFTA, Article 1136(5).

55 NAFTA, Article 1136(2),(6).

Often, the disputes have involved what some would consider pure domestic or public policy issues. For instance, Methanex, a Canadian company, brought an action against the USA claiming US$970 million in current and future income losses allegedly suffered as a result of the State of California's phasing-out of methyl-tertiary-butyl ether, a gasoline additive with potential health and environmental risks.[56] The public often consider that such issues—in this case California's regulation of a potentially hazardous gasoline additive—should be subjected solely to domestic lawmaking. On the other hand, investors often consider that such legislation could be enacted for protectionist reasons (under the guide of health and safety protection), or that the measures nevertheless impact upon their investment. While the Methanex claim was dismissed,[57] a claim brought by Metalclad, a US company engaged in waste disposal, was successful in its dispute with Mexico as a result of the latter's failure to grant Metalclad a permit to open a waste disposal facility (Metalclad was awarded over US$1 million).[58] Metalclad prevailed largely because although it had secured all required permits from Mexican federal authorities to construct and operate the facility (and in fact seemingly had been induced by the Mexican Government to invest and open the facility), action on the part of the local authorities prevented the facility from opening.

Another case involving environmental policy was initiated against the Canadian government by a US company, SD Myers, which claimed $20 000 000 in damages arising from Canada's ban on the export of PCB (polychlorinated biphenyls) waste.[59] The tribunal found against the Canadian Government, holding that its reason for implementing the ban was to protect Canadian industry, rather than the environment. Canada unsuccessfully applied for judicial review, seeking to have the award set aside on public policy grounds.

Following the Vienna Convention, tribunals have tried to avoid inconsistencies not through the literal interpretation of NAFTA provisions, but by applying them in their wider commercial, environmental or other contexts. Panels have also used contextual methods of interpretation. They have taken account of the nature and effect of governmental action and have juxtaposed governmental claims of sovereignty and public policy against private claims of per se arbitrariness, or of unequal and unfair treatment vis-à-vis local companies and individuals. The jurisprudence over the issue of expropriation is perhaps the most interesting, if not controversial, and is further explored below.

---

56 *Methanex Corporation v United States of America*, In the Matter of an Arbitration under Chapter 11 of the North American Free Trade Agreement and the UNCITRAL Arbitration Rules, Final Award of the Tribunal, 7 August 2005, available at [www.naftaclaims.com/disputes_us_6.htm].

57 After six years, the claim was dismissed on the grounds that the arbitral tribunal lacked jurisdiction under Article 1110 because the measures in question did not 'relate to' Methanex. The tribunal added that, had it had such jurisdiction, it would have dismissed the claim on the merits. Methanex was also required to pay the defendant's legal and arbitration costs.

58 *Metalclad Corp v United Mexican States*, Final Award, NAFTA/ICSID(AF) Tribunal, Case No ARB(AF)/97/1, 30 August 2000, 40 *ILM* 36 (2001), notes 95 and 172. The Government of Mexico appealed the award which was, in significant measure, upheld by the British Columbia Supreme Court.

59 See *SD Myers Inc v Canada*, NAFTA/UNCITRAL Tribunal, Partial Award, 13 November 2000, 40 *ILM* 1408 (2001), also available at [www.naftalaw.org] (Myers) and (Myers Dissent); *Attorney-General of Canada v SD Myers, Inc*, Court File No T-80-03 (Myers Judgment).

'Expropriation' under Chapter 11

The jurisprudence resulting from the interpretation of expropriation in Chapter 11 tribunals has not been entirely consistent. 'Expropriation' was accorded its widest interpretation in the *Metalclad* case.[60] In contrast, both the *Myers* and *Pope & Talbot* cases interpreted expropriation restrictively.[61] In two comparatively recent cases, *Methanex* and *Thunderbird*, the tribunals dismissed the claims somewhat summarily.[62]

The *Metalclad* tribunal not only found a breach of Article 1110 but also interpreted expropriation expansively and made a significant compensation award. It stated:

> Thus, expropriation under NAFTA includes not only open, deliberate and acknowledged takings of property, such as outright seizure or formal or obligatory transfer of title in favor of the host State, but also covert or incidental interference with the use of property which has the effect of depriving the owner, in whole or in significant part, of the use or reasonably-to-be-expected economic benefit of property even if not necessarily to the obvious benefit of the host State.[63]

Despite the fact that the decision was given a restrictive application and despite the absence of authority for the statement above, the expansive reach given to expropriation is frequently cited as authority; but it is also discredited. Other tribunals have avoided deciding on grounds of expropriation, preferring to locate their decision in some other Chapter 11 violation, such as Article 1105,[64] or by treating the case as a breach of contract by a local authority.[65]

Further cases have purported to redefine the reach of Article 1110, particularly by limiting it. For example, the tribunal in the *Pope & Talbot* case maintained that:

> Regulations can indeed be characterized in a way that would constitute creeping expropriation ... Indeed, much creeping expropriation could be conducted by regulation, and a blanket exception for regulatory measures would create a gaping loophole in international protection against expropriation.[66]

---

60 See *Metalclad Corp v United Mexican States*, Final Award, NAFTA/ICSID(AF)Tribunal, Case No ARB(AF)/97/1, 30 August 2000, 40 *ILM* 36 (2001).

61 *Attorney-General of Canada v SD Myers, Inc*, Court File No T-80-03 (2001); *Pope & Talbot, Inc v Canada*, Interim Merits Award, 26 June 2000, 40 *ILM* 258 (2001).

62 See *Methanex Corporation v United States of America*, In the Matter of an Arbitration under Chapter 11 of the NAFTA and the UNCITRAL Arbitration Rules, Final Award of the Tribunal, 7 August 2005, available at [www.naftaclaims.com/disputes_us_6.htm] (while the decision was technically based on the tribunal not having jurisdiction under Article 1110, the tribunal went out of its way to state that, even if it had the jurisdiction, it would have rejected the merits of the claims). See also *International Thunderbird Gaming Corporation v Mexico*, UNCITRAL (NAFTA), Arbitral Award, 26 January 2006, available at [http://ita.law.uvic.ca/documents/ThunderbirdAward.pdf] (the claimant's arguments were rejected on the basis of a lack of reasonable expectations).

63 *Metalclad* above note 60 at para 103.

64 See *Loewen Group, Inc and Raymond L Loewen v United States of America*, ICSID Case No ARB(AF)/98/3 (26 June 2003). In this case, the tribunal dismissed the expropriation claim against the US Government.

65 See *Azinian v The United Mexican States*, Notice of Arbitration, filed 10 March 1997; Final Award issued 1 November 1999, available at [www.naftalaw.com]. For documents filed in this case, see [www.naftalaw.org]. In this case, the tribunal declined to treat a breach of contract as an expropriation.

66 *Pope & Talbot* above note 61 at para 99.

However, the *Pope & Talbot* tribunal insisted that, to be a violation of Article 1110, the interference had to be substantial under international law:[67]

> The test is whether that interference is sufficiently restrictive to support a conclusion that the property has been 'taken' from the owner ... Action that is confiscatory, or that prevents, unreasonably interferes with or unduly delays, effective enjoyment of an alien's property.[68]

As a result, the tribunal found that no expropriation had arisen; there had not been any nationalisation, no substantial loss of control, and the claimant continued to operate as a profitable business despite the regulations.[69]

In *Myers*, the tribunal adopted a similar approach towards expropriation, emphasising the need for a high degree of interference to constitute a finding of expropriation, as distinct from government regulation. In effect, while 'expropriations tend to involve the deprivation of property rights; regulations [tend to involve] a lesser interference'.[70] It elaborated:

> An expropriation usually amounts to a lasting removal of the ability of an owner to make use of its economic rights although it may be that, in some contexts and circumstances it would be appropriate to view a deprivation as amounting to an expropriation, even if it were partial or temporary.[71]

The *Feldman* case highlighted, not the degree of deprivation, but the factual distinction between expropriation and regulation:

> Article 1110 deals not only with direct takings, but indirect expropriations and measures 'tantamount to expropriation', which potentially encompass a variety of government regulatory activity that may significantly interfere with an investor's property rights.[72]

The tribunal concluded, in light of the earlier *Azinian* decision:

> not all government regulatory activity that makes it difficult or impossible for an investor to carry out a particular business, change in the law or change in the application of existing laws that makes it uneconomical to continue a particular business, is an expropriation under Article 1110.[73]

The tribunal, considering the government conduct in light of its context and in particular in light of the Restatement of Law, held that it had not engaged in an expropriation under Article 1110(1).[74] While it declined to consider that the government had violated the public purpose, non-discriminatory and due process

---

67 Ibid at paras 96, 102.

68 Ibid at para 102.

69 Ibid at para 101, 104. For arguments along comparable lines, see *Myers*, above note 59 at paras 285–6.

70 *Myers* above note 59 at para 282.

71 Ibid at para 283.

72 *Feldman* v *Mexico*, ICSID Case No ARB(AF)/99/1, (16 December 2002) at para 100, available at [www.worldbank.org/icsid/cases/feldman_mexico-award-en.PDF]; referring to *Azinian v The United Mexican States*, Notice of Arbitration, filed 10 March 1997; Final Award issued 1 November 1999, available at [www.naftalaw.com].

73 Ibid at para 112.

74 Ibid at para 135.

criteria in that article, it reflected on the virtue of determining whether the government had violated minimum standards of treatment.[75]

Finally, both *Pope & Talbot* and *Feldman* returned to examining whether the government had sufficiently interfered with the investment to constitute a confiscation. However, they both held that interference must impact upon the investor's business as a whole, as distinct from a part of it. If the latter, the interference will not be 'sufficient' to constitute a taking in violation of the NAFTA.[76]

Commentary

Despite the fact that Chapter 11 tribunals reasonably consistently hold that an expropriation occurs only when the government interference is substantial, it is still not clear how much interference is substantial in fact. If one takes a narrow view, substantial interference ought to be construed restrictively, on a strict construction of Chapter 11, and perhaps secondarily in deference to governments exercising their police powers or in regulating property. If a tribunal takes a wider view, substantial interference may be assessed in two very different ways: according to the kind and according to the degree of interference. The problem with relying on the *kind* of interference to determine whether a government taking amounts to expropriation is that it is unduly open-ended, and it is difficult to second-guess how tribunals might reach that determination in a complex set of facts. Relying on the *degree* of interference is perhaps a more reliable predictor, except that some tribunals are likely to treat degrees of government taking differently according to their conception of 'substantial' interference.

11.4.2 AUSFTA

Australia's FTA with the USA is probably its most important, and as such was heavily scrutinised, both in terms of its effect on trade and in regard to investment. The following extract details not only the importance of the investment relationship between Australia and the USA, but also reviews each party's negotiating objectives, and the outcomes and impact of the agreement.

Thomas Westcott, 'Foreign Investment Issues in the Australia–United States Free Trade Agreement'[77]

Bilateral investment relationship

The United States accounts for almost 30 per cent of total Foreign Direct Investment (FDI) in Australia, making it the largest source of FDI. As at 31 December 2003, the total stock of US FDI in Australia was $70.9 billion. The next largest direct investors were the UK with $52.7 billion and Japan with $18.2 billion. Significantly, Australia has a larger stock of FDI in the US than they do here, with $78 billion invested as at 31 December 2003. This is more than twice the level of Australian-sourced FDI in any other country [UK $34.3 billion, NZ $21.8 billion].

75 Ibid at para 141.

76 Feldman, above 72 at para 152.

77 Available at [www.treasury.gov.au/documents/958/pdf/06_foreign_investment_policy_ausfta.pdf].

Current FDI levels reflect a shift in the historical trend of capital flows; Australia has always relied on significant amounts of foreign capital, but has not traditionally had high direct investment outflows. In 2001 Australia's stock of direct investment in the US was higher for the first time than the stock of US direct investment in Australia: $88.8 billion compared to $60.1 billion. In 2002, the stock of Australian FDI in the US was $70.2 billion compared to a US stock of $63.6 billion in Australia. Services trade figures give further evidence of the maturing of the bilateral trade and investment relationship. In 2003–04, Australian services exports to the US totaled nearly $4.5 billion while the US exported nearly $6.2 billion worth of services to Australia. These figures highlight the strength of the bilateral services and investment relationship and the value of an investment agreement that provides even greater certainty and improved dynamic linkages.

...

Negotiating objectives

...

Australia sought an enhanced treaty framework to govern investment flows, whilst looking for opportunities to reduce the impediments that licensing requirements, standards or other regulations in the United States impose on Australian investors and service providers. For example, improved access was sought in specific sectors, including ferries. In addition, Australia opposed inclusion of provisions that allow investors to initiate claims against the host state for breaches of investment provisions (investor–state dispute settlement provisions). Australia also looked to ensure that full account was taken of Australia's foreign investment policy and the need for appropriate policies to encourage foreign investment, while addressing community concerns about foreign ownership of Australian assets.

American objectives were set out in the Trade Promotion Authority provisions contained in the *Trade Act 2002* which gave the US administration guidance on issues to be covered in FTAs. From this, the Department of the United States Trade Representative (USTR) developed an agreed 'template' text which forms the basis of each US bilateral negotiation. More detailed investment objectives were set out in a letter from the USTR to Congress in late 2002 indicating the US sought, *inter alia*, modification of the national interest provisions of Australia's foreign investment legislation.

Investment obligations and market access

INVESTMENT ACCESS—NEGOTIATED OUTCOMES

Consistent with the requirements of the US Congressional mandate embodied in the Trade Promotion Authority, negotiations on improved investment access did not begin until the fourth negotiating round in October 2003, following the report of the US Trade Commission assessment of the potential impact of the agreement, and the substantive discussion of options did not effectively commence until the fifth round in December 2003.

In the context of the overall dynamics of the negotiations, the achievement of market access gains for foreign investors was a high priority for US negotiators. In particular, the US argued that the absence of pre-establishment screening in the US produced a market access imbalance that disadvantaged US investors. The US starting point preferred outcome was to exempt US investors fully from the application of Australia's foreign investment screening arrangements and/or from the application of the national interest test—or at least to narrow the interpretation of the latter effectively to issues of national security only.

The negotiations therefore presented an opportunity for the Government to consider the scope for liberalisation of Australia's foreign investment policy regime. However, the Government remained committed to retaining key elements of the existing framework, which it considered served Australia's interests well. In particular, it was not prepared to concede any erosion of the principle of a broad national interest test or of pre-establishment screening of all significant foreign acquisitions of existing Australian companies or assets. Australia's preferred approach, therefore, was to explore the scope for an agreement based on increased screening thresholds, while preserving the existing national interest test.

The terms of the deal on investment market access were finalised in early February 2004. Pre-establishment screening based on a national interest test was retained, while the dollar threshold above which US investments in non-sensitive sectors would require notification was significantly increased. This reflected the judgment that, in all but an identifiable set of sensitive sectors, national interest concerns were closely correlated with the value of the assets concerned and had historically only been raised by cases where the assets were valued significantly above the existing $50 million threshold. This outcome should reduce the number of investors requiring Foreign Investment Review Board approval while preserving the Government's right to continue to screen US investments of major significance against the national interest test.

The following amendments in relation to United States-sourced investment came into effect on 1 January 2005:

- exemption from the *Foreign Acquisitions and Takeovers Act* 1975 (Cwlth) of acquisitions of interests in financial sector companies as defined by the *Financial Sector (Shareholdings) Act 1998*;
- introduction of a screening threshold of $800 million, indexed annually to the GDP implicit price deflator, for acquisitions of interests in Australian businesses in non-sensitive sectors;
- introduction of a screening threshold of $50 million, indexed annually to the GDP implicit price deflator, for acquisitions of interests in Australian businesses in defined sensitive sectors. The sensitive sectors are:
    - media;
    - telecommunications;
    - transport, including airports, port facilities, rail infrastructure, international and domestic aviation and shipping services provided either within, or to and from, Australia;
    - the supply of training or human resources or the development, manufacture or supply of military goods, equipment or technology to the Australian or other defence forces;
    - the development, manufacture or supply of goods, equipment or technologies able to be used for a military purpose;
    - the development, manufacture or supply of, or provision of services relating to, encryption and security technologies and communications systems; and
    - the extraction of (or holding of rights to extract) uranium or plutonium, or the operation of nuclear facilities;
- introduction of a minimum screening threshold of $50 million, indexed annually to the GDP implicit price deflator, for acquisitions by entities in which a United States federal or state government has a prescribed interest;
- introduction of a screening threshold of $800m, indexed annually to the GDP implicit price deflator, for acquisitions of interests in non-residential developed commercial property (other than accommodation facilities); and
- removal of existing policy-based screening requirements for the establishment of new Australian businesses.

Of these changes, the introduction of a distinction between sensitive and non-sensitive sectors is arguably most significant. This is a change from the previously established practice whereby certain investments—media, newspapers, foreign government investments—are treated as 'more sensitive' through policy, but not subject to different treatment under the FATA [*Foreign Acquisitions and Takeovers Act*].

The agreement no longer to screen US investments in financial sector companies (FSCs) covered by the *Financial Sector (Shareholdings) Act 1998* under the FATA, streamlines the previous dual process whereby foreign investment in the shares of FSCs was subject to a national interest test under both pieces of legislation. A side letter to the agreement makes it clear that the principle announced by the Treasurer in April 1997, viz that any large-scale transfer of the Australian ownership of the financial system to foreign hands would be considered contrary to the national interest, will continue to apply. The FATA will still apply to non-share transactions in FSCs.

The removal of the current policy requiring notification for new business (greenfields) US investments over $10 million reflects the fact that such investments do not generally raise national interest concerns akin to the foreign acquisition of existing economic assets but rather add directly to the economy's capacity to provide goods and services both for domestic consumption and export. Moreover, whereas foreign investment screening of new businesses has in the past been used to assist in the enforcement of acceptable environmental standards and heritage rules, Australia now has separate effective and comprehensive national legislation for this purpose. The agreement includes a commitment to conduct a review, within 18 months of entry into force, of options to exempt passive portfolio investment from the Act and to minimise the screening of internal corporate reorganisations and foreign-to-foreign takeovers. Australia also made a commitment to provide prior warning to the US authorities, subject to the consent of the investor, should a US acquisition of an Australian business or assets raise issues likely to require action by the Australian Government to reject, unwind or impose conditions. All Australia's existing sectoral foreign investment restrictions were preserved under the agreement.

The outcome outlined above represents the first liberalisation of investment policy to come about through trade negotiations, and is arguably a far more significant package of reforms than is ever likely to have been agreed in more traditional multilateral negotiations. Moreover, while the package was negotiated in the context of an FTA, which necessarily focuses attention on the market access 'concessions' each party agrees to grant to the other, these reforms are expected to provide net benefits to the Australian economy. These expected benefits will come through the impact of reduced compliance costs and, to some extent, a lower equity risk premium for foreign investors in Australia, with a consequent positive impact on the level of inwards FDI and related dynamic benefits over time.

Quantifying such benefits has been the subject of considerable analysis and debate elsewhere and is beyond the scope of this article. Nevertheless, consistent with the lessons from previous rounds of trade liberalisation, it is reasonable to anticipate that the primary beneficiary of liberalisation will be the economy that liberalises—in this case, Australia.

THE PROVISIONS OF THE INVESTMENT CHAPTER

The 17 articles of the investment chapter—Chapter 11 of the agreement—fall into the following categories: definitions and scope; non-discrimination obligations; investment protection; limitations on government measures; and dispute settlement procedures. The chapter's structure is broadly consistent with the NAFTA model and though similar to the Singapore–Australia FTA (SAFTA) text in many respects, it differs in the treatment of investments in the services sector.

The chapter's scope is set, in part, by an asset-based definition of 'investment' as:

> every asset that an investor owns or controls, directly or indirectly, that has the characteristics of an investment, including such characteristics as the commitment of capital or other resources, the expectation of gain or profit, or the assumption of risk [Article 11.17].

The asset-based formulation used is narrower than the Australia–Singapore approach which doesn't limit the forms of debt covered. Though in principle an asset-based definition is more expansive than an enterprise-based approach to investment that focuses on FDI, the definition used is narrowed in scope by requiring that an asset 'have the characteristics of an investment'. This is intended to limit the scope of 'investment' to prevent expropriation claims regarding, for example, permits to pollute and grazing rights on federal land. Other existing OECD agreements adopt a narrower definition of 'capital movements' and FDI. However, the narrower definition used in this agreement differs from that used in Australia's bilateral investment treaties where the maximum level of protection is sought for Australian investments in other countries. Other than the definition of investment, the scope of the investment chapter is determined by coverage of the pre-establishment and post-establishment stages of investment as qualified by 'negative list' style annexes.

Chapter 11 guarantees the investors of each party non-discrimination and prompt and adequate compensation in the event of expropriation of an investment. Non-discrimination principles are captured in Article 11.3: National Treatment, 11.4: Most Favoured Nation (MFN) Treatment, and 11.5: Minimum Standard of Treatment, with limited exceptions to these contained in annexes. Of note is the fact that this is the first FTA investment chapter that Australia has concluded with post-establishment MFN and a minimum standard of treatment obligation.

Agreement to include an MFN provision is unsurprising but significant as it commits Australia to extending to the US any future favourable treatment granted to another treaty partner. Neither Singapore nor Australia had sought to include an MFN article in SAFTA, in part reflecting the fact that both countries were separately negotiating or considering negotiating with the US and in part reflecting Singapore's membership of the preferential ASEAN group.

The chapter also sets out the minimum standard of treatment to be afforded to investors of each party. It defines the customary international minimum standard of treatment of aliens as the minimum standard of treatment to be applied. The provision provides greater clarity to what is meant by 'fair and equitable treatment' and 'full protection and security'. This language is responsive to perceived problems with outcomes in various NAFTA cases and reflects the subsequent NAFTA Free Trade Commission binding interpretation issued in July 2001. The expropriation provision provides a guarantee that parties will not directly expropriate or nationalise a covered investment, nor indirectly expropriate through equivalent measures except where such measures are non-discriminatory, enacted for a public purpose in accordance with due process of law, and where there is payment of prompt, adequate and effective compensation. Chapter 11 also provides guidance on the sorts of actions that may constitute indirect expropriation and contains a commitment that the expropriation article is not to affect normal governmental regulatory activity.

In addition to these non-discrimination and expropriation principles, chapter 11 also guarantees investors the right to transfer freely investments (including capital, profits etc) into and out of the country. The right of free transfers is subject to the application of domestic laws relating to bankruptcy, insolvency, issuing and dealing securities, criminal offences and so forth. Australia agreed to eschew a balance of payments exception to the free transfers principle previously used in its FTAs on the basis that Australia acknowledged that it could never envisage invoking this exception to block transfers from the US. However, the Australian Treasurer subsequently made it clear in a letter to his counterpart, US Treasury Secretary Snow, that Australia continues to see a role for capital and exchange controls in limited and extreme circumstances by some countries and that the International Monetary Fund, rather than bilateral trade negotiations, was the appropriate forum in which to resolve differences of view regarding the future role for such controls in the context of potential balance of payments difficulties.

The performance requirements provision (Article 11.9) regulates conditional incentives and other requirements imposed by governments as a condition of an investment approval. This provision extends the WTO Trade-Related Investment Measures Agreement by covering measures in the services sector as well as the goods sector. The provision prohibits requirements relating to the transfer of technology and the exclusive supply to specific markets as well as domestic sales targets.

Australia agreed to limit the use of performance requirements, recognising that certain performance requirements can distort trade and investment flows. The provision gives Australia a binding guarantee restricting the use of such requirements by governments in the US which might adversely affect the interests of Australian companies, or Australian trade and investment interests. At the same time, the provision does not affect the right of governments to regulate the operation of enterprises in their jurisdiction for any public policy purpose, including environmental and health and safety concerns.

The investment chapter is arguably most notable, however, for the absence of investor–state dispute settlement provisions. The US's stated objective on investment dispute resolution procedures was that the agreement: provide procedures to resolve disputes between US and Australian investors that are in keeping with the goals of making such procedures expeditious, fair and transparent.

However, Australia was strongly of the view that an agreement between two developed countries with advanced legal systems and an established rule of law does not require an additional avenue for investors to pursue their rights outside the domestic legal system. Notwithstanding the evolution of US treaty language to give greater guidance to arbitration panels, there remains continuing discomfort over NAFTA jurisprudence.

The eventual agreement not to incorporate investor–state dispute settlement provisions reflected an acknowledgement by both parties of the robustness of their respective domestic legal systems, along with provision, should circumstances change in future, for either party to initiate discussions to review this outcome, but without prejudicing the outcome of such possible future discussions. One important implication of the omission of investor–state dispute settlement provisions is that decisions by the Treasurer on foreign investment cases will not be subject to international arbitration when no similar rights are available under domestic law.

Conclusion

The primary focus in most FTAs has been trade liberalisation. A 2003 Productivity Commission study found evidence that FDI responds significantly to the investment provisions of FTAs. Moreover, the study did not find evidence of trade diversion that might be expected from companies relocating from a low-cost to a higher cost (FTA partner) host country. The study also concludes that FDI responds more significantly to preferential FTAs than to bilateral investment treaties, which have tended to be more narrowly focused on investment protection. This suggests a greater role for FTAs in encouraging reform of investment regulations and in opening capital markets, including for FDI.

Negotiating FTAs necessarily involves trade-offs in arriving at an agreed liberalisation of domestic policy settings, even though experience strongly indicates that such reforms inevitably benefit the economy which undertakes the reform. Australia's foreign investment policy has been periodically reviewed and liberalised since its inception in the mid-1970s. The latest reforms are expected to bring further benefits to Australia, while reaffirming the Government's responsibility to review significant and sensitive foreign investments to ensure they are in the national interest. Chapter 11 of the agreement will be important in shaping Australia's future investment agreements, though negotiators must be prepared to depart from this text where appropriate in future negotiations. This offers no immediate solution to potential difficulties associated with divergent treaties containing different rules and processes. Australia continues to support efforts to develop FTA and investment treaty best practice through plurilateral forums such as APEC and the OECD, and multilaterally in the WTO.

... ...

11.4.3 Multilateral agreements on investment

Due to the number of BITs being negotiated, significant differences sometimes exist between agreements as to, *inter alia*, levels of protection, standards and enforcement options. These differences, in addition to inconsistent tribunal determinations, create uncertainty and confusion among investors as well as governments. In order to add certainly and predictability into international investment through the addition of uniform standards, as perhaps as a way to influence or increase (or decrease) 'world' standards, the idea of negotiating a multilateral agreement on investment (MAI) is often posed and discussed. The OECD is the latest organisation to attempt to negotiate such an agreement. The OECD efforts, which began in 1995, were heavily criticised by certain developed and developing countries, as well as by civil society for developmental, environmental or other public policy reasons.[78] For this reason, and despite the conclusion of a draft MAI, the OECD discontinued the negotiations in 1998.[79] There is no doubt that efforts to spur the negotiation of an MAI will again resurface in the future.

78 For detailed analysis of the failed OECD attempt at negotiating an MAI, see J Kurtz, 'A General Investment Agreement in the WTO? Lessons from Chapter 11 of NAFTA and the OECD Multilateral Agreement on Investment' (2002) 23 *University of Pennsylvania Journal of International Economic Law* 713; R Dattu, 'A Journey from Havana to Paris: The Fifty-Year Quest for the Elusive MAI' (2000) 24 *Fordham International Law Journal* 295.

79 See OECD, The Multilateral Agreement on Investment Draft Consolidated Text', available at [www1.oecd.org/daf/mai/pdf/ng/ng987r1e.pdf].

11.5 Arbitrating investment disputes

The chapter has focused thus far on the macro-political, economic and legal environment surrounding FDI and, in particular, attempts at regulating and also liberalising investment internationally. Discussion now shifts to dispute resolution, especially specific processes that are available to parties involved in an investment dispute. As we will see, the liberalisation of international investment law has given rise to a range of institutions and mechanisms by which investors can bring actions against host states for allegedly infringing legal rights accorded to foreign investors by law.

A primary mechanism for the resolution of investor–state investment disputes is by recourse to international commercial arbitration. As mentioned above, there are three primary arbitration facilities used to arbitrate international investment disputes: the ICSID,[80] the ICSID Additional Facility[81] and the UNCITRAL.[82]

11.5.1 The ICSID

The most significant multilateral development in the resolution of investment disputes can be traced back to the establishment of the ICSID in 1965. Affiliated with the World Bank, it provides facilities for the conciliation and arbitration of investment disputes between foreign investors and host governments. Arbitration under the ICSID is located in Washington DC, at the premises of the World Bank.

Key to the ICSID are the principles and processes it sets out for the settlement of investment disputes, including entrenching the regime of international arbitration to resolve investment disputes.[83] The ICSID not only provides multilateral legitimacy to the settlement of investment disputes, but it also serves as a protocol that states could incorporate into their BITs without having to rely on the domestic courts of other states in resolving investment disputes.

ICSID arbitrations are widely used and are incorporated by reference into a variety of regional and bilateral trade agreements. Some ICSID cases are widely publicised, including those involving states that are parties to the NAFTA.[84] ICSID arbitrations

80 On the ICSID generally, see [www.worldbank.org/icsid].

81 ICSID Additional Facility Rules are available at the World Bank website, available at [http:www .worldbank.org/icsid/basic-doc-archive/9.htm].

82 UNCITRAL Arbitration Rules, GA Res 31/98, UN UNCITRAL, 99th Plen Mtg (15 December 1996) (UNCITRAL Rules), also available at [www.uncitral.org/pdf/english/texts/ arbitrationarb-rules/.pdf]. See generally J Paulson & G Petrochilos, *Revision of the UNCITRAL Arbitration Rules*, available at [www.uncitral.org/pdf/english/news/arbrules_report.pdf].

83 Convention on the Settlement of Investment Disputes Between States and Nationals of Other States, 18 March 1965, 17 UST 1270, TIAS No 6090, available at [http://www.worldbank.org/icsid].

84 See for example *Mondev International Ltd v United States of America*, ICSID Case No ARB (AF)/99/2 (Award) (11 October 2002). This case held that the protection accorded by Article 1105(1) of the NAFTA against governmental interference extended to contract claims. See also *Société Générale de Surveillance SA v Islamic Republic of Pakistan*, ICSID Case No ARB/01/13, Decision on Jurisdiction dated 6 August 2003 at para 167 ('under general international law, a violation of a contract entered into by a State with an investor of another State, is not, by itself, a violation of international law').

have also added to the jurisprudence on international investment law, such as by extending a government taking to include by contract.[85]

11.5.2 The ICSID Additional Facility

The ICSID Additional Facility was established in 1978 to provide effective access to the ICSID dispute resolution regime. The ICSID Additional Facility regime has rules that are different from the ICSID. In particular, they accommodate disputes in which only one party to the ICSID, whether the host government or the investor from a member country, is a disputant.

The ICSID and the ICSID Additional Facility rules both provide that the tribunal hold its first session within 60 days from the date of constituting the tribunal, or as otherwise agreed to by the parties. However, all the other timelines are within the discretion of the panel and are ordinarily reached in consultation with the ICSID Secretary General as well as the parties themselves.

11.5.3 The UNCITRAL

The UNCITRAL was established in 1966 to harmonise and unify international trade law. Functioning through working groups on specific projects, its Arbitration Rules were devised specifically to provide member parties with a unified and ordered method of arbitrating disputes. In particular, the UNCITRAL Rules establish a procedural framework for the process of international arbitration. These rules are widely adopted and incorporated into various international trade and investment agreements between states and also involving private parties. They are easy to adopt, since they can be used by any party regardless of membership of or affiliation with any international association.[86]

The UNCITRAL Rules provide for the parties to exchange pleadings within 45 days of the initiation of proceedings. However, they do not stipulate further timelines, such as the duration of hearings, although they do permit the panel to extend the timelines.[87] The problem is that, absent definitive timelines, proceedings may be dilatory unless the arbitrators proceed with expedition.

The UNCITRAL Rules are also discussed in Chapter 10 of this book.

11.5.4 Distinctive features

Each of these arbitration regimes has its own distinctive procedures. What they share is the credence they accord to international commercial arbitration as a regime for the resolution of investment disputes in particular. They emphasise the value of choosing

---

85 See Mondev, ibid. See also N Rubins & NS Kinsella, *International Investment, Political Risk and Dispute Resolution: A Practitioner's Guide*, Oceana Publications, New York, 2005, p 234.

86 On this mission of the UNCITRAL, see Working Group on Arbitration and Conciliation on the Work of its Forty-second Session (New York, 10–14 January 2005), A/CN.9/573, available at [http://uncitral.org].

87 See UNCITRAL Arbitration Rules, Article 23.

expert arbitrators and according them with sufficient discretion, both in running arbitration proceedings and in arriving at awards. Both the ICSID Additional Facility Rules and the UNCITRAL Rules permit arbitral tribunals to establish procedural orders to govern the conduct of arbitration proceedings. However, the ICSID Additional Facility Rules require the tribunal to apply the agreement of the parties on procedural matters, while the UNCITRAL Rules do not so circumscribe the authority of arbitrators. In further contrast, the UNCITRAL Rules provide for confidential hearings unless the parties agree otherwise. As we will see below, Chapter 11 of the NAFTA allows for investment arbitration under all three arbitration regimes, but it expressly provides for the publication of the award as an exception to the confidentiality of arbitration awards under the UNCITRAL Rules.

Awards under all three arbitration regimes are reached by a majority of the arbitrators. The problem is that two arbitrators may agree on an award, but differ on its quantification. This is a particular issue under the UNCITRAL Rules, in which the arbitrators may reach a majority decision but fail to agree on the award of damages. The UNCITRAL Rules render the losing party responsible for costs which may also include legal fees if they are claimed throughout the proceedings. The panel retains wide latitude in assessing party-to-party costs. There is no authority provided to administer such costs, although the parties may designate an authority to do so.[88]

The ICSID and the ICSID Additional Facility leave costs largely in the hands of the panels, subject to guidelines established by the ICSID Administrative Council. As a matter of practice, the ICSID generally commences proceedings by requiring the parties to make an advance deposit to defray costs, usually in equal shares. The risk is that one party may decline to do so, forcing the other to advance the full amount in order to proceed. The result is that one party can significantly impede the panel process.[89]

11.5.5 Principled jurisprudence

A key issue in the development of international investment is the need for a principled foundation and a coherent jurisprudence through which tribunals apply those principles to particular investment disputes. The difficulty is in grounding those principles in a uniform body of international investment law and ensuring that they are consistently construed by international tribunals hearing such cases.

11.5.5a 'Fair and equitable treatment'

'Fair and equitable treatment' is a central concept in the protection of private investments in international investment law. The problem lies in uncertainty over the nature and limits of such treatment—the extent to which states are entitled to accord less-than-equal treatment on grounds of national public policy. In issue, too, is whether

88 See UNCITRAL Arbitration Rules, Article 40.

89 See ICSID Basic Documents, Administrative and Financial Regulations, available at [www.worldbank.org/icsid].

treatment that would otherwise be deemed to be unfair, in discriminating against particular foreign investors or foreign investors generally, is rendered 'fair' by virtue of a transcendent principle of national law.

Nor is the jurisprudence on fair and equitable treatment entirely coherent. The problem is that the concepts themselves are general in nature; tribunals conceive of them differently in light of their different jurisprudential backgrounds, their conception of the interface between national and international law, and the degree of deference they show to state sovereignty on the one hand and the importance they place on creating a level playing field for international investors on the other.[90] Typifying these issues are a series of cases commencing with the ICSID award in *Maffezini v Kingdom of Spain*.[91] In that case, the tribunal restricted the application of the applicable MFN clause. More specifically, the tribunal contended that an MFN clause should not 'override public policy considerations that the contracting parties might have envisaged as fundamental conditions for their acceptance of the agreement in question', Applying this argument to the exhaustion of local remedies, the Tribunal held:

> if one contracting party has conditioned its consent to arbitration on the exhaustion of local remedies ... this requirement could not be bypassed by invoking the most favored nation clause in relation to a third-party agreement that does not contain this element since the stipulated condition reflects a fundamental rule of international law ... This conclusion is compelled by the consideration that it would upset the finality of arrangements that many countries deem important as a matter of public policy ... [A] distinction has to be made between the legitimate extension of rights and benefits by means of the operation of the clause, on the one hand, and disruptive treaty-shopping that would play havoc with the policy objectives of underlying specific treaty provisions, on the other hand.[92]

The tribunal expressed concern that allowing a party to use an MFN clause in order to negate the specific agreement contained in an applicable BIT would violate the public policy directed at the finality of an agreement. It would also override the will of the contracting parties in agreeing to 'national treatment.'

11.5.5b Legitimate expectations

Central to a determination of 'fair and equitable treatment' is the need to determine the investor's 'legitimate expectations'. Not unlike the common law of estoppel, an investor's legitimate expectations can be grounded in light of variable conduct by

---

90 On the fair and equitable treatment standard in investment treaties, see for example N Rubins & NS Kinsella, *International Investment, Political Risk and Dispute Resolution: A Practitioner's Guide*, Oceana Publications, New York, 2005, p 212; C Schreuer, 'Fair and Equitable Treatment in Arbitral Practice' (2005) 6 *J World Trade & Inv* 357.

91 ICSID Case No ARB/97/7, Award on the Merits, 13 November 2000, at [http://ita.law.uvic.ca/documents/Maffezini-Award- English.pdf] at para 64; *MTD Equity Sdn Bhd & MTD Chile SA v Chile*, ICSID Case No ARB/01/7, 25 May 2004, available at [http://ita.law.uvic.ca/documents/MTD-Award.pdf] at para 178; IA Laird, 'MTD Equity Sdn Bhd and MTD Chile SA v Republic of Chile—Recent Developments in the Fair and Equitable Treatment Standard' in *Transnational Dispute Management*, October 2004, vol 1, issue 4.

92 Ibid at para 63.

host states upon which foreign investors reasonably rely. Such conduct may vary from express representations made by a host state, its course of dealings giving rise to such a reasonable expectation, and the statements and opinions expressed by administrative agencies on the applicability of national law, to the general regulatory framework upon which an investor reasonably relies.[93]

As an illustration, in the *Thunderbird* case, the tribunal held that, while the Government of Mexico had made a representation upon which claimant investor Thunderbird had relied, that conduct was only actionable if it created 'reasonable and justifiable expectations on the part of the investor'.[94] The tribunal found that the government's representation had not generated any legitimate expectation upon which the claimant could reasonably have relied.

The legitimacy of the investor's expectations is evaluated according to an objective standard, which by definition is variable in application. In *Saluka v Czech Republic*, the tribunal explicitly rejected a subjective standard, stating:

> the scope of the Treaty's protection of foreign investment against unfair and inequitable treatment cannot exclusively be determined by foreign investors' subjective motivations and considerations. Their expectations, in order for them to be protected, must rise to the level of legitimacy and reasonableness in light of the circumstances.[95]

Equally difficult is arriving at a balance between the legitimate expectations of foreign investors and the justifiable interests of host states. In *Saluka v Czech Republic*, the tribunal opined:

> No investor may reasonably expect that the circumstances prevailing at the time the investment is made remain totally unchanged. In order to determine whether frustration of the foreign investor's expectations was justified and reasonable, the host State's legitimate right subsequently to regulate domestic matters in the public interest must be taken into consideration as well.[96]

The problem, again, is in establishing a principled legal foundation upon which to base the expectations of investors on the one hand, and objective criteria by which to assess whether the governmental action may reasonably override those expectations on the other.

---

93 On such 'legitimate expectations', see *Saluka Investments BV (The Netherlands) v The Czech Republic*, Partial Award dated 17 March 2006, at [http://ita.law.uvic.ca/documents/Saluka-PartialawardFinal.pdf] at para 304; *Waste Management, Inc v The United Mexican States*, ICSID Case No ARB(AF)/00/3 (NAFTA), Final Award, 30 April 2004, available at [http://ita.law.uvic.ca/documents/laudo_ingles.pdf] at para 98; *International Thunderbird Gaming Corporation v Mexico*, UNCITRAL (NAFTA), Arbitral Award, 26 January 2006, available at [http://ita.law.uvic.ca/documents/ThunderbirdAward.pdf] at para 147; GAMI *Investments Inc v The Government of the United Mexican States*, Final Award of 15 November 2004 (UNCITRAL Arbitration), available at [http://ita.law.uvic.ca/documents/Gami.pdf] at para 100.

94 Ibid at para.304.

95 See *Saluka* above note 93 at para 304.

96 Ibid at para 300. But cf *CME Czech Republic BV v The Czech Republic*, Partial Award of 13 September 2001, 9 ICSID Reports 12. See also *Técnicas Medioambientales Tecmed, SA v United Mexican States*, ICSID Case No ARB (AF)/00/2, Award dated 29 May 2003, available at [http://ita.law.uvic.ca/documents/Tecnicas_001.pdf] at para 160.

11.5.6 Review of awards

Arbitral awards in investment cases, in the regimes studied, are generally not subject to appeal to domestic courts. However, they may be subject to review by the tribunal itself, in which it determines whether it has erred in making its awards. An arbitral award may also be reviewed by an arbitral 'court' that is responsible for the interpretation, revision or annulment of that award. Alternatively, the award may be subject to review before a court of law.

Several questions arise. What is the basis for review under the applicable arbitral regime and applicable law? What are the standards of review that are applied? How do they diverge from one another? What are the consequences of such reviews? And, in particular, how might courts determine the applicable remedy?

11.5.6a The ICSID

The ICSID provides for a review of an investment award by a Challenge Committee, which is set up specifically for the purpose of such a review.

The grounds under which the Challenge Committee can conduct a review are restricted and fall well short of an appeal. However, it is significantly empowered, including the ability to modify or nullify the award, albeit on limited procedural grounds. Resort to domestic courts is not an option under the ICSID, as there are an entirely internally generated system of rules governing the establishment, determination and review of arbitration awards.

The grounds for a challenge of an ICSID investment award include:

- The panel was not properly constituted;
- The panel manifestly exceeded its powers;
- There was corruption on the part of a panel member;
- There was a serious departure from a fundamental rule of procedure; or
- The award failed to state the reasons on which it was based.

In the past, ICSID Challenge Committees have interpreted these rules for challenge expansively, leading to a number of challenges. Given the floodgate problems that arose, some more recent ICSID Challenge Committees have declined to hear challenges, although this is not consistently the case.

Under the ICSID, either party can also request that an award be annulled by an ad hoc Challenge Committee. ICSID Challenge Committees traditionally interpreted these rules liberally and permitted a series of challenges. While this practice has dissipated, the ICSID challenge process is still viewed as being proactive.

11.5.6b The UNCITRAL and ICSID Additional Facility

Consistent with international commercial arbitration practice, neither the ICSID nor the ICSID Additional Facility Arbitration Rules provide for any appeal on the merits of the case. They limit jurisdiction to review based on the interpretation of awards, to redressing procedural irregularities, and to correct arithmetic and other clerical errors. They do not determine whether or not to enforce, modify or annul an award on the merits. Consistent with international arbitration practice, the UNCITRAL and ICSID Additional Facility awards may be challenged under the commercial arbitration laws of the place of arbitration.

11.5.7 The backlash

A backlash against international regulation of investor practice, including resort to arbitration as distinct from domestic courts, is based on concern that states will cede their sovereignty to private panels that reach decisions in disregard of state interests, and subject countries to intrusive and opportunistic investor practice. The spectre is raised of international investors that, not unlike multinational gobbling giants, use private methods of arbitration to fetter states, subjecting them to global corporate excess. The alternative is to cement state-controlled regulation of investor practice consistent with the immediate social concerns of the affected state and enforced through domestic courts.[97]

11.6 Conclusion

Australian investors have various legal factors to consider in making direct investment decisions. Among these is the law that will apply to their investment practices. Despite the notion that there is an international body of investment law, customary in origins and glossed by multilateral, regional and bilateral treaties, the international law governing investments is a morass of disparate parts. A simplistic response is that the application of a domestic system of law to govern foreign investment provides clarification only by acknowledging that any body of international law that is inclusive of domestic law is likely to be diverse in nature and effect. Even if one accepts that the resolution of investment disputes is significantly influenced by regionalism, such as by the investment law prevailing among the parties to the EU and the NAFTA, the result is rather different regional investment law and practice.

For example, the foundation of EU investment law rests upon a highly integrated body of principles, rules and procedures governing investment, administered by centralised institutions. This integrated and centralised approach is evident in the self-effectuating EU doctrines of 'direct applicability' and 'direct effect'.[98] Equally

---

97 While the argument is usually couched in terms of side-stepping local courts, critics have argued that Chapter 11 tribunal decisions could prevail over local courts. See D Krueger, 'The Combat Zone: *Mondev International, Ltd v United States* and the Backlash against NAFTA Chapter 11' (2003) 21 *BU Int'l LJ* 399 (arguing that, but for a technical time bar, the *Mondev* tribunal might have prevailed over US judicial decisions, but acknowledging that in both the *Mondev* and *Loewen* cases (see above note 64), the tribunals were reluctant to hold the government liable in conflict with the decisions of domestic US courts).

98 It is arguable that the NAFTA negotiators, rather than having ceded sovereignty, adopted ADR to resolve disputes. It is more accurate to state that, in adopting Chapter 11 of the NAFTA, each NAFTA party conceded the application of its domestic law and resorted to its domestic courts in favour of an independent arbitral process grounded in principles of international investment law.

distinctive of the EU is the right of investors to access national courts of EU member states.[99] In contrast, Chapter 11 of the NAFTA represents a rather decentralised regional agreement; it relies on ad hoc awards arrived at by an assortment of arbitral panels; there is limited attempt under the NAFTA to seek conceptual uniformity or the integration of law and practice. Judicial review of Chapter 11 decisions is at best a patchwork quilt. There is also no centralised court system that seeks to unify investment law. In so far as domestic laws apply, they serve less to explain the international jurisprudence on investment than to 'domesticate' investment decision making.

Australian investors need to appreciate that significant legal implications can arise when they invest in foreign states. There is some guidance in the small number of FTAs and BITs to which Australia has subscribed. Australia and most of its trade partners can also resolve some disputes involving investment at the WTO; however, as described above, this is very limited. Australian investors also need to be cognisant of the domestic investment laws that prevail in host states, as well as the extent to which domestic tribunals purport to exercise jurisdiction over foreign investors and their investments. Historically, there was good reason to be concerned that governments in some developing states might construe their authority to expropriate the property of foreign investors expansively, on broad public policy grounds. This chapter has also shown that Australian investors ought to recognise that highly developed states are also often empowered by their domestic laws to expropriate foreign investments on national interest grounds. The US domestic law on investment, for example, grants extensive authority to the US Government to expropriate foreign investments, while at the same time purporting to comply with international investment law. The recent trading climate resulting from the financial crisis has also accentuated the tension between the desire of states to liberalise trade and their preoccupation with protecting vested local interests. How this tension is played out over the ensuing decades will have a significant impact on FDI, including by Australians abroad.

Questions

With regard to the case study at the beginning of this chapter:

1 Is there an international investment law? What is the governing law?
2 a Explain the various philosophies regarding the benefits or detriments of FDI.
  b What impact do BITs or FTAs have on these philosophies?
3 What are some of the factors a company must consider when deciding whether to invest abroad?
4 What are the primary arguments states can invoke to justify their regulation of FDI?
5 What kinds of investment disputes involving Australian parties are likely to arise in the immediate future?

99 The problem under the EU regime is that access to the EU is not 'as of right', but is subject to particular treaty provisions that vary from treaty to treaty.

6 What is an 'expropriation'? Provide an example of an 'expropriation'.
7 What is the distinction between a 'direct' and an 'indirect' 'expropriation'?
8 What international bodies/institutions are primarily responsible for resolving international investment disputes?
9 What role, if any, does the Australian judiciary have in deciding international investment disputes?
10 a Why does the AUSFTA with the USA not contain Chapter 11-type provisions?
   b What effect does this have on investment considerations?
11 What are the primary issues which tribunals and/or courts should take account in deciding international investment disputes?
12 Can private parties bring actions directly against states/governments before international tribunals/institutions?
13 What are the primary arguments investors can invoke to protect their 'rights' from the exercise of 'powers' by those states?
14 a How would you advise FISHCO to proceed?
   b Is there any recourse for FISHCO if California stops the construction of the fishing farm facilities?
15 a Would California stopping the construction of the fishing farm facility be an expropriation?
   b If so, what would be the appropriate forum?
   c What remedy would be available to FISHCO?
   d Would your answer differ if FISHCO were a Canadian company?
   e What if the AUSFTA contained NAFTA Chapter 11-type provisions providing for investor–state tribunals?
16 a Are the tax breaks promised to FISHCO by the former government compliant with international law?
   b Which law might be relevant?
   c Who could complain?

PART VI

Dispute Resolution

CHAPTER 12

dispute resolution: courts

You are employed as assistant to the Director of International Sales at WOOLTHINGS INTERNATIONAL. WOOLTHINGS is a large international company based in Adelaide that sells designer woollen products, primarily in Asian markets. Your manager is currently negotiating on behalf of WOOLTHINGS to supply woollen clothing to Clothesfit, an international chain of clothing stores based in the United Arab Emirates. Both WOOLTHINGS and Clothesfit are public companies. Should the contract be concluded, it would involve supplying woollen clothing designed specifically for Clothesfit's global market. Anticipated annual gross revenue from such a contract is approximately AUD$60 million. Your manager anticipates a five-year renewable contract. WOOLTHINGS has annual gross sales of AUD$400 million. Clothesfit's gross annual sales exceed AUD$1.2 billion.

Your manager knows that you are studying international business law. She has asked you to prepare a memorandum of questions and issues relating to these matters that she can raise in her meeting with the Manager of the Legal Department as they prepare the draft terms of the proposed contract. She is particularly concerned about the risk of any disputes arising, and ensuring that WOOLTHINGS is legally protected through, among other provisions, a suitable choice of jurisdiction and law clause in the contract. She has told you that if this contract is concluded, it will be the largest entered into by WOOLTHINGS to date; that Clothesfit is known to drive a hard bargain; and that WOOLTHINGS's greatest asset is its reputation for producing quality goods in a competitive international market for woollen products.

12.1 Introduction

This chapter initiates discussion on how disputes may arise, alternative methods of resolving them, and making effective choices among those alternatives. The chapter concentrates on resolving international commercial disputes before courts of law.

By the end of this chapter, readers should have an idea about how a party can resolve a trade or investment dispute before an Australian court, in light of Australian law, including Australia's international rights and obligations. The analysis contained in this chapter concentrates on approaches adopted by Australian courts towards choice of laws and jurisdiction, and the application of foreign law to a dispute. It considers issues of sovereignty and the enforcement of judicial decisions by Australian and foreign courts. The chapter also reflects on the extraterritorial reach of such decisions in light of state sovereignty and local public policy on the one hand, and the principles of comity and international law on the other.

Chapter 13 then discusses an 'alternative' choice of jurisdiction to domestic courts of law, in particular the choice of international commercial arbitration, with a focus on investment disputes.

12.2 Choice of process

Freedom of contract allows the parties not only to choose the forum that will hear any dispute between them, but also the law that will apply to any dispute. The parties are also free to choose the process by which their dispute will be heard. For example, the parties may include a clause in their contract that, should a dispute arise, they will first attempt to resolve it through mediation. Their decision constitutes a choice of process, which may include further choices as to how such mediation should be conducted (not limited to making a choice of arbitration or submitting their dispute to a domestic court in a particular jurisdiction).

What is important to note is that mediation may actually be a preliminary stage in a process that may end up with litigation. In the recent Federal Court decision in *Armacel Pty Ltd v Smurfit Stone Container Corporation*,[1] the contract in dispute included both the choice of New South Wales as the applicable jurisdiction and law, and that the parties should attempt to resolve their dispute by mediation in Sydney. Accordingly, the parties were to first attempt to resolve their conflict themselves through the facilitation of a mediator, and only failing that to have recourse to the courts. So it is more correct to state that in choosing mediation the parties choose to resolve disputes through processes that *precede* litigation. Their idealised result in making such a choice may be to settle their dispute without having to resort to litigation. Their purpose may be to reduce the costs, time, disruption of their respective businesses, and publicity associated with dispute resolution, while conceivably trying to preserve their commercial relationship.

Whether parties choose to adopt mediation or some other method of dispute resolution preceding litigation depends on the particular relationship between the parties, their needs and expectations both of themselves and of each other, and how they engage in settlement. Their choice also involves recognition of the risks of making such a choice, as when mediation is protracted and costly, and is ultimately followed by even more protracted and costly litigation. Parties are also free to choose particular substitutes for litigation. For example, they may choose arbitration in accordance with the rules of a particular arbitration association; their rationale may be that an arbitrator is likely to have more commercial expertise than most courts of law, and that this expertise is needed to resolve their dispute. Furthermore, an arbitrator may operate more expeditiously than a court that is hampered by rules of evidence and procedure. The parties may also believe that an arbitral award will be widely recognised and enforced in international law. Finally, in choosing to arbitrate

1 [2008] FCA 592.

under the rules of a selected arbitration association, they may have resort to a widely used and tried and tested process of dispute resolution in international commerce.

What is important to recognise is that parties have many choices to consider in deciding how conflicts between them should be resolved. No one choice is perfect; no alternative is likely to be suited to every case.

John Levingston, 'Choice of Law, Jurisdiction and ADR Clauses'

6th Annual Contract Law Conference, 26–28 February 2008, p 10[2]

INTERNATIONAL APPROACH BY AUSTRALIAN COURTS AND APPLICATION OF FOREIGN LAW

The potential disadvantage for a party caused by conflict of laws and jurisdiction is ameliorated by the international approach adopted by Australian courts towards international commercial disputes. This is despite the common law rule that Australian courts do not know foreign law.

However, Australian courts have no difficulty accepting evidence and proof of foreign law, and in applying it. This is usually done as an expert opinion based on specialized knowledge set out in an affidavit from a practitioner qualified in the jurisdiction. Though questions of foreign law are decided by the judge.

A typical foreign law clause in international trade is: *This agreement is governed by the law of England;* which may appear in international agreements concerning export commodities, charter parties and other shipping documents, international payments and marine insurance. English law is assumed to be the same as Australian law (and in some areas it is, such as in regard to bills of exchange and marine insurance), unless there is evidence to the contrary. In some Australian export trades, an English governing law clause appears for no reason other than it has been used in those trades for over 100 years.

Further, Australian courts are sometimes prepared to consider and apply decisions beyond the traditional common law developed by English courts. This is particularly evident in the law of Admiralty and Equity in which Australian courts have recognised the need to adopt an international approach in the interpretation of Conventions consistent with foreign courts dealing with the same issue. This approach is reinforced by *forum non-conveniens*, stay applications and anti-suit injunctions.

… … …

12.3 Litigating before Australian courts

Through litigation, the parties bring an international trade dispute before a domestic Australian court. In choosing to submit a dispute to the domestic courts of Australia, the parties make a *choice of jurisdiction*; namely, to have their dispute heard by courts in that jurisdiction, including before the courts of a particular state in Australia. In choosing the law that applies to their dispute, the parties make a *choice of law*; namely, to have their dispute decided in accordance with that or some other law.

2 Available at [www.lexisnexis.com.au/aus/products/upFront/documents/Choiceoflaw_jurisdictionandADRclausespaper.pdf].

Often parties to international commercial disputes make the same choice of jurisdiction and choice of law, such as by agreeing to submit their dispute to an Australian Federal or Supreme Court to decide in accordance with local law. However, the choice of law need not coincide with the choice of jurisdiction, as when the parties choose to have their dispute resolved before the Supreme Court of New South Wales but have a foreign law, such as the law of a particular state in the USA, as their choice of law. Alternatively, a local court in exercising jurisdiction may decide in accordance with the domestic law governing the choice of law to apply foreign law. Conversely, a local court may decide not to apply foreign law, despite it being the choice of law of the parties, on public policy or other grounds.

12.3.1 Choice of jurisdiction

While a choice of forum or jurisdiction clause will usually provide for a dispute to be heard by a particular court in a specific jurisdiction, it might also provide for a particular procedure by which a dispute will be heard.

There are various reasons for parties making choices of jurisdiction:

- One or both parties may conduct business in that jurisdiction;
- The jurisdiction may be geographically proximate to the parties, such as in the place where they conduct business or most witnesses reside, or it may be close to such a place, or otherwise conveniently located for the purpose of resolving a dispute;
- The parties may choose a jurisdiction because of the reputation of courts within that jurisdiction, their perception of impartiality there, the absence of bias or corruption, the transparency of proceedings, and the expeditious conduct of hearings; they may be familiar with those courts and confident in their ability to resolve commercial disputes in a manner that is recognised and enforced by foreign courts; the choice of a 'convenient' choice of forum is referred to as a *forum conveniens* clause.

In practice, the parties to international commercial transactions may resort to domestic courts for various 'practical' reasons:

- The tradition of domestic courts in resolving particular types of international commercial disputes;
- The nature, development and significance of the substantive law in that forum particularly as it applies to the industry or transaction at issue;
- The past experience of other parties with those courts;
- The familiarity and level of comfort of the parties with the rules of evidence and procedure applied by those courts;
- The manner in which those courts have functioned in the past;
- The recognition they have accorded to international business transactions;
- The extent to which their rules of evidence and procedure have been deemed 'progressive' in nature;
- The manner in which they have applied local law or public policy to international disputes;
- The recognition they have accorded to foreign law; and
- The likelihood of their decisions being recognised internationally and enforced by foreign courts.

The choice of a domestic court may also be a matter of convenience, including:

- The proximity of one or more parties to those domestic courts;
- The fact that one or more parties conduct business there; or
- The fact that no party has a vested interest in choosing such courts.

A party may also choose a jurisdiction for less credible reasons. One party may be in a dominant bargaining position that enables it to insist on its choice of jurisdiction in the place at which it conducts business, where its witnesses are located, or before courts with which it is most familiar and whose proceedings it may be able to influence. The other party may simply have to take it or leave it.

In limited circumstances, a court may decline to enforce the choice of jurisdiction of the parties on the grounds that:

- The choice was made in bad faith, or that the consent to that choice was vitiated by fraud, duress, oppression, undue influence or unconscionable conduct;
- The choice conflicts with the mandatory law of the forum, such as the law governing anticompetitive behaviour; or
- The choice conflicts with the forum's public policy.

Another rationale by which courts may decline to enforce the parties' choice of jurisdiction is that the choice undermines the court's 'personal jurisdiction'. This rationale is problematic because it denies the freedom of the parties to make a choice of jurisdiction; it may also over-extend the public policy of the forum court. In addition, courts that adopt this stance may be perceived as acting parochially:

- They may superimpose that choice of forum in disregard of the reasonable expectations of the parties;
- They may employ subjective reasoning in reaching decisions; and/or
- They may misapply the terms of business contracts, including subverting the consent of the parties.

Arguably, courts that adopt such a recourse undermine, not only predictability in contracting, but also the public policy by which choice of jurisdiction and law are intended to sanctify the freedom of parties to contract.

A related problem arises when one or both parties engage in 'forum shopping'. This occurs when parties 'shop' for jurisdictions that are sympathetic to their interests. That shopping may include jurisdictions:

- That are more proximate to one party's business offices, executives and witnesses than are alternative jurisdictions;
- Where the rules of evidence and procedure are expected to favour that party; or
- Whose courts are likely to invoke local public policies in favour of that party.

Alternatively, a party may forum-shop in order to inconvenience the other party, for example:

- By raising that other party's costs of bringing witnesses to the forum;
- By engaging in dilatory tactics so as to prolong a dispute; or
- By driving up the other party's costs.

Finally, parties to international business transactions may fail to make a choice of jurisdiction. In that case, a court to which one party brings a dispute has to determine whether it has jurisdiction to hear that matter and, if so, on what grounds it may exercise that jurisdiction. In the absence of a forum selection clause, the court may still determine that it has jurisdiction; for example, on the grounds that both parties reside there, or have their principal places of business there; or alternatively, that they are otherwise 'substantially' connected to that jurisdiction.

If a court determines that it has jurisdiction, it will ordinarily apply the procedural law of that forum to the dispute, including its domestic rules of evidence and procedure. It may also apply the substantive law of the forum on grounds that it is the *lex loci contractus*; that is, 'the law of the place where the contract was made'. Such a judicial determination may arise in particular if the contract giving rise to the dispute was formed there.

In assuming jurisdiction, a court may apply the *lex fori*—'the law of the forum'—with or without taking account of that forum's conflict of law rules. If it does take account of these conflict of law rules, it may apply the forum's substantive law on the grounds that its conflict of law rules so prescribe. Alternatively, it may apply the law of another forum on the same grounds.

12.3.2 Choice of law

> The realm of the conflict of laws is a dismal swamp, filled with quaking quagmires, and inhabited by learned but eccentric professors who theorize about mysterious matter in a strange and incomprehensible jargon.[3]

Parties that make a choice of law decide which—among competing—laws ought to apply to their dispute. The guiding principle is that such choices are voluntarily made and exercised in good faith.

Parties to international business contracts may make varied choices. For example, they may adopt a choice of forum, but not a choice of law. A 'good reason' for them not making a choice of law may be on account of their intention to conduct all future business dealings in the same jurisdiction, or their expectation that courts in that jurisdiction will apply domestic law as the 'law of the place of contracting' to any dispute. However, that 'good reason' may become a 'bad reason' should their place of contracting change, as when forum law changes, or where forum courts apply foreign law on the grounds that the performance of the contract is 'substantially connected' to the law of another place.

Parties to disputes may encounter both difficulty and cost in having to 'prove' foreign laws that may well be conceptually, substantively and procedurally different from domestic law. Courts may also encounter difficulties in having to establish and then apply the substantive law of another state. They may ascertain foreign law by taking judicial notice of that law, and this may occur if the substantive law of that other state is comparable to the law of the forum, as when the common law on the formulation, performance and termination of a contract is comparable under Australian and English common law.

---

3 D Prosser, 'Interstate Publication' (1953) 51 *Michigan Law Review* 959 at 971.

These complications grow when the parties or their witnesses misconstrue foreign law and the court, in turn, misapplies that law. This occurs especially when the foreign law is complex, when it is grounded in policies and principles that vary significantly from those that apply in the forum, or when it includes statutes or regulations that have a history which the forum court has difficulty comprehending. Also, a party may adduce evidence of foreign law that is erroneous, the other party may fail to remedy that impression, and/or the court may simply misunderstand the representations made by the parties or their witnesses about the nature of that foreign law.

Courts that misunderstand the substantive law of another state may also make characterisation errors; for example, they may fail to differentiate between rights entrenched in foreign constitutions and 'ordinary' rights. They may misunderstand the difference between procedural and substantive law, as well as the application of each. Courts may also misconstrue concepts in foreign legal systems, such as by conflating common law principles of contract law with civil law principles of obligations. For example, Australian judges may conceive of principles of 'consent' in contract and 'duty of care' in tort quite differently from the conception of 'obligations' adopted by civil law judges in France or Germany.

Australian courts may diverge significantly from foreign courts in the rules of evidence and procedure they apply, such as in determining the admissibility and sufficiency of evidence. They may also differ over the entitlement of a party to obtain specific performance or an injunction against an alleged legal wrong; over the extent of redress arising from an alleged breach of contract; on limits placed on the movement of property out of the jurisdiction; and on the extent of the prohibition on the destruction of documents evidencing violation of a trade practice. They may treat the cause (reason) for contracting in civil law comparably to the 'consideration' ('bargained-for-exchange') for contracting in common law; and they may fail to differentiate between an ordinary legal duty of good faith and a fiduciary duty of the 'utmost good faith'.

These conceptual problems in understanding and applying foreign law are not peculiar to disputes in which the parties have failed to exercise choices of law. They are endemic to situations in which domestic courts are required to decide cases on the basis of foreign law.

These conceptual problems may be simplified by international codes and conventions governing business practice, such as the convention on the International Sale of Goods (CISG), that attempt to arrive at uniform principles governing international business practice. However, they may also be complicated by the different ways in which such international codes and conventions are interpreted. These codes are also usually far from exhaustive, and they are sometimes outpaced by changes in international business practice. In addition, not all states are signatories to the international conventions giving rise to such codes, and domestic courts may well apply particular sections in such codes differently.

A quite different problem in making a choice of law is that domestic courts charged with jurisdiction may decline to apply foreign law, such as if an Australian court insists on applying domestic law on the grounds that it is required to do so by legislation, or because foreign law is perceived to be unreasonable or in conflict with domestic public policy, even if the contract provides for the application of that foreign law. For example, however 'international' a trade dispute may be, it may still be challenged before an Australian court for violating the *Trade Practices Act 1974* (Cth), leading to ACCC investigations and s 155 notices. If that court hears a dispute over anticompetitive conduct, it may apply the relevant *Contracts Review Act* dealing with unfair trade practice, the *Trade Practices Act* to regulate deceptive, misleading and unconscionable conduct, and the relevant *Fair Trading Act* to ensure that the conduct of trade is fair. The construction that it attributes to a 'misleading', 'deceptive' or 'unconscionable' trade practice may also diverge from the construction accorded to those practices under foreign law.

As we will see later in this chapter, the divergence between domestic and foreign law may pose significant problems in practice. For example, Australian courts may permit ordinary damages for anticompetitive conduct. In contrast, US courts may award treble damages under their antitrust legislation, particularly under the *Sherman Antitrust Act 1890*. Particular difficulties may arise if US courts not only assert jurisdiction, but also apply 'punitive' damages extraterritorially and well in excess of damages awarded by Australian courts.

12.4 'Exclusive' jurisdiction

Let us assume that one of the parties submits the same dispute to a foreign court in a country in which that party conducts business, or where some of the property in dispute is located. What if that foreign court accepts jurisdiction? What if that foreign court chooses to apply its domestic law to the dispute? And what if that domestic law diverges from the law in Australia?

These issues are not academic; they arise in commercial practice. What makes them difficult to answer is the realisation that foreign courts, not unlike Australian courts, may be influenced by their own local public policies; they may apply their own domestic legislation, sometimes as a matter of compulsion and other times as a convenience; and they may also decline to defer to the 'exclusive' jurisdiction or choice of foreign law because they accord primacy to domestic over foreign interests.

Let us take a practical example. What if the parties provide by contract that the law in New South Wales should be the exclusive law of the transaction and that any dispute should be decided in that jurisdiction? What if one party to that contract applies to a Federal District Court in the USA to resolve the same dispute, claiming that US law applies to the transaction? What if that US District Court accepts jurisdiction and decides the matter in accordance with US law? What might an Australian court do about it, should the unsuccessful party bring the matter before that Australian court?

Illustrating the judicial dilemma faced by Australian courts is the recent decision of the Federal Court of Australia in *Armacel Pty Ltd v Smurfit Stone Container Corporation*.[4] That case involved a dispute between Armacel Pty Ltd, an Australian company, and

4 [2008] FCA 592.

Smurfit Stone Container Corporation, a US company. The agreement provided that New South Wales law would prevail in the event of a conflict between its law and the law of the jurisdiction in which the equipment which was the subject of a licensing agreement was located.

The key issue revolved around this dispute resolution clause in the intellectual property licensing agreement:

> This Agreement must be read and construed according to the laws of the State of New South Wales, Australia and the parties submit to the jurisdiction of that State. If any dispute arises between the Licensor and the Licensee in connection with this Agreement or the Technology, the parties will attempt to mediate the dispute in Sydney, [New South Wales,] Australia.

One party, Smurfit, instituted proceedings in a US District Court. The other party, Armacel instituted proceedings shortly afterwards before the Federal Court of Australia on the same matter.

The US District Court applied the US conflicts of law principle of contract interpretation, and held that Australia was not the exclusive licensing jurisdiction. That court also dismissed Armacel's motion to dismiss the US proceedings for want of jurisdiction.

Based on that decision, Smurfit applied for a stay of proceedings before the Federal Court of Australia on grounds that Australia was not the appropriate forum; that is, on the grounds of *forum non conveniens*.

Judge Jacobson on the Federal Court of Australia declined to allow Armacel to re-argue the question of whether the jurisdiction clause in the licensing agreement provided for exclusive Australian jurisdiction. Judge Jacobson held that the agreement ought to have been interpreted in light of New South Wales law, as the governing law of the contract; but that it would be improper to permit proceedings on the same issues to take place in Australia; and that the US District Court decision prevented or estopped such proceedings. Had estoppel not applied, the New South Wales jurisdiction would have been exclusive, even though the jurisdiction clause was not exclusive on its face.

Judge Jacobson gave due consideration to the facts that the parties had negotiated at arm's length; they intended to provide for certainty in choosing the place at which their dispute would be litigated; they agreed to compulsory mediation in New South Wales; and their agreement had sought to avoid requiring a New South Wales court to apply the law of another jurisdiction as the location of the relevant equipment. He maintained too that submitting to 'the jurisdiction of [New South Wales]' included the exercise by the Federal Court of federal jurisdiction in the State of New South Wales.

Despite staying the Federal Court proceedings, Judge Jacobson held that Armacel could apply to lift the stay should developments in the US District Court render such an application appropriate. He referred in particular to Armacel's claims under the Australian *Trade Practices Act* that Smurfit had engaged in misrepresentations while negotiating the licensing agreement, but accepted expert evidence from Smurfit's US counsel that such claims could be brought in the US proceedings. However, Judge Jacobson also held that, should the US Court decline to apply the *Trade Practices Act*, it might be appropriate to lift the stay before the Australian Federal Court.

Finally, Judge Jacobson made the stay conditional on Smurfit filing an appearance in the Australian proceedings and participating in mediation in Sydney, in compliance with the licensing agreement, which Smurfit had previously declined to do:

> 95. It is prima facie vexatious and oppressive to commence a proceeding in an Australian court if another action is already pending between the same parties, raising the same issues in another country. The existence of simultaneous proceedings with respect to the same controversy is a highly relevant consideration but it does not necessarily follow that there should be a stay of the Australian proceedings: *Henry v Henry* at 591–592; *CSR v Cigna* at 389ff.
>
> 96. The test to be applied is whether having regard to the controversy as a whole, the Australian proceedings are vexatious or oppressive in the *Voth* sense: *CSR v Cigna* at 401. The considerations include which forum can provide more effectively for complete resolution of the matters in controversy, which proceeding was commenced first and the stage that each of the proceedings has reached: *Henry v Henry* at 592.
>
> 97. Plainly, the fact that the United States proceedings were first in point of time is a relevant consideration. Moreover, for the reasons referred to by Lord Woolf in *Messier Dowty* at [34]–[42], I do not consider that I should approach the question with an adverse pre-disposition to the claim for negative declaratory relief: *Challenger Group Holdings Ltd v Concept Equity Pty Ltd* [2005] NSWSC 374 at [42]–[43]. This issue in the US District Court is not hypothetical. Our courts should be slow to criticise the approach of the foreign court to the question of negative declaratory relief. It must be a matter of discretion in all the circumstances. Moreover, the US District Court has held that it does have jurisdiction and no point was raised in the Pennsylvania proceeding about negative declaratory relief.
>
> 98. The essential question which seems to me to arise is whether Armacel would be able to obtain the relief it seeks under the *Trade Practices Act* in the proceedings in the US District Court. This question turns substantially upon whether the District Court has 'supplemental jurisdiction' over the trade practices claims under 28 USC SS 1367. I will set out the text of that section as an annexure to my reasons for judgment.

This decision is not remarkable on its face. However, it does demonstrate that, no matter how seemingly self-evident the choice of an Australian jurisdiction and law might be, an Australian court may defer to a foreign court that assumes jurisdiction over the matter. It may do so on the grounds that the foreign court has jurisdiction, that it has properly discharged it, and that it would be inappropriate for an Australian court to re-hear the matter. In favour of Australian courts so determining is the assertion that Australian judges should defer to foreign judgments, except on grounds of public policy or in accordance with the principles of natural justice.

A countervailing concern is that parties to an international commercial transaction will ignore the 'exclusive' jurisdiction and choice of the law expressed in the contract and will shop for a sympathetic forum. A related concern is that a foreign forum may arrive at a determination in disregard to the choice of law chosen by the parties and at variance with the determination that a domestic court might have reached, had it been charged with jurisdiction.

Armacel Pty Ltd v Smurfit Stone Container Corporation displays this tension between upholding an exclusive jurisdiction clause and respecting the exercise of jurisdiction and choice of law of a foreign court. It also demonstrates the tension between staying domestic proceedings on the grounds of discouraging duplication in litigation and domestic public policy in retaining jurisdiction.

Finally, the decision illustrates the ambivalence that some Australian courts may feel. On the one hand, they may reluctantly decline to accept jurisdiction because a foreign court has dealt with the matter. On the other hand, they may instruct the parties to perform residual duties in the domestic jurisdiction that they had assumed by contract but failed to perform. In *Armacel*, Judge Jacobson stayed domestic proceedings, but at the same time instructed the parties to participate in proceedings before the Federal Court of Australia and to submit to mediation, as was provided for by the contract.

12.5 The principle of *forum non conveniens*

In jurisdictions that subscribe to the principle of *forum non conveniens*, a court can dismiss a case on the grounds that the dispute is better adjudicated in a different forum. In effect, the court determines both that the forum is 'not convenient' and, by way of contrast, that another forum is 'convenient'.

The principle of *forum non conveniens* is based on the notion that the forum may not be a 'convenient' place to hear a dispute. The law governing *forum non conveniens* is complicated by the issue, not simply of whether the forum is 'convenient' or 'inconvenient', but whether it is the 'most suitable' forum, to the exclusion of others. Further complicating the analysis is the more recent practice of courts to decide based on whether the forum was 'clearly inappropriate'.

The High Court of Australia rejected the 'most suitable' forum test in *Oceanic Sun Line Special Shipping Co v Fay*[5]and in *Voth v Manildra Flour Mills*.[6] Instead, the High Court devised its own 'clearly inappropriate forum' test, in effect by eliminating 'clearly inappropriate forums' rather than all other forums.

In applying the *forum non conveniens* test, Australian courts tend to compare foreign versus local options in deciding which forum is the 'most appropriate'. For example, in a wrongful dismissal case, the court may only dismiss a case on the grounds of *forum non conveniens* if the defendant is able to establish that it is 'oppressed' or 'harassed' by the plaintiff's choice of Australia as the forum for bringing a legal action. The result is that it is very difficult for Australian defendants to obtain a dismissal from their own courts on the grounds of *forum non conveniens*. In *Regie National des Usines Renault SA v Zhang*,[7] the High Court reaffirmed the 'clearly inappropriate forum' test in Australian law. However, it also stated that, even when the law of a foreign country had to be applied to decide a dispute, Australia would not be a 'clearly inappropriate' forum for hearing the matter.

5 (1988) 165 CLR 197.

6 (1990) 71 CLR 538.

7 (2002) 210 CLR 491.

The problem is to identify what criteria Australia courts will invoke in differentiating between a 'clearly appropriate' and a 'clearly inappropriate' forum, as arose before the UK Court of Appeal in *Spiliada Maritime Corp v Cansulex Ltd.*[8] This difficulty is accentuated in cases in which Australian courts are faced with complex choice of law problems, such as in relation to allegedly negligent omissions giving rise to asbestos-related injuries arising overseas.[9]

The underlying difficulty is that Australian courts also do not agree upon the parameters of the law of the place of the tort. Consider the example of *Puttick v Fletcher Challenge Forests Pty Ltd.*[10] In that case, the High Court considered whether Victoria was a *forum non conveniens* in an action in which the plaintiff, a resident in Victoria, sued the holding company of his former employer, a company resident in New Zealand, for negligence.

The trial court in *Puttick* held that the applicable law was that of New Zealand and that Victoria was a 'clearly inappropriate forum'. On appeal, a majority of the Court of Appeal dismissed the appeal and held that the relevant law was that of New Zealand. The plaintiff appealed to the High Court of Australia, which unanimously allowed the appeal, holding that it was not yet possible to decide whether the law of New Zealand was the applicable law. All that the Court of Appeal could decide was that the law of New Zealand was arguably the law that governed the dispute. Assuming that the dispute was governed by New Zealand law, the High Court held that the defendant had not established that Victoria was a clearly inappropriate forum to try the dispute. Geographical proximity, similarities between legal systems and legislation for the determination of some trans-Tasman litigation led to the inference that Victoria was potentially an appropriate forum.

The court held that the orders of the trial judge should be set aside and that the defendant's original summons be dismissed with costs.

What does this decision of the High Court mean in practice? For one thing, it is unlikely that an Australian court will apply the principle of *forum non conveniens* to exclude its jurisdiction in a torts case based on negligence. What can also reasonably be assumed is that such a determination may be influenced by the kind and degree of connection between the subject matter in dispute and Australia, but that even a limited connection might suffice.

12.6 Proving foreign law

Foreign law lies at the heart of private international law. After all, a true conflict of law cannot be resolved unless and until the content of foreign law is established. Despite this, the pleading and proof of foreign law remain among the most under-explored topics in Australian private international law. In light of the High Court of Australia's significant

8 [1987] 1 AC 460.

9 See for example *James Hardie Industries v Hall* (1998) 43 NSWLR 554; [1998] NSWSC 434; *James Hardie Industries v Grigor* (1998) 45 NSWLR 20; [1998] NSWSC 266; *Amaca Pty Ltd v Frost* [2006] NSWCA 173. Under Australian law, the applicable law in such negligence cases is the law of the place of the tort: see *Regie National des Usines Renault SA v Zhang* (2002) 210 CLR 491; [2002] HCA 10.

10 [2007] VSCA 264.

> change of direction on choice of law since 2000, most notably in cases such as *John Pfeiffer Pty Ltd v Rogerson*, *Regie Nationale des Usines Renault SA v Zhang* and *Neilson v Overseas Projects Corporation of Victoria Ltd*, it is all the more important to answer some of the basic questions about the pleading and proof of foreign law. Who pleads foreign law? What law do they plead? Are they obliged to do so? How do they prove its content? When can local law be applied in the place of foreign law? ... Australian courts take a more robust and pragmatic approach to these issues than might be supposed. In particular, the so-called presumption of identity is a label that masks a much richer and more complex reality.[11]

International commercial disputes are often complex in themselves. Expecting parties to such disputes to prove foreign law adds yet a further layer of complexity. That complexity is most apparent in establishing the manner and extent to which foreign law ought to pleaded, determined and applied to the satisfaction—and comprehension—of a domestic court.

This is not to suggest that Australian courts are fundamentally suspicious of foreign law. Nor is it to suggest that they will disregard the choice of foreign law in international commercial agreements. In fact, they may well enforce choice of law clauses providing for the application of foreign law to a dispute. The problem is rather that it may be both costly and difficult for a party to prove foreign law. Domestic courts in Australia, as elsewhere, may also misunderstand the subtleties of foreign law. In addition, not only may the parties themselves misunderstand the nature and application of the foreign law, domestic courts may also do so, even in the face of extensive testimony on the nature and applicability of that foreign law.

The general principle is that, if the content of foreign law is in issue, it must be established by the party relying on it as a matter of fact, not as a question of law. In effect, the party purporting to rely on foreign law must first plead it and then prove it to the satisfaction of the Australian court.

As a functional matter, courts historically limit the requirement to prove foreign law by applying a 'presumption of similarity'—known as a 'presumption identity'. According to this presumption, foreign law is presumed to be similar to local law unless a party proves to the contrary. One result of this presumption is that the Australian courts usually apply Australian law as the default rule. Parties to international commercial transactions, in turn, may well accept this default rule because it avoids them having to suffer the inconvenience and cost of proving foreign law as a fact to the satisfaction of an Australian court.

Still, the presumption of similarity is not binding. There are instances in which Australian courts have insisted on being apprised of foreign law.[12] There are also recent cases in which Australian courts have denied relief on the grounds that a party failed to prove foreign law. In *National Auto Glass Supplies (Australia) Pty Ltd v Nielsen & Moller Autoglass (NSW) Pty Ltd*,[13] Judge Graham of the Federal Court of Australia raised more pervasive doubt over the applicability of the New South Wales

---

11 J McComish, 'Pleading and Proving Foreign Law in Australia' (2007) 31(2) *Melbourne University Law Review* 400 at 400.

12 See for example *Damberg v Damberg* (2001) 52 NSWLR 492.

13 [2007] FCA 1625 at para 41.

law of defamation to a case otherwise governed by Hong Kong and mainland Chinese law. In denying the applicants relief because they had failed to prove that foreign law, he stated:

> the general presumption that, in the absence of evidence to the contrary, foreign law is the same as Australian law is not inflexible. Where the law of the forum is governed by a statute and the law within Australia is itself lacking in uniformity, I doubt whether it could be presumed that the defamation law in China, including the Special Administrative Region of Hong Kong, is the same as it is in New South Wales.
>
> In the absence of evidence as to the relevant defamation law in the Special Administrative Region of Hong Kong and in the remainder of the People's Republic of China or at least that part where [the recipient] was located at the time when he received the ... email, I do not consider that any award of damages should be made referable to the transmission of the ... email to [the recipients in Hong Kong and China]. The relevant defamation law (if any) has not been proven.
>
> While the default application of Australian law is usually just and convenient, there are certain areas of law in which this default application should be overridden because it would be unfair or anomalous, especially so when local law is idiosyncratic. Although some judges have applied Australian defamation law by default in other cases governed by foreign law, defamation is an area of law which differs markedly around the world, and until the recent uniform *Defamation Acts*, the law of NSW was particularly idiosyncratic even in comparison with the other Australian States. Thus, it could hardly be said that the 'presumption of similarity' was a realistic or fair approximation of the actual content of foreign law in this case.
>
> Note: Although the common law 'place of publication' choice of law rule continues to apply in Australia regarding defamatory material published overseas (see *Dow Jones v. Gutnick*), the uniform *Defamation Acts* altered the rule applicable to material published within Australia so as to apply the law of the 'Australian jurisdictional area with which the harm occasioned by the publication as a whole has its closest connection'.

This decision raises doubts about the circumstances in which Australian courts may decline to apply the 'presumption of similarity'. It also focuses on the extent to which parties that fail to plead foreign law may be denied a legal remedy. Parties to international trade agreements therefore have to consider several strategic considerations, including when, how and to what extent they ought they to rely on and plead foreign law. If parties are to plead foreign law, they need to consider the most effective way in which to present it in court: in direct evidence, by recourse to expert testimony on foreign law, or by resort to foreign legal representation. They also need to demonstrate to the satisfaction of the court that the foreign law so pleaded will lead to a remedy that is more applicable to the dispute than Australian law would be.

The parties to an international commercial dispute should also appreciate that common law courts, for the most part, better understand the common law, while civil law courts better comprehend the trappings of civil law. For the parties to dabble with the law of another legal system may be a risky affair. For example, whether the defaulting party to an international commercial transaction gave 'good consideration' for a promise is quite different from whether there was a 'good reason' or *causa* for so contracting in civil law. Similarly, the ambivalence in some common law jurisdictions about whether a party is subject to a duty to negotiate in good faith is decided far more coherently in German law under the well-developed principle of 'fault on contracting', or *culpa in contrahendo*.

As a further illustration, punitive damages—seldom available for breach of contract in common law—may be available for the breach of an obligation in civil law, while common law remedies—such as reliance, restitution or expectation damages, specific performance and injunctions—may lack exact equivalents in civil law.

Nor are these legal differences restricted to differences between common law systems such as Australia and civil law systems such as Germany. Countries with similar legal traditions, such as the USA and Australia, may diverge significantly in both the nature and application of their laws, For example, the practice of some US courts of awarding treble damages in antitrust litigation, such as under the *Sherman Antitrust Act 1890*, is markedly in contrast to the more conservative approach of Australian courts in limiting damages generally. In addition, US courts are far more likely to tolerate extensive pretrial discovery and protracted courtroom procedures than are Australian courts.

12.6.1 Procedure versus substance

Courts may use the same concepts while attributing different meanings to them. For example, common law courts in Australia and the USA may have comparable views about matters of 'procedure' and matters of 'substance'. However, they may differ over whether a issue is procedural or substantive in nature, such as in quantifying damages in choice of law cases. The following extract from Russell Weintraub further elaborates:

Russell J Weintraub, 'Choice of Law for Quantification of Damages: A Judgment of the House of Lords Makes a Bad Rule Worse'

(2007) 42 *Texas International Law Journal* 311 at 314[14]

'Procedural' is a term used in many contexts. It may refer to the rules that govern the workings of the forum's courts—pleading, preserving objections for appeal, discovery. In the United States it may refer to a federal court's freedom to apply a federal rule when the court has subject-matter jurisdiction because of the parties' diversity of citizenship and is applying state, not federal, law to 'substantive' issues. Or, as indicated above, a 'procedural' issue might be one for which the forum court will not engage in its usual choice-of-law analysis, but will simply apply its own rule.

Justice Frankfurter said it as well as anyone: Matters of 'substance' and matters of 'procedure' are much talked about in the books as though they defined a great divide cutting across the whole domain of law. But, of course, 'substance' and 'procedure' are the same key-words to very different problems. Neither 'substance' nor 'procedure' represents the same invariants. Each implies different variables depending upon the particular problem for which it is used.

Therefore, in deciding when to apply the 'procedural' label in the context of choice of law, the question is: what justifies a forum in insisting on applying its local rule when under the forum's

14 Discussing *Harding v Wealands* [2006] HL 32.

choice-of-law rule the law of another jurisdiction applies to all 'substantive' issues? The proper standard is one that balances the difficulty of finding and applying the foreign rule against the likelihood that applying the forum's rule will affect the result in a manner that will induce forum shopping. Pleading, serving process, preserving objections for appeal, and similar issues relating to the day-to-day operation of courts are properly labeled 'procedural' for choice-of-law purposes. Flouting those rules will affect the outcome, but an attorney is not likely to choose one forum over another to take advantage of such housekeeping provisions. Discovery rules require more balancing. A forum that permits massive pre-trial discovery is likely to attract plaintiffs. US-style discovery is one of the reasons that American forums are magnets for the aggrieved and injured of the world. Nevertheless, it would be unthinkable to require US judges and lawyers to learn and apply foreign discovery rules. Discovery is properly labeled 'procedural' for choice-of-law purposes.

... ...

12.7 Enforcing foreign judgments

12.7.1 Introduction

The historical basis for the enforcement of a foreign judgment lies in the principle of the 'comity of nations'—*comitas gentium* —and is grounded in natural law thinking.[15] Over the past century, the principle has shifted to a legal duty; namely, that the defendant owes a legal duty to pay the debt, as expressed by the judgment. For a judgment to be enforced, it is necessary for the court making the judgment to be of 'competent jurisdiction'. It is necessary too for that court to have jurisdiction to enforce the defendant's legal duty in accordance with the conflict of law rules of the forum. Also necessary is the need to take account of statutory requirements that may impact upon the manner in which, and the extent to which, judges are able to enforce such a judgment.[16]

12.7.2 Problems with enforcement

The fact that a foreign court has pronounced judgment does not conclude the matter, since it is necessary to enforce that judgment and enforcement may well pose difficulties in foreign jurisdictions.

These problems are especially germane for Australian courts. At issue is the need to harmonise law beyond a patchwork of different principles governing the enforcement of foreign judgments. It is also necessary to recognise that national and regional regulatory regimes inevitably conceive of enforcement disparately and sometimes inconsistently.

---

15 See for example P Durack, 'Australia: Conflicts and Comity', in J Lacey (ed), *Act of State and Extraterritorial Reach: Problems of Law and Policy*, ABA Section of International Law and Practice, Chicago, 1983, p 47.

16 See *Adams v Cape Industries Plc* [1990] 1 Ch 433, in which the UK Court of Appeal attempted to enforce the judgment of a Texan court against a UK company whose subsidiaries were engaged in asbestos mining in South Africa. The court concluded, per Slade, Mustill and Gibson JJ, that the basis of a foreign judgment resided in the 'obligation' owed by the debtor.

Even though Australian law reflects a somewhat procedural approach towards the enforcement of foreign judgments generally, both the federal courts and the Supreme Court of New South Wales have sought to enforce foreign judgments on more substantive grounds, consistent with the Principles and Rules of Transnational Civil Procedure adopted by the International Institute for the Unification of Private Law (UNIDROIT) and the American Law Institute (ALI). Arriving at complete uniformity, however, is wishful thinking and remains elusive.[17]

The current situation in Australia in regard to the enforcement of foreign judgments is unsatisfactory from several perspectives:

- The *Foreign Judgments Act 1991* (Cth) provides for the enforcement of foreign judgments in only a select number of countries, and these do not include most of Australia's largest trade partners.
- Enforcement at common law entails significant cost, as the party purporting to enforce a foreign judgment ordinarily incurs the cost and time involved in initiating fresh proceedings and, according to some courts taking their lead from English courts, may need to re-litigate the entire case.
- There are few pervasive multilateral treaties that provide for the enforcement of foreign judgments. This is in stark contrast to the enforcement of foreign arbitral awards, discussed in the next chapter. Not only are international arbitral awards enforced under Part II of the *International Arbitration Act 1974* (Cth), and the widely adopted 1958 Convention on the Recognition and Enforcement of Foreign Arbitral Awards, they do not require the adoption of special procedures for enforcement, or the rehearing of an arbitration case.

12.7.3 The *Foreign Judgments Act*

The enforcement of foreign judgments in Australia may occur at common law or under the *Foreign Judgments Act*. At common law, a creditor armed with a foreign judgment may initiate fresh proceedings, either on the basis of the unsatisfied foreign judgment, or by virtue of the original cause of action. If the latter, the creditor will be prevented from raising any defence that was, or could have been, raised in the foreign proceedings.[18]

Under s 6 of the *Foreign Judgments Act*, an Australian court need not establish jurisdiction over the person against whom the judgment is being enforced. All that is required under the Act is that the foreign judgment be registered.

However far-reaching the jurisdiction of an Australian court may appear to be under the *Foreign Judgments Act*, it does not reach judgments in all countries. The list in s 5(1) is extensive, but is by no means exhaustive. Commonwealth jurisdictions—such as the UK, New Zealand and some provinces in Canada—are well-represented, as well as leading

---

17 See American Law Institute/UNIDROIT, The Principles and Rules of Transnational Civil Procedure and their Application to New South Wales, Final Draft, November 2004.

18 See *Blair & Perpetual Trustee Co Ltd v Curran* (1939) 62 CLR 464; *Port of Melbourne Authority v Anshun Pty Ltd* (1981) 147 CLR 589.

European countries such as France and Germany, along with Japan. But there are notable absences from the list among Australia's primary trading partners. For example, no federal or state courts in the USA are listed; nor are China or India. In addition, the list is oddly selective, such as in the recognition accorded to superior and inferior courts in Alberta, British Columbia and Manitoba, but not elsewhere in Canada. The result is that enforcing judgments is inevitably complicated by jurisdictional problems arising from such disparities.

It is also noteworthy that some foreign judgments are unenforceable at common law in Australia, notably prohibitions on enforcing penal,[19] appropriation[20] or other public laws, or giving effect to laws directed at public policy in the foreign state.[21] Part 2 of the *Foreign Judgments Act* also restricts the type of judgments that may be enforced to 'enforceable money judgments',[22] which include a judgment payable in 'an amount of money, other than ... taxes or other charges of a similar nature; or a fine or other penalty'. Further provision is made for setting aside a judgment whose enforcement 'would be contrary to public policy'.[23]

12.7.4 Jurisdiction over foreign judgments

Jurisdiction to proceed on a foreign judgment is similar at common law to jurisdiction under the *Foreign Judgments Act*.[24] Jurisdiction to proceed is based on either:

- The residence or presence of the judgment debtor in the forum at the time when proceedings are commenced;[25] or
- Express submission by the judgment debtor to the jurisdiction of the foreign court,[26] or voluntary submission, so long as the purpose extends beyond contesting jurisdiction or protecting property.[27]

Both the common law and the *Foreign Judgments Act* provide that a foreign judgment cannot be registered if it has not finally determined the dispute between the parties.[28] All that is required is that the matter has been finally determined, referred to as *res judicata*,

19 *Huntington v Attrill* [1893] AC 150; *Government of India, Ministry of Finance (Revenue Division) v Taylor* [1955] 1 All ER 292.

20 *Oppenheimer v Cattermole* [1976] AC 249.

21 See *Attorney-General (United Kingdom) v Heinemann Publishers Australia Pty Ltd (No 2)* 'The Spycatcher Case' (1988) 165 CLR 3.

22 Section 3(1).

23 Section 7(2)(a)(ix).

24 Section 7(2)(a)(iv) also provides for setting aside the registration of a judgment on the grounds that 'the courts of the country of the original court had no jurisdiction in the circumstances of the case'. However, s 7(3)(a) deems that the foreign court has jurisdiction when the judgment debtor voluntarily submits to the jurisdiction, agrees prior to the proceedings to be subject to the jurisdiction, or either resides in, or has its principal place of business in the jurisdiction at the time when proceedings were commenced.

25 See *Herman v Meallin* (1891) 8 WN (NSW) (natural persons); *Adams v Cape Industries Plc* [1990] Ch 433 (corporations).

26 See *Vogel v R & A Kohnstamm Ltd* [1973] QB 133.

27 *Foreign Judgments Act*, s 11.

28 *Castrique v Imrie* (1870) LR 4 HL 429; FJA s 5(4)(a).

whether or not it might become the subject of an appeal or be set aside as a default judgment after the date of application for enforcement as a foreign judgment.

The enforcement of foreign judgments is subject to substantive requirements. Under s 15 of the *Service and Execution of Process Act 1992* (Cth), the judgment debtor must be present at the time of service in the jurisdiction or anywhere in Australia. However, under the Supreme Court Rules of New South Wales, Part 10, rule 1A(1)(v), a judgment debtor outside Australia can be served.

12.7.5 Defences against enforcement of foreign judgments

Common law and statutory defences against the enforcement of a foreign judgment include a fraud committed on the foreign court, the denial of natural justice to the judgment debtor and enforcement that is against the public policy of the forum.

12.7.5a The fraud defence

In Australia, the fraud defence against the enforcement of a foreign judgment is available on the discovery since the judgment of something material that provides a ground for setting it aside for fraud (so long as the party did not know of the fraud at the time of the hearing).[29] This rule varies from the established English law rule in *Abouloff v Oppenheimer & Co*[30] that a foreign judgment can be set aside for fraud even without discovering something material since the conclusion of the hearing.

12.7.5b The denial of justice defence

Both the common law and the *Foreign Judgments Act* provide a defence to enforcement on grounds that there was a denial of justice in the foreign judgment, relating to bias, impartiality or incompetence of the foreign tribunal affecting the defendant's right to present its case or receive a fair hearing.[31]

12.7.5c Violation of public policy

The enforcement of a foreign judgment may be contrary to the public policy of the forum, although the nature of an applicable 'public policy' is somewhat unclear. It would seem that, while procedural public policy concerns are conceived as the denial of justice, 'public policy' in this context relates primarily to foreign laws that in substance are deemed to violate fundamental principles of natural justice or due process of law, as these are conceived in Australia. A further justification, albeit less clear, is that foreign judgments may be based on foreign law that, while not violative of natural justice, conflict with local public policy, such as in relation to competition law.[32]

29 See *Wentworth v Rogers (No 5)* [1986] 6 NSWLR 534 at 538.

30 (1882) 10 QBD 295.

31 *Adams v Cape Industries plc* [1990] Ch 433; *Foreign Judgment Act*, s 7(2)(a)(v).

32 *Kuwait Airways Corp v Iraqi Airways Corp* [2002] UKHL 19 at [16] per Lord Nicholls. See also *Foreign Judgment Act*, s 7(2)(a)(xi).

12.7.6 Overturning a foreign judgment

Finally, the enforcement by a domestic court of a foreign judgment may be short-lived. A domestic court may decline to enforce it if that foreign judgment is subsequently overturned.[33]

12.7.7 Enforcing judgments in foreign courts

Enforcing an Australian judgment in the courts of some of Australia's largest trading parties may also give rise to difficulties, primarily on public policy grounds. This is clearly the case in the USA. However, not dissimilar restrictions on enforcement arise in Japan, where the Code of Civil Procedure subjects enforcement of foreign judgments to 'the public order or good morals of Japan'.[34] Even in Australia, the statutory protection that is accorded to foreign judgments under the *Foreign Judgments Act* is circumscribed by local public policy considerations.

12.7.8 Conclusion

The enforcement of foreign judgments in Australia poses a number of problems, not least the cost and time needed to enforce them, including in some cases, re-hearing the dispute. The law governing enforcement of foreign judgments reflects these problems, although the same issues arise in other jurisdictions as well. These problems are especially pronounced in England, where a foreign judgment may well need to be re-litigated.

The future of the enforcement of foreign judgments remains largely unclear. Few countries are likely to enforce all foreign judgments as of right—there are too many risks that such judgments might violate local public policy or natural justice. However, there is need for greater uniformity in the treatment of foreign judgments, including through multilateral agreement on their treatment, not unlike the New York Convention's recognition and enforcement of foreign arbitral awards. The stumbling block lies in the reluctance of many states to surrender their sovereignty to foreign tribunals, coupled with concern to preserve local public policy.

A compromise would be to conclude a multilateral treaty in which foreign judgments are subject to scrutiny to ensure that they satisfy threshold requirements. If they pass the threshold, they ought to be registered as enforceable in those jurisdictions in which application for enforcement is made.

Unless and until such a compromise is reached, the parties to international commercial transactions must recognise that being armed with a foreign judgment is not determinative in itself. There is need also for the enforcement of that judgment which, at its worst, may involve re-litigating the case.

---

33 See *Benefit Strategies Group Inc v Prider* [2007] SASC 250.

34 See L Gamertsfelder, 'Cross Border Litigation: Exploring the Difficulties Associated with Enforcing Australian Money Judgments in Japan' (1998) 17 *Australian Bar Review* 161.

12.8 Sovereignty and extraterritoriality

12.8.1 Introduction

States that exercise jurisdiction over activities outside their borders raise two related questions:

1 The extent to which they impinge upon the sovereignty of the country in which the activity took place; and
2 The extent to which they impinge upon the activities of nationals who are affected by such extraterritorial measures.

At a practical level, the growth of extraterritorial laws that impinge on sovereignty is inevitable in an increasingly interdependent community of states. Powerful states, like the USA, employ extraterritorial legislation as a combined measure of both public policy and foreign policy. Other states follow suit in reaction to such policy, either as a reflection of their own policy objectives, or functionally in response to immediate political and economic ends.

What has resulted is a rather unsystematic body of extraterritorial laws across the global community, with diverse characteristics and implications. Australian individuals and companies are directly impacted by such developments insofar as they are subject to prospective liability abroad. Australians and their trade partners are also affected by the extent to which Australia has endorsed extraterritorial legislation and applied it in Australia.[35]

12.8.2 The principle of comity

'Extraterritoriality' encompasses two different types of laws:

1 Laws that regulate the conduct of nationals abroad; and
2 Laws that regulate the conduct by non-nationals outside the country making the laws.

One objection to such extraterritoriality is that it violates principles of comity, by which states are bound to respect each other's territoriality as members of the community of nations.[36]

The principle of comity supposedly operates at different levels. At a principled level, it serves as a constraint on the unbridled exercise of extraterritoriality by establishing a threshold of treatment that states are expected to accord other states and their subjects. At a practical level, comity lacks defining characteristics; it is general in its scope of application, and it is more persuasive than mandatory in reach. It may also be used as a weapon by more politically and economically powerful nations against those who are less so. As such, comity may well be disregarded in the face of self-interest.

---

35 But see OECD, *Revised Recommendation of the Council: Concerning Co-Operation between Member Countries on Anticompetitive Practices Affecting International Trade* (1995) C(95) 130. Note that these recommendations have only persuasive authority and are not binding on any party.

36 See generally I Brownlie, *Principles of Public International Law*, Oxford University Press, Oxford, 5th ed, 1988, p 289.

At a business level, however, it is important to appreciate that states—even powerful ones—may respond to the perceived demands for comity, significantly because they may not want to be seen as violating minimal standards of reciprocal respect for other states and their subjects.[37]

12.8.3 The principles of territoriality

The principle of comity is offset by principles of territoriality; not least that the territorial sovereignty of states is limited by the requirement that one state not be compelled to surrender its sovereignty to another state.[38]

Under traditional principles of territoriality, states are prohibited from enforcing their laws in the territory of another state without the authority of that other state. Exceptions to this principle include the fact that states are subject to international law prohibiting crimes against humanity. However, there are arguably fewer limits on state sovereignty than the regulation of criminal conduct by individuals according to the criminal laws of Australia.[39]

The principle of strict state territoriality inevitably conflicts with the countervailing interest of countries to exercise extraterritorial 'sovereignty' in order to protect their trading interests and those of their nationals, including by resort to expansive extraterritorial measures.[40] The functional basis behind the exercise of such extraterritorial jurisdiction lies in the face of the supposedly 'indivisible' power of states and their territorial integrity.

12.8.4 Balancing territoriality against extraterritoriality

There are few clear guidelines in balancing territorial laws against extraterritorial laws. Some states have constructed their own rules. For example, the American Law Institute maintains that the authority of states to act extraterritorially is circumscribed by the 'effect' of the foreign activities upon the state purporting to exercise extraterritorial jurisdiction and the 'reasonableness' of that exercise:[41]

---

37 See generally H Maier, 'Resolving Extraterritorial Conflicts, or "There and Back Again"' (1984) 25 *Virginia Journal of International Law* 7 at 23; AV Lowe, 'The Problems of Extraterritorial Jurisdiction: Economic Sovereignty and the Search for a Solution' (1985) 34 *International & Comparative Law Quarterly* 724; P Durack, 'Extraterritorial Application of United States Law' (Paper presented at the American Bar Association, New Orleans, 12 August 1981), reprinted in AV Lowe, *Extraterritorial Jurisdiction: An Annotated Collection of Legal Materials*, Grotius Publications, Cambridge, 1983, pp 91–2.

38 See *SS Lotus (France v Turkey)* [1927] PCIJ (ser A), No 10 at 18–19.

39 See I Shearer, 'Jurisdiction'. in S Blay, R Piotrowicz & M Tsamenyi (eds), *Public International Law: An Australian Perspective*, Oxford University Press, Melbourne, 1997, pp 162–4; FA Mann, 'The Doctrine of Jurisdiction in International Law Revisited after Twenty Years', in FA Mann (ed), *Further Studies in International Law*, Oxford University Press, Oxford, 1990 p 4.

40 See for example the UK's *Protection of Trading Interests Act 1980*, c 11 and Canada's *Foreign Extraterritorial Measures Act*, RSC 1985, c F-29.

41 See *Restatement (Third) of the Law: The Foreign Relations Law of the United States* (1987). See also H Maier, 'Jurisdictional Rules in Customary International Law', in K Meessen (ed), *Extraterritorial Jurisdiction in Theory and Practice*, Kluwer Law Publishers, Deventer, 1996, p 65.

- The first principle, concentrating on the 'effect' of the foreign activities, is rooted in the early US case of *United States v Aluminum Co of America (Alcoa)*.[42] Its deficiency is that it denies the sovereignty of the state in which the extraterritorial authority is exercised.
- The second principle, that the exercise of that extraterritoriality must be reasonable, is enunciated in cases such as *Timberlane Lumber Co v Bank of America*[43] and *Mannington Mills v Congoleum Corp*.[44] It attempts to ameliorate the effect of an extraterritorial exercise by taking account of competing interests, including both domestic and foreign. Its deficiency lies in the fact that such an interest analysis inevitably defies predictability. There are often multiple interests; each can be accorded different weights, and each can be valued differently in relation to the others.

The combined 'effects' and 'reasonableness' approach also lacks a principled foundation. A real risk is that, all too often, it will be in the 'interest' of the state exercising extraterritorial jurisdiction to assert that its 'interests' are 'reasonable' in trumping the countervailing 'interests' of a foreign country.[45]

12.8.5 Extraterritorial legislation: competition laws

Extraterritorial legislation is most frequently used by developed countries in extending the extraterritorial reach of their competition laws, in particular to regulate allegedly anticompetitive conduct domestically, but also abroad. For example, it is in the national interests of Australia to control anticompetitive behaviour that undermines the public order of the country, including by regulating the conduct of business abroad of its nationals, corporations, subsidiaries and agents that has an impact upon the country.[46]

The scope of extraterritorial legislation directed against anticompetitive behaviour varies significantly from country to country. Australia adopts a minimalist standard of intervention. In particular, it claims jurisdiction only over anticompetitive behaviour when the affected corporation is resident or carries on business in Australia, or is a citizen or ordinarily resident of Australia.[47]

Regarding Australia's primary trade partners, the EU applies a comparable position to Australia, albeit more expansively construed by European tribunals.[48]

---

42 148 F 2d 416 (2nd Cir 1945).

43 549 F 2d 597 (9th Cir 1976).

44 595 F 2d 1287 (3rd Cir 1979).

45 See generally H Maier, 'Interest Balancing and Extraterritorial Jurisdiction' (1983) 31 *American Journal of Comparative Law* 579 at 589–90. See also Note, 'Predictability and Comity: Toward Common Principles of Extraterritorial Jurisdiction' (1985) 98 *Harvard Law Review* 1310 at 1324–5.

46 See for example *Trade Practices Act 1974* (Cth); *Treaty Establishing the European Economic Community*, opened for signature 25 March 1957, 298 UNTS 3, Articls 85–6 (entered into force 1 January 1959) (*Treaty of Rome*); *Act Against Restraints on Competition 1957* (Federal Republic of Germany); *Monopolies and Mergers Act 1965* (UK).

47 For example s 5(1) and (2) of the *Trade Practices Act 1974* (Cth) extends Part IV, IVA and V of the Act. See also E Jardine, 'Extra-Territorial Enforcement of Australian Anti-Trust Legislation: Australian Meat Holdings Pty Ltd v Trade Practices Commission' (1990) 12 *Sydney Law Review* 652.

48 See E Jardine, 'An Agreement between Australia and the European Union on Trade Practices: A Proposal' (1996) 4 *Trade Practices Law Journal* 67.

In contrast, the USA exercises a far more expansive extraterritorial jurisdiction than Australia, allowing private individuals to sue foreign corporations for treble damages for allegedly anticompetitive behaviour that adversely affects the claimant.[49] These differences, tracing back to the *Westinghouse* cases (see below, Section 12.8.7), has given rise to tensions between Australia and the USA over the extraterritorial reach of antitrust legislation and has led to retaliatory blocking under Australian law.[50]

12.8.6 Trade sanctions

Extraterritorial legislation is also used as a form of trade sanction, notably through primary trade boycotts that forbid nationals and corporations from trading with boycotted states, or secondary boycotts intended to deter third party countries from trading with 'target' nations. The purpose behind trade sanctions generally is to produce change in the political and economic practices of foreign countries, directed at human rights reform, national security, or more tenuously, as foreign policy weapons. Political in nature, the use of trade sanctions is controversial but continually practised, particularly by the USA.[51]

Trade sanctions are best recalled in attempts by the global community to outlaw the apartheid regime in South Africa, and to isolate the military junta in Fiji, the Kadafi Government in Libya, the nuclear regimes in North Korea and Iran, and the dictatorship of Mugabe in present-day Zimbabwe.

A significant weapon, trade sanctions are also viewed as controversial because of their uneven use, tolerance shown to political excesses of 'allies', and allegedly punitive or excessive responses to others.[52]

Governments and their national courts may accord trade, political and other sanctions a restrictive or an expansive scope of application.[53] For example, US authorities have sometimes interpreted the principle of nationality expansively to include both parents

49 See *Restatement (Third) of the Law: The Foreign Relations Law of the United States* (1987), ss 402, 403, 415.

50 See for example *United States v Aluminum Co of America*, 148 F 2d 416 (2nd Cir, 1945). For critical responses from Australians, see G Triggs, 'Extraterritorial Reach of United States Anti-Trust Legislation: The International Law Implications of the Westinghouse Allegations of a Uranium Producers' Cartel' (1979) 12 *Melbourne University Law Review* 250 at 257; L Maher, 'Antitrust Fall-Out: Tensions in the Australian–American Relationship' (1982) 13 *Federal Law Review* 105; W Pengilley, 'Extraterritorial Effects of United States Commercial and Antitrust Legislation: A View From "Down Under"' (1983) 16 *Vanderbilt Journal of Transnational Law* 833; E Khoo, 'The Reach of US Antitrust Law and its Effect on Australia' (1994) 14 *Queensland Lawyer* 134 at 257.

51 See for example A Lowenfeld, 'Economic Sanctions: A Look Back and a Look Ahead' (1990) 88 *Michigan Law Review* 1930 at 1930; A Lowenfeld, *Trade Controls For Political Ends*, 2nd edn, Bender, New York,1983; M Malloy, *Economic Sanctions and US Trade*, Little, Brown & Co, 1990, pp 3–31; B Carter, *International Economic Sanctions*, The Falmer Press, 1988, p 4.

52 See for example B Carter, 'International Economic Sanctions: Improving the Haphazard US Legal Regime' (1987) 75 *California Law Review* 1162 at 1165; D Santeusanio, 'Extraterritoriality and Secondary Boycotts: A Critical and Legal Analysis of United States Foreign Policy' (1998) 21 *Suffolk Transnational Law Review* 367 at 368.

53 See for example V Lowe, 'The Problems of Extraterritorial Jurisdiction: Economic Sovereignty and the Search for a Solution' (1985) 34 *International and Comparative Law Quarterly* 724 at 726.

and subsidiaries of US companies, even when those companies are primarily owned by foreign interests and incorporated or organised under the laws of foreign countries.[54] Nor is the extraterritorial reach of US legislation limited to trade sanctions. In a controversial series of asbestos cases involving CSR Limited, US courts purported to exert extraterritorial jurisdiction over CSR on grounds that it sold asbestos fibre to a US manufacturer which, in turn, caused asbestos-related injuries among US nationals. US law has also exerted extraterritorial jurisdiction over foreign incorporated companies that use goods or services acquired in the USA, even when those companies do not conduct business directly in the US.

The authority of the US Government to exercise extraterritorial jurisdiction, however questionable in international law, is increasingly justified by US domestic legislation. While the authority of the US President to impose sanctions in an emergency was largely restricted to trading with an enemy nation or its nationals, *The International Emergency Economic Powers Act of 1977* accords the President wide latitude to impose restrictions on overseas financial transactions or to freeze foreign assets. A particular purpose is to extend export controls (discussed in Chapter 7) to the military application of US technology, although the scope of the legislation appears to include the use of that technology for commercial as distinct from military purposes. One can well question the legitimacy—and predictability—of such extraterritoriality under the principle of the comity of nations, but it is important for Australian interests to appreciate the practical significance of such US export controls.[55] Such was the experience in 1982 when an Australian company, Santos Ltd, had to engage in a corporate restructuring in response to a US trade-imposed boycott of a French company, Dresser France, that was a supplier of Santos in the construction of a pipeline.

Equally powerful, but less legally challengeable, are secondary boycotts, by which a third party country complies with the boycott of a 'target' country rather than face trade or other sanctions itself. Secondary boycotts are not legally objectionable on their face because they do not directly restrict trading with a target state. They are objectionable, however, for purporting to direct the foreign policy of a third party country, its nationals and corporations. From a business perspective, they can give rise to significant economic dislocation, including a trickle-down impact on third party countries, their nationals and corporations.[56]

12.8.7 'Blocking' legislation

Blocking legislation is a form of retaliation for foreign extraterritorial legislation. The problem with blocking legislation generally is that it has expanded from retaliation directed at redressing the application of extraterritorial laws to specific industries, parties

54 See for example LJ Kutten & B Murphy, *An Overview of United States Export Controls*, Aspen Publishers Inc, Deventer, 1988, pp 6–7.

55 See for example Note, 'Predictability and Comity: Toward Common Principles of Extraterritorial Jurisdiction' (1985) 98 *Harvard Law Review* 1310 at 1317. See generally H Fenton, 'United States Antiboycott Laws: An Assessment of Their Impact Ten Years after Adoption' (1987) 10 *Hastings International and Comparative Law Review* 211 at 215–17.

56 See generally V Lowe, 'US Extraterritorial Jurisdiction: The *Helms-Burton* and *D'Amato Acts*' (1997) 46 *International and Comparative Law Quarterly* 378.

and conduct to general acts of retaliation that are unrelated to those specific circumstances. A related problem is that blocking legislation has evolved into an expression of foreign policy goals that are less retaliatory than directive in both intent and effect.

The USA is a significant target of such retaliation. Specific targets include US legislation that:

- Prevents the enforcement of foreign judgments;
- Prohibits compliance with the orders of foreign governments;
- Prohibits giving evidence or producing documents in foreign legal proceedings; and
- Seeks to recover assets in retaliation against the execution of foreign judgments ('clawback' legislation).[57]

Australian blocking legislation is contained in the *Foreign Proceedings (Excess of Jurisdiction) Act 1984* (Cth). This legislation was enacted in response to litigation in the USA, arising from the drastic fall in uranium prices in the 1960s. In response, uranium producers lobbied for the US Government to place an embargo on imported uranium, which reduced world demand by two-thirds. In response to this fall in demand, and to stabilise world prices, Australia, the UK, France, Canada and South Africa formed a cartel to limit and allocate the production and sale of uranium outside the USA. The result was that uranium prices increased dramatically during the early and mid-1970s. This price increase placed pressure on the largest US supplier of uranium, Westinghouse Electric Corporation, to meet local US supply needs, given its dependence on foreign producers. As a result, it brought an antitrust suit claiming treble damages against 29 US and foreign corporations, including four corporations operating primarily in Australia. It alleged that the cartel had caused the dramatic price rise and was responsible for its inability to meet its domestic supply obligations.

12.8.8 Responses to the USA

The problem with attempts to block the extraterritorial reach of US antitrust law is not only the availability of treble damages against a defendant under US law, but the extent to which extraterritoriality is imbedded in US law. For example, the Constitution of the USA itself empowers Congress to 'regulate Commerce with foreign Nations, and among the several States': Article I, s 8, clause 3. In addition, some US laws with extraterritorial reach give rise to both civil and criminal penalties, including imprisonment. Most invasive is the *Sherman Act 1890*. Section 1 of that Act prohibits 'every contract, combination in the form of trust or otherwise, or conspiracy, in restraint of trade or commerce among the several states, or with foreign nations'. The act has extraterritorial impact, with s 2 imposing criminal penalties: 'every person who shall monopolise, or attempt to monopolise ... any part of the trade or commerce among the several states, or with foreign nations, shall be deemed guilty of a felony'.[58] US courts, in turn, have

57 See generally V Lowe, 'The Problems of Extraterritorial Jurisdiction: Economic Sovereignty and the Search for a US Extraterritorial Jurisdiction' (1985) 34 *International and Comparative Law Quarterly* 724 at 727; W Pengilley, 'United States Trade and Antitrust Laws: A Study of International Legal Imperialism from *Sherman to Helms-Burton*' (1998) 6 *Competition and Consumer Law Journal* 187 at 212–13.

58 See generally W Pengilley, 'United States Trade and Antitrust Laws: A Study of International Legal Imperialism from *Sherman* to *Helms-Burton*' (1998) 6 *Competition and Consumer Law Journal* 187.

construed the *Sherman Act* expansively to reach individuals, corporations and public entities both inside and outside the USA.

In addition to a plethora of private suits, the *Sherman Act* has led to criminal and civil proceedings brought by the Attorney-General or the Federal Trade Commission, with multimillion dollar damage awards, injunctive relief and even imprisonment.[59]

Illustrating the extraterritorial reach of US antitrust law, in the *Westinghouse* cases, the US Department of Justice established its own antitrust investigation, including a grand jury charged with determining whether the international uranium cartel, including Australia, ought to be subject to criminal prosecution. The investigation included attempts to secure evidence through discovery orders extending to, among other places, Australia. The Australian Government was not consulted or given advance notice of such investigations. However, it barred company employees from entering the USA in order to avoid personal liability. The Australian Government also initiated retaliatory legislation, namely, the *Foreign Proceedings (Prohibition of Certain Evidence) Act 1976* (Cth). This act authorised the Attorney-General of Australia, *inter alia*, to prohibit the production of documents or giving evidence in foreign proceedings if that foreign country acted contrary to international law and the principles of comity.

Partly as a result of Australia's retaliating legislation, the four Australian defendants declined to appear. In response, the US District Court entered default judgments against them and provided Westinghouse with injunctive relief to freeze their assets in the USA. These default judgments and injunctions, in turn, gave rise to further retaliatory legislation in Australia—the *Foreign Antitrust Judgment (Restriction of Enforcement) Act 1979* (Cth), which empowered the Attorney-General to declare a foreign judgment unenforceable in Australia if it violated international law or comity and had a detrimental effect upon Australian trade or commerce.[60]

The ensuing fractious litigation lasted well into the 1980s. The 'problem' was most effectively resolved, in the end, less due to the litigation than from a dramatic fall in the global demand for uranium due to the availability of alternative sources of energy.[61]

---

59 The *Sherman Act* is only part of the extraterritorial apparatus of the US Government. Other legislation includes the *Federal Trade Commission Act*, 15 USC §§ 41–58 (1997) and the *Clayton Act*, 15 USC §§ 12–27 (1997). Neither act gives rise to criminal penalties, but they are far-reaching all the same. The *Clayton Act* is directed against price discrimination (§13), exclusive dealing contracts (§ 14), and, especially, mergers and acquisitions giving rise to monopolies or otherwise drastically reducing competition (§ 18). The *Federal Trade Commission Act* prohibits unfair competition and unfair or deceptive acts or practices that affect commerce, and includes 'cease and desist' orders: see 15 USC § 45(b) (1997). See also generally C Canenbley (ed), *Enforcing Antitrust against Foreign Enterprises*, Kluwer, Deventer, 1981, p 7.

60 See L Maher, 'Time, Uranium and the Legislative Process' (1978) 9 *Federal Law Review* 399.

61 See further LE Trakman, 'Winner Take Some: Loss Sharing and Commercial Impracticability' (1985) 69 *Minnesota L Rev* 471–519; W Pengilley, 'United States Trade and Antitrust Laws: A Study of International Legal Imperialism from *Sherman to Helms-Burton*' (1998) 6 *Competition and Consumer Law Journal* 187 at 851–60; P Joskow, 'Commercial Impossibility, the Uranium Market and the Westinghouse Case' (1977) 6 *Journal of Legal Studies* 119; W Eagan, 'The Westinghouse Uranium Contracts: Commercial Impracticability and Related Matters' (1980) 18 *American Business Law Journal* 281.

12.8.9 Treaties governing extraterritoriality

Concluding different forms of treaties may help to curb both the assertion of extraterritorial jurisdiction by treaty partners and also establish processes by which to resolve differences arising from the exercise of such extraterritoriality.

12.8.9a Treaties of cooperation

Treaties of peace, goodwill and friendship are common in the international community, serving as stand-alone agreements or to buttress economic pacts, notably bilateral and regional agreements. Treaties may also entertain controversial topics, such as anticompetition, or 'anti-trust' issues. Prominent among these treaties is the treaty between the Government of Australia and the Government of the United States, Relating to Cooperation on Antitrust Matters (the 'Antitrust Cooperation Agreement').

In functional terms, these 'diplomatic' treaties may do little more than pay lip-service to the virtue of cooperation among countries. However, they may also be useful in setting up protocols for notifying a state about impending extraterritorial legislation, as well as setting out a process of consultation. An illustration of such a process is provided for in Chapter 20 of the North American Free Trade Agreement between the USA, Canada and Mexico.[62]

Particular issues for negotiation and settlement include, among others, efforts by the trade partners of the USA to constrain the extraterritorial application of the *Helms-Burton Act*, directed at protecting US economic and political interests abroad. Another persistent issue has been the efforts of the USA and Canada to resolve the persistent softwood lumber dispute between them arising from the alleged sale of Canadian softwood lumber at less than fair market value in the USA.[63]

Under the Antitrust Cooperation Agreement, Australia and the USA should each notify the other of governmental policies that may have antitrust implications in the other state, including an impact on national interests. Following such notification, the notifying party may request consultations if it believes that the antitrust policies of the other have an adverse impact on its interests (see Article 1). The effectiveness of such measures varies according to the extent to which each party's interests are primary, and the capacity and willingness of each to notify the other and redress the interests of that other. Linked to such capacity is the political and economic power each party has to assert its interests, to invoke countervailing measures such as blocking legislation, or to engage in other tactics beyond diplomacy in order to secure compliance. For example, in the *Westinghouse* litigation, when some Australian parties declined to submit to the jurisdiction of US courts on the grounds that US law was extraterritorial in application, violative of the principles of comity and contrary to international law and the failure

62 See LE Trakman (assisted by K Jadeja), *Dispute Settlement under the NAFTA: Manual and Sourcebook*, Transnational Publishers, New York, 1997.

63 See 'Sanctions: NAFTA Designates Confer on Complaint Against Helms-Burton Under Chapter 20' (1996) 13 *International Trade Reporter* 1093. See also JG Castel, *Extraterritoriality in International Trade: Canada and United States of America Practices Compared*, Butterworths, Toronto, 1988, p 51.

to resolve the issue through diplomatic measures, the Attorney-General of Australia initiated blocking legislation.[64]

Diplomatic intervention is unlikely to be effective in the face of conflict. It involves compromise; it may take time to accomplish; and just as it eventuates, it can evaporate, leaving the parties with the status quo. As a matter of practice, it is not a direct alternative to blocking legislation.

12.8.9b Trade treaties

Some new bilateral and regional trade and investment agreements provide for ways of redressing issues arising from extraterritoriality. Most pronounced among these measures are principles upon which states agree to treat the nationals of other states. According to the General Agreement on Tariffs and Trade (GATT) established in 1947, member states agreed to provide one another most-favoured nation treatment, including receiving no less-favoured 'advantage, favour, privilege or immunity' than that which is provided to any other party. There are exceptions to this principle, notably on the grounds of national security, and to permit states to enter into regional agreements that accord different treatment to the regional parties. The GATT also provides for a process of negotiation and consultation by which parties can resolve their differences over such treatment.

These facilities for cooperation continue under the auspices of the World Trade Organization (WTO), as the successor to the GATT. The extent to which the WTO constrains the action of states, such as the extraterritorial measures of the USA under the *Helms-Burton* legislation, remains unclear. The probability is that powerful countries such as the USA and regional trading blocs such as the EU will either tailor their extraterritorial legislation to mesh, however uncomfortably, with the exceptions to multilateral treaties, while multilateral trade sanctions will be invoked against so-called 'rogue' countries.[65]

A particular weakness associated with regional and bilateral agreements directed at negotiated settlements of extraterritoriality is that individuals are not parties to such agreements. They can exert pressure on their respective governments to intervene, but these governments may well take the view that it is not in the national interest to so intervene. The Antitrust Cooperation Agreement between Australia and the USA provides, in Article 6, that the Australian government can request that the US government participate in private litigation, and also report to the court on the substance

64 See P Durack, 'Australia: Conflicts and Comity', in J Lacey (ed), *Act of State and Extraterritorial Reach: Problems of Law and Policy*, ABA Section of International Law and Practice, Chicago, 1983, p 43; G Triggs, 'Extraterritorial Reach of United States Anti-Trust Legislation: The International Law Implications of the Westinghouse Allegations of a Uranium Producers' Cartel' (1979) 12 *Melbourne University Law Review* 250 at 272; P Durack, 'Extraterritorial Application of United States Law' (Paper presented at the American Bar Association, New Orleans, 12 August 1981), reprinted in AV Lowe, *Extraterritorial Jurisdiction: An Annotated Collection of Legal Materials*, Grotius Publications, Cambridge, 1983, p 94.

65 See for example 'Memorandum of Understanding Concerning the US *Helms-Burton Act* and the US *Iran and Libya Sanctions Act* (European Union–United States)' (1997) 36 *ILM* 529. The act permits US citizens to bring private actions against persons who have 'trafficked' in confiscated property, and provides for successful plaintiffs to be awarded treble damages.

and outcome of intergovernmental consultations. Such intervention in litigation in the USA is not contemplated, however, in the absence of prior consultations between the parties. Nor is there any assurance that the US Government will properly or fully represent the interests of the Australian Government in such litigation.

States that do not comply with such multilateral treaties may well argue that such treaties are too general to offer specific guidance, are ineffective as measures of control, and that the national interest justifying extraterritorial laws ought to prevail.[66]

12.9 Conclusion

Preparing to litigate an international business dispute involves significant strategic and legal considerations that should be addressed at the outset. Particular attention should be paid to the nature of the relationship between the parties, as well as prospective reasons as to why it might fail during the course of a contractual relationship. Parties to international business dealings may prefer to contract on the basis of good faith, hoping that such litigation will not eventuate to mar their pre-existing relationship. However, they cannot be sure that a conflict will not arise; and being prepared for such a contingency is an attribute of international business dealings.

The written contract is an important means of regulating of the relationship between the parties. Contracts deal with such material terms as the price and quality of goods and services and the duration of the relationship. However, strategic legal consideration should also be given to contract clauses that set out the courts of a particular country or state that has jurisdiction to hear a dispute arising between the parties, known as 'choice of jurisdiction' clauses. Further consideration should be given to the laws of a particular country or state that apply to that contract, known as 'choice of law' clauses.

Parties to international business relationships also need to recognise that international business contracting is complicated by legal differences in the laws of different countries in which such relationships arise. For example, a domestic court charged with jurisdiction to hear a dispute may be required to apply the law of a foreign country. As a result, that domestic court may require that such foreign law be proven to its satisfaction. Also, a court may reach a decision that is it unable to enforce because the assets affected by its decision are in another jurisdiction. In such a case, the successful party may need to secure a foreign judgment enforcing the judicial decision in its favour. Complicating such decisions is the need to appreciate that courts may decline to enforce foreign judgments for various reasons, such as on the grounds of public policy or of state sovereignty.

Many of these issues are left to lawyers to resolve. However, it is especially important that parties who engage in international business relationships are aware of these issues, are capable of developing strategies to deal with them, and are able to properly direct lawyers in negotiating, contracting and resolving disputes arising on account of them.

---

66 See LE Trakman, 'The Proliferation of Free Trade Agreements: Bane or Beauty?' (2008) 42 *Journal of World Trade* 367; see also M Asaro, 'The *Iran and Libya Sanctions Act of 1996*: A Thorn in the Side of the World Trading System' (1997) 23 *Brooklyn Journal of International Law* 505 at 515–27.

Questions

With regard to the case study at the beginning of this chapter:

1 What considerations should you take into account in advising a client whether to adopt a judicial, arbitral or other dispute resolution option?

2 a How would you advise in choosing among alternative dispute resolution options, not limited to arbitration?

b How would you advise in choosing among different dispute resolution options before courts of law?

3 Under what circumstances, if any, should you advise your client to adopt an 'exclusive forum agreement'?

4 a What considerations should you take into account in advising your clients on the adoption of a 'choice of law' provision?

b In providing such advice, should you try to identify the single 'best' choice of law?

5 What considerations are likely to influence an Australian court in determining whether the forum is 'convenient' or 'inconvenient' under the *forum non conveniens* principle?

6 What considerations are likely to influence Australian courts in determining whether to recognise and enforce a foreign judgment?

7 a What are the risks in having to 'prove' foreign law?

b What are the most effective ways to limit such risks?

8 a What is the distinction in judicial proceedings between 'procedural' and 'substantive' issues?

b How consistently do courts apply this distinction?

9 What problems arise in enforcing foreign judgments before Australian courts?

10 Describe the tension between the sovereignty of states and the extra-territorial application of their laws.

11 On what issues would you advise the Director of International Sales at WOOLTHINGS to concentrate in negotiating the contract with Clothesfit? Provide reasons for your advice.

12 You have since been informed that WOOLTHINGS has stated that it is only willing to negotiate a three-year 'initial' supply contract for approximately half of the supplies, which is two years short of the five-year contract originally anticipated and would generate less than half the revenues anticipated from that five-year contract. It provides as reasons that it 'prefers to try out new suppliers before committing to a longer term agreement'. What strategic advice would you give to your manager regarding how WOOLTHINGS might respond to this statement?

13 What factors should WOOLTHINGS consider in proposing 'choice of jurisdiction' and 'choice of law' clauses to govern its contract with Clothesfit?

14 How would you draft a 'choice of jurisdiction' and a 'choice of law' clause?

CHAPTER 13

dispute resolution: arbitration

SEAGOODS Industries, an international company based in Sydney, Australia, shipped a large container of frozen Pacific Salmon by sea to Paris, France, in May 2009. In June 2009, the recipient company, FASHIONFOODS PARIS, sent an email stating in particular: 'Container has arrived. However, on checking at Customs, the Salmon is contaminated and not fit for high-end consumption by our customers. As a result, we have refused to accept delivery of the consignment. We hereby cancel the contract'. SEAGOODS Industries responded the following day, stating: 'Container was fully sealed, insulated and frozen throughout shipment. Our agent on board the container ship checked the container regularly and found no adverse conditions as you describe. As a result, we dispute your contention that the shipment was in any way defective. We also dispute your right to cancel the contract. The contract specifically provides that disputes in relation to performance of the contract are to be resolved by arbitration under the UNCITRAL Arbitration Rules'. FASHIONFOODS PARIS responded: 'We will not accept delivery of defective goods. We agree that the contract provides for binding arbitration under the UNCITRAL Rules and are pleased to proceed under them'.

13.1 Introduction

This chapter is devoted to the nature, form and operation of international commercial arbitration. The purpose is to explore the different characteristics of arbitration, including how it works in practice. For convenience, the chapter roughly follows the structure of the United Nations Commission on International Trade Law (UNCITRAL) Model Law (1985). The chapter is punctuated with discussion, ranging from how the parties may make choices about arbitration—including whether or not to adopt all of the Model Law—to the nature and significance of those choices.

There are many differences in the nature and operation of arbitration, significant variations in the conduct of arbitration hearings, and equally telling divergences in the nature and form of arbitration awards. However, in all cases, arbitration is a process that is guided by the dictates of commercial practice within the confines of law. Except in the limited circumstances in which the parties choose to have their dispute resolved by amiable resolution or according to the dictates of fairness under Article 33(2) of the UNCITRAL Rules,[1] arbitration is less about balancing the interests of the parties than about applying principled and legally acceptable norms to commercial disputes. The fact that arbitrators may apply those norms differently in complex commercial arbitrations in light of the particular context does not detract from the requirement that arbitrators decide in accordance with law, unless the parties prescribe otherwise.

13.2 Alternative dispute resolution: the basics

13.2.1 Resolving disputes 'efficiently'

> Timing can be the most crucial part of dispute resolution ... Early intervention and advice is absolutely critical in saving cost and time. The more time that goes by, the less serious the people you're dealing with think you are. In some places there are strict procedural requirements and delay could mean losing your rights ... Early intervention may even help to settle disputes. Often, if it's a dispute over trying to recover money, a well-drafted letter from a lawyer will actually produce a result if it happens promptly.[2]

A key issue in choosing the form and operation of dispute resolution—such as through a clause in a contract providing for negotiation, mediation, arbitration and/or litigation—is the inferred efficiency of the process chosen. In the ideal world, the parties choose a process of dispute resolution that is time- and cost-effective and that is suited to their particular needs, relationship, trade, or industry, and that avoids prolonged conflict. Besides the situation in which one party protracts a conflict as a business tactic, an essential consideration at the outset is whether the parties are properly informed about the dispute resolution options that are available to them, the way in which different arbitration institutions function, their perceived virtues and deficiencies, and how they operate in relation to specific disputes.

Each choice, as in any other process of conflict avoidance and resolution, involves value judgments about the nature and suitability of that choice to resolve their differences. This raises uncertainty as to how parties ought to make choices and how they should conduct their business dealings—including conflicts—in light of them.

In making a choice among dispute resolution options at the time of contracting and before a dispute arises, the parties cannot reasonably anticipate that a dispute will eventuate, or the form it will assume. In fact, they will usually contract on the assumption that a dispute will not arise. As a result, they may regard the choice of a

1 Deciding by *amiable compositeur* (amiable composition) and *ex aequo et bono* (equally and fairly) presupposes that arbitrators reach decisions, not by operation of law, but according to that which they consider to be fair to the parties in the circumstances. See further LE Trakman, 'Ex Aequo et Bono: De-mystifying An Ancient Concept' (2008) 8(2) *Chicago Journal of International Law* 621.

2 'International Dispute Resolution', 9 January 2008: [www.dynamicbusiness.com/articles/articles-export/international-dispute-resolution.html].

dispute resolution clause as peripheral to their immediate interests, and avoid protracted negotiation over its incorporation in their contract. Preferring to adopt an affirmative outlook, they may be more intent on negotiating over more immediate issues, such as price and terms of delivery.

While the desire of parties not to deal with conflict at the time of entering into agreements does not preclude them from doing so at the time of a dispute, the hazard is that having to choose the process that will govern their dispute at the time of its eventuation may be fraught with difficulty, not least of all that the dispute itself may discourage them from choosing an opportune means of resolving it. The alternative is to be suitably apprised in advance about dispute resolution options and ways of choosing among them. A business client may well be advised about the prospect of early intervention in resolving a dispute in order to improve reduce costs and save time later.

13.2.2 What are the 'alternatives'?

Alternative dispute resolution (ADR) is the name for dispute resolution processes and techniques that are 'alternative' to resorting to domestic courts of law. These methods serve as essentially private methods of dispute resolution. They ordinarily avoid both the formality and publicity associated with litigation before domestic courts of law.

The first 'alternative' includes methods of dispute resolution by which the parties resolve their own conflicts. For example, the parties negotiate to resolve a dispute themselves; or they do so through the facilitation of a mediator or conciliator. The ideal result is that the parties will reach an agreed compromise by which they can reduce the costs, time, disruption of business and publicity associated with dispute resolution, while preserving their commercial relationship through mutual cooperation in reaching a negotiated settlement of their differences.

Whether such an ideal result can be realised depends significantly on the particular relationship between the parties, the needs and expectations they have both of themselves and of each other, and how they engage in negotiated settlement. Just as a negotiation may succeed in producing a lasting peace between the parties, it may also fail them at a crucial time in their relationships and business cycle. Also, a mediator or conciliator appointed by the parties to help them to facilitate a negotiation may falter, and no settlement may eventuate. Alternatively, the agreement that results may favour one party over the other; or it may regress into default by a party because its terms are uneconomic, unfair, or both.

A further alternative to litigation before domestic courts is to have resort to international commercial arbitration. In arbitration proceedings, the parties choose the arbitration and arbitral proceedings. However, unlike negotiation, mediation and conciliation proceedings, it is the arbitrator and not the parties who reaches the ultimate decision. The rationale in support of international commercial arbitration is that an arbitrator appointed by the parties may have the commercial expertise to resolve the dispute in a more time- and cost-effective manner than by resort to a domestic court. This assumption may be correct. However, there is no assurance that this will eventuate, since the arbitration may itself be protracted and costly and, conceivably, commercially unrealistic.

It is important to appreciate the key attributes of different methods of dispute resolution that the parties might choose, as well as how they may work in particular cases. Among other considerations are:

- The nature of the relationship between the parties;
- Their past experience with dispute avoidance and resolution (not limited to their particular relationship);
- The type of trade or industry in which they do business;
- The dispute resolution options available to them;
- The perceived cost and convenience of each option; and
- Their willingness to adopt one or more of those options.

13.3 International commercial arbitration

13.3.1 What is arbitration?

Arbitration arises when the parties to a dispute agree to submit it to a neutral third party—an arbitrator—for resolution. The arbitrator is responsible for hearing their respective positions and for reaching a decision, known as an arbitral award. The award reached is binding upon the parties and enforceable in law.

Arbitration proceedings are generally private. They are held at a venue, time and place that are convenient for the parties and the appointed arbitrator or arbitrators; and both the arbitration proceedings and the arbitral award are usually confidential.

Arbitral proceedings are usually less formal than proceedings before domestic courts of law, and arbitrators usually participate actively in arbitral proceedings—in admitting and hearing evidence, examining witnesses and arriving at the appropriate award.

Arbitration is rooted in the consent of the parties. The choice of arbitration is ordinarily made by the parties in their contract (through a 'choice of arbitration' clause), or else adopted by them as ad hoc arbitration at the time of a dispute. In choosing arbitration, the parties ordinarily bind themselves to respect the arbitration award and to comply with it.

Choosing arbitration entails choosing an arbitrator as well as a process of arbitrating, either directly or through an arbitration association. Typically, arbitration associations such as the Australian Centre for International Commercial Arbitration (ACICA) offer a 'model' clause, by which the parties can both choose to have their dispute regulated by that association, including the choice of an association arbitrator.

Ordinarily, in choosing arbitration, the parties forego the submission of their dispute to a domestic court of law. However, a party to an arbitration process may sometimes challenge an arbitration award in court on grounds that may also be deemed actionable by that court.

The arbitrator chosen by the parties is expected to reach a decision or award, independently of the parties. To ensure the arbitrator's impartiality and the transparency of arbitral proceedings, the arbitrator's fees are usually determined in advance, either through agreement between the arbitral panel and the parties, or by the arbitration association that the parties choose to administer the arbitration, or by the arbitrators themselves in accordance with such governing rules as Article 38 of the UNCITRAL Rules.[3]

While the form and process of arbitration may differ markedly according to the context and the rules of arbitration chosen by the parties, usually the arbitrator will hear the positions of the respective parties, including written and oral evidence in support of those positions. The award reached by the arbitrator is usually binding and enforceable if the country where the arbitration is held is a signatory to the New York Convention on the Enforcement and Recognition of Foreign Arbitration Awards 1958 (the 'New York Convention'). Australia is such a signatory.[4]

The choice of arbitration often occurs along a continuum. For example, the parties first attempt negotiations to avoid a dispute, then turn to conciliation or mediation to resolve a dispute, and finally to arbitration as a last resort.

The conception of arbitration as 'rent-a-judge' is uncharitable—arbitrators are usually experts either in commercial law generally, or in the specific trade or industry with which the parties are associated.

13.3.2 Why choose international commercial arbitration?

International commercial arbitration has a long history, tracing back to Medieval Europe, and possibly before, to the practices of merchants engaged in the sale of goods and services over land and sea. It arises when the parties to a commercial dispute across national boundaries agree to submit that dispute to a neutral third party arbitrator who, on appointment, is responsible for deciding it in an expert manner.

The rationale for choosing arbitration is that the parties to international commercial transactions deal with one another at arm's length. They may mistrust the application of the domestic law of one party over that of the other. They may also be able to choose among arbitration regimes, based on their respective needs and interests. They may wish to adopt a process of dispute settlement that is both private and confidential, as distinct from the public process associated with judicial hearings before domestic courts of law.[5]

As discussed above, the most common method by which parties choose arbitration is by incorporating an arbitration clause into their contract. That clause usually specifies the nature of their choice of arbitration, the rules governing the appointment of an arbitral tribunal, the conduct of the tribunal proceedings and the binding force of the ensuing award. The parties may provide in detail for the appointment and remuneration of an arbitrator or arbitrators, the manner in which the hearing is to be conducted and the nature of the arbitral award. More often, however, the parties simply provide for arbitration in general, adopting the rules of a particular arbitration association to govern their particular dispute.

---

3 These rules are included in full at the end of this chapter.

4 For detailed discussion of the New York Convention, see text supra at page 33 below.

5 On confidentiality in international commercial arbitration, see LE Trakman, 'Confidentiality in International Commercial Arbitration' (2002) 18 *Arbitration International* 1–18.

Most often, the parties will adopt a standard-form arbitration clause in their contract, without detailed discussion of its virtues or pitfalls. They will do so in part because they believe that, in the vast majority of instances, no arbitration will eventuate. However, if their assumption proves to be wrong, their unwise choice of arbitration may prove to be both a dilatory and costly price of doing business.

Alternatively, the parties may base their choice of international commercial arbitration on the particular needs of the parties. For example, they may incorporate a distinct arbitration clause, or they may choose an arbitration association based on its reputation, or because they feel comfortable with its procedures. One or both of the parties may also have used that arbitration regime in the past and be satisfied that, if invoked, it is sufficiently workable to resolve their business disputes. The choice of international commercial arbitration may also reflect compromise between the parties. For example, one party may make a concession to the other in the choice of arbitration because conceding in that choice is deemed to be acceptable, or because that compromise may be counterbalanced by concessions received from the other party.

The parties may make a choice of international commercial arbitration for different reasons. For example, they may adopt the rules of reputable international arbitration associations with which they are familiar, and choose their arbitrator from a roster of qualified persons provided by that association. A perceived benefit of international commercial arbitration may be that it is widely practised in relation to international commercial disputes. It is extensively recognised in law, including through arbitration legislation in Australia and the decisions of Australian courts that enforce arbitral awards.

It is also extensively recognised internationally, through multilateral, regional and bilateral treaties. Part of the modern international law merchant (known as the *Lex Mercatoria*), it is governed by international rules such as the UNCITRAL Rules. It is also embodied in the UNCITRAL Model Law, promulgated by the United Nations Commission on International Trade Law in 1985 and adopted by many trading nations.

In an ideal world, if international commercial arbitration is to be respected, it is important that the arbitration agreement be recognised by both parties and enforced before domestic courts. In effect, in choosing arbitration the parties elect that:

- Neither will disregard the provision for arbitration agreement;
- Neither will submit a dispute to a court of law in disregard of the agreement; and
- Neither will 'shop' in pursuit of a sympathetic forum to avoid the application of an arbitration agreement.

In furthering these ends, it is important that domestic courts do not hear disputes in disregard of the arbitration agreement, save insofar as public policy or the rules of natural justice or due process justify it.[6]

13.3.3 International commercial arbitration in Australia

Resolving international disputes may require that arbitrators in Australia or applying Australian law have a detailed understanding, not only of the law governing

6 On these public policy requirements, see s 19 of the *International Arbitration Act 1974* (Cth), discussed in the next section.

international arbitration, but also the procedural and substantive law that might apply to such disputes. For example, as a procedural matter, evidence that is deemed admissible in another jurisdiction may be deemed inadmissible before Australian courts on the grounds that it is excluded as extrinsic or parol evidence. It is also important to assess how domestic courts might construe a binding and enforceable contract in determining whether one party to a dispute has defaulted and, in particular, in determining the applicable remedy. Australian courts, too, may adopt dissimilar methods of interpretation to a dispute. For example, they may interpret an agreement in accordance with its literal words, or more contextually in light of the practices of the parties, trade usages and customs, including international treaties, conventions and decisions of international tribunals. They may also conceive of arbitration in general, and international commercial arbitration in particular.

International commercial arbitration is the subject of legal recognition in Australia, notably under the *International Arbitration Act 1974* (Cth) (IAA). Section 16 of that act adopts the UNCITRAL Model Law, which serves as an international standard by which to frame international arbitration agreements.[7] The IAA provides the parties with further flexibility. Section 22 allows them to choose their own arbitration regime, opting out of the UNCITRAL Model Law if they choose. Part 3 of the IAA provides the parties with further options, notably in enforcing interim measures and consolidating arbitral proceedings. Section 19 of the IAA also clarifies the nature, manner and application of 'public policy' to international commercial arbitration. An arbitral award is in conflict with the public policy of Australia 'if it is manifestly contrary to widely accepted principles of public policy'.[8] As further evidence of Australia's endorsement of the international arbitration regime, Part II of the IAA implements the New York Convention to which Australia acceded without reservation. The IAA also extends the application of the New York Convention to all external territories. In addition, according to Part IV of the IAA, Australia is a signatory to the International Centre for Settlement of Investment Disputes (ICSID) governing the arbitration of investment disputes.

Australian courts generally permit parties to an international commercial dispute to adapt arbitral procedures to their perceived business environment. However, this choice cannot be exercised in contravention of the principles of natural justice or due process of law. Among these principles are the right of each party to have due notice of an arbitration hearing, to present its case or answer the case presented by the other party, and to be treated fairly in the course of deliberations.

Australian courts protect the right of the parties to international commercial transactions to choose arbitration to resolve disputes in a fair, impartial, expeditious and cost-effective manner. They treat international arbitration awards as final and binding, and decline to disturb the findings of arbitrators except on public policy grounds or to prevent a denial of natural justice.

---

7 See [http://interarb.com/clout/mal.htm].

8 But see R Pryles, 'Reflections on Transnational Public Policy' (2007) 24 *Journal of International Arbitration* 8.

International commercial arbitration is also supported by both governmental and non-governmental organisations. For example, the National Alternative Dispute Resolution Advisory Council (NADRAC) is an independent body that advises the Australian Attorney-General on the development of high-quality, economic and efficient ways of resolving disputes without the need for a judicial decision, including by resort to commercial arbitration.[9]

While arbitration was historically restricted in Australia to building and construction disputes, in the past several decades it has grown to encompass multi-sector industries, from trade to investment, and encompassing parties from across Asia and further internationally. Arbitration clauses in international trade and investment contracts are also extensively employed, with parties to international transactions adopting arbitration, rather than relying on domestic courts in Australia or abroad, or, for that matter, domestic arbitration. International commercial arbitration has also evolved due to its improved image as an efficient, expert and low-cost method of resolving commercial disputes. This image is a notable result of cases such as the *Anaconda Operation v Fluor Australia Pty Ltd*,[10] in which arbitration proceedings were notably short, and the arbitrators confined the examination of witnesses and subjected the submission of documentary evidence to tight timelines.

Adding to the legal and practical recognition of international commercial arbitration in Australia is the evolution of its international arbitration centres. Notable among these is the growth of the ACICA, with revised arbitration rules adopted in 2005 modelled on the UNCITRAL Arbitration Rules of 1985. Significant too was the establishment in 2007 of the Australian Maritime and Transport Arbitration Commission (AMTAC) to provide maritime and transportation arbitration services, notably in response to Australia's global importance as a maritime trading nation.

What follows is an analysis of the key features and application of international commercial arbitration, seen in part through the prism of the UNCITRAL Model Law.

13.4 The scope of the UNCITRAL Model Law

The UNCITRAL Model Law on International Commercial Arbitration is widely utilised in international arbitration. Not only is it administered by many international arbitration associations, it is also incorporated into domestic legal systems, including in Australia.

The Model Law is important in ensuring the application of widely accepted rules and practices to govern global commerce, as distinct from local laws that might be perceived to promote the interests of one party over the other. It also avoids the impact of domestic laws that might be considered ill-suited to an international transaction, producing a harsh, one-sided, or impractical result.

---

9 See [www.nadrac.gov.au].

10 Conducted before Paulsson QC, Uff QC and Naughton QC in 2002.

Article 1 of the Model Law affords a wide scope of application to international commercial arbitration, as follows:

> (3) An arbitration is international if:
>
> (a) the parties to an arbitration agreement have, at the time of the conclusion of that agreement, their places of business in different States; or
>
> (b) one of the following places is situated outside the State in which the parties have their places of business:
>
> (i) the place of arbitration if determined in, or pursuant to, the arbitration agreement;
>
> (ii) any place where a substantial part of the obligations of the commercial relationship is to be performed or the place with which the subject-matter of the dispute is most closely connected; or
>
> (c) the parties have expressly agreed that the subject-matter of the arbitration agreement relates to more than one country.
>
> (4) For the purposes of paragraph (3) of this article:
>
> (a) if a party has more than one place of business, the place of business is that which has the closest relationship to the arbitration agreement;
>
> (b) if a party does not have a place of business, reference is to be made to his habitual residence.
>
> (5) This Law shall not affect any other law of this State by virtue of which certain disputes may not be submitted to arbitration or may be submitted to arbitration only according to provisions other than those of this Law.

International commercial transactions may be linked to various jurisdictions among which the parties may have preferences. Article 1 of the Model Law, dealing with 'scope of application', provides for a variety of places of arbitration, including in accordance with the arbitration agreement, such as:

- The place at which a substantive part of the obligations under the contract are to be performed;
- The place at which the subject matter of the contract is most closely connected; and
- The place the parties have agreed should apply to their agreement.

If the parties have more than one place of business, the applicable place may be that which has the closest relationship to the arbitration agreement. Should the parties not have a place of business, the parties' 'habitual place of business' may apply. All this is helpful to the parties, but raises the spectre of their having to make a choice among competing alternatives, basing that choice on sound reasons and the ability to substantiate them, and to live with the consequences.

Should the parties choose the place of arbitration, it is important that they do so in light of their discrete circumstances, including their geographic location, economic position and relationship. They may want to make a choice that reduces their costs, such as the costs of travel to distant hearings and the cost of disrupting their businesses when key executives are summonsed to testify before arbitrators in locations that are distant from their ordinary places of business.

The parties also have a range of practical concerns in choosing the form of international arbitration itself. For example, the choice of London, Paris, New York, or, more regionally, Hong Kong as the place of arbitration may appeal to many parties because each is a recognised centre of international commercial arbitration. Each is home to leading international arbitration associations; each can provide immediate access to established arbitration services including arbitrators; and each is a signatory of the New York Convention. At the same time, one or more of the parties may shy away from choosing any of these locations as the place of arbitration. Part of that reluctance may be attributed to the sheer cost of holding arbitrations in expensive urban centres. Another part may be political. A non-US party may be reluctant to choose the International Center of Dispute Resolution of the American Arbitration Association (AAA) in New York because of concern that such a choice may unduly favour a US party to the dispute, whether it does so or not. A non-European may be reluctant to choose arbitration before the International Chamber of Commerce (ICC), emanating from Paris, for similar reasons.

Further concerns may arise not simply because the place of arbitration is familiar to one party, but because another party is uncomfortable with that choice precisely because of that familiarity. Given that there is no perfect choice of arbitration, the parties may want to reach agreement over the place of arbitration prior to a dispute, with the least dissension and without alienating another party. Choosing a neutral place of arbitration may have a shared appeal, because no one party can claim a special affinity or advantage in that place. It may be conveniently located; for example, equidistant from the place of business of both parties. The arbitral *situs* may also offer sophisticated arbitration services. However, its location advantages may be outweighed by countervailing concerns, such as those relating to the jurisdiction exercised by courts over arbitration there.

13.4.1 The arbitration agreement

Article 7(1) of the UNCITRAL Model Law—'Definition and form of arbitration agreement'—states as follows:

> 'Arbitration agreement' is an agreement by the parties to submit to arbitration all or certain disputes which have arisen or which may arise between them in respect of a defined legal relationship, whether contractual or not. An arbitration agreement may be in the form of an arbitration clause in a contract or in the form of a separate agreement.

Parties are usually advised to make a choice of arbitration at the time of agreement, including the selection of both an arbitration association and its applicable rules of arbitration. Issues that influence such choices include, among others, the type of dispute, trade, or industry in issue, the history of and relationship between the parties, the commercial experience of the arbitrator chosen and, if the arbitrator is under the aegis of an arbitration association, its reputation and standing.

Most international, regional and domestic arbitration associations provide model arbitration clauses from which the parties can choose in whole or part. The benefit of making such a choice is the fact that such model clauses are tried and tested. Parties should be aware, however, that model arbitration clauses are also ways in which arbitration associations seek to attract customers, that their model clauses may be self-serving, and that they may embody rules of procedure that ill-suit the parties. It is important, therefore, for the parties to consider alternative choices of arbitration, including the perceived benefits and pitfalls of each. The most common way in which parties choose arbitration is by adopting either a standardised or a tailored arbitration clause in their contract. This clause may be devised to stand alone, serving as the exclusive means of dispute resolution chosen by the parties. Alternatively, the parties may choose arbitration along a continuum of dispute resolution options, for example by providing by contract first for mediation and, only failing that, for arbitration.

The arbitration clause may provide for arbitration in extensive detail, including the manner in which an arbitrator is to be appointed, the rules and procedures governing conduct of the arbitration, arbitral costs, and the binding nature of the award. Alternatively, the arbitration clause may adopt the rules and procedures of an established arbitration association. In this latter instance, the rules of that association will govern the appointment of the arbitrator(s), and the rules governing the administration of arbitration, from initiation to conclusion.

In recent years, arbitration associations increasingly provide for ad hoc arbitration. This allows the parties to choose the nature and form of arbitration they prefer, often at the time of a dispute. The clause may also be suitably adapted to their particular needs and circumstances, notably for expedited or fast-track arbitral proceedings. Established arbitration associations are keen for parties making such choices to use their facilities and services, such as their offices as an arbitration venue, their translation services and their rules of arbitration, suitably adapted to meet the ad hoc needs of the parties.

13.4.2 Formal requirements

Article 7(2) of the UNCITRAL Model Law—'Definition and form of arbitration agreement'—states as follows:

> The arbitration agreement shall be in writing. An agreement is in writing if it is contained in a document signed by the parties or in an exchange of letters, telex, telegrams or other means of telecommunication which provide a record of the agreement, or in an exchange of statements of claim and defence in which the existence of an agreement is alleged by one party and not denied by another. The reference in a contract to a document containing an arbitration clause constitutes an arbitration agreement provided that the contract is in writing and the reference is such as to make that clause part of the contract.

Both the UNCITRAL Model Law and the New York Convention stipulate that arbitration agreements must be in writing. Article II(2) of the New York Convention also requires that the agreement must either be signed by both parties or contained in an exchange of letters or telegrams. The UNCITRAL Model Law is more liberal, and includes any means of telecommunication constituting a permanent record of an agreement to arbitrate. Should an arbitration agreement be subject to the IAA, as distinct from the UNCITRAL Model Law, the definition of 'agreement in writing' is prescribed by the New York Convention.

In *Comandate Marine Corp v Pan Australia Shipping*,[11] the Federal Court held that an arbitration clause included in an exchange of signed letters between the parties fulfilled the requirement for an arbitration agreement to be 'in writing'. The court also established a flexible standard of interpreting arbitration agreements, holding that the words 'all disputes arising out of this contract' were sufficiently wide to include claims of misleading and deceptive conduct in forming a contract under the

11 [2006] FCAFC 192.

Trade Practices Act 1974 (Cth). The construction of the Federal Court was echoed by the House of Lords in *Fiona Trust & Holding Corp v Privalov*.[12]

Australian courts have held that arbitration agreements may confer a right on just one party to commence arbitration.[13] This is consistent with established practice in the construction industry, as well as in banking and finance.

13.4.3 Drafting arbitration clauses

Drafting arbitration clauses requires an understanding of arbitration options, as well as different methods of drafting such clauses.

One option is for the parties to draft a detailed arbitration clause which purports to deal exhaustively with different aspects of arbitration, from the choice of arbitration and arbitrators, to the rules governing arbitration proceedings, to costs, and to the nature and form of the award itself. Parties who adopt this option may draw upon their own existing practice, or practice in their trade or industry to determine how to devise such clauses, or they may craft them *de novo* to suit their circumstances.

A party in a distinctive trade or industry that regularly engages in international commercial transactions may have an incentive to model an arbitration clause on its own specific experience, or that of others in its trade. For example, the parties may be engaged in a complex industry or transaction in which the services of a highly specialised form of arbitration with special powers and unique procedures are considered suitable. This may arise, for example, in intellectual property disputes that involve complex determinations, drawing on engineering sophistication or other expertise.

In most cases, drafting detailed arbitration clauses *de novo* is not worth the time and cost, given the existence of established arbitration options that can be incorporated into international trade agreements by reference. For example, parties may prefer to rely on the model arbitration clause of an international arbitration centre, such as ACICA, because its model clause is the subject of recognised methods of interpretation, and is enforceable before both international tribunals and domestic courts of law. This does not mean that the parties should blindly adopt such model clauses; their particular circumstances may justify otherwise, such as when different associations adopt different cost and fee schedules in complex disputes.

The following are considerations (among others) in drafting arbitration clauses.

First, the clause should accommodate the peculiarities of the transaction or parties in issue, including their disparate preferences. Drafting a *sui generis* arbitration clause that another party is unlikely to accept, or that will require extensive negotiation, may not be worth the time and effort involved. Choosing an established or model arbitration clause—for example, one drafted by ACICA or the ICC, with which both parties may be familiar or otherwise concur—may be a preferable alternative. Regional factors, such as the location of both parties in the Asian region, may be a significant factor in choosing a regional arbitration association like the Hong Kong International Arbitration Centre. That choice may be based on the ease of access to that association, its 'neutral'

---

12 [2007] UKHL 40.

13 See for example *PMT Partners v Australian National Parks & Wildlife Service* [1995] HCA 36.

location, or the fact that international arbitration providers like the ICC or the AAA are less accessible and generally involve higher costs than regional centres.

Second, the arbitration clause should take account of different kinds of arbitration clauses; for example by adopting a model arbitration clause or providing for ad hoc arbitration. Parties also need to consider adopting trade- or industry-specific arbitration clauses, such as referring intellectual property disputes to the World Intellectual Property Organization (WIPO).

Third, the arbitration clauses should take account of the particular relationship and parties involved, such as when one or both parties have a distinctive view of the value of a particular arbitration option or conversely, the disutility of other options.

13.4.4 Choice of arbitrators

Article 11 of the UNCITRAL Model Law—'Appointment of arbitrators'—states as follows:

> (1) No person shall be precluded by reason of his nationality from acting as an arbitrator, unless otherwise agreed by the parties.
>
> (2) The parties are free to agree on a procedure of appointing the arbitrator or arbitrators, subject to the provisions of paragraphs (4) and (5) of this article.
>
> (3) Failing such agreement,
>
> (a) in an arbitration with three arbitrators, each party shall appoint one arbitrator, and the two arbitrators thus appointed shall appoint the third arbitrator; if a party fails to appoint the arbitrator within thirty days of receipt of a request to do so from the other party, or if the two arbitrators fail to agree on the third arbitrator within thirty days of their appointment, the appointment shall be made, upon request of a party, by the court or other authority specified in article 6;
>
> (b) in an arbitration with a sole arbitrator, if the parties are unable to agree on the arbitrator, he shall be appointed, upon request of a party, by the court or other authority specified in article 6.
>
> (4) Where, under an appointment procedure agreed upon by the parties,
>
> (a) a party fails to act as required under such procedure, or
>
> (b) the parties, or two arbitrators, are unable to reach an agreement expected of them under such procedure, or
>
> (c) a third party, including an institution, fails to perform any function entrusted to it under such procedure,
>
> any party may request the court or other authority specified in article 6 to take the necessary measure, unless the agreement on the appointment procedure provides other means for securing the appointment.
>
> (5) A decision on a matter entrusted by paragraph (3) or (4) of this article to the court or other authority specified in article 6 shall be subject to no appeal. The court or other authority, in appointing an arbitrator, shall have due regard to any qualifications required of the arbitrator by the agreement of the parties and to such considerations as are likely to secure the appointment of an independent and impartial arbitrator and, in the case of a sole or third arbitrator, shall take into account as well the advisability of appointing an arbitrator of a nationality other than those of the parties.

The parties are free to appoint arbitrators of their own choosing to govern their dispute, as well as the number of arbitrators. Arbitrators are usually chosen because of their expertise in the applicable trade or industry (as well as their expertise in arbitration itself).

Ordinarily, the parties choose either one or three arbitrators; Articles 10 and 11 of the Model Law presuppose that the parties will choose three arbitrators. The parties usually choose one arbitrator each, while the third arbitrator is chosen by the party-appointed arbitrators, the applicable arbitration association, or, failing agreement on appointment, by a court of law. This is in contrast with s 6 of the New South Wales *Commercial Arbitration Act 1984* (CAA), which provides for the choice of a single arbitrator in domestic arbitration.

Where the parties fail to agree on the number of arbitrators to be appointed, the appointment process for arbitrators will generally be provided by the institutional rules of an applicable arbitration association or, conceivably, by domestic legislation applicable to international arbitration. For all other circumstances, Article 11 of the Model Law and s 8 of the CAA prescribe a procedure for the appointment of arbitrators.

As a general principle, the arbitrators are chosen to resolve particular disputes, not to conduct business or trade on behalf of parties who are in conflict. However, arbitrators may be appointed to make commercial decisions when doing so relates to the resolution of a dispute.

Australian law does not ordinarily prescribe any special procedure for the appointment of arbitrators in multiparty disputes. If a multiparty dispute is likely to arise under a contract, it is advisable for the parties to agree on a set of arbitration rules that contain particular provisions for the appointment of arbitrators, such as under the ACICA arbitration rules (Article 11).

Criteria governing the appointment of an arbitrator include reputation and subject expertise. Commercial arbitrators are usually expected to have a combination of sophisticated legal experience, a firm grasp of commerce and international trade law, and a capacity to grasp the complexities of the particular case. As a result, a variety of international and national organisations provide arbitration training, such as the Chartered Institute of Arbitrators based in London, which has Australian headquarters in Sydney. Courses can also be taken through (among other reputable international associations) the ICC, based in Paris; the London Court of International Arbitration, based in London; and the International Center for Dispute Resolution of the AAA in New York. The parties may also have resort to various arbitration associations in the region. Notably among these are the Hong Kong International Arbitration Centre (HKIAC) and the Singapore International Arbitration Centre (SIAC).

Arbitration appointees are generally required to sign a disclosure demonstrating that they are independent of the parties, that they are impartial between them and otherwise not in conflict of interest, and that they will treat the arbitration proceedings as confidential. Their appointment is not subject to appeal to a court of law, except by agreement of the parties, or on their failure to exercise jurisdiction. In the latter instance, the arbitral tribunal has authority to rule on the nature and limits of its own jurisdiction, such as under Article 21 of the UNCITRAL Rules.

Australian law does not require that an arbitrator be licensed or otherwise qualified to serve in that capacity. Nor are arbitrators disqualified on such formal grounds as citizenship, residency or nationality. However, arbitrators can be challenged on grounds of bias, conflict of interest or other lack of independence, or for incapacity. Regarding disclosure obligations, Article 12 of the UNCITRAL Model Law requires that arbitrators disclose any circumstance that is likely to raise reasonable doubt as to their impartiality or lack of independence. This duty of disclosure continues throughout the course of the arbitration.

Article 12 of the Model Law allows any party to challenge the appointment of an arbitrator on the grounds of an alleged lack of independence, or a lack of qualification or expertise to act. For the former, the test is one of 'reasonable apprehension'. In *Livesey v New South Wales Bar Association*,[14] the court held that an arbitrator would be removed if a party to the proceedings, or a fair-minded and informed lay observer, might in the circumstances reasonably apprehend a lack of impartiality (the informed lay observer should have knowledge of the facts of the case and the level of sophistication of a member of the general business community, as distinct from having any particular legal knowledge).

Arbitrators may also be challenged for the manner in which they conduct the hearings; for example not acting impartially or independently, denying parties the reasonable opportunity to present their case, or exceeding their arbitral jurisdiction. In some instances, these concerns may be justified and upheld before the governing body of an arbitration association, such as the ICC Court or the London Court of International Arbitration, or on review by a domestic court of law.

However, domestic courts are reluctant to interfere with arbitration proceedings or awards, save in the presence of grave abuse. Usually, domestic courts:

- Defer to the choice of the parties to submit their disputes to international arbitration, as well as to the parties' choice of arbitral proceedings;
- Respect the commercial expertise of the arbitrators in relation to the subject matter in dispute and the process of arbitration itself;
- Avoid allowing themselves to be used by unsuccessful parties to engage in after-the-fact forum shopping, looking for a sympathetic court to review and overturn arbitration awards;
- Are wary not to reward unsuccessful parties who invoke procedural objections to arbitration proceedings in order to jettison adverse arbitration award; and
- Respect arbitral awards by treating them as binding and enforceable.

Arbitrators are also not usually liable before Australia courts for negligent conduct in the hearing of a dispute. For example, s 28 of the IAA provides that arbitrators are not liable for negligence in their conduct as arbitrators, which is also reflected in s 51 of the CAA. However, they are liable for fraud, as outlined in Article 44 of the ACICA arbitration rules.

13.4.5 Representation in arbitration

The parties to an international commercial arbitration are free to engage in arbitration with or without representation. Section 29(2) of the IAA specifically provides that a party to arbitration may:

- Represent itself;
- Choose a legal practitioner from any jurisdiction to represent it; or
- Choose anyone at its discretion to represent it.

---

14 (1983) 151 CLR 294.

This is in notable contrast with domestic arbitration, notably s 20(1) of the CAA, in which the choice of a representative in arbitration proceedings is subject to a variety of requirements.

As a matter of practice, parties to international commercial arbitration are invariably represented by lawyers who may have a combination of attributes in their professional backgrounds—they may be established litigators; they may have past experience as counsel in arbitration proceedings or as arbitrators; and/or they may be specialists in the trade or industry in question. In complex arbitrations, parties are often represented by teams of lawyers, who together combine these different backgrounds and experiences.

In highly specialised cases, the parties may include specialist representatives, such as actuaries or accountants in complex accounting cases. In complex intellectual property cases, the parties may include representatives who are engineers or IT experts. These specialist representatives may not only advise the parties on technical matters, they may also assist in preparing documentation, including claims and defences. Subject to the terms of reference of the arbitration itself, they may participate to varying degrees in the preparation of, examination and cross-examination of witnesses.

13.4.6 The jurisdiction of arbitrators

Article 16 of the UNCITRAL Model Law—'Competence of arbitral tribunal to rule on its jurisdiction'—states as follows:

> (1) The arbitral tribunal may rule on its own jurisdiction, including any objections with respect to the existence or validity of the arbitration agreement. For that purpose, an arbitration clause which forms part of a contract shall be treated as an agreement independent of the other terms of the contract. A decision by the arbitral tribunal that the contract is null and void shall not entail *ipso jure* the invalidity of the arbitration clause.
>
> (2) A plea that the arbitral tribunal does not have jurisdiction shall be raised not later than the submission of the statement of defence. A party is not precluded from raising such a plea by the fact that he has appointed, or participated in the appointment of, an arbitrator. A plea that the arbitral tribunal is exceeding the scope of its authority shall be raised as soon as the matter alleged to be beyond the scope of its authority is raised during the arbitral proceedings. The arbitral tribunal may, in either case, admit a later plea if it considers the delay justified.
>
> (3) The arbitral tribunal may rule on a plea referred to in paragraph (2) of this article either as a preliminary question or in an award on the merits. If the arbitral tribunal rules as a preliminary question that it has jurisdiction, any party may request, within thirty days after having received notice of that ruling, the court specified in article 6 to decide the matter, which decision shall be subject to no appeal; while such a request is pending, the arbitral tribunal may continue the arbitral proceedings and make an award.

An arbitral tribunal may rule on its own jurisdiction, including on the validity of the arbitration agreement and the contract to which the arbitral agreement pertains. This often arises when an arbitration tribunal examines a putative contract and determines whether clauses selecting the place of arbitration and the law to be applied are valid. In international arbitration, the arbitrator is expressly empowered to determine whether or not an arbitration agreement exists under Article 16(1) of the Model Law.

Of note, an arbitration tribunal may nullify the contract which provides for arbitration, while upholding and applying the arbitration clause which is contained in that contract.

An objection to the jurisdiction of an arbitral tribunal is subject to procedural guidelines, and should usually be raised prior to the submission of the statement of defence. Similarly, a claim that the tribunal has acted *ultra vires* should be raised directly after that authority has been exercised. The arbitral tribunal may entertain such a plea as a preliminary question, or in its award. If it deals with the issue as a preliminary question, a party can ordinarily challenge that preliminary ruling before a court of law.

In New South Wales, the arbitrator to a domestic dispute can determine whether or not an arbitration agreement is void *ab initio* only if the parties so agree. If the parties do not agree, the arbitrator is usually expected to adjourn proceedings and submit the question to the courts for determination. According to the High Court, an agreement to arbitrate can also be severed from the contract.[15]

Article 8(1) of the Model Law provides that, if a case is already proceeding through arbitration, a court will not ordinarily accept jurisdiction over the matter unless it is apparent that the arbitration agreement is void, or the arbitration as set up is unlikely to give rise to a legally supportable result. Thus, if any of the parties objects to the jurisdiction of the court, the court will usually stay proceedings subject to the continuation of the arbitration.

13.4.7 The place of arbitration

Article 20 of the UNCITRAL Model Law—'Place of arbitration'—states as follows:

> (1) The parties are free to agree on the place of arbitration. Failing such agreement, the place of arbitration shall be determined by the arbitral tribunal having regard to the circumstances of the case, including the convenience of the parties.
>
> (2) Notwithstanding the provisions of paragraph (1) of this article, the arbitral tribunal may, unless otherwise agreed by the parties, meet at any place it considers appropriate for consultation among its members, for hearing witnesses, experts or the parties, or for inspection of goods, other property or documents.

As a general principle the parties are free to choose the place of arbitration, as provided under Article 1 of the Model Law. Should they fail to exercise that choice, the arbitral tribunal may make the choice, taking account of what is convenient for the parties. For example, Article 20 of the Model Law includes the convenience of the parties as a criterion in making that choice.

Arbitrators may conduct hearings in whole or part on site; for example, where a disputed construction project is located. They may also decide, in consultation with the parties, upon the duration of proceedings.

13.4.8 The arbitrability of a dispute

A dispute must be arbitrable; that is, the matters in dispute must be capable of being resolved through arbitration. Article 1 of the Model Law conceives of arbitrability

---

15 See *Codelfa Construction v State Rail Authority (NSW)* (1982) 149 CLR 337.

expansively—as long as the matter in dispute is commercial and international (Article 1(1) and (3)), it is arbitrable. What complicates the scope of arbitrability is the difficulty of defining it before a dispute occurs and before a ruling has been made on such arbitrability.

From an arbitrator's perspective, an issue may be deemed not to be arbitrable on procedural grounds; for example, because it falls outside of the jurisdiction of arbitration in general or outside of the purview of the current arbitration in particular. A matter may also not be arbitrable because it raises substantive issues that are deemed not to be the subject of arbitration. At the most general, these issues may be deemed not to relate to substantive issues that are of an 'international commercial' nature. At their most particular, these issues may be deemed to fall outside of the purview of the specific arbitration or outside the purview of arbitration more generally. As an example of the latter, arbitrators are not expected to determine criminal liability, as such matters are generally within the realm of domestic or international criminal courts.

The determination that a matter is not arbitrable may also arise because it involves issues and parties that are not the subject of the arbitration agreement, such as disputes involving third party contracts. A matter may also not be arbitrable because it falls within the jurisdiction of a court of law, such as in regulating anticompetitive conduct in accordance with domestic law, or for public policy grounds.

Australian law is increasingly, but not uniformly, receptive in relation to the arbitrability of commercial disputes. The practice of some Australian courts is to hold that a matter is arbitrable even if it deals with delicate domestic public policy issues, such as those that arise in competition law, or in bankruptcy and insolvency proceedings.[16] In addition, Australian courts have held that various matters arising under trade practices legislation are arbitrable. For example, the New South Wales Court of Appeal has held that consumer protection issues under the *Trade Practices Act* are capable of settlement by arbitration.[17] Australian courts have also held that disputes over misleading and deceptive conduct under s 52 of the *Trade Practices Act* are arbitrable.[18]

In contrast, some Australian courts are willing to challenge the arbitrability of matters that impinge on public policy in the area of anticompetitive behaviour. For example, despite the presence of arbitration agreements, several courts have exercised jurisdiction over disputes involving Part IV of the *Trade Practices Act* on anticompetitive behaviour.[19]

In disputes involving multiple claims, some Australian courts have also determined that only some of the claims are arbitrable. In effect, they have stayed proceedings in respect of those matters that are arbitrable, retaining jurisdiction over other matters which they deem not to be arbitrable.[20] Other Australian courts have avoided the issue of

16 See for example *Tanning Research Laboratories v O'Brien* (1990) 64 ALJR 211, reported in *Yearbook of Commercial Arbitration XV* (1991), pp 521–9.

17 See for example *IBM Australia v National Distribution Services* (1991) 22 NSWLR 466.

18 See for example *Francis Travel Marketing v Virgin Atlantic Airways* (1996) 39 NSWLR 160; *Hi-Fert v Kiukiang Maritime Carriers* (1998) 159 ALR 142.

19 See *Petersville v Peters (WA)* (1997) ATPR 41-566; *Alstom Power v Eraring Energy* (2004) ATPR 42-009.

20 See for example *Hi-Fert and Tanning Research Laboratories v O'Brien* (1990) 169 CLR 332; *Transfield v Pacific Hydro Limited* [2006] VSC 175.

arbitrability, concentrating instead on whether the arbitration agreement was sufficiently broad in its scope of application to cover the matter in dispute.[21]

Given that arbitrators are expected to rule on the limits of their own jurisdiction, it is for them in the first instance to determine whether a matter before them is arbitrable. However, parties may challenge that determination in court on the grounds that all or some of the matters raised were not arbitrable. In that case, a judicial declaration that a matter is not arbitrable might arise after the fact and in accordance with the reasons provided by that court.

13.4.9 The conduct of arbitration

Article 23(1) of the UNCITRAL Model Law—'Statements of claim and defence'—states as follows:

> Within the period of time agreed by the parties or determined by the arbitral tribunal, the claimant shall state the facts supporting his claim, the points at issue and the relief or remedy sought, and the respondent shall state his defence in respect of these particulars, unless the parties have otherwise agreed as to the required elements of such statements. The parties may submit with their statements all documents they consider to be relevant or may add a reference to the documents or other evidence they will submit.

Following the Model Law, in preparing for arbitration proceedings, each party to an international commercial dispute is required to state its claim or defence in respect of the issues, unless the parties have otherwise agreed upon the facts or issues in dispute. Should a claimant fail to communicate a statement of claim, the arbitral tribunal may terminate proceedings. Should the defendant fail to communicate a statement of defence, the arbitral tribunal may continue proceedings in the absence of the defendant, or treat such failure as an admission of a claim. Should any party fail to appear in proceedings, or fail to adduce documents, the tribunal may continue proceedings.

There is no uniform method by which arbitrators ought to conduct proceedings, unlike uniform rules of evidence and procedure that are applied by domestic courts. What is required are procedures that provide the parties to arbitration with due process safeguards. In particular, the parties must be provided with the opportunity to present their arguments, and to be treated equally and in accordance with the applicable law.

The arbitral award ought also to be based on the information presented at the hearing, and not on the basis of extraneous considerations beyond its purview. This does not imply that arbitrators are prohibited from taking account of considerations beyond the oral or written evidence presented during the course of arbitral proceedings; rather, it implies that their primary basis for deciding should be grounded in the documentary and oral testimony of witnesses, the parties and their representatives, submitted during the course of arbitration proceedings.

Part of the reason for choosing arbitration is the assumption that international commercial arbitrators have commercial expertise, they understand the significance of international comity, and they have an extensive knowledge of the international law merchant, including the significance of international conventions, treaties and customs.

21 See for example *ACD Tridon Inc v Tridon Australia* [2002] NSWSC 896.

At a formal level, arbitral tribunals are usually expected to work with the parties to establish and apply procedures that are cost- and time-effective, and that provide the claimant with an opportunity to file a claim, and the defendant with an opportunity to file a response. The tribunal may establish the applicable procedures to govern arbitration hearings through a preliminary conference or hearing with the parties, or by other means. These proceedings are ordinarily intended to identify the issues in dispute, to determine if the parties can agree upon particular facts or issues, and to establish the manner in which to conduct the hearing itself.

The nature of arbitration hearings varies significantly from arbitration to arbitration. The conduct of proceedings may be influenced considerably by the arbitration agreement, the authority that is vested in the arbitrators, the commercial issues in dispute, the usages and practices in the applicable industry, and the background of the arbitral tribunal itself.

In some cases, arbitral tribunals resort to preliminary hearings as a matter of course. There, some matters are dispensed with, others are clarified, and instructions are given to the parties with regard to their claims and responses respectively. These preliminary hearings may take place at the place of arbitration, or else at another place or places, at the convenience of the parties, the arbitral tribunal or witnesses. The arbitral tribunal may also stipulate for discovery, including for example that the tribunal make a site visit to the place of business of one or another party.

The date and duration of the full hearing are usually prescribed in advance. The tribunal may specify the location and duration of the hearing, the issues that will be dealt with at that hearing, and the timelines for the parties to submit documentation in preparation for that hearing. For example, the tribunal may require that the claimant set out the relevant issues (including details of the claim), and provide relevant documentary evidence, a list of witnesses and issues for determination at the hearing, and timelines within which to adduce such evidence. The tribunal may give the defendant similar instructions. Some tribunals may set out requirements or guidelines to govern the format, content and length of the claim or defence.

General guidelines for international commercial arbitration include that proceedings should be conducted in a transparent manner. To ensure that their conduct is beyond reproach, the arbitrators should make full disclosure of any circumstances that might reasonably be construed as placing them in a position of conflict of interest, such as having a personal or professional relationship with a party directly, through a member of family, a partner or associate. They should be cautious not to provide cause to an unsuccessful party seeking grounds upon which to challenge an arbitral award.[22]

Arbitral tribunals may invoke institutional rules, such as those contained in the Model Law, to impede parties from disrupting proceedings. For example, they may find a party in default under Article 25 of the Model Law for failing, 'without sufficient cause', to communicate a statement of claim under Article 25(a) or a defence under Article 25(b). Should a party 'fail to appear at a hearing or to produce documentary evidence, the

22 See LE Trakman, 'The IBA Guidelines on Conflict of Interest in International Commercial Arbitration'(2007) 10 *International Arbitration Law Review* 124.

arbitral tribunal may continue the proceedings and make the award on the evidence before it' (Article 25(c)).

13.4.10 Rules of evidence and procedure

Arbitrators are not bound by the rules of evidence and procedure that constrain domestic courts of law. Both domestic and international arbitrators enjoy significant latitude in determining the admissibility, relevance, materiality and weight of the evidence in arbitral proceedings.[23]

Article 19 of the Model Law permits the arbitrators to ignore the domestic laws of evidence in an international case. Thus, unlike a court—which will always apply the local laws on civil procedure, including the law of evidence—arbitrators may apply those laws that they deem most relevant and appropriate in determining the admissibility, relevance, materiality and weight of evidence, including in discharging the burden of proof.

As a result, arbitral tribunals may approach arbitral hearings quite differently to a court, depending on the nature of the dispute, the parties and the preferred evidentiary approach adopted by the tribunal. For example, the arbitral tribunal may:

- Prescribe a limited time period, such as several days, a week or more—for a formal hearing;
- Stipulate requirements to govern the hearing, including the nature of proceedings, provision for documentary and oral testimony;
- Insist on reviewing documentary testimony and witnesses lists, among others, in advance of the hearing, and prescribe proceedings in light of that testimony;
- Prescribe the format of the hearing in advance, the permissible mix of documentary and oral testimony, the permissible manner of examining witnesses, and the amount of time during which each party may present its case.

Arbitrators also adapt proceedings to the discrete needs of the dispute and the parties, in compliance with law but also in accordance with attributes they accord to international commercial arbitration. These attributes are usually conceived of as the holding of hearings that:

- Are more informal than before courts of law;
- Are less constrained by the strict rules of evidence and procedure that are apposite to courts of law;
- Facilitate awards that combine commercial efficacy with legal enforceability; and
- Are cost-effective for the parties and not subject to undue delay.

Typically, arbitral proceedings in common law jurisdictions, such as before the AAA in New York, are likely on average to be longer in duration and involve more oral testimony, cross-examination and discovery than arbitral hearings in civil law jurisdictions, such as before the ICC in Paris, in which hearings are usually less adversarial and more inquisitorial than in the common law tradition. However, none of these general assumptions are necessarily so. Arbitrators with a civil law background

23 See for example Article 19(2) of the UNCITRAL Model Law and s 19(3) of the CAA.

who are appointed to preside over arbitral hearings in New York may rely more on documentary than oral testimony and more on inquisitorial than adversarial hearings. Even common law arbitrators may follow this recourse, simply because they believe that civil law traditions are preferable, or that they are more suited to the case at hand.

In practice, arbitrators in international arbitration are guided by the institutions that are adopted (expressly or by reference) by the specific arbitration association under which they are appointed, such as by the ACICA arbitration rules. For example, arbitrators may adhere to general standards governing international arbitration established by the International Bar Association's Rules on the Taking of Evidence. These rules are endorsed by the ACICA arbitration rules in the absence of express agreement between the parties or rulings by the appointed arbitrator(s) to the contrary.

International arbitration may also be influenced, to varying degrees, by the rules of evidence and procedure adopted by domestic courts, such as by Australian courts. This may arise by operation of law, by agreement between the parties, by stipulation of the arbitral tribunal, or simply by virtue of the background and training of the representatives of the parties or the arbitrator in a judicial system.

The tendency for arbitration to replicate judicial proceedings is accentuated in Australia, in which domestic arbitration in particular is sometimes conducted in a somewhat comparable manner to judicial proceedings. For example, witnesses often are sworn in, examined and cross-examined by lawyers, not unlike before domestic courts.

The practice of arbitration replicating judicial decisions may also be due to the fact that international commercial arbitrators themselves may rely on domestic courts, such as under Article 27 of the Model Law which provides that an arbitral tribunal or a party with the approval of the arbitral tribunal may request assistance from a competent court in taking evidence. In addition, the court so approached is likely to apply its own rules in hearing that evidence within its competence.

At their most dubious, arbitration hearings may take too long. They may be subject to unduly lengthy delays. Hearings may be protracted; witness lists may grow; excessive extensions may be given to the parties to produce documents or witnesses; and the ensuing arbitral award may be convoluted or impractical to enforce. The parties can help to avoid such difficulties by being deliberative in their choice of both arbitration and arbitrators; while arbitrators should be vigilant to avoid protracted and costly hearings. A particular problem is that many arbitrators are lawyers licensed to practice in a particular domestic jurisdiction; the result is that they may conceive of their role as 'judicial', which may not be warranted in the arbitral context.

13.4.11 The authority of arbitrators

Article 34 of the UNCITRAL Model Law—'Applicable law, *amiable compositeur*'—states as follows:

> (1) The Arbitral Tribunal shall apply the law designated by the parties as applicable to the substance of the dispute. Failing such designation by the parties, the Arbitral Tribunal shall apply the rules of law which it considers applicable.
>
> (2) The Arbitral Tribunal shall decide as *amiable compositeur* or *ex aequo et bono* only if the parties have, in writing, expressly authorized the Arbitral Tribunal to do so and if the law applicable to the arbitral procedure permits such arbitration.

(3) In all cases, the Arbitral Tribunal shall decide in accordance with the terms of the contract and shall take into account the usages of the trade applicable to the transaction.

Arbitration proceedings are generally subject to law. The arbitrators are bound by the law applicable to the dispute, such as the substantive law governing the formation, performance and termination of the contract. Arbitral proceedings are also subject to law in the manner in which they are conducted and in the right of the parties to procedural justice, including to receive a fair hearing, to have access to relevant documentation, to present arguments in support of a claim or defence, and to an award that complies with the rules governing the conduct of arbitration and the applicable law. Article 18 of the Model Law specifically provides that the parties shall be treated equally and given a full opportunity to present their case.

In limited instances, the parties may agree that an arbitrator should decide disputes through amiable composition or according to that which they consider is 'fair and just', as distinct from that which the law requires them to decide. The general view is that arbitration proceedings should only be conducted in such a manner in exceptional circumstances, based on the peculiarities of the dispute, the distinct background and qualifications of the arbitrator and the concern of the parties that the otherwise applicable law may be unduly rigid or simply silent on the issues. Parties may also choose to have their disputes so resolved because of their confidence in the ability of the arbitrator(s) to decide fairly; or simply because the parties are unable to agree upon an applicable law.[24]

Arbitration conducted by amiable composition or according to the arbitrator's conception of 'fairness and justness' is growing in practice. It is the source of study by international associations such as the ICC and the London Court of International Arbitration. It is also viewed as part of a modern international law merchant, which is cosmopolitan in nature, transcends the law of any one jurisdiction, and is embodied in principles of comity, as distinct from formal principles of law.

Resistance to such arbitration includes the concern that arbitrators who are not subject to judicial review may abuse their discretion and ultimately undermine the credibility of international commercial arbitration itself.

13.4.12 Treatment of parties

Article 18 of the UNCITRAL Model Law—'Equal treatment of parties'—states as follows:

> The parties shall be treated with equality and each party shall be given a full opportunity of presenting his case.

Arbitration proceedings are bound by procedures attributed to the rules of natural justice. The arbitral tribunal is required to provide each party with adequate time in which to present its case and to treat each party equally. Some tribunals may treat such equality formally, such as providing the representatives of the parties with equal time to present their party's cases.

24 See LE Trakman, 'Ex Aequo et Bono: De-mystifying an Ancient Concept' (2008) 8(2) *Chicago Journal of International Law* 621.

The tribunal is also required to treat the parties in a substantively equal manner. Such equality entails equal treatment in the latitude given to each in adducing evidence and examining witnesses, including in addressing the tribunal.

While an arbitral tribunal should not assist a party in presenting its case (unlike some courts that might assist unrepresented consumers in actions against legally represented suppliers), an arbitrator may censure one party for conduct it considers improper, including in relation to another party.

Arbitrators may also adopt constraints to ensure that the parties are treated equally (at least formally), such as by using a clock to provide each party with the same time limits in which to present or answer a case, and also to ensure that proceedings are expeditious. The tribunal may also adopt substantive rules to ensure that the parties are treated fairly in the admission and weighing of evidence.

The tribunal may redress abuse in the conduct of arbitral hearings by ruling against a party who is impeding the arbitral process, by rejecting a claim or defence as spurious, or by making an award that takes account of vexatious or other improper conduct.

13.4.13 Stay of judicial proceedings

Article 8 of the UNCITRAL Model Law—'Arbitration agreement and substantive claim before court'—states as follows:

> (1) A court before which an action is brought in a matter which is the subject of an arbitration agreement shall, if a party so requests not later than when submitting his first statement on the substance of the dispute, refer the parties to arbitration unless it finds that the agreement is null and void, inoperative or incapable of being performed.
> (2) Where an action referred to in paragraph (1) of this article has been brought, arbitral proceedings may nevertheless be commenced or continued, and an award may be made, while the issue is pending before the court.

Article 8 of the Model Law provides for a stay of judicial proceedings where there is a valid arbitration agreement, so long as a party requests the stay before making its first substantive submission on the substance of the dispute.

Section 7(2) of the IAA specifically incorporates by reference the New York Convention, providing for a stay of judicial proceedings in regard to specified matters that are suited to resolution by arbitration. These matters are listed in s 7(1) of the IAA. The primary purpose of the section is to ensure that a stay of proceedings is permitted under the New York Convention in regard to international commercial arbitration, but not in regard to purely domestic arbitration. In contrast, the Model Law has no such qualifications in regard to a stay of judicial proceedings.

Given the generality of Article 8 of the Model Law and the specific provisions of s 7(2) of the IAA, it is unclear how courts will apply each section in specific cases. As a general rule, Australian courts are likely to stay proceedings on an application of a party in the presence of a valid international arbitration agreement.[25]

However, Australian courts are likely to limit the scope of the IAA, including by declining to stay proceedings, in order to comply with domestic legislation that restricts the application of international arbitration. For example, s 11 of the *Carriage of Goods*

25 See for example *Shanghai Foreign Trade Corporation v Sigma Metallurgical Company* (1996) 133 FLR 417.

by Sea Act 1991 (Cth) nullifies an arbitration agreement in a bill of lading or similar document relating to the international carriage of goods to and from Australia, unless the designated seat of the arbitration is in Australia. Section 43 of the *Insurance Contracts Act 1984* (Cth) and s 19 of the *Insurance Act 1902* (NSW) also render an arbitration agreement void unless it is concluded after the dispute arose. This limitation now appears to apply to both insurance and reinsurance contracts.[26] Similar limitations on the scope of arbitration are included in s 7C of the *Home Building Act 1989* (NSW).

13.4.14 Confidentiality of proceedings

The general principle that arbitration is a confidential private process established by the parties is a widely held tenet of international commercial arbitration. This principle also guides arbitrators in establishing procedures that ensure confidentiality, such as in the private manner in which hearings are conducted.[27]

However, the extent of confidentiality in arbitration proceedings is not uniform among different arbitration associations. Nor is confidentiality consistently conceived and applied by domestic systems of law. In particular, Australian courts have declined to adopt the stricter principles of confidentiality that are adopted by courts elsewhere, notably in the UK. The High Court of Australia held in *Esso Australia Resources v Plowman*[28] that, while arbitral proceedings and hearings are private (in not being open to the public), not all documents voluntarily produced by a party during the course of an arbitration are confidential. This ruling amounts to a rejection of the principle, adopted by courts in other jurisdictions including the UK, that by agreeing to arbitrate the parties impliedly agree upon confidentiality. The position under Australian law is potentially troubling, given that confidentiality is an important hallmark of international commercial arbitration. However, the High Court of Australia did provide that the parties can expressly agree that documents produced in the arbitration be kept confidential.

The result of the High Court decision is that parties to international commercial arbitration are advised to make express provision for confidentiality in their arbitration agreement. This may be in relation to all aspects of the arbitration, or the parties may expressly agree upon the confidentiality of specific aspects of that arbitration, such as in relation to specific documentation, and require the parties and witnesses to sign confidentiality orders.

13.4.15 Interim measures

Article 9 of the UNCITRAL Model Law—'Arbitration agreement and interim measures by court'—states as follows:

> It is not incompatible with an arbitration agreement for a party to request, before or during arbitral proceedings, from a court an interim measure of protection and for a court to grant such measure.

The UNCITRAL Model Law permits an arbitral tribunal to make any interim orders or grant such interim relief as it deems appropriate in light of the subject matter

---

26 See *HIH Casualty & General Insurance Limited (in liquidation) v Wallace* (2006) NSWSC 1150.

27 On confidentiality in arbitration, see LE Trakman, 'Confidentiality in International Commercial Arbitration' (2002) 18 *Arbitration International* 1–18.

28 (1995) 183 CLR 10.

in dispute. Article 9 states that, before or during arbitral proceedings, a party may request that a court grant interim measures, and the court may make such a grant. It is unclear whether Australian courts will grant interim measures of protection in support of foreign arbitrations, as Article 1(2) of the Model Law expressly allows Article 9 to be applied to arbitrations in a foreign *situs*.[29] There appears to be no case law on the subject at this time in Australia. However, given similarities between Australian, Singaporean and UK arbitration laws, Australian courts may follow the High Court of Singapore in *Front Carriers v Atlantic Shipping Corp*,[30] which granted an interim measure of protection under an asset preservation order in support of foreign arbitration proceedings in UK.

Parties to an arbitration agreement may also choose to apply s 23 of the IAA on additional provisions, allowing courts to enforce interim measures of protection under Article 17 of the Model Law, not unlike awards under Chapter VIII of the Model Law.

Finally, international arbitration in Australia may be impacted to varying degrees by the domestic law governing interim orders. For example, under s 23 of the CAA, an arbitrator is free to make interim awards unless the parties stipulate to the contrary in their arbitration agreement; while s 47 of the CAA grants courts comparable powers to make interlocutory orders in arbitration as in judicial proceedings.

13.4.16 The form of the award

Article 31 of the UNCITRAL Model Law—'Form and contents of award'—states as follows:

> (1) The award shall be made in writing and shall be signed by the arbitrator or arbitrators. In arbitral proceedings with more than one arbitrator, the signatures of the majority of all members of the arbitral tribunal shall suffice, provided that the reason for any omitted signature is stated.
> (2) The award shall state the reasons upon which it is based, unless the parties have agreed that no reasons are to be given or the award is an award on agreed terms under article 30.
> (3) The award shall state its date and the place of arbitration as determined in accordance with article 20(1). The award shall be deemed to have been made at that place.
> (4) After the award is made, a copy signed by the arbitrators in accordance with paragraph (1) of this article shall be delivered to each party.

Article 17 of the Model Law empowers arbitral tribunals to make interim orders to protect the subject matter of the dispute, such as granting an injunction to prevent one party from disposing of property.

Arbitration proceedings ordinarily conclude with the arbitral tribunal issuing a final award, often preceded by one or more interim awards. The length of time permitted before such an award is issued is primarily left to the arbitral tribunal, so long as this does not lead to so inordinate a delay as to constitute the denial of natural justice.

---

29 Article 1(2) states: 'The provisions of this Law, except articles 8, 9, 35 and 36, apply only if the place of arbitration is in the territory of this State'.

30 [2006] SGHC 127.

The Model Law does not provide timelines within which an award should be rendered, but it does provide for formalities in rendering the award that address the interests of natural justice. For example, the award must be in writing; signed by at least a majority of the arbitrators; contain reasons; provide the date and place of the arbitration; and be delivered to all parties to the proceedings (Article 31). These requirements, in turn, are more onerous than in respect of domestic arbitration, such as under s 20 of the CAA, where there is no express requirement for the award to identify the date or place of arbitration, or that the award should be in writing.

Nor are commercial arbitration awards, in either domestic and international arbitration, subject to statutory time limits. Under Article 32 of the Model Law, a delay in rendering an award will not lead to the termination of the arbitral proceedings. However, a party may conceivably apply to a domestic court for a determination that the arbitrator be disqualified for being 'unable to perform his function or for any other reason fail[ing] to act without undue delay' under Article 14(1).

Article 29 of the Model Law provides that any decision of the arbitral tribunal must be reached by a majority of the tribunal. If a decision cannot be reached, it provides that the presiding arbitrator's ruling prevails in regard to procedural—but not substantive—matters. Presumably, the inability of the majority to reach a decision on a substantive matter that is material to the award is a ground to challenge the award, or the absence of one, before a court of law. Of note, s 15 of the CAA authorises a presiding arbitrator to rule on both procedural and substantive matters, should a majority of the tribunal be unable to agree.

13.4.17 The content of the award

An arbitration award that complies with the applicable law is binding on the parties and enforceable in law. In addition, arbitral awards usually are expected to include reasons for the decisions reached, but providing such reasons is not required in all cases. Article 31(2) of the Model Law provides that an award 'shall state the reasons upon which it is based, unless the parties have agreed that no reasons are to be given'. The Model Law understandably does not elaborate upon the nature and detail in which such reasons should be expressed, and the nature of awards are likely to vary from case to case. Parties to an international arbitration may forego such reasons in fast-track proceedings or for strategic reasons.

The nature and content of an arbitral award may vary significantly according to the nature of the arbitration agreement, the rules of an arbitration association or the ad hoc rules adopted by the parties, and the nature of applicable law. The award may also be affected by, among other factors, particular stipulations in the agreement between the parties (not limited to the arbitration clause), arbitration practice in the arbitral *situs*, the nature of the commercial dispute, and the legal background of the parties, their representatives and the arbitrators themselves.

EXAMPLE: An arbitral award in a civil law jurisdiction—or an award rendered by an arbitrator trained in civil law—may be deductive, working from general legal principle to the specific facts.

It may also concentrate on the applicable principle of law and less upon judicial precedent. For example, arbitral awards by the ICC in Paris are likely to embody the distinctly civil legal tradition as developed and applied by the ICC Court.

An arbitral award in a common law jurisdiction—or rendered by a common law arbitrator—may be inductive, reasoning from the particular facts to general principles of law, with significant reliance placed on case law. For example, arbitral awards made by common law arbitrators appointed by the International Center for Dispute Resolution of the AAA usually reflect inductive common law traditions, including a detailed analysis of the facts and extensive reliance on case law

13.4.18 The impact of legal traditions on commercial arbitration

Leon Trakman, 'Legal Traditions and International Commercial Arbitration' (2006) 17(1) *American Review of International Arbitration* 1

Emanating from diffuse economic, social and political environments, parties contemplating international commercial arbitration today can choose from a range of sophisticated instruments that suggest what, when and how to arbitrate disputes. They can choose arbitration forums and rules based on the perceived stability of the applicable arbitral systems, the development of their jurisprudence and their record of successfully concluded and enforced arbitrations. Parties can also choose from an increasing number of national and regional arbitration centers that accommodate different legal traditions and respond differently to disparate legal cultures. They can adopt a variety of arbitration clauses, duly adapted to meet their particular needs [at 29–31].

...

Codes, laws and guidelines governing international commercial arbitration developed by such organizations as the International Court of Arbitration ('ICA'), the International Bar Association ('IBA') and the International Chamber of Commerce ('ICC') have been drafted against the background of common-law and civil-law values. In balancing these two great legal traditions, it was assumed that together they represent a composite legal tradition governing international commercial arbitration. The result of that assumption was decades of fine work enshrining international arbitration doctrines, principles, and rules of law and procedures that blend these two important legal traditions. From the doctrine of freedom of contract to specific rules of evidence and procedures that govern arbitral hearings, the international arbitration community has sought to maintain the respected legal traditions that lawyer-arbitrators and counsel find familiar and comfortable [at 1].

...

A stereotypical conclusion is that international commercial arbitration, along with the lawyer-arbitrators and counsel who serve it, emanates primarily from an amalgam of civil and common law traditions that are unified by international organizations like the ICC. Certainly there is truth to this stereotype. At a formal level, international arbitration codes, laws and practices have evolved in some measure out of civil and common law traditions that are unified in part by international organizations

> like the ICC. Their pervasive impact upon modern arbitration is reinforced by the realization that traditional business interests served by arbitration have converged at the leading trading cities of Europe and North America where the civil and common-law systems prevail. Consistent with this observation, premier international arbitration centers—the International Chamber of Commerce, the American Arbitration Association and the London Court of International Arbitration—are located in Paris, New York and London respectively. Further imbedding civil and common-law influences is the fact that international commercial arbitrators and counsel alike are drawn significantly from common and civil-law ranks. In addition, arbitrators from Latin America to Japan and China share codes of obligations of one form or another that trace back to civil-law roots and which form a primary source of their legal systems [at 13–14].
>
> ... ...

13.4.19 The review of an arbitration award

Article 34 of the UNCITRAL Model Law—'Application for setting aside as exclusive recourse against arbitral award Form and contents of award'—states as follows:

> (1) Recourse to a court against an arbitral award may be made only by an application for setting aside in accordance with paragraphs (2) and (3) of this article.
>
> (2) An arbitral award may be set aside by the court specified in article 6 only if:
>
> (a) the party making the application furnishes proof that:
>
> (i) a party to the arbitration agreement referred to in article 7 was under some incapacity; or the said agreement is not valid under the law to which the parties have subjected it or, failing any indication thereon, under the law of this State; or
>
> (ii) the party making the application was not given proper notice of the appointment of an arbitrator or of the arbitral proceedings or was otherwise unable to present his case; or
>
> (iii) the award deals with a dispute not contemplated by or not falling within the terms of the submission to arbitration, or contains decisions on matters beyond the scope of the submission to arbitration, provided that, if the decisions on matters submitted to arbitration can be separated from those not so submitted, only that part of the award which contains decisions on matters not submitted to arbitration may be set aside; or
>
> (iv) the composition of the arbitral tribunal or the arbitral procedure was not in accordance with the agreement of the parties, unless such agreement was in conflict with a provision of this Law from which the parties cannot derogate, or, failing such agreement, was not in accordance with this Law; or
>
> (b) the court finds that:
>
> (i) the subject-matter of the dispute is not capable of settlement by arbitration under the law of this State; or
>
> (ii) the award is in conflict with the public policy of this State.
>
> (3) An application for setting aside may not be made after three months have elapsed from the date on which the party making that application had received the award or, if a request had been made under article 33, from the date on which that request had been disposed of by the arbitral tribunal.
>
> (4) The court, when asked to set aside an award, may, where appropriate and so requested by a party, suspend the setting aside proceedings for a period of time determined by it in order to give the arbitral tribunal an opportunity to resume the arbitral proceedings or to take such other action as in the arbitral tribunal's opinion will eliminate the grounds for setting aside.

The UNCITRAL Model Law provides that an application to set aside the award before a domestic court, including in Australia, must be made within three months of the date of the award. The party so applying must be able to establish at least one of the following factors:

- The arbitration agreement was void or at least unenforceable;
- The arbitrator(s) were not properly appointed;
- The party challenging the award was not given sufficient notice to properly prepare its case;
- The award dealt with issues beyond the parties' agreement; or
- There was a conflict between the award and the mandatory public policy, or *ordre public*, of the state in which enforcement of the award was sought. For example, courts in New South Wales may decline to enforce an arbitral award on the grounds that it conflicts with the *Contracts Review Act 1980*. They may rule that unfair trade practices conflict with the *Trade Practices Act 1974* (Cth) in regulating deceptive, misleading and unconscionable conduct, or with the *Fair Trading Acts*. They may also apply mandatory domestic public policy on the grounds that a party to an arbitration has engaged in misleading and deceptive trade practices, or has otherwise acted unconscionably.

Most common law courts are nevertheless reluctant to challenge arbitration awards. For example, in *Lesotho Highlands Development Authority v Impregilo SpA*,[31] the House of Lords heard a challenge to an arbitration award under the rules of the ICC. A majority expressed reluctance to review both the procedures and application of the award—the concern of the majority being to ensure that arbitration was not only binding on the parties, but also final. The court sought to maintain a 'free-standing' system of 'one-stop adjudication', in which the choice of law and procedure rests first with the parties themselves, and thereafter with the arbitrators hearing their dispute.

Article 36 of the Model Law provides that an arbitral award is recognised and enforced 'irrespective of the country in which it was made'. It stipulates that an award can be challenged only if a party to the arbitration agreement:

> was under some incapacity; or the said agreement is not valid under the law to which the parties have subjected it or … under the law of the country where the award was made; or if party against whom the award was invoked was not given proper notice of the appointment of an arbitrator or of the arbitral proceedings or was otherwise unable to present his case.

One effect of Article 36, among others, is to extend the enforceability of arbitration awards made in countries that are not parties to the New York Convention.

In applying Articles 35 and 36 of the Model Law, the Federal Court in *Sharrment Pty Ltd v Official Trustee in Bankruptcy*[32] denied that the parties to an arbitration had the right to avoid the effect of an award by sheltering themselves behind the artificial personality

31 [2005] UKHL 43.

32 (1988) 18 FCR 449.

of different corporate structures. Insofar as the award is binding on the parent company or its shareholders, it is also binding upon those seeking to hide behind a corporate veil.

The application of public policy to arbitral awards is by no means definitive. Courts may diverge over the kinds and degrees of public policy and how they construe it. They may differ in response to an injunction against a party to stop an alleged legal wrong, redress a breach of contract, the movement of property out of the jurisdiction, or the destruction of documents evidencing violation of a trade law. They may also vary in determining the category or quantum of damages to redress a breach of a restrictive contract practice.

In addition, domestic courts may interpret domestic statutory law differently. For example, Australian courts may decline to enforce an arbitration award on the grounds that a party to international commercial arbitration has violated the *Trade Practices Act*; or they may sanction an ACCC investigation and a s155 notice before domestic courts.

13.4.20 Costs

Article 38 of the UNCITRAL Model Law provides for costs:

> The arbitral tribunal shall fix the costs of arbitration in its award. The term 'costs' includes only:
>
> (a) The fees of the arbitral tribunal to be stated separately as to each arbitrator and to be fixed by the tribunal itself in accordance with article 39;
> (b) The travel and other expenses incurred by the arbitrators;
> (c) The costs of expert advice and of other assistance required by the arbitral tribunal;
> (d) The travel and other expenses of witnesses to the extent such expenses are approved by the arbitral tribunal;
> (e) The costs for legal representation and assistance of the successful party if such costs were claimed during the arbitral proceedings, and only to the extent that the arbitral tribunal determines that the amount of such costs is reasonable
> (f) Any fees and expenses of the appointing authority as well as the expenses of the Secretary-General of the Permanent Court of Arbitration at The Hague.

There is no definitive rule in regard to the costs of arbitration, or the party who is responsible to bear those costs. The UNCITRAL Rules provide in Article 38 that the arbitral tribunal itself fix the costs in its award, specifying not only the nature of these costs, but that the amount must be 'reasonable' under Article 39.

In most cases, costs of arbitration include:

- The time that members of the arbitral tribunal spend in preparing for, hearing and writing the arbitral award;
- The expenses of members of the arbitral tribunal, such as travel, administrative support and other disbursements;
- The costs and expenses of expert witnesses; and, sometimes
- The costs of legal representation.

Further costs may include the fees charged by the Permanent Court of International Arbitration under Article 38(f) of the UNCITRAL Rules, or of an applicable arbitration association such as the ICC, the London Court of International Arbitration, or the AAA. It may also include any tax levied on arbitration within an applicable *situs*.

As a general but not universal rule, the party who loses the arbitration is responsible for bearing most if not all of the applicable arbitration costs. That general rule is preserved in Article 40(1) of the UNCITRAL Rules, subject to the apportionment of those costs between the parties, including sharing them equally, taking into account the circumstances of the case.

A determination of costs is usually contained within the arbitral award itself, such as under Article 38 of the UNCITRAL Rules. A decision on costs may be the subject of a separate award; in complex commercial cases, costs may be allocated variously according to the amount in dispute, the nature and form of proceedings (such as in preliminary, interim, or differently structured hearings) and other relevant circumstances.

In some cases, arbitration associations rather than specific arbitrators may determine and allocate costs, according to a schedule of costs prescribed by the administering authority chosen by the parties, or by an arbitration court such as the Secretary-General of the Permanent Court of International Arbitration under Article 41(3) of the UNCITRAL Rules, or by the ICC Court in ICC arbitrations. However, even in these circumstances, costs are usually based on the complexity of the case, its duration, and the time and cost spent by the tribunal preparing for and hearing it, as well as the fees and costs of expert witnesses.

The parties can usually apply to the arbitral tribunal making a determination on costs, for example to correct a typographical or computation error in the award. This is provided for under Article 36 of the UNCITRAL Rules. Should a party wish to challenge an award of costs on the grounds that it is excessive or is unfairly apportioned between the parties however, such a challenge may conceivably be lodged with the tribunal the parties have chosen to administer their dispute or, failing that, with a court of law on jurisdictional grounds, including that the tribunal has acted *ultra vires*. Such a jurisdictional challenge will not be readily entertained.

Given that international commercial arbitration is a private and usually confidential process and arises in many different settings, including in rather complex cases, it is difficult to arrive at reliable estimates of costs of the 'average' arbitration. It is also difficult to compare these costs to the costs of an 'average' civil suit before a domestic court of law. Given these considerations, the fact that arbitration associations may provide average cost data is not reliable. What can be reasonably supposed is that trained, experienced and expert commercial arbitrators are likely to be cost-conscious, expeditious in their proceedings, and commercially focused in making their awards, including on costs. So too, arbitration associations seeking to secure repeat business might also want to sponsor cost-effective arbitral proceedings. After all, a significant reason for parties choosing international commercial arbitration is to minimise costs in the parties' quest for commercially expedient processes and results. Whether or not the parties are justified in relying on these expectations in concluding arbitration agreements depends on the circumstances.

13.4.21 Arbitration awards and the courts

There is no ordinary right to appeal an award of an international arbitration tribunal on errors of law. However, under Article 34 (2) of the Model Law, reproduced above, a party may seek an order from a court to have an arbitral award set aside for a violation of natural justice or due process of law, or for violating public policy. Section 19 of the IAA includes (among such grounds) evidence of fraud, corruption or breach of natural justice in making the award. In key respects, the Model Law and the IAA both embody grounds to review arbitration awards under the New York Convention.

The grounds for challenging domestic arbitration awards before Australian courts are wider than the grounds for challenging international awards. For example, the CAA allows a domestic arbitration award to be challenged on questions of law (s 38(2)) with the consent of all parties to the arbitration, or by special leave of the court (s 38(4)), or when the arbitrator has engaged in improper conduct (s 42). However, courts will only grant such leave in the case of domestic arbitrations if the question of law has a substantial effect on the rights of one or more parties to the arbitration, and only in the face of a manifest error of law (CAA, s 38(5)).[33] The parties may expressly agree to exclude these extended grounds for challenging an arbitration award before a court of law.

13.5 The recognition and enforcement of arbitration awards

The New York Convention is an internationally recognised law by which arbitration awards are enforced among states that are signatories to it. Australia is such a signatory state.

The New York Convention provides significant benefits to parties to international arbitration agreements by ensuring that arbitration awards are respected across national boundaries. This recognition of arbitration awards is significant where it is necessary to enforce an award—such as by attaching property in a jurisdiction in which the courts may not recognise a foreign judicial decision, but will recognise an arbitration award that is in compliance with the New York Convention.

Australian courts are unlikely to interfere with the appointment of an arbitrator, the conduct of arbitral hearings, or the rendering of an arbitral award.[34] However, they might intervene on the specific request of a party to the arbitration or by operation of law in limited circumstances set out in the UNCITRAL Model Law itself:

- They may grant interim protective measures under Article 9.
- They may appoint an arbitrator where the parties or the two party-appointed arbitrators have failed to agree on the appointment of an arbitrator under Articles 11(3) and (4).
- They may determine the legitimacy of a challenge to an arbitrator if so requested by the challenging party under Article 13(3).
- They may decide whether the mandate of an arbitrator should be terminated under Article 14 on the request of a party.

---

33 See for example *Giles v GRS Constructions* (2002) 81 SASR 575; *Pioneer Shipping v BTP Tioxide* [1982] AC 724.

34 For more detail on Australian arbitrations, see [www.australianarbitration.com/international-arbitration-law].

- They may decide on the jurisdiction of the arbitral tribunal in situations where that tribunal has ruled on a plea as a preliminary question, and in which a party to the arbitration has requested the court to make a final determination on its jurisdiction under Article 16(3).
- They may assist in taking evidence under Article 27.
- They may set aside an arbitral award under Article 34(2).
- In domestic arbitration, Australian courts have the additional discretion to stay proceedings (CAA, s 53), to review an award for errors of law (CAA, s 38) and to issue subpoenas on the application by a party (CAA, s 17.)

In addition, courts may decline to enforce international arbitration awards on grounds specified in the New York Convention itself. That Convention specifically enables domestic courts to nullify awards, on the grounds of both procedural irregularity and domestic public policy, including under Article 34 of the Model Law.

Section 8 of the IAA implements Australia's obligations under Article V of the New York Convention to recognise foreign arbitral awards as though they were rendered by an Australian court. Article 25 of the Model Law provides for recognition to international awards made in Australia in a manner comparable to the recognition that s 33 of the CAA accords to domestic arbitral awards.

Australian courts have generally supported the extensive application of the New York Convention. As a result, they have accorded a high level of recognition and enforcement to international arbitration awards. Such recognition usually arises when Australian courts stay judicial proceedings pending the outcome of international commercial arbitration.[35]

Australian courts are less likely to enforce interlocutory or procedural orders made by an arbitral tribunal.[36] However, parties wishing to avoid this result may resort to s 23 of the IAA (optional provisions), which allows for the enforcement of interim measures under Part VIII of the Model Law.

Despite their readiness to recognise arbitral awards under the New York Convention, Australian courts may still scrutinise awards to determine whether they are enforceable in fact under the Convention. For example, an Australian court may determine that the issue adduced in the award falls outside the purview of the arbitration clause, outside the arbitral purview, and within the jurisdiction of a court of law.[37] Australian courts may also hold that a party to an arbitration agreement has waived the right to arbitration by participating in litigation dealing with matters otherwise falling within the purview of arbitration.[38]

Australian courts may also construe international commercial arbitration restrictively in the face of peremptory domestic laws. For example, they will decline to enforce an arbitration agreement or award that purports to exclude the operation of the *Trade*

---

35 See for example *Origin Energy Resources v Benaris International NV* [2002] TASSC 50; *CTA International Pty Limited v Sichuan Changhong Electric Co Limited* [2002] VSC 374.

36 See for example *Resort Condominiums International v Bolwell* (1993) 118 ALR 655.

37 See *ACD Tridon v Tridon Australia* [2002] NSWSC 896; *Transfield Philippines Inc v Luzon Hydro Corp* [2002] VSC 215.

38 See *Comandate Marine Corp v Pan Australia Shipping Pty Ltd* [2006] FCA 1246 (1 September 2006).

Practices Act 1974 (Cth). In *Clough Engineering Limited v Oil & Natural Gas Corporation Limited*,[39] the Federal Court maintained that the *Trade Practices Act* is a 'public policy statute' that cannot be excluded by agreement.

Australian judges may conceivably avoid the application of such 'public policy statutes' in finding that the proper law of the contract is not Australian, or that the transaction is significantly connected to other jurisdictions, justifying the application of foreign law that is not subject to comparable public policy.[40] Of note, in *Comandate Marine Corp v Pan Australia Shipping Pty Ltd*,[41] the Federal Court recognised that, insofar as the parties to a binding arbitration agreement choose foreign law, an Australian court will not apply the *Trade Practices Act* if the arbitrators determine that it does not apply.

Several important inferences arise from the application of Australian law to international commercial arbitration. If the parties want to avoid domestic 'public policy', they ought to adopt foreign law. If they wish domestic law to apply, they ought to appreciate the extent to which domestic law is mandatory. However they frame their agreements, they should recognise the risk that an Australian court may hold that they have waived their right to arbitrate, or that they are prevented from raising an arbitration agreement if that party has filed suit or participated in litigation on a related issue in a court of law.

13.6 The UNCITRAL Arbitration Rules 1976

This section deals with the widely recognised UNCITRAL Arbitration Rules 1976. Currently in force, these rules are shortly to be replaced by the UNCITRAL Arbitration Rules 2009. The extracts below provide useful background.

Gavin Griffith and Andrew D Mitchell, 'Contractual Dispute Resolution in International Trade: The UNCITRAL Arbitration Rules (1976) and the UNCITRAL Conciliation Rules (1980)' (2002) 3 *Melbourne International Law Journal* 184

III. UNCITRAL ARBITRATION RULES (1976)

The [UNCITRAL] Arbitration Rules have become the most widely accepted set of procedures for ad hoc arbitrations. However, it is important to note that arbitral institutions can still play a role under the Arbitration Rules. The Arbitration Rules leave it open to the parties to designate an arbitral institution as an 'appointing authority' that can be called upon, for example, to assist the parties where they cannot agree upon an arbitrator. In addition, in some arbitral institutions, such as the

39 [2007] FCA 881.

40 See for example *Transfield v Pacific Hydro Limited* [2006] VSC 175.

41 [2006] FCAFC 192.

International Chamber of Commerce and the American Arbitration Association, the parties may substitute the Arbitration Rules for the institution's own rules.

...

C. OVERVIEW OF THE ARBITRATION RULES

The Arbitration Rules are comprised of 41 articles grouped into four sections relating to the different stages of an arbitral proceeding. The following overview tracks those four sections to provide a flavour of the key elements of the Arbitration Rules and place them in the context of commercial arbitration practice.

1. INTRODUCTORY RULES: SECTION I

... The Arbitration Rules include a Model Arbitration Clause, which parties can include in their written contracts to satisfy the writing requirement and determine the scope of the arbitrator's role. The Model Arbitration Clause is drafted in a broad inclusionary manner to permit the resolution of all disputes concerning the contract. The Arbitration Rules also note that the parties may wish to consider adding to their contract details as to: the appointing authority; the number of arbitrators; the place of arbitration; and the language of arbitration. It is good practice to include *at least* these elements in any arbitration clause.

The Arbitration Rules are expressly subject to mandatory domestic laws (namely, domestic laws out of which the parties cannot contract). While inconsistencies between domestic laws and the Arbitration Rules are rare, they do arise. For example, domestic law may provide that challenges to the appointment of an arbitrator are within the exclusive jurisdiction of the court, regardless of the procedure set out in the Arbitration Rules or otherwise agreed to by the parties.

...

Under the Arbitration Rules, the parties may be represented by persons of their choice, provided that the names and addresses of those persons are communicated to the other party.

2. COMPOSITION OF THE ARBITRAL TRIBUNAL: SECTION II

A fundamental principle in international commercial arbitration is the impartiality and independence of the arbitrator, and the Arbitration Rules require that all arbitrators be both impartial and independent. Impartiality means the arbitrator must not be biased or prejudiced in favour of one party or issue. Independence means the arbitrator must have no financial connection or relationship with either of the parties.

...

The Arbitration Rules state that a party may only challenge an arbitrator where circumstances exist that give rise to justifiable doubts as to the arbitrator's impartiality or independence. Further, a party can only challenge an arbitrator appointed by that party for reasons that come to light after the appointment has been made.

...

Apart from a challenge, if an arbitrator dies, resigns, refuses to act or becomes incapable of acting, they must be replaced. The Arbitration Rules set out particular procedures for the appointment of another arbitrator in these circumstances.

If the presiding arbitrator is replaced at any stage, the entire arbitration hearings must be repeated. If any other arbitrator is replaced, the arbitral tribunal has discretion whether to continue as a truncated tribunal or to repeat the arbitration hearings with another arbitrator. This decision will be affected by practical considerations relating to the stage of the proceedings reached and the sensitivity of the parties to further delay.

3. ARBITRAL PROCEEDINGS: SECTION III

Unlike proceedings in national courts, there are no set rules of procedure for international commercial arbitrations. They are conducted in accordance with the agreement of the parties, subject to mandatory laws of the place of arbitration and the requirements of international commercial arbitration conventions. Under the Arbitration Rules, the parties transfer control of the proceedings to the arbitral tribunal once it is established.

...

The Arbitration Rules contain certain procedural safeguards for the parties. Each party must be treated equally and given a proper opportunity to present its case. The parties must also exchange a statement of claim and a statement of defence. The arbitral tribunal determines whether any further documents, evidence or exhibits are required from the parties. However, the Arbitration Rules provide that if the arbitral tribunal appoints an expert, the parties must have the opportunity to interrogate the expert.

...

A common feature of international commercial arbitration is objection to jurisdiction. The jurisdiction of arbitral tribunals is limited by the agreement of the parties, and may be further limited by national laws that declare that certain matters must be heard by their courts. Examples of jurisdictional questions include: the validity of the arbitration clause or agreement; whether the arbitral tribunal is properly constituted; whether the matters submitted to arbitration fall within the arbitration clause or agreement; and whether those matters are arbitrable. The 'inherent' power of arbitral tribunals to decide their jurisdiction (the doctrine of Competence/Competence) is made explicit in the Arbitration Rules. Of course, this power cannot be used to oust the jurisdiction of the relevant national court, which holds the ultimate power to decide jurisdictional questions.

If a party objects to the jurisdiction of the arbitral tribunal, it is important that it makes a formal objection promptly. The Arbitration Rules require that such objections 'be raised not later than in the statement of defence or, with respect to a counter-claim, in the reply to the counter-claim.' Although this suggests that the right to object is lost after this stage in the proceedings, whether the right has been waived will depend upon the applicable national law. On the other hand, a party who knows that the Arbitration Rules have not been complied with and who fails to object promptly to the non-compliance, is deemed to have waived its right to object.

4. THE AWARD: SECTION IV

International commercial arbitration often involves more than one system of law. Different laws may govern:

(a) the proceedings of the arbitral tribunal (the *lex arbitri*);
(b) the recognition and enforcement of the award; and
(c) the issues in dispute (the 'applicable law').

...

Arbitral tribunals must be able to make a 'final award' that resolves any outstanding issues before the tribunal. However, it is possible for a number of awards to be made during the course of an arbitral proceeding. The Arbitration Rules state that an arbitral tribunal is also entitled to make interim, interlocutory and partial awards. Thus in response to a challenge to its jurisdiction, an arbitral tribunal may resolve this threshold question by making a partial award. There may be other discrete issues which can also be addressed by a partial award to simplify the proceedings. Interim measures for protection ... are examples of partial awards.

...

The costs of a commercial arbitration can be very high. They are often substantially greater than proceedings in a domestic court because of the need to pay for the arbitral tribunal, administrative costs and accommodation expenses.

Under the Arbitration Rules, the arbitral tribunal fixes its own costs, which are restricted to: the fees of each arbitrator, including travel and other expenses; the costs of expert advice and other assistance; the travel and other expenses of witnesses approved by the tribunal; the costs of legal representation of the successful party to the extent approved by the tribunal; and the fees and expenses of the appointing authority.

...

E. INFLUENCE AND ACCEPTANCE OF THE ARBITRATION RULES

... According to the experience of the Arbitration Rules in international tribunals and private arbitrations, the sensible level of discretion afforded to the arbitral tribunal as well as their international and neutral nature make the Arbitration Rules one of the best approaches to resolving international trade law disputes. They have proven to be practical and flexible enough to meet the enormously different needs of parties in particular disputes.

... ...

At this stage, it is worth reproducing the full text of The UNCITRAL Arbitration Rules 1976.

UNCITRAL Arbitration Rules 1976

Section I: Introductory rules

SCOPE OF APPLICATION

ARTICLE 1

1. Where the parties to a contract have agreed in writing that disputes in relation to that contract shall be referred to arbitration under the UNCITRAL Arbitration Rules, then such disputes shall be settled in accordance with these Rules subject to such modification as the parties may agree in writing.
2. These Rules shall govern the arbitration except that where any of these Rules is in conflict with a provision of the law applicable to the arbitration from which the parties cannot derogate, that provision shall prevail.

MODEL ARBITRATION CLAUSE

Any dispute, controversy or claim arising out of or relating to this contract, or the breach, termination or invalidity thereof, shall be settled by arbitration in accordance with the UNCITRAL Arbitration Rules as at present in force.

Note—Parties may wish to consider adding:

(a) The appointing authority shall be ... (name of institution or person);

(b) The number of arbitrators shall be ... (one or three);

(c) The place of arbitration shall be ... (town or country);

(d) The language(s) to be used in the arbitral proceedings shall be ...

NOTICE, CALCULATION OF PERIODS OF TIME

ARTICLE 2

1. For the purposes of these Rules, any notice, including a notification, communication or proposal, is deemed to have been received if it is physically delivered to the addressee or if it is delivered at his habitual residence, place of business or mailing address, or, if none of these can be found after making reasonable inquiry, then at the addressee's last-known residence or place of business. Notice shall be deemed to have been received on the day it is so delivered.
2. For the purposes of calculating a period of time under these Rules, such period shall begin to run on the day following the day when a notice, notification, communication or proposal is received. If the last day of such period is an official holiday or a non-business day at the residence or place of business of the addressee, the period is extended until the first business day which follows. Official holidays or non-business days occurring during the running of the period of time are included in calculating the period.

NOTICE OF ARBITRATION

ARTICLE 3

1. The party initiating recourse to arbitration (hereinafter called the 'claimant') shall give to the other party (hereinafter called the 'respondent') a notice of arbitration.
2. Arbitral proceedings shall be deemed to commence on the date on which the notice of arbitration is received by the respondent.
3. The notice of arbitration shall include the following:
   (a) A demand that the dispute be referred to arbitration;
   (b) The names and addresses of the parties;
   (c) A reference to the arbitration clause or the separate arbitration agreement that is invoked;
   (d) A reference to the contract out of or in relation to which the dispute arises;
   (e) The general nature of the claim and an indication of the amount involved, if any;
   (f) The relief or remedy sought;
   (g) A proposal as to the number of arbitrators (ie one or three), if the parties have not previously agreed thereon.
4. The notice of arbitration may also include:
   (a) The proposals for the appointments of a sole arbitrator and an appointing authority referred to in article 6, paragraph 1;

(b) The notification of the appointment of an arbitrator referred to in article 7;

(c) The statement of claim referred to in article 18.

REPRESENTATION AND ASSISTANCE

ARTICLE 4

The parties may be represented or assisted by persons of their choice. The names and addresses of such persons must be communicated in writing to the other party; such communication must specify whether the appointment is being made for purposes of representation or assistance.

Section II: Composition of the arbitral tribunal

NUMBER OF ARBITRATORS

ARTICLE 5

If the parties have not previously agreed on the number of arbitrators (ie one or three), and if within fifteen days after the receipt by the respondent of the notice of arbitration the parties have not agreed that there shall be only one arbitrator, three arbitrators shall be appointed.

APPOINTMENT OF ARBITRATORS (ARTICLES 6 TO 8)

ARTICLE 6

1. If a sole arbitrator is to be appointed, either party may propose to the other:

   (a) The names of one or more persons, one of whom would serve as the sole arbitrator; and

   (b) If no appointing authority has been agreed upon by the parties, the name or names of one or more institutions or persons, one of whom would serve as appointing authority.

2. If within thirty days after receipt by a party of a proposal made in accordance with paragraph 1 the parties have not reached agreement on the choice of a sole arbitrator, the sole arbitrator shall be appointed by the appointing authority agreed upon by the parties. If no appointing authority has been agreed upon by the parties, or if the appointing authority agreed upon refuses to act or fails to appoint the arbitrator within sixty days of the receipt of a party's request therefor, either party may request the Secretary-General of the Permanent Court of Arbitration at The Hague to designate an appointing authority.

3. The appointing authority shall, at the request of one of the parties, appoint the sole arbitrator as promptly as possible. In making the appointment the appointing authority shall use the following list-procedure, unless both parties agree that the list-procedure should not be used or unless the appointing authority determines in its discretion that the use of the list-procedure is not appropriate for the case:

   (a) At the request of one of the parties the appointing authority shall communicate to both parties an identical list containing at least three names;

   (b) Within fifteen days after the receipt of this list, each party may return the list to the appointing authority after having deleted the name or names to which he objects and numbered the remaining names on the list in the order of his preference;

   (c) After the expiration of the above period of time the appointing authority shall appoint the sole arbitrator from among the names approved on the lists returned to it and in accordance with the order of preference indicated by the parties;

(d) If for any reason the appointment cannot be made according to this procedure, the appointing authority may exercise its discretion in appointing the sole arbitrator.

4. In making the appointment, the appointing authority shall have regard to such considerations as are likely to secure the appointment of an independent and impartial arbitrator and shall take into account as well the advisability of appointing an arbitrator of a nationality other than the nationalities of the parties.

ARTICLE 7

1. If three arbitrators are to be appointed, each party shall appoint one arbitrator. The two arbitrators thus appointed shall choose the third arbitrator who will act as the presiding arbitrator of the tribunal.
2. If within thirty days after the receipt of a party's notification of the appointment of an arbitrator the other party has not notified the first party of the arbitrator he has appointed:
   (a) The first party may request the appointing authority previously designated by the parties to appoint the second arbitrator; or
   (b) If no such authority has been previously designated by the parties, or if the appointing authority previously designated refuses to act or fails to appoint the arbitrator within thirty days after receipt of a party's request therefor, the first party may request the Secretary-General of the Permanent Court of Arbitration at The Hague to designate the appointing authority. The first party may then request the appointing authority so designated to appoint the second arbitrator. In either case, the appointing authority may exercise its discretion in appointing the arbitrator.
3. If within thirty days after the appointment of the second arbitrator the two arbitrators have not agreed on the choice of the presiding arbitrator, the presiding arbitrator shall be appointed by an appointing authority in the same way as a sole arbitrator would be appointed under article 6.

ARTICLE 8

1. When an appointing authority is requested to appoint an arbitrator pursuant to article 6 or article 7, the party which makes the request shall send to the appointing authority a copy of the notice of arbitration, a copy of the contract out of or in relation to which the dispute has arisen and a copy of the arbitration agreement if it is not contained in the contract. The appointing authority may require from either party such information as it deems necessary to fulfil its function.
2. Where the names of one or more persons are proposed for appointment as arbitrators, their full names, addresses and nationalities shall be indicated, together with a description of their qualifications.

CHALLENGE OF ARBITRATORS (ARTICLES 9 TO 12)

ARTICLE 9

A prospective arbitrator shall disclose to those who approach him in connexion with his possible appointment any circumstances likely to give rise to justifiable doubts as to his impartiality or independence. An arbitrator, once appointed or chosen, shall disclose such circumstances to the parties unless they have already been informed by him of these circumstances.

ARTICLE 10

1. Any arbitrator may be challenged if circumstances exist that give rise to justifiable doubts as to the arbitrators impartiality or independence.
2. A party may challenge the arbitrator appointed by him only for reasons of which he becomes aware after the appointment has been made.

ARTICLE 11

1. A party who intends to challenge an arbitrator shall send notice of his challenge within fifteen days after the appointment of the challenged arbitrator has been notified to the challenging party or within fifteen days after the circumstances mentioned in articles 9 and 10 became known to that party.
2. The challenge shall be notified to the other party, to the arbitrator who is challenged and to the other members of the arbitral tribunal. The notification shall be in writing and shall state the reasons for the challenge.
3. When an arbitrator has been challenged by one party, the other party may agree to the challenge. The arbitrator may also, after the challenge, withdraw from his office. In neither case does this imply acceptance of the validity of the grounds for the challenge. In both cases the procedure provided in article 6 or 7 shall be used in full for the appointment of the substitute arbitrator, even if during the process of appointing the challenged arbitrator a party had failed to exercise his right to appoint or to participate in the appointment.

ARTICLE 12

1. If the other party does not agree to the challenge and the challenged arbitrator does not withdraw, the decision on the challenge will be made:
   (a) When the initial appointment was made by an appointing authority, by that authority;
   (b) When the initial appointment was not made by an appointing authority, but an appointing authority has been previously designated, by that authority;
   (c) In all other cases, by the appointing authority to be designated in accordance with the procedure for designating an appointing authority as provided for in article 6.
2. If the appointing authority sustains the challenge, a substitute arbitrator shall be appointed or chosen pursuant to the procedure applicable to the appointment or choice of an arbitrator as provided in articles 6 to 9 except that, when this procedure would call for the designation of an appointing authority, the appointment of the arbitrator shall be made by the appointing authority which decided on the challenge.

REPLACEMENT OF AN ARBITRATOR

ARTICLE 13

1. In the event of the death or resignation of an arbitrator during the course of the arbitral proceedings, a substitute arbitrator shall be appointed or chosen pursuant to the procedure provided for in articles 6 to 9 that was applicable to the appointment or choice of the arbitrator being replaced.

2. In the event that an arbitrator fails to act or in the event of the de jure or de facto impossibility of his performing his functions, the procedure in respect of the challenge and replacement of an arbitrator as provided in the preceding articles shall apply.

REPETITION OF HEARINGS IN THE EVENT OF THE REPLACEMENT OF AN ARBITRATOR

ARTICLE 14

If under articles 11 to 13 the sole or presiding arbitrator is replaced, any hearings held previously shall be repeated; if any other arbitrator is replaced, such prior hearings may be repeated at the discretion of the arbitral tribunal.

Section III: Arbitral proceedings

GENERAL PROVISIONS

ARTICLE 15

1. Subject to these Rules, the arbitral tribunal may conduct the arbitration in such manner as it considers appropriate, provided that the parties are treated with equality and that at any stage of the proceedings each party is given a full opportunity of presenting his case.
2. If either party so requests at any stage of the proceedings, the arbitral tribunal shall hold hearings for the presentation of evidence by witnesses, including expert witnesses, or for oral argument. In the absence of such a request, the arbitral tribunal shall decide whether to hold such hearings or whether the proceedings shall be conducted on the basis of documents and other materials.
3. All documents or information supplied to the arbitral tribunal by one party shall at the same time be communicated by that party to the other party.

PLACE OF ARBITRATION

ARTICLE 16

1. Unless the parties have agreed upon the place where the arbitration is to be held, such place shall be determined by the arbitral tribunal, having regard to the circumstances of the arbitration.
2. The arbitral tribunal may determine the locale of the arbitration within the country agreed upon by the parties. It may hear witnesses and hold meetings for consultation among its members at any place it deems appropriate, having regard to the circumstances of the arbitration.
3. The arbitral tribunal may meet at any place it deems appropriate for the inspection of goods, other property or documents. The parties shall be given sufficient notice to enable them to be present at such inspection.
4. The award shall be made at the place of arbitration.

LANGUAGE

ARTICLE 17

1. Subject to an agreement by the parties, the arbitral tribunal shall, promptly after its appointment, determine the language or languages to be used in the proceedings. This

determination shall apply to the statement of claim, the statement of defence, and any further written statements and, if oral hearings take place, to the language or languages to be used in such hearings.

2. The arbitral tribunal may order that any documents annexed to the statement of claim or statement of defence, and any supplementary documents or exhibits submitted in the course of the proceedings, delivered in their original language, shall be accompanied by a translation into the language or languages agreed upon by the parties or determined by the arbitral tribunal.

STATEMENT OF CLAIM

ARTICLE 18

1. Unless the statement of claim was contained in the notice of arbitration, within a period of time to be determined by the arbitral tribunal, the claimant shall communicate his statement of claim in writing to the respondent and to each of the arbitrators. A copy of the contract, and of the arbitration agreement if not contained in the contract, shall be annexed thereto.
2. The statement of claim shall include the following particulars:
   (a) The names and addresses of the parties;
   (b) A statement of the facts supporting the claim;
   (c) The points at issue;
   (d) The relief or remedy sought.

The claimant may annex to his statement of claim all documents he deems relevant or may add a reference to the documents or other evidence he will submit.

STATEMENT OF DEFENCE

ARTICLE 19

1. Within a period of time to be determined by the arbitral tribunal, the respondent shall communicate his statement of defence in writing to the claimant and to each of the arbitrators.
2. The statement of defence shall reply to the particulars (b), (c) and (d) of the statement of claim (article 18, para 2). The respondent may annex to his statement the documents on which he relies for his defence or may add a reference to the documents or other evidence he will submit.
3. In his statement of defence, or at a later stage in the arbitral proceedings if the arbitral tribunal decides that the delay was justified under the circumstances, the respondent may make a counter-claim arising out of the same contract or rely on a claim arising out of the same contract for the purpose of a set-off.
4. The provisions of article 18, paragraph 2, shall apply to a counter-claim and a claim relied on for the purpose of a set-off.

AMENDMENTS TO THE CLAIM OR DEFENCE

ARTICLE 20

During the course of the arbitral proceedings either party may amend or supplement his claim or defence unless the arbitral tribunal considers it inappropriate to allow such amendment having regard to the delay in making it or prejudice to the other party or any other circumstances. However, a claim may not be amended in such a manner that the amended claim falls outside the scope of the arbitration clause or separate arbitration agreement.

PLEAS AS TO THE JURISDICTION OF THE ARBITRAL TRIBUNAL

ARTICLE 21

1. The arbitral tribunal shall have the power to rule on objections that it has no jurisdiction, including any objections with respect to the existence or validity of the arbitration clause or of the separate arbitration agreement.
2. The arbitral tribunal shall have the power to determine the existence or the validity of the contract of which an arbitration clause forms a part. For the purposes of article 21, an arbitration clause which forms part of a contract and which provides for arbitration under these Rules shall be treated as an agreement independent of the other terms of the contract. A decision by the arbitral tribunal that the contract is null and void shall not entail *ipso jure* the invalidity of the arbitration clause.
3. A plea that the arbitral tribunal does not have jurisdiction shall be raised not later than in the statement of defence or, with respect to a counter-claim, in the reply to the counterclaim.
4. In general, the arbitral tribunal should rule on a plea concerning its jurisdiction as a preliminary question. However, the arbitral tribunal may proceed with the arbitration and rule on such a plea in their final award.

FURTHER WRITTEN STATEMENTS

ARTICLE 22

The arbitral tribunal shall decide which further written statements, in addition to the statement of claim and the statement of defence, shall be required from the parties or may be presented by them and shall fix the periods of time for communicating such statements.

PERIODS OF TIME

ARTICLE 23

The periods of time fixed by the arbitral tribunal for the communication of written statements (including the statement of claim and statement of defence) should not exceed forty-five days. However, the arbitral tribunal may extend the time-limits if it concludes that an extension is justified.

EVIDENCE AND HEARINGS (ARTICLES 24 AND 25)

ARTICLE 24

1. Each party shall have the burden of proving the facts relied on to support his claim or defence.
2. The arbitral tribunal may, if it considers it appropriate, require a party to deliver to the tribunal and to the other party, within such a period of time as the arbitral tribunal shall decide, a summary of the documents and other evidence which that party intends to present in support of the facts in issue set out in his statement of claim or statement of defence.
3. At any time during the arbitral proceedings the arbitral tribunal may require the parties to produce documents, exhibits or other evidence within such a period of time as the tribunal shall determine.

ARTICLE 25

1. In the event of an oral hearing, the arbitral tribunal shall give the parties adequate advance notice of the date, time and place thereof.
2. If witnesses are to be heard, at least fifteen days before the hearing each party shall communicate to the arbitral tribunal and to the other party the names and addresses of the witnesses he intends to present, the subject upon and the languages in which such witnesses will give their testimony.
3. The arbitral tribunal shall make arrangements for the translation of oral statements made at a hearing and for a record of the hearing if either is deemed necessary by the tribunal under the circumstances of the case, or if the parties have agreed thereto and have communicated such agreement to the tribunal at least fifteen days before the hearing.
4. Hearings shall be held in camera unless the parties agree otherwise. The arbitral tribunal may require the retirement of any witness or witnesses during the testimony of other witnesses. The arbitral tribunal is free to determine the manner in which witnesses are examined.
5. Evidence of witnesses may also be presented in the form of written statements signed by them.
6. The arbitral tribunal shall determine the admissibility, relevance, materiality and weight of the evidence offered.

INTERIM MEASURES OF PROTECTION

ARTICLE 26

1. At the request of either party, the arbitral tribunal may take any interim measures it deems necessary in respect of the subject-matter of the dispute, including measures for the conservation of the goods forming the subject-matter in dispute, such as ordering their deposit with a third person or the sale of perishable goods.
2. Such interim measures may be established in the form of an interim award. The arbitral tribunal shall be entitled to require security for the costs of such measures.
3. A request for interim measures addressed by any party to a judicial authority shall not be deemed incompatible with the agreement to arbitrate, or as a waiver of that agreement.

EXPERTS

ARTICLE 27

1. The arbitral tribunal may appoint one or more experts to report to it, in writing, on specific issues to be determined by the tribunal. A copy of the expert's terms of reference, established by the arbitral tribunal, shall be communicated to the parties.
2. The parties shall give the expert any relevant information or produce for his inspection any relevant documents or goods that he may require of them. Any dispute between a party and such expert as to the relevance of the required information or production shall be referred to the arbitral tribunal for decision.
3. Upon receipt of the expert's report, the arbitral tribunal shall communicate a copy of the report to the parties who shall be given the opportunity to express, in writing, their opinion on the report. A party shall be entitled to examine any document on which the expert has relied in his report.

4. At the request of either party the expert, after delivery of the report, may be heard at a hearing where the parties shall have the opportunity to be present and to interrogate the expert. At this hearing either party may present expert witnesses in order to testify on the points at issue. The provisions of article 25 shall be applicable to such proceedings.

DEFAULT

ARTICLE 28

1. If, within the period of time fixed by the arbitral tribunal, the claimant has failed to communicate his claim without showing sufficient cause for such failure, the arbitral tribunal shall issue an order for the termination of the arbitral proceedings. If, within the period of time fixed by the arbitral tribunal, the respondent has failed to communicate his statement of defence without showing sufficient cause for such failure, the arbitral tribunal shall order that the proceedings continue.
2. If one of the parties, duly notified under these Rules, fails to appear at a hearing, without showing sufficient cause for such failure, the arbitral tribunal may proceed with the arbitration.
3. If one of the parties, duly invited to produce documentary evidence, fails to do so within the established period of time, without showing sufficient cause for such failure, the arbitral tribunal may make the award on the evidence before it.

CLOSURE OF HEARINGS

ARTICLE 29

1. The arbitral tribunal may inquire of the parties if they have any further proof to offer or witnesses to be heard or submissions to make and, if there are none, it may declare the hearings closed.
2. The arbitral tribunal may, if it considers it necessary owing to exceptional circumstances, decide, on its own motion or upon application of a party, to reopen the hearings at any time before the award is made.

WAIVER OF RULES

ARTICLE 30

A party who knows that any provision of, or requirement under, these Rules has not been complied with and yet proceeds with the arbitration without promptly stating his objection to such non-compliance, shall be deemed to have waived his right to object.

Section IV The award

DECISIONS

ARTICLE 31

1. When there are three arbitrators, any award or other decision of the arbitral tribunal shall be made by a majority of the arbitrators.
2. In the case of questions of procedure, when there is no majority or when the arbitral tribunal so authorizes, the presiding arbitrator may decide on his own, subject to revision, if any, by the arbitral tribunal.

FORM AND EFFECT OF THE AWARD

ARTICLE 32

1. In addition to making a final award, the arbitral tribunal shall be entitled to make interim, interlocutory, or partial awards.
2. The award shall be made in writing and shall be final and binding on the parties. The parties undertake to carry out the award without delay.
3. The arbitral tribunal shall state the reasons upon which the award is based, unless the parties have agreed that no reasons are to be given.
4. An award shall be signed by the arbitrators and it shall contain the date on which and the place where the award was made. Where there are three arbitrators and one of them fails to sign, the award shall state the reason for the absence of the signature.
5. The award may be made public only with the consent of both parties.
6. Copies of the award signed by the arbitrators shall be communicated to the parties by the arbitral tribunal.
7. If the arbitration law of the country where the award is made requires that the award be filed or registered by the arbitral tribunal, the tribunal shall comply with this requirement within the period of time required by law.

APPLICABLE LAW, AMIABLE COMPOSITEUR

ARTICLE 33

1. The arbitral tribunal shall apply the law designated by the parties as applicable to the substance of the dispute. Failing such designation by the parties, the arbitral tribunal shall apply the law determined by the conflict of laws rules which it considers applicable.
2. The arbitral tribunal shall decide as *amiable compositeur* or *ex aequo et bono* only if the parties have expressly authorized the arbitral tribunal to do so and if the law applicable to the arbitral procedure permits such arbitration.
3. In all cases, the arbitral tribunal shall decide in accordance with the terms of the contract and shall take into account the usages of the trade applicable to the transaction.

SETTLEMENT OR OTHER GROUNDS FOR TERMINATION

ARTICLE 34

1. If, before the award is made, the parties agree on a settlement of the dispute, the arbitral tribunal shall either issue an order for the termination of the arbitral proceedings or, if requested by both parties and accepted by the tribunal, record the settlement in the form of an arbitral award on agreed terms. The arbitral tribunal is not obliged to give reasons for such an award.
2. If, before the award is made, the continuation of the arbitral proceedings becomes unnecessary or impossible for any reason not mentioned in paragraph 1, the arbitral tribunal shall inform the parties of its intention to issue an order for the termination of the proceedings. The arbitral tribunal shall have the power to issue such an order unless a party raises justifiable grounds for objection.
3. Copies of the order for termination of the arbitral proceedings or of the arbitral award on agreed terms, signed by the arbitrators, shall be communicated by the arbitral tribunal to the parties.

Where an arbitral award on agreed terms is made, the provisions of article 32, paragraphs 2 and 4 to 7, shall apply.

INTERPRETATION OF THE AWARD

ARTICLE 35

1. Within thirty days after the receipt of the award, either party, with notice to the other party, may request that the arbitral tribunal give an interpretation of the award.
2. The interpretation shall be given in writing within forty-five days after the receipt of the request. The interpretation shall form part of the award and the provisions of article 32, paragraphs 2 to 7, shall apply.

CORRECTION OF THE AWARD

ARTICLE 36

1. Within thirty days after the receipt of the award, either party, with notice to the other party, may request the arbitral tribunal to correct in the award any errors in computation, any clerical or typographical errors, or any errors of similar nature. The arbitral tribunal may within thirty days after the communication of the award make such corrections on its own initiative.
2. Such corrections shall be in writing, and the provisions of article 32, paragraphs 2 to 7, shall apply.

ADDITIONAL AWARD

ARTICLE 37

1. Within thirty days after the receipt of the award, either party, with notice to the other party, may request the arbitral tribunal to make an additional award as to claims presented in the arbitral proceedings but omitted from the award.
2. If the arbitral tribunal considers the request for an additional award to be justified and considers that the omission can be rectified without any further hearings or evidence, it shall complete its award within sixty days after the receipt of the request.
3. When an additional award is made, the provisions of article 32, paragraphs 2 to 7, shall apply.

COSTS (ARTICLES 38 TO 40)

ARTICLE 38

The arbitral tribunal shall fix the costs of arbitration in its award. The term 'costs' includes only:

(a) The fees of the arbitral tribunal to be stated separately as to each arbitrator and to be fixed by the tribunal itself in accordance with article 39;

(b) The travel and other expenses incurred by the arbitrators;

(c) The costs of expert advice and of other assistance required by the arbitral tribunal;

(d) The travel and other expenses of witnesses to the extent such expenses are approved by the arbitral tribunal;

(e) The costs for legal representation and assistance of the successful party if such costs were claimed during the arbitral proceedings, and only to the extent that the arbitral tribunal determines that the amount of such costs is reasonable;

(f) Any fees and expenses of the appointing authority as well as the expenses of the Secretary-General of the Permanent Court of Arbitration at The Hague.

ARTICLE 39

1. The fees of the arbitral tribunal shall be reasonable in amount, taking into account the amount in dispute, the complexity of the subject-matter, the time spent by the arbitrators and any other relevant circumstances of the case.
2. If an appointing authority has been agreed upon by the parties or designated by the Secretary-General of the Permanent Court of Arbitration at The Hague, and if that authority has issued a schedule of fees for arbitrators in international cases which it administers, the arbitral tribunal in fixing its fees shall take that schedule of fees into account to the extent that it considers appropriate in the circumstances of the case.
3. If such appointing authority has not issued a schedule of fees for arbitrators in international cases, any party may at any time request the appointing authority to furnish a statement setting forth the basis for establishing fees which is customarily followed in international cases in which the authority appoints arbitrators. If the appointing authority consents to provide such a statement, the arbitral tribunal in fixing its fees shall take such information into account to the extent that it considers appropriate in the circumstances of the case.
4. In cases referred to in paragraphs 2 and 3, when a party so requests and the appointing authority consents to perform the function, the arbitral tribunal shall fix its fees only after consultation with the appointing authority which may make any comment it deems appropriate to the arbitral tribunal concerning the fees.

ARTICLE 40

1. Except as provided in paragraph 2, the costs of arbitration shall in principle be borne by the unsuccessful party. However, the arbitral tribunal may apportion each of such costs between the parties if it determines that apportionment is reasonable, taking into account the circumstances of the case.
2. With respect to the costs of legal representation and assistance referred to in article 38, paragraph (e), the arbitral tribunal, taking into account the circumstances of the case, shall be free to determine which party shall bear such costs or may apportion such costs between the parties if it determines that apportionment is reasonable.
3. When the arbitral tribunal issues an order for the termination of the arbitral proceedings or makes an award on agreed terms, it shall fix the costs of arbitration referred to in article 38 and article 39, paragraph 1, in the text of that order or award.
4. No additional fees may be charged by an arbitral tribunal for interpretation or correction or of its award under articles 35 to 37.

DEPOSIT OF COSTS

ARTICLE 41

1. The arbitral tribunal, on its establishment, may request each party to deposit an equal amount as an advance for the costs referred to in article 38, paragraphs (a), (b) and (c).

2. During the course of the arbitral proceedings the arbitral tribunal may request supplementary deposits from the parties.
3. If an appointing authority has been agreed upon by the parties or designated by the Secretary-General of the Permanent Court of Arbitration at The Hague, and when a party so requests and the appointing authority consents to perform the function, the arbitral tribunal shall fix the amounts of any deposits or supplementary deposits only after consultation with the appointing authority which may make any comments to the arbitral tribunal which it deems appropriate concerning the amount of such deposits and supplementary deposits.
4. If the required deposits are not paid in full within thirty days after the receipt of the request, the arbitral tribunal shall so inform the parties in order that one or another of them may make the required payment. If such payment is not made, the arbitral tribunal may order the suspension or termination of the arbitral proceedings.
5. After the award has been made, the arbitral tribunal shall render an accounting to the parties of the deposits received and return any unexpended balance to the parties.

... ...

13.7 Conclusion

International commercial arbitration is not a panacea. The parties to a dispute are not assured that, in choosing international commercial arbitration, their dispute will be resolved in a time- or cost-effective manner. Even a diligent choice of arbitration procedures or arbitrators may lead to protracted costs or delays for reasons not readily foreseen by the parties at the time they adopted their arbitration clause. International commercial arbitration may also fail to satisfy the expectations of one or both parties. The arbitral award may be cumbersome and ill-suited to the commercial context.

Nor are the parties assured that international arbitrators have the requisite commercial expertise or arbitral skill to manage an arbitral hearing and arrive at an award that is both commercially viable and in compliance with law. What the parties do have in choosing international commercial arbitration, however, is the opportunity to exercise a choice as to the manner in which their disputes are to be resolved, including choosing both arbitrators and arbitral processes, and without being confined by domestic courts and local public policy. How effective their choices are in fact is ordinarily the product of their skill in choosing arbitral processes and the manner in which the arbitrators chosen acquit themselves.

International commercial arbitration may drive up the costs of conflict and delay resolution, and this may be what one party seeks as part of its strategy in its arbitral dispute with another. No matter how well meaning arbitrators may be, no matter how equally they may treat the parties to an arbitration, and no matter how efficiently they may administer arbitral hearings, they may encounter one or more parties who are undisciplined, disingenuous or both in making a claim or presenting a defence.

However, these criticisms can be directed at any decision-making process. Arbitration is a measure of free choice. In exercising such a choice, it is incumbent on the parties to choose the nature and form of arbitration that applies most effectively to their dispute. Should they make an unwise election, they ought to assume at least some responsibility for the ensuing results. Should they make a wise choice and still be disappointed, a greater degree of fault may lie with the arbitrator, arbitration association, one or more third parties, or simply to happenstance.

The risk of making a bad choice of dispute resolution is not peculiar to international commercial arbitration. That risk arises under any system of dispute resolution. Nor should primacy be given to the perception of the losing party that arbitration has failed. In a winner-take-all arbitral system, one party inevitably loses. That is exactly what arbitration entails. One reason for choosing it lies in the decisiveness of a winner-take-all remedy, as well as in the virtue of an arbitrator so deciding.

Questions

With regard to the case study at the beginning of this chapter:

1. What is international commercial arbitration?
2. What is the difference between ad hoc and institutionalised arbitration?
3. What issues should one consider in choosing arbitration?
4. What should be included in an arbitration clause?
5. When should an arbitration clause be invoked?
6. When is an international arbitration award final and binding?
7. What strengths and weaknesses are associated with international commercial arbitration?
8. Why arbitrate? Why not litigate?
9. What is the primary significance of the choice of arbitration under the UNCITRAL Arbitration Rules, as distinct from arbitration under the domestic rules set out in the IAA?
10. What might happen if one party to a dispute declines to proceed under the UNCITRAL Rules?
11. If you were asked to provide FASHIONFOODS PARIS with an arbitration strategy to deal with its conflict with SEAGOODS, what advice would you give?
12. If you were asked to provide SEAGOODS with an arbitration strategy, what advice would you give?

Index